THE FIVE BOOKS OF MOSES

THE
FIVE BOOKS
OF MOSES

Genesis, Exodus, Leviticus, Numbers, Deuteronomy

STANDARD EDITION

A NEW TRANSLATION WITH INTRODUCTIONS,
COMMENTARY, AND NOTES BY

EVERETT FOX

SCHOCKEN BOOKS
NEW YORK

Parts of this work were originally published as *In the Beginning* (Genesis)
in 1983, *Now These Are the Names* (Exodus) in 1986, and *Genesis and Exodus*
in 1990 by Schocken Books Inc.

Grateful acknowledgment is made to The Schocken Institute for
Jewish Research of The Jewish Theological Seminary of America in
Jerusalem for permission to reproduce on p. 11 the frontispiece of
The Schocken Bible (Jerusalem, Schocken Library, ms. 14940),
an illuminated manuscript circa 1300, South Germany.

Library of Congress Cataloging-in-Publication Data

Bible. O.T. Pentateuch. English. Fox. 1995.
The five books of Moses : Genesis, Exodus, Leviticus, Numbers,
Deuteronomy : a new translation with introductions, commentary,
and notes / by Everett Fox.
p.   cm.
ISBN 0-8052-4140-x
1. Bible.   O.T.   Pentateuch—Commentaries.   I. Fox,   Everett.
II. Title.
BS1223.A3F68   1995

222'.105209—dc20   95-10143
                                                      CIP

PRODUCTION STAFF

Kathy Grasso   Robert Rosenbaum
Production Manager   Copy Editor

Fearn Cutler   Angie Chiu
Design Director   Production Assistant

M. Susan Norton   Altie Karper
Production Editor   Managing Editor

Book design by Maura Fadden Rosenthal

Manufactured in the United States of America
2 4 6 8 9 7 5 3 1

In memory of my father,
Barnett S. Fox (1906–1963)
and
In honor of the eightieth birthday of my mother,
Lillian Fox Levmore

Psalm 15

CONTENTS

CONTENTS

LEVITICUS: NOW HE CALLED

NUMBERS: IN THE WILDERNESS

DEUTERONOMY: THESE ARE THE WORDS

Translator's Preface

> ... read the Bible as though it were something entirely unfamiliar, as
> though it had not been set before you ready-made. . . . Face the book with
> a new attitude as something new. . . . Let whatever may happen occur be-
> tween yourself and it. You do not know which of its sayings and images
> will overwhelm and mold you. . . . But hold yourself open. Do not believe
> anything a priori; do not disbelieve anything a priori. Read aloud the
> words written in the book in front of you; hear the word you utter and let
> it reach you.
>
> —*adapted from a lecture of Martin Buber, 1926*

THE PURPOSE OF THIS WORK IS TO DRAW THE READER INTO THE WORLD OF THE
Hebrew Bible through the power of its language. While this sounds simple
enough, it is not usually possible in translation. Indeed, the premise of almost all
Bible translations, past and present, is that the "meaning" of the text should be
conveyed in as clear and comfortable a manner as possible in one's own language.
Yet the truth is that the Bible was not written in English in the twentieth or even
the seventeenth century; it is ancient, sometimes obscure, and speaks in a way
quite different from ours. Accordingly, I have sought here primarily to echo the
style of the original, believing that the Bible is best approached, at least at the beginning, on its own terms. So I have presented the text in English dress but with a
Hebraic voice.

The result looks and sounds very different from what we are accustomed to
encountering as the Bible, whether in the much-loved grandeur of the King James
Version or the clarity and easy fluency of the many recent attempts. There are no
old friends here; Eve will not, as in old paintings, give Adam an apple (nor will she
be called "Eve"), nor will Moses speak of himself as "a stranger in a strange land,"
as beautiful as that sounds. Instead, the reader will encounter a text which challenges him or her to rethink what these ancient books are and what they mean,
and will hopefully be encouraged to become an active listener rather than a passive receiver.

This translation is guided by the principle that the Hebrew Bible, like much of the
literature of antiquity, was meant to be read aloud, and that consequently it must
be translated with careful attention to rhythm and sound. The translation therefore tries to mimic the particular rhetoric of the Hebrew whenever possible, preserving such devices as repetition, allusion, alliteration, and wordplay. It is

intended to echo the Hebrew, and to lead the reader back to the sound structure and form of the original.

Such an approach was first espoused by Martin Buber and Franz Rosenzweig in their monumental German translation of the Bible (1925–1962) and in subsequent interpretive essays. *The Five Books of Moses* is in many respects an offshoot of the Buber-Rosenzweig translation (hereafter abbreviated as B-R). I began with their principles: that translations of individual words should reflect "primal" root meanings, that translations of phrases, lines, and whole verses should mimic the syntax of the Hebrew, and that the vast web of allusions and wordplays present in the text should be somehow perceivable in the target language (for a full exposition in English, see now Buber and Rosenzweig 1994). In all these areas I have taken a more moderate view than my German mentors, partly because I think there are limitations to these principles and partly because recent scholarship points in broader directions. As a result, my translation is on the whole less radical and less strange in English than B-R was in German. This, however, does not mean that it is less different from conventional translations, or that I have abandoned the good fight for a fresh look at the Bible's verbal power.

Buber and Rosenzweig based their approach on the Romantic nineteenth-century notion that the Bible was essentially oral literature written down. In the present century there have been Bible scholars who have found this view attractive; on the other hand, there has been little agreement on how oral roots manifest themselves in the text. One cannot suggest that the Bible is a classic work of oral literature in the same sense as the *Iliad* or *Beowulf.* It does not employ regular meter or rhyme, even in sections that are clearly formal poetry. The text of the Bible that we possess is most likely a mixture of oral and written materials from a variety of periods and sources, and recovering anything resembling original oral forms would seem to be impossible. This is particularly true given the considerable chronological and cultural distance at which we stand from the text, which does not permit us to know how it was performed in ancient times.

A more fruitful approach, less dependent upon theories whose historical accuracy is unprovable, might be to focus on the way in which the biblical text, *once completed,* was copied and read. Recent research reveals that virtually all literature in Greek and Roman times—the period when the Hebrew Bible was put into more or less the form in which it has come down to us (but not the period of its composition)—was read aloud. This holds for the process of copying or writing, and also, surprisingly, for solitary reading. As late as the last decade of the fourth century, Saint Augustine expressed surprise at finding a sage who read silently. Such practices and attitudes seem strange to us, for whom the very definition of a library, for instance, is a place where people have to keep quiet. But it was a routine in the world of antiquity, as many sources attest.

So the Bible, if not an oral document, is certainly an aural one; it would have been read aloud as a matter of course. But the implications of this for understanding the text are considerable. The rhetoric of the text is such that many passages and sections are understandable in depth only when they are analyzed *as they are heard.* Using echoes, allusions, and powerful inner structures of sound, the text is often able to convey ideas in a manner that vocabulary alone cannot do. A few illustrations may suffice to introduce this phenomenon to the reader; it will be encountered constantly throughout this volume.

Sound plays a crucial role in one of the climactic sequences in Genesis, Chapters 32–33. Jacob, the protagonist, has not seen his brother Esau for twenty years. Now a rich and successful adult, he is on his way back to Canaan after a long exile. He sends messengers to forestall Esau's vengeance—for twenty years earlier, Jacob had stolen the birthright and the blessing which Esau felt were rightly his own. When Jacob finds out that his brother "is already coming . . . and four hundred men are with him" (32:7), he goes even further, preparing an elaborate gift for Esau in the hopes of appeasing his anger. The text in vv.21–22 presents Jacob's thoughts and actions (the translation is taken from the New English Bible):

> for he thought, "I will appease him with the present that I have sent on
> ahead, and afterwards, when I come into his presence, he will perhaps re-
> ceive me kindly." So Jacob's present went on ahead of him. . . .

This is an accurate and highly idiomatic translation of the Hebrew, and the reader will notice nothing unusual about the passage as it reads in English. The sound of the Hebrew text, on the other hand, gives one pause. It is built on variations of the word *panim,* whose basic meaning is "face," although the Hebrew uses it id- iomatically to encompass various ideas. (Note: in Hebrew, the sound *p* is pro- nounced as *ph* under certain circumstances.) If the text is translated with attention to sound, its quite striking oral character emerges (italics mine):

> For he said to himself:
> I will wipe (the anger from) his *face (phanav)*
> with the gift that goes ahead of my *face; (le-phanai)*
> afterward, when I see his *face, (phanav)*
> perhaps he will lift up my *face! (phanai)*
> The gift crossed over ahead of his *face.* . . . *(al panav)*

Comparison of these two English versions is instructive. In the New English Bible, as in most other contemporary versions, the translators are apparently con- cerned with presenting the text in clear, modern, idiomatic English. For example, they render the Hebrew *yissa phanai* as "receive me kindly." The N.E.B. translates the *idea* of the text; at the same time it translates *out* the sound by not picking up on the repetition of *panim* words.

What does the reader gain by hearing the literalness of the Hebrew? And what is lost by the use of its idiomatic meaning? As mirrored in the second translation, it is clear that our text is signaling something of significance. The motif of "face" (which might be interpreted as "facing" or "confrontation") occurs at crucial points in the story. The night before his fateful meeting with Esau, as he is left to ponder the next day's events, Jacob wrestles with a mysterious stranger—a divine being. After Jacob's victory, the text reports (32:31):

> Yaakov called the name of the place: Peniel/*Face of God*,
> for: I have seen God,
> *face to face*,
> and my life has been saved.

The repetition suggests a thematic link with what has gone before. One could interpret that once the hero has met and actually bested this divine being, his coming human confrontation is assured of success. Thus upon meeting Esau at last, Jacob says to him (33:10):

> For I have, after all, seen your *face*, as one sees the *face* of God,
> and you have been gracious to me.

It could be said that in a psychological sense the meetings with divine and human adversaries are a unity, the representation of one human process in two narrative episodes. This is accomplished by the repetition of the word *panim* in the text.

The above interpretation depends entirely on sound. Once that focus is dropped, either through the silent reading of the text or a standard translation, the inner connections are simply lost and the reader is robbed of the opportunity to make these connections for himself. Clearly there is a difference between translating what the text means and translating what it says.

While the Jacob passages use the sound of a specific word to indicate an important motif in the narrative, there are other cases where sound brings out structure, and the structure itself conveys the principal idea of the passage. A striking example of this is found at the beginning of Genesis. God's first acts of creation in 1:3–5 are portrayed in a highly ordered fashion, suggesting that creation itself is orderly, and this idea is the thematic backbone of the whole chapter. We are meant to experience the orderliness of God's activity through the sensuality of the language and through the particular way in which the text speaks. A translation keyed to the sound of the Hebrew reads:

> God said: Let there be light! And there was light.
> God saw the light: that it was good.
> God separated the light from the darkness.
> God called the light: Day! and the darkness he called: Night!

The four occurrences of "God" plus verb accomplish the narrator's goal, and give·
a tone to the creation account that makes it akin to poetry. In contrast, virtually
all modern translations treat the passage as prose, rendering it into clear written
English but simultaneously removing its inner structure. What remains is a statement of what is taking place in the narrative, but without its underlying thrust.
Again the New English Bible:

> God said, "Let there be light," and there was light; and God saw that the
> light was good, and he separated light from darkness. He called the light
> day, and the darkness night.

This translation is cast in good English style. For just that reason two occurrences of "God" have been omitted, and the passage consequently reads
smoothly—so smoothly that one glides past it as if creation were the same as any
other narrated action. But what has been lost is the characteristic oral ring of the
text, and simultaneously its intent to say something beyond the content of words
alone.

Another example of translating with an ear to the sound and structure of the
original, this time from the book of Exodus, comes from the dramatic story of
the Sea of Reeds (14:11–12). The newly freed Israelites find themselves pursued by
their former masters, the Pharaoh and his army; with their backs to the Sea, they
panic, and bitterly harangue their would-be deliverer, Moses. The present translation, attempting to reflect the repetition and structure of the original, yields the
following:

> they said to Moshe:
> Is it because there are no graves in Egypt
> that you have taken us out to die in the wilderness?
> What is this that you have done to us, bringing us out of Egypt?
> Is this not the very word that we spoke to you in Egypt,
> saying: Let us alone, that we may serve Egypt!
> Indeed, better for us serving Egypt
> than our dying in the wilderness!

This passage demonstrates several aspects of a rhetorical translation method, if
we may so term it: the laying out of the text in "cola" or lines meant to facilitate
reading aloud (more on this below); the repetition of words—"Egypt" five times
and "wilderness" twice—to stress the irony of the Israelites' predicament (as they
see it, Egypt means life, and the wilderness, certain death); and the double use of
"serve," the very word that Moses constantly drummed into Pharaoh's ears in the
early part of the book to denote the Israelites' desire to go and worship their God

("Send free my people, that they may serve me"). If we juxtapose the above translation with that found in, say, the New International Version, the importance of this approach to the text becomes clear:

> They said to Moses, "Was it because there were no graves in Egypt that you brought us to the desert to die? What have you done to us by bringing us out of Egypt? Didn't we say to you in Egypt, 'Leave us alone; let us serve the Egyptians'? It would have been better for us to serve the Egyptians than to die in the desert!"

Here the rhetorical force of the Hebrew has been ignored. The Hebrew text does not transpose "desert to die" to "die in the desert" at the end of the passage (the word order repeats in the original, for emphasis); it does not distinguish in sound between "Egypt" and "Egyptians"; and it certainly does not read like standard colloquial prose. Indeed, all of Chapter 14 of Exodus demonstrates the Bible's use of an intermediate form between poetry and prose, a form designed to instruct as well as to inspire.

But it is not only in narrative that the rhetoric of biblical language makes itself felt. Fully half of the book of Exodus is law or instruction, and one can find there further examples of the importance of sound structure in the Bible. Take, for instance, the law concerning the protection of widows and orphans (22:23–24). This time I shall present the text first through the eyes of the Jerusalem Bible:

> You must not be harsh with the widow, or with the orphan; if you are harsh with them, they will surely cry out to me, and be sure that I shall hear their cry; my anger will flare and I shall kill you with the sword, your own wives will be widows, your own children orphans.

This is powerful language, especially in a law code. But the Hebrew text goes much farther, utilizing as it does a double form of the verb rarely found in multiple sequence:

> Any widow or orphan you are not to afflict.
> Oh, if you afflict, afflict them . . . !
> For (then) they will cry, cry out to me,
> and I will hearken, hearken to their cry,
> my anger will flare up
> and I will kill you with the sword,
> so that your wives become widows, and your children,
>   orphans!

Here the text is in effect slowed down by the division into lines, and the verb forms are isolated to underscore their unique rhetoric. The effect of the whole is to focus attention on this particular law among a host of others.

2

Once the spokenness of the Bible is understood as a critical factor in the translation process, a number of practical steps become necessary which constitute radical changes from past translation practices. Buber and Rosenzweig introduced three such major innovations into their work: the form in which the text is laid out, the reproduction of biblical names and their meanings, and the "leading-word" technique by means of which important repetitions in the Hebrew are retained in translation.

First, as is obvious from the excerpts quoted above, the translated text is printed in lines resembling blank verse. These "cola" are based primarily on spoken phrasing. In Buber's view, each unit represents simultaneously a unit of breathing and of meaning, thus illustrating the deep connection between form and content in the Hebrew Bible. While current scholars, myself included, would not agree with Buber that the text's rhetoric necessarily corresponds to "breathing," cola divisions do facilitate reading aloud and make it possible for the listener to sense the text's inner rhythm—and only at that point can the text begin to deliver its message with full force.

Cola do not correspond to the traditional verse divisions found in printed Bibles. Those divisions are of late origin (perhaps from the ninth century, in written form), and were adopted for the sake of reference. Jews and Christians have used them in roughly the same form since the middle ages. Cola, on the other hand, arise from the experience of reading the Hebrew text aloud and of feeling its spoken rhythms. The specific divisions used in this volume are somewhat arbitrary; each reader will hear the text differently. My line divisions are sometimes identical to B-R, but often are not; they sometimes correspond to the punctuation laid down by Jewish tradition (the Masoretic accents or *trop*), but not always. What is most important, however, is that the practice of dividing the text into lines points away from the apprehension of the Bible as a written book and restores the sense of it as spoken performance.

Second, personal and place names generally appear in Hebrew forms throughout this translation. Thus, for example, the Hebrew *Moshe* is retained instead of Moses, *Kayin* instead of Cain, *Rivka* instead of Rebecca, and *Bil'am* instead of Balaam. This practice stems from the central role that names play in biblical stories (as often in literature). In biblical Israel as throughout the ancient world, names are often meant to give clues about their bearer's personality or fate. The meaning of a name is often explained outright in the text itself. In *The Five Books of Moses* this is represented by a slash in the text, as in the following example (Gen. 30:23–24):

> She said:
> God has removed/*asaf*
> my reproach.
> And she called his name: Yosef,
> saying:
> May YHWH add/*yosef*
> another son to me.

The name here is a play on words, hinting at Joseph's eventual fate (he will be a son "removed" and "added," that is, lost and found by his family). By retaining the Hebrew sounds in translation, a meaningful portion of the narrative is thus moved from footnotes, where it appears in most modern translations, back to the body of the text. That this is important is demonstrated by the fact that virtually every major (usually male) character in Genesis has his name explained in this manner.

It should be noted that such interpretations of names in the Bible are not based on philological derivations, that is, on scientific etymology. The name Jacob/Yaakov, for instance, which is understood in Gen. 25 as "Heel-Holder" and in Chapter 27 as "Heel-Sneak," probably held the original meaning of "may (God) protect." But the biblical writers were not so much concerned with what a name originally meant as they were with its sound, and with the associations inherent in that sound. Therefore what is important in our example is that "Yaakov" recalls *ekev*, "heel." This kind of interpretation is known as "folk etymology" or "popular etymology." A similar phenomenon appears in the naming of Moses (Ex. 2:10).

A third important technique with which biblical literature often conveys its message, and which must influence the translation of the text, is what Buber called the "leading-word" (*Leitwort*) principle. Key ("leading") words are repeated within a text to signify major themes and concerns, like recurring themes in a piece of music (hence the similarity of Buber's term to composer Richard Wagner's word *Leitmotif*). A leading-word operates on the basis of sound: the repetition of a word or word root encourages the listener to make connections between diverse parts of a story (or even of a book), and to trace a particular theme throughout. This is not to be seen, however, as a static process. A leading-word may appear in different forms and contexts, with changed meaning, thus lending a sense of movement and development to the text and its characters. One example may be cited here; others appear throughout this book.

Buber's essay, "Abraham the Seer," traces the biblical tradition's portrayal of Abraham through the use of key words and phrases in the text. Chief among these is the verb "to see" (Hebrew *ra'o*), which appears constantly in the Abraham narratives and which tells us something significant about both the man himself and how he is meant to be remembered. At the outset of Abraham's journey to Canaan, which signals his entry into biblical tradition as an independent personality, God sends him off to a land that he will "let him see" (12:1). Arriving in the land, Abraham is granted a communication from God, expressed by the phrase "YHWH was seen by Avram . . ." (12:7). God subsequently promises the land to him and his descendants ("see from the place that you are . . . for all the land that you see, to you I give it and to your seed, for the ages" [13:15]). "Seeing" comes to the fore in the story of Abraham's concubine Hagar; her encounter with God's messenger ends with her addressing a "God of Seeing" (16:13). Further meetings between Abraham and God (17:1, 18:1) likewise express themselves visually, with the latter scene, where God announces Isaac's impending birth at Abraham's tent, almost unique in the Bible for its bold picture of God appearing directly to human beings. Finally, with the great test of Abraham in Chapter 22, the "Binding of Isaac," the theme of seeing is brought to a climax. Buber describes the use of the leading-word in that passage, summarizing how it rounds out the entire Abraham cycle:

> It appears here more often than in any previous passage. Abraham sees the place where the act must be accomplished, at a distance. To the question of his son, he replies that God will provide ("see to") the lamb for the burnt offering. In the saving moment he lifts up his eyes and sees the ram. And now he proclaims over the altar the name that makes known the imperishable essence of this place, Mount Moriah: YHWH Will See. . . . God sees man, and man sees God. God sees Abraham, and tests him by seeing him as the righteous and "whole" man who walks before his God (17:1), and now, at the end of his road, he conquers even this final place, the holy temple mountain, by acting on God's behalf. Abraham sees God with the eye of his action and so recognizes Him, just as Moses, seeing God's glory "from behind," will recognize Him as Gracious and Merciful.*

Buber goes one step further in his analysis of the leading-word *see:* he views it as a clue to the biblical concept of Abraham's role in history. Taking the hint from I Sam. 9:9 ("the prophet of our day was formerly called a seer"), he posits that the Bible wants us to understand Abraham as the spiritual father of the later prophets. Abraham, then, is preeminent as the first man in the Bible of whom it is reported that God "was seen by him."

Such an understanding of the role of leading-words as crucial to biblical style rarely makes itself felt in translation. Bible translators are reluctant to reproduce repetitions of Hebrew words in the text because they are generally fearful of creating a tedious English style. However, once one abandons the idea of the Bible as

---

* Martin Buber, *On the Bible: Eighteen Studies,* edited by Nahum N. Glatzer (New York: Schocken Books, 1982), p. 42.

primarily a written work, the repetitiveness of leading-words becomes a signal rather than a stumbling block, freeing the reader to experience the dynamic manner in which the Bible expresses itself. That this sometimes entails a loss of nuance in the translation (where "see" in Hebrew may signify "perceive" or "understand" in a particular passage, for instance) is a price that must be paid; yet such a translation may in fact retain more of the breadth of the Hebrew than is immediately apparent.

A final word needs to be said about the leading-word technique. It may serve a purpose in the text beyond conveying meaning: it may play a structural role, unifying sections that have been culled from different sources within biblical Israel to form a composite account. The ancient redactors of the Bible apparently crafted the material they received into an organic whole. Using such means as leading-word repetition, they in effect created a new literature in which deep relationships exist between the parts of the whole.

The above three translation techniques—setting out the text in cola, transliterating and explaining Hebrew names, and reproducing leading-words—form the crux of an approach to the Bible's spokenness, but there are other methods used by the text to the same end. Three are particularly worthy of mention: wordplay, allusion, and what I have termed small-scale repetition.

The Bible uses wordplay to make a point forcefully, especially in prophetic passages or those with a prophetic flavor. In Gen. 40:13 and 19, for instance, Joseph predicts that the king of Egypt will end the imprisonment of two of his courtiers. When the cupbearer is to be restored to his former position, Joseph says,

> in another three days
> Pharaoh will lift up your head. . . .

In contrast, when Joseph predicts that the chief baker will be executed, the text reads:

> in another three days Pharaoh will lift up your head
> from off you. . . .

By beginning both statements with the same phrasing, the narrator is able to heighten the impact of "from off you" on both audience and victim.

A powerful example of the second device, allusion, occurs near the beginning of Exodus. Baby Moses, floating precariously yet fetus-like on the Nile, is one of the enduring images in the book, as children have long attested. Modern English readers, however, are seldom aware that the Hebrew word for Moses's floating cradle—rendered by virtually all standard translations as "basket"—is the same as the one used in Gen. 6:14ff. to describe Noah's famous vessel (*teiva*). Preserving the connection between the two, as I have tried to do in the Exodus passage with "little-ark" (and which, incidentally, the authors of the King James Version did with "ark"), is to keep open the play of profound meaning that exists between the two stories.

Finally, we may give an example of small-scale repetition. Unlike the leading-word technique, this is limited to a brief report and is used to express one specific idea. In Gen. 6:11–13, for instance, it illustrates an important biblical concept: just punishment. Three times in the passage we hear the word "ruin," indicating what human evil has done to the world; the fourth time (v.13) it appears in a causative form, to show that God retaliates in exactly the same terms, measure for measure.

> Now the earth had gone to *ruin* before God; the earth was filled with
>   wrongdoing.
> God saw the earth, and here: it had gone to *ruin,*
> for all flesh had *ruined* its way upon the earth.

> God said to Noah:
> An end of all flesh has come before me,
> for the earth is filled with wrongdoing through them;
> here, I will bring *ruin* upon them, along with the earth.

The Bible is fond of this technique, which it uses in a number of narratives that deal with human misbehavior (e.g., the Tower of Babel story in Gen. 11). It is another example of how the form in which the text is cast goes a long way toward expressing its intent.

From the above examples it may appear that it is not difficult to carry out the Buber-Rosenzweig principles in a translation. In practice, however, the translator who wishes to bring the language spoken by his audience into consonance with the style of the Hebrew text runs the risk of doing violence to that language, forced as he or she is into "hebraizing" the language. There will of necessity be a certain strangeness and some awkward moments in such a translation. Buber and Rosenzweig themselves came under fire for creating a strange new kind of German in their work; one critic in 1933 accused them of "unusual affectations." My renditions of the Torah books, while limited in what they wreak with the English language both by my cautiousness and by the less pliable nature of English (than German), have been liable to similar characterization, especially in the legal sections.

This problem, however, is inherent in this kind of undertaking, and I have accepted its risks willingly. In the last generation there have been any number of clear, smooth-reading translations of the Bible, all aimed at making the text readily accessible to the reader. I have taken a different road, arguing (along with Buber and Rosenzweig) that the reader must be prepared to meet the Bible at least halfway and must become an active participant in the process of the text, rather than a passive listener. To this end, there is no alternative but to force the language of the translation to become the instrument through which the Hebraic voice of the text speaks.

I have taken pains to illustrate some of the rhetorical devices that emerge from an oral reading of the text in order to indicate the direction taken in *The Five Books of Moses*. A concluding observation must be made. Every critic knows, or should know, that art defies categorization and exact description. We try to understand what makes a masterpiece tick, whether it be a painting, a piece of music, or a work of literature, yet in the end our analyses fall silent before the greatness and subtlety of the work itself. The techniques that I have described above must remain suggestive rather than definitive; they point out a direction rather than speak directly. Biblical narratives do not end with the phrase "The moral of the story is . . . ," any more than biblical laws overtly spell out their assumptions. Translating with attention to sound therefore may help to preserve not only the message of the text but also its ambiguity and open-endedness. In that persona the Bible has been familiar to Jewish and Christian interpreters, who for centuries have sought to fill in the gaps and resolve the difficulties in the text by means of their own ingenuity. This volume is aimed at helping present-day readers to share in that experience.

3

Reading the Bible in the literary, rhetorical manner I have just explicated is grounded in certain assumptions about the text. *The Five Books of Moses* stays close to the basic "masoretic" text-type of the Torah, that is, the vocalized text that has been with us for certain for about a millennium. Deviations from that form, in the interest of solving textual problems, are duly mentioned in the Notes. In following the traditional Hebrew text, I am presenting to the English reader an unreconstructed book, but one whose form is at least verifiable in a long-standing tradition. This translation, therefore, is not a translation of some imagined "original" text, or of the Torah of Moses' or Solomon's or even Jeremiah's time. These documents, could they be shown to have existed for certain or in recognizable form, have not been found, and give little promise of ever being found. *The Five Books of Moses* is, rather, a translation of the biblical text as it might have been known in the formative, postbiblical period of Judaism and early Christianity (the Roman era). As far as the prehistory of the text is concerned, readers who have some familiarity with biblical criticism will note that in my Commentary I have made scant reference to the by-now classic dissection of the Torah into clear-cut prior "sources" (designated J, E, P, and D by the Bible scholars of the past century). Such analysis has been dealt with comprehensively by others (cf., for instance, Levine on the book of Numbers). In addition, it remains a theoretical construct, and the nature of biblical texts militates against recovering the exact process by which the Bible came into being. In any event, virtually all the standard introductions to the Bible deal with this topic; beyond these, readers may find Friedman (1989) of particular clarity and usefulness.

Given the text that I am using, what has interested me here is chiefly the final form of the Torah books, how they fit together as artistic entities, and how they have combined traditions to present a coherent religious message. This was surely the goal of the final "redactor(s)," but it was not until recently a major goal of biblical scholars. While, therefore, I am not committed to refuting the tenets of source criticism in the strident manner of Benno Jacob and Umberto Cassuto, I have concentrated in this volume on the "wholeness" of biblical texts, rather than on their growth out of fragments. My Commentary is aimed at helping the reader to search for unities and thematic development.

At the same time, in recent years I have found it increasingly fascinating to encounter the text's complex layering. It appears that every time a biblical story or law was put in a new setting or redaction, its meaning, and the meaning of the whole, must have been somewhat altered. A chorus of different periods and concerns is often discernible, however faintly. Sometimes these function to "deconstruct" each other, and sometimes they actually create a new text. In offering a rendition that does not try to gloss over stylistic differences, I hope that this book will make it possible for an inquisitive reader to sense that process at work. As far as analysis of the text in this manner is concerned, I would recommend to the reader the brilliant work of Greenstein (1985a) and Damrosch (1987).

4

Some readers may wonder whether *The Five Books of Moses* is merely an English translation of B-R. It is not. Although B-R served as the theoretical basis for my work, I have found it necessary to modify their approach in the present setting. There are a number of reasons for this.

For one, Bible scholarship has made notable advances since Buber's heyday (Rosenzweig had already died in 1929). Although he completed the German translation in 1961, and kept abreast of work in the field, it must be said that Buber did not greatly modify the text of the Pentateuch translation, philologically speaking, between 1930 when the second edition appeared and the revised printings of the mid-1950s. It seemed imperative to me to bring the work of postwar biblical philology to bear on the English translation, rather than relying solely on Buber's etymologies. Some of the changes in this area have been cited in the Notes to the text (as "B-R uses . . .").

Second, in the attempt to make the German translation mirror the Hebrew original Rosenzweig did not hesitate to either create new German words or reach back into the German literature of past ages to find forms suitable for rendering certain Hebrew expressions. To perform a corresponding feat in English would simply not work; the language is not flexible, and usages change so quickly that

an artful appeal to the past seems futile except for the benefit of linguistic historians. While I have endeavored to produce an English text that reflects the style of
biblical Hebrew, I have in the main shied away from pushing the language beyond
reasonable and comprehensible limits.

There are other significant deviations from B-R here. I have used a different
rendering of the name of God, which had been a distinctive B-R trademark (for
an explanation, see "On the Name of God and Its Translation"). I have sometimes
opted for different line divisions, based on my own hearing of the Hebrew; in-
dented purely poetic passages, a practice not followed by B-R in narrative texts;
read a large number of clauses differently from a grammatical or syntactical point
of view; and loosened the practice, sometimes overdone in B-R, of reproducing a
Hebrew root by a single English one wherever it occurs.

It will be noted that I have included here one element that many readers felt
was sorely lacking in B-R: notes and commentary. Every translation of the Bible
implies a commentary, but few have included one with the text. *The Five Books of
Moses* especially requires such an apparatus, both to explain its translation technique and to show how it may be used fruitfully in interpreting the Bible. Read in
conjunction with the text, the explanatory material presents a methodology for
studying and teaching the Bible.

Finally, there is the personal aspect of this work. It was conceived as an act of
homage to the B-R translation; at the beginning, I desired solely (and rashly) to
bring their accomplishment over into English. It was therefore a labor of love, and
despite the amount of work involved, a relatively safe one; I did not, at least initially, have to make my own decisions about the biblical text. I should certainly
never have undertaken my own translation at that stage.

But working on a project of this nature inevitably leads to things that are not
predictable at the outset. It happened exactly as Rosenzweig wrote about his own
involvement: like a seduction. It soon became apparent that, not only could I not
in good conscience do to English what especially Rosenzweig had done to
German, but I was also beginning to find my own voice as creator and scholar in
the translation. Thus—although this was not my original intention—I am quite
aware that in this book I am presenting a piece of myself as well as an approach
to the Bible for English readers.

This having been said, *The Five Books of Moses* is still very much in the B-R tradition. It retains the general approach of its predecessor, exclusive of those principles that are dependent on the form and character of the German language. It is
therefore the child of B-R, with all the links and independent features that a par-
ent-child relationship implies. It may also be seen as an attempt to bring the work
of B-R into a new era of Bible scholarship, and as an artistic endeavor in its own
right.

5

The Five Books of Moses is heavily indebted to B-R, but one may also view it in a more contemporary context. Over the past two decades, there has been an explosion of "literary" study of the Bible. Numerous scholars have turned their attention to the form and rhetoric of the biblical text, concentrating on its finished form rather than on trying to reconstruct history or the development of the text. Such an approach is hardly new. Already in late antiquity, Jewish interpretation of the Bible often centered around the style and precise wording of the text, especially as heard when read aloud. Similarly, the medieval Jewish commentators of Spain and France showed great sensitivity to the linguistic aspects of the Bible. In both cases, however, no systematic approach was developed; literary interpretation remained interwoven with very different concerns such as homiletics, mysticism, and philosophy.

It has remained for twentieth-century scholars, reacting partly against what they perceived to be the excessive historicizing of German Bible scholarship, to press for a literary reading of the Bible. Early pioneers in this regard include Umberto Cassuto, Buber and (later) Meir Weiss in Israel, and Benno Jacob (who was consulted frequently during the writing of B-R) in Germany. More recently we might mention James Muilenberg (who labeled his holistic approach "Rhetorical Criticism"), Edwin Good, James Ackerman, and Robert Alter in the U.S.; and J. P. Fokkelman in Holland. These names are now the tip of the iceberg, and one can speak of a whole school of interpreters in a literary or rhetorical vein. The reader will find a number of stimulating studies listed in "Suggestions for Further Reading."

The Five Books of Moses is akin to many of these efforts, and has benefited directly from them. Although I began my work independently of the literary movement, I have come to feel a kinship with it, and regard my text as one that may be used to study the Bible in a manner consistent with its findings. At the same time, I am not committed to throwing out historical scholarship wholesale. It would be a mistake to set up the two disciplines in an adversarial relationship, as has often been done. The Hebrew Bible is by nature a complex and multi-faceted literature, in both its origins and the history of its use and interpretation. No one "school" can hope to illuminate more than part of the whole picture, and even then, one's efforts are bound to be fragmentary. Probably, only a synthesis of all fruitful approaches available into a fully interdisciplinary methodology will provide a satisfactory overview of the biblical text (see Greenstein 1989). In this respect, approaching the Bible is analogous to dealing with the arts in general, where a multitude of disciplines from aesthetics to the social and natural sciences is needed to flesh out the whole. I hope that *The Five Books of Moses* will make a contribution toward this process, by providing an English text, and an underlying reading of the Hebrew, that balances what has appeared previously.

There is another more recent movement in biblical studies which deserves both mention and study. As of this writing, feminist Bible criticism has come into its own. A substantial number of thoughtful and thought-provoking studies have appeared in recent years that examine the portrayal and position of women in biblical texts. One of the glaring gaps in previous Bible scholarship—and one of the difficult issues for contemporary readers of the Bible—lies in coming to terms with the social/sexual milieu assumed by the text. Wrestling with this issue is an appropriate complement to the other types of text-wrestling that have taken place throughout the ages. I have tried to present some of the findings of feminist criticism on the text, and I have listed some appropriate recent works in "Suggestions for Further Reading."

6

To what extent can any translation of the Bible be said to be more "authentic" than another? Because of lack of information about the various original audiences of our text, the translator can only try to be as faithful as the information will allow. This is particularly true where a work as universally known as the Bible is concerned. Even if the precise circumstances surrounding its writing and editing were known, the text would still be affected by the interpretations of the centuries. It is as if a Beethoven symphony were to be performed on period instruments, using nineteenth-century performance techniques: would it still sound as fresh and radical to us as it did in Beethoven's own day? Thus I would suggest that it is almost impossible to reproduce the Bible's impact on its contemporaries; all that the translator can do is to perform the task with as much honesty as possible, with a belief in one's artistic intuition and a consciousness of one's limitations.

Yet how are we to distinguish the point where explication ends and personal interpretation begins? From the very moment of the Bible's editing and promulgation, there began the historical process of interpretation, a process which has at times led to violent disagreement between individuals and even nations. Everyone who has ever taken the Bible seriously has staked so much on a particular interpretation of the text that altering it has become close to a matter of life and death. Nothing can be done about this situation, unfortunately, and once again the translator must do the best he or she can. Art, by its very nature, gives rise to interpretation—else it is not great art. The complexity and ambiguity of great literature invites interpretation, just as the complexities and ambiguities of its interpreters encourage a wide range of perspectives. The Hebrew Bible, in which very diverse material has been juxtaposed in a far-ranging collection spanning centuries, rightly or wrongly pushes the commentator and reader to make inner connections and draw overarching conclusions. My interpretations in this book stem from this state of affairs. I have tried to do my work as carefully and as conscientiously as I can, recognizing the problems inherent in this kind of enterprise. I hope the result is not too far from what the biblical editors had intended.

My ultimate goal in this volume has been to show that reading the Hebrew Bible is a process, in the same sense that performing a piece of music is a process. Rather than carrying across ("translating") the content of the text from one linguistic realm to another, I have tried to involve the reader in the experience of giving it back ("rendering"), of returning to the source and recreating some of its richness. My task has been to present the raw material of the text as best I can in English, and to point out some of the method that may be fruitfully employed in wrestling with it.

Buber and Rosenzweig translated the Bible out of the deep conviction that language has the power to bridge worlds and to redeem human beings. They both, separately and together, fought to restore the power of ancient words and to speak modern ones with wholeness and genuineness. Despite the barriers in their own lives—Buber's early disappointments, Rosenzweig's struggle with German idealism and later with a terrible paralysis that left him unable to speak—they each came to see dialogue as a central fact of interhuman and human-divine relations.

The era in which we live, seventy years after the first appearance of the Buber-Rosenzweig *Im Anfang* (Genesis), is, however, heir to many decades of a very different experience. Since 1933, but beginning certainly well before, the Western world has experienced the debasement and trivialization of human language, and thus of divine language as well. From Stalin's and Hitler's speeches, to Orwell's visions, to the reality of Vietnam War jargon and on to the babble of television and advertising, words seem to have lost their elemental meaningfulness in a way that the optimistic nineteenth century into which Buber and Rosenzweig were born could not have dared to believe. In this situation, can a translation of ancient books, even though they are from the Bible, have anything to say, or are they merely a "message from a dead man," to use Kafka's poignant expression?

Yet Buber and Rosenzweig knew that language lives only in the mouths of speakers, human beings who face each other and who at every moment of conversation and contact literally translate for one another. The reading of the Bible is hopefully a cultural means for reawakening that conversation, for in the struggle to understand and apply these texts, one may come to perceive the importance of real words. A Bible translation should be the occasion for reaffirming the human desire to speak and be heard, for encouraging people to view their lives as a series of statements and responses—conversations, really. In sending the reader back to the text, the Buber-Rosenzweig Bible sought to counter the deadness of contemporary language and contemporary living which were all too apparent at the turn of the century, even before war and genocide began to take their toll. As we approach the end of that century, the same problems remain, altered further by the present revolution in communications. Amid the overcrowded air of cyberspace, the Hebrew Bible may still come to tell us that we do not live by bread alone, and that careful and loving attention to ancient words may help us to form the modern ones that we need.

Everett Fox
Clark University
Worcester, Massachusetts
January 1995
Shevat 5755

I have mentioned that this book should be understood as a performance. Nevertheless, at the present time I have made only a few changes, preferring to leave a more substantial revision—and citation of some excellent articles and books that have appeared in the meantime—for the future. At the same time, I wish to acknowledge the helpful suggestions of a number of scholars: Bernard Levinson (in "Recovering the Lost Original Meaning of *ve-lo' tekhasseh 'alav* [Deuteronomy 13:9]," *Journal of Biblical Literature* 115:4, Winter 1996); Judith Romney Wegner (Deut. 6:7); Marc Brettler (Gen. 22); and Robert Alter, in *Genesis: Translation and Commentary* (New York: W. W. Norton and Co., 1996).

Worcester, Massachusetts
January 1997

ACKNOWLEDGMENTS

IT IS AN IMPOSSIBLE TASK TO ADEQUATELY THANK ALL THOSE WHO HAVE HELPED IN THIS long-term project, in ways great and small. I will therefore have to content myself with mentioning mostly the more recent recipients of my gratitude, with apologies to others for omitting their names.

First and foremost I should like to thank Professor Edward L. Greenstein of the Jewish Theological Seminary of America, who since before the onset of the Schocken project has given me encouragement, used my material in teaching, and been overly generous with his time and expert advice, particularly philological. He has articulated the rationale for this translation in his writings, and has been a solid support and appropriately meticulous critic in many conversations over the years. Beginning with the book of Exodus, he has also served as painstaking chief reader of my manuscript; I have adopted numerous suggestions of his in both the text and the accompanying material. Our discussions on many words (such as *nidda* in Lev. 12:2 and *yovel* in Lev. 25:10) proved decisive for me. That said, all responsibility for what appears in these pages is mine alone.

Bonny Fetterman at Schocken Books has supplied endless patience, good cheer, and creative solutions to nasty logistical problems of production. Her counsel and support go back many years, and were crucial in getting me through the long haul. Arthur Samuelson, who originally signed me for this project, has returned to Schocken exactly in time to handle the final product's entry into the world. I am glad to have his energy and expertise on board.

Professor Steven Hall, as a graduate student at Brandeis University, was of considerable help to me in procuring secondary materials, particularly on Leviticus and Numbers.

Being on sabbatical in 1993–94 in Israel afforded me the opportunity for a final push on the last three books. I wish to thank the staff at Hebrew Union College in Jerusalem for their kindness in providing me with a well-supplied and quiet library in which to work near my home; the Hebrew University Library was of course also quite helpful. I am also grateful to Avivah Zornberg for the opportunity to attend weekly study sessions with her; her mastery of midrashic and medieval material and their profundities helped to stimulate my rather "plain meaning"-oriented brain in ways which may not be apparent in my text but which are there nevertheless. Lastly, I have the sad task of expressing gratitude too late in print to Joy Ungerleider Mayerson, who died in 1994. As head of the Dorot Foundation, she was kind enough to supply me with a grant for the year to finish this work. As a patroness of many important cultural and religious activities and institutions, she will be profoundly missed.

I am deeply grateful to all those who over the years have written me or communicated verbally about their experiences using my texts in various settings. This concentrated use of the material—whether in college classes on the humanities, religious schools, synagogue or church services, or private or family study groups—has been a prime influence on my desire and ability to forge ahead with this work.

Several colleagues deserve mention here for stimulating my thinking and for sharing in the spirit of the project. I should like to thank Professor Lawrence Rosenwald for the wonderful experience of collaborating on the translation and presentation of *Scripture and Translation,* Buber and Rosenzweig's collected essays on the Bible and its rendering into German. I am also grateful to Professors Susan Handelman and Lewis Glinert for their insights over the past year, and to Drs. F. J. Hoogewoud and Martin Kessler for introducing me to the work of Dutch scholars, kindred spirits in their approach to the biblical text.

Two scholars were particularly gracious as this project came to a close: Professor Marc Brettler, who shared with me the galleys of his fine study, *The Creation of History in Ancient Israel*, and suggested various materials relating to the book of Deuteronomy; and Professor Jeffrey Tigay, who permitted me to see a draft version of his major new commentary on Deuteronomy (to appear as the final volume of the *JPS Torah Commentary* series). In connection with the latter, I wish also to thank Dr. Ellen Frankel of the Jewish Publication Society for her quick and helpful response.

I continue to benefit greatly from my colleagues in the Department of Foreign Languages and Literatures at Clark University; their warmth and collegiality around issues of language, identity, and culture are a source of nourishment to me. I wish also to thank the university administration for faculty development funds that they provided me early in the process of translating the final three books.

I am grateful to many friends who over the years have followed my work with interest and encouragement. Chief among these is William Novak, whose meaningful support and advice have stretched from 1971 to the present.

I would like to thank my children, Akiva, Leora, and Ezra, who have had to put up with a father whose brain may often have seemed to be in another millennium. Most of all, I would like to acknowledge the help of my wife, Cherie Koller-Fox, who has seen this project through since 1971, and has had to live with my none-too-easy journey through this work. Our conversations on the text and categories of Leviticus in particular have helped immeasurably to clarify my thinking on biblical issues. *Now He Called* is for her, with love.

Finally, praise to the One who has helped me survive, and sustained me, and brought me to this moment.

ON THE NAME OF GOD
AND ITS TRANSLATION

THE READER WILL IMMEDIATELY NOTICE THAT THE PERSONAL NAME OF THE BIBLICAL God appears in this volume as "YHWH." That is pretty standard scholarly practice, but it does not indicate how the name should be pronounced. I would recommend the use of traditional "the LORD" in reading aloud, but others may wish to follow their own custom. While the visual effect of "YHWH" may be jarring at first, it has the merit of approximating the situation of the Hebrew text as we now have it, and of leaving open the unsolved question of the pronunciation and meaning of God's name. Some explanation is in order.

The name of God has undergone numerous changes in both its writing and translation throughout the history of the Bible. At an early period the correct pronunciation of the name was either lost or deliberately avoided out of a sense of religious awe. Jewish tradition came to vocalize and pronounce the name as "Adonai," that is, "the/my Lord," a usage that has remained in practice since late antiquity. Another euphemism, regularly used among Orthodox Jews today, is "Ha-Shem," literally, "The Name."

Historically, Jewish and Christian translations of the Bible into English have tended to use "Lord," with some exceptions (notably, Moffatt's "The Eternal"). Both old and new attempts to recover the "correct" pronunciation of the Hebrew name have not succeeded; neither the sometimes-heard "Jehovah" nor the standard scholarly "Yahweh" can be conclusively proven.

For their part, Buber and Rosenzweig sought to restore some of what they felt was the name's ancient power; early drafts of their Genesis translation reveal a good deal of experimentation in this regard. They finally settled on a radical solution: representing the name by means of capitalized personal pronouns. The use of YOU, HE, HIM, etc., stemmed from their conviction that God's name is not a proper name in the conventional sense, but rather one which evokes his immediate presence. Buber and Rosenzweig—both of whom wrote a great deal about their interpretation (see Buber and Rosenzweig 1994) based it on their reading of Ex. 3:14, a text in which another verbal form of YHWH appears, and which they translated as "I will be-there howsoever I will be-there" (i.e., my name is not a magical handle through which I can be conjured up; I am ever-present). For more on this passage, and the name, see the Commentary and Notes in the text below.

The B-R rendering has its attractiveness in reading aloud, as is demonstrated by recordings of Buber reading his text, but it is on doubtful grounds etymologically. It also introduces an overly male emphasis through its constant use of "HE," an emphasis which is not quite so pronounced in the Hebrew. For these reasons, and out of a desire to reflect the experience of the Hebrew reader, I have followed the practice of transcribing the name as Yhwh.

Readers who are uncomfortable with the maleness of God in these texts may wish to substitute "God" for "he" in appropriate passages. While, as a translator, I am committed to reproducing the text as faithfully as I can, it is also true that the ancient Hebrews viewed God as a divinity beyond sexuality, and modern readers as well may see fit to acknowledge this.

GUIDE TO THE PRONUNCIATION
OF HEBREW NAMES

THE PRECISE PRONUNCIATION OF BIBLICAL HEBREW CANNOT BE DETERMINED WITH certainty. The following guide uses a standard of pronunciation which is close to that of modern Hebrew, and which will serve for the purpose of reading the text aloud.

a (e.g., Adam, Avraham, Aharon) as in f*a*ther (never as in b*a*t)
e or *ei* (e.g., Lea, Levi, Rahel, Esav) as the *a* in c*a*pe (never as the *e* in b*e*)
o (e.g., Edom, Lot, Moshe) as in st*o*ne (never as in h*o*t)
u (e.g., Luz, Zevulun, Shur) as in B*u*ber (never as in s*u*n)

When *e* occurs in both syllables of a name (e.g., Hevel, Peleg), it is generally pronounced as the *e* in t*e*n. In such cases the first syllable is the accented one; generally speaking, Hebrew accents the last syllable.

When *e* is the second letter of a name (e.g., Devora, Yehuda, Betzalel), it is often pronounced as the *a* in *a*go.

kh (e.g., Hanokh, Yissakhar) is to be sounded like the *ch* in Johann Sebastian Ba*ch*.

h (e.g., Havva, Het, Hur) most often indicates Hebrew *het*, pronounced less heavily than *kh* but not as English *h*. I have removed the *h* from names (e.g., Yehuda for Judah) to avoid confusion in this regard.

The system for transcribing Hebrew words used in this volume follows the above model, rather than standard scholarly practice (e.g., *k-r-v* instead of *qrb*, *sh-r-tz* instead of *šrṣ*), in the interests of the general reader. For this reason, I also do not distinguish here between the Hebrew letters *alef* and *ayin* in transcription, even though technically their pronunciations differ. I have, however, added an apostrophe when the lack of one might lead the reader to mispronounce the word (e.g., Se'ir, Be'er).

Some well-known names in the text have been transcribed in their traditional English spelling. These include Canaan (Heb. *Kenaan*), Egypt (*Mitzrayim*), Israel (*Yisrael*), Jordan (*Yarden*), Pharaoh (*Par'o*), and Sinai (*Seenai*). Otherwise, I have indicated the familiar English forms of the names in the Notes, under the rubric "Trad. English. . . ."

TO AID THE READER OF GENESIS AND EXODUS

GIVEN THE ILLUSTRIOUS PREDECESSORS THAT ANY TRANSLATOR OF GENESIS AND Exodus follows, I have not tried to provide here either a comprehensive commentary or an all-encompassing system of notes. Rather, I have sought to suggest some fruitful avenues for thought and discussion in the Commentary, and to provide such information in the Notes as will be helpful to the nonspecialist. Naturally, the selection of material for these purposes is entirely mine; others might single out different details and different aspects of the text.

Since I have espoused a "rhetorical" approach to biblical texts in my work, I have decided to limit myself largely to literary remarks in the Commentary: indicating themes and motifs as they appear and are developed in these books and elsewhere in the Bible; pointing out structural aspects of the text; and treating issues of character development in the narrative. I have by and large eschewed historical issues, and those pertaining to the origins and textual history of Genesis and Exodus. These matters, which are highly theoretical and subject to detailed and often heated scholarly discussion, are treated comprehensively in standard works such as Speiser (1964) for Genesis and Childs (1974) for Exodus (see also the volumes of the Jewish Publication Society's *The Torah Commentary,* currently appearing). More detailed information on the ancient Near Eastern background and parallels to Genesis and Exodus can be found in Cassuto (1967, 1972/1974) and Sarna (1966, 1986). Readers whose interest is primarily archaeological will seek works such as Mazar (1990).

בראשית

—◦◦◦—

Genesis

—◦◦◦—

At the Beginning

ON THE BOOK OF GENESIS
AND ITS STRUCTURE

THE TEXT OF GENESIS SEEMS TO SPEAK WITH MANY VOICES. FOR A BOOK WHOSE BASIC arrangement is chronological, tracing the history of a single family, it exhibits a good deal of discontinuity on the surface. Here time flows uniformly, there it takes startling jumps; fragments are followed by more or less full-blown tales; genres alternate, from mythic to genealogical to folkloristic. In addition, scholars often portray Genesis as a collection of historically diverse materials that were compiled by scribes for whom deviating from received tradition was anathema. Hence the repetitions, the inconsistencies, and the irregular pacing.

Is Genesis then, at best, a collection of stories related to the origins of Israel, with most of its seams still showing? Such an assessment does not do justice to what must have been a complex process of addition and growth or to the final product. An overview of the book does produce a certain scheme; at some point in the text's history a coherent picture must have begun to emerge from the disparate materials handed down. For the modern reader, utilizing the Buber-Rosenzweig method of focusing on repeating words and key themes as the text presents them may make it possible to generalize about the organization of the book and also to speculate on its overall intent in the form in which it has come down to us.

On its most obvious level Genesis is a book about origins. It seeks to link the origin of the people of Israel with that of the world, relating in the process how various human characteristics and institutions arose.

On the surface this parallels much of ancient literature and folklore. All peoples are interested in their own beginnings, picturing them in a way which validates their present existence. Genesis, however, is different in that, like the rest of the Torah, it downplays the heroic element of the people's origins and in its place stresses God's role in them. Moreover the one great omission—the origin of God—establishes from the beginning a unique basis for a tribal chronicle. From Genesis and subsequent books we learn primarily about God's relationship to the people and what he expects of them; almost everything else is subordinated to this purpose.

Preliminarily one can speak of at least seven major themes whose recurrence establishes their importance in the book:

1. *Origins:* Of the world, of humanity, and of the people of Israel.
2. *Order/Meaning in History:* By means of stylized or patterned chronology—reliance on certain round numbers such as 3, 7, and 40—it is suggested that human events are not random but somehow planned.

3. *Blessing:* From creation onward God bestows blessings on his creatures in general and on the fathers and mothers of Israel in particular.
4. *Covenant:* God concludes agreements with human beings.
5. *God Punishes Evildoing:* God is provoked to anger not by his capriciousness but by human failure to uphold justice and morality.
6. *Sibling Conflict, with the Younger Usually Emerging the Victor:* The order of nature (primacy of the firstborn) is overturned, demonstrating that God, not nature, is the ruling principle in human affairs.
7. *Testing:* God tests those who are to carry forth his mission; the result is the development of moral character.

Superseding these important themes, which occur throughout the Bible in various forms, is the dominant one of *continuity*, represented by the unifying word in Genesis *toledot* ("begettings"). The word appears eleven times, often accompanied by long genealogical lists. The names may deflect attention from what is central to Genesis. The major thrust of the book would seem to be toward human fecundity, following the early divine command to "bear fruit and be many" (1:28), and pointing toward the eventual fecundity of the people of Israel (which will only be realized in the book of Exodus). Such an emphasis seems appropriate in a book about origins.

Ironically, however, the undercurrent in Genesis points not to life and its continuation, but rather to its threatened extinction. In story after story the protagonist, his people, and occasionally the entire world are threatened. In at least one case (Avraham) a perfectly legal and natural solution is found—the birth of Yishmael as his heir—only to be rejected by God in favor of a more difficult one: a son born to an elderly woman.

It is clear that the stress on continuity and discontinuity has one purpose: to make clear that God is in control of history. Human fertility and continuity in history come not from magical rites or from the arbitrary decisions of the gods, but from a God who bases his rule on justice. Nature disappears as a ruling factor in human affairs, replaced by a principle of morality which is unshakable precisely because it comes from a God who is beyond the rules of nature.

But the result is a book which abounds in tension. From the beginnings of human history (Chap. 4) we encounter contradictions and opposites, whether on a small scale (fertility and barrenness) or a large one (promise and delayed fulfillment). Nowhere is this so clear as in the dramatic high point of the book, Chap. 22. As Avraham stands with knife upraised, the entire enterprise of Genesis hangs in the balance. But the entire book is replete with such tensions and continuity-threatening situations. There are barren wives, brothers vowing to kill brothers, cities and even a world being destroyed by an angry God. The main characters of Genesis thus emerge as survivors, above all else. Noah sets the pattern, but he is merely the first, and too passive an example. The Patriarchs must brave hostile foreigners, bitter intrafamily struggles, and long wanderings before they can find peace.

While by the end of the book many of the tensions have been resolved, one conspicuously has not: God's promise of the land of Canaan. As the book ends, "in Egypt," we are left to ponder how this God, who keeps his promises to "those who love him" (Ex. 20:6), will bring the people back to their land—a land inhabited by someone else and in which the Children of Israel own only a burial site. Yet despite the tension, we may assume from the experiences of the Patriarchs that God will indeed "take account of" the Israelites (50:24), that he will take whatever ill has been planned against them and "plan-it-over for good" (50:20).

A word should also be said here about hero traditions. In the great epics of the ancient world the hero often stands as a lonely figure. He must overcome obstacles, fight monsters, acquire helpers (whether women, "sidekicks," or magic objects); and his triumph in the end signals man's triumph over his archenemy, Death. Every battle won, every obstacle hurdled, is psychologically a victory for us, the audience, a cathartic release from our own frustrating battle against death.

The Bible sees things rather differently. Death is also overcome, but not only by the individual's struggle. It is rather through the covenant community, bound together by God's laws and his promises, that the heroic vision is lived out. Despite the triumphs of the characters in Genesis, it is really in the book of Exodus that the great battle scenes (the plagues in Egypt, the Red Sea) and meetings with the divine (Mount Sinai) take place. And it is therefore God himself who is most properly the "hero" of these stories. No major character in Genesis achieves success without depending fully on God, and the standards that are held up to them are ultimately seen as God's own, to be imitated by imperfect humankind.

The book of Genesis falls naturally into four large sections. The first, usually termed the "Primeval History" (Chaps. 1–11), begins with creation and progresses through the early generations of humanity, ending in Mesopotamia. The second (Chaps. 12 through 25:18) is the cycle of stories concerning Avraham, the father of the people of Israel. Part III (Gen. 25:19 through Chap. 36) deals in the main with stories about his grandson Yaakov. The final section (Chaps. 37–50) is the tale of Yosef and of how the Children of Israel came to live in Egypt (thus paving the way for the book of Exodus).

The following skeletal outline will lay out some of the interesting structural features of the book. There is an elemental symmetry that emerges from the four sections; further comments, especially about how the sections cohere, will be found in the explanatory material accompanying the text in this volume.

    I. Chosen Figure (Noah)
       Sibling Hatred (Kayin–Hevel), with sympathy for youngest
       Family Continuity Threatened (Hevel murdered)

Ends with Death (Haran, Terah; Sarai barren)
  Humanity Threatened (Flood)
  Ends Away from Land of Israel ("In Harran")

II. Chosen Figure (Avraham)
  Sibling Hatred (Yishmael–Yitzhak) Implied, with sympathy for
    youngest
  Family Continuity Threatened (Sarai barren, Yitzhak almost
    sacrificed)
  Ends with Death (Sara, Avraham)
    Rivalry Between Wives (Hagar–Sarai)
    Barren Wife (Sarai)
    Wife–Sister Story (Chaps. 12 and 20)
    Ends with Genealogy of Non-Covenant Line (Yishmael)

III: Chosen Figure (Yaakov)
  Sibling Hatred (Esav–Yaakov), with sympathy for youngest
  Family Continuity Threatened (Yaakov almost killed)
  Ends with Death (Devora, Rahel, Yitzhak)
    Rivalry Between Wives (Lea–Rahel)
    Barren Wife (Rahel)
    Wife–Sister Story (Chap. 26)
    Ends with Genealogy of Non-Covenant Line (Esav)

IV. Chosen Figure (Yosef)
  Sibling Hatred (Brothers–Yosef), with sympathy for youngest
  Family Continuity Threatened (Yehuda's sons die; Yosef almost
    killed; family almost dies in famine)
  Ends with Death (Yaakov, Yosef)
    Humanity Threatened (Famine)
    Ends Away from Land of Israel ("In Egypt")

There is of course great variety within this bare structure; each version of a motif has its own special characteristics and emphases. Yet the patterning observed above gives the book a general coherence, above and beyond differences. It also demonstrates a conscious hand at work, one concerned about the texture of the book as a whole and able, despite the possible rigidity of what had been handed down, to shape the received material into a plastic and breathing unity.

Two general observations about Genesis will round out the picture here. First, as the book progresses there is a tendency for the style of the literature to become smoother. The abrupt changes and sometimes fragmentary nature of the material in Part I, and the vignettes built around Avraham's life in Part II, give way to a greater coherence and concentration in Part III, and finally to a relatively flowing and psychologically complete narrative in Part IV. Along with this, the characters in the latter half of the book seem to be more changeable and human, in contrast to Noah and Avraham, who often appear almost perfect models of piety.

Second, contact with God becomes less and less direct as Genesis moves on. Avraham's dreams and visions seem a far cry from Adam's conversations with God in the garden (although see Chap. 18); Yaakov's encounters with God are less frequent than Avraham's; and finally, Yosef never has a conversation with God, although he receives dream interpretations from him. This process of distancing may reflect an often-observed tendency in religions to think of primeval times as a "golden age" of closeness between gods and men, as contrasted to today (whenever one is writing), when humankind finds itself tragically distant from the divine and in need of communication.

PART I

THE PRIMEVAL HISTORY

(1–11)

THE COLLECTION OF STORIES WHICH FORMS PART I OF GENESIS HAS BEEN ASSEMBLED for a number of purposes:

1. History is traced from the creation of the world, in a direct line, down to Avraham, father of the People of Israel. Through use of the leading-word *toledot*, "begettings," we are meant to view him as the logical end point in God's preliminary plan in history.

2. The nature of God, as he will appear throughout the Hebrew Bible, is firmly established. He is seen as a Creator who is beyond fate, nature, and sexuality; as an all-powerful orderer and giver of meaning to history; as a bestower of blessing to living creatures; as a giver of choice to human beings; as a just punisher of evil and, simultaneously, a merciful ruler; and as a maker of covenants. The one quality of God which does not unfold until the Patriarchal stories (Parts II-IV) is his shaping of human destiny through focusing on the People of Israel. It is portrayed as the logical outcome of the characteristics just mentioned.

3. It appears that the Mesopotamian origins of Israel are reflected in such narratives as the Creation, the Flood, and the Tower of Babel, and are transformed or repudiated in the biblical versions. What in the older culture appears arbitrary and chaotic has been changed in the Bible into stories that stress morality and order. Further, human beings in Genesis Chapters 1–11, despite their failure to live up to God's expectations, are nevertheless considered capable of doing so, in contrast to the Mesopotamian view that humankind was created merely to be slaves to the gods.

4. Like virtually all other creation stories, Part I is concerned with the origin of the world and its institutions. Chapter 1 expounds on the origins of earth, sky, vegetation, animals, and human beings (as well as the Sabbath); Chapter 2, of sexuality, death, pain in childbirth, and work; Chapter 4, of sin, hatred, and murder, as well as of cities and crafts; Chapter 6, of giants; and Chapter 10, of nations (including the low status of the Canaanites) and languages.

In sum, Part I serves as a fitting Prologue, not only to Genesis but to the entire Bible. The reader's chief task in interpreting it is to be able to determine the reason for the inclusion of any one section into the whole.

God as Creator (1:1–2:4a): Three principal themes emerge from the great creation account with which Genesis opens. The first is the total and uncompromised power of God as creator; the second, the intrinsic order and balance of the created world; and the third, humankind's key position in the scheme of creation. These themes are brought home as much by the form in which they are presented as by their actual mention.

God (Heb. *elohim,* a generic term) is introduced into the narrative without any description of origins, sex, or limitations of power. As the only functioning character of the chapter, he occupies center stage. There is no opposition, no resistance to his acts of creation, which occur in perfect harmony with his express word.

As a sign of both God's total control and his intent, the world unfolds in symmetrical order. The division of God's labor into six days, plus a seventh for rest, itself indicates a powerful meaningfulness at work, as well as providing the external structure for the narrative. Interpreters have tended to divide these into either three groups of two days or two groups of three, with always the same results: a balanced and harmonious whole. In addition, the number seven is significant (as it will be elsewhere in the Bible) as a symbol of perfection, not only in Israel but in the ancient world in general.

The narrative uses several repeating words and phrases to both unify the story and underscore the theme of order. These include "God said," "Let there be. . . ," "God saw that it was good," "It was so," and "There was setting, there was dawning. . . ."

A

I:I ┌ t the beginning of God's creating
of the heavens and the earth,

1 **At the beginning**…:This phrase, which has long been the focus of debate among grammarians, is traditionally read: "In the beginning God created the heavens and the earth." B-R agrees, I have followed several medieval commentators, and most moderns, in my rendition. **creating**: Indicative of God's power and not used in reference to humans, although later in the chapter such words as "make" and "form" do appear. **the heavens and the earth:** Probably a merism—an inclusive idiom meaning "everything" or "everywhere"—such as in Hamlet's "There are more things in heaven and earth…."

The text is so formed as to highlight the creation of humankind. Although in each previous day "God said" is the keynote, suggesting forethought as well as action, here (v.26) God fully spells out his intentions, as it were, thinking out loud. Humanity, created in the divine "image," is to hold sway over the rest of creation. Only with the addition of humankind is God able to survey his newly formed world and to pronounce it "exceedingly good" (v.31).

At least two motifs appear in this chapter which will become important later in Genesis. The three occurrences of "blessing" (1:22, 1:28, 2:3) point to a central idea in the Patriarchal stories. In addition the concept of order and its logical conclusion—that history makes sense—figures prominently in the familial histories of the book. This is accomplished largely by the meaningful use of numbers, as above.

The entire account concludes (2:1–3) with a tightly structured poem. "God," "the seventh day," "work," and "made" are mentioned three times, "finished," "ceased," and "all" twice; and "created" returns, echoing 1:1, to round out the whole creation narrative.

The postscript (2:4a; some scholars align it with what follows in Chap. 2 instead) introduces the key structural phrase of Genesis, "These are the begettings...." It may also indicate the polemical intent of the creation story. Rosenzweig understood the verse to contrast "begetting," i.e., sexual creation as it occurs in non-Israelite myths, with the "true" creation.

In that vein, a final word needs to be said about extrabiblical evidence. As has often been pointed out, Gen. 1 is unmistakably reacting against prevailing Near Eastern cosmogonies of the time. Most of the cultures surrounding ancient Israel had elaborate creation stories, highlighting the birth, sexuality, and violent uprisings of the gods. As we indicated at the outset, the concept of God presented here militates against such ideas, arguing chiefly out of omission and silence. (It should also be noted that in poetic books such as Isaiah, Job, and Psalms, a tradition about violent conflict at creation has been preserved.) The Genesis narrative has taken such old mythological motifs as battles with the primeval (female) waters or with sea monsters and eliminated or neutralized them. What remains is both utterly simple and radical in its time.

◆

2   when the earth was wild and waste,
    darkness over the face of Ocean,
    rushing-spirit of God hovering over the face of the waters—

3   God said: Let there be light! And there was light.
4   God saw the light: that it was good.
    God separated the light from the darkness.
5   God called the light: Day! and the darkness he called: Night!
    There was setting, there was dawning: one day.

6   God said:
    Let there be a dome amid the waters,
    and let it separate waters from waters!
7   God made the dome
    and separated the waters that were below the dome from the
        waters that were above the dome.
    It was so.
8   God called the dome: Heaven!
    There was setting, there was dawning: second day.

9   God said:
    Let the waters under the heavens be gathered to one place,
    and let the dry land be seen!
    It was so.

---

2 **when the earth** . . . : Gen. 1 describes God's bringing order out of chaos, not creation from noth-
ingness. **wild and waste:** Heb. *tohu va-vohu,*
indicating "emptiness." **Ocean:** The primeval waters, a common (and usually divine) image in ancient Near Eastern mythology. **rushing-spirit:**
Others, "wind." The Hebrew word *ruah* can mean
both "spirit" and "wind." See Ps. 33:6. **hovering:**
Or "flitting." The image suggested by the word (see
Deut. 32:11) is that of an eagle protecting its young.

3–5 **God said . . . God saw . . . God separated . . .
God called:** Here, from the outset of the story, the
principle of order is stressed, through the rhythmic
structure of "God" plus verb, four times.

4 **God saw . . . that it was good:** The syntax is em-

phatic; others use "God saw how good it was." The
phrase is reminiscent of ancient Near Eastern descriptions of a craftsman being pleased with his
work. **separated:** The verb occurs four more times
early in the chapter (vv.6, 7, 14, 18), and further
points to the motif of order.

5 **setting . . . dawning:** The Heb. terms *erev* and
boker are rather more specific than the usual
"evening" and "morning." Elsewhere I have used
"sunset" and "daybreak"; the latter would have
clashed with "day" in these lines.

6 **dome:** Heb. *raki'a,* literally a beaten sheet of
metal.

8 **Heaven!:** The sky.

10 God called the dry land: Earth! and the gathering of the waters
   he called: Seas!
   God saw that it was good.
11 God said:
   Let the earth sprout forth with sprouting-growth,
   plants that seed forth seeds, fruit trees that yield fruit, after their
   kind, (and) in which is their seed, upon the earth!
   It was so.
12 The earth brought forth sprouting-growth,
   plants that seed forth seeds, after their kind,
   trees that yield fruit, in which is their seed, after their kind.
   God saw that it was good.
13 There was setting, there was dawning: third day.

14 God said:
   Let there be lights in the dome of the heavens, to separate the
   day from the night,
   that they may be for signs—for set-times, for days and years,
15 and let them be for lights in the dome of the heavens, to provide
   light upon the earth!
   It was so.
16 God made the two great lights,
   the greater light for ruling the day and the smaller light for ruling
   the night,
   and the stars.
17 God placed them in the dome of the heavens
18 to provide light upon the earth, to rule the day and the night, to
   separate the light from the darkness.
   God saw that it was good.
19 There was setting, there was dawning: fourth day.

---

11 **sprout forth with sprouting-growth . . . seed forth seeds . . . fruit trees . . . fruit:** The three sound doublets create a poetic effect in God's pronouncement. Note that they are not repeated by the narrator in verse 12. See also v.20, ". . . swarm with a swarm . . ." **after their kind:** Here as in a number of passages in the translation I have shifted some words that occur in the singular (especially collectives) for the sake of clarity. See, for example, 6:3, 5.
14 **lights:** In the sense of "lamps." **for signs—for set-times . . . :** Hebrew difficult.

20 God said:
Let the waters swarm with a swarm of living beings, and let fowl
fly above the earth, across the dome of the heavens!

21 God created the great sea-serpents
and all living beings that crawl about, with which the waters
swarmed, after their kind,
and all winged fowl after their kind.
God saw that it was good.

22 And God blessed them, saying:
Bear fruit and be many and fill the waters in the seas,
and let the fowl be many on earth!

23 There was setting, there was dawning: fifth day.

24 God said:
Let the earth bring forth living beings after their kind,
herd-animals, crawling things, and the wildlife of the earth after
their kind!
It was so.

25 God made the wildlife of the earth after their kind, and the herd-
animals after their kind, and all crawling things of the soil after
their kind.
God saw that it was good.

26 God said:
Let us make humankind, in our image, according to our likeness!
Let them have dominion over the fish of the sea, the fowl of the
heavens, animals, all the earth, and all crawling things that
crawl about upon the earth!

27 So God created humankind in his image,
in the image of God did he create it,
male and female he created them.

---

21 **great sea-serpents:** The rebellious primeval mon-
ster of Ps. 74:13 (and common in ancient Near Eastern myth) is here depicted as merely another one of
God's many creations.

22 **And God blessed them:** The first occurrence in
Genesis of the key motif of blessing, which recurs
especially throughout the Patriarchal stories. **Bear
fruit and be many and fill:** Heb. *peru u-revu u-mil'u.*

26 **in our image:** The "our" is an old problem. Some
take it to refer to the heavenly court (although, not
surprisingly, no angels are mentioned here).

27 **God created humankind:** The narrative breaks
into verse, stressing the importance of human beings. "Humankind" (Heb. *adam*) does not specify
sex, as is clear from the last line of the poem.

Garden and Expulsion (2:4b–3:24): From the perspective of God in Chap. 1, we now switch to that of humankind (note how the opening phrase in 2:4b, "earth and heaven," reverses the order found in 1:1). This most famous of all Genesis stories contains an assortment of mythic elements and images which are common to human views of prehistory: the lush garden, four central rivers located (at least partially) in fabled lands, the mysterious trees anchoring the garden (and the world?), a primeval man and woman living in unashamed nakedness, an animal that talks, and a God who converses regularly and intimately with his creatures. The narrative presents itself, at least on the surface, as a story of origins. We are to learn the roots of human sexual feelings, of pain in childbirth, and how the anomalous snake (a land creature with no legs) came to assume its present form. Most strikingly, of course, the story seeks to explain the origin of the event most central to human consciousness: death.

The narrative unfolds through a series of contrasts: good and evil, life and death, heaven and earth, give and take, knowledge and ignorance, humans and animals, hiding and revealing. Some of these concepts appear literally as key words in the text. The characters also appear through contrasts: man as God's image and as dust, woman as helper and hinderer, the snake as shrewd and (after the curse) lowly.

A further focus is provided by the echoing of the word "eat," whose connotation changes from sustenance/bounty (2:9, 16) to prohibition (2:17) to misunderstanding (3:1–5) and disobedience (3:6, 11–13), and finally to curse (3:14, 17, 19). Such a flexible use of words sets up a rhythmic drama which, as much of Genesis, bears resemblance to poetry rather than to prose.

Part I of the story (Chap. 2) sets the stage in the garden, focusing on *Adam,* "Everyman" (see *Cambridge Bible Commentary,* Gen. I–II). God is here regularly called "YHWH, God," a rare designation which may suggest a preexpulsion view of the wholeness of God as well as of humankind. Man continues his status as "God's image" (1:26–27), imitating the divine act of giving names (1:5, 8, 10). He is also nevertheless a creature of the dust, both at the beginning (2:7) and end (3:19) of the story.

The bridge to Part II (Chap. 3) is deftly accomplished by linking two identical-sounding words in the Hebrew, *arum* (here, "nude" and "shrewd"). The choice of the snake as the third character is typically ancient Near Eastern (it is so used in other stories about death and immortality, such as the *Gilgamesh Epic* from Mesopotamia). Some interpreters have seen sexual overtones in this choice as well. Yet a plain reading of the text need not overemphasize the snake, who disappears as a personality once the fatal fruit has been eaten.

The ending of the story has also raised questions of interpretation. Buber was among those who see in the act of expulsion from the garden a deed of mercy rather than one of fear or jealousy. Certainly a creature whose first act upon ac-

28 God blessed them,
God said to them:
Bear fruit and be many and fill the earth
and subdue it!
Have dominion over the fish of the sea, the fowl of the heavens,
and all living things that crawl about upon the earth!

29 God said:
Here, I give you
all plants that bear seeds that are upon the face of all the earth,
and all trees in which there is tree fruit that bears seeds,
for you shall they be, for eating;

30 and also for all the living things of the earth, for all the fowl of
the heavens, for all that crawls about upon the earth in which
there is living being—
all green plants for eating.
It was so.

31 Now God saw all that he had made,
and here: it was exceedingly good!
There was setting, there was dawning: the sixth day.

2:1 Thus were finished the heavens and the earth, with all of their
array.

2 God had finished, on the seventh day, his work that he had made,
and then he ceased, on the seventh day, from all his work that he
had made.

3 God gave the seventh day his blessing, and he hallowed it,
for on it he ceased from all his work, that by creating, God had
made.

4 These are the begettings of the heavens and the earth: their
being created.

At the time of YHWH, God's making of earth and heaven,

---

29 **I give you:** "You" in the plural.
30 **all green plants for eating:** Human beings in their original state were not meat-eaters. For the change, see 9:3ff.
31 **exceedingly good . . . the sixth day:** The two qualifiers "exceedingly" and "the" are deviations from the previous expressions in the story, and underscore the sixth day (when humankind was created)

as the crowning achievement of creation (or else serve as a summary to the whole).
2:3 **gave . . . his blessing:** Or "blessed," here expanded in English for rhythmical reasons. **by creating, God had made:** Hebrew difficult. Buber's working papers show numerous attempts at a solution.
4b YHWH For a discussion of the name of God and its translation and pronunciation, see p. xxix.

quiring new "knowledge" is to cover himself up poses no threat to the Creator. The text, like its late successor, the book of Job, may be suggesting that in the human sphere, unlike the divine, knowledge and mortality are inextricably linked. This is a tragic realization, but it is also the world as human beings know it.

Although the specifics of this story are never again referred to in the Hebrew Bible, and are certainly not crucial for the rest of Genesis, one general theme *is* central to the Bible's worldview. This is that rebellion against or disobedience toward God and his laws results in banishment/estrangement and, literally or figuratively, death. Thus from the beginning the element of *choice,* so much stressed by the Prophets later on, is seen as the major element in human existence.

All this said, it should be recognized that the garden story, like many biblical texts, has been the subject of endless interpretation. One line of thought takes the psychological point of view. The story resembles a vision of childhood and of the transition to the contradictions and pain of adolescence and adulthood. In every way—moral, sexual, and intellectual—Adam and Havva are like children, and their actions after partaking of the fruit seem like the actions of those who are unable to cope with newfound powers. The resolution of the story, banishment from the garden, suggests the tragic realization that human beings must make their way through the world with the knowledge of death and with great physical difficulty. At the same time the archetypal man and woman do not make the journey alone. They are provided with protection (clothing), given to them by the same God who punished them for their disobedience. We thus symbolically enter adulthood with the realization that being turned out of Paradise does not mean eternal rejection or hopelessness.

5 no bush of the field was yet on earth,
  no plant of the field had yet sprung up,
  for YHWH, God, had not made it rain upon earth,
  and there was no human/*adam* to till the soil/*adama*—

6 but a surge would well up from the ground and water all the face
    of the soil;

7 and YHWH, God, formed the human, of dust from the soil,
  he blew into his nostrils the breath of life
  and the human became a living being.

8 YHWH, God, planted a garden in Eden/Land-of-Pleasure, in the
    east,
  and there he placed the human whom he had formed.

9 YHWH, God, caused to spring up from the soil
  every type of tree, desirable to look at and good to eat,
  and the Tree of Life in the midst of the garden
  and the Tree of the Knowing of Good and Evil.

10 Now a river goes out from Eden, to water the garden,
   and from there it divides and becomes four stream-heads.

11 The name of the first one is Pishon/Spreader—that is the one
     that circles through all the land of Havila, where gold is;

12 the gold of that land is good, there too are bdellium and the
     precious-stone carnelian.

13 The name of the second river is Gihon/Gusher—that is the one
     that circles through all the land of Cush.

14 The name of the third river is Hiddekel/Tigris—that is the one
     that goes to the east of Assyria.
   And the fourth river—that is Perat/Euphrates.

---

5 **human/*adam* . . . soil/*adama*:** The sound connection, the first folk etymology in the Bible, establishes the intimacy of humankind with the ground (note the curses in 3:17 and 4:11). Human beings are created from the soil, just as animals are (v.19). Some have suggested "human . . . humus" to reflect the wordplay.

6 **surge:** Or "flow."

8 **Eden/Land-of-Pleasure:** For another use of the Hebrew root, see 18:12. The usage here may be a folk etymology; Speiser translates it as "steppe."

9 **Tree of Life:** Conferring immortality on the eater of its fruit. **Knowing of Good and Evil:** Interpreters disagree on the meaning of this phrase. It could be a merism (as in "knowledge from A to Z"—that is, of everything), or an expression of moral choice.

10 **stream-heads:** Branches or tributaries.

12 **bdellium . . . carnelian:** Identification uncertain; others suggest, for instance, "lapis" and "onyx."

15 YHWH, God, took the human and set him in the garden of Eden,
   to work it and to watch it.
16 YHWH, God, commanded concerning the human, saying:
   From every (other) tree of the garden you may eat, yes, eat,
17 but from the Tree of the Knowing of Good and Evil—
   you are not to eat from it,
   for on the day that you eat from it, you must die, yes, die.

18 Now YHWH, God, said:
   It is not good for the human to be alone,
   I will make him a helper corresponding to him.
19 So YHWH, God, formed from the soil every living-thing of the
      field and every fowl of the heavens
   and brought each to the human, to see what he would call it;
   and whatever the human called it as a living being, that became
      its name.
20 The human called out names for every herd-animal and for the
      fowl of the heavens and for every living-thing of the field,
   but for the human, there could be found no helper
      corresponding to him.
21 So YHWH, God, caused a deep slumber to fall upon the human,
      so that he slept,
   he took one of his ribs and closed up the flesh in its place.
22 YHWH, God, built the rib that he had taken from the human into
      a woman
   and brought her to the human.
23 The human said:
      This-time, she-is-it!
      Bone from my bones,

15 **work:** A different Hebrew word (here, *avod*) from the one used in 2:2–3 (*melakha*).
16 **eat, yes, eat:** Heb. *akhol tokhel*, literally, "eating you may eat." Others use "you may freely eat"; I have followed B-R's practice of doubling the verb throughout, which retains the sound as well as the meaning. In this passage, as in many instances, I have inserted the word "yes" for rhythmical reasons.
17 **die, yes, die:** Others use "surely die."
18 **It is not good:** In contrast to the refrain of Gen. I,

"God saw that it was good." **corresponding to:** Lit. "opposite." The whole phrase (Heb. *ezer kenegdo*) could be rendered "a helping counterpart." At any rate, the Hebrew does not suggest a subordinate position for women.
20 **called out:** Or "gave." **for the human:** Others use "for Adam" or "for a man."
21 **ribs:** Or possibly "sides," paralleling other ancient peoples' concept of an original being that was androgynous.

flesh from my flesh!
She shall be called Woman/*Isha,*
for from Man/*Ish* she was taken!

24 Therefore a man leaves his father and his mother and clings to
his wife,
and they become one flesh.

25 Now the two of them, the human and his wife, were nude, yet
they were not ashamed.

3:1 Now the snake was more shrewd than all the living-things of the
field that YHWH, God, had made.
It said to the woman:
Even though God said: You are not to eat from any of the
trees in the garden . . . !

2 The woman said to the snake:
From the fruit of the (other) trees in the garden we may eat,

3 but from the fruit of the tree that is in the midst of the garden,
God has said:
You are not to eat from it and you are not to touch it,
lest you die.

4 The snake said to the woman:
Die, you will not die!

5 Rather, God knows
that on the day that you eat from it, your eyes will be opened
and you will become like gods, knowing good and evil.

6 The woman saw
that the tree was good for eating
and that it was a delight to the eyes,
and the tree was desirable to contemplate.
She took from its fruit and ate
and gave also to her husband beside her,
and he ate.

---

23 **She:** Lit. "this-one."
3:1 **Even though God said:** Others use "Did God really
say . . . ?" **in the garden . . . !:** Such an uncompleted
phrase, known as aposeopesis, leaves it to the reader
to complete the speaker's thought which in the

Bible is usually an oath or a threat (see also, for instance, 14:23, 21:23, 26:29, 31:50).
5 **you:** Plural. **like gods:** Or "like God."

7   The eyes of the two of them were opened
and they knew then
that they were nude.
They sewed fig leaves together and made themselves loincloths.

8   Now they heard the sound of YHWH, God, (who was) walking
about in the garden at the breezy-time of the day.
And the human and his wife hid themselves from the face of
YHWH, God, amid the trees of the garden.

9   YHWH, God, called to the human and said to him:
Where are you?

10 He said:
I heard the sound of you in the garden and I was afraid, because I
am nude,
and so I hid myself.

11 He said:
Who told you that you are nude?
From the tree about which I command you not to eat,
have you eaten?

12 The human said:
The woman whom you gave to be beside me, she gave me from
the tree,
and so I ate.

13 YHWH, God, said to the woman:
What is this that you have done?
The woman said:
The snake enticed me,
and so I ate.

14 YHWH, God, said to the snake:
Because you have done this,
damned be you from all the animals and from all the living-
things of the field;

---

7 **then:** Added in English to avoid a "knew-nude" rhyme.

8 **breezy-time:** Evening. **face of YHWH:** The "face" or presence of God is a dominating theme in many biblical stories and in the book of Psalms. People

seek God's face or hide from it; God reveals it to them or hides it from them.

12 **gave to be:** Put. "Give" has been retained here, despite its awkwardness, as a repeating word in the narrative.

upon your belly shall you walk and dust shall you eat, all the days
of your life.

15 I put enmity between you and the woman, between your seed
and her seed:
they will bruise you on the head, you will bruise them in the
heel.

16 To the woman he said:
I will multiply, multiply your pain (from) your pregnancy,
with pains shall you bear children.
Toward your husband will be your lust, yet he will rule over you.

17 To Adam he said:
Because you have hearkened to the voice of your wife
and have eaten from the tree about which I commanded you,
saying:
You are not to eat from it!
Damned be the soil on your account,
with painstaking-labor shall you eat from it, all the days of your
life.

18 Thorn and sting-shrub let it spring up for you,
when you (seek to) eat the plants of the field!

19 By the sweat of your brow shall you eat bread,
until you return to the soil,
for from it you were taken.
For you are dust, and to dust shall you return.

20 The human called his wife's name: Havva / Life-giver!
For she became the mother of all the living.

21 Now YHWH, God, made Adam and his wife coats of skins and
clothed them.

---

15 **seed:** Offspring, descendants.

17 **painstaking-labor:** Heb. *itzavon*. Man and woman
receive equal curses (see v.16, "pain . . . pains").

18 **sting-shrub:** Heb. *dardar;* thistle ("thorns and this-
tles" suggests an alliteration not found in the Hebrew).

20 **Havva:** Trad. English "Eve."

21 **God . . . clothed them:** Once punishment has been
pronounced, God cares for the man and the
woman. Both aspects of God comprise the biblical
understanding of his nature, and they are not exclusive of each other.

The First Brothers (4:1–16): With the story of Kayin and Hevel the narrative points both forward and backward. For the first time the major Genesis themes of struggle and sibling hatred, and discontinuity between the generations, make their appearance. In addition the concept of *sin* is introduced (Rosenzweig), having not appeared by name previously.

One may observe significant links to the garden story. Once again human beings are given a choice; once again disregarding the warning leads to death and estrangement from God; and once again the primal bond between humanity and the soil is ruptured. Chapter 3 is directly recalled by the use of specific wording: God echoes the curse he had put on the woman (3:16) in his warning to Kayin (4:7), and "Where is Hevel your brother?" (4:9) brings to mind "Where are you?" (3:9), which had been addressed to Kayin's father.

The text is punctuated by the use of "brother," a meaningful seven times, as well as by changing connotations of the word "face" (Kayin, unable to bring about a lifting of his own face, becomes estranged from God's). Repetition also helps to convey the harshness of Kayin's punishment: he is exiled to the "land of Nod/Wandering" (v.16), for which we have been prepared by the "wavering and wandering" of verses 12 and 14.

Although this story may well have originated as a tale of enmity between two ways of life (farmer and shepherd), or in another context, it has obviously been transformed into something far more disturbing and universal.

22 YHWH, God, said:
Here, the human has become like one of us, in knowing good
   and evil.
So now, lest he send forth his hand
and take also from the Tree of Life
and eat
and live throughout the ages . . . !
23 So YHWH, God, sent him away from the garden of Eden, to work
   the soil from which he had been taken.
24 He drove the human out
and caused to dwell, eastward of the garden of Eden,
the winged-sphinxes and the flashing, ever-turning sword
to watch over the way to the Tree of Life.

4:1 The human knew Havva his wife,
she became pregnant and bore Kayin.
She said:
Kaniti / I-have-gotten
a man, as has YHWH!
2 She continued bearing—his brother, Hevel.
Now Hevel became a shepherd of flocks, and Kayin became a
   worker of the soil.

3 It was, after the passing of days
that Kayin brought, from the fruit of the soil, a gift to YHWH,
4 and as for Hevel, he too brought—from the firstborn of his flock,
   from their fat-parts.
YHWH had regard for Hevel and his gift,
5 for Kayin and his gift he had no regard.
Kayin became exceedingly upset and his face fell.

---

22 **one of us:** See note on 1:26. **throughout the ages:**
Or "for the eons"; others use "forever."
24 **winged-sphinxes:** Mythical ancient creatures, also
represented on the Ark of the Covenant (Ex. 25:18).
"Cherubim," the traditional English rendering, has
come to denote chubby, red-cheeked baby angels in
Western art, an image utterly foreign to the ancient
Near East.
4:1 **knew:** Intimately; a term for sexual intercourse.
Kayin: Trad. English "Cain." The name means

"smith" (see also v.22, below). **I-have-gotten:** Others
use "I have created." **as has YHWH:** Hebrew difficult.
2 **Hevel:** The name suggests vapor, steam, i.e.,
"something transitory" (see the opening of the
book of Ecclesiastes: *havel havalim*).
3 **gift:** Heb. *minha,* usually referring to sacrifices of
grain.
4 **fat-parts:** I.e., the choicest.

The Line of Kayin (4:17–26): From whole stories the text turns to several brief accounts, some of which are clearly fragments. The first of these deals with origins: of cities, of certain crafts, and of worship. The former two are associated (perhaps negatively) with Kayin's line. The only personality in these texts about whom we learn anything is Lemekh—and his "saying" (vv.23–24) seems hopelessly obscure. Some interpreters have understood it as a challenge to God, and thus believe that it has been included here as an example of the wickedness typical of the generations that preceded the Flood.

The names of Adam and Havva's son and grandson (vv.25–26) are sad reminders of Hevel's death—a personal touch in an otherwise prosaic section of narrative.

From Adam to Noah (5): The extraordinary numbers in this section are significant, not so much for their length as for their message. Cassuto has tried to fit them into a defined scheme, showing that the purpose, and achieved effect, of our text is to convey that human history follows a meaningful pattern. Pride of place on the list is occupied by the seventh member, Hanokh, who is portrayed as the first man of God. He serves as a preparation for Noah, who also "walks in accord with God" (6:9). Hanokh's life span, 365 years, exemplifies the number scheme of Genesis: as an expression of numerical perfection (the number of days in a year), it symbolizes moral perfection.

6 YHWH said to Kayin:
Why are you so upset? Why has your face fallen?

7 Is it not thus:
If you intend good, bear-it-aloft,
but if you do not intend good,
at the entrance is sin, a crouching-demon,
toward you his lust—
but you can rule over him.

8 Kayin said to Hevel his brother . . .
But then it was, when they were out in the field
that Kayin rose up against Hevel his brother
and he killed him.

9 YHWH said to Kayin:
Where is Hevel your brother?
He said:
I do not know. Am I the watcher of my brother?

10 Now he said:
What have you done!
A sound—your brother's blood cries out to me from the soil!

11 And now,
damned be you from the soil,
which opened up its mouth to receive your brother's blood from
your hand.

12 When you wish to work the soil
it will not henceforth give its strength to you;
wavering and wandering must you be on earth!

13 Kayin said to YHWH:
My iniquity is too great to be borne!

14 Here, you drive me away today from the face of the soil,
and from your face must I conceal myself,
I must be wavering and wandering on earth—

---

7 **Is it not thus . . . :** Hebrew obscure. **bear-it-aloft:** Others use "there is forgiveness," "there is uplift." **toward you his lust—/ but you can rule over him:** Recalling God's words to Havva in 3:16.

8 **Kayin said . . . :** The verse appears incomplete. Ancient versions add "Come, let us go out into the field."

10 **A sound:** Or "Hark!"

now it will be
that whoever comes upon me will kill me!

15 YHWH said to him:
No, therefore,
whoever kills Kayin, sevenfold will it be avenged!
So YHWH set a sign for Kayin,
so that whoever came upon him would not strike him down.

16 Kayin went out from the face of YHWH
and settled in the land of Nod/Wandering, east of Eden.

17 Kayin knew his wife;
she became pregnant and bore Hanokh.
Now he became the builder of a city
and called the city's name according to his son's name,
    Hanokh.

18 To Hanokh was born Irad,
Irad begot Mehuyael,
Mehuyael begot Metushael,
Metushael begot Lemekh.

19 Lemekh took himself two wives,
the name of the (first) one was Ada, the name of the second was
    Tzilla.

20 Ada bore Yaval,
he was the father of those who sit amidst tent and herd.

21 His brother's name was Yuval,
he was the father of all those who play the lyre and the pipe.

22 And Tzilla bore as well—Tuval-Kayin,
burnisher of every blade of bronze and iron.
Tuval-Kayin's sister was Naama.

23 Lemekh said to his wives:
    Ada and Tzilla, hearken to my voice,

---

15 **a sign:** The exact appearance of the sign is not specified. It is a warning and a protection, not the punishment itself (which is exile).
17 **Now he:** "He" refers to Kayin.
18 **Mehuyael begot:** Heb. *Mehiyael.*

19 **Ada . . . Tzilla:** The names suggest "dawn" and "dusk" (Gaster).
20 **father:** Ancestor or founder.
22 **burnisher . . . :** Or "craftsman of every cutting-edge of copper and iron."

wives of Lemekh, give ear to my saying:
Aye—a man I kill for wounding me,
a lad for only bruising me!

24 Aye—if sevenfold vengeance be for Kayin,
then for Lemekh, seventy-sevenfold!

25 Adam knew his wife again, and she bore a son.
She called his name: Shet/Granted-One!
meaning: God has granted me another seed in place of Hevel,
for Kayin killed him.

26 To Shet as well a son was born,
he called his name: Enosh/Mortal.

At that time they first called out the name of YHWH.

5:1 This is the record of the begettings of Adam/Humankind.
At the time of God's creating humankind,
in the likeness of God did he then make it,

2 male and female he created them
and gave blessing to them
and called their name: Humankind!
on the day of their being created.

3 When Adam had lived thirty and a hundred years,
he begot one in his likeness, according to his image,
and called his name Shet.

4 Adam's days after he begot Shet were eight hundred years, and
he begot (other) sons and daughters.

5 And all the days that Adam lived were nine hundred years
and thirty years,
then he died.

6 When Shet had lived five years and a hundred years, he begot
Enosh,

---

26 **called out the name of** YHWH I.e., worshiped God.

5:1 **At the time . . . :** The language is reminiscent of
the earlier poem in 1:27. In this case, however, the
Hebrew creates a rhyming effect. The cola of the
poem here end thus: *bera'am / otam / shemam:*
Adam / hibare'am. Such a rhyming scheme is rare in
biblical Hebrew, and usually endows a passage with
particular significance (see also, for instance, II Sam.
12:11).

7 and Shet lived after he begot Enosh seven years and eight
hundred years, and begot (other) sons and daughters.

8 And all the days of Shet were twelve years and nine hundred
years, then he died.

9 When Enosh had lived ninety years, he begot Kenan,

10 and Enosh lived after he begot Kenan fifteen years and eight
hundred years, and begot (other) sons and daughters.

11 And all the days of Enosh were five years and nine hundred
years,
then he died.

12 When Kenan had lived seventy years, he begot Mehalalel,

13 and Kenan lived after he begot Mehalalel forty years and eight
hundred years, and begot (other) sons and daughters.

14 And all the days of Kenan were ten years and nine hundred
years,
then he died.

15 When Mehalalel had lived five years and sixty years, he begot
Yered.

16 and Mehalalel lived after he begot Yered thirty years and eight
hundred years, and begot (other) sons and daughters.

17 And all the days of Mehalalel were ninety-five years and eight
hundred years,
then he died.

18 When Yered had lived sixty-two years and a hundred years, he
begot Hanokh,

19 and Yered lived after he begot Hanokh eight hundred years, and
begot (other) sons and daughters.

20 And all the days of Yered were sixty-two years and nine hundred
years,
then he died.

21 When Hanokh had lived sixty-five years, he begot Metushelah,

---

18 **Hanokh:** Trad. English "Enoch."

22 and Hanokh walked in accord with God after he begot
    Metushelah three hundred years, and begot (other) sons and
    daughters.

23 And all the days of Hanokh were sixty-five years and three
    hundred years.

24 Now Hanokh walked in accord with God,
    then he was no more,
    for God had taken him.

25 When Metushelah had lived eighty-seven years and a hundred
    years, he begot Lemekh,

26 and Metushelah lived after he begot Lemekh eighty-two years
    and seven hundred years, and begot (other) sons and
    daughters.

27 And all the days of Metushelah were sixty-nine years and nine
    hundred years,
    then he died.

28 When Lemekh had lived eighty-two years and a hundred years,
    he begot a son.

29 He called his name: Noah!
    saying:
    Zeh yenahamenu / May this-one comfort-our-sorrow
    from our toil, from the pains of our hands
    coming from the soil, which Yhwh has damned.

30 And Lemekh lived after he begot Noah ninety-five years and five
    hundred years, and begot (other) sons and daughters.

31 And all the days of Lemekh were seventy-seven years and seven
    hundred years,
    then he died.

---

22 **and Hanokh walked in accord with God . . . three hundred years:** The variation from the rigid formulations of this chapter draws attention to this key figure, the first pious man (similarly with Noah, 5:29). "Walked in accord with God" means walked in God's ways, led a righteous life.

24 **then he was no more:** He died. Later interpreters found the phrase ambiguous, and fantastic postbiblical legends arose concerning Hanokh (see Ginzberg).

31 **seventy-seven years and seven hundred years:** As in 4:24, a man named Lemekh is linked to multiples of seven.

Antiquity and the Preparation for the Flood (6:1–8): The final pre-Flood section of the text includes a theme common to other ancient tales: the biological mixing of gods and men in dim antiquity. Perhaps this fragment, which initially seems difficult to reconcile with biblical ideas about God, has been retained here to round out a picture familiar to ancient readers, and to recall the early closeness of the divine and the human which, according to many cultures, later dissolved. It is also possible that the episode serves as another example of a world that has become disordered, thus providing further justification for a divinely ordered destruction.

The stage is set for the Flood by means of a powerful sound reference. In 5:29 Noah was named, ostensibly to comfort his elders' "sorrow" over human "pains" in tilling the soil. Here (6:6), however, the meaning of the name has been ironically reversed. The one who was supposed to bring comfort only heralds God's own being "sorry" and "pained" (vv. 6–7). A similar ironic wordplay, where the audience knows what the name-bestower does not, occurs in Ex. 2:3; curiously, the hero of that passage, the baby Moses, is also connected with an "ark"—the term for the little basket in which he is set adrift.

32 When Noah was five hundred years old,
Noah begot Shem, Ham, and Yefet.

6:1 Now it was when humans first became many on the face of the
soil

and women were born to them,

2 that the divine beings saw how beautiful the human women
were,

so they took themselves wives, whomever they chose.

3 YHWH said:

My rushing-spirit shall not remain in humankind for ages, for
they too are flesh;

let their days be then a hundred and twenty years!

4 The giants were on earth in those days,
and afterward as well,
when the divine beings came in to the human women
and they bore them (children)—
they were the heroes who were of former ages, the men of
name.

5 Now YHWH saw

that great was humankind's evildoing on earth

and every form of their heart's planning was only evil all the day.

6 Then YHWH was sorry

that he had made humankind on earth,

and it pained his heart.

7 YHWH said:

I will blot out humankind, whom I have created, from the face of
the soil,

6:2 **divine beings:** Or "godlings."

3 **for they too are flesh:** Hebrew difficult. The text uses the singular. **a hundred and twenty years:** Some early interpreters take this to specify a "grace period" for humanity before the Flood. The text seems to be setting the limits of the human life span.

4 **came in to:** The common biblical term for sexual intercourse. The concept, also expressed in Arabic, is of the man entering the woman's tent for the purposes of sex.

5 **now YHWH saw ... evildoing:** In contrast to the refrain of Chapter 1, "God saw that it was good." **every form of their heart's planning:** This lengthy phrase indicates human imagination (Speiser: "every scheme that his mind devised"). "Heart" (Heb. *lev* or *levav*) often expresses the concept of "mind" in the Bible.

7 **man to beast:** Or "human to animal."

The Deluge (6:9–8:19): The biblical account of the Flood is replete with echoes and allusions which point to three clear motifs: God's justice, the totality of punishment, and a new beginning patterned after Gen. I.

The first of these is brought out in 6:11–13: the repetition of the word "ruin" indicates not only the sorry state of society but also the principle of just retaliation, for God is to "bring ruin" upon the earth (v.13).

The totality of the disaster is conveyed by the repeated use of the word "all" in 7:21–23, as well as by the completeness of the list of those destroyed (7:21–23). Humans, as befits their place in the order of creation, appear last, but actually it is they who drag virtually all of creation down with them. This reflects a deeply held biblical idea that human action directly affects the orderly and otherwise neutral functioning of nature.

There are striking parallels between the Flood narrative and the creation account of Chap. I. Just as the animals were created, each "according to its kind," their rescue, both in boarding and leaving the Ark, is similarly worded. "Ocean" and the great "rushing-wind" which existed at creation (1:2) return here, the former to signify a lapse into chaos and the latter, the restoration of order and peace (7:11, 8:1). Finally, after the Flood (9:1–3) Noah is blessed in wording that recalls Adam's blessing in 1:28–30. The world thus begins anew, with the implication of some hope for the future.

Repetition emphasizes other aspects of the story's message. In general the word-stem "live" occurs constantly throughout the text, highlighting the rescue and renewal of life as well as its destruction. Noah's obedience, another major theme, is indicated by variations on the phrase "according to all that God commanded him, so he did" (6:22). Of rhythmical, almost ritual-sounding import is the phrase "you and your sons and your wife and your sons' wives."

Our story has often been compared, with much justification, to the several Mesopotamian Flood accounts (e.g., in the *Gilgamesh* and *Atrahasis* epics), with which it shares a great deal of detail. At one time scholars were quick to concentrate on the parallels, but the differences are now recognized as being much more significant. In general one may say that in contrast to the earlier (Mesopotamian) versions the biblical one is unambiguous in both tone and intent. It has been placed in Genesis to exemplify a God who judges the world according to human behavior, punishes evil and rescues the righteous. This is a far cry from the earlier accounts, where the gods plan the destruction of the world for reasons that are unclear (or in one version, because humankind's noise is disturbing the sleep of the gods), and where the protagonist, Utnapishtim, is saved as the result of a god's favoritism without any moral judgments being passed.

from man to beast, to crawling thing and to the fowl of the
heavens,
for I am sorry that I made them.

8 But Noah found favor in the eyes of YHWH.

9 These are the begettings of Noah.
Noah was a righteous, wholehearted man in his generation,
in accord with God did Noah walk.

10 Noah begot three sons: Shem, Ham, and Yefet.

11 Now the earth had gone to ruin before God, the earth was filled
with wrongdoing.

12 God saw the earth, and here: it had gone to ruin,
for all flesh had ruined its way upon the earth.

13 God said to Noah:
An end of all flesh has come before me,
for the earth is filled with wrongdoing through them;
here, I am about to bring ruin upon them, along with the earth.

14 Make yourself an Ark of *gofer* wood,
with reeds make the Ark,
and cover it within and without with a covering-of-pitch.

15 And this is how you are to make it:
Three hundred cubits the length of the Ark, fifty cubits its
breadth, and thirty cubits its height.

16 A skylight you are to make for the Ark, finishing it to a cubit upward.
The entrance of the Ark you are to set in its side;
with a lower, a second, and a third deck you are to make it.

---

9 **righteous:** A term with legal connotations; "in the right" or "just." **righteous, wholehearted:** Foreshadowing Avraham, of whom similar vocabulary will be used (17:1). "Whole" (below "wholly-sound") is used of animals fit for sacrifice. Others, "perfect" or "unblemished."

11–12 **Now the earth . . . :** A poetic summary of the situation.

11 **before God:** In his sight.

12 **God saw the earth, and here: it had gone to ruin:** A bitter echo of 1:31, "Now God saw all that he had made, / and here: it was exceedingly good!"

13 **has come before me:** Has been determined by me.

14 **Ark:** English as well as Hebrew etymology points to a box or chest, not strictly a boat. God, not human engineering, is the source of survival in the story. *gofer:* Identification unknown. **reeds:** Reading Heb. *kanim* for traditional text's *kinnim* ("compartments").

15 **cubits:** A cubit equaled a man's forearm in length, about 17½ inches.

16 **skylight:** Hebrew obscure, including the end of the phrase.

◆ 17 As for me,

here, I am about to bring on the Deluge, water upon the earth,
to bring ruin upon all flesh that has rush of life in it, from under
the heavens,
all that is on earth will perish.

18 But I will establish my covenant with you:
you are to come into the Ark, you and your sons and your wife
and your sons' wives with you,

19 and from all living-things, from all flesh, you are to bring two
from all into the Ark, to remain alive with you.
They are to be a male and a female (each),

20 from fowl after their kind, from herd-animals after their kind,
from all crawling things of the soil after their kind,
two from all are to come to you, to remain alive.

21 As for you,
take for yourself from all edible-things that are eaten and gather
it to you,
it shall be for you and for them, for eating.

22 Noah did it,
according to all that God commanded him, so he did.

7:1 YHWH said to Noah:
Come, you and all your household, into the Ark!
For you I have seen as righteous before me in this generation.

2 From all (ritually) pure animals you are to take seven and seven
(each), a male and his mate,
and from all the animals that are not pure, two (each), a male
and his mate,

---

17 **Deluge:** Heb. *mabbul.* Others suggest the more conventional word "Flood," but the term may be an Assyrian loan-word.

18 **covenant:** An agreement or pact, most notably (in the Bible) one between God and individuals or between him and the people of Israel.

7:2 **(ritually) pure:** An anachronism, referring to later Israelite laws about sacrifice and eating. **seven and seven each:** The contradiction between this and 6:19 has led scholars to posit two different sources for the story. **male:** Lit. "a man."

3 and also from the fowl of the heavens, seven and seven (each),
    male and female,
  to keep seed alive upon the face of all the earth.

4 For in yet seven days
  I will make it rain upon the earth for forty days and forty nights
  and will blot out all existing-things that I have made, from the
    face of the soil.

5 Noah did it, according to all that Y{\small HWH} had commanded him.

6 Noah was six hundred years old when the Deluge occurred,
    water upon the earth;

7 and Noah came, his sons and his wife and his sons' wives with
    him, into the Ark before the waters of the Deluge.

8 From the pure animals and from the animals that are not pure
    and from the fowl and all that crawls about on the soil—

9 two and two (each) came to Noah, into the Ark, male and female,
  as God had commanded Noah.

10 After the seven days it was
   that the waters of the Deluge were upon the earth.

11 In the six hundredth year of Noah's life, in the second
     New-Moon, on the seventeenth day after the New-Moon,
   on that day:
       then burst all the well-springs of the great Ocean
       and the sluices of the heavens opened up.

12 The torrent was upon the earth for forty days and forty nights.

13 On that very day came Noah, and Shem, Ham, and Yefet, Noah's
   sons, and Noah's wife and his three sons' wives with them,
   into the Ark,

---

4 **in yet seven days:** Seven days from now. **forty:**
Used in the Bible to denote long periods of time;
also a favorite patterned number.

11 **then burst . . . :** Cassuto (1972) suggests that the
poetic verses here and elsewhere in the Flood

story are fragments of an Israelite epic. See also
9:11, 15. **well-springs . . . sluices:** The normal
sources of rain function here without any restraint (Cassuto). **Ocean:** The world returns to the
primeval chaos of 1:2.

14   they and all wildlife after their kind, all herd-animals after their
          kind, all crawling things that crawl upon the earth after their
          kind, all fowl after their kind, all chirping-things, all winged-
          things;

15   they came to Noah, into the Ark, two and two (each) from all
          flesh in which there is the rush of life.

16   And those that came, male and female from all flesh they came,
          as God had commanded him.
          YHWH closed (the door) upon him.

17   The Deluge was forty days upon the earth.
          The waters increased and lifted the Ark, so that it was raised
          above the earth;

18   the waters swelled and increased exceedingly upon the earth, so
          that the Ark floated upon the face of the waters.

19   When the waters had swelled exceedingly, yes, exceedingly over
          the earth, all high mountains that were under all the heavens
          were covered.

20   Fifteen cubits upward swelled the waters, thus the mountains
          were covered.

21   Then expired all flesh that crawls about upon the earth—fowl,
          herd-animals, wildlife, and all swarming things that swarm
          upon the earth,
          and all humans;

22   all that had the breath of the rush of life in their nostrils,
          all that were on firm-ground, died.

23   He blotted out all existing-things that were on the face of the soil,
          from man to beast, to crawling thing and to fowl of the heavens,
          they were blotted out from the earth.
          Noah alone remained, and those who were with him in the Ark.

24   The waters swelled upon the earth for a hundred and fifty days.

---

16 **YHWH closed:** Another sign of God's control over
the events (and of his protection of Noah).

17–20 **increased . . . swelled and increased exceedingly . . . swelled exceedingly, yes, exceedingly . . . swelled:** The structure here mirrors
the action: the surging and growing of the waters.

18 **swelled:** Lit. "grew mighty." **floated:** Lit. "went."

22 **firm-ground:** Heb. *harava*, lit. "dry-land." Hebrew
has two words for "dry" (*harev* and *yavesh*), while
English uses only one.

23 **blotted out:** Twice repeated, echoing God's
promise in 6:7.

8:1 But God paid mind to Noah and all living-things, all the animals
that were with him in the Ark,
and God brought a rushing-wind across the earth, so that the
waters abated.

2 The well-springs of Ocean and the sluices of the heavens were
dammed up,
and the torrent from the heavens was held back.

3 The waters returned from upon the earth, continually advancing
and returning,
and the waters diminished at the end of a hundred and fifty days.

4 And the Ark came to rest in the seventh New-Moon, on the
seventeenth day after the New-Moon, upon the mountains
of Ararat.

5 Now the waters continued to advance and diminish until the
tenth New-Moon.
On the tenth, on the first day of the New-Moon, the tops of the
mountains could be seen.

6 At the end of forty days it was: Noah opened the window of
7 the Ark that he had made, / and sent out a raven;
it went off, going off and returning, until the waters were
dried up from upon the earth.

8 Then he sent out a dove from him, to see whether the waters had
subsided from the face of the soil.

9 But the dove found no resting-place for the sole of her foot,
so she returned to him into the Ark,
for there was water upon the face of all the earth.
He sent forth his hand and took her, and brought her to him into
the Ark.

10 Then he waited yet another seven days
and sent out the dove yet again from the Ark.

8:1 **paid mind:** More than merely "remembered."
rushing-wind: Reminiscent of the "rushing-spirit
of God" at creation.

3,5 **advancing and returning . . . advance and diminish:** Again, as in 7:17–20, the motion of the waters is
suggested by means of sound.

7 **sent out:** Or "released."

8 **dove:** This bird is portrayed in the Bible as beautiful
(even pure) and delicate. From this passage, of
course, stems the popular use of the dove as the
symbol of peace.

Aftermath (8:20–9:19): The passages immediately following the Flood narrative speak of a God who is remarkably receptive to a human kind of change. From having been "sorry" that he created humankind (6:6), he now evinces a change of heart about the entire issue of evil, conceding human imperfections (8:21). In a wonderfully structured declaration, where "never again" moves in position from the middle to the beginning of the phrase (8:21–22), God as it were chooses to restrain his own ability to radically disturb the processes of nature. Where later on in Genesis the human characters exhibit the capacity to change, here it is God himself.

The blessing in 9:1–3 establishes Noah as a kind of second Adam (and it might be noted that chronologically Noah is the first man born after Adam dies). It repeats the basic formulation of the blessing in 1:28–30, with an important exception: meat-eating is now to be allowed, as part of God's concession to human nature. Previously only the plant world had been accessible to humankind for food. However—and this very word punctuates the text twice in 9:4–5—there is to be an accounting for willful bloodshed, as if to suggest that the eating of meat is being permitted only under strict conditions. To underscore the importance of this concept, the section about bloodshed uses the vocabulary of creation: human beings are made "in the image of God."

With vv.8 and 9 the key concept of "covenant" appears for the first time in the Bible. It is accompanied, as is usual in the Bible, by a symbol or "sign" (in this case, the rainbow). We are led back to the creation story again, as other biblical texts speak of the Sabbath as a "sign of the covenant" between God and Israel (e.g., Ex. 31:12–17).

The sixfold repetition of the phrase "never again" provides a thematic unity in these passages.

◆ 11 The dove came back to him at eventime,
and here—a freshly plucked olive leaf in her beak!
So Noah knew
that the waters had subsided from upon the earth.

12 Then he waited yet another seven days
and sent out the dove,
but she returned to him again no more.

13 And so it was in the six hundred and first year, in the beginning-
month, on the first day of the New-Moon,
that the waters left firm ground upon the earth.
Noah removed the covering of the Ark and saw:
here, the face of the soil was firm.

14 Now in the second New-Moon, on the twenty-seventh day after
the New-Moon, the earth was (completely) dry.

15 God spoke to Noah, saying:

16 Go out of the Ark, you and your wife, your sons and your sons'
wives with you.

17 All living-things that are with you, all flesh—fowl, animals, and
all crawling things that crawl about upon the earth,
have them go out with you,
that they may swarm on earth, that they may bear fruit and
become many upon the earth.

18 So Noah went out, his sons, his wife, and his sons' wives with
him,

19 all living-things—all crawling things, and all fowl, all that crawl
about upon the earth,
according to their clans they went out of the Ark.

20 Noah built a slaughter-site to Yhwh.
He took from all pure animals and from all pure fowl
and offered up offerings upon the slaughter-site.

---

13 **left firm ground:** Or "were fully dried up" (see note
to 7:22).
19 **clans:** Classifications.
20 **slaughter-site:** Etymologically the word *mizbe'ah*
hearkens back to a time when such sites were used

mainly for animal sacrifice; the Bible cites other
uses such as libations and cereal offerings. **offered
up:** The Hebrew verb (*'alo*) implies upward movement.

◆ 21 Now YHWH smelled the soothing savor
and YHWH said in his heart:
I will never curse the soil again on humankind's account, since
what the human heart forms is evil from its youth;
I will never again strike down all living-things, as I have done;
22 (never) again, all the days of the earth, shall

sowing and harvest,
cold and heat,
summer and winter,
day and night
ever cease!

9:1 Now God blessed Noah and his sons and said to them:
Bear fruit and be many and fill the earth!
2 Fear-of-you, dread-of-you shall be upon all the wildlife of the
earth and upon all the fowl of the heavens,
all that crawls on the soil and all the fish of the sea—
into your hand they are given.
3 All things crawling about that live, for you shall they be, for eating,
as with the green plants, I now give you all.
4 However: flesh with its life, its blood, you are not to eat!
5 However, too: for your blood, of your own lives, I will demand-
satisfaction—
from all wild-animals I will demand it,
and from humankind, from every man regarding his brother,
demand-satisfaction for human life.
6 Whoever now sheds human blood,
for that human shall his blood be shed,
for in God's image he made humankind.
7 As for you—bear fruit and be many, swarm on earth and become
many on it!
8 God said to Noah and to his sons with him, saying:

---

21 **smelled the soothing savor:** Conveyed by the
sound in Hebrew, *va-yarah et re'ah ha-niho'ah.* **evil
from its youth:** That is, evil already begins in what
we might call adolescence. But Speiser renders it
"from the start."

22 **sowing and harvest . . . :** The solemn promise is
expressed in verse.
9:6 **Whoever . . . :** A poem that plays on the sounds of
"humankind" (*adam*) and "blood" (*dam*): *Shofekh
dam ha-adam/ ba-adam damo yishafekh.* **for that
human:** Or "by humans."

9 As for me—here, I am about to establish my covenant with you
and with your seed after you,
10 and with all living beings that are with you: fowl, herd-animals,
and all the wildlife of the earth with you;
all those going out of the Ark, of all the living-things of the
earth.
11 I will establish my covenant with you:
All flesh shall never be cut off again by waters of the Deluge,
never again shall there be Deluge, to bring the earth to ruin!
12 And God said:
This is the sign of the covenant which I set
between me and you and all living beings that are with you, for
ageless generations:
13 My bow I set in the clouds,
so that it may serve as a sign of the covenant between me and
the earth.
14 It shall be:
when I becloud the earth with clouds
and in the clouds the bow is seen,
15 I will call to mind my covenant
that is between me and you and all living beings—all flesh: never
again shall the waters become a Deluge, to bring all flesh to
ruin!
16 When the bow is in the clouds,
I will look at it,
to call to mind the age-old covenant
between God and all living beings—
all flesh that is upon the earth.
17 God said to Noah:
This is the sign of the covenant that I have established between
me and all flesh that is upon the earth.

18 Noah's sons who went out of the Ark were Shem, Ham, and Yefet.
Now Ham is the father of Canaan.

18 **Now Ham is the father of Canaan:** See repetition
in the story to follow, vv.20–27.

Drunkenness and Nakedness (9:20–29): From the lofty poetry of God's blessings and promises, we encounter an all-too-brief description of a bizarre event. The soil, which evidently has not entirely shaken off its primeval curse, proves once again to be a source of trouble. The nature of the crime mentioned here ("seeing the father's nakedness") has been variously interpreted; Buber and others see in it a reference to the sexual "immorality" of the Canaanites, which the Israelites found particularly abhorrent. This would explain the emphasis on the *son* of the culprit in the story, rather than on the perpetrator.

A similar undistinguished ancestry is traced in Chap. 19, referring to the incestuous origins of Israel's neighbors and frequent enemies, the Moabites and Ammonites.

The Table of the Nations (10): Genesis, with its typically ancient Near Eastern emphasis on "begettings," now traces the development of humanity from the sons of Noah. The key formula throughout is "their lands, their nations." Commentators have noted numerical unity in the list, citing a total of seventy nations (once repetitions are omitted) laid out in multiples of seven. That number, as we have indicated, represents the concept of totality and perfection in the Bible. Thus the stage is set for the Babel story of the next chapter, with its condemnation of humanity's attempt to forestall the divinely willed "scattering" into a well-ordered world.

Many of the names in this chapter have been identified (see Speiser), but some are still not known with certainty. Israel is conspicuous in its absence; despite the biblical narrative's ability to trace Israel's origins, those origins are meant to be seen not solely in biological terms but rather in terms of God's choice. Similarly, Israel arises from women who begin as barren—thus pointing to divine intervention in history, rather than the perfectly normal account that we have here.

19 These three were Noah's sons, and from these were scattered
abroad all the earth-folk.

20 Now Noah was the first man of the soil; he planted a vineyard.
21 When he drank from the wine, he became drunk and exposed
himself in the middle of his tent.
22 Ham, the father of Canaan, saw his father's nakedness and told
his two brothers outside.
23 Then Shem and Yefet took a cloak, they put it on the shoulders
of the two of them,
and walked backward, to cover their father's nakedness.
—Their faces were turned backward, their father's nakedness
they did not see.

24 Now when Noah awoke from his wine, it became known (to
him) what his littlest son had done to him.
25 He said:
Damned be Canaan,
servant of servants may he be to his brothers!
26 And he said:
Blessed be YHWH, God of Shem,
but may Canaan be servant to them!
27 May God extend/*yaft*
Yefet,
let him dwell in the tents of Shem,
but may Canaan be servant to them!

28 And Noah lived after the Deluge three hundred years and fifty
years.
29 And all the days of Noah were nine hundred years and fifty years,
then he died.

10:1 Now these are the begettings of the sons of Noah,
Shem, Ham, and Yefet.
Sons were born to them after the Deluge.

24 **littlest:** Or "youngest," difficult in the light of v.18.   26 **to them:** Others use "to him."

The Unfinished Citadel (11:1–9): At its most obvious, in an isolated context, this famous story is about the overweening pride of man, as represented by his technology. God's actions here recall the ending of the garden story, where humanity was also within reach of the divine.

Yet more is involved than a threat. Buber felt that this episode has been inserted at this point to show that humanity has failed again, as at the time of the Flood. It has not spread out and divided into nations, as in Chap. 10. The failure paves the way for a new divine plan, which is to be realized through one man (Avraham) and his descendants.

Structurally, the story is a tiny literary masterpiece. It utilizes numerous plays on sound which make meaningful and often ironic linkages between sections and ideas in the text. Most significant is how the general message—that God's response occurs in exactly the same terms as the human challenge (i.e., divine justice)—is transmitted by means of form. Fokkelman has provided a detailed study; it will suffice here to indicate only the outline. The divine "Come-now!" of v.7 clearly stands as an answer to humankind's identical cry in vv.3 and 4. In addition humans, who congregated in order to establish a "name" and to avoid being "scattered over the face of all the earth" (v.4), are contravened by the action of God, resulting in the ironic name "Babble" and a subsequent "scattering" of humanity (v.9). The text is thus another brilliant example of biblical justice, a statement about a worldview in which the laws of justice and morality are as neatly balanced as we like to think the laws of nature are.

There is an important cultural background to the story. "Shinar" refers to Mesopotamia, and the "tower," undoubtedly, to the ubiquitous *ziggurratu* (now unearthed by archeologists) which served as man-made sacred mountains (i.e., temples). By portraying an unfinished tower, by dispersing the builders, and by in essence making fun of the mighty name of Babylon, the text functions effectively to repudiate the culture from which the people of Israel sprang (Avram's "Ur" of 11:28 was probably the great Mesopotamian metropolis). From Chap. 12 on, a new worldview is created.

Noah to Avram (11:10–32): Here are enumerated another ten generations, making the orderly connection between the origins of the world (Noah was viewed as a second Adam) and the origins of the people of Israel. The life spans are considerably shorter than those of Chap. 5, yet some sort of careful number scheme seems evident here as well (see Cassuto 1972).

Beginning with v.26 we are introduced to Avram, with little hint of what is to come in his momentous life. For the moment he is only a son, a brother, and a husband, and a man whose early life is marked principally by the death of the old world (Haran and Terah), with little hope for the new (his wife is barren).

2 The Sons of Yefet are Gomer and Magog, Madai, Yavan and
Tuval, Meshekh and Tiras.

3 The Sons of Gomer are Ashkenaz, Rifat, and Togarma.

4 The Sons of Yavan are Elisha and Tarshish, Cittites and
Dodanites.

5 From these the seacoast nations were divided by their lands,
each one after its own tongue:
according to their clans, by their nations.

6 The Sons of Ham are Cush and Mitzrayim, Put and Canaan.

7 The Sons of Cush are Seva and Havila, Savta, Ra'ma, and
Savtekha;
the Sons of Ra'ma—Sheva and Dedan.

8 Cush begot Nimrod; he was the first mighty man on earth.

9 He was a mighty hunter before YHWH,
therefore the saying is:
Like Nimrod, a mighty hunter before YHWH.

10 His kingdom, at the beginning, was Bavel, and Erekh, Accad and

11 Calne, in the land of Shinar;
from this land Ashur went forth and built Nineveh—along with

12 the city squares and Calah, / and Resen between Nineveh and
Calah—that is the great city.

13 Mitzrayim begot the Ludites, the Anamites, the Lehavites,

14 the Naftuhites, / the Patrusites, and the Casluhites, from where
the Philistines come, and the Caftorites.

15/16 Canaan begot Tzidon his firstborn and Het, / along with the

17 Yevusite, the Amorite and the Girgashite, / the Hivvite,

18 the Arkite and the Sinite, / the Arvadite, the Tzemarite and the
Hamatite.
Afterward the Canaanite clans were scattered abroad.

10:2 **Sons:** Here, and later, it may mean "descendants."

4 **Dodanites:** Some read "Rodanites," following I Chron. 1:7.

6 **Mitzrayim:** The biblical name for Egypt (the modern Egyptian name is *Misr*).

8 **mighty man:** Three times here; clearly Nimrod was well known as an ancient hero.

10 **Calne:** Some read *cullana,* "all of them."

11 **city squares:** Some read this as a name, "Rehovot-Ir."

14 **Casluhites . . . Caftorites:** Some reverse the order; the Bible often speaks of the origins of the Philistines in Caftor (Crete).

15 **Yevusite, etc.:** Collective names.

19 And the Canaanite territory went from Tzidon, then as you
    come toward Gerar, as far as Gaza, then as you come toward
    Sedom and Amora, Adma, and Tzevoyim, as far as Lasha.
20 These are the Sons of Ham after their clans, after their tongues,
    by their lands, by their nations.

21 (Children) were also born to Shem,
    the father of all the Sons of Ever (and) Yefet's older brother.
22 The Sons of Shem are Elam and Ashur, Arpakhshad, Lud, and
    Aram.
23 The Sons of Aram are Utz and Hul, Geter and Mash.
24 Arpakhshad begot Shelah, Shelah begot Ever.
25 Two sons were born to Ever:
    the name of the first one was Peleg/Splitting, for in his days the
    earth-folk were split up,
    and his brother's name was Yoktan.
26/27 Yoktan begot Almodad and Shelef, Hatzarmavet and Yera,/
28/29   Hadoram, Uzal and Dikla,/ Oval, Avimael and Sheva,/ Ofir,
    Havila, and Yovav—all these are the Sons of Yoktan.
30 Now their settlements went from Mesha, then as you come
    toward Sefar, to the mountain-country of the east.
31 These are the Sons of Shem after their clans, after their tongues,
    by their lands, after their nations.

32 These are the clan-groupings of the Sons of Noah, after their
    begettings, by their nations.
    From these the nations were divided on earth after the Deluge.

11:1 Now all the earth was of one language and one set-of-words.
2 And it was when they migrated to the east that they found a val-
    ley in the land of Shinar and settled there.
3 They said, each man to his neighbor:
    Come-now! Let us bake bricks and let us burn them well-burnt!
    So for them brick-stone was like building-stone, and raw-bitumen
    was for them like red-mortar.

11:1 **language:** Lit. "lip."
3 **so . . . brick-stone . . . :** An explanation of Mesopotamian building techniques for the Hebrew audience. The text plays on sound (*levena . . . le-aven,
hemer . . . la-homer*). **raw-bitumen:** Asphalt, used
for making cement.

4 Now they said:
 Come-now! Let us build ourselves a city and a tower, its top in
  the heavens,
 and let us make ourselves a name,
 lest we be scattered over the face of all the earth!
5 But YHWH came down to look over the city and the tower that
  the humans were building.
6 YHWH said:
 Here, (they are) one people with one language for them all, and
  this is merely the first of their doings—
 now there will be no barrier for them in all that they scheme to do!
7 Come-now! Let us go down and there let us baffle their
  language,
 so that no man will understand the language of his neighbor.
8 So YHWH scattered them from there over the face of all the earth,
 and they had to stop building the city.
9 Therefore its name was called Bavel/Babble,
 for there YHWH baffled the language of all the earth-folk,
 and from there, YHWH scattered them over the face of all the earth.

10 These are the begettings of Shem:
 Shem was a hundred years old, then he begot Arpakhshad, two
  years after the Deluge,
11 and Shem lived after he begot Arpakhshad five hundred years,
  and begot (other) sons and daughters.
12 Arpakhshad lived thirty-five years, then he begot Shelah,
13 and Arpakhshad lived after he begot Shelah three years and four
  hundred years, and begot (other) sons and daughters.
14 Shelah lived thirty years, then he begot Ever,
15 and Shelah lived after he begot Ever three years and four hundred years, and begot (other) sons and daughters.
16 When Ever had lived thirty-four years, he begot Peleg,
17 and Ever lived after he begot Peleg thirty years and four hundred
  years, and begot other (sons) and daughters.

---

4 **make . . . a name:** That is, make sure that we and our works will endure.
10 **two years after the Deluge:** Possibly a typical pop-ular way of telling time (see Amos 1:1, "two years after the earthquake").

18 When Peleg had lived thirty years, he begot Re'u,

19 and Peleg lived after he begot Re'u nine years and two hundred
years, and begot other (sons) and daughters.

20 When Re'u had lived thirty-two years, he begot Serug,

21 and Re'u lived after he begot Serug seven years and two hundred
years, and begot (other) sons and daughters.

22 When Serug had lived thirty years, he begot Nahor,

23 and Serug lived after he begot Nahor two hundred years, and
begot (other) sons and daughters.

24 When Nahor had lived twenty-nine years, he begot Terah,

25 and Nahor lived after he begot Terah nineteen years and a
hundred years, and begot (other) sons and daughters.

26 When Terah had lived seventy years, he begot Avram, Nahor,
and Haran.

27 Now these are the begettings of Terah:
Terah begot Avram, Nahor, and Haran;
and Haran begot Lot.

28 Haran died in the living-presence of Terah his father in the land
of his kindred, in Ur of the Chaldeans.

29 Avram and Nahor took themselves wives;
the name of Avram's wife was Sarai,
the name of Nahor's wife was Milca—daughter of Haran, father
of Milca and father of Yisca.

30 Now Sarai was barren, she had no child.

31 Terah took Avram his son and Lot son of Haran, his son's son,
and Sarai his daughter-in-law, wife of Avram his son,
they set out together from Ur of the Chaldeans, to go to the land
of Canaan.
But when they had come as far as Harran, they settled there.

32 And the days of Terah were five years and two hundred years,
then Terah died,
in Harran.

---

26 **Avram:** Trad. English "Abram."
28 **in the living-presence of Terah his father:** During
his father's lifetime. **Chaldeans:** An anachronism;
see Speiser.
30 **barren, she had no child:** This doubling is charac-

teristic of biblical style (formal poetry in the Bible
uses parallelism of lines).
31 **Harran:** An important city and center of moon
worship, like Ur. The name means "crossroads."

THE PATRIARCHAL NARRATIVES

THE STORIES ABOUT THE FATHERS AND MOTHERS OF ISRAEL, AS A COLLECTION, ARE almost contrapuntal in their richness. Life experiences are repeated and common themes recur; yet at the same time there is a remarkable variety of personalities.

Two prominent themes throughout are God's promises (of land and descendants) and his blessing. The texts revolve around the question of whether and how God will fulfill his promises, and how people will effect the transfer of the blessing. Each generation portrayed in the narratives must deal with the inherent tensions raised by these questions, since their resolution does not occur easily.

The stories are also marked by each figure's struggle to develop a concept of the religious life, of "walking in accord with God." Each one carves out his own distinct path, to arrive at a mature understanding of what it means to be a father of the people of Israel. In order to bring about such an understanding, God apparently "tests" them in both obvious and more oblique ways, often against a backdrop of bitter sibling rivalry. One also observes a physical unsettledness about the Patriarchs' quest; only Yitzhak is spared the wanderings that occur so regularly in the stories.

Rather interestingly, although the texts purport to be about "fathers," it is God himself who most consistently fits that role for the characters. God acts *in loco parentis* for each of the Patriarchs, always, significantly, after the loss of the human father. He first appears to Avraham after the death of Terah; to Yitzhak after that of Avraham; to Yaakov after he leaves home (and a seemingly dying father); and he helps Yosef directly, after he has left his father's home.

Numbers play an important role in the Patriarchal stories, as they did in Part I. It has been pointed out (see Sarna 1966) that the life spans of the Patriarchs fit into a highly ordered pattern. Avraham lives for 175 years, equaling 7×5^2; Yitzhak, for 180 years, equaling 5×6^2; and Yaakov, for 147 years, or 3×7^2. This is unmistakably a purposeful scheme, meant to convey that human history is orderly and meaningful. Similarly an examination of the stories reveals that Avraham lives for 75 years in the lifetime of his father and 75 years in the lifetime of his son, while Yaakov spends 20 years away from his father, with Yosef roughly following suit in the next generation.

Last, it should be noted that the Patriarchal stories in various details anticipate the later Exodus of the Israelites from Egypt. The specific references will be mentioned in the Notes.

PART II

AVRAHAM

(12–25:18)

ALTHOUGH AVRAHAM IS THE BIOLOGICAL FATHER OF ISRAEL, THE DIVERSE TRADITIONS about him which have been collected and connected to form a cycle of stories give evidence of much more. The cycle portrays an active *Homo religiosis* who converses with God, sometimes with an air of doubt and questioning, who proclaims God's name at various sacred sites, who is concerned about justice and the treatment of the oppressed, and who makes dramatic life decisions without flinching. The stories thus reveal struggle, despite the fact that Avraham often appears to be the "perfect" man, always obeying God's bidding and prospering.

Buber (1982), noting the unifying effect of the verb "see" throughout the cycle, understood Avraham as the father of the Prophets of Israel (formerly called "seers"). He also viewed the cycle as based around the series of tests that Avraham must undergo, tests quite different, we might add, from the labors of Hercules and other such ancient challenges.

Other than "see," a number of leading-words launch the major concerns of the Patriarchs: "bless," "seed," and "land." At the same time the cycle contains previously encountered motifs, albeit with interesting refinements: punishment for sin (this time, with human questioning), intimacy with God (here through visions), and sibling rivalry (with more complex results than murder). Above all we note the singling out of one man to perform the will of God, a man very different from the rather passive Noah.

Avraham stands at the core of the entire book of Genesis, as his experiences will in many ways be reflected in those who follow him. At the core of both the book and the cycle looms the disturbing Chapter 22, which brings together and resolves, for the moment, the major themes encountered so far.

The Call and the Journey (12:1–9): The Avraham cycle begins decisively, with a command from God to leave the past behind and go to an unnamed land. Prominent in this speech, clearly, is the concept of blessing, which will be realized by the gifts of land (Canaan) and seed (Yitzhak, the son).

The classic mythological motif of the journey, where the hero meets such dangers as monsters and giants, has here been avoided. All that the text wishes us to know about is God's speech and Avram's immediate obedience; as in Chap. 22, all other details of the actual trip have been omitted.

12:1 YHWH said to Avram:
Go-you-forth
from your land,
from your kindred,
from your father's house,
to the land that I will let you see.

2 I will make a great nation of you
and will give-you-blessing
and will make your name great.
Be a blessing!

3 I will bless those who bless you,
he who curses you, I will damn.
All the clans of the soil will find blessing through you!

4 Avram went, as YHWH had spoken to him, and Lot went with
him.
And Avram was five years and seventy years old when he went
out of Harran.

5 Avram took Sarai his wife and Lot his brother's son, all their
property that they had gained, and the persons whom they had
made-their-own in Harran,
and they went out to go to the land of Canaan.
When they came to the land of Canaan,

6 Avram passed through the land, as far as the Place of Shekhem,
as far as the Oak of Moreh.
Now the Canaanite was then in the land.

7 YHWH was seen by Avram and said:
I give this land to your seed!
He built a slaughter-site there to YHWH who had been seen by
him.

12:1 **kindred:** Others use "birthplace."
3 **find blessing:** Or "seek to be blessed (as you)."
5 **property . . . gained:** Heb. *rekhusham . . . rakhashu.*
6 **Place:** Possibly with the implication of "sacred
place." **Oak:** Some read "valley." **Moreh:** Some, like
Buber, interpret this as "sage." **the Canaanite:** The

peoples inhabiting the land at the time of the Israelite conquest under Joshua; see also 13:7.
7 **was seen:** Others use "appeared to," which is more
comfortable in English. "See" has been kept here as
a leading word in the Avraham cycle.

The Wife—I (12:10–20): Almost immediately upon his arrival in the promised land Avram is forced to leave it. It will be his son Yitzhak's task to remain there on a more permanent basis.

This is the first of three such stories which are practically identical (see Chaps. 20 and 26). All pose a challenge for the interpreter. An honored man of God seeks to save his own skin by passing his wife off as his sister; in each case the Patriarch emerges safely and with increased wealth.

Speiser has tried to use the analogy of Hurrian (i.e., from Harran) law in which a wife can be elevated to the status of "sister" as one element in the expansion of her status. The legal background, however, is unclear and may not be decisive here. Coming as it does after God's promise to biologically found "a great nation" (v.2) through Avram, the story in its first version is probably best understood as an example of God's protection not only of the key male figure, but of the Matriarch as well. Harming Sarai, or even the threat of violating her sexuality, brings with it divine punishment. In addition the story also enables Avram to expand his wealth—itself a sign of God's favor and the Patriarch's importance or "weightiness" (see Polzin 1975).

8   He moved on from there to the mountain-country, east of Bet-El,
    and spread his tent, Bet-El toward the sea and Ai toward the east.
    There he built a slaughter-site to YHWH
    and called out the name of YHWH.

9   Then Avram journeyed on, continually journeying to the Negev.

10 Now there was a famine in the land,
    and Avram went down to Egypt, to sojourn there,
    for the famine was heavy in the land.

11 It was when he came near to Egypt that he said to Sarai his wife:
    Now here, I know well that you are a woman fair to look at.

12 It will be, when the Egyptians see you and say: She is his wife,
    that they will kill me, but you they will allow to live.

13 Pray say that you are my sister
    so that it may go well with me on your account, that I myself
        may live thanks to you.

14 It was when Avram came to Egypt, that the Egyptians saw how
        exceedingly fair the woman was;

15 when Pharaoh's courtiers saw her, they praised her to Pharaoh,
    and the woman was taken away into Pharaoh's house.

16 It went well with Avram on her account,
    sheep and oxen, donkeys, servants and maids, she-asses and
        camels, became his.

17 But YHWH plagued Pharaoh with great plagues, and also his
        household, because of Sarai, Avram's wife.

18 Pharaoh had Avram called, and said:
    What is this that you have done to me!
    Why did you not tell me that she is your wife?

19 Why did you say: She is my sister?
    —So I took her for myself as a wife.
    But now, here is your wife, take her and go!

20 So Pharaoh put men in charge of him, who escorted him and his
        wife and all that was his.

---

8   **toward the sea:** West.
9   **the Negev:** The "dry," southern portion of the land
    of Israel.
10 **sojourn:** To reside temporarily, as an alien.
    heavy: Severe.

15 Pharaoh: Heb. Par'o. This is an Egyptian title,
    "(Lord of) the Great House," and not a name.

Lot; The Land (13): We return to the theme of the land. Not for the last time, Avram's nephew Lot is used as a foil. Their "parting" shows how Lot makes a bad choice—the "wicked and sinful" area of Sedom and Amora—while Avram settles "in the land of Canaan," which had been promised to him. From here (vv.14ff.), Avram is given God's twofold promise again, with that of descendants being spelled out more vividly this time.

This section is linked to the previous one by the repetition of the phrase "he and his wife and all that was his."

13:1 Avram traveled up from Egypt, he and his wife and all that was
    his, and Lot with him, to the Negev.

2 And Avram was exceedingly heavily laden with livestock, with
    silver and with gold.

3 He went on his journeyings from the Negev as far as Bet-El, as far
    as the place where his tent had been at the first, between Bet-El
    and Ai,

4 to the place of the slaughter-site that he had made there at the
    beginning.
    There Avram called out the name of YHWH.

5 Now also Lot, who had gone with Avram, had sheep and oxen
    and tents.

6 And the land could not support them, to settle together,
    for their property was so great that they were not able to settle
    together.

7 So there was a quarrel between the herdsmen of Avram's
    livestock and the herdsmen of Lot's livestock.
    Now the Canaanite and the Perizzite were then settled in the
    land.

8 Avram said to Lot:
    Pray let there be no quarreling between me and you, between my
    herdsmen and your herdsmen,
    for we are brother men!

9 Is not all the land before you?
    Pray part from me!
    If to the left, then I to the right,
    if to the right, then I to the left.

10 Lot lifted up his eyes and saw all the plain of the Jordan—
    how well-watered was it all, before YHWH brought ruin upon
    Sedom and Amora,
    like YHWH's garden, like the land of Egypt, as you come toward
    Tzo'ar.

13:2 **heavily laden:** Rich.
8 **brother men:** Relatives.
9 **before you:** Possibly a legal term concerning boundaries. **left . . . right:** North and south.

10 YHWH **brought ruin:** See Chap. 19. **Sedom and Amora:** Trad. English "Sodom and Gomorrah."

War and Rescue (14): Abruptly Avram is presented in a new light: that of successful warrior (see Muffs). Consistent with his character as we will come to know it, he stands by his kinsman, acts intrepidly, and refuses the spoils of war. Equally important, he is respected by foreigners, a theme that will return both in Genesis and later. Perhaps this very different story has been included here as part of the early sections of the cycle in order to establish Avram's status and stature. He is no longer merely a wanderer but well on the road to becoming a powerful local figure.

Whether the events described in this chapter are historical or part of an elaborate symbolic or mythical scheme has been the subject of debate among biblical scholars. The issue, barring unexpected archeological finds, is likely to remain unsolved.

The story is constructed around a geographical framework, using the formula "—that is now *x*—" to identify older sites for a contemporary audience. The one place which is *not* identified, the "Shalem" of verse 18, may well be Jerusalem. If so, this would substantiate the city's claim to holiness. Historically it was not conquered until King David's reign in the tenth century B.C.E.

11 So Lot chose for himself all the plain of the Jordan.
   Lot journeyed eastward, and they parted, each man from the
      other:
12 Avram settled in the land of Canaan, while Lot settled in the
      cities of the plain, pitching-his-tent near Sedom.
13 Now the men of Sedom were exceedingly wicked and sinful
      before YHWH.
14 YHWH said to Avram, after Lot had parted from him:
   Pray lift up your eyes and see from the place where you are,
      to the north, to the Negev, to the east, to the Sea:
15 indeed, all the land that you see, I give it to you
   and to your seed, for the ages.
16 I will make your seed like the dust of the ground,
   so that if a man were able to measure the dust of the ground, so
      too could your seed be measured.
17 Up, walk about through the land in its length and in its breadth,
   for I give it to you.
18 Avram moved-his-tent and came and settled by the oaks of
      Mamre, which are by Hevron.
   There he built a slaughter-site to YHWH.

14:1 Now it was in the days of Amrafel king of Shinar, Aryokh king of
      Ellasar, Kedorla'omer king of Elam, and Tidal king of Goyim:
   2 They prepared for battle against Bera king of Sedom, Birsha king
      of Amora, Shinav king of Adma, Shemever king of Tzevoyim,
      and the king of Bela—that is now Tzo'ar.
   3 All these joined together in the valley of Siddim/Limestone—
      that is now the Sea of Salt.
   4 For twelve years they had been subservient to Kedorla'omer,
      and in the thirteenth year they had revolted,
   5 but then in the fourteenth year came Kedorla'omer and the kings
      who were with him,
      they struck the Refa'ites in Ashterot-Karnayim, the Zuzites

14:3 **The Sea of Salt:** The Dead Sea.

6   in Ham, the Emites in Shaveh-Kiryatayim, / and the
Horites in their hill-country of Se'ir near El Paran,
which is by the wilderness.

7 As they returned, they came to En Mishpat / Judgment Spring—
that is now Kadesh,
and struck all the territory of the Amalekites and also the
Amorites, who were settled in Hatzatzon-Tamar.

8 Then out marched the king of Sedom, the king of Amora, the
king of Adma, the king of Tzevoyim, and the king of Bela—
that is now Tzo'ar;
they set-their-ranks against them in war in the valley of Siddim,

9 against Kedorla'omer king of Elam, Tidal king of Goyim,
Amrafel king of Shinar, and Aryokh king of Ellasar—
four kings against the five.

10 Now the valley of Siddim is pit after pit of bitumen,
and when the kings of Sedom and Amora fled, they flung
themselves therein,
while those who remained fled to the hill-country.

11 Now they took all the property of Sedom and Amora and all
their food, and went away,

12 and they took Lot and all his property—the son of Avram's
brother—and went away,
for he had settled in Sedom.

13 One who escaped came and told Avram the Hebrew—
he was dwelling by the Oaks of Mamre the Amorite, brother of
Eshcol and brother of Aner,
they were Avram's covenant-allies.

14 When Avram heard that his brother had been taken prisoner,
he drew out his retainers, his house-born slaves, eighteen and
three hundred, and went in pursuit as far as Dan.

---

10 **bitumen:** Asphalt. **flung themselves:** Others use
"fell."

12 **—the son of Avram's brother—** : The Hebrew
places the phrase after "property," not after "Lot,"

as would be comfortable in English. **for he had settled:** The story abounds in similar explanatory
phrases, which could almost be put in parentheses.

14 **brother:** Kinsman.

15   He split up (his forces) against them in the night, he and his
         servants, and struck them and pursued them as far as Hova,
         which is to the north of Damascus.

16   But he returned all the property, and he also returned his brother
         Lot and his property, and also the women and the (other)
         people.

17   The king of Sedom went out to meet him upon his return from
         the strike against Kedorla'omer and against the kings that were
         with him, to the valley of Shaveh—that is now the King's
         Valley.

18   Now Malki-Tzedek, king of Shalem, brought out bread and wine,
         —for he was priest of God Most-High,

19   and gave him blessing and said:
      Blessed be Avram by God Most-High,
      Founder of Heaven and Earth!

20   And blessed be God Most-High,
      who has delivered your oppressors into your hand!
      He gave him a tenth of everything.

21   The king of Sedom said to Avram:
      Give me the persons, and the property take for yourself.

22   Avram said to the king of Sedom:
      I raise my hand in the presence of YHWH, God Most-High,
      Founder of Heaven and Earth,

23   if from a thread to a sandal-strap—if I should take from anything
         that is yours . . . !
      So that you should not say: I made Avram rich.

24   Nothing for me!
      Only what the lads have consumed,
      and the share of the men who went with me—Aner, Eshcol, and
         Mamre,
      let them take their share.

---

15 **north:** Lit. "left."
18 **Malki-Tzedek:** Trad. English "Melchizedek." The
    name is a Hebrew one, and the character appears
    as if from nowhere. **Shalem:** Identified with the
    later Jerusalem. **God Most-High:** Heb. *El Elyon*.

20 **a tenth:** Like the tithe later given to Israelite priests.
22 **I raise my hand:** I swear.
23 **from a thread to a sandal-strap:** As in "from A to
    Z," or "anything at all."
24 **lads:** Servants.

The Covenant between the Pieces (15): Amid scenes of great drama and almost mystery, a number of significant motifs are presented: (1) Avram's expressions of doubt that God will keep his promise about descendants (thus heightening the tension and final miracle of Yitzhak's birth); (2) the linking of the Patriarch to the event of the Exodus centuries later; and (3) the "cutting" of a covenant, in a manner well known in the ancient world. This last motif, especially with its setting of "great darkness" and "night-blackness," takes Avram far beyond the earlier figure of Noah into a special and fateful relationship with God.

15:1 After these events YHWH's word came to Avram in a vision,
saying:
Be not afraid, Avram,
I am a delivering-shield to you,
your reward is exceedingly great.

2 Avram said:
My Lord, YHWH,
what would you give me—
for I am going (to die) accursed,
and the Son Domestic of My House is Damascan Eliezer.

3 And Avram said further:
Here, to me you have not given seed,
here, the Son of My House must be my heir.

4 But here, YHWH's word (came) to him, saying:
This one shall not be heir to you,
rather, the one that goes out from your own body, he shall be heir
to you.

5 He brought him outside and said:
Pray look toward the heavens and count the stars,
can you count them?
And he said to him:
So shall your seed be.

6 Now he trusted in YHWH,
and he deemed it as righteous-merit on his part.

7 Now he said to him:
I am YHWH
who brought you out of Ur of the Chaldeans
to give you this land, to inherit it.

15:1 **YHWH's word came:** A formula often used by the Prophets. Avram is portrayed as their spiritual ancestor (Buber, 1982).

2 **accursed:** Heb. *ariri;* B-R uses "bare-of-children."
Son Domestic ... Damascan: Hebrew difficult. The translation here reflects the play on sound (Heb. *ben meshek ... dammesek*).

3 **Son of My House:** The chief servant, who could inherit the estate in certain circumstances. Note the play on "son": the Hebrew here is *ben beti,* while *ben* alone means "son." **heir:** Three times here, indicating Avram's main concern.

6 **he deemed it:** "He" refers to God.

7 **who brought you out:** Like the later "I am YHWH your God, who brought you out of the land of Egypt" (Ex. 20:2). The language is undoubtedly intentional.

The Firstborn Son (16): In the face of Sarai's inability to bear children, Avram is given the legitimate option of producing an heir through her maid, Hagar. Somewhat embarrassing to later interpreters, this practice was nevertheless common in the ancient Near East (see also 30:3ff., 30:9ff.). Hagar abuses her temporarily exalted position (as her son Yishmael apparently does in a parallel story, in Chap. 21), but is saved by God's intervention. The motif of "affliction" is continued from Chap. 15 (here, in vv.6, 9, and 11); also mentioned three times is God's "hearkening" (hence the name Yishmael/God Hearkens). Buber understood this vocabulary to allude to the Exodus story, which in its early chapters uses the same terms.

Although Yishmael is not ultimately the chosen heir, he is nonetheless protected by God (see 21:20) and is eventually made into "a great nation" (17:20), as befits a child of Avram.

8 But he said:
My Lord, YHWH,
by what shall I know that I will inherit it?

9 He said to him:
Fetch me a calf of three, a she-goat of three, a ram of three, a
turtle-dove, and a fledgling.

10 He fetched him all these.
He halved them down the middle, putting each one's half toward
its neighbor,
but the birds he did not halve.

11 Vultures descended upon the carcasses,
but Avram drove them back.

12 Now it was, when the sun was coming in ,
that deep slumber fell upon Avram—
and here, fright and great darkness falling upon him!

13 And he said to Avram:
You must know, yes, know
that your seed will be sojourners in a land not theirs;
they will put them in servitude and afflict them
for four hundred years.

14 But the nation to which they are in servitude—I will bring
judgment on them,
and after that they will go out with great property.

15 As for you, you will go to your fathers in peace;
you will be buried at a good ripe-age.

16 But in the fourth generation they will return here,
for the iniquity of the Amorite has not reached full-measure.
heretofore.

17 Now it was, when the sun had come in,
that there was night-blackness,

8 **But he said:** Avram, having just demonstrated trust
in v.6, now expresses deep doubt. **inherit:** Or "possess."

9 **of three:** I.e., three years old, and presumably mature and ritually fit for sacrifice.

12 **deep slumber:** Not conventional sleep, it is almost
always sent by God in the Bible (see 2:21, for example). The result here is "fright and great darkness. "

13 **afflict:** Looking toward the "affliction" of the Israelites in Egypt (Ex. 1:11, 12).

15 **ripe-age:** Lit. "grayness" or "hoariness."

16 **But in the fourth generation . . . :** God here speaks
of the future conquest of Canaan by Avram's descendants. The natives (here termed "Amorites")
are viewed as having forfeited their right to the land
by their immorality (see Lev. 18:25–8).

◆ and here, a smoking oven, a fiery torch
that crossed between those pieces.

18 On that day
Yʜᴡʜ cut a covenant with Avram,
saying: I give this land to your seed,
from the River of Egypt to the Great River, the river Euphrates,

19 the Kenite and the Kenizzite and the Kadmonite,

20 and the Hittite and the Perizzite and the Refa'ites,

21 and the Amorite and the Canaanite and the Girgashite and the
Yevusite.

16:1 Now Sarai, Avram's wife, had not borne him (children).
She had an Egyptian maid—her name was Hagar.

2 Sarai said to Avram:
Now here, Yʜᴡʜ has obstructed me from bearing;
pray come in to my maid,
perhaps I may be built-up-with-sons through her!
Avram hearkened to Sarai's voice:

3 Sarai, Avram's wife, took Hagar the Egyptian-woman, her maid,
at the end of ten years of Avram's being settled in the land of
Canaan,
and gave her to her husband Avram as a wife for him.

4 He came in to Hagar, and she became pregnant.
But when she saw that she was pregnant, her mistress became of
light-worth in her eyes.

5 Sarai said to Avram:
The wrong done me is upon you!
I myself gave my maid into your bosom,
but now that she sees that she is pregnant, I have become of
light-worth in her eyes.
May Yʜᴡʜ see-justice-done between me and you!

18 **cut:** Concluded; the usage is influenced by the act of
cutting animals by the parties involved, as in this
story.

19 **the Kenite . . . :** Canaanite tribes, here presented as
a round ten in number.

16:1 **built-up-with-sons:** Heb. *ibbane*, a play on *bano*
(build) and *ben* (son).

3 **wife:** Or "concubine."

4 **became of light-worth in her eyes:** A Hebrew
idiom. JPS: "was lowered in her esteem."

6 Avram said to Sarai:
   Here, your maid is in your hand, deal with her however seems
        good in your eyes.
   Sarai afflicted her, so that she had to flee from her.

7 But YHWH's messenger found her by a spring of water in the
        wilderness, by the spring on the way to Shur.

8 He said:
   Hagar, Sarai's maid, whence do you come, whither are you
        going?
   She said:
   I am fleeing from Sarai my mistress.

9 YHWH's messenger said to her:
   Return to your mistress and let yourself be afflicted under her
        hand!

10 And YHWH's messenger said to her:
    I will make your seed many, yes, many, it will be too many to
        count!

11 And YHWH's messenger said to her:
    Here, you are pregnant,
    you will bear a son;
    call his name: Yishmael/God Hearkens,
    for God has hearkened to your being afflicted.

12 He shall be a wild-ass of a man,
    his hand against all, hand of all against him,
    yet in the presence of all his brothers shall he dwell.

13 Now she called the name of YHWH, the one who was speaking to
        her:
    You God of Seeing!

---

6 **afflicted:** Or "abused," "maltreated."

7 **YHWH's messenger:** Traditionally "angel," but the
English word stems from the Greek *angelos,* which
also means "messenger." In Genesis God's messengers seem to be quite human in appearance, and are
sometimes taken for God himself (see 18:2ff.).

10 **too many to count:** Apparently fulfilling God's

blessing and promise to Avram in 15:5. Until 17:16,
nothing indicates that Yishmael is not Avram's long-
awaited heir.

11 **Yishmael:** Trad. English "Ishmael."

13 **Have I actually gone on seeing . . . :** Heb. obscure.
Hagar possibly is expressing surprise that she survived her encounter with God.

69

The Covenant of Circumcision (17): As Plaut notes, up to this point the covenant between God and Avram has been rather one-sided. In this chapter Avram is given
a command to perform—not only of circumcision, but to be moral and upright
(v.1, expanded in 18:19). Circumcision is but the symbol of the ongoing imperative
to do "what is just."

In many societies circumcision has been connected directly to puberty and
marriage, usually taking place (as it does here to Yishmael) at around the age
of thirteen. Our passage's moving back of the rite essentially to birth is a daring
reinterpretation, at once defusing the act of exclusively sexual content while at
the same time suggesting that the covenant, a lifelong commitment, is nevertheless passed down biologically through the generations. The males of the tribe are
not simply made holy for marriage. They bear the mark upon their bodies as a sacred reminder of their mission.

The chapter echoes with repetition: "exceedingly, exceedingly" (vv.6 and 20,
referring to the fruitfulness of Avram's descendants), "you and your seed after
you" (vv.7, 10; see also v.19), "for the ages" (covenant and land, vv.7, 8, 13, 19), and
"into your generations" (vv.7, 9, 12).

Preparatory to Avram's assumption of fatherhood—of an individual and of a
people—his name is changed (v.5), as is that of Sarai (v.15). This act is of the utmost significance in the biblical world. Since a person's name was indicative of
personality and fate, the receiving of a new one signified a new life or a new stage
in life. Similarly, Yaakov (and in a sort of coronation, Yosef) will undergo a change
of name. Such a practice still survives among kings and popes.

For she said:
Have I actually gone on seeing here
after his seeing me?
14 Therefore the well was called:
Well of the Living-One Who-Sees-Me.
Here, it is between Kadesh and Bered.

15 Hagar bore Avram a son,
and Avram called the name of the son whom Hagar bore:
Yishmael.
16 Avram was eighty years and six years old when Hagar bore
Yishmael to Avram.

17:1 Now when Avram was ninety years and nine years old
Yhwh was seen by Avram and said to him:
I am God Shaddai.
Walk in my presence! And be wholehearted!
2 I set my covenant between me and you,
I will make you exceedingly, exceedingly many.
3 Avram fell upon his face.
God spoke with him,
saying:
4 As for me,
here, my covenant is with you,
so that you will become the father of a throng of nations.
5 No longer shall your name be called Avram,
rather shall your name be Avraham,
for I will make you *Av Hamon Goyyim*/Father of a Throng of
Nations!

17:1 **Ninety years and nine years:** Thirteen years have elapsed since the events of the previous chapter. Now that Yishmael is entering puberty, God can no longer conceal that he is not the promised heir. See vv.16, 18. **Shaddai:** Hebrew obscure. Traditionally translated "Almighty"; others use "of the mountains." In Genesis the name is most often tied to promises of human fertility, as in v.2. **Walk . . . be**

wholehearted: Contrasted to Noah (6:9), Avram is a genuine religious man who lives his faith actively.
2 **set:** Heb. *va-ettena*. The root *n-t-n* is repeated throughout the chapter (as "make" in vv.5 and 6, and as "give" in vv.8 and 16).
4 **throng:** The word suggests the sound of a crowd, rather than merely a large number.
5 **Avraham:** Trad. English "Abraham."

6 I will cause you to bear fruit exceedingly, exceedingly,
I will make nations of you,
(yes,) kings will go out from you!

7 I establish my covenant between me and you and your seed after
you, throughout their generations as a covenant for the ages,
to be God to you and to your seed after you.

8 I will give to you and to your seed after you, the land of your
sojournings, all the land of Canaan, as a holding for the ages,
and I will be God to them.

9 God said to Avraham:
As for you,
you are to keep my covenant, you and your seed after you,
throughout their generations.

10 This is my covenant which you are to keep, between me and you
and your seed after you:
every male among you shall be circumcised.

11 You shall circumcise the flesh of your foreskin,
so that it may serve as a sign of the covenant between me and
you.

12 At eight days old, every male among you shall be circumcised,
throughout your generations,
whether house-born or bought with money from any foreigner,
who is not your seed.

13 Circumcised, yes, circumcised shall be your house-born and your
money-bought (slaves),
so that my covenant may be in your flesh as a covenant for the
ages.

14 But a foreskinned male,
who does not have the foreskin of his flesh circumcised,
that person shall be cut off from his kinspeople—
he has violated my covenant!

8 **I will be God to them:** Often reiterated as part of the biblical covenant (e.g., 28:21).
12 **house-born or bought with money:** I.e., slaves.

The entire household, as an extension of the man's personality, is to be brought into the covenant.

15 God said to Avraham:
As for Sarai your wife—you shall not call her name Sarai,
for Sara/Princess is her name!
16 I will bless her, and I will give you a son from her,
I will bless her
so that she becomes nations,
kings of peoples shall come from her!
17 But Avraham fell on his face and laughed,
he said in his heart:
To a hundred-year-old man shall there be (children) born ?
Or shall ninety-year-old Sara give birth?
18 Avraham said to God:
If only Yishmael might live in your presence!
19 God said:
Nevertheless,
Sara your wife is to bear you a son,
you shall call his name: Yitzhak/He Laughs.
I will establish my covenant with him as a covenant for the ages,
for his seed after him.
20 And as for Yishmael, I hearken to you:
Here, I will make him blessed, I will make him bear fruit, I will
make him many, exceedingly, exceedingly—
he will beget twelve (tribal) leaders, and I will make a great
nation of him.
21 But my covenant I will establish with Yitzhak, whom Sara will
bear to you at this set-time, another year hence.
22 When he had finished speaking with Avraham,
God went up, from beside Avraham.

15 **you shall not call her name Sarai:** Significantly, Sara is the only woman in the Bible to have her name changed by God.
16 **so that she becomes nations:** Sara in essence shares the blessing of God. She is not merely the biological means for its fulfillment.
17 **laughed:** Laughter becomes the key word of most of the stories about Yitzhak.
19 **Yitzhak:** Trad. English "Isaac."

20 **make him blessed ... make him bear fruit ... make him many:** Heb. *berakhti oto ve-hifreiti oto ve-hirbeiti oto.* **twelve princes:** Thus equaling the twelve sons/tribes of Israel?
21 **another year:** Not nine months (Sara does not immediately become pregnant). Again the events seem to take place in a realistic framework, rather than in a strictly supernatural one.

73

Visit and Promise (18:1–15): The announcement of Sara's impending child is set in the familiar ancient garb of a tale about divine travelers who visit an old couple. Central, as is usual in folklore, is the idea of hospitality, emphasized in the text by the threefold use of "pray" (please) (vv.3–4), "pass on/by" (vv.3–5), and by Avraham's flurry of activity (he himself "runs" twice, "hastens" three times, and "fetches" four times in serving his guests).

The Great Intercession (18:16–33): With v.17 the narrative is interrupted, and there begins a remarkable scene in which man confronts God. As if to emphasize the importance of this encounter, the text presents God as thinking out loud, and using the intimate term "know" (see 4:1) to describe his relationship to Avraham. And Avraham, the man through whom the nations "will find blessing" (v.18; see 12:3), the progenitor of "a great . . . nation" (v.18; see 12:2) that will see in justice its great goal, is now confronted with an urgent question of justice. While Avraham seems to be testing God in this story, it may in fact be precisely the reverse that is intended. Perhaps here more than anywhere else in the entire cycle (with the possible exception of Chap. 22), Avraham appears as the worthy father of his people, the one who will "charge his sons and his household . . . to do what is right and just" (v.19). Without this story Avraham would be a man of faith but not a man of compassion and moral outrage, a model consistent with Moses and the Prophets of Israel.

The tightly structured, almost formal dialogue allows us to focus totally on the issue at hand. Predominating as refrains are the words "innocent" and "guilty," along with the expected versions of "just/justice" that pervade Avraham's remarks.

23 Avraham took Yishmael his son and all those born in his house
   and all those bought with his money,
all the males among Avraham's household people,
and circumcised the flesh of their foreskins on that same day,
as God had spoken to him.

24 Avraham was ninety-nine years old when he had the flesh of his
   foreskin circumcised,

25 and Yishmael his son was thirteen years old when he had the flesh
   of his foreskin circumcised.

26 On that same day
were circumcised Avraham and Yishmael his son,

27 and all his household people, whether house-born or
   money-bought from a foreigner, were circumcised with him.

18:1 Now YHWH was seen by him by the oaks of Mamre
   as he was sitting at the entrance to his tent at the heat of the day.

2 He lifted up his eyes and saw:
here, three men standing over against him.
When he saw them, he ran to meet them from the entrance to
   his tent and bowed to the earth

3 and said:
My lords,
pray if I have found favor in your eyes,
pray do not pass by your servant!

4 Pray let a little water be fetched, then wash your feet and recline
   under the tree;

5 let me fetch (you) a bit of bread, that you may refresh your
   hearts,
then afterward you may pass on—

22 **God went up, from beside Avraham:** Perhaps a formula used to signify the end of the conversation.

23 **on that same day:** Underlining Avraham's customary obedience. **as God had spoken to him:** Like Noah in 6:22, 7:5, and 7:9, Avraham scrupulously follows God's commands without question (so too in 21:4 and 22:3).

18:1 **entrance to his tent:** Also used in vv.2 and 10, it may hint at the important events being portrayed: the "entrance to the tent" is often a sacred spot in subsequent books of the Bible.

2 **three men:** See note on 16:7. **over against him:** Heb. *alav* could mean "over" or "next to" him.

3 **My lords:** Some use "My Lord."

4 **wash your feet:** Customary for weary travelers in the ancient world.

for you have, after all, passed your servant's way!
They said:
Do thus, as you have spoken.

6   Avraham hastened into his tent to Sara and said:
Make haste! Three measures of choice flour! Knead it, make
bread-cakes!

7   Avraham ran to the oxen,
he fetched a young ox, tender and fine, and gave it to a
serving-lad, that he might hasten to make it ready;

8   then he fetched cream and milk and the young ox that he had
made ready, and placed it before them.
Now he stood over against them under the tree while they ate.

9   They said to him:
Where is Sara your wife?
He said:
Here in the tent.
Now he said:

10   I will return, yes, return to you when time revives,
and Sara your wife will have a son!
Now Sara was listening at the entrance to the tent, which was
behind him.

11   And Avraham and Sara were old, advanced in days,
the way of women had ceased for Sara.

12   Sara laughed within herself, saying:
After I have become worn, is there to be pleasure for me? And my
lord is old!

13   But YHWH said to Avraham:
Now why does Sara laugh and say: Shall I really give birth, now
that I am old?

14   Is anything beyond YHWH?
At that set-time I will return to you, when time revives, and Sara
will have a son.

---

10 **when time revives:** An idiom for "next year." B-R
uses "at the time of life-bestowing."

11 **the way of women:** The menstrual period.
12 **pleasure:** Sexual.

15 Sara pretended (otherwise), saying:
No, I did not laugh.
For she was afraid.
But he said:
No, indeed you laughed.

16 The men arose from there, and looked down upon the face of
Sedom,
and Avraham went with them to escort them.

17 Now YHWH had said to himself:
Shall I cover up from Avraham what I am about to do?

18 For Avraham is to become, yes, become a nation great and
mighty (in number),
and all the nations of the earth will find blessing through him.

19 Indeed, I have known him,
in order that he may charge his sons and his household after him:
they shall keep the way of YHWH,
to do what is right and just,
in order that YHWH may bring upon Avraham what he spoke
concerning him.

20 So YHWH said:
The outcry in Sedom and Amora—how great it is!
And their sin—how exceedingly heavily it weighs!

21 Now let me go down and see:
if they have done according to its cry that has come to me—
destruction!
And if not—
I wish to know.

22 The men turned from there and went toward Sedom,
but Avraham still stood in the presence of YHWH.

23 Avraham came close and said:
Will you really sweep away the innocent along with the guilty?

24 Perhaps there are fifty innocent within the city,

21 **destruction:** Some read "altogether (according to its cry)."
22 **but Avraham still stood in the presence of YHWH:** Some manuscripts read "But YHWH still stood in the presence of Avraham." The subject of the sentence has been reversed by scribes who were uncomfortable with the passage's human portrayal of God.

The End of Sedom and Amora (19): The detailed and colorful story of Lot in Sedom and in flight from it adds a great deal to the Avraham cycle. On the one hand there is the portrayal of Lot's continuing his uncle's tradition of hospitality (vv.1–3), even to the extent of being willing to sacrifice his own daughters' virginity. On the other hand Lot comes across as timid (vv.7–8) and fearful (vv.18–20). In fact the word "pray" (which we noted in Chap. 18 as a "hospitality term," and which serves that function in verse 2 here as well) is used later in this chapter in a way that almost suggests whining. He thus once again brings Avraham's personality into sharper focus.

The crimes of Sedom and Amora are at last indicated more openly: abuse of the sacred duty of hospitality, and sexual immorality (v.5). The latter theme returns at the end of the story, with the incestuous incident that takes place at the instigation of Lot's daughters.

The story uses some stylized vocabulary. In v.13, the messengers talk of "bringing ruin," just as we encountered in the Flood narrative (6:13). The narrative also gives negative twists to words which were positive in the previous chapter: "know" and "just" are changed to indicate illicit sex (v.5) and a condemnation of the alien Lot (v.9, "act-the-judge and adjudicate"). Here too, "door/entrance" is transformed from a place of contact with God to one of confrontation with men.

The account of the destruction itself is terse and mysterious, but it also reveals the predicament of an all-too-human man, Lot.

The final section of the Sedom and Amora story recounts the origins of two of Israel's neighbors, the Moabites and Ammonites. As traditional enemies, they are not treated very kindly, any more than was the ancestor of the Canaanites in 9:20–27.

◆ will you really sweep it away?
Will you not bear with the place because of the fifty innocent
    that are in its midst?

25 Heaven forbid for you to do a thing like this,
to deal death to the innocent along with the guilty,
that it should come about: like the innocent, like the guilty,
Heaven forbid for you!
The judge of all the earth—will he not do what is just?

26 YHWH said:
If I find in Sedom fifty innocent within the city,
I will bear with the whole place for their sake.

27 Avraham spoke up, and said:
Now pray, I have ventured to speak to my Lord,
and I am but earth and ashes:

28 Perhaps of the fifty innocent, five will be lacking—
will you bring ruin upon the whole city because of the five?
He said:
I will not bring ruin, if I find there forty-five.

29 But he continued to speak to him and said:
Perhaps there will be found there only forty!
He said:
I will not do it, for the sake of the forty.

30 But he said:
Pray let not my Lord be upset that I speak further:
Perhaps there will be found there only thirty!
He said:
I will not do it, if I find there thirty.

31 But he said:
Now pray, I have ventured to speak to my Lord:
Perhaps there will be found there only twenty!
He said:
I will not bring ruin, for the sake of the twenty.

---

25 **Heaven forbid:** Lit. "May you have a curse," an ironic turn of phrase in this situation. **like the innocent, like the guilty:** Or "innocent and guilty alike."

26 **bear with:** Or "bear the sin."

27 **earth and ashes:** Heb. *afar va-efer*, traditionally "dust and ashes." The phrase, while common in English, is used in the Bible again only in Job (30:19, 42:6).

32 But he said:
Pray let my Lord not be upset that I speak further just this one
time:
Perhaps there will be found there only ten!
He said:
I will not bring ruin, for the sake of the ten.
33 YHWH went, as soon as he had finished speaking to Avraham, and
Avraham returned to his place.

19:1 The two messengers came to Sedom at sunset,
as Lot was sitting at the gate of Sedom.
When Lot saw them, he arose to meet them and bowed low,
brow to the ground
2 and said:
Now pray, my lords,
pray turn aside to your servant's house,
spend the night, wash your feet;
(starting-early) you may go on your way.
They said:
No, rather we will spend the night in the square.
3 But he pressed them exceedingly hard,
so they turned in to him and came into his house.
He made them a meal-with-drink and baked flat-cakes, and they
ate.
4 They had not yet lain down, when the men of the city, the men
of Sedom, encircled the house,
from young lad to old man, all the people (even) from the
outskirts.
5 They called out to Lot and said to him:
Where are the men who came to you tonight?
Bring them out to us, we want to know them!
6 Lot went out to them, to the entrance, shutting the door behind
him

33 **YHWH went:** See note on 17:22.

19:5 **we want to know them:** The meaning is unmistakably sexual.

7 and said:
  Pray, brothers, do not be so wicked!
8 Now pray, I have two daughters who have never known a man,
  pray let me bring them out to you, and you may deal with them
    however seems good in your eyes;
  only to these men do nothing,
  for they have, after all, come under the shadow of my roof-beam!
9 But they said:
  Step aside!
  and said:
  This one came to sojourn and (wants to) judge, play-the-judge?!
  Now we will do worse to you than (to) them!
  And they pressed exceedingly hard against the man, against Lot,
    and stepped closer to break down the door.
10 But the men put out their hand and brought Lot in to them,
    into the house, and shut the door.
11 And the men who were at the entrance to the house, they struck
    with dazzling-light—(all men) great and small,
  so that they were unable to find the entrance.
12 The men said to Lot:
  Whom else have you here—a son-in-law, sons, daughters?
  Bring anyone whom you have in the city out of the place!
13 For we are about to bring ruin on this place,
  for how great is their outcry before YHWH!
  And YHWH has sent us to bring it to ruin.
14 Lot went out to speak to his sons-in-law, those who had taken his
    daughters (in marriage), and said:
  Up, out of this place, for YHWH is about to bring ruin on the city!
  But in the eyes of his sons-in-law, he was like one who jests.
15 Now when the dawn came up,
  the messengers pushed Lot on, saying:

8 **pray let me bring them out to you . . . :** For a similar story, see Judg. 19. There the offer of rape is accepted by the townspeople.
9 **judge, play-the-judge:** Heb. *va-yishpot shafot.*

10 **the men:** The messengers.
11 **(all men) great and small:** Lit. "from small to
  great."

Up, take your wife and your two daughters who are here,
lest you be swept away in the iniquity of the city!

16 When he lingered,
the men seized his hand, his wife's hand, and the hand of his two
daughters
—because YHWH's pity was upon him—
and, bringing him out, they left him outside the city.

17 It was, when they had brought him outside, that (one of them)
said:
Escape for your life, do not gaze behind you, do not stand still
anywhere in the plain:
to the hill-country escape, lest you be swept away!

18 Lot said to them:
No, pray, my lord!

19 Now pray, your servant has found favor in your eyes,
you have shown great faithfulness in how you have dealt with
me, keeping me alive—
but I, I am not able to escape to the hill-country,
lest the wickedness cling to me, and I die!

20 Now pray, that town is near enough to flee to, and it is so tiny;
pray let me escape there—is it not tiny?—and stay alive!

21 He said to him:
Here then, I lift up your face in this matter as well,
by not overturning this town of which you speak.

22 Make haste, escape there,
for I am not able to do anything until you come there.
Therefore the name of the town was called: Tzo'ar / Tiny.

23 (Now) the sun was going out over the earth as Lot came to
Tzo'ar.

24 But YHWH rained down brimstone and fire upon Sedom and
Amora, coming from YHWH, from the heavens,

---

17 **Escape:** Heb. *himmalet,* used five times here. Perhaps it is a pun on Lot's name; he is "the escaper" in a number of situations.
19 **lest the wickedness cling to me:** The expression of an idea common to many cultures: that evil is like a disease, a physical rather than purely moral entity.
20 **tiny:** Or "a trifle."

21 **lift up your face:** A similar Assyrian phrase means "save" or "cheer." **overturning:** Overthrowing. The word is used later in the Bible to describe the fate of the two cities again (e.g., Lam. 4:6).
22 **I am not able . . . until you come there:** In deference to Avraham (see v.29).

25 he overturned those cities and all of the plain, all those settled in
   the cities and the vegetation of the soil.

26 Now his wife gazed behind him, and she became a pillar of salt.

27 Avraham started-early in the morning to the place where he had
   stood in YHWH's presence,

28 he looked down upon the face of Sedom and Amora and upon
   the whole face of the plain-country
   and saw:
   here, the dense-smoke of the land went up like the dense-smoke
   of a furnace!

29 Thus it was, when God brought ruin on the cities of the plain,
   that God kept Avraham in mind and sent out Lot from the
   overturning,
   when he overturned the cities where Lot had settled.

30 Lot went up from Tzo'ar and settled in the hill-country, his two
   daughters with him,
   for he was afraid to settle in Tzo'ar.
   So he settled in a cave, he and his two daughters.

31 Now the firstborn said to the younger:
   Our father is old,
   and there is no man in the land to come in to us as befits the way
   of all the earth!

32 Come, let us have our father drink wine and lie with him
   so that we may keep seed alive by our father.

33 So they had their father drink wine that night,
   then the firstborn went in and lay with her father—
   but he knew nothing of her lying down or her rising up.

34 It was on the morrow that the firstborn said to the younger:
   Here, yesternight I lay with father.
   Let us have him drink wine tonight as well,
   then you go in and lie with him,

---

26 **she became a pillar of salt:** An old folklore motif of
what happens when humans see God (or his actions), made popular by the many mineral pillars in
the region around the Dead Sea.

The Wife—II (20): The second occurrence of "The Matriarch Protected" comes immediately before the story of Yitzhak's birth, as if to emphasize God's hand in the process one more time. In this long variation on the theme, God is most active and Avraham most revealing of his past. He emerges from danger as a man who clearly enjoys God's full protection and bounty.

The story almost draws a web of magic around Sara. Avimelekh is nearly killed by God, and Sara's childlessness is inflicted upon all the women in the king's household—even though there is not the slightest doubt of his innocence (he "had not come near her").

Yitzhak Born (21:1–8): Two principal ideas punctuate this climax for which we have waited since Chap. 12: God keeps his promises (hence the poem in v.1), and the key word in the stories about Yitzhak: "laughter" (here the result of the actual birth).

so that we may keep seed alive by our father.

35 They had their father drink wine that night as well,
then the younger arose and lay with him,
but he knew nothing of her lying down or her rising up.

36 And Lot's two daughters became pregnant by their father.

37 The firstborn bore a son and called his name: Mo'av/By Father,
he is the tribal-father of Mo'av of today.

38 The younger also bore a son, and called his name: Ben-
Ammi/Son of My Kinspeople,
he is the tribal-father of the children of Ammon of today.

20:1 Avraham traveled from there to the Negev, and settled between
Kadesh and Shur, sojourning in Gerar.

2 Avraham said of Sara his wife: She is my sister.
So Avimelekh king of Gerar sent and had Sara taken.

3 But God came to Avimelekh in a dream of the night and said to
him:
Here, you must die because of the woman whom you have
taken,
for she is a wedded wife!

4 Avimelekh had not come near her. He said:
My Lord,
Would you kill a nation, though it be innocent?

5 Did he not say to me: She is my sister,
and also she, she said: He is my brother!
With a whole heart and with clean hands have I done this.

6 God said to him in the dream:
I also know that it was with a whole heart that you did this,
and so I also held you back from being at fault against me,
therefore I did not let you touch her.

7 But now, return the man's wife
—indeed, he is a prophet, he can intercede for you—

---

35 **but he knew nothing . . . :** The repetition of the
phrase from v.33 is meant either to absolve Lot or to
ridicule him.
37 **Mo'av:** Trad. English "Moab."
20:3 **wedded wife:** Heb. *be'ulat ba'al.*

5 **With a whole heart:** Lit. "In the wholeness of my
heart."
6 **being at fault:** Or "sinning," which is perhaps too
theological a translation.

and live!

But if you do not return her:

know that you must die, yes, die, you and all that is yours!

8 Early in the morning Avimelekh called all his servants,

he spoke all these words in their ears, and the men became
exceedingly afraid.

9 Then Avimelekh had Avraham called and said to him:

What have you done to us?

In what did I fail you,

that you have brought me and my kingdom into such great fault?

Deeds which are not to be done, you have done to me!

10 And Avimelekh said to Avraham:

What did you foresee, that you did this thing?

11 Avraham said:

Indeed, I said to myself:

Surely there is no awe of God in this place,

they will kill me on account of my wife!

12 Then, too, she is truly my sister, my father's daughter,

however not my mother's daughter—so she became my wife.

13 Now it was, when the power-of-God caused me to roam from my
father's house,

that I said to her:

Let this be the faithfulness that you do me:

in every place that we come, say of me: He is my brother.

14 Avimelekh took sheep and oxen, servants and maids, and gave
them to Avraham,

and returned Sara his wife to him.

15 Avimelekh said:

Here, my land is before you,

settle wherever seems good in your eyes.

---

8 **morning:** Heb. *boker* sometimes has this more general meaning.
11 **awe:** Others, "fear."
13 **roam:** A word which in Genesis suggests a wandering that is nevertheless directed by God. See 21:14 and 37:15 for other examples. This passage gives us a fascinating glimpse of Avraham's own perception of the events in Chap. 12. It is not unusual for the biblical storyteller to give out informa-tion in this manner (in a later speech of the protagonist). **faithfulness:** Or "favor."

16 And to Sara he said:
Here, I have given a thousand pieces of silver to your brother,
here, it shall serve you as a covering for the eyes for all who are
with you
and with everyone, that you have been decided for.
17 Avraham interceded with God
and God healed Avimelekh: his wife and his slave-women, so that
they gave birth.
18 For YHWH had obstructed, obstructed every womb in
Avimelekh's household
on account of Sara, the wife of Avraham.

21:1 Now YHWH took account of Sara as he had said,
YHWH dealt with Sara as he had spoken.
2 Sara became pregnant and bore Avraham a son in his old age,
at the set-time of which God had spoken to him.
3 And Avraham called the name of his son, who was born to him,
whom Sara bore to him:
Yitzhak/He Laughs.
4 And Avraham circumcised Yitzhak his son at eight days old, as
God had commanded him.
5 Avraham was a hundred years old when Yitzhak his son was born
to him.
6 Now Sara said:
God has made laughter for me,
all who hear of it will laugh for me.
7 And she said:
Who would have declared to Avraham:
Sara will nurse sons?
Well, I have borne him a son in his old age!
8 The child grew and was weaned,
and Avraham made a great drinking-feast on the day that Yitzhak
was weaned.

---

16 **a covering for the eyes:** Hebrew obscure; apparently it has legal connotations (see also "decided for" at the end of the verse).
18 **YHWH had obstructed:** On account of Sara, the "obstructed" one of 16:2.

21:6 **laugh for me:** Out of joy or disbelief. Some suggest "laugh at."

Yishmael Banished (21:9–21): Once Yitzhak has been born, separation must be made between heir and firstborn. Despite Avraham's obvious love for him, Yishmael must leave; his mother must repeat her ordeal of Chap. 16 as well. Nonetheless the text emphasizes that God is there "with the lad" (v.20); twice the Yishmael motif of "God hearkening" resounds (v.17); and God promises that the boy will eventually attain the same exalted status as his brother (vv.13, 18).

Structurally, this brief tale foreshadows the next chapter, the ordeal of Yitzhak. It speaks of a journey into the unknown, a child at the point of death, the intervention of God's "messenger," the parent's sighting of the way out, and the promise of future blessing. Of course the differences between the two stories are equally important.

9 Once Sara saw the son of Hagar the Egyptian-woman, whom
     she had borne to Avraham, laughing. . . .
10 She said to Avraham:
     Drive out this slave-woman and her son,
     for the son of this slave-woman shall not share-inheritance with
       my son, with Yitzhak!
11 The matter was exceedingly bad in Avraham's eyes because of
     his son.
12 But God said to Avraham:
     Do not let it be bad in your eyes concerning the lad and
       concerning your slave-woman;
     in all that Sara says to you, hearken to her voice,
     for it is through Yitzhak that seed will be called by your (name).
13 But also the son of the slave-woman—a nation will I make of
     him,
     for he too is your seed.
14 Avraham started-early in the morning,
     he took some bread and a skin of water
     and gave them to Hagar—placing them upon her shoulder—
       together with the child and sent her away.
     She went off and roamed in the wilderness of Be'er-Sheva.
15 Now when the water in the skin was at an end, she threw the
     child under one of the bushes,
16 and went and sat by herself, at-a-distance, as far away as a
     bowshot,
     for she said to herself:
     Let me not see the child die!
     So she sat at-a-distance, and lifted up her voice and wept.
17 But God heard the voice of the lad,
     God's messenger called to Hagar from heaven and said to her:
     What ails you, Hagar? Do not be afraid,
     for God has heard the voice of the lad there where he is.

9 **laughing:** Perhaps mockingly. The theme of
Yitzhak's life continues.
11 **bad in Avraham's eyes:** Displeasing or upsetting to
him.

12 **seed will be called:** I.e., your line will be continued.
14 **Be'er-Sheva:** Trad. English "Beersheba."

Treaty (21:22–34): This interlude, which usefully separates the life threats to Avraham's two sons (for a similar example, see I Sam. 25), is one of many scenes demonstrating Avraham's relationship with local princes.

18 Arise, lift up the lad and grasp him with your hand,
for a great nation will I make of him!

19 God opened her eyes, and she saw a well of water;
she went, filled the skin with water, and gave the lad to drink.

20 And God was with the lad as he grew up,
he settled in the wilderness, and became an archer, a bowman.

21 He settled in the wilderness of Paran, and his mother took him a
wife from the land of Egypt.

22 It was at about that time that Avimelekh, together with Pikhol
the commander of his army, said to Avraham:
God is with you in all that you do.

23 So now, swear to me here by God:
If you should ever deal falsely with me, with my progeny and my
posterity . . . !
Rather, faithfully, as I have dealt with you, deal with me, and with
the land in which you have sojourned.

24 Avraham said:
I so swear.

25 But Avraham rebuked Avimelekh
because of a well of water that Avimelekh's servants had seized.

26 Avimelekh said:
I do not know who did this thing,
nor have you ever told me, nor have I heard of it apart from
today.

27 So Avraham took sheep and oxen and gave them to Avimelekh,
and the two of them cut a covenant.

28 Then Avraham set seven ewe-lambs of the flock aside.

29 Avimelekh said to Avraham:
What mean these seven ewe-lambs that you have set aside?

30 He said:
Indeed, these seven ewe-lambs you should take from my hand,
so that they may be a witness for me that I dug this well.

---

23 **with my progeny and my posterity:** Heb. *u-le-nini*
u-le-nekhdi.

30 **take:** Accept.

The Great Test (22): This story is certainly one of the masterpieces of biblical literature. In a famous article by Erich Auerbach it is remarked how biblical style as exemplified here, in contradistinction to that of Homer and other epic bards, eschews physical and psychological details in favor of one central preoccupation: a man's decision in relation to God. The result of this style is a terrible intensity, a story which is so stark as to be almost unbearable.

Chap. 22 is a tale of God's seeming retraction of his promise (of "seed") to Avraham. The fact that other issues may be involved here (i.e., Israel's rejection of local and widely practiced ideas of child sacrifice) may be quite beside the point. Coming just one chapter after the birth of the long-awaited son, the story completely turns around the tension of the whole cycle and creates a new, frightening tension of its own. The real horror of the story lies in this threatened contradiction to what has gone before.

Most noticeable in the narrative is Avraham's silence, his mute acceptance of, and acting on, God's command. We are told of no sleepless night, nor does he ever say a word to God. Instead he is described with a series of verbs: starting-early, saddling, taking, splitting, arising, going (v.3; similarly in vv.6 and 9–10). Avraham the bargainer, so willing to enter into negotiations with relations (Chap. 13), allies (Chap. 14), local princes (Chap. 20), and even God himself (Chap. 18), here falls completely silent.

The chapter serves an important structural function in the Avraham cycle, framing it in conjunction with Chap. 12. The triplet in v.2 ("Pray take your son,/ your only-one,/ whom you love") recalls "from your land/ from your kindred/ from your father's house" in 12:1; "go-you-forth" and "the land that I will tell you of" (v.2; the latter, three times in the story) similarly point back to Avraham's call (12:1, "Go-you-forth . . . to the land that I will let you see"). There he had been asked to give up the past (his father); here, the future (his son). Between the two events lies Avraham's active life as man of God, ancestor, and intercessor. After this God will never speak with him again.

In many ways this story is the midpoint of Genesis. It brings the central theme of continuity and discontinuity to a head in the strongest possible way. After Moriyya, we can breathe easier, knowing that God will come to the rescue of his chosen ones in the direst of circumstances. At the same time we are left to ponder the difficulties of being a chosen one, subject to such an incredible test.

The story is also the paradigmatic narrative of the entire book. The Patriarch passes the test, and we know that the fulfillment of the divine promise is assured. Yet there is an ominous note: love, which occurs here by name for the first time, leads almost to heartbreak. So it will be for the rest of Genesis.

31 Therefore that place was called Be'er-Sheva/Well of the Seven-
    Swearing,
   for there the two of them swore (an oath).
32 Thus they cut a covenant in Be'er-Sheva.
   Then Avimelekh and Pikhol the commander of his army arose
   and returned to the land of the Philistines.
33 Now he planted a tamarisk in Be'er-Sheva
   and there he called out the name: YHWH God of the Ages.
34 And Avraham sojourned in the land of the Philistines for many
    days.

22:1 Now after these events it was
    that God tested Avraham
    and said to him:
    Avraham!
    He said:
    Here I am.
  2 He said:
    Pray take your son,
    your only-one,
    whom you love,
    Yitzhak,
    and go-you-forth to the land of Moriyya/Seeing,
    and offer him up there as an offering-up
    upon one of the mountains
    that I will tell you of.
  3 Avraham started-early in the morning,
    he saddled his donkey,
    he took his two serving-lads with him and Yitzhak his son,
    he split wood for the offering-up
    and arose and went to the place that God had told him of.

33 **tamarisk:** A tree rarely mentioned in the Bible, it may indicate a holy place, similar to the oaks where Avraham dwells earlier. **God of the Ages:** A name unique to this passage.
34 **Philistines:** Another anachronism. The Philistines appear first in the days of the Conquest (Joshua and Judges).
22:1 **after these events:** Others use "Some time after-

ward." **Here I am:** A term frequently used to convey readiness, usually in relation to a superior's command or address.
2 **Yitzhak:** The name is left until the end of the phrase, to heighten tension. Similarly, see 27:32. **Moriyya:** Trad. English "Moriah." The mountain here is later identified with the site of Solomon's Temple.

4 On the third day Avraham lifted up his eyes
and saw the place from afar.

5 Avraham said to his lads:
You stay here with the donkey,
and I and the lad wish to go yonder,
we wish to bow down and then return to you.

6 Avraham took the wood for the offering-up,
he placed them upon Yitzhak his son,
in his hand he took the fire and the knife.
Thus the two of them went together.

7 Yitzhak said to Avraham his father, he said:
Father!
He said:
Here I am, my son.
He said:
Here are the fire and the wood,
but where is the lamb for the offering-up?

8 Avraham said:
God will see-for-himself to the lamb for the offering-up,
my son.
Thus the two of them went together.

9 They came to the place that God had told him of;
there Avraham built the slaughter-site
and arranged the wood
and bound Yitzhak his son
and placed him on the slaughter-site atop the wood.

10 And Avraham stretched out his hand,
he took the knife to slay his son.

11 But YHWH's messenger called to him from heaven
and said:

---

5 **bow down:** Worship.
6, 8 **Thus the two of them went together:** Between these two statements is Avraham's successful deflection of Yitzhak's question, and perhaps the hint of a happy ending.
7 **fire:** I.e., a torch or brand.

8 **see-for-himself:** Or "select." See the name of the mountain in verse 14, "YHWH Sees." **offering-up,/ my son:** One might read it with a dash instead of a comma, to preserve what may be an ironic answer.
10 **slay:** A verb used to describe animal sacrifice; the throat is slit.

Avraham! Avraham!
He said:
Here I am.

12 He said:
Do not stretch out your hand against the lad,
do not do anything to him!
For now I know
that you are in awe of God—
you have not withheld your son, your only-one, from me.

13 Avraham lifted up his eyes and saw:
here, a ram was caught behind in the thicket by its horns!
Avraham went,
he took the ram
and offered it up as an offering-up in place of his son.

14 Avraham called the name of that place: YHWH Sees.
As the saying is today: On YHWH's mountain (it) is seen.

15 Now YHWH's messenger called to Avraham a second time from
heaven

16 and said:
By myself I swear
—YHWH's utterance—
indeed, because you have done this thing, have not withheld your
son, your only-one,

17 indeed, I will bless you, bless you,
I will make your seed many, yes, many,
like the stars of the heavens and like the sand that is on the shore
of the sea;
your seed shall inherit the gate of their enemies,

18 all the nations of the earth shall enjoy blessing through your
seed,
in consequence of your hearkening to my voice.

13 **a ram caught behind:** Most ancient versions read "one/a ram caught."

16 **YHWH's utterance:** A phrase often found in the Prophetic books. See note on 15:1.

17 **indeed, I will bless you:** Avra-ham has received such blessings before, but never before "because you have hearkened to my voice" (v.18). **inherit the gate:** I.e., possess or take the city.

18 **all the nations . . . :** See 12:3.

Purchase and Burial (23): Even though he is now secure in God's covenant, Avraham must still live and function in the human world. His purchase of a burial plot for Sara shows us once more his dealings with his neighbors, here as their equal, and also establishes at last his legal foothold in Canaan, albeit with a small piece of land. The long conversations and considerable formality of the chapter, which are not unusual in an ancient Near Eastern context, contrast with the extreme brevity of the previous chapter.

The narrative strikes a curious balance between the emotional reality of the situation (e.g., the repetition of "dead," "presence," and "bury") and the requirements of legal procedure ("Hear me," "give title," and "holding").

◆ 19 Avraham returned to his lads,
they arose and went together to Be'er-Sheva.
And Avraham stayed in Be'er-Sheva.

20 Now after these events it was, that it was told to Avraham, saying:
Here, Milca too has borne, sons to Nahor your brother:

21 Utz his firstborn and Buz his brother, Kemuel father of

22 Aram, / and Cesed, Hazo, Pildash, Yidlaf, and Betuel.

23 Now Betuel begot Rivka.—
These eight Milca bore to Nahor, Avraham's brother.

24 And his concubine—her name was Re'uma—bore too: Tevah,
Gaham, Tahash, and Maakha.

23:1 Now Sara's life was one hundred years and twenty years and
seven years, (thus) the years of Sara's life.

2 Sara died in Arba-Town, that is now Hevron, in the land of
Canaan.
Avraham set about to lament for Sara and to weep over her;

3 then Avraham arose from the presence of his dead
and spoke to the Sons of Het, saying:

4 I am a sojourner settled among you;
give me title to a burial holding among you,
so that I may bury my dead from my presence.

5 The Sons of Het answered Avraham, saying to him:

6 Hear us, my lord!
You are one exalted by God in our midst—
in the choicest of our burial-sites you may bury your dead,
no man among us will deny you his burial-site
for burying your dead!

---

19 **Avraham returned:** The fact that Yitzhak is not mentioned here has given rise to speculation for centuries (see Shalom Spiegel, *The Last Trial*). The omission may simply arise from the fact that Yitzhak as a personality is not important to the story, which is first and foremost a test of Avraham.
23 **Rivka:** Trad. English "Rebecca."
23:1 **(thus) the years of Sara's life:** She is the only biblical woman whose life span is given, again as a sign of importance.

3 **Sons of Het:** Or "Hittites," not to be confused with the great Hittite empire in Asia Minor. Here the name describes a Canaanite group.
4 **a sojourner:** Even after many years, Avraham is still acutely aware of his nonnative status in the land.
5–6 **saying to him:/ Hear us:** Others use "saying:/ No, hear us."
6 **one exalted:** Others use "a prince."

The Betrothal Journey (24): The last full episode of the Avraham cycle is the longest in the book. Its leisurely pace, attention to detail, and concentration on speeches as well as action belie the importance of what is being recounted: the finding of a wife for Yitzhak, who is biologically to continue the line. Yet after all that has happened in the previous chapters, we know that this will be taken care of by God. That is implied in Avraham's assured "he himself [God] will send his messenger on before you" (v.7).

Many meeting/betrothal scenes in the Bible take place at a well (e.g., Yaakov, Moshe); this was probably a literary convention (see Culley 1976b and Alter 1981 for a discussion of the significance of such a phenomenon). Like other crucial moments in Avraham's life the chapter involves a journey, albeit one made by his emissary. It is therefore natural that the key words of the chapter are "go," "journey," and "grant success." "Take" also appears frequently, as the biblical term often used for "marry."

7 Avraham arose,
he bowed low to the People of the Land, to the Sons of Het,
8 and spoke with them, saying:
If it be then according to your wish
that I bury my dead from my presence,
hear me and interpose for me to Efron son of Tzohar,
9 that he may give me title to the cave of Makhpela, that is his, that
is at the edge of his field,
for the full silver-worth let him give me title in your midst for a
burial holding.
10 Now Efron had a seat amidst the Sons of Het,
and Efron the Hittite answered Avraham in the ears of the Sons
of Het,
of all who had entry to the council-gate of his city,
saying:
11 Not so, my lord, hear me!
The field I give to you,
and the cave that is therein, to you I give it;
before the eyes of the Sons of My People I give it to you—
bury your dead!
12 Avraham bowed before the People of the Land
13 and spoke to Efron in the ears of the People of the Land, saying:
But if you yourself would only hear me out!
I will give the silver-payment for the field,
accept it from me,
so that I may bury my dead there.
14 Efron answered Avraham, saying to him:
15 My lord—hear me!
A piece of land worth four hundred silver weight,
what is that between me and you!
You may bury your dead!

---

7 **People of the Land:** Possibly a title indicating nota-
bles, not, as in later usage, the "common folk."

10 **of all who had entry:** Similar to "People of the
Land"—the aristocrats.

16 Avraham hearkened to Efron:
Avraham weighed out to Efron the silver-worth
of which he had spoken in the ears of the Sons of Het—
four hundred silver weight at the going merchants' rate.

17 Thus was established the field of Efron, that is in Makhpela, that
faces Mamre,
the field as well as the cave that is in it, and the trees that were in
all the field, that were in all their territory round about,

18 for Avraham as an acquisition,
before the eyes of the Sons of Het, of all who had entry to the
council-gate of his city.

19 Afterward Avraham buried Sara his wife
in the cave of the field of Makhpela, facing Mamre, that is now
Hevron, in the land of Canaan.

20 Thus was established the field as well as the cave that is in it for
Avraham as a burial holding, from the Sons of Het.

24:1 Now Avraham was old, advanced in days,
and Yhwh had blessed Avraham in everything.

2 Avraham said to his servant, the elder of his household, who
ruled over all that was his:
Pray put your hand under my thigh!

3 I want you to swear by Yhwh, the God of Heaven and the God of
Earth,
that you will not take a wife for my son from the women of the
Canaanites, among whom I am settled;

4 rather, you are to go to my land and to my kindred, and take a
wife for my son, for Yitzhak.

5 The servant said to him:
Perhaps the woman will not be willing to go after me to this land;
may I then bring your son back there,
back to the land from which you once went out?

20 **established:** Others use "made over."
24:2 **put your hand under my thigh:** A symbol used in
taking of an oath (see also 47:29). The use of "thigh"
might allude to a curse of childlessness as the punishment for not keeping the oath.

5 **back there:** The Hebrew text has "there" in the next
line; it has been moved up in the English text for reasons of style. The word occurs four times in vv.5–8,
as a signal of what is most important to Avraham:
that his son must stay in the land of Canaan.

6 Avraham said to him:
Watch out that you do not ever bring my son back there!

7 YHWH, the God of Heaven,
who took me from my father's house and from my kindred,
who spoke to me,
who swore to me, saying:
I give this land to your seed—
he himself will send his messenger on before you,
so that you take a wife for my son from there.

8 Now if the woman is not willing to go after you,
you will be clear from this sworn-oath of mine,
only: You are not to bring my son back there!

9 The servant put his hand under the thigh of Avraham his lord,
and swore to him (an oath) about this matter.

10 The servant took ten camels from his lord's camels and went, all
kinds of good-things from his lord in his hand.
He arose and went to Aram Of-Two-Rivers, to Nahor's town.

11 He had the camels kneel outside the town at the water well
at setting time, at the time when the water-drawers go out,

12 and said:
YHWH, God of my lord Avraham,
pray let it happen today for me, and deal faithfully with my lord
Avraham!

13 Here, I have stationed myself by the water spring as the women
of the town go out to draw water.

14 May it be
that the maiden to whom I say: Pray lower your pitcher that I
may drink,
and she says: Drink, and I will also give your camels to drink—
let her be the one that you have decided on for your servant, for
Yitzhak,
by means of her may I know that you have dealt faithfully with
my lord.

---

7 **I give this land to your seed:** Quoting 12:7.
10 **Aram Of-Two-Rivers:** Others leave untranslated,
"Aram-Naharayim."

11 **setting time:** Sunset. **water-drawers:** Female.
12 **let it happen:** Or "let it go well."

15 And it was: Not yet had he finished speaking,
   when here, Rivka came out,
   —she had been born to Betuel, son of Milca, wife of Nahor,
      brother of Avraham—
   her pitcher on her shoulder.

16 The maiden was exceedingly beautiful to look at,
   a virgin—no man had known her.
   Going down to the spring, she filled her pitcher and came up
      again.

17 The servant ran to meet her and said:
   Pray let me sip a little water from your pitcher!

18 She said:
   Drink, my lord!
   And in haste she let down her pitcher on her arm and gave him
      to drink.

19 When she had finished giving him to drink, she said:
   I will also draw for your camels, until they have finished drinking.

20 In haste she emptied her pitcher into the drinking-trough,
   then she ran to the well again to draw,
   and drew for all his camels.

21 The man kept staring at her,
   (waiting) silently to find out whether YHWH had granted success
      to his journey or not.

22 It was, when the camels had finished drinking,
   that the man took a gold nose-ring, a half-coin in weight, and two
      bracelets for her wrists, ten gold-pieces in weight,

23 and said:
   Whose daughter are you? Pray tell me!
   And is there perhaps in your father's house a place for us to spend
      the night?

24 She said to him:
   I am the daughter of Betuel, son of Milca, whom she bore to
      Nahor.

25 And she said to him:

---

25 **Yes, there is straw:** Not until Rivka has extended the offer of hospitality (and enthusiastically, with the triple "yes") is the servant sure that "YHWH has granted success to my journey." Hospitality, once again, is the determinant, over and above beauty or virginity.

Yes, there is straw, yes, plenty of fodder with us, (and) yes, a place
    to spend the night.

26 In homage the man bowed low before YHWH

27 and said:

Blessed be YHWH, God of my lord Avraham,

who has not relinquished his faithfulness and his trustworthiness
    from my lord!

While as for me, YHWH has led me on the journey to the house
    of my lord's brothers!

28 The maiden ran and told her mother's household according to
    these words.

29 Now Rivka had a brother, his name was Lavan.

Lavan ran to the man, outside, to the spring:

30 and it was,

as soon as he saw the nose-ring, and the bracelets on his sister's
    wrists,

and as soon as he heard Rivka his sister's words, saying: Thus the
    man spoke to me,

that he came out to the man—there, he was still standing by the
    camels, by the spring—

31 and said:

Come, you who are blessed by YHWH, why are you standing
    outside?

I myself have cleared out the house and a place for the camels!

32 The man came into the house and unbridled the camels,

they gave straw and fodder to the camels

and water for washing his feet and the feet of the men that were
    with him.

33 (Food) was put before him to eat, but he said:

I will not eat until I have spoken my words.

He said: Speak!

34 He said:

I am Avraham's servant.

---

27 **his faithfulness and his trustworthiness:** Others
combine and translate as "steadfast kindness." The
phrase is often found in the Psalms, describing God.
brothers: Relatives.

29 **Lavan:** Trad: English "Laban." He will be a key figure in the story of Rivka's son Yaakov.

34 **He said . . . :** The servant's speech diplomatically
omits certain emotional details of Avraham's
speech, most notably his warning against Yitzhak
himself's going back "there."

35 YHWH has blessed my lord exceedingly, so that he has become
    great,
    he has given him sheep and oxen, silver and gold, servants and
        maids, camels and donkeys.
36 Sara, my lord's wife, bore my lord a son after she had grown old,
    and he has given him all that is his.
37 Now my lord had me swear, saying:
    You are not to take a wife for my son from the women of the
        Canaanites, in whose land I am settled!
38 No! To my father's house you are to go, to my clan,
    and take a wife for my son.
39 I said to my lord:
    Perhaps the woman will not go after me!
40 He said to me:
    YHWH, in whose presence I have walked, will send his messenger
        with you,
    he will grant success to your journey,
    so that you take a wife for my son from my clan and from my
        father's house.
41 Only then will you be clear from my oath-curse:
    When you come to my clan,
    if they do not give her to you, you will be clear from my
        oath-curse.
42 Now I came to the well today and said:
    YHWH, God of my lord Avraham,
    pray, if you wish to grant success to the journey on which I am
        going,
43 here: I have stationed myself by the water spring;
    may it be
    that the girl who comes out to draw,
    to whom I say: Pray give me a little water from your pitcher to
        drink,
44 and she says to me: You drink, and I will also draw for your
        camels—

---

40 **will send his messenger:** Speaking figuratively.
41 **oath-curse:** Changed from Avraham's simple

"sworn-oath," perhaps because it is reported from
the servant's point of view.

let her be the woman whom YHWH has decided on for the son of
   my lord.

45 (And) I, even before I had finished speaking in my heart,
here, Rivka came out, her pitcher on her shoulder,
she went down to the spring and drew.
I said to her: Pray give me to drink!

46 In haste she let down her pitcher from herself and said:
Drink, and I will also give your camels to drink.
I drank, and she also gave the camels to drink.

47 Then I asked her, I said: Whose daughter are you?
She said: The daughter of Betuel, son of Nahor, whom Milca
   bore to him.
I put the ring on her nose and the bracelets on her wrists,

48 and in homage I bowed low before YHWH, and blessed YHWH,
   God of my lord Avraham,
who led me on the true journey to take the daughter of my lord's
   brother for his son.

49 So now, if you wish to deal faithfully and truly with my lord, tell
   me,
and if not, tell me,
that I may (know to) turn right or left.

50 Lavan and Betuel answered, they said:
The matter has come from YHWH;
we cannot speak anything to you evil or good.

51 Here is Rivka before you,
take her and go, that she may be a wife for the son of your lord,
as YHWH has spoken.

52 It was
when Avraham's servant heard their words, that he bowed to the
   ground before YHWH.

53 And the servant brought out objects of silver and objects of gold
   and garments, and gave them to Rivka,
and he gave presents to her brother and to her mother.

---

50 **YHWH:** The family apparently worships the God of
Avraham, in addition to others (see 31:19, 30).

53 **objects of silver and . . . gold and garments:** A
stock biblical phrase (see, similarly, Ex. 3:22) for
wealth or presents.

Avraham's Descendants and Death (25:1–18): Avraham's death is bracketed by two passages dealing with his offspring: first, through Ketura (a concubine), and then through Hagar (Yishmael's line). God's promise is on the way to fulfillment, although Yitzhak is as yet childless and only a small portion of the land has been permanently acquired.

54 They ate and drank, he and the men that were with him, and
    spent the night.
When they arose at daybreak, he said:
Send me off to my lord.

55 But her brother and her mother said:
Let the maiden stay with us a few days, perhaps ten—after that
    she may go.

56 He said to them:
Do not delay me, for YHWH has granted success to my journey;
send me off, that I may go back to my lord.

57 They said:
Let us call the maiden and ask (for an answer from) her own
    mouth.

58 They called Rivka and said to her:
Will you go with this man?
She said:
I will go.

59 They sent off Rivka their sister with her nurse, and Avraham's
    servant with his men,

60 and they gave Rivka farewell-blessing and said to her:
Our sister, may you become thousandfold myriads!
May your seed inherit the gate of those who hate him!

61 Rivka and her maids arose, they mounted the camels and went
    after the man.
The servant took Rivka and went away.

62 Now Yitzhak had come from where you come to the Well of the
    Living-One Who-Sees-Me—for he had settled in the Negev.

63 And Yitzhak went out to stroll in the field around the turning of
    sunset.
He lifted up his eyes and saw: here, camels coming!

64 Rivka lifted up her eyes and saw Yitzhak;

---

55 **a few days, perhaps ten:** Some interpret as "a year
or ten months."

59 **with her nurse:** Yitzhak's life as the father of his people begins with the marriage arranged in this chapter; curiously, when he dies in Chap. 35, the nurse
dies as well, perhaps to hint that Rivka dies too.

60 **May your seed inherit the gate:** See Avraham's
blessing in 22:17. Again, the matriarch shares in the
blessing.

62 **Well of the Living-One:** Already a site of God's activity (16:14).

63 **stroll:** Hebrew obscure; some use "ponder."

◆ 65 she got down from the camel and said to the servant:
Who is the man over there that is walking in the field to meet us?
The servant said:
That is my lord.
She took a veil and covered herself.

66 Now the servant recounted to Yitzhak all the things that he had
done.

67 Yitzhak brought her into the tent of Sara his mother,
he took Rivka and she became his wife, and he loved her.
Thus was Yitzhak comforted after his mother.

25:1 Now Avraham had taken another wife, her name was Ketura.

2 She bore him Zimran and Yokshan, Medan and Midyan, Yishbak
and Shuah.

3 Yokshan begot Sheva and Dedan,
Dedan's sons were the Ashurites, the Letushites, and the
Leummites.

4 Midyan's sons (were) Efa, Efer, Hanokh, Avida, and Eldaa.
All these (were) Ketura's sons.

5 But Avraham gave over all that was his to Yitzhak.

6 And to the sons of the concubines that Avraham had, Avraham
gave gifts, and he sent them away from Yitzhak his son while
he was still alive, eastward, to the Eastland.

7 Now these are the days and years of the life of Avraham, which
he lived:

8 A hundred years and seventy years and five years, then he expired.
Avraham died at a good ripe-age, old and satisfied (in days),
and was gathered to his kinspeople.

9 Yitzhak and Yishmael his sons buried him, in the cave of
Makhpela, in the field of Efron son of Tzohar the Hittite, that
faces Mamre,

10 the field that Avraham had acquired from the Sons of Het.
There were buried Avraham and Sara his wife.

---

67 **Sara:** As the story opened with Yitzhak's father in his last active moments, it closes with the memory of his mother. Yitzhak is on his own.
25:7 **days and years:** Lit. "days of the years."

8 **A hundred years . . . :** See "The Patriarchal Narratives," p.51. **satisfied:** Or "full." For the complete expression, see 35:29.

11 Now it was after Avraham's death, that God blessed Yitzhak his
son.
And Yitzhak settled by the Well of the Living-One Who-Sees-Me.

12 Now these are the begettings of Yishmael son of Avraham,
whom Hagar the Egyptian-woman, Sara's maid, bore to
Avraham.

13 And these are the names of the sons of Yishmael, by their names
after (the order of) their begettings:

14 Yishmael's firstborn, Nevayot; and Kedar, Adbe'el, Mivsam,
Mishma, Duma, Massa,

15 Hadad and Teima, Yetur, Nafish and Kedma.

16 These are the sons of Yishmael, these their names, in their
villages and in their corrals,
twelve leaders for their tribes.

17 And these are the years of the life of Yishmael: a hundred years
and thirty years and seven years, then he expired.
He died and was gathered to his kinspeople.

18 Now they dwelt from Havila to Shur, which faces Egypt, back to
where you come toward Assyria;
in the presence of all his brothers did (his inheritance) fall.

11 **God blessed Yitzhak:** This is the first detail reported
about Yitzhak after his father's death—lest there be
any doubt about the continuation of God's care.
16 **corrals:** Others (including Buber) use "circled encampments." **twelve princes:** See 17:20.

18 **did (his inheritance) fall:** Hebrew difficult. Others
interpret negatively, "made raids against" or "fell
upon" (his kinsmen).

YAAKOV

(25:19–36:43); See also 37–50

BEFORE COMMENTING ON THE YAAKOV CYCLE, IT IS APPROPRIATE TO CONSIDER WHY HIS father Yitzhak, the second of the Patriarchs, receives no true separate group of stories on his own.

Yitzhak functions in Genesis as a classic second generation—that is, as a transmitter and stabilizing force, rather than as an active participant in the process of building the people. There hardly exists a story about him in which he is anything but a son and heir, a husband, or a father. His main task in life seems to be to take roots in the land of Canaan, an admittedly important task in the larger context of God's promises in Genesis. What this means, unfortunately, is that he has almost no personality of his own. By Chapter 27, a scant two chapters after his father dies, he appears as (prematurely?) old, blind in both a literal and figurative sense, and as we will see, he fades out of the text entirely, only to die several chapters, and many years, later.

The true dynamic figure of the second generation here is Rivka. It is she to whom God reveals his plan, and she who puts into motion the mechanism for seeing that it is properly carried out. She is ultimately the one responsible for bridging the gap between the dream, as typified by Avraham, and the hard-won reality, as realized by Yaakov.

Avraham is a towering figure, almost unapproachable as a model in his intimacy with God and his ability to hurdle nearly every obstacle. Adding to this the fact that Yitzhak is practically a noncharacter, and that Yosef, once his rise begins, also lacks dimension as a personality, it becomes increasingly clear that it is Yaakov who emerges as the most dynamic and most human personality in the book. The stories about him cover fully half of Genesis, and reveal a man who is both troubled and triumphant. Most interestingly, he, and not Avraham, gives his name to the people of Israel.

Distinctive themes of the cycle include physical struggle, deception, and confrontation. These are expressed through the key words of Yaakov's name ("Heel-Holder" and "Heel-Sneak," then Yisrael, "God-Fighter"), "deceive" and similar words, and "face." Also recurring are the terms "love," "bless," "firstborn-right," and "wages/hire" (one word in Hebrew). The cycle is structured partly around etiologies (folk explanations of place-names and personal names) and also around Yaakov's use of stones in several of the stories.

Continuing from the Avraham cycle are such earlier themes as wandering, sibling rivalry, the barren wife, wives in conflict, the renaming of the protagonist, God perceived in dreams and visions; and particular geographical locations such as Bet-El, Shekhem, and the Negev (Cassuto 1974).

Finally, it should be mentioned that the Yaakov stories are notable in the manner in which they portray the two levels of biblical reality: divine and human. Throughout the stories human beings act according to normal (though often strong) emotions, which God then uses to carry out his master plan. In this cycle one comes to feel the interpretive force of the biblical mind at work, understanding human events in the context of what God wills. It is a fascinating play between the ideas of fate and free will, destiny and choice—a paradox which nevertheless lies at the heart of the biblical conception of God and humankind.

Rivka's Children (25:19–34): Two stories of sibling confrontation begin the Yaakov cycle. From the first, vv. 19–28, all the necessary conditions are introduced for what is to come: struggle in the womb (foreshadowing Yaakov's wrestling match in Chap. 32, the structural resolution of this earlier one), God's plan for the younger son to outdo the older one, the importance of names as clues to personalities, and parental preference. This last point seals the fate of the two boys.

The second story (vv.29–34) is Yaakov's first act of stealth, and sets the pattern for his whole life. Note at the same time the text's emphasis on Esav's role (v.34), "Thus did Esav despise the firstborn-right."

As before, these episodes point in two temporal directions. Esav resembles Yishmael, the man of the bow; and parental preference will launch the initially tragic action in the Yosef story (Chap. 37).

19 Now these are the begettings of Yitzhak, son of Avraham.
Avraham begot Yitzhak.

20 Yitzhak was forty years old when he took Rivka daughter of
Betuel the Aramean, from the country of Aram, sister of
Lavan the Aramean, for himself as a wife.

21 Yitzhak entreated YHWH on behalf of his wife, for she was barren,
and YHWH granted-his-entreaty:
Rivka his wife became pregnant.

22 But the children almost crushed one another inside her,
so she said:
If this be so,
why do I exist?
And she went to inquire of YHWH.

23 YHWH said to her:
Two nations are in your body,
two tribes from your belly shall be divided;
tribe shall be mightier than tribe,
elder shall be servant to younger!

24 When her days were fulfilled for bearing, here: twins were in her
body!

25 The first one came out ruddy, like a hairy mantle all over,
so they called his name: Esav/Rough-One.

26 After that his brother came out, his hand grasping Esav's heel,
so they called his name: Yaakov/Heel-Holder.
Yitzhak was sixty years old when she bore them.

27 The lads grew up:
Esav became a man who knew the hunt, a man of the field,
but Yaakov was a plain man, staying among the tents.

25:20 **forty years old:** Another schematic number.
Twenty years later (see v.26), his wife will bear him
children. **Aramean:** Three times in this verse the
root "Aram" confirms what we learned in the previous chapter—the importance of family and lineage
here. **country of Aram:** Others leave this untranslated, as "Padan-Aram."

22 **almost crushed:** Others use "struggled." **inquire:**
Consult an oracle. Note that there is no indication
that Yitzhak is aware of what God wants.

23 **tribes:** Heb. *le'ummim,* a poetic term for "peoples."
24 **here:** The text speaks from the point of view of the
onlookers, not of Rivka, who is perfectly aware that
she has twins.
25 **Esav:** Trad. English "Esau." **Rough-One:** A conjec-
tural interpretation from Arabic *'athaya.*
26 **Yaakov:** Trad. English "Jacob." **Heel-Holder:** A
popular reinterpretation of the name Yaakov, which
may have meant originally "May (God) protect."
27 **plain:** Hebrew unclear. Others use "simple."

In the Land (26:1–6): As we have suggested, there is no true collection of stories about Yitzhak. That is, virtually nowhere does Yitzhak appear in a tale where, as a distinct individual, he is a central character. And unlike Yaakov and Yosef, Yitzhak never directly receives his father's blessing. This is bestowed by God, and one gets the impression that even Avraham does not deal with his son as an individual. This is not surprising, given Yitzhak's function in his father's life.

For the narrative, his main purpose, as we have stressed above, is simply to remain in the land (note the repetition of the word "land" in this section). It is almost as if Avraham, the man who lives in the shadow of sacred trees, plants one in the person of his son. In this chapter Yitzhak is forbidden to go beyond the borders of Canaan. Even his death, so seemingly out of place in Chap. 35, occurs after Yaakov has returned home from his wanderings: only when it is assured that there will be continuity in the land is he allowed to die—despite the fact that as a result the text must leave him blind and dying for twenty years.

28 Yitzhak grew to love Esav, for (he brought) hunted-game for his
    mouth,
    but Rivka loved Yaakov.

29 Once Yaakov was boiling boiled-stew,
    when Esav came in from the field, and he was weary.
30 Esav said to Yaakov:
    Pray give me a gulp of the red-stuff, that red-stuff,
    for I am so weary!
    Therefore they called his name: Edom / Red-One.
31 Yaakov said:
    Sell me your firstborn-right here-and-now.
32 Esav said:
    Here, I am on my way to dying, so what good to me is a
    firstborn-right?
33 Yaakov said:
    Swear to me here-and-now.
    He swore to him and sold his firstborn-right to Yaakov.
34 Yaakov gave Esav bread and boiled lentils;
    he ate and drank and arose and went off.
    Thus did Esav despise the firstborn-right.

26:1 Now there was a famine in the land, aside from the former
    famine which there had been in the days of Avraham,
    so Yitzhak went to Avimelekh, king of the Philistines, to Gerar.
2 And YHWH was seen by him and said:
    Do not go down to Egypt;
    continue to dwell in the land that I tell you of,
3 sojourn in this land, and I will be with you and will give you
    blessing—
    for to you and to your seed I give all these lands

---

28 **(he brought) hunted-game:** Hebrew difficult.
29 **boiling boiled-stew:** This phrase may connote plotting, as in our English "cook up," "brew," "concoct," or "stir up" trouble. Other forms of the Hebrew denote "insolence" or "intentional evil."
31 **here-and-now:** Others use "at once"; apparently a legal term.

34 **he ate . . . :** Esav's impulsive personality is brilliantly portrayed by the use of four rapid-fire verbs. **despise:** Others use "belittle."
26:1 **a famine . . . Yitzhak went to Avimelekh:** Parallel to the story in Chap. 20.

The Wife—III (26:7–11): Here is the final "Yitzhak version" of the tale, constructed around the same king whom Avraham had encountered in Chap. 20. Its individual coloring is supplied by the "laughing-and-loving" of v.8, playing on Yitzhak's name. Otherwise, just as in the following episode, he is merely repeating his father's experience.

Blessing (26:12–33): Confirmation of Yitzhak's status as heir comes in vv.12–14, in the form of material blessings (already referred to immediately after Avraham's death, 25:11). It will be Yaakov's task to reclaim and continue the spiritual side of the tradition.

The first episode is centered around not Yitzhak but Avraham. The phrase "his father" reverberates; and Avimelekh returns. In the second episode, Avraham's treaty with that king (Chap. 21) is replayed, with the same result as before: an explanation of the name Be'er-Sheva.

and will fulfill the sworn-oath that I swore to Avraham your
father:

4 I will make your seed many, like the stars of the heavens,
and to your seed I will give all these lands;
all the nations of the earth shall enjoy blessing through your
seed—

5 in consequence of Avraham's hearkening to my voice
and keeping my charge: my commandments, my laws, and my
instructions.

6 So Yitzhak stayed in Gerar.

7 Now when the men of the place asked about his wife, he said:
She is my sister,
for he was afraid to say: my wife—
(thinking): Otherwise the people of the place will kill me on
account of Rivka, for she is beautiful to look at.

8 But it was, when he had been there a long time,
that Avimelekh, king of the Philistines, looked out through a
window
and saw: there was Yitzhak laughing-and-loving with Rivka his
wife!

9 Avimelekh had Yitzhak called and said:
But here, she must be your wife!
Now how could you say: She is my sister?
Yitzhak said to him:
Indeed, I said to myself: Otherwise I will die on account of her!

10 Avimelekh said:
What is this that you have done to us!
One of the people might well have lain with your wife,
and then you would have brought guilt upon us!

---

5 **in consequence of Avraham's hearkening . . . :**
The blessing mirrors 22:17ff. **my commandments . . . :** These are not specified; this is probably
a poetic phrase describing a general idea.

8 **laughing-and-loving:** Heb. *metzahek,* which can
mean laughter or sexual activity. Trad. English
"sporting."

◆ 11 Avimelekh commanded the entire people, saying:
Whoever touches this man or his wife must be put to death, yes,
death!

12 Yitzhak sowed in that land, and reaped in that year a hundred
measures;
thus did Yhwh bless him.

13 The man became great, and went on, went on becoming greater,
until he was exceedingly great:

14 he had herds of sheep and herds of oxen and a large retinue-of-
servants,
and the Philistines envied him.

15 And all the wells which his father's servants had dug in the days
of Avraham his father, the Philistines stopped up and filled
with earth.

16 Avimelekh said to Yitzhak:
Go away from us, for you have become exceedingly more mighty
(in number) than we!

17 So Yitzhak went from there, he encamped in the wadi of Gerar
and settled there.

18 Yitzhak again dug up the wells of water which had been dug in
the days of Avraham his father, the Philistines having stopped
them up after Avraham's death,
and he called them by the names, the same names, by which his
father had called them.

19 Yitzhak's servants also dug in the wadi, and found there a well of
living water.

20 Now the shepherds of Gerar quarreled with the shepherds of
Yitzhak, saying: The water is ours!
So he called the name of the well: Esek/Bickering, because they
had bickered with him.

---

11 **touches:** Or "harms."
12 **reaped:** Lit. "attained."
17 **there:** The word occurs seven times through v.25. It

may be a counterpoint to Chap. 24's usage, or to
stress that Yitzhak stays in the land.
19 **wadi:** An often-dry riverbed. **living water:** fresh-
water.

21 They dug another well, and quarreled also over it,
so he called its name: Sitna/Animosity.

22 He moved on from there and dug another well, but they did not
quarrel over it,
so he called its name: Rehovot/Space,
and said: Indeed, now YHWH has made space for us, so that we
may bear fruit in the land!

23 He went up from there to Be'er-Sheva.

24 Now YHWH was seen by him on that night and said:
I am the God of Avraham your father.
Do not be afraid, for I am with you,
I will bless you and will make your seed many, for the sake of
Avraham my servant.

25 He built a slaughter-site there
and called out the name of YHWH.
He spread his tent there, and Yitzhak's servants excavated a well
there.

26 Now Avimelekh went to him from Gerar, along with Ahuzzat his
aide and Pikhol the commander of his army.

27 Yitzhak said to them:
Why have you come to me?
For you hate me and have sent me away from you!

28 They said:
We have seen, yes, seen that YHWH has been with you,
so we say: Pray let there be an oath-curse between us, between us
and you,
we want to cut a covenant with you:

29 If ever you should deal badly with us . . . !
Just as we have not harmed you and just as we have only dealt
well with you and have sent you away in peace—
you are now blessed by YHWH!

30 He made them a drinking-feast, and they ate and drank.

---

26 **aide:** Lit. "friend."
30 **they ate and drank:** The cutting of a covenant is often accompanied by a meal in biblical and other societies.

Deceit and Blessing (26:34–28:9): Of all the stories of Genesis, this is perhaps the most brilliantly staged. Nowhere is the narrative so vivid as here, and nowhere, even including Chap. 22, is the tension so masterfully drawn out.

Despite the fact that the story line is a simple one, involving deception and the "taking" of the blessing, the text is imbued with great subtlety. Most striking is the sensuality it invokes: seven times we hear of "game," six of the "delicacy" (or "tasty-dish"), and three times Yitzhak "feels" Yaakov (who "comes close" four times). In fact the story makes use of all five of the senses. One sense—that of sight—is defective, and on that deficiency will turn the action of the story. Yet another level of meaning is apparent: "to see" in ancient Israel, as in many cultures, was a term connected to prophetic powers, as we observed regarding Avraham. So here, ironically, Yitzhak's blindness leads to both deception and to the proper transferral of the blessing.

Structurally the story is framed by two references to Esav and his wives: 26:34–35 prepares the way for his loss of the blessing, by showing that he has alienated himself from his parents (and broken Avraham's charge to Yitzhak in 24:3), and 28:6–9 finds Esav obeying his father and making a rather pathetic attempt to reassure himself of his love.

Some of the story's motifs will return later. The threefold "as he loves" looks to the crucial role that the theme of "love" will play later on in Genesis (as well as being a key to the story itself). The general theme of nonrecognition will return with an interesting twist in the Yosef novella (especially in Chaps. 42–44).

31 Early in the morning they swore (an oath) to one another;
   then Yitzhak sent them off, and they went from him in peace.

32 Now it was on that same day
   that Yitzhak's servants came and told him about the well that
      they had been digging,
   they said to him: We have found water!

33 So he called it: Shiv'a / Swearing-Seven;
   therefore the name of the city is Be'er-Sheva until this day.

34 When Esav was forty years old, he took to wife Yehudit daughter
      of B'eri the Hittite and Ba'semat daughter of Elon the Hittite.

35 And they were a bitterness of spirit to Yitzhak and Rivka.

27:1 Now when Yitzhak was old and his eyes had become too dim for
      seeing,
   he called Esav, his elder son, and said to him:
   My son!
   He said to him:
   Here I am.

2 He said:
   Now here, I have grown old, and do not know the day of my
      death.

3 So now, pray pick up your weapons—your hanging-quiver and
      your bow,
   go out into the field and hunt me down some hunted-game,

4 and make me a delicacy, such as I love;
   bring it to me, and I will eat it,
   that I may give you my own blessing before I die.

5 Now Rivka was listening as Yitzhak spoke to Esav his son,
   and so when Esav went off into the fields to hunt down hunted-
      game to bring (to him),

6 Rivka said to Yaakov her son, saying:
   Here, I was listening as your father spoke to Esav your brother,
      saying:

---

34 **forty years old:** The same age that his father was at
   the time of his marriage.
27:4 **delicacy:** See 25:28. Yitzhak is tied to the senses, a
trait that he prizes in Esav. **my own blessing:** Or
"my special blessing." Heb. *nefesh* frequently means
"self" or "personality."

7 Bring me some hunted-game and make me a delicacy, I will eat it
and give you blessing before YHWH, before my death.

8 So now, my son, listen to my voice, to what I command you:

9 Pray go to the flock and take me two fine goat kids from there,
I will make them into a delicacy for your father, such as he loves;

10 you bring it to your father, and he will eat,
so that he may give you blessing before his death.

11 Yaakov said to Rivka his mother:
Here, Esav my brother is a hairy man, and I am a smooth man,

12 perhaps my father will feel me—then I will be like a trickster in
his eyes,
and I will bring a curse and not a blessing on myself!

13 His mother said to him:
Let your curse be on me, my son!
Only: listen to my voice and go, take them for me.

14 He went and took and brought them to his mother, and his
mother made a delicacy, such as his father loved.

15 Rivka then took the garments of Esav, her elder son, the choicest
ones that were with her in the house,

16 and clothed Yaakov, her younger son;
and with the skins of the goat kids, she clothed his hands and the
smooth-parts of his neck.

17 Then she placed the delicacy and the bread that she had made in
the hand of Yaakov her son.

18 He came to his father and said:
Father!
He said:
Here I am. Which one are you, my son?

19 Yaakov said to his father:
I am Esav, your firstborn.
I have done as you spoke to me:

7 **before YHWH:** Note that Rivka adds these words to
her husband's.
9 **take:** Fetch (see also vv.13, 14, 45).
13 **Let your curse be on me:** Ominously, Rivka disappears from the narrative after v.46.
18 **Which one are you:** Three times—here, in v.21, and
in v.24—the father asks for assurances about the
son's identity. **my son:** This phrase reverberates
throughout the story, underlining the confusion
over the identity of the sons.
19 **Esav, your firstborn:** From the first word the lie is
blatant; contrast Esav's tension-filled reply to the
same question in v.32.

Pray arise, sit and eat from my hunted-game,
that you may give me your own blessing.

20 Yitzhak said to his son:
How did you find it so hastily, my son?
He said: Indeed, YHWH your God made it happen for me.

21 Yitzhak said to Yaakov:
Pray come closer, that I may feel you, my son,
whether you are really my son Esav or not.

22 Yaakov moved closer to Yitzhak his father.
He felt him and said:
The voice is Yaakov's voice, the hands are Esav's hands—

23 but he did not recognize him, for his hands were like the hands of
Esav his brother, hairy.
Now he was about to bless him,

24 when he said:
Are you he, my son Esav?
He said:
I am.

25 So he said: Bring it close to me, and I will eat from the hunted-
game of my son,
in order that I may give you my own blessing.
He put it close to him and he ate,
he brought him wine and he drank.

26 Then Yitzhak his father said to him:
Pray come close and kiss me, my son.

27 He came close and kissed him.
Now he smelled the smell of his garments
and blessed him and said:
See, the smell of my son
is like the smell of a field
that YHWH has blessed.

---

20 **made it happen:** An appropriate expression to use
with Yitzhak; see 24:12.

23 **hairy:** In the end Yitzhak relies more on the sense of
touch than on his hearing. Yet the latter is usually re-

garded as the source of truth in the Bible (see Deut.
4:12, for example).

27 **a field:** Fitting for Esav, the "man of the field"
(25:27).

28 So may God give you
from the dew of the heavens,
from the fat of the earth,
(along with) much grain and new-wine!

29 May peoples serve you,
may tribes bow down to you;
be master to your brothers,
may your mother's sons bow down to you!
Those who damn you, damned!
Those who bless you, blessed!

30 Now it was, when Yitzhak had finished blessing Yaakov,
yes it was—Yaakov had just gone out, out from the presence of
Yitzhak his father—
that Esav his brother came back from his hunting.

31 He too made a delicacy and brought it to his father.
He said to his father:
Let my father arise and eat from the hunted-game of his son,
that you may give me your own blessing.

32 Yitzhak his father said to him:
Which one are you?
He said:
I am your son, your firstborn, Esav.

33 Yitzhak trembled with very great trembling
and said:
Who then was he
that hunted down hunted-game and brought it to me—I ate it all
before you came
and I gave him my blessing!
Now blessed he must remain!

34 When Esav heard the words of his father,
he cried out with a very great and bitter cry,

---

29 **Those who bless you, blessed!:** Perhaps hearkening back to God's speech to Avraham in 12:3. Note that this blessing, at least in this particular wording, is never spoken to Yitzhak.

32 **Esav:** The exact identification is put off until the end of the sequence, heightening the drama. Similarly, see 22:2.

33 **blessed he must remain:** Once uttered, the words of blessing cannot be rescinded.

33, 34 **very great:** Movingly, the father's terror and the son's anguish mirror one another via use of the same phrase (Heb. *ad me'od,* which is rare).

and said to his father:
Bless me, me also, father!

35 He said:
Your brother came with deceit and took away your blessing.

36 He said:
Is that why his name was called Yaakov/Heel-Sneak? For he has
   now sneaked against me twice:
My firstborn-right he took, and now he has taken my blessing!
And he said:
Haven't you reserved a blessing for me?

37 Yitzhak answered, saying to Esav:
Here, I have made him master to you,
and all his brothers I have given him as servants,
with grain and new-wine I have invested him—
so for you, what then can I do, my son?

38 Esav said to his father:
Have you only a single blessing, father?
Bless me, me also, father!
And Esav lifted up his voice and wept.

39 Then Yitzhak his father answered, saying to him:
   Behold, from the fat of the earth
     must be your dwelling-place,
     from the dew of the heavens above.

40   You will live by your sword,
     you will serve your brother.
     But it will be
     that when you brandish it,
     you will tear his yoke from your neck.

41 Now Esav held a grudge against Yaakov because of the blessing
   with which his father had blessed him.

36 **Heel-Sneak:** In effect, Esav puts a curse on his brother's name, which will be removed only in 32:29, twenty years later. **he has now sneaked against me:** Or "cheated me."

37 **invested:** Or "sustained."

39 **Behold, from the fat of the earth:** Some interpret this negatively as "Behold, *away* from the fat of the earth. . . ."

40 **brandish:** I.e., a sword; Hebrew obscure.

Yaakov Sets Out (28:10–22): Yaakov's journey takes him not only to a foreign land, but to the portals of adulthood. It begins fittingly with a dream vision, so that we will know from the start that God is with him. In fact Yaakov always encounters God at crucial life junctures, at the point of journeys (31:3—leaving Aram; 32:25ff.—meeting Esav; 35:1— returning to Bet-El; 35:9ff.—the homecoming; and 46:2ff.—on the way to Egypt).

The setting for this particular encounter is highly unusual, especially when compared to the generally nongeographical nature of the revelations to Avraham. The idea of a sacred site ("place," a biblical word with these connotations, occurs three times) is strongly suggested. The notion of a ladder or ramp (or "gateway," v.17) between the divine and human worlds is well known in ancient stories. A variation of the theme occurs in 32:2–3, where Yaakov sees "messengers" again in an "encounter"; these two stories frame the middle of the entire cycle.

As Yaakov enters his adult life, he resembles both his grandfather Avraham, the visionary, and his son Yosef, the dreamer.

Esav said in his heart:
Let the days of mourning for my father draw near
and then I will kill Yaakov my brother!

42 Rivka was told of the words of Esav, her elder son.
She sent and called for Yaakov, her younger son,
and said to him:
Here, Esav your brother is consoling himself about you, with (the
thought of) killing you.

43 So now, my son, listen to my voice:
Arise and flee to Lavan my brother in Harran,

44 and stay with him for some days, until your brother's fury has
turned away,

45 until his anger turns away from you and he forgets what you did
to him.
Then I will send and have you taken from there—
for should I be bereaved of you both in a single day?

46 So Rivka said to Yitzhak:
I loathe my life because of those Hittite women;
if Yaakov should take a wife from the Hittite women—like these,
from the women of the land,
why should I have life?

28:1 So Yitzhak called for Yaakov,
he blessed him and commanded him, saying to him:
You are not to take a wife from the women of Canaan;

2 arise, go to the country of Aram, to the house of Betuel, your
mother's father,
and take yourself a wife from there, from the daughters of Lavan,
your mother's brother.

3 May God Shaddai bless you,
may he make you bear fruit and make you many,
so that you become a host of peoples.

---

41 **Let the days . . . :** That is, wait until my father
dies!

44 **days:** May be an idiomatic usage meaning "years."

45 **Then I will send:** This never occurs in the later
course of the story.

28:2 **arise, go to the country of Aram:** It is curious that
Yitzhak sends his son on a journey that he himself
had been forbidden to undertake.

4 And may he give you the blessing of Avraham,
to you and to your seed with you,
for you to inherit the land of your sojournings,
which God gave to Avraham.
5 So Yitzhak sent Yaakov off;
he went to the country of Aram, to Lavan son of Betuel the
Aramean,
the brother of Rivka, the mother of Yaakov and Esav.

6 Now Esav saw
that Yitzhak had given Yaakov farewell-blessing and had sent him
to the country of Aram, to take himself a wife from there,
(and that) when he had given him blessing, he had commanded
him, saying: You are not to take a wife from the women of
Canaan!
7 And Yaakov had listened to his father and his mother and had
gone to the country of Aram.
8 And Esav saw
that the women of Canaan were bad in the eyes of Yitzhak his
father,
9 so Esav went to Yishmael and took Mahalat daughter of Yishmael
son of Avraham, sister of Nevayot, in addition to his wives as a
wife.

10 Yaakov went out from Be'er-Sheva and went toward Harran,
11 and encountered a certain place.
He had to spend the night there, for the sun had come in.
Now he took one of the stones of the place
and set it at his head
and lay down in that place.
12 And he dreamt:
Here, a ladder was set up on the earth,
its top reaching the heavens,
and here: messengers of God were going up and down on it.

4 **seed . . . land:** Again the two elements of the blessing given to Avraham.
5 **Yaakov and Esav:** In the end, the oracle to Rivka is
confirmed, with younger son superseding elder.

12 **Here:** The word (three times) emphasizes the immediacy of the report; it is the vocabulary of
dreams, as in 37:7 (Andersen). **ladder:** Others use
"ramp" or "stairway."

13 And here:
YHWH was standing over against him.
He said:
I am YHWH,
the God of Avraham your father and the God of Yitzhak.
The land on which you lie
I give to you and to your seed.

14 Your seed will be like the dust of the earth;
you will burst forth, to the Sea, to the east, to the north, to the
Negev.
All the clans of the soil will find blessing through you and
through your seed!

15 Here, I am with you,
I will watch over you wherever you go
and will bring you back to this soil;
indeed, I will not leave you
until I have done what I have spoken to you.

16 Yaakov awoke from his sleep
and said:
Why,
YHWH is in this place,
and I, I did not know it!

17 He was awestruck and said:
How awe-inspiring is this place!
This is none other than a house of God,
and that is the gate of heaven!

18 Yaakov started-early in the morning,
he took the stone that he had set at his head
and set it up as a standing-pillar
and poured oil on top of it.

19 And he called the name of the place: Bet-El/House of God—
however, Luz was the name of the city in former times.

---

13 **over against:** See note to 18:2.
the land, etc.: Once again Yaakov receives the blessing of Avraham "his father" (!). See 13:14–16.

18 **standing-pillar:** A stone marker, common to the
culture of the region.

19 **Bet-El:** Trad. English "Beth El."

Arrival in Aram (29:1–14): As one might expect from the usual biblical pattern, Yaakov meets his bride-to-be at a well. As in other ancient stories (see also Ex. 2:15–17) the hero performs a feat of physical strength, this time with a large stone—continuing the use of stones as a motif in the Yaakov stories.

Lavan is once again the chief representative of the family, as he was in the betrothal account of Chap. 24.

20 And Yaakov vowed a vow, saying:
   If God will be with me
   and will watch over me on this way that I go
   and will give me food to eat and a garment to wear,
21 and if I come back in peace to my father's house—
   YHWH shall be God to me,
22 and this stone that I have set up as a standing-pillar shall become a
      house of God,
   and everything that you give me
   I shall tithe, tithe it to you.

29:1 Yaakov lifted his feet and went to the land of the Easterners.
   2 He looked around him, and there: a well in the field, and there
      were three herds of sheep crouching near it,
   for from that well they used to give the herds to drink.
   Now the stone on the mouth of the well was large,
   3 so when all the herds were gathered there,
   they used to roll the stone from the mouth of the well, give the
      sheep to drink, and put the stone back on the mouth of the
      well in its place.
   4 Now Yaakov said to them:
   Brothers, where are you from?
   They said:
   We are from Harran.
   5 He said to them:
   Do you know Lavan, son of Nahor?
   They said:
   We know him.
   6 He said to them:
   Is all well with him?
   They said:
   It is well—
   and here comes Rahel his daughter with the sheep!

21 **in peace:** Or "safely." This functions as a key word in the Yaakov cycle, extending into the Yosef story as well. Yaakov, the "sneak" and wanderer, seeks peace and safety; he does not find it until the end of his life, albeit in a foreign land.
22 **tithe:** See note to 14:20.

29:1 **lifted his feet:** Colloquially, "picked up and went."
5 **We know him:** Biblical Hebrew expresses the idea "yes" by repeating the words of the question. See also v.6 and 24:58.
6 **Rahel:** Trad. English "Rachel." The name means "ewe."

Deception Repaid (29:15–30): The language of the text here, as well as the tenor of the situation, suggest that the Bible has set up Yaakov's punishment for having stolen Yitzhak's blessing from his brother. "Deceived" (v.25) and "younger . . . firstborn" (v.26) echo the Chap. 27 narrative, and provide another example of biblical justice.

7 He said:
Indeed, it is still broad daylight,
it is not time to gather in the livestock,
so give the sheep to drink and go back, tend them.

8 But they said:
We cannot, until all the herds have been gathered;
only then do they roll the stone from the mouth of the well, and
then we give the sheep to drink.

9 While he was still speaking with them,
Rahel came with the sheep that were her father's
—for she was a shepherdess.

10 Now it was when Yaakov saw Rahel, the daughter of Lavan
and the sheep of Lavan his mother's brother,
that Yaakov came close,
he rolled the stone from the mouth of the well
and gave drink to the sheep of Lavan his mother's brother.

11 Then Yaakov kissed Rahel, and lifted up his voice and wept.

12 And Yaakov told Rahel
that he was her father's brother
and that he was Rivka's son.
She ran and told her father.

13 Now it was, as soon as Lavan heard the tidings concerning
Yaakov, his sister's son,
that he ran to meet him, embraced him and kissed him, and
brought him into his house.
And he recounted all these events to Lavan.

14 Lavan said to him:
Without doubt you are my bone, my flesh!
And he stayed with him the days of a Renewing-of-the-Moon.

15 Lavan said to Yaakov:
Just because you are my brother, should you serve me for
nothing?
Tell me, what shall your wages be?

---

7 **to gather in:** For the night.
10 **his mother's brother:** Three times here, to accentuate the familial ties.

12 **brother:** Relative (so also v.15).
14 **Renewing-of-the-Moon:** Heb. *hodesh,* a month.

Love, Jealousy, and Children (29:31–30:24): The narrative now demonstrates (1) how Yaakov prospers in exile, increasing both in wealth and in progeny, and thus (2) how God fulfills his promise to the Patriarchs to "make them many." Characteristically for the Bible, this takes place as a result of human emotions: the jealousy of two sisters who are married to the same man. The emotions, interestingly, are portrayed largely through the names given to Yaakov's sons. In the end Lea seems to be the victor, at least in the terms of a culture that prizes the production of male children; she becomes the mother of fully half of the sons of Israel (Redak).

16 Now Lavan had two daughters: the name of the elder was Lea,
   the name of the younger was Rahel.

17 Lea's eyes were delicate, but Rahel was fair of form and fair to
   look at.

18 And Yaakov fell in love with Rahel.
   He said:
   I will serve you seven years for Rahel, your younger daughter.

19 Lavan said:
   My giving her to you is better than my giving her to another
      man;
   stay with me.

20 So Yaakov served seven years for Rahel,
   yet they were in his eyes as but a few days, because of his love for
      her.

21 Then Yaakov said to Lavan:
   Come-now, (give me) my wife, for my days-of-labor have been
      fulfilled,
   so that I may come in to her.

22 Lavan gathered all the people of the place together and made a
   drinking-feast.

23 Now in the evening
   he took Lea his daughter and brought her to him,
   and he came in to her.

24 Lavan also gave her Zilpa his maid,
   for Lea his daughter as a maid.

25 Now in the morning:
   here, she was Lea!
   He said to Lavan:
   What is this that you have done to me!
   Was it not for Rahel that I served you?
   Why have you deceived me?

---

16 **Lea:** Or "Le'a," trad. English "Leah." The name
means "wild cow."

17 **delicate:** Others use "weak." Either the term is
meant negatively or else Lea is being praised for one
attribute but Rahel for total beauty.

18 **seven:** Aside from forty, this is the other schematic
number found often in Genesis and elsewhere (for
instance, as the basic number of the biblical calendar, in days, months, and years).

19 **with me:** Or "in my service," "under me."

26 Lavan said:
Such is not done in our place, giving away the younger before the
firstborn;
27 just fill out the bridal-week for this one, then we shall give you
that one also,
for the service which you will serve me for yet another seven
years.
28 Yaakov did so—he fulfilled the bridal-week for this one,
and then he gave him Rahel his daughter as a wife.
29 Lavan also gave Rahel his daughter Bilha his maid,
for her as a maid.
30 So he came in to Rahel also,
and he loved Rahel also,
more than Lea.
Then he served him for yet another seven years.

31 Now when YHWH saw that Lea was hated,
he opened her womb,
while Rahel was barren.
32 So Lea became pregnant and bore a son;
she called his name: Re'uven/See, a Son!
for she said:
Indeed, YHWH has seen my being afflicted,
indeed, now my husband will love me!
33 She became pregnant again and bore a son,
and said:
Indeed, YHWH has heard that I am hated,
so he has given me this one as well!
And she called his name: Shim'on/Hearing.
34 She became pregnant again and bore a son,
and said:
Now this time my husband will be joined to me,
for I have borne him three sons!
Therefore they called his name: Levi/Joining.

---

21 **fulfilled:** I.e., over, completed.
31 **hated:** Others use "rejected," "unloved."

32 **Re'uven:** Trad. English "Reuben."
33 **Shim'on:** Trad. English "Simeon."

35 She became pregnant again and bore a son,
and said:
This time I will give thanks to YHWH!
Therefore she called his name: Yehuda / Giving-Thanks.
Then she stopped giving birth.

30:1 Now when Rahel saw that she could not bear (children) to
Yaakov,
Rahel envied her sister.
She said to Yaakov:
Come-now, (give) me children!
If not, I will die!

2 Yaakov's anger flared up against Rahel,
he said:
Am I in place of God,
who has denied you fruit of the body?

3 She said:
Here is my slave-girl Bilha;
come in to her,
so that she may give birth upon my knees, so that I too may be
built-up-with-sons through her.

4 She gave him Bilha her maid as a wife,
and Yaakov came in to her.

5 Bilha became pregnant and bore Yaakov a son.

6 Rahel said:
God has done-me-justice; yes, he has heard my voice!
He has given me a son!
Therefore she called his name: Dan / He-Has-Done-Justice.

7 And Bilha, Rahel's maid, became pregnant again and bore a
second son to Yaakov.

8 Rahel said:
A struggle of God have I struggled with my sister; yes, I have
prevailed!
So she called his name: Naftali / My Struggle.

---

35 **Yehuda:** Trad. English "Judah."
30:2 **Yaakov's anger flared up:** The usual biblical expression for anger; lit. "Yaakov's nostril(s) flamed."

3 **give birth upon my knees:** An idiom for legal adoption (here, by Rahel).

Yaakov in Exile: Stealth and Prosperity (30:25–32:1): The long account of how Yaakov outwits Lavan rounds out the portrait of his personality: he is a man at once clever, successful, and harassed. The text goes to great lengths to describe both men in behavior and thought, and we are given enough dialogue to be able to understand their motivations. The repeating words point to major themes: "serve," "wages," "face" (which will become central to the whole cycle by Chap. 32), and a whole vocabulary of trickery: "steal" (with the variations "be stealthy" and "steal the wits"), "take away" (see Chap. 27), "snatch," and "rob."

9 Now when Lea saw that she had stopped giving birth,
she took Zilpa her maid and gave her to Yaakov as a wife.

10 Zilpa, Lea's maid, bore Yaakov a son.

11 Lea said:
What fortune!
So she called his name: Gad/Fortune.

12 And Zilpa, Lea's maid, bore a second son to Yaakov.

13 Lea said:
What happiness!
For women will deem me happy.
So she called his name: Asher/Happiness.

14 Now Re'uven went in the days of the wheat-harvest and found
some love-apples in the field,
and brought them to Lea his mother.
Rahel said to Lea:
Pray give me (some) of your son's love-apples!

15 She said to her:
Is your taking away my husband such a small thing
that you would now take away my son's love-apples?
Rahel said:
Very well, he may lie with you tonight in exchange for your son's
love-apples.

16 So when Yaakov came home from the fields in the evening, Lea
went out to meet him and said:
You must come in to me,
for I have hired, yes, hired you for my son's love-apples.
So he lay with her that night.

17 And God hearkened to Lea,
so that she became pregnant and bore Yaakov a fifth son.

---

13 **What happiness:** Others use "Happy am I!"
14 **love-apples:** Heb. *duda'im;* a plant believed to have
aphrodisiac powers. Others use "mandrakes."

15 **taking away:** The theme of "taking," so prominent
in Chap. 27, returns, in the context of sibling rivalry
again.

18 Lea said:

God has given me my hired-wages,

because I gave my maid to my husband!

So she called his name: Yissakhar/There-Is-Hire.

19 Once again Lea became pregnant, and she bore a sixth son to
Yaakov.

20 Lea said:

God has presented me with a good present,

this time my husband will prize me—

for I have borne him six sons!

So she called his name: Zevulun/Prince.

21 Afterward she bore a daughter, and called her name Dina.

22 But God kept Rahel in mind,

God hearkened to her and opened her womb,

23 so that she became pregnant and bore a son.

She said:

God has removed/*asaf*

my reproach!

24 So she called his name: Yosef,

saying:

May Yhwh add/*yosef*

another son to me!

25 Now it was, once Rahel had borne Yosef, that Yaakov said to
Lavan:

Send me free, that I may go back to my place, to my land,

26 give over my wives and my children,

for whom I have served you,

and I will go.

Indeed, you yourself know my service that I have served you!

---

18 **hired-wages:** "Wages" recurs as a theme through-out this part of the Yaakov cycle (Fokkelman). It is perhaps a veiled portrayal of the events of Yaakov's adulthood as "payment" for what he did to his brother. **Yissakhar:** Trad. English "Issachar."

20 **this time my husband will prize me:** Lea's six pregnancies and birthings are bracketed by this verse and 29:32, "Now my husband will love me." **Zevulun:** Trad. English "Zebulun."

23–24 **removed . . . add:** Yosef's naming prefigures his destiny as a son lost and found.

24 **Yosef:** Trad. English "Joseph."

26 **give over my wives and my children:** In the law of the region, slaves did not retain control of their families. Does this suggest something about Yaakov's treatment by Lavan? (Speiser)

27 Lavan said to him:
Pray, if I have found favor in your eyes . . .
I have become wealthy,
and YHWH has blessed me on account of you.

28 And he said: Specify the wages due you from me, and I will give
you payment.

29 He said to him:
You yourself know
how I have served you,
and how it has gone with your livestock in my charge.

30 For you had but few before me,
and they have since burst out into a multitude.
Thus has YHWH blessed you at my every step!
But now, when may I too do something for my household?

31 He said:
What shall I give you?
Yaakov said:
You are not to give me anything—
only do this thing for me,
then I will return, I will tend your flock, I will keep watch:

32 Let me go over your whole flock today
removing from there every speckled and dappled head;
and every dark head among the lambs, and each dappled and
speckled-one among the goats—they shall be my wages.

33 And may my honesty plead for me on a future day:
when you come-to-check my wages (that are) before you,
whatever is not speckled or dappled among the goats, or dark
among the lambs,
it will be as though stolen by me.

34 Lavan said:
Good, let it be according to your words.

---

27 **Pray, if I have found:** Or "May I now find." **I have
become wealthy,/ and YHWH . . . :** Some interpret
this as "I have divined that YHWH. . . ."

32 **Let me go:** Some read "Go." **every speckled . . . :**
This would appeal to Lavan, since such animals
would be in the minority.

◆ 35 And on that (very) day he removed the streaked and dappled he-
goats

and every speckled and dappled she-goat, every one that had any
white on it,

and every dark-one among the lambs,

and handed them over to his sons.

36 Then he put a three-days' journey between himself and Yaakov.

Now Yaakov was tending Lavan's remaining flock.

37 Yaakov took himself rods from moist poplar, almond, and plane
trees

and peeled white peelings in them, exposing the white that was
on the rods,

38 then he presented the rods that he had peeled in the gutters, in
the water troughs where the flock would come to drink, in
front of the flock.

Now they would be in heat as they came to drink;

39 thus the flock came to be in heat by the rods,

and the flock bore streaked, speckled, and dappled (young).

40 But the sheep, Yaakov set apart,

and gave position among the flock to each streaked-one and every
dark-one among Lavan's flocks;

thus he made special herds for himself, but did not make them for
Lavan's flock.

41 So it was that whenever the robust flock-animals were in heat,

Yaakov would put the rods in sight of the flock-animals, in the
gutters, to make them be in heat next to the rods.

42 But when the flock-animals were feeble, he would not put them
there.

And so it was that the feeble-ones became Lavan's, and the
robust-ones, Yaakov's.

---

35 **white:** Heb. *lavan.* Also the word "poplar" in v.37 is a
play on Lavan (*livne*). The conniving father-in-law is
tricked with words resembling his own name.

39 **by the rods:** Folk belief holds that what the animals

see as they mate will influence the color of their offspring.

40 **gave position:** Following the interpretation of
Fokkelman.

43 The man burst-forth-with-wealth exceedingly, yes, exceedingly, he
  came to have many flock-animals and maids and servants, and
  camels and donkeys.

31:1 Now he heard the words of Lavan's sons, (that they) said:
  Yaakov has taken away all that was our father's,
  and from what was our father's he has made all this weighty-
    wealth!
2 And Yaakov saw by Lavan's face:
  here, he was no longer with him as yesterday and the day-before.
3 And YHWH said to Yaakov:
  Return to the land of your fathers, to your kindred!
  I will be with you!
4 So Yaakov sent and had Rahel and Lea called to the field, to his
  animals,
5 and said to them:
  I see by your father's face:
  indeed, he is no longer toward me as yesterday and the day-
    before.
  But the God of my father has been with me!
6 You yourselves know that I have served your father with all my
  might,
7 but your father has cheated me and changed my wages ten times
  over,
  yet God has not allowed him to do me ill.
8 If he said thus: The speckled-ones shall be your wages,
  all the animals would bear speckled-ones,
  and if he said thus: The streaked-ones shall be your wages,
  all the animals would bear streaked-ones.
9 So God has snatched away your father's livestock and given them
  to me.

43 **he came to have many flock-animals:** Like his father (26:14) and grandfather (12:16).
31:1 **he was no longer with him:** Others use "Lavan's
manner toward him was no longer. . . ."
3 **land of your fathers . . . your kindred:** Here, unlike 12:1, the land is Canaan, not Harran! **I will be
with you:** Heb. *ehye immakh*, interpreted here and

throughout by B-R as "I will be-there with you,"
stressing that it is God's presence that is indicated by
the verb *hyh*, "to be." See especially Ex. 3:14.
4 **to the field:** As a place where such conversations
would be certain to be private.
7 **ten times:** Many times.

10 Now it was at the time of the animals' being in heat
  that I lifted up my eyes and saw in a dream:
  here, the he-goats that mount the animals—streaked, speckled,
    and spotted!
11 And God's messenger said to me in the dream: Yaakov!
  I said: Here I am.
12 He said:
  Pray lift up your eyes and see:
  All the he-goats that mount the animals—streaked, speckled, and
    spotted!
  For I have seen all that Lavan is doing to you.
13 I am the God of Bet-El,
  where you anointed the pillar,
  where you vowed a vow to me.
  So now, arise,
  get out of this land,
  return to the land of your kindred!
14 Rahel and Lea answered him, they said to him:
  Do we still have a share, an inheritance in our father's house?
15 Is it not as strangers that we are thought of by him?
  For he has sold us and eaten up, yes, eaten up our purchase-price!
16 Indeed, all the riches that God has snatched away from our
    father—
  they belong to us and to our children.
  So now, whatever God has said to you, do!
17 So Yaakov arose, he lifted his children and his wives onto the
    camels
18 and led away all his livestock, all his property that he had gained,
  the acquired-livestock of his own acquiring which he had gained
    in the country of Aram,
  to come home to Yitzhak his father in the land of Canaan.
19 Now Lavan had gone to shear his flock;
  Rahel, meanwhile, stole the *terafim* that belonged to her father.

---

10 **Now it was . . . in a dream:** Several times in this chapter we hear of important events secondhand, in speech rather than in action. See note to 20:13. **streaked, speckled, and spotted:** Heb. *akuddim,* *nekuddim, u-veruddim.* The rhyme (rare in biblical Hebrew) suggests a vision or a dream.

19 *terafim:* Hebrew obscure; apparently some sort of idols. Others use "household gods."

20 Now Yaakov stole the wits of Lavan the Aramean,
by not telling him that he was about to flee.

21 And flee he did, he and all that was his;
he arose and crossed the River, setting his face toward the
hill-country of Gil'ad.

22 Lavan was told on the third day that Yaakov had fled;

23 he took his tribal-brothers with him and pursued him, a seven-
days' journey,
and caught up with him in the hill-country of Gil'ad.

24 But God came to Lavan the Aramean in a dream of the night
and said to him:
Be on your watch
lest you speak to Yaakov, be it good or ill!

25 When Lavan caught up with Yaakov,
—Yaakov had pegged his tent in the mountains, and Lavan along
with his brothers had pegged (his tent) in the hill-country
of Gil'ad—

26 Lavan said to Yaakov:
What did you mean to do
by stealing my wits and leading my daughters away like captives
of the sword?

27 Why did you secretly flee and steal away on me, without even
telling me,
—for I would have sent you off with joy and with song, with
drum and with lyre—

28 and you did not even allow me to kiss my grandchildren and my
daughters?
You have done foolishly now!

29 It lies in my hand's power to do (all of) you ill!
But yesterday night the God of your father said to me, saying:
Be on your watch
from speaking to Yaakov, be it good or ill!

---

20 **stole the wits:** Fooled, hoodwinked.   28 **kiss:** Upon leaving; "kiss good-bye."
24 **be it good or ill:** Lit. "from good to ill."

30 Well now, you had to go, yes, go, since you longed, longed for
    your father's house—
Why did you steal my gods?

31 Yaakov answered and said to Lavan:
Indeed, I was afraid, for I said to myself: Perhaps you will even
    rob me of your daughters!

32 With whomever you find your gods—he shall not live;
here in front of our brothers, (see if) you recognize anything of
    yours with me, and take it!
Yaakov did not know that Rahel had stolen them.

33 Lavan came into Yaakov's tent and into Lea's tent and into the
    tents of the two maids, but he did not find anything.
Then he went out of Lea's tent and came into Rahel's tent.

34 Now Rahel had taken the *terafim* and had put them in the basket-
    saddle of the camels, and had sat down upon them.
Lavan felt all around the tent, but he did not find anything.

35 She said to her father:
Do not let upset be in my lord's eyes that I am not able to rise
    in your presence,
for the manner of women is upon me.
So he searched, but he did not find the *terafim*.

36 Now Yaakov became upset and took up quarrel with Lavan,
Yaakov spoke up, saying to Lavan:
What is my offense, what is my sin,
that you have dashed hotly after me,

37 that you have felt all through my wares?
What have you found from all your household-wares?
Set it here in front of your brothers and my brothers,
that they may decide between us two!

38 It is twenty years now that I have been under you:
your ewes and your she-goats have never miscarried,
the rams from your flock I never have eaten,

---

30 **you had to go:** Or "Suppose you had to go."
31 **Indeed, I was afraid:** Yaakov seems to be explaining why he "had to go" first, and then answering Lavan's question in v. 32.
32 **with me:** In my possession.

34 **sat down upon them:** Ridiculing the pagan gods, at least to the audience. **felt all around:** Recalling the "feeling" of Yitzhak in Chap. 27.
35 **manner of women:** The menstrual period.
37 **felt all through:** Or "rifled."

39 none torn-by-beasts have I ever brought you—
   I would make good the loss,
   at my hand you would seek it,
   stolen by day or stolen by night.
40 (Thus) I was:
   by day, parching-heat consumed me, and cold by night,
   and my sleep eluded my eyes.
41 It is twenty years for me now in your house:
   I have served you fourteen years for your two daughters, and six
        years for your animals,
   yet you have changed my wages ten times over.
42 Had not the God of my father,
   the God of Avraham and the Terror of Yitzhak,
   been-there for me,
   indeed, you would have sent me off now, empty-handed!
   But God has seen my being afflicted and the toil of my hands,
   and yesterday night he decided.
43 Lavan gave answer, he said to Yaakov:
   The daughters are my daughters,
   the children are my children,
   the animals are my animals—
   all that you see, it is mine!
   But to my daughters—what can I do to them today, or to their
        children whom they have borne?
44 So now, come,
   let us cut a covenant, I and you,
   and let (something here) serve as a witness between me and you.
45 Yaakov took a stone and erected it as a standing-pillar.
46 And Yaakov said to his brothers:
   Collect stones!
   They fetched stones and made a mound.
   And they ate there by the mound.

39 **seek:** I.e., seek restitution.
41 **twenty years:** Yosef will be away from Yaakov for
   approximately the same period of time.
42 **Terror:** The intent of the Hebrew is unclear; it

could be something like "Yitzhak's champion" or
"the One who inspired terror in Yitzhak."
43 **to my daughters:** Others use "for my daughters."
46 **And they ate:** See note to 26:30.

Preparations for Esav (32:2–24): As if to portend something momentous, Yaakov's first act upon setting out for home is an encounter with "messengers of God." From this starting point everything is subsequently a matter of "two camps" (v.8) or two levels: the divine and the human. This is the key to understanding the meeting between Yaakov and his brother in its entirety: Yaakov will have to deal with God before he can resolve his problem with Esav.

With an obsequiousness whose language reflects both the culture and the emotional setting, Yaakov prepares a gift for Esav, but finds to his dismay that his brother is "coming to meet him," with seemingly hostile intent. Once again stealth (or at least extreme caution) is the rule, with Yaakov taking elaborate precautions.

47 Now Lavan called it: *Yegar Sahaduta,*
while Yaakov called it: Gal-Ed.

48 Lavan said:
This mound is witness between me and you from today.
Therefore they called its name: Gal-Ed/Mound-Witness,

49 and also: Mitzpa/Guardpost,
because he said:
May Y H W H keep guard between me and you, when we are
hidden from one another!

50 If you should ever afflict my daughters,
if you should ever take wives besides my daughters . . . !
No man is here with us,
(but) see, God is witness between me and you!

51 And Lavan said to Yaakov:
Here is this mound, here is the pillar that I have sunk between me
and you:

52 witness is this mound, witness is the pillar
that I will not cross over this mound to you
and you will not cross over this mound and this pillar to me,
for ill!

53 May the God of Avraham and the God of Nahor keep-justice
between us—the God of their father.
And Yaakov swore by the Terror of his father Yitzhak.

54 Then Yaakov slaughtered a slaughter-meal on the mountain
and called his brothers to eat bread.
They ate bread and spent the night on the mountain.

32:1 Lavan started-early in the morning, kissed his grandchildren and
his daughters and blessed them,
and Lavan went to return to his place.

2 As Yaakov went on his way,
messengers of God encountered him.

---

47 *Yegar Sahaduta:* Aramaic for "Mound-Witness" (Yaakov's Gal-Ed of the next verse). Aramaic was the lingua franca of the area from the First Millennium B.C.E. on, and is still spoken in some Syrian villages.
49 **when we are hidden:** Even when I cannot verify your behavior.
50 **God:** Or "a god."
54 **bread:** Or more generally, "food."
32:1 **Lavan (started-early)...:** The verse numbering follows the Hebrew; some English translations number 32:1 as 31:55.

3 Yaakov said when he saw them:
This is a camp of God!
And he called the name of that place: Mahanayim/Double-
Camp.

4 Now Yaakov sent messengers on ahead of him to Esav his
brother in the land of Se'ir, in the territory of Edom,
5 and commanded them, saying:
Thus say to my lord, to Esav:
Thus says your servant Yaakov:
I have sojourned with Lavan and have tarried until now.
6 Ox and donkey, sheep and servant and maid have become mine.
I have sent to tell my lord, to find favor in your eyes.
7 The messengers returned to Yaakov, saying:
We came to your brother, to Esav—
but he is already coming to meet you, and four hundred men are
with him!
8 Yaakov became exceedingly afraid and was distressed.
He divided the people that were with him and the sheep and the
oxen and the camels into two camps,
9 saying to himself:
Should Esav come against the one camp and strike it, the camp
that is left will escape.
10 Then Yaakov said:
God of my father Avraham,
God of my father Yitzhak,
O YHWH,
who said to me: Return to your land, to your kindred, and I will
deal well with you!—
11 Too small am I for all the faithfulness and trust that you have
shown your servant.
For with only my rod did I cross this Jordan, and now I have
become two camps.

7 **four hundred men:** A considerable fighting force.
Even if the number is schematic (as ten times forty),
it still represents something formidable.
11 **Too small:** This is the first indication of the change

in Yaakov's personality. Now he relies on God (although he still uses his wits, by diplomatically and
strategically preparing for his meeting with Esav).

12 Pray save me from the hand of my brother, from the hand of
    Esav!
    For I am in fear of him,
    lest he come and strike me down, mothers and children alike!

13 But you, you have said:
    I will deal well, well with you,
    I will make your seed like the sand of the sea, which is too much
        to count!

14 Spending the night there that night,
    he took a gift from what was at hand, for Esav his brother:

15 she-goats, two hundred, and kids, twenty,
    ewes, two hundred, and rams, twenty,

16 nursing camels and their young, thirty,
    cows, forty, and bulls, ten,
    she-asses, twenty, and colts, ten;

17 he handed them over to his servants, herd by herd separately,
    and said to his servants:
    Cross on ahead of me, and leave room between herd and herd.

18 He charged the first group, saying:
    When Esav my brother meets you
    and asks you, saying: To whom do you belong, where are you
        going, and to whom do these ahead of you belong?

19 Then say:
    —to your servant, to Yaakov, it is a gift sent to my lord, to Esav,
    and here, he himself is also behind us.

20 Thus he charged the second, and thus the third, and thus all that
        were walking behind the herds, saying:
    According to this word shall you speak to Esav when you come
        upon him:

21 You shall say: Also—here, your servant Yaakov is behind us.
    For he said to himself:
    I will wipe (the anger from) his face
    with the gift that goes ahead of my face;

---

13 **you have said:** I.e., you have promised. See also
note on 31:10. **like the sand:** In fact, this is God's
promise to Avraham, in 22:17.

15: **she-goats . . . :** The gift is a special one, promising
increase (females with their young).

The Mysterious Stranger: Struggle at the Yabbok (32:25–33): Unexpectedly there is a break in the narrative. The stage has been set for something mysterious to happen with a nighttime backdrop and accented references to "crossing" (vv.23–24), which clearly refers to more than just the river.

The great wrestling scene at the Yabbok both symbolizes and resolves beforehand Yaakov's meeting with Esav, much as Shakespeare's prebattle dream scenes (e.g., *Julius Caesar, Richard III, Macbeth*) will do with his characters. Struggle, the motif already introduced in the mother's womb (Chap. 25), returns here, but that is not the only consideration. At issue is Yaakov's whole life and personality, which despite his recent material successes are still under the pall of Esav's curse (27:36). Central, then, is the change of name in v.29, which suggests both a victorious struggle and the emergence of a new power. This is further supported by the Hebrew plays on sound: *Y'KB* (Yaakov), *YBK* (Yabbok), and *Y'BK* (wrestling).

The story may have originated as the well-known tale of a hero fighting a river divinity, but it clearly has been transformed into something much broader by its position and vocabulary.

On the mysterious aspects of both the story and the name Israel, see Geller.

afterward, when I see his face,
perhaps he will lift up my face!

22 The gift crossed over ahead of his face,
but he spent the night on that night in the camp.

23 He arose during that night,
took his two wives, his two maids, and his eleven children
to cross the Yabbok crossing.

24 He took them and brought them across the river; he brought
across what belonged to him.

25 And Yaakov was left alone—
Now a man wrestled with him until the coming up of dawn.

26 When he saw that he could not prevail against him,
he touched the socket of his thigh;
the socket of Yaakov's thigh had been dislocated as he wrestled
with him.

27 Then he said:
Let me go,
for dawn has come up!
But he said:
I will not let you go
unless you bless me.

28 He said to him:
What is your name?
And he said: Yaakov.

29 Then he said:
Not as Yaakov/Heel-Sneak shall your name be henceforth
uttered,
but rather as Yisrael/God-Fighter,

---

21 **lift up my face:** Or "be gracious to me."
23 **Yabbok:** A traditional natural boundary, it creates a wild gorge which is the perfect setting for this incident.
25 **left alone:** In a psychological sense Yaakov has not yet crossed the river.
26 **touched:** Perhaps in homage, for the injury had already occurred (Ehrlich).
27 **dawn has come up:** In folklore, supernatural beings often must disappear with the break of day.

28-29 **What is your name? . . . Not as Yaakov:** As if to say "You cannot be blessed with such a name!" The "man" in effect removes Esav's curse.
29 **God-Fighter:** The name may actually mean "God fights." Buber further conjectured that it means "God rules," containing the kernel of ancient Israel's concept of itself, but he retained "Fighter of God" in the translation.

Resolution (33:1–17): Once the Yabbok crisis is past, there is hope for reconciliation of the brothers. Even so, Yaakov exercises caution, behaving like a man who is presenting tribute to a king. The narrative is brought full circle in vv.10 and 11, where "face" is once again highlighted and where Yaakov's gift is termed a "token-of-blessing." At last the tension of Yaakov's early life seems resolved.

for you have fought with God and men
and have prevailed.

30 Then Yaakov asked and said:
Pray tell me your name!
But he said:
Now why do you ask after my name?
And he gave him farewell-blessing there.

31 Yaakov called the name of the place: Peniel/Face of God,
for: I have seen God,
face to face,
and my life has been saved.

32 The sun rose on him as he crossed by Penuel,
and he was limping on his thigh.

33 —Therefore the Children of Israel do not eat the sinew that is on
the socket of the thigh until this day,
for he had touched the socket of Yaakov's thigh at the sinew.

33:1 Yaakov lifted up his eyes and saw:
there was Esav coming, and with him, four hundred men!
He divided the children among Lea, Rahel, and the two maids:

2 he put the maids and their children first,
Lea and her children behind them,
and Rahel and Yosef behind them,

3 while he himself advanced ahead of them.
And he bowed low to the ground seven times, until he had come
close to him, to his brother.

4 Esav ran to meet him,
he embraced him, flung himself upon his neck, and kissed him.
And they wept.

5 Then he lifted up his eyes and saw the women and the children,
and said:

---

29 **God and men:** Others use "beings divine and human."

30 **Now why do you ask:** In folklore the name of a divine being is often withheld, for to know it would be to acquire power over him. See also Judg. 13:18: "Now why do you ask after my name? For it is wondrous!"

31 **Peniel/Face of God:** See v.21, and 33:10, for the important allusions.

32 **The sun rose:** A sign of favor. **Penuel:** A variant spelling of Peniel.

33 **sinew:** The sciatic nerve.

Home: Peace and Violence (33:18–34:31): "Yaakov came home in peace to the city of Shekhem" (33:18) continues the theme of resolution. Not only has Esav accepted his gift, but Yaakov has arrived home safely, in fulfillment of his prayer in 28:21. Like Avraham he purchases land; again like him he builds an altar.

Chap. 34, however, shatters the newly created atmosphere of security and peace ("peaceably disposed" in v.21 is a bitter twist). Whereas Avraham and Yitzhak had been able to conclude treaties with the inhabitants of Canaan, Yaakov winds up in the opposite position. The text implies, as usual, that Canaanite sexual behavior is odious (v.7, "such [a thing] is not to be done!"), and this provides the spring for the action. Interestingly, Yaakov's sons act somewhat like their father had, "with deceit" (v.13); and love once again leads to an unfortunate end.

The vengefulness and brutality of Yaakov's sons in this story anticipates their later behavior in the Yosef story (Chap. 37); surprisingly, it is for the present crime and not the sale of Yosef that their father condemns them on his deathbed (49:5–7).

The chapter is notable for the latitude it allows its characters to express their thoughts and emotions: Shekhem's desire and love, the sons' anger and cunning, the Hivvites' gullibility and greed, and Yaakov's fear. Like other stories in the Yaakov cycle, it presents us with a somewhat ambiguous situation, where right and wrong are not always simple and the putative heroes are not always heroic.

What are these to you?

He said:

—the children with whom God has favored your servant.

6 Then the maids came close, they and their children, and bowed
low.

7 Then Lea and her children came close and bowed low.

Afterward Yosef and Rahel came close and bowed low.

8 He said:

What to you is all this camp that I have met?

He said:

—to find favor in my lord's eyes.

9 Esav said:

I have plenty, my brother, let what is yours remain yours.

10 Yaakov said:

No, I pray!

Pray, if I have found favor in your eyes,

then take this gift from my hand.

For I have, after all, seen your face, as one sees the face of God,

and you have been gracious to me.

11 Pray take my token-of-blessing that is brought to you,

for God has shown me favor—for I have everything.

And he pressed him, so he took it.

12 Then he said:

Let us travel on, and I will go on at your side.

13 But he said to him:

My lord knows

that the children are frail,

and the sheep and the oxen are suckling in my care;

if we were to push them for a single day, all the animals would
die!

14 Pray let my lord cross on ahead of his servant,

while as for me, I will travel slowly,

33:8 **What to you is:** I.e., What does it mean to you?

9 **my brother:** The phrase suggests that they are now reconciled.

◆ at the pace of the gear ahead of me and at the pace of the
children,
until I come to my lord, at Se'ir.

15 Esav said:
Pray let me leave with you some of the people who are mine.
But he said:
For what reason?
May I only find favor in my lord's eyes!

16 So Esav started back that same day on his journey to Se'ir,

17 while Yaakov traveled to Succot.
He built himself a house there, and for his livestock he made sheds.
Therefore they called the name of the place: Succot/Sheds.

18 Yaakov came home in peace to the city of Shekhem, which is in
the land of Canaan,
on his homecoming from the country of Aram,
and he encamped facing the city.

19 And he acquired the piece of territory where he had spread out
his tent, from the Sons of Hamor, Shekhem's father, for a
hundred lambs'-worth.

20 There he set up a slaughter-site
and called it:
El/God, the God of Yisrael!

34:1 Now Dina, Lea's daughter, whom she had borne to Yaakov, went
out to see the women of the land.

2 And Shekhem son of Hamor the Hivvite, the prince of the land,
saw her:
he took her and lay with her, forcing her.

3 But his emotions clung to Dina, Yaakov's daughter—he loved the
girl,
and he spoke to the heart of the girl.

---

15 **leave with you:** Or "station with you," "put at your
disposal." **mine:** Lit. "with me." **For what reason?:**
Yaakov still seems cautious.
19 **he acquired:** Like his grandfather Avraham, Yaakov
must purchase the land. **lambs'-worth:** Hebrew obscure.

34:1 **to see:** To visit.
2 **Hamor:** Heb. "donkey." Some take the name to
prove that they were donkey-drivers, while others
see it as an insult to the character. **forcing:** Or
"humbling."

4 So Shekhem said to Hamor his father, saying:
Take me this girl as a wife!

5 Now Yaakov had heard that he had defiled Dina his daughter,
but since his sons were with his livestock in the fields, Yaakov
kept silent until they came home.

6 Hamor, Shekhem's father, went out to Yaakov, to speak with him.

7 But Yaakov's sons came back from the fields when they heard,
and the men were pained, they were exceedingly upset,
for he had done a disgrace in Israel by lying with Yaakov's
daughter,
such (a thing) is not to be done!

8 Hamor spoke with them, saying:
My son Shekhem—
his emotions are so attached to your daughter,
(so) pray give her to him as a wife!

9 And make marriage-alliances with us:
give us your daughters, and our daughters take for yourselves,

10 and settle among us!
The land shall be before you:
settle down, travel about it, obtain holdings in it!

11 And Shekhem said to her father and to her brothers:
May I only find favor in your eyes!
However much you say to me, I will give-in-payment,

12 to whatever extreme you multiply the bride-price and the
marriage-gift,
I will give however much you say to me—
only give me the girl as a wife!

13 Now Yaakov's sons answered Shekhem and Hamor his father
with deceit,
speaking (thus) because he had defiled Dina their sister,

7 **disgrace:** A different Hebrew word from the one
rendered "disgraced" in 15:2.
8 **his emotions are so attached:** Speiser uses "has his
heart set on." **pray give:** The repetition of "give"
suggests a greediness on their part.

10 **travel about:** Or "trade."
13 **with deceit:** Another example of a key word in the
Yaakov stories; see 27:35 and 29:25.

Home: Blessing and Death (35): Several brief notices round out Yaakov's return to Canaan. First (vv.1–7) there is the return to Bet-El, where he builds an altar and has the "foreign" gods of his household people put away—thus fulfilling his promise in Chap. 28. This passage is built upon the Hebrew word *El,* God (related actually to an earlier Northwest Semitic name for a god).

Apparently a second version of Yaakov's name change is recorded in vv.9–15. As in the case of Avraham, seed and land are promised by God. The land can be given to him and "to your seed after you" only upon his return.

Finally, spread out through the chapter are the accounts of three deaths: Devora, Rivka's nurse (v.8—a veiled reference to Rivka's own death?), Rahel (vv.16–20), and finally Yitzhak (vv.28–29). Yaakov's youth is over, with the dramatic break with those close to him in that period.

14 they said to them:
   We cannot do this thing,
   give our sister to a man who has a foreskin,
   for that would be a reproach for us!
15 Only on this (condition) will we comply with you:
   if you become like us, by having every male among you
      circumcised.
16 Then we will give you our daughters, and your daughters we will
      take for ourselves,
   and we will settle among you, so that we become a single people.
17 But if you do not hearken to us, to be circumcised,
   we will take our daughter and go.
18 Their words seemed good in the eyes of Hamor and in the eyes
      of Shekhem son of Hamor,
19 and the young man did not hesitate to do the thing,
   for he desired Yaakov's daughter.
   Now he carried more weight than anyone in his father's house.
20 When Hamor and Shekhem his son came back to the gate of
      their city,
   they spoke to the men of their city, saying:
21 These men are peaceably disposed toward us;
   let them settle in the land and travel about in it,
   for the land is certainly wide-reaching enough for them!
   Let us take their daughters as wives for ourselves, and let us give
      them our daughters.
22 But only on this (condition) will the men comply with us, to
      settle among us, to become a single people:
   that every male among us be circumcised, as they are
      circumcised.
23 Their acquired livestock, their acquired property and all their
      beasts—will they not then become ours?!
   Let us only comply with them, that they may settle among us!

19 **desired:** Not the same Hebrew term as in 2:9.   21 **peaceably disposed:** Or "friendly," "honest."
carried more weight: I.e., was more respected.

♦ 24 So they hearkened to Hamor and to Shekhem his son, all who go
out (to war) from the gate of his city:
all the males were circumcised, all who go out (to war) from the
gate of his city.
25 But on the third day it was, when they were still hurting,
that two of Yaakov's sons, Shim'on and Levi, Dina's full-brothers,
took each man his sword,
they came upon the city (feeling) secure, and killed all the males,
26 and Hamor and Shekhem his son they killed by the sword.
Then they took Dina from Shekhem's house and went off.
27 Yaakov's (other) sons came up upon the corpses and plundered
the city,
because they had defiled their sister.
28 Their sheep, their oxen, their donkeys—whatever was inside the
city and out in the field, they took,
29 all their riches, all their little-ones and their wives they captured
and plundered,
as well as all that was in the houses.
30 But Yaakov said to Shim'on and to Levi:
You have stirred-up-trouble for me,
making me reek among the settled-folk of the land, the
Canaanites and the Perizzites!
For I have menfolk few in number;
they will band together against me and strike me,
and I will be destroyed, I and my household!
31 But they said:
Should our sister then be treated like a whore?

35:1 Now God said to Yaakov:
Arise,
go up to Bet-El and stay there,
and construct a slaughter-site there
to the God/*El* who was seen by you when you fled from Esav
your brother.

24 **all who go out . . . :** I.e., all able-bodied men.

25 **Shim'on and Levi:** They are condemned for this incident by Yaakov in 49:5–7.

2 Yaakov said to his household and to all who were with him:
Put away the foreign gods that are in your midst!
Purify yourselves! Change your garments!

3 Let us arise and go up to Bet-El,
there I will construct a slaughter-site
to the God who answered me on the day of my distress
—he was with me on the way that I went!

4 So they gave Yaakov all the foreign gods that were in their hand,
along with the sacred-rings that were in their ears,
and Yaakov concealed them under the oak/*ela* that is near
Shekhem.

5 Then they moved on.
Now a dread from God lay upon the towns that were around
them,
so that they did not pursue Yaakov's sons.

6 So Yaakov came back to Luz, which is in the land of Canaan—
that is now Bet-El—he and all the people that were with him.

7 There he built a slaughter-site
and called the place:
Godhead/*El* of Bet-El!
For there had the power-of-God been revealed to him, when he
fled from his brother.

8 Now Devora, Rivka's nurse, died.
She was buried below Bet-El, beneath the oak;
they called its name: Allon Bakhut/Oak of Weeping.

9 God was seen by Yaakov again, when he came back from the
country of Aram,
and he gave him blessing:

10 God said to him:
Yaakov is your name,
Yaakov shall your name be called no more,

35:2 **Change your garments:** Speiser translates this as
"Put on new clothes."
8 **Rivka's nurse, died:** See note to 24:59.

9ff. **God was seen . . . :** Apparently a different version
of the Peniel story of Chap. 32.

Re'uven (35:21–22): The following tiny fragment, concerning Re'uven's usurping his father's concubine, serves to presage his fall as firstborn later on. Such an act had symbolic value in biblical society; Avshalom (Absalom) sleeps with David's concubines as a sign of rebellion and a desire to attain the crown (II Sam. 16:21–22).

Esav's Descendants (36): The complicated genealogies and dynasties of this chapter close out the first part of the Yaakov cycle, strictly speaking. Fitting in the context of a society which lay great store by kinship and thus by careful remembering of family names, it may also indicate the greatness of Yitzhak's line, as Chap. 25 had earlier done for Avraham. Certainly the lists give evidence of a time when the Edomites were more than merely Israel's neighbors, assuming great importance in historical recollection (Speiser).

for your name shall be Yisrael!
And he called his name: Yisrael!

11 God said further to him:
I am God Shaddai.
Bear fruit and be many!
Nation, yes, a host of nations shall come from you,
kings shall go out from your loins!

12 The land
that I gave to Avraham and to Yitzhak,
to you I give it,
and to your seed after you I give the land.

13 God went up from beside him, at the place where he had spoken
with him.

14 And Yaakov set up a standing-pillar at the place where he had
spoken with him, a pillar of stone,
he poured out a poured-offering on it and cast oil upon it.

15 And Yaakov called the name of the place where God had spoken
with him:
Bet-El/House of God!

16 They departed from Bet-El.
But when there was still a stretch of land to come to Efrat,
Rahel began to give birth,
and she had a very hard birthing.

17 It was, when her birthing was at its hardest,
that the midwife said to her:
Do not be afraid,
for this one too is a son for you!

18 It was, as her life was slipping away
—for she was dying—

11–12 **I am God Shaddai . . . :** See God's words to Avra-ham in 17:6.

13 **at the place where he had spoken with him:** The phrase occurs three times here and subsequently, probably to emphasize the sanctity of Bet-El.

17 **this one too is a son:** This seems to be a breach birth, since the midwife already knew that it was a son when "her birthing was at its hardest"—that is, before the child had fully emerged.

18 **her life was slipping away:** Or "her life-breath was leaving (her)," paralleling a similar expression in Ugaritic.

that she called his name: Ben-Oni/Son-of-My-Woe.
But his father called him: Binyamin/Son-of-the-Right-Hand.

19 So Rahel died;
she was buried along the way to Efrat—that is now Bet-Lehem.

20 Yaakov set up a standing-pillar over her burial-place,
that is Rahel's burial pillar of today.

21 Now Yisrael departed and spread his tent beyond Migdal-
Eder/Herd-Tower.

22 And it was when Yisrael was dwelling in that land: Re'uven went
and lay with Bilha, his father's concubine.
And Yisrael heard—

Now the sons of Yaakov were twelve:

23 The sons of Lea: Yaakov's firstborn, Re'uven; Shim'on, Levi and
Yehuda, Yissakhar and Zevulun.

24 The sons of Rahel: Yosef and Binyamin.

25 The sons of Bilha, Rahel's maid: Dan and Naftali.

26 The sons of Zilpa, Lea's maid: Gad and Asher.
These (were) Yaakov's sons, who were born to him in the
country of Aram.

27 Yaakov came home to Yitzhak his father at Mamre, in the city of
Arba—that is now Hevron,
where Avraham and Yitzhak had sojourned.

28 And the days of Yitzhak were a hundred years and eighty

29 years, / then Yitzhak expired.
He died and was gathered to his kinspeople, old and satisfied in
days.
Esav and Yaakov his sons buried him.

36:1 And these are the begettings of Esav—that is Edom.

2 Esav took his wives from the women of Canaan:
Ada, daughter of Elon the Hittite, and Oholivama, daughter

---

18 **But his father called him: Binyamin:** Given the
power of names, it would not have been considered
proper for a child to begin life with a name such as
the one Rahel gives him. **Binyamin:** Trad. English
"Benjamin."

19 **Bet-Lehem:** Trad. English "Bethlehem."

29 **Then Yitzhak expired:** See the Commentary on
26:1-6.

3   of Ana (and) granddaughter of Tziv'on the Hivvite, / and
     Ba'semat, daughter of Yishmael and sister of Nevayot.

4   Ada bore Elifaz to Esav,
    Ba'semat bore Re'uel,

5   Oholivama bore Ye'ush, Ya'lam, and Korah.
    These are Esav's sons, who were born to him in the land of
     Canaan.

6   Esav took his wives, his sons and his daughters, and all the
     persons in his household,
    as well as his acquired-livestock, all his animals, and all his
     acquisitions that he had gained in the land of Canaan,
    and went to (another) land, away from Yaakov his brother;

7   for their property was too much for them to settle together,
    the land of their sojourning could not support them, on account
     of their acquired-livestock.

8   So Esav settled in the hill-country of Se'ir—Esav, that is Edom.

9   And these are the begettings of Esav, the tribal-father of Edom, in
    the hill-country of Se'ir:

10   These are the names of the sons of Esav:
    Elifaz son of Ada, Esav's wife, Re'uel, son of Ba'semat, Esav's
     wife.

11   The sons of Elifaz were Teiman, Omar, Tzefo, Ga'tam, and
    Kenaz.

12   Now Timna was concubine to Elifaz son of Esav, and she bore
    Amalek to Elifaz.
    These are the sons of Ada, Esav's wife.

13   And these are the sons of Re'uel: Nahat and Zerah, Shamma and
    Mizza.
    These were the sons of Ba'semat, Esav's wife.

14   And these were the sons of Oholivama, daughter of Ana, (and)
    granddaughter of Tziv'on (and) Esav's wife:
    She bore Ye'ush and Ya'lam and Korah to Esav.

15   These are the families of Esav's sons:

36:7 **for their property was too much:** Again recalling
Avraham, in his conflict with Lot (13:6).
14 **Tziv'on:** The name means "hyena." Such animal

names have long been popular in the region and
occur a number of times in this chapter (Vawter).
15 **families:** Others use "chieftains."

◆   From the sons of Elifaz, Esav's firstborn, are: the Family Teiman, the Family Omar, the Family Tzefo, the Family

16   Kenaz,/ the Family Korah, the Family Ga'tam, the Family Amalek;

these are the families from Elifaz in the land of Edom, these are the sons of Ada.

17 And these are the Children of Re'uel, Esav's son: the Family Nahat, the Family Zerah, the Family Shamma, the Family Mizza;

these are the families from Re'uel in the land of Edom, these the Children of Ba'semat, Esav's wife.

18 And these are the Children of Oholivama, Esav's wife: the Family Ye'ush, the Family Ya'lam, the Family Korah;

these are the families from Oholivama, daughter of Ana, Esav's wife.

19 These are the Children of Esav and these are their families.
—That is Edom.

20 These are the sons of Se'ir the Horite, the settled-folk of the land:

21 Lotan and Shoval and Tziv'on and Ana and Dishon and Etzer and Dishan.

These are the Horite families, the Children of Se'ir in the land of Edom.

22 The sons of Lotan were Hori and Hemam, and Lotan's sister was Timna.

23 And these are the sons of Shoval: Alvan and Manahat and Eval, Shefo and Onam.

24 And these are the sons of Tziv'on: Ayya and Ana.
—That is the Ana who found the *yemim* in the wilderness, as he was tending the donkeys of Tziv'on his father.

25 And these are the sons of Ana: Dishon—and Oholivama was Ana's daughter.

26 And these are the sons of Dishon: Hemdan and Eshban and Yitran and Ceran.

24 *yemim:* Hebrew obscure; some use "hot-springs," "lakes."

26 **Dishon:** The traditional text uses "Dishan," but see I Chron. 1:41.

27 These are the sons of Etzer: Bilhan and Zaavan and Akan.

28 These are the sons of Dishan: Utz and Aran.

29 These are the Horite families: the Family Lotan, the Family

30   Shoval, the Family Tziv'on, the Family Ana,/ the Family
     Dishon, the Family Etzer, the Family Dishan.
     These are the families of the Horites, according to their families
     in the land of Se'ir.

31 Now these are the kings who served as king in the land of Edom,
     before any king of the Children of Israel served as king:

32 In Edom, Bela son of Be'or was king; the name of his city was
     Dinhava.

33 When Bela died, Yovav son of Zerah of Botzra became king in
     his stead.

34 When Yovav died, Husham from the land of the Teimanites
     became king in his stead.

35 When Husham died, Hadad son of Bedad became king in his
     stead—who struck Midyan in the territory of Mo'av, and the
     name of his city was Avit.

36 When Hadad died, Samla of Masreka became king in his stead.

37 When Samla died, Sha'ul of Rehovot-by-the-River became king in
     his stead.

38 When Sha'ul died, Baal-Hanan son of Akhbor became king in his
     stead.

39 When Baal-Hanan son of Akhbor died, Hadar became king in his
     stead; the name of his city was Pa'u, and the name of his wife,
     Mehetavel daughter of Matred, daughter of Mei-Zahav.

40 Now these are the names of the families from Esav, according to
     their clans, according to their local-places, by their names:

41 The Family Timna, the Family Alvan, the Family Yetet,/ the
     Family Oholivama, the Family Ela, the Family

42   Pinon,/ the Family Kenaz, the Family Teiman, the Family

43   Mivtzar,/ the Family Magdiel, the Family Iram.
     These are the families of Edom according to their settlements in
     the land of their holdings.

     That is Esav, the tribal-father of Edom.

PART IV

YOSEF

(37–50)

THE STORIES ABOUT THE LAST PATRIARCH FORM A COHERENT WHOLE, LEADING SOME to dub it a "novella." It stands well on its own, although it has been consciously and artfully woven together into both the Yaakov cycle and the entire book.

Initially the tale is one of family emotions, and it is in fact extreme emotions which give it a distinctive flavor. All the major characters are painfully expressive of their feelings, from the doting father to the spoiled son, from the malicious brothers to the lustful wife of Potifar, from the nostalgic adult Yosef to the grief-stricken old Yaakov. It is only through the subconscious medium of dreams, in three sets, that we are made to realize that a higher plan is at work which will supersede the destructive force of these emotions.

For this is a story of how "ill"—with all its connotations of fate, evil, and disaster—is changed to good. Despite the constant threat of death to Yosef, to the Egyptians, and to Binyamin, the hidden, optimistic thrust of the story is "life," a word that appears in various guises throughout. Even "face," the key word of the Yaakov cycle which often meant something negative, is here given a kinder meaning, as the resolution to Yaakov's life.

A major subtheme of the plot is the struggle for power between Re'uven and Yehuda. Its resolution has implications that are as much tribal as personal, for the tribe of Yehuda later became the historical force in ancient Israel as the seat of the monarchy.

Although many details of the narrative confirm Egyptian practices, those practices actually reflect an Egypt considerably later than the period of the Patriarchs (Redford). Of interest also is the prominence of the number five in the story, a detail that is unexplained but that gives some unity to the various sections of text.

In many ways the Yosef material repeats elements in the Yaakov traditions. A long list could be compiled, but let us at least mention here sibling hatred, exile of the hero, foreign names, love and hate, dreams, and deception—even so detailed as to duplicate the use of a goat-kid. But its focusing on a classic rags-to-riches plot, with the addition of a moralistic theme, make the Yosef story a distinctive and always popular tale, accessible in a way that the more difficult stories of the first three parts of Genesis are not.

Young Yosef: Love and Hate (37): As has been the pattern with the Avraham and Yaakov cycles, the opening chapter here introduces the key themes of the entire story. These include the father's love, the power of words, dreams, "ill" as a key word (here denoting evil intent but eventually encompassing misfortune, among other concepts), and of course, the brothers' hatred, which at first glance is the motivating force behind the action.

But the initial blame for what happens clearly lies with the father (vv.3–4), and is made unbearable by Yosef's own behavior. In point of fact he is largely responsible for his own downfall, bearing tales about his brothers (v.2) even before Yaakov's preference for him is noted. His insistence on telling his dreams to his brothers must be galling, particularly the second time (v.9), coming as it does after the report that "they hated him still more for his dreams" (v.8).

The key word of the chapter, not surprisingly, is "brother," culminating in Yehuda's ironic words (v.27): "let not our hand be upon him, for he is our brother. . . ." Shortly afterward Yosef, their "(own) flesh," is sold into slavery and probable death.

37:1 Yaakov settled in the land of his father's sojournings,
in the land of Canaan.

2 These are the begettings of Yaakov.

Yosef, seventeen years old, used to tend the sheep along with his
brothers,
for he was serving-lad with the sons of Bilha and the sons of
Zilpa, his father's wives.
And Yosef brought a report of them, an ill one, to their father.

3 Now Yisrael loved Yosef above all his sons,
for he was a son of old age to him,
so he made him an ornamented coat.

4 When his brothers saw that it was he whom their father loved
above all his brothers,
they hated him,
and could not speak to him in peace.

5 Now Yosef dreamt a dream, and told it to his brothers
—from then on they hated him still more—,

6 he said to them:
Pray hear this dream that I have dreamt:

7 Here,
we were binding sheaf-bundles out in the field,
and here, my sheaf arose, it was standing upright,
and here, your sheaves were circling round and bowing down to
my sheaf!

37:2 **begettings:** In the sense of "family history." As noted above, the Yosef story is a continuation of the Yaakov saga. **seventeen:** Together with 47:28, this provides another example of numerical balance in these stories (see the Commentary on "The Patriarchal Narratives," p. 51). Yosef lives with Yaakov for the first seventeen years of his life and for the last seventeen of his father's. **along with his brothers:** A hint that he would one day "shepherd" (rule) his brothers? The Hebrew is open to that interpretation (Redford). **brought a report:** Or "gossip." Although the doting father's love is crucial, it seems really to be Yosef's own behavior (which precedes the information about his coat) that causes his abuse by the brothers.

3 **ornamented:** Hebrew obscure; B-R uses "ankle-length."

4 **hated:** Such a violent emotion nevertheless has once before (with Lea in 29:31) led not to disaster but to the fulfillment of the divine plan (there, the hatred results in the competition to have children). **in peace:** Or "civilly"—again the key Yaakov word, "peace."

6 **hear:** Which can also mean "understand" in biblical Hebrew.

◆ 8 His brothers said to him:
Would you be king, yes, king over us?
Or would you really rule, yes, rule us?
From then on they hated him still more—for his dreams, for his
words.

9 But he dreamt still another dream, and recounted it to his
brothers,
he said:
Here, I have dreamt still (another) dream:
Here,
the sun and the moon and eleven stars were bowing down to me!

10 When he recounted it to his father and his brothers,
his father rebuked him and said to him:
What kind of dream is this that you have dreamt!
Shall we come, yes, come, I, your mother and your brothers,
to bow down to you to the ground?

11 His brothers envied him,
while his father kept the matter in mind.

12 Now his brothers went to tend their father's sheep in Shekhem.

13 Yisrael said to Yosef:
Are not your brothers tending sheep in Shekhem?
Come, I will send you to them!
He said to him:
Here I am.

14 And he said to him:
Come, pray, look into the well-being of your brothers and into
the well-being of the sheep,
and bring me back word.

---

8 **king, yes, king . . . rule, yes, rule:** The doubling
might reflect the brothers' astonishment and bitterness. See also v. 10.

10 **your mother:** The fact that she had died in Chap. 35
does not detract from the symbol of the dream.

11 **remembered:** Or "kept in mind."

12 **Shekhem:** In our text this city's name (three times

here) reminds the reader of the disastrous events of
Chap. 34.

13 **Come:** Repeated in vv.20 and 27; it is ironically
Yaakov's decision to send Yosef to his brothers that
sets this part of the plot into action.

14 **well-being:** Heb. *shalom,* translated as "peace" in v.4
and elsewhere.

So he sent him out from the valley of Hevron, and he came to
    Shekhem.
15 And a man came upon him—here, he was roaming in the field;
the man asked him, saying:
What do you seek?
16 He said:
I seek my brothers,
pray tell me where they are tending-sheep.
17 The man said:
They have moved on from here,
indeed, I heard them say: Let us go to Dotan.
Yosef went after his brothers and came upon them in Dotan.
18 They saw him from afar,
and before he had gotten near them, they plotted-cunningly
    against him to cause his death.
19 They said each man to his brother:
Here comes the master dreamer!
20 So now, come, let us kill him and throw him into one of these
    pits
and say: An ill-tempered beast has devoured him!
Then we will see what becomes of his dreams!
21 When Re'uven heard it he tried to rescue him from their hand, he
    said:
Let us not take his life!
22 And Re'uven said to them:
Do not shed blood!
Throw him into this pit that is in the wilderness,
but do not lay a hand upon him!
—in order that he might save him from their hand, to return him
    to his father.

23 So it was, when Yosef came to his brothers,
that they stripped Yosef of his coat,
the ornamented coat that he had on,

---

15 **a man:** Possibly another divine messenger (like the "man" in 32:25). See also the note to "roaming" in 20:13.
19 **the master dreamer:** Lit. "that master of dreams."

20 **ill-tempered:** Others, "wild."
21 **take his life:** Lit. "strike him mortally."

Yehuda and Tamar (38): Chap. 38 has been the subject of many discussions, for it seems to be out of place. It interrupts the story of Yosef at a crucial dramatic spot, and is not chronologically fully consistent with it (Yehuda ages considerably; then we return to Yosef as a seventeen-year-old). Some feel that the suspension in the drama helps to raise tension; others argue that this is the only possible place to put an important tradition about the important brother. While these and other arguments may have their merit, one may discern some significant thematic connections as well, both within the context of the Yosef story and of Genesis as a whole.

The episode first of all demonstrates the growth of Yehuda as a character who is central to the Yosef novella. Already in Chap. 37 he had demonstrated active leadership, albeit in a questionable cause. There he actually saved Yosef's life, in contrast to Re'uven's unsuccessful and ultimately self-centered rescue attempt. As the one who basically assumes responsibility, he will be made to undergo an inner development in the narrative, and again becomes the one to take charge of the youngest son (Binyamin, in Chaps. 43 and 44). The missing piece that begins to explain his nobility in this regard (Chap. 44) is the present chapter. Yehuda here learns what it is to lose sons, and to want desperately to protect his youngest. Although his failure to marry off Tamar to the youngest son leads to public humiliation (twice, actually), his response shows that he immediately accepts blame: "She is in-the-right more than I" (v.26). Such an interpretation is further confirmed by the restriction of the word "pledge" to here and 43:9. Yehuda has learned what it means to stake oneself for a principle.

Only after we have been informed of Yehuda's change can the narrative resume with Chap. 39. True to biblical thinking, redemption may start only after the crime has been punished (e.g., the Samson story, where the hero's hair begins to grow immediately after his imprisonment).

Actually the chronology works out quite well. We are told via 41:46, 53–54, that about twenty years elapse between the sale of Yosef and his meetings with the brothers in Egypt; this often signifies a period in biblical parlance and could encompass a generation or a bit less. Since Yehuda was quite possibly a father already in Chap. 37, the present story could well end just before the events reported in Chap. 43—in other words, Yehuda reaches full inner maturity just in time.

The other function of this story seems to be to carry out the major theme of Genesis as we have presented it: continuity and discontinuity between the generations. What is at stake here is not merely the line of one of the brothers, but the line which (as the biblical audience must have been fully aware) will lead to royalty—King David was a descendant of Peretz of v.29. This should not be surprising in a book of origins; we noted the possible mention of Jerusalem in 14:18. Apparently a popular early theme, connected as we have noted to the power of God in history, continuity/discontinuity is repeated in somewhat similar circum-

24 and took him and cast him into the pit.
Now the pit was empty—no water in it.
25 And they sat down to eat bread.

They lifted up their eyes and saw:
there was a caravan of Yishmaelites coming from Gil'ad,
their camels carrying balm, balsam, and ladanum,
traveling to take them down to Egypt.
26 Now Yehuda said to his brothers:
What gain is there
if we kill our brother and cover up his blood?
27 Come, let us sell him to the Yishmaelites—
but let not our hand be upon him,
for he is our brother, our flesh!
And his brothers listened to him.

28 Meanwhile, some Midyanite men, merchants, passed by;
they hauled up Yosef from the pit
and sold Yosef to the Yishmaelites, for twenty pieces-of-silver.
They brought Yosef to Egypt.

29 When Re'uven returned to the pit:
here, Yosef was no more in the pit!
He rent his garments
30 and returned to his brothers and said:
The child is no more!
And I—where am I to go?

31 But they took Yosef's coat,
they slew a hairy goat
and dipped the coat in the blood.
32 They had the ornamented coat sent out
and had it brought to their father and said:
We found this;

25 **bread:** Or "food."
29 **rent his garments:** The tearing of clothing was a
customary sign of mourning.

30 **And I . . . :** Heb. *va-ani, ana ani va.* The sound expresses the emotions.   **where am I to go:** I.e., what
will become of me?

179

stances in the book of Ruth (which contains the only other mention of "beget-tings" outside of Genesis and Num.3:1).

The narrator has woven Chaps. 38 and 37 together with great skill. Again a man is asked to "recognize" objects, again the use of a kid, and again a brother (this time a dead one) is betrayed.

pray recognize
whether it is your son's coat or not!

33 He recognized it
and said:
My son's coat!
An ill-tempered beast has devoured him!
Yosef is torn, torn-to-pieces!

34 Yaakov rent his clothes,
he put sackcloth on his loins
and mourned his son for many days.

35 All his sons and daughters arose to comfort him,
but he refused to be comforted.
He said:
No,
I will go down to my son
in mourning, to Sheol!
Thus his father wept for him.

36 Meanwhile, the Midyanites had sold him into Egypt
to Potifar, Pharaoh's court-official,
Chief of the (palace) Guard.

38:1 Now it was at about that time
that Yehuda went down, away from his brothers
and turned aside to an Adullamite man—his name was Hira.

2 There Yehuda saw the daughter of a Canaanite man—his name
was Shua,
he took her (as his wife) and came in to her.

---

32 **pray recognize:** See 27:23, where Yitzhak did not "recognize" Yaakov. Yaakov's youth returns to haunt him, in a sense.

33 **My son's coat:** With the omission of "It is," the shock is conveyed more dramatically. Some ancient versions, however, include the phrase. **An ill-tempered beast . . . torn-to-pieces:** The Hebrew breaks into verse structure, with three word-beats per line: *haya ra'a akhalat'hu/ tarof toraf Yosef* (Alter 1981).

34 **many days:** Possibly "years"; at any rate, longer than a normal mourning period (in the Bible, thirty or seventy days) (Jacob).

35 **Sheol:** The biblical underworld; others (and B-R) use "the grave."

36 **Midyanites:** The Hebrew has "Medanites." **court-official:** Lit. "eunuch," a common ancient Near Eastern title for such a position. Originally the term was applied literally, although later on the person was not necessarily a eunuch.

38:1 **away from his brothers:** More than geography seems to be meant. Yehuda begins to change as a person here, in preparation for Chap. 44. Note that the place Adullam assonates with Arabic (*'adula*) "to turn aside."

3　She became pregnant and bore a son, and he called his name: Er.

4　She became pregnant again and bore a son, and she called his
　　　name: Onan.

5　Once again she bore a son, and she called his name: Shela.
　　Now he was in Ceziv when she bore him.

6　Yehuda took a wife for Er, his firstborn—her name was Tamar.

7　But Er, Yehuda's firstborn, did ill in the eyes of YHWH, and
　　YHWH caused him to die.

8　Yehuda said to Onan:
　　Come in to your brother's wife, do a brother-in-law's duty by her,
　　to preserve seed for your brother!

9　But Onan knew that the seed would not be his,
　　so it was, whenever he came in to his brother's wife, he let it go
　　　to ruin on the ground,
　　so as not to provide seed for his brother.

10　What he did was ill in the eyes of YHWH,
　　and he caused him to die as well.

11　Now Yehuda said to Tamar his daughter-in-law:
　　Sit as a widow in your father's house
　　until Shela my son has grown up.
　　For he said to himself:
　　Otherwise he will die as well, like his brothers!
　　So Tamar went and stayed in her father's house.

12　And many days passed.

　　Now Shua's daughter, Yehuda's wife, died.
　　When Yehuda had been comforted,
　　he went up to his sheep-shearers, he and his friend Hira the
　　　Adullamite, to Timna.

5　**Ceziv:** The Hebrew root connotes "lying."

6　**Tamar:** The name means "date palm."

6–7　**firstborn:** Perhaps parallel to the ineffectual firstborn, Re'uven, of the previous chapter.

7　**(did) ill:** I.e., he was evil, although we are not told
specifically how.

8　**a brother-in-law's duty:** It was a well-known practice in biblical times that if a man died without leaving an heir, it was the obligation of his nearest of kin
(usually his brother) to marry the widow and sire a
son—who would then bear the name of the deceased man (Deut. 25:5–10).

10　**What he did was ill:** Onan dies because he does not
fulfill his legal obligation to continue his brother's
line. The later interpretation, that his crime was
masturbation ("onanism"), has no basis in this text.

11　**Otherwise he will die:** Folk belief often regarded a
woman who had outlived two husbands as a bad risk
in marriage. The emotion here—a father's fear of
losing a young son—will return as central in 42:36.

13 Tamar was told, saying:
Here, your father-in-law is going up to Timna to shear his sheep.

14 She removed her widow's garments from her,
covered herself with a veil and wrapped herself,
and sat down by the entrance to Enayim/Two-Wells, which is on
the way to Timna,
for she saw that Shela had grown up, yet she had not been given
to him as a wife.

15 When Yehuda saw her, he took her for a whore, for she had
covered her face.

16 So he turned aside to her by the road and said:
Come-now, pray let me come in to you—
for he did not know that she was his daughter-in-law.
She said:
What will you give me for coming in to me?

17 He said:
I myself will send out a goat kid from the flock.
She said:
Only if you give me a pledge, until you send it.

18 He said:
What is the pledge that I am to give you?
She said:
Your seal, your cord, and your staff that is in your hand.
He gave them to her and then he came in to her—and she
became pregnant by him.

19 She arose and went away,
then she put off her veil from her and clothed herself in her
widow's garments.

20 Now when Yehuda sent the goat kid by the hand of his friend the
Adullamite, to fetch the pledge from the woman's hand,
he could not find her.

18 **seal . . . cord . . . staff:** Individual objects of identification in the ancient Near East, particularly the
seal, which served to sign documents. See Speiser.

Yosef: Rise and Fall (39): This chapter prefigures Yosef's eventual rise to power and simultaneously chronicles his lowest point, literally and figuratively. The two strands of the plot are woven together into a pattern of success/authority → imprisonment → success/authority. This also mirrors the larger story, which progresses from favorite son → slavery → viceroy of Egypt. The integration takes place partly through the medium of a key word, "hand"—which also occurred four times at the end of Chap. 38 and thus acts as a further textual connector. Yosef's success is tied six times to the phrase "in his hands" (vv.3, 4, 6, 8, 22, 23); he is thrown into prison because of the garments that he left in his mistress's "hands" (vv.12, 13). Similarly, the movement of the chapter is mirrored in the word "eyes," which is linked first to the theme of authority (v.4), then to the attempted seduction (v.7), and finally to authority again (v.21) (Alter).

The chapter also repeats the phrase "And it was" (in one form or another) some twelve times, as a distinct stylistic pattern.

Yosef's temporary downfall occurs here for reasons beyond literary balance or suspense. It is in a very real sense the punishment for the bratty behavior of his adolescence. Once again words (this time not his own) get him into trouble (vv.17, 19), as they did in 37:8. And once again a garment is displayed as proof of a fabricated crime.

21 He asked the people of her place, saying:
  Where is that holy-prostitute, the one in Two-Wells by the
      road?
  They said:
  There has been no holy-prostitute here!
22 So he returned to Yehuda and said:
  I could not find her; moreover, the people of the place said:
      There has been no holy-prostitute here!
23 Yehuda said:
  Let her keep them for herself, lest we become a laughing-stock.
  Here, I sent her this kid, but you, you could not find her.

24 Now it was, after almost three New-Moons
  that Yehuda was told, saying:
  Tamar your daughter-in-law has played-the-whore,
  in fact, she has become pregnant from whoring!
  Yehuda said:
  Bring her out and let her be burned!
25 (But) as she was being brought out,
  she sent a message to her father-in-law, saying:
  By the man to whom these belong I am pregnant.
  And she said:
  Pray recognize—
  whose seal and cords and staff are these?
26 Yehuda recognized them
  and said:
  She is in-the-right more than I!
  For after all, I did not give her to Shela my son!
  And he did not know her again.

27 Now it was, at the time of her birthing, that here: twins were in
      her body!

21 **holy-prostitute:** Or "cult prostitute," one attached
to a shrine in Canaan. Sex in the ancient world was
often linked to religion (as part of fertility rites), although the Hebrews sought to sever the tie.

27ff. **Now it was . . . :** The scene here rather strikingly
recalls Yaakov and Esav at birth: twins, the hand
reaching out, and the struggle to be first.

◆ 28 And it was, as she was giving birth, that (one of them) put out a
      hand;
   the midwife took and tied a scarlet thread on his hand, saying:
   This one came out first.
29 But it was, as he pulled back his hand, here, his brother came out!
   So she said:
   What a breach you have breached for yourself!
   So they called his name: Peretz/Breach.
30 Afterward his brother came out, on whose hand was the scarlet
      thread.
   They called his name: Zerah.

39:1 Now when Yosef was brought down to Egypt,
   Potifar, an official of Pharaoh, and chief of the guard, an
      Egyptian man, acquired him from the hand of the Yishmaelites
      who brought him down there.
 2 But YHWH was with Yosef, so that he became a man of success:
   while he was in the house of his lord the Egyptian,
 3 his lord saw that YHWH was with him,
   so that whatever he did, YHWH made succeed in his hands.
 4 Yosef found favor in his eyes, and he waited upon him;
   he appointed him over his house, and everything belonging to
      him he placed in his hands.
 5 And it was, from when he had appointed him over his house and
      over everything that belonged to him,
   that YHWH blessed the Egyptian's house because of Yosef;
   YHWH's blessing was upon everything that belonged to him, in
      the house and in the fields.

29 **breach:** Not in the sense of a "breach birth."
30 **Zerah:** Possibly connoting "red of dawn"—connecting with the scarlet thread of v.28 (and possibly
   paralleling Esav, who was also known as Edom, the
   "Red One").

39:1 **Potifar . . . :** The narrative resumes exactly, almost
   literally, where it had left off in 37:36.
 2 **a man of success:** Or "a man blessed by success."
 4 **over his house:** Foreshadowing Yosef's eventual
   position and title (41:40).

6 So he left everything that was his in Yosef's hands,
> not concerning himself about anything with him there, except
>> for the bread that he ate.
> Now Yosef was fair of form and fair to look at.

7 Now after these events it was
> that his lord's wife fixed her eyes upon Yosef
> and said:
> Lie with me!
8 But he refused,
> he said to his lord's wife:
> Look, my lord need not concern himself with anything in the
>> house, with me here,
> and everything that belongs to him, he has placed in my hands.
9 He is no greater in this house than I
> and has withheld nothing from me
> except for yourself,
> since you are his wife.
> So how could I do this great ill?
> I would be sinning against God!
10 Now it was, as she would speak to Yosef day after day, that he
>> would not hearken to her, to lie beside her, to be with her—
11 so it was, on such a day,
> when he came into the house to do his work,
> and none of the house-people was there in the house—
12 that she grabbed him by his garment, saying:
> Lie with me!
> But he left his garment in her hand and fled, escaping outside.
13 Now it was, when she saw that he had left his garment in her
>> hand and had fled outside,

6 **left:** Consigned; see also v.13 for a play on words. **except for the bread that he ate:** Since the Egyptians did not eat with foreigners (see, for instance, 43:32). **fair of form and fair to look at:** The only other person in the Bible described in exactly these words is Rahel, Yosef's mother (29:17). We are thus given an indirect clue about the source of Yaakov's doting behavior in the Yosef story.
9 **sinning:** Or "at fault." **against God:** From this point on, it is clear that Yosef is no longer the spoiled brat of Chap. 37. At key points in his life he consistently makes mention of God as the source of his success and good fortune (40:8; 41:16; 45:5, 7, 9).
10 **to lie beside her, to be with her:** A curious expression. Why does not the text say, as in v.7, "to lie with her"? There is an additional irony: "to be with" usually refers to God (see v.2, for example).

The Rise to Power: Dreams (40:1–41:52): Continued are the themes of Yosef's success in adversity and skill in interpreting dreams (yet his father and brother, and not he, had done the interpreting in Chap. 37!). In Chap. 37 dreams had brought about his downfall; here (Chap. 40) they will help the cupbearer and in Chap. 41 ultimately save a country, his family, and himself. Yosef's self-assurance and reliance on God, already evident in 39:9, here mean that it will not be long before he stands at the pinnacle.

Yosef's dramatic rise to power is an old and favorite motif in folklore. The text colorfully presents Pharaoh's dreams, in great detail, especially in his emotional retelling. All the more striking then is Yosef's simple interpretation (41:23–27).

14 that she called in her house-people and said to them, saying:
See! He has brought to us
a Hebrew man to play around with us!
He came to me, to lie with me,
but I called out with a loud voice,

15 and it was, when he heard that I lifted up my voice and called out
that he left his garment beside me and fled, escaping outside!

16 Now she kept his garment beside her, until his lord came back to
the house.

17 Then she spoke to him according to these words, saying:
There came to me the Hebrew servant whom you brought to us,
to play around with me;

18 but it was, when I lifted up my voice and called out,
that he left his garment beside me and fled outside.

19 Now it was, when his lord heard his wife's words which she spoke
to him,
saying: According to these words, your servant did to me!—
that his anger flared up;

20 Yosef's lord took him and put him in the dungeon house,
in the place where the king's prisoners are imprisoned.
But while he was there in the dungeon house,

21 YHWH was with Yosef and extended kindness to him:
he put his favor in the eyes of the dungeon warden.

22 And the dungeon warden put in Yosef's hands all the prisoners
that were in the dungeon house;
whatever had to be done there, it was he that did it.

23 The dungeon warden did not need to see to anything at all in his
hands,
since YHWH was with him,
and whatever he did, YHWH made succeed.

---

14 **play around:** A sexual reference; or it might mean
"laugh at." (Translated laughing-and-loving in 26:8.)
15 **beside:** Three times here, the word perhaps sug-

gests to the audience that Yosef's garment is all that
she will ever get "to lie beside her."
20 **dungeon:** Hebrew obscure.
21 **kindness:** Or "faithfulness," "loyalty." See 32:11.

189

40:1 Now after these events it was
that the cupbearer and the baker of the king of Egypt fell afoul of
their lord, the king of Egypt.

2 Pharaoh became infuriated with his two officials, with the chief
cupbearer and the chief baker,

3 and he placed them in custody in the house of the chief of the
guard, in the dungeon house, the place where Yosef was
imprisoned.

4 The chief of the guard appointed Yosef for them, that he should
wait upon them.
They were in custody for many days.

5 And then the two of them dreamt a dream, each man his own
dream, in a single night,
each man according to his dream's interpretation,
the cupbearer and the baker of the king of Egypt, who were
imprisoned in the dungeon house.

6 When Yosef came to them in the morning and saw them, here,
they were dejected!

7 So he asked Pharaoh's officials who were with him in custody in
the house of his lord, saying:
Why are your faces in such ill-humor today?

8 They said to him:
We have dreamt a dream, and there is no interpreter for it!
Yosef said to them:
Are not interpretations from God?
Pray recount them to me!

9 The chief cupbearer recounted his dream to Yosef, he said to
him:
In my dream—
here, a vine was in front of me,

40:1 **the cupbearer and the baker of the king of Egypt:** The Hebrew has "the cupbearer of the king of Egypt and the baker," a common construction in biblical Hebrew.

2 **cupbearer:** Others use "butler."

4 **appointed Yosef:** As Potifar had "appointed him over his house" (39:4).

5 **interpretation:** Or "meaning."

8 **Are not interpretations from God:** Foreshadowing 41:16, "Not I! / God will answer . . . ."

10 and on the vine, three winding-tendrils,
   and just as it was budding, the blossom came up,
   (and) its clusters ripened into grapes.

11 Now Pharaoh's cup was in my hand—
   I picked the grapes
   and squeezed them into Pharaoh's cup
   and put the cup in Pharaoh's palm.

12 Yosef said to him:
   This is its interpretation:
   The three windings are three days—

13 in another three days
   Pharaoh will lift up your head,
   he will restore you to your position
   so that you will put Pharaoh's cup in his hand (once more),
   according to the former practice, when you were his cupbearer.

14 But keep me in mind with you, when it goes well for you,
   pray deal kindly with me and call me to mind to Pharaoh,
   so that you have me brought out of this house.

15 For I was stolen, yes, stolen from the land of the Hebrews,
   and here too I have done nothing
   that they should have put me in the pit.

16 Now when the chief baker saw that he had interpreted for good,
   he said to Yosef:
   I too, in my dream—
   here, three baskets of white-bread were on my head,

17 and in the uppermost basket, all sorts of edibles for Pharaoh,
       baker's work,
   and birds were eating them from the basket, from off my head.

18 Yosef gave answer, he said:
   This is its interpretation:
   The three baskets are three days—

---

11 **Pharaoh's cup:** The cup was a common symbol of fate in the ancient Near East.

13 **lift up your head:** A parallel expression in Assyrian means "release" or "pardon."

14 **with you:** Possibly stressing the personal nature of the plea.

15 **stolen:** The Yaakov motif of Chaps. 30–31.

16 **white-bread:** Others use "wicker."

17ff. **eating:** In Pharaoh's dreams of Chap. 41, "eating up" comes to symbolize the disaster of famine.

19 in another three days
   Pharaoh will lift up your head
   from off you,
   he will hang you on a tree,
   and the birds will eat your flesh from off you.

20 And thus it was, on the third day,
   Pharaoh's birthday,
   that he made a great drinking-feast for all his servants,
   and he lifted up the head of the chief cupbearer and the head of
      the chief baker amidst his servants:

21 he restored the chief cupbearer to his cupbearership,
   so that he put the cup in Pharaoh's palm (once more),

22 but the chief baker he hanged,
   just as Yosef had interpreted to them.

23 But the chief cupbearer did not keep Yosef in mind,
   he forgot him.

41:1 Now at the end of two years'-time it was
   that Pharaoh dreamt:
   here, he was standing by the Nile-Stream,

2 and here, out of the Nile, seven cows were coming up,
   fair to look at and fat of flesh,
   and they grazed in the reed-grass.

3 And here, seven other cows were coming up after them out of
      the Nile,
   ill to look at and lean of flesh,
   and they stood beside the other cows on the bank of the Nile.

4 Then the cows ill to look at and lean of flesh ate up
   the seven cows fair to look at, the fat-ones.
   Pharaoh awoke.

5 He fell asleep and dreamt a second time:

---

19 **hang . . . on a tree:** Others use "impale on a stake."
23 **he forgot him:** Here, as in Potifar's house, initial success gives way to failure and continued imprisonment.

41:1 **two years'-time:** Lit. "two years of days."
2 **cows:** in later (Ptolemaic) Egyptian inscriptions, as here, cows represent years.

here, seven ears-of-grain were going up on a single stalk, fat and
good,

6   and here, seven ears, lean and scorched by the east wind, were
springing up after them.

7   Then the lean ears swallowed up
the seven ears fat and full.
Pharaoh awoke,
and here: (it was) a dream!

8   But in the morning it was, that his spirit was agitated,
so he sent and had all of Egypt's magicians and all of its wise-
men called.
Pharaoh recounted his dream to them,
but no one could interpret them to Pharaoh.

9   Then the chief cupbearer spoke up to Pharaoh, saying:
I must call my faults to mind today!

10   Pharaoh was once infuriated with his servants
and placed me in custody, in the house of the chief of the guard,
myself and the chief baker.

11   And we dreamt a dream in a single night, I and he,
we dreamt each-man according to the interpretation of his
dream.

12   Now there was a Hebrew lad there with us, a servant of the chief
of the guard;
we recounted them to him, and he interpreted our dreams to us,
for each-man according to his dream he interpreted.

13   And thus it was: As he interpreted to us, so it was—
I was restored to my position, and he was hanged.

14   Pharaoh sent and had Yosef called.
They hurriedly brought him out of the pit;
he shaved, changed his clothes, and came before Pharaoh.

15   Pharaoh said to Yosef:
I have dreamt a dream, and there is no interpreter for it!

---

5 **fat and good:** Referring to the ears of grain.

8 **his dream:** The two dreams function as one, as
Yosef explains.

But I have heard it said of you
that you but need to hear a dream in order to interpret it!

16 Yosef answered Pharaoh, saying:
Not I!
God will answer what is for Pharaoh's welfare.

17 Pharaoh spoke to Yosef:
In my dream—
here, I was standing on the bank of the Nile,

18 and here, out of the Nile were coming up seven cows,
fat of flesh and fair of form,
and they grazed in the reed-grass.

19 And here, seven other cows were coming up after them,
wretched and exceedingly ill of form and lank of flesh,
in all the land of Egypt I have never seen their like for ill-
    condition!

20 Then the seven lank and ill-looking cows ate up
the first seven cows, the fat-ones.

21 They entered their body, but you would not know that they had
    entered their body, for they were as ill-looking as at the
    beginning!
Then I awoke.

22 And I saw (again) in my dream:
here, seven ears were going up on a single stalk, full and good,

23 and here, seven ears, hardened, lean, and scorched by the east
    wind, were springing up after them.

24 Then the lean ears swallowed up
the seven good ears!
Now I have spoken with the magicians, but there is no one that
    can tell me the answer!

25 Yosef said to Pharaoh:
Pharaoh's dream is one.
What God is about to do, he has told Pharaoh.

---

19 **in all the land . . . I have never seen their like:**
Pharaoh's description of his dream is more vivid
than the narrator's (vv.1–4).

25 **is one:** Or "has a single meaning."

26 The seven good cows
   are seven years,
   the seven good ears
   are seven years,
   the dream is one.
27 And the seven lank and ill-looking cows that were coming up
     after them
   are seven years,
   and the seven ears, hollow and scorched by the east wind,
   will be seven years of famine!
28 That is the word that I spoke to Pharaoh:
   what God is about to do, he has let Pharaoh see.
29 Here,
   seven years are coming
   of great abundance in all the land of Egypt.
30 But seven years of famine will arise after them,
   when all the abundance in the land of Egypt will be forgotten.
   The famine will destroy the land,
31 and you will not know of that abundance in the land
   because of that famine afterward,
   for it will be exceedingly heavy.
32 Now as for the twofold repetition of the dream to Pharaoh: it
     means that the matter is determined by God,
   and God is hastening to do it.
33 So now, let Pharaoh select a discerning and wise man,
   and set him over the land of Egypt.
34 Let Pharaoh do this: let him appoint appointed-overseers for the
     land,
   dividing the land of Egypt into five parts during the seven years
     of abundance.

26ff. **The seven good cows . . . :** Yosef's interpretation is highly structured. The rhetoric emphasizes the last line of v.27: after hearing "*x* are seven years," three times, we hear "*x* will be seven years of famine!" See above, 40:19, where "Pharaoh will lift up your head" is followed by "from off you."

34 **let him appoint appointed-overseers:** We already know that Yosef is a man often entrusted with responsibility—"appointed" (39:4, 40:4). **dividing . . . into five parts:** Hebrew obscure. B-R uses "arm (the land of Egypt)."

Famine: The Brothers Come (41:53–42:38): Worldwide famine creates the backdrop for the family drama that is about to unfold. The ancients understood famine as sent by the gods, often as punishment; and the events of our text suggest that God is indeed the prime mover here. We are again presented with the characters of Chap. 37, all of whom have somehow changed. Yaakov emerges as more pitiful than ever (a shadow of the wrestler at the Yabbok), Yosef as powerful governor, not only of all Egypt but of his family's destiny as well, and the brothers, remarkably, are repentant (42:21–22). We also see Yosef's emotional side for the first time. He weeps in 42:24, as he will do three times again (43:30; 45:2, 14–15).

35 Let them collect all kinds of food from these good years that are
    coming,
    and let them pile up grain under Pharaoh's hand as food-
    provisions in the cities, and keep it under guard.
36 So the provisions will be an appointed-reserve for the land
    for the seven years of famine that will occur in the land of Egypt,
    so that the land will not be cut off by the famine.
37 The words seemed good in Pharaoh's eyes and in the eyes of all
    his servants,
38 and Pharaoh said to his servants:
    Could we find another like him, a man in whom is the spirit of a
    god?
39 Pharaoh said to Yosef:
    Since a god has made you know all this,
    there is none as wise and discerning as you;
40 you shall be the One Over My House!
    To your orders shall all my people submit;
    only by the throne will I be greater than you!
41 Pharaoh said further to Yosef:
    See, I place you over all the land of Egypt!
42 And Pharaoh removed his signet-ring from his hand and placed it
    on Yosef's hand,
    he had him clothed in linen garments and put the gold chain
    upon his neck;
43 he had him mount the chariot of his second-in-rank, and they
    called out before him: *Avrekh!*/Attention!
    Thus he placed him over all the land of Egypt.
44 Pharaoh said to Yosef:
    I am Pharaoh,
    but without you, no man shall raise hand or foot in all the land of
    Egypt!

---

35 **hand:** I.e., supervision.
36 **the land:** I.e., its people.
37 **The words seemed good:** Words now bring about
   Yosef's rise to power.
40 **the One Over My House:** A title similar to that of
   Yosef's steward in 43:16ff. **submit:** Hebrew obscure. **only by the throne:** Similar to Yosef's situ-

ation in Potifar's house, "He is no greater in this
house than I" (39:9)—but he withholds his wife.
41ff. **all the land of Egypt:** A refrain here, pointing to
   Yosef's power.
43 *Avrekh*/**Attention:** Hebrew unclear. Some suggest
   that it is Hebrew for "bend the knee," others that it
   resembles an Assyrian title.

45 Pharaoh called Yosef's name: *Tzafenat Pane'ah*/The God Speaks
and He Lives.

He gave him Asenat, daughter of Poti Fera, priest of On, as a
wife.

And Yosef's (influence) went out over all the land of Egypt.

46 Now Yosef was thirty years old when he stood in the presence of
Pharaoh, king of Egypt.

Yosef went out from Pharaoh's presence and passed through all
the land of Egypt.

47 In the seven years of abundance the land produced in handfuls.

48 And he collected all kinds of provisions from those seven years
that occurred in the land of Egypt,

and placed provisions in the towns.

The provisions from the fields of a town, surrounding it, he
placed in it (as well).

49 So Yosef piled up grain like the sand of the sea, exceedingly
much, until they had to stop counting, for it was uncountable.

50 Now two sons were born to Yosef, before the year of famine
came,

whom Asenat, daughter of Poti Fera, priest of On, bore to him.

51 Yosef called the name of the firstborn: Menashe/He-Who-
Makes-Forget,

meaning: God has made-me-forget all my hardships, all my
father's house.

52 And the name of the second he called: Efrayim/Double-Fruit,

meaning: God has made me bear fruit in the land of my
affliction.

53 There came to an end the seven years of abundance that had
occurred in the land of Egypt,

---

45 *Tzafenat-Pane'ah*/The God Speaks and He Lives:
An Egyptian name which is appropriate to the story.
Yosef lives, and through him so do Egypt, his family,
and the future People of Israel. **Yosef's influence:**
Perhaps an idiom, or merely "Yosef went out."

46 **thirty:** Yosef will be in power for eighty years
(2×40), another patterned number.

51 **Menashe:** Trad. English "Menasseh." **made-me-
forget:** Yet he does not forget for long, any more
than the cupbearer did (Chap. 41).

52 **bear fruit . . . affliction:** Two expressions from the
stories about the Patriarchs.

54ff. **Famine occurred in all lands:** The repetition of
"all" here brings home the totality of the famine.

54 and there started to come the seven years of famine, as Yosef had
said.
Famine occurred in all lands, but in all the land of Egypt there
was bread.
55 But when all the land of Egypt felt the famine, and the people
cried out to Pharaoh for bread,
Pharaoh said to all the Egyptians:
Go to Yosef, whatever he says to you, do!
56 Now the famine was over all the surface of the earth.
Yosef opened up all (storehouses) in which there was (grain), and
gave-out-rations to the Egyptians,
since the famine was becoming stronger in the land of Egypt.
57 And all lands came to Egypt to buy rations, to Yosef,
for the famine was strong in all lands.

42:1 Now when Yaakov saw that there were rations in Egypt,
Yaakov said to his sons:
Why do you keep looking at one another?
2 And he said:
Here, I have heard that there are rations in Egypt,
go down there and buy us rations from there,
that we may live and not die.
3 So Yosef's brothers went down, ten (of them),
to buy some rationed grain from Egypt.
4 But Binyamin, Yosef's brother, Yaakov would not send with his
brothers,
for he said: Lest harm befall him!
5 The sons of Yisrael came to buy rations among those that came,
for the famine was in the land of Canaan.
6 Now Yosef was the governor over the land, it was he who
supplied rations to all the people of the land.
And Yosef's brothers came and bowed low to him, brow to the
ground.

42:2 **that we may live and not die:** This becomes a refrain in the story, alternating in meaning between
Yosef's family (here and 43:8) and the Egyptians
(47:19).

4 **Yosef's brother:** His full brother, as opposed to the
others who were half-brothers.

7 When Yosef saw his brothers, he recognized them,
but he pretended-no-recognition of them and spoke harshly with
them.
He said to them:
From where do you come?
They said: From the land of Canaan, to buy food-rations.

8 Now although Yosef recognized his brothers, for their part, they
did not recognize him.

9 And Yosef was reminded of the dreams that he had dreamt of
them.
He said to them:
You are spies!
It is to see the nakedness of the land that you have come!

10 They said to him: No, my lord!
Rather, your servants have come to buy food-rations.

11 We are all of us the sons of a single man,
we are honest,
your servants have never been spies!

12 But he said to them:
No!
For it is the nakedness of the land that you have come to see!

13 They said:
Your servants are twelve,
we are brothers,
sons of a single man in the land of Canaan:
the youngest is with our father now,
and one is no more.

14 Yosef said to them:
It is just as I spoke to you, saying: You are spies!

7 **recognized:** Ironically recalling the brothers' "Pray
recognize" of 37:32. **pretended-no-recognition:**
Others use "pretended to be a stranger."
9 **nakedness:** Vulnerability (strategically).

11 **honest:** They will be, by the end of the chapter
(Redford).
13 **twelve:** At last they think of themselves as a unit,
"we are brothers!"

15 Hereby shall you be tested:
As Pharaoh lives!
You shall not depart from this (place)
unless your youngest brother comes here!

16 Send one of you to fetch your brother,
while (the rest of) you remain as prisoners.
Thus will your words be tested, whether there is truth in you or
not—
as Pharaoh lives, indeed, you are spies!

17 He removed them into custody for three days.

18 Yosef said to them on the third day:
Do this, and stay alive,
for I hold God in awe:

19 if you are honest,
let one of your brothers be held prisoner in the house of your
custody,
and as for you, go, bring back rations for the famine-supply of
your households.

20 Then bring your youngest brother back to me,
so that your words will be proven truthful, and you will not die.
They (prepared to) do so.

21 But they said, each man to his brother:
Truly,
we are guilty:
concerning our brother!
—that we saw his heart's distress
when he implored us,
and we did not listen.
Therefore this distress has come upon us!

22 Re'uven answered them, saying:
Did I not say to you, say: Do not sin against the child!

---

16 **tested:** Heb. *bahan,* a different root from the word translated "tested" *(nissa)* in 22:1. Interestingly, the English "test" and the Hebrew *bhn* originally meant the refining of metals, separating pure from impure. **or not—:** Or "(in you.)/ If not . . . ."

21 **guilty:** Perhaps it is the phrase "youngest brother" in Yosef's words (v.20) that jars their memory. They must now show responsibility to their father, which they had evaded in Chap. 37. **distress. . . . distress:** Another example of justice in the Bible: the punishment fits the crime.

22 **Re'uven:** A replay of Chap. 37, with Re'uven again making extravagant but ineffective declarations. Once again Yehuda will emerge in charge.

The Test (43–44): Yosef's testing of his brothers is masterful, not only because of the plan itself, but also because of the depth of emotion that the text evokes in its characterizations. It demonstrates how well the whole story has been integrated into the Yaakov material, for here as well as there long conversations are used to reveal complex passions.

Some have questioned the morality of Yosef's actions, seeing that the aged Yaakov might well have died while the test was progressing, without ever finding out that Yosef had survived. But that is not the point of the story. What it *is* trying to teach (among other things) is a lesson about crime and repentance. Only by recreating something of the original situation—the brothers are again in control of the life and death of a son of Rahel—can Yosef be sure that they have changed. Once the brothers pass the test, life and covenant can then continue.

But you would not listen,
so for his blood—now, (satisfaction) is demanded!

23 Now they did not know that Yosef was listening, for a translator
was between them.

24 But he turned away from them and wept.
When he was able to return to them, he spoke to them and had
Shim'on taken away from them, imprisoning him before their
eyes.

25 Then Yosef commanded that they fill their vessels with grain
and return their silver-pieces into each man's sack,
and give them victuals for the journey.
They did so for them.

26 Then they loaded their rations onto their donkeys and went from
there.

27 But as one opened his sack to give his donkey fodder at the night-
camp,
he saw his silver—there it was in the mouth of his pack!

28 He said to his brothers:
My silver has been returned—yes, here in my pack!
Their hearts gave way, and they trembled to one another, saying:
What is this that God has done to us?

29 They came home to Yaakov their father, in the land of Canaan,
and told him all that had befallen them, saying:

30 The man, the lord of the land, spoke harshly with us,
he took us for those that spy on the land!

31 Now we said to him: We are honest, we have never been spies!

32 We are twelve, brothers all, sons of our father:
one is no more, and the youngest is now with our father in the
land of Canaan.

33 Then the man, the lord of the land, said to us:
Hereby shall I know whether you are honest:

23 **translator:** Interpreter.
24 **imprisoning:** Or "fettering." **before their eyes:**
As opposed to the sale of Yosef where their presence is not mentioned, strictly speaking.
25 **they fill:** "They" refers to Yosef's servants. **silver-
pieces:** Yosef had been sold for silver (37:28).

30 **The man:** Used eight times of Yosef in Chaps.
42–44, perhaps out of ironic anonymity. **harshly:**
Paralleling their earlier attitude: they "could not
speak to him in peace" (37:4).

Leave one of your brothers with me,

and as for the famine-supply of your households, take it and go.

34 But bring your youngest brother back to me,

so that I may know that you are not spies, that you are honest.

(Then) I will give your brother back to you, and you may travel
about the land.

35 But it was, when they emptied their sacks: there was each man's
silver pouch in his sack!

They looked at their silver pouches, they and their father, and
became frightened.

36 Yaakov their father said to them:

It is I that you bereave!

Yosef is no more,

Shim'on is no more,

now you would take Binyamin—

upon me has all this come!

37 Re'uven said to his father, saying:

My two sons you may put to death

if I do not bring him back to you!

Place him in my hands, and I myself will return him to you.

38 But he said:

My son is not to go down with you!

For his brother is dead,

and he alone is left!

Should harm befall him on the journey on which you are going,
you will bring down my gray hair in grief to Sheol!

43:1 But the famine was heavy in the land.

2 And so it was, when they had finished eating the rations that they
had brought from Egypt,

that their father said to them:

Return, buy us some food-rations.

---

37 **My two sons:** Re'uven is again spouting nonsense.
I myself will return him: But he did not in 37:22
(Ackerman 1982).
38 **My son is not to go down. . . . you will bring
down my gray hair in grief:** Yaakov will indeed "go

down," but to Egypt, not to Sheol, to meet his
"dead" son. The latter part of the phrase is basically
repeated in 44:29 and 44:31, as a key to the father's
feelings. **he alone is left:** Of his mother Rahel (see
44:20).

3 But Yehuda said to him, saying:
  The man warned, yes, warned us,
  saying: You shall not see my face unless your brother is with you.
4 If you wish to send our brother with us, we will go down and
      buy you some food-rations.
5 But if you do not wish to send him, we will not go down,
  for the man said to us: You shall not see my face unless your
      brother is with you.
6 Yisrael said:
  Why did you deal so ill with me, by telling the man that you have
      another brother?
7 They said:
  The man asked, he asked about us and about our kindred,
  saying: Is your father still alive? Do you have another brother?
  So we told him, according to these words.
  Could we know, know that he would say: Bring your brother
      down?
8 Yehuda said to Yisrael his father:
  Send the lad with me,
  and we will arise and go,
  that we may live and not die,
  so we, so you, so our little-ones!
9 I will act as his pledge,
  at my hand you may seek him!
  If I do not bring him back to you
  and set him in your presence,
  I will be culpable-for-sin against you all the days (to come).
10 Indeed, had we not lingered, we would indeed have been back
      twice already!

43:3 **my face:** The great confrontation theme of the
  Yaakov stories returns.
4–5 **send:** Or "release," "let go."
  9 **I will act as his pledge/ at my hand you may seek**

him: Echoing Yaakov's own language of responsibility in 31:39 ("I would make good the loss/ at my
hand you would seek it"). **in your presence:** Literally "before your face."

11 Yisrael their father said to them:
If it must be so, then, do this:
Take some of the produce of the land in your vessels
and bring them down to the man as a gift:
a little balsam, a little honey, balm and ladanum, pistachio nuts
and almonds.

12 And silver two times over take in your hand;
and the silver that was returned in the mouth of your packs,
return in your hand,
perhaps it was an oversight.

13 And as for your brother, take him!
Arise, return to the man,

14 and may God Shaddai give you mercy before the man,
so that he releases your other brother to you, and Binyamin as
well.
And as for me—if I must be bereaved, I must be bereaved!

15 The men took this gift, silver two times over they took in their
hand
and Binyamin as well.
They arose and went down to Egypt
and stood in Yosef's presence.

16 When Yosef saw Binyamin with them,
he said to the steward of his house:
Bring the men into the house, slaughter some slaughter-animals
and prepare them,
for it is with me that these men shall eat at noon.

17 The man did as Yosef had said, the man brought the men into
Yosef's house.

---

11 **Take:** Three times, culminating in the pathetic "And as for your brother, take him!" (v.13). **balsam . . . honey, balm and ladanum, pistachio nuts and almonds:** Another example of concealment in the story. The list includes the cargo of the caravan that carried Yosef away (37:25).

12 **two times over . . . oversight:** Heb. *mishne . . . mishge.*

14 **God Shaddai:** Yaakov uses the same term for God as did his father, when Yaakov left for Aram (28:3). **bereaved:** Echoing the fears of his mother Rivka (27:45).

18 But the men were frightened that they had been brought into
  Yosef's house, and said:
  It is because of the silver that was returned in our packs before
    that we have been brought here,
  for (them to) roll upon us, and fall upon us,
  and take us into servitude, along with our donkeys!
19 They came close to the man, to the steward of Yosef's house, and
    spoke to him at the entrance to the house,
20 they said:
  Please, my lord!
  We came down, came down before to buy food-rations,
21 but it was, when we came to the night camp and opened our
    packs,
  there was each man's silver in the mouth of his pack, our silver by
    its (exact) weight—
  but (here) we have returned it in our hand!
22 And other silver as well we have brought down in our hand, to
    buy food.
  We do not know who put back our silver in our packs!
23 He said:
  It is well with you, do not be afraid!
  Your God, the God of your father, placed a treasure in your packs
    for you—(for) your silver has come in to me.
  And he brought Shim'on out to them.
24 Then the man had the men come into Yosef's house
  and gave them water so that they might wash their feet
  and gave them fodder for their donkeys.
25 They prepared the gift, until Yosef came back at noon,
  for they understood that they were to eat bread there.
26 When Yosef came into the house, they brought him the gift that
    was in their hand, into the house,
  and bowed down to him, to the ground.

18 **roll upon us:** Others use "attack us." **roll upon us, and fall upon us:** The rhythm reflects the brothers' emotional anguish.

23 **has come in:** I.e., I have received full payment.

27 He asked after their welfare and said:
   Is your old father well, of whom you spoke?
   Is he still alive?

28 They said:
   Your servant, our father, is well, he is still alive—
   and in homage they bowed low.

29 He lifted up his eyes and saw Binyamin his brother, his mother's
      son,
   and he said:
   Is this your youngest brother, of whom you spoke to me?
   And he said:
   May God show you favor, my son!

30 And in haste—for his feelings were so kindled toward his brother
      that he had to weep—
   Yosef entered a chamber and wept there.

31 Then he washed his face and came out, he restrained himself, and
      said:
   Serve bread!

32 They served him by himself and them by themselves and the
      Egyptians who were eating with him by themselves,
   for Egyptians will not eat bread with Hebrews—for that is an
      abomination for Egyptians.

33 But they were seated in his presence:
   the firstborn according to his rank-as-firstborn and the youngest
      according to his rank-as-youngest.
   And the men stared at each other in astonishment over it.

34 He had courses taken to them from his presence,
   and Binyamin's course was five times greater than all their
      courses.
   Then they drank and became drunk with him.

---

27 **well:** Or "at peace"—as before, a key element of the
   Yaakov stories.
29 **Is this:** Or "So this is."
34 **five times:** Others use "many times." Yet the promi-

nence of the number five throughout the Yosef
story, as noted above, should not be overlooked.

44:1 Now he commanded the steward of his house, saying:
Fill the men's packs with food, as much as they are able to carry,
and put each man's silver in the mouth of his pack.

2 And my goblet, the silver goblet, put in the mouth of the
youngest's pack, along with the silver for his rations.
He did according to Yosef's word which he had spoken.

3 At the light of daybreak, the men were sent off, they and their
donkeys;

4 they were just outside the city—they had not yet gone far—when
Yosef said to the steward of his house:
Up, pursue the men, and when you have caught up with them,
say to them:
Why have you paid back ill for good?

5 Is not this (goblet) the one that my lord drinks with?
And he also divines, yes, divines with it!
You have wrought ill in what you have done!

6 When he caught up with them, he spoke those words to them.

7 They said to him:
Why does my lord speak such words as these?
Heaven forbid for your servants to do such a thing!

8 Here, the silver that we found in the mouth of our packs, we
returned to you from the land of Canaan;
so how could we steal silver or gold from the house of your lord?

9 He with whom it is found among your servants, he shall die,
and we also will become my lord's servants!

10 He said:
Now as well, according to your words, so be it:
he with whom it is found shall become my servant, but you shall
be clear.

11 With haste each-man let down his pack to the ground, each-man
opened his pack.

44:2 **my goblet:** The ensuing scene is somewhat parallel
to Rahel's theft of the *terafim* (compare v.9 with
31:32).

5 **divines:** Cups were used in predicting the future in
the ancient Near East; see note to 40:11. The diviner
would examine the shapes made by insoluble liquids, such as oil in water. **You have wrought ill:**
Resembling Laban's accusation against Yaakov,
"You have done foolishly" (31:28).

10 **clear:** Of punishment.

12 and then he searched: with the eldest he started and with the
    youngest he finished—
  and the goblet was found in Binyamin's pack!

13 They rent their clothes,
  each-man loaded up his donkey, and they returned to the city.

14 Yehuda and his brothers came into Yosef's house
  —he was still there—
  and flung themselves down before him to the ground.

15 Yosef said to them:
  What kind of deed is this that you have done!
  Do you not know that a man like me can divine, yes, divine?

16 Yehuda said:
  What can we say to my lord?
  What can we speak, by what can we show ourselves innocent?
  God has found out your servants' crime!
  Here we are, servants to my lord, so we, so the one in whose
    hand the goblet was found.

17 But he said:
  Heaven forbid that I should do this!
  The man in whose hand the goblet was found—he shall become
    my servant,
  but you—go up in peace to your father!

18 Now Yehuda came closer to him and said:
  Please, my lord,
  pray let your servant speak a word in the ears of my lord,
  and do not let your anger flare up against your servant,
  for you are like Pharaoh!

19 My lord asked his servants, saying: Do you have a father or
  (another) brother?

---

16 **your servants' crime:** Of selling Yosef?

17 **But he said:** "He" is Yosef. **this:** Enslaving all of the brothers.

18 **Now Yehuda . . . said . . . :** Yehuda's great speech, masterful in its rhetoric, is chiefly aimed at stirring up sympathy for the father; it contains the word "father" fourteen times. Binyamin, whose appearance actually causes Yosef great anguish, is hardly treated as a personality at all. **you are like Pharaoh:** Lit. "like you is like Pharaoh."

20 And we said to my lord: We have an old father
and a young child of his old age,
whose brother is dead,
so that he alone is left of his mother,
and his father loves him.

21 And you said to your servants: Bring him down to me, I wish to
set my eyes upon him.

22 But we said to my lord:
The lad cannot leave his father,
were he to leave his father, he would die.

23 But you said to your servants: If your youngest brother does not
come down with you, you shall not see my face again.

24 Now it was, when we went up to your servant, my father, we told
him my lord's words,

25 and our father said: Return, buy us some food-rations.

26 But we said: We cannot go down;
if our youngest brother is with us, then we will go down,
for we cannot see the man's face if our youngest brother is not
with us.

27 Now your servant, my father, said to us:
You yourselves know
that my wife bore two to me.

28 One went away from me,
I said: For sure he is torn, torn-to-pieces!
And I have not seen him again thus far.

29 Now should you take away this one as well from before my face,
should harm befall him, you will bring down my gray hair in
ill-fortune to Sheol!

30 So now,
when I come back to your servant, my father, and the lad is not
with us,
—with whose life his own life is bound up!—

---

22 **he would die:** "He" refers to Yaakov, although the Hebrew is somewhat ambiguous.

28 **thus far:** A hint that Yosef is still alive, or perhaps a tiny expression of hope.

30 **life:** Heb. *nefesh,* also "emotions" or "feelings."

Reconciliation (45): In revealing his true identity at last, Yosef makes two points: first, that it was all part of God's plan; and second, that the family must immediately prepare for migration to Egypt. Thus the personal story is intertwined with the national one, and the text therefore gives limited time and space to psychological details. The motif of God's plan is stressed by the repetition of "God sent me" (vv.5, 7, 8), while the anticipated bounties of settling in Egypt are brought out by the threefold "good-things of Egypt" (vv.18, 20, 23) and by the repeated exhortation to "come" (vv.18, 19).

31 it will be, that when he sees that the lad is no more, he will die,
and your servant will have brought down the gray hair of your
servant, our father, in grief to Sheol!

32 For your servant pledged himself for the lad to my father,
saying: If I do not bring him back to you, I will be culpable-for-sin
against my father all the days (to come).

33 So now,
pray let your servant stay instead of the lad, as servant to my
lord,
but let the lad go up with his brothers!

34 For how can I go up to my father, when the lad is not with me?
Then would I see the ill-fortune that would come upon my
father!

45:1 Yosef could no longer restrain himself in the presence of all who
were stationed around him,
he called out:
Have everyone leave me!
So no one stood (in attendance upon) him when Yosef made
himself known to his brothers.

2 He put forth his voice in weeping:
the Egyptians heard, Pharaoh's household heard.

3 Then Yosef said to his brothers:
I am Yosef. Is my father still alive?
But his brothers were not able to answer him,
for they were confounded in his presence.

4 Yosef said to his brothers:
Pray come close to me!
They came close.
He said:
I am Yosef your brother, whom you sold into Egypt.

5 But now, do not be pained,
and do not let upset be in your eyes that you sold me here!

31 **our father:** Is Yehuda unknowingly including
Yosef?

45:5 **(upset):** At each other, or referring to each individual's feelings of guilt.

Migration to Egypt (45:16–47:12): Yaakov's descent to Egypt involves three meetings: with God, with Yosef, and with Pharaoh. The first is God's final revelation to Yaakov. God had previously forbidden Yitzhak to go to Egypt during a famine (26:1–2), but his son may now go as part of the divine plan, his people's destiny. The blessing given to Avraham's children (particularly to Yishmael) is repeated in 46:3, and God will be "with" Yaakov (46:4) on this journey as he has been on others.

The meeting between father and long-lost son is brief but powerful, returning as it does to the "face" motif (46:30). Immediately afterward Yosef gives the family advice on how to demonstrate their usefulness to the Egyptians, and one is struck by the precariousness of their situation in even this best of circumstances.

Yaakov's brief audience with Pharaoh is both moving and pathetic. The Patriarch sums up his life in depressing terms, and it becomes clear that long life (he believes his own to be short), in addition to wealth and fertility, is considered a sign of divine favor.

The actual migration is sketched in a few brief strokes. The list of names in 46:8–27 has been constructed on patterned numbers, with a total of seventy.

For it was to save life that God sent me on before you.

6 For it is two years now that the famine has been in the midst of
the land,
and there are still another five years in which there shall be no
plowing or harvest.

7 So God sent me on before you
to make you a remnant on earth,
to keep you alive as a great body-of-survivors.

8 So now,
it was not you that sent me here, but God!
He has made me Father to Pharaoh and lord of all his household
and ruler over all the land of Egypt.

9 Make haste, go up to my father and say to him:
Thus says your son, Yosef:
God has made me lord of all Egypt;
come down to me, do not remain!

10 You shall stay in the region of Goshen, you shall be near me,
you and your sons and the sons of your sons,
your sheep, your oxen, and all that is yours.

11 I will sustain you there,
for there are still five years of famine left
—lest you be as disinherited, you and your household and all that
is yours.

12 Here, your eyes see, as well as my brother Binyamin's eyes, that it
is my mouth that speaks to you!

13 So tell my father of all the weight I carry in Egypt, and of all that
you have seen,
and make haste, bring my father down here!

14 He flung himself upon his brother Binyamin's neck and wept,
and Binyamin wept upon his neck.

15 Then he kissed all his brothers and wept upon them.
After this his brothers spoke with him.

---

11 **as disinherited:** Or "reduced-to-poverty."
13 **all the weight I carry:** I.e., my importance.

15 **his brothers spoke with him:** Which they could
not do "in peace" in 37:4.

◆ 16 The news was heard in Pharaoh's household, they said:
Yosef's brothers have come!
It was good in Pharaoh's eyes and in the eyes of his servants.

17 And Pharaoh said to Yosef:
Say to your brothers:
Do this—
load your animals and go,
come back to the land of Canaan;

18 fetch your father and your households
and come to me!
I will give you the good-things of the land of Egypt,
so that you will eat of the fat of the land!

19 And you, you have been commanded:
Do this—
take you wagons from the land of Egypt for your little ones and
your wives,
and carry your father down
and come!

20 Let not your eyes look-with-regret on your household-wares,
for the good-things of all the land of Egypt—they are yours!

21 The sons of Yisrael did so,
Yosef gave them wagons in accordance with Pharaoh's orders
and gave them victuals for the journey.

22 To all of them, each man, he gave changes of clothes,
but to Binyamin he gave three hundred pieces-of-silver and five
changes of clothes,

23 and to his father he sent in like manner:
ten donkeys, carrying the good-things of Egypt,
and ten she-asses, carrying grain and bread,
and food for his father, for the journey.

16 **come:** The verb focuses toward Pharaoh's invitation to follow: "Yosef's brothers have come!" (v.16) to "and come to me" (v.18) to "and come!" (v.19).
18 **good-things:** More precisely, "best-things" ("good" has been retained here to indicate a major theme of the story: good and ill).

20 **Let not your eyes look-with-regret:** Possibly "Do not stint."
22 **but to Binyamin he gave:** The original situation (Chap. 37) is set up once more; this time the brothers do not react adversely to the youngest son's being favored.

24 Then he sent off his brothers, and they went;
   he said to them:
   Do not be agitated on the journey!

25 They went up from Egypt and came to the land of Canaan, to
   Yaakov their father,

26 and they told him, saying:
   Yosef is still alive!
   Indeed, he is ruler of all the land of Egypt!
   His heart failed,
   for he did not believe them.

27 But when they spoke to him all of Yosef's words which he had
      spoken to them,
   and when he saw the wagons that Yosef had sent to carry him
      down,
   their father Yaakov's spirit came to life.

28 Yisrael said:
   Enough!
   Yosef my son is still alive;
   I must go and see him before I die!

46:1 Yisrael traveled with all that was his
   and came to Be'er-Sheva,
   and he slaughtered slaughter-offerings to the God of his father
      Yitzhak.

2 And God said to Yisrael in visions of the night,
   he said:
   Yaakov! Yaakov!
   He said:
   Here I am.

3 Now he said:
   I am *El*/God,
   the God of your father.
   Do not be afraid of going down to Egypt,
   for a great nation will I make of you there.

---

27 **Yosef's words:** In Chap. 37 his words were damaging, but here they are life-giving.
46:2 **Yaakov! Yaakov!:** Doubled as in 22:11 and other

moments of dramatic revelations in the Bible (e.g.,
Ex. 3:4).

4 I myself
will go down with you to Egypt,
and I myself
will bring you up, yes, up again.
And Yosef will lay his hand on your eyes.

5 Yaakov departed from Be'er-Sheva.
Yisrael's sons carried Yaakov their father, their little-ones and
their wives in the wagons that Pharaoh had sent for carrying
him,
6 and they took their acquired-livestock and their property that
they had gained in the land of Canaan
and came to Egypt,
Yaakov and all his seed with him,
7 his sons and the sons of his sons with him, his daughters and the
daughters of his sons;
all his seed he brought with him to Egypt.

8 Now these are the names of the Sons of Israel who came to
Egypt:
Yaakov and his sons:
Yaakov's firstborn was Re'uven.
9 Re'uven's sons: Hanokh, Pallu, Hetzron, and Carmi.
10 Shim'on's sons: Yemuel, Yamin, Ohad, Yakhin, and Tzohar, and
Sha'ul the son of the Canaanite-woman.
11 Levi's sons: Gershon, Kehat, and Merari.
12 Yehuda's sons: Er, Onan, Shela, Peretz, and Zerah,
but Er and Onan had died in the land of Canaan.
And Peretz's sons were Hetzron and Hamul.
13 Yissakhar's sons: Tola, Puvva, Yov, and Shimron.
14 Zevulun's sons: Sered, Elon, and Yahl'el.
15 These are the sons of Lea, whom she bore to Yaakov in the
country of Aram, and also Dina his daughter;
all the persons among his sons and daughters were thirty-three.

---

4 **lay his hand on your eyes:** I.e., be present at your
death.
8 **Now these are the names . . . :** This phrase opens
the book of Exodus, making that book a resumption of the Genesis narrative.

16 Gad's sons: Tzifyon and Haggi, Shuni and Etzbon, Eri, Arodi, and
    Ar'eli.
17 Asher's sons: Yimna, Yishva, Yishvi, and Beri'a, and Serah their
    sister.
    And Beri'a's sons: Hever and Malkiel.
18 These are the sons of Zilpa, whom Lavan had given to Lea his
    daughter,
    she bore these to Yaakov: sixteen persons.
19 The sons of Rahel, Yaakov's wife: Yosef and Binyamin.
20 To Yosef there were born in the land of Egypt—whom Asenat,
    daughter of Poti Fera, priest of On, bore to him: Menashe and
    Efrayim.
21 Binyamin's sons: Bela, Bekher and Ashbel, Gera and Naaman, Ahi
    and Rosh, Muppim, Huppim, and Ard.
22 These are the sons of Rahel, who were born to Yaakov,
    all the persons were fourteen.
23 Dan's sons: Hushim.
24 Naftali's sons: Yahtze'el, Guni, Yetzer, and Shillem.
25 These are the sons of Bilha, whom Lavan had given to Rahel his
    daughter,
    she bore these to Yaakov: all the persons were seven.
26 All the persons who came with Yaakov to Egypt, those going out
    from his loins, aside from the wives of Yaakov's sons:
    all the persons were sixty-six.
27 Now Yosef's sons, who had been born to him in Egypt: the
    persons were two.
    (Thus) all the persons of Yaakov's household who came to Egypt
    were seventy.

28 Now Yehuda he had sent on ahead of him, to Yosef,
    to give directions ahead of him to Goshen.
    When they came to the region of Goshen,
29 Yosef had his chariot harnessed and went up to meet Yisrael his
    father, to Goshen.
    When he caught sight of him

27 **seventy:** Once again, the "perfect" number.

Yosef the Life-Giver (47:13–26): The events of this section are not attested historically in Egyptian records. Perhaps they have been included here to confirm Yosef's stature as Rescuer, not only of his family but of all Egypt as well (see note to 42:2). The description of Yosef's power is now complete: just as the brothers were ready to "become my lord's servants" (44:9), so now are the Egyptians (47:25).

Some have seen the episode as an ironic reversal of what is to come in Exodus, with the Egyptians' enslavement of the Israelites; if so, this interlude may have been an amusing one to ancient Israelite audiences.

The text uses the repetition of the phrase "to/for Pharaoh" to effectively paint the legal transaction.

◆ he flung himself upon his neck
and wept upon his neck continually.

30 Yisrael said to Yosef:
Now I can die,
since I have seen your face, that you are still alive!

31 Yosef said to his brothers and to his father's household:
I will go up, so that I may tell Pharaoh and say to him:
My brothers and my father's household, who were in the land of
Canaan, have come to me.

32 The men are shepherds of flocks,
indeed, they have always been livestock men,
and their sheep and their oxen, all that is theirs, they have
brought along.

33 Now it will be, when Pharaoh has you called and says: What is it
that you do?

34 Then say: Your servants have always been livestock men, from
our youth until now, so we, so our fathers—
in order that you may settle in the region of Goshen.
For every shepherd of flocks is an abomination to the Egyptians.

47:1 So Yosef came and told Pharaoh, he said:
My father and my brothers, their sheep and their oxen and all
that is theirs, have come from the land of Canaan,
and here, they are in the region of Goshen!

2 Now from the circle of his brothers he had picked out five men
and had set them in Pharaoh's presence.

3 Pharaoh said to his brothers:
What is it that you do?
They said to Pharaoh:
Your servants are shepherds of flocks, so we, so our fathers.

4 And they said to Pharaoh:
It is to sojourn in the land that we have come,
for there is no grazing for the flocks that are your servants',

---

33 **What is it that you do:** What is your occupation?
34 **every shepherd . . . is an abomination to the
Egyptians:** Speiser understands this as a reference
to the Hyksos "shepherd kings," who as foreigners
ruled Egypt in the mid-Second Millennium (until
they were driven out).

47:4 **It is to sojourn:** Are they still sensitive to the accusation in 42:12, "For it is the nakedness of the land
that you have come to see"?

for the famine is heavy in the land of Canaan.
So now,
pray let your servants settle in the region of Goshen!

5 Pharaoh said to Yosef, saying:
(So) your father and your brothers have come to you:

6 the land of Egypt is before you;
in the goodliest-part of the land, settle your father and your
brothers,
let them settle in the region of Goshen.
And if you know that there are able men among them,
make them chiefs of livestock over what is mine.

7 Yosef brought Yaakov his father and had him stand in Pharaoh's
presence.
And Yaakov gave Pharaoh a blessing-of-greeting.

8 Pharaoh said to Yaakov:
How many are the days and years of your life?

9 Yaakov said to Pharaoh:
The days and years of my sojourn are thirty and a hundred years;
few and ill-fated have been the days and years of my life,
they have not attained the days and years of my fathers' lives in
the days of their sojourn.

10 Yaakov gave Pharaoh a blessing-of-farewell
and went out from Pharaoh's presence.

11 So Yosef settled his father and his brothers,
giving them holdings in the land of Egypt,
in the goodliest-part of the land, in the region of Ra'meses, as
Pharaoh had commanded.

12 Yosef sustained his father, his brothers, and his father's entire
household with bread, in proportion to the little-ones.

13 But bread there was none in all the land,
for the famine was exceedingly heavy,
and the land of Egypt and the land of Canaan were exhausted by
the famine.

---

8 **days and years:** See the note to 25:7.   9 **in the days of:** Others use "during."

14 Yosef had collected all the silver that was to be found in the land
of Egypt and in the land of Canaan, from the rations that they
had bought,
and Yosef had brought the silver into Pharaoh's house.

15 When the silver in the land of Egypt and in the land of Canaan
had run out,
all the Egyptians came to Yosef, saying:
Come-now, (let us have) bread!
Why should we die in front of you, because the silver is gone?

16 Yosef said:
Come-now, (let me have) your livestock, and I will give you
(bread) for your livestock, since the silver is gone.

17 So they brought their livestock to Yosef, and Yosef gave them
bread (in exchange) for the horses, the sheep-livestock, the
oxen-livestock, and the donkeys;
he got-them-through with bread (in exchange) for all their
livestock in that year.

18 But when that year had run out, they came back to him in the
second year and said to him:
We cannot hide from my lord
that if the silver has run out and the animal-stocks are my lord's,
nothing remains for my lord except for our bodies and our soil!

19 Why should we die before your eyes, so we, so our soil?
Acquire us and our soil for bread,
and we and our soil will become servants to Pharaoh.
Give (us) seed-for-sowing
that we may live and not die,
that the soil may not become desolate!

20 So Yosef acquired all the soil of Egypt for Pharaoh
—for each of the Egyptians sold his field, for the famine was
strong upon them—
and the land went over to Pharaoh.

21 As for the people, he transferred them into the cities, from one
edge of Egypt's border to its other edge.

---

17 **got-them-through:** Lit. "led them."

21 **transferred them:** Hebrew difficult; some read "en-slaved them."

Yosef's Sons Blessed (48): Yaakov, near to death, blesses his grandsons (Rahel's!) in moving terms, bringing full circle many of the motifs of his life. Elder and younger sons are switched by the blind Patriarch, who this time, though, is one who is fully aware of their identities. As in both literature and life, a dying man sees both past (here) and future (the next chapter) with great clarity, as in a vision.

22 Only the soil of the priests he did not acquire,
  for the priests had a prescribed-allocation from Pharaoh, and they
    ate from their allocation which Pharaoh had given them,
  therefore they did not sell their soil.
23 Yosef said to the people:
  Now that I have acquired you and your soil today for Pharaoh,
  here, you have seed, sow the soil!
24 But it shall be at the ingatherings, that you shall give a fifth to
    Pharaoh,
  the four other parts being for you
  as seed for the field and for your eating-needs, for those in your
    households, and for feeding your little-ones.
25 They said:
  You have saved our lives!
  May we find favor in my lord's eyes: we will become servants to
    Pharaoh.
26 And Yosef made it a prescribed-law until this day, concerning the
    soil of Egypt: For Pharaoh every fifth part!
  Only the soil of the priests, that alone did not go over to Pharaoh.

27 Now Yisrael stayed in the land of Egypt, in the region of Goshen;
  they obtained holdings in it, bore fruit, and became exceedingly
    many.
28 And Yaakov lived in the land of Egypt for seventeen years.
  And the days of Yaakov, the years of his life, were seven years and
    a hundred and forty years.
29 Now when Yisrael's days drew near to death,
  he called his son Yosef and said to him:
  Pray, if I have found favor in your eyes,
  pray put your hand under my thigh—
  deal with me faithfully and truly:
  pray do not bury me in Egypt!
30 When I lie down with my fathers,
  carry me out of Egypt, and bury me in their burial-site!

24 **a fifth:** Here is the ubiquitous "five" again.

He said:
I will do according to your words.

31 But he said:
Swear to me!
So he swore to him.
Then Yisrael bowed, at the head of the bed.

48:1 Now after these events it was
that they said to Yosef:
Here, your father has taken sick!
So he took his two sons with him, Menashe and Efrayim. . . .

2 When they told Yaakov, saying: Here, your son Yosef is coming to
you,
Yisrael gathered his strength and sat up in the bed.

3 Yaakov said to Yosef:
God Shaddai was seen by me
in Luz, in the land of Canaan;
he blessed me

4 and he said to me:
Here, I will make you bear fruit and will make you many,
and will make you into a host of peoples;
I will give this land to your seed after you, as a holding for the
ages!

5 So now,
your two sons who were born to you in the land of Egypt
before I came to you in Egypt,
they are mine,
Efrayim and Menashe,
like Re'uven and Shim'on, let them be mine!

6 But your begotten sons, whom you will beget after them,
let them be yours;
by their brothers' names let them be called, respecting their
inheritance.

48:5 **they are mine:** As it were, adopted. **Efrayim and
Menashe:** Note how Yaakov reverses the order of
birth; see vv.14, 17–19.

7 While I—
when I came back from that country,
Rahel died on me,
in the land of Canaan,
on the way, with still a stretch of land left to come to Efrat.
There I buried her, on the way to Efrat—that is now Bet-Lehem.

8 When Yisrael saw Yosef's sons, he said:
Who are these?

9 Yosef said to his father:
They are my sons, whom God has given me here.
He said:
Pray take them over to me, that I may give-them-blessing.

10 Now Yisrael's eyes were heavy with age, he was not able to see.
He brought them close to him,
and he kissed them and embraced them.

11 Yisrael said to Yosef:
I never thought to see your face (again),
and here, God has let me see your seed as well!

12 Yosef took them from between his knees
and they bowed low, their brows to the ground.

13 Yosef took the two of them,
Efrayim with his right-hand, to Yisrael's left,
and Menashe with his left-hand, to Yisrael's right,
and brought them close to him.

14 But Yisrael stretched out his right-hand and put it on the head of
Efrayim—yet he was the younger!—
and his left-hand on the head of Menashe;
he crossed his arms, although Menashe was the firstborn.

15 Then he blessed Yosef and said:
The God
in whose presence my fathers walked,
Avraham and Yitzhak,
the God

---

7 **Rahel died on me:** The memory is still painful to Yaakov, even after many years.

11 **your face:** The final and most powerful occurrence of the term.

Yaakov's Testament and Death (49): In this ancient piece of poetry, Yaakov addresses his sons, not as they are, but as they will be. There is little resemblance, for instance, between the Binyamin as the beloved and protected youngest son of the Yosef story and the preying wolf of v.27, but the Benjaminites were later to be known for their military skills. Scholars have therefore seen the entire poem as a retrojection of Israel as it came to be on the days of the Patriarchs.

As in the fuller Yosef narrative, the first three sons are quickly disqualified from active leadership, paving the way for the rise of Yehuda (the tribe from which sprang David and the royal house of Israel). Despite this, Yosef still receives the richest blessing.

The chapter is textually among the most difficult in the Torah. Many passages are simply obscure, leaving the translator to make at best educated guesses.

who has tended me
ever since I was (born), until this day—
16 the messenger
who has redeemed me from all ill-fortune,
may he bless the lads!
May my name continue to be called through them
and the name of my fathers, Avraham and Yitzhak!
May they teem-like-fish to (become) many in the midst of the
land!
17 Now when Yosef saw that his father had put his right hand on
Efrayim's head,
it sat ill in his eyes,
and he laid hold of his father's hand, to turn it from Efrayim's
head to Menashe's head.
18 Yosef said to his father:
Not so, father, indeed, this one is the firstborn, place your hand
on his head!
19 But his father refused and said:
I know, my son, I know—
he too will be a people, he too will be great,
yet his younger brother will be greater than he, and his seed will
become a full-measure of nations!
20 So he blessed them on that day,
saying:
By you shall Israel give-blessings, saying:
God make you like Efrayim and Menashe!
Thus he made Efrayim go before Menashe.
21 Then Yisrael said to Yosef:
Here, I am dying,
but God will be with you,
he will have you return to the land of your fathers.

---

15 **tended:** Or "shepherded."
16 **redeemed me from all ill-fortune:** Despite his words in 47:9, perhaps Yaakov achieves a measure of peace in the end. **my name continue to be called**

through them: My line continue through them.
teem-like-fish: Others use "become teeming (multitudes)."
19 **I know:** Though blind, Yaakov knows exactly what he is doing, unlike his father in Chap. 27.

22 And I, I give you
    one portion over and above your brothers,
    which I took away from the Amorite,
    with my sword, with my bow.

49:1 Now Yaakov called his sons and said:
    Gather round, that I may tell you
    what will befall you in the aftertime of days.

2   Come together and hearken, sons of Yaakov,
       hearken to Yisrael your father.

3   Re'uven,
       my firstborn, you,
       my might, first-fruit of my vigor!
       Surpassing in loftiness, surpassing in force!
4   Headlong like water—surpass no more!
       For when you mounted your father's bed,
       then you defiled it—he mounted the couch!

5   Shim'on and Levi,
       such brothers,
       wronging weapons are their ties-of-kinship!
6   To their council may my being never come,
       in their assembly may my person never unite!
       For in their anger they kill men,
       in their self-will they maim bulls.
7   Damned be their anger, that it is so fierce!
       Their fury, that it is so harsh!
       I will split them up in Yaakov,
       I will scatter them in Yisrael.

---

22 **one portion over and above:** Hebrew unclear. We do not know to what event Yaakov is referring in this entire verse. **took away:** Others use "will take," "must take."

49:4 **when you mounted . . . :** Alluding to 35:21–22.
  5 **ties-of-kinship:** Hebrew obscure. Others use "weapons," "swords" (B-R uses "mattocks").
  6 **in their anger they kill men:** See 34:25–26.

8   Yehuda,
>   you—your brothers will praise you,
>   your hand on the neck of your enemies!
>   Your father's sons will bow down to you.

9   A lion's whelp, Yehuda—
>   from torn-prey, my son, you have gone up!
>   He squats, he crouches,
>   like the lion, like the king-of-beasts,
>   who dares rouse him up?

10   The scepter shall not depart from Yehuda,
>   nor the staff-of-command from between his legs,
>   until they bring him tribute,
>   —the obedience of peoples is his.

11   He ties up his foal to a vine,
>   his young colt to a crimson tendril;
>   he washes his raiment in wine,
>   his mantle in the blood of grapes;

12   his eyes, darker than wine,
>   his teeth, whiter than milk.

13   Zevulun,
>   on the shore of the sea he dwells;
>   he is a haven-shore for boats,
>   his flank upon Tzidon.

14   Yissakhar,
>   a bone-strong donkey,
>   crouching among the fire-places.

15   When he saw how good the resting-place was,
>   and how pleasant was the land,
>   he bent his shoulder to bearing
>   and so became a laboring serf.

---

8 **Yehuda . . . enemies:** Heb. *yehuda/ atta yodukha ahikha/ yadekha al oref oyevekha.*

9 **lion:** Eventually the symbol of the (Judahite) monarchy.

10 **until they bring . . . :** Hebrew difficult; others use "until Shiloh comes." The phrase is an old and unsolved problem for interpreter and translator alike.

11 **colt:** Of a donkey.

13 **Tzidon:** Sidon, the important Phoenician city (north of Israel).

15 **laboring serf:** The Hebrew *mas 'oved* denotes forced labor.

16   Dan,
       his people will mete-out-judgment,
       (to all) of Israel's branches together.
17   May Dan be a snake on the wayside,
       a horned-viper on the path,
       who bites the horse's heels
       so that his rider tumbles backward.

18   I wait-in-hope for your deliverance, O YHWH!

19   Gad,
       goading robber-band will goad him,
       yet he will goad at their heel.

20   Asher,
       his nourishment is rich,
       he gives forth king's dainties.

21   Naftali,
       a hind let loose,
       he who gives forth lovely fawns.

22   Young wild-ass,
       Yosef,
       young wild-ass along a spring,
       donkeys along a wall.
23   Bitterly they shot at him,
       the archers assailed him,
24   yet firm remained his bow,
       and agile stayed his arms and hands—
       by means of the hands of Yaakov's Champion,
       up there,
       the Shepherd, the Stone of Yisrael.

---

16 **mete-out-judgment:** Others use "will endure."
18 **I wait-in-hope . . . :** Either a deathbed cry or possibly the cry of a falling rider (see the preceding line) (Ehrlich).

19 **goad:** Lit. "attack"; a play on "Gad" (Heb. *gad gedud yegudennu*).
24 **arms and hands:** Lit. "arms of his hands."

25 By your father's God—
 may he help you,
 and Shaddai,
 may he give-you-blessing:
 Blessings of the heavens, from above,
 blessings of Ocean crouching below,
 blessings of breasts and womb!

26 May the blessings of your father transcend
 the blessings of mountains eternal,
 the bounds of hills without age.
 May they fall upon the head of Yosef,
 on the crown of the consecrated-one among his brothers.

27 Binyamin,
 a wolf that tears-to-pieces!
 In the morning he devours prey,
 and then, in the evening, divides up the spoil.

28 All these are the tribes of Israel, twelve,
 and this is what their father spoke to them;
 he blessed them,
 according to what belonged to each as blessing, he blessed them.

29 And he commanded them, saying to them:
 I am now about to be gathered to my kinspeople;
 bury me by my fathers,
 in the cave that is in the field of Efron the Hittite,

30 at the cave that is in the field of Makhpela, that faces Mamre, in
 the land of Canaan.
 —Avraham had acquired that field from Efron the Hittite, as a
 burial holding.

31 There they buried Avraham and Sara his wife,
 there they buried Yitzhak and Rivka his wife,
 there I buried Lea—

---

25 **Shaddai:** Once again connected to fertility (note the content of the following lines). **give-you-bless-ing:** Just as Yaakov had blessed Yosef's sons, so Yosef is the only one of the twelve brothers to whom Yaakov applies the term.

26 **mountains:** Reading *hararei* for the traditional Hebrew *horei*, "parents" on the basis of Hab. 3:6.

28 **tribes:** Heb. *shevatim*, "staffs," which symbolized the tribes.

31 **Lea:** Not called "my wife." Again the old feelings remain vivid.

Yaakov's Burial (50:1–14): The funeral of Yaakov seems to presage the Exodus from Egypt—here with Pharaoh's permission and a large royal escort (including "chariots and horsemen," who in several generations will pursue Yaakov's descendants into the sea).

Interestingly, the *Iliad* also ends with an elaborate burial scene. The contrast is instructive: the Homeric epic celebrates the deeds and mourns the lost youth of a hero (Hector); Genesis reflects Yosef's standing at court and the desire to bury Yaakov in the land of Canaan, in the family plot. Note too that Genesis has two more scenes, tending to lessen the impact of this impressive funeral sequence.

The End of the Matter (50:15–26): Drawing out the tension inherent in the Patriarchs' family relationships to the very end, the text repeats an earlier situation in Yaakov's life—his brother's feelings of "grudge" and threats to kill him—in the guise of his sons' fears toward Yosef. Here, however, there can be no question of personal vengeance, since Yosef sees the brothers' betrayal of him as but part of a larger purpose. In his words of v.20, "God planned-it-over for good . . . to keep many people alive," the text resolves two of the great hanging issues that have persisted throughout Genesis: sibling hatred and the threat to generational continuity.

Left hanging, of course, is the issue of the promised land, since the narrative concludes "in Egypt," but these final chapters lead to the assurance that God will "take account" (vv.24–25) of the Sons of Israel, as they are soon to be termed.

32 an acquisition, the field and the cave that is in it, from the Sons of
 Het.

33 When Yaakov had finished commanding his sons,
 he gathered up his feet onto the bed and expired,
 and was gathered to his kinspeople.

50:1 Yosef flung himself on his father's face,
 he wept over him and kissed him.
2 Then Yosef charged his servants, the physicians, to embalm his
 father,
 and the physicians embalmed Yisrael.
3 A full forty days were required for him,
 for thus are fulfilled the days of embalming.
 And the Egyptians wept for him for seventy days.
4 Now when the days of weeping for him had passed,
 Yosef spoke to Pharaoh's household, saying:
 Pray, if I have found favor in your eyes,
 pray speak in the ears of Pharaoh, saying:
5 My father had me swear, saying:
 Here, I am dying—
 in my burial-site which I dug for myself in the land of Canaan,
 there you are to bury me!
 So now,
 pray let me go up, bury my father, and return.
6 Pharaoh said:
 Go up and bury your father, as he had you swear.
7 So Yosef went up to bury his father;
 and with him went up all of Pharaoh's servants,
 the elders of his household and all the elders of the land of
 Egypt,
8 all of Yosef's household,
 his brothers and his father's household.
 Only their little-ones, their sheep, and their oxen did they leave
 behind in the region of Goshen.

---

33 **expired:** Omitted are the "old and satisfied in days"
 that were applied to his father and grandfather.

9 And along with him went up chariots as well, and horsemen as
well—

the company was an exceedingly heavy one.

10 They came as far as Goren Ha-Atad/Bramble Threshing-Floor,
which is in (the country) across the Jordan,

and there they took up lament, an exceedingly great and heavy
lament,

and he held mourning for his father, for seven days.

11 Now when the settled-folk of the land, the Canaanites, saw the
mourning at Bramble Threshing-Floor,

they said:

This is such a heavy mourning/*evel* for Egypt!

Therefore its name was called: Meadow/*avel* of Egypt,

which is in (the country) across the Jordan.

12 So his sons did thus for him, as he had commanded them:

13 his sons carried him back to the land of Canaan

and buried him in the cave in the field of Makhpela.

—Avraham had acquired that field as a burial holding from Efron
the Hittite, (the field) facing Mamre.

14 Then Yosef returned to Egypt,

he and his brothers and all who had gone up with him to bury his
father,

after he had buried his father.

15 When Yosef's brothers saw that their father was dead, they said:

What if Yosef holds a grudge against us

and repays, yes, repays us for all the ill that we caused him!

16 So they charged Yosef, saying:

Your father commanded before his death, saying:

17 Say thus to Yosef:

Ah, pray forgive your brothers' offense and their sin, that they
caused you ill!

50:9 **heavy:** Three times through v.11. The root *k-b-d* connotes "honor," "importance," "weight," and is central here perhaps to emphasize the respect shown to
Yaakov.

13 **the cave in the field of Makhpela:** Despite God's
continual promise of the land throughout the book,
this is practically all that the Patriarchs possess at the
end of Genesis.

◆ Now, pray forgive the offense of the servants of your father's God!
Yosef wept as they spoke to him.

18 And his brothers themselves came, they flung themselves down
    before him and said:
Here we are, servants to you!

19 But Yosef said to them:
Do not be afraid! For am I in place of God?

20 Now you, you planned ill against me,
(but) God planned-it-over for good,
in order to do (as is) this very day—
to keep many people alive.

21 So now, do not be afraid!
I myself will sustain you and your little-ones!
And he comforted them and spoke to their hearts.

22 So Yosef stayed in Egypt, he and his father's household.
Yosef lived a hundred and ten years;

23 Yosef saw from Efrayim sons of the third generation,
and also the sons of Makhir son of Menashe were born on
    Yosef's knees.

24 Yosef said to his brothers:
I am dying,
but God will take account, yes, account of you,
he will bring you up from this land
to the land about which he swore
to Avraham, to Yitzhak, and to Yaakov.

25 Yosef had the Sons of Israel swear, saying:
When God takes account, yes, account of you,
bring my bones up from here!

26 And Yosef died, a hundred and ten years old.
They embalmed him and they put him in a coffin
in Egypt.

---

22 **a hundred and ten years:** The ideal Egyptian life span.

23 **born on Yosef's knees:** Considered his own; see 30:3.

24 **brothers:** Presumably meant in the sense of "family."

25 **Sons of Israel:** They are no longer merely the sons of one man but are now on their way to becoming a people.

שְׁמוֹת

———◦◦◦———

EXODUS

———◦◦◦———

NOW THESE ARE
THE NAMES

ON THE BOOK OF EXODUS
AND ITS STRUCTURE

THE BOOK OF EXODUS IS ISRAEL'S SECOND BOOK OF ORIGINS. GENESIS HAD CONCERNED itself with the beginnings of the world, of human beings and their institutions, and of the people of Israel as a tribal family. Exodus continues this thrust as it recounts the origin of the people on a religious and political level (here inseparable as concepts). A number of biblical ideas receive their fullest early treatment in this book: God's acting directly in history; making himself "known" to both Israelites and foreigners; covenant as a reciprocal agreement between God and humans; law as an expression of total worldview; and the use of sacred structure (Tabernacle or "Dwelling") as a vehicle for and expression of perceived truths about the world. In addition, several biblical institutions make their first appearance in Exodus: Passover, Sabbath, rudimentary leadership/government, and cult/priesthood. All this is presented in a general narrative framework, raising the question as to whether what we have here is story or history. Is Exodus a fanciful reconstruction of what happened to Moshe (Moses) and his generation, riddled with anachronisms? Or is it a faithful and reliable handing-down of eyewitness data which only the cynical or irreligious would doubt?

For the first position there are several supports. We possess virtually no extrabiblical references to the events recorded in our book, either in Egypt or elsewhere. Then, too, there seem to be inconsistencies of time within the story (Chaps. 16 and 18 appear to presuppose laws which were given later), and patterns within the telling of the tale that are too symmetrical (the Plagues) or too stereotyped (the constant use of stylized language) to be simple reporting of fact. Finally, Exodus is lacking in the citation of personal and geographical names, especially as compared to the books that precede and follow (Genesis and Numbers).

For the second position, that of Exodus as a reliable historical record, there exist no methods of proof other than evaluation of literary form—that is, accepting that oral literature is able to preserve facts without later coloration. But even if it could be shown that Exodus is oral literature—an evaluation which is too sweeping, given the present form of the book—modern scholarship has come to cast doubt on the absolute historical reliability of oral tradition (see Vansina).

Despite these observations, there is still something unsettling about writing Exodus off as a work of fiction, however pious that fiction may have been. For the rest of the Hebrew Bible abounds in emotional references to the experience of the exodus. At every stage of biblical literature, that experience is invoked for the purpose of directing behavior (see especially Judg. 2, I Sam. 8, II Sam. 7, II Kings

17, Neh. 9, and Ps. 78; and most of Deuteronomy is rhetorically grounded in it). The entire structure and emotional force of biblical law rest upon such exhortations as "A sojourner you are not to oppress:/you yourselves know (well) the feelings of the sojourner,/for sojourners were you in the land of Egypt" (Ex. 23:9) and such situations as that of the Hebrew serf (Ex. 21:2ff.). Apparently the experience of the exodus period was crucial in forming the group consciousness of the Israelites, and ever since it has provided a model from which both later Judaism and Christianity were to draw frequently and profoundly.

A hypothetical analogy, based on American history, may help to shed light on the historicity of Exodus. Imagine a book based on the following outline: first, a section on the American Revolution, with some biographical material on a few of the Founding Fathers, focusing mostly on the outbreak of the war and key battles; second, a description of the Constitutional Convention, including some of the more important speeches and discussions; third, the text of the Constitution itself; and finally, L'Enfant's original blueprints for the building of the new capital, Washington, D.C., interspersed with accounts of the first few presidents' inaugural addresses. What would be the underlying message of such a book? We are certainly dealing here with more than a straight journalistic description of the events, more than a legalistic discussion of constitutional law, and more than a technical presentation for architects. Such a book would actually be presenting the ideals of America's self-image: a nation founded on the willingness to fight for particular rights against Old World tyranny, established under democratic laws based on reason and providing governmental checks and balances, and whose ideals would be embodied in the construction of a brand-new, centrally located capital city that used classically grounded forms of architecture to express grace and reason as the basis for the new society.

Now this portrayal is very simplistic, but it gets its point across (and I would be willing to wager that, somewhere in this country, there exists a school textbook written along these lines). In a similar manner, although with much more weight given to God's role in the process, the book of Exodus unfolds. The dramatic story of Israel's deliverance from bondage, coupled with Moshe's own early development, is only the first part of the book, and accounts for less than half of it. It is followed by several stories of desert wanderings, and then by a presentation of the covenant made between God and Israel at Sinai, against a stunning natural backdrop. The second half of the book enumerates a series of laws which constitute the covenant, and the details of construction of a portable sanctuary designed both to symbolize and actually to accommodate God's presence among the Israelites (with the interruption of a major rebellion). So, like our theoretical American model, Exodus conveys far more than information about events. It is, rather, the narration of a worldview, a laying out of different types of texts bearing the *meaning* of Israel's historical experience.

I stress the word "experience" because that is what is at stake here. Human memory is always selective. We remember what we wish to remember, giving weight to particular emotions, sometimes over and above the facts (or, as the poet

Maya Angelou puts it autobiographically, "The facts sometimes obscure the truth"). The same thing appears to be true of group memory. What a people remembers of substance is not nearly as important as how they process their experience.

In our Exodus text one can perceive a characteristically Israelite process at work. The book emerges as a mix of historical recollection, mythical processing, and didactic retelling, what Buber and others have called a "saga." What is preserved in the book of Exodus, therefore, is a Teaching (Heb. *Tora*) based on a set of experiences, which became history for ancient Israel. Hence, to understand better the workings of the book, we need to turn to its themes and its structure. This will be more fruitful than trying to find the exact location of the Sea of Reeds or Mount Sinai, or the "Lost Ark," or Moshe's burial site— of whose location "no man has knowledge until this day" (Deut. 34:6). These have all receded into archeological oblivion. What has survived of ancient Israel is its approach to history and to life, and its literature. In that sense, the book of Exodus is an attempt to distill history and to learn from it, using echoes from the past to shape the present and the future.

When we turn to a closer consideration of the structure of Exodus, we must proceed on the assumption that a work of art stems from both artful and unconscious design. Therefore, any structuring of such a book can only be hypothetical and must not limit itself to ironclad categories.

With that said, a number of potential divisions of our book present themselves. The first emerges from a close look at the subject matter of the text. Strikingly, Exodus appears to be arranged in groups of a few chapters each (bearing in mind that the chapter divisions are historically late), resulting in the following scheme:

1. Prologue in Egypt (Chap. 1)
2. Moshe's Early Life and Call (Chaps. 2–4)
3. Moshe's Mission in Egypt (5:1–7:13)
4. The First Nine Plagues (7:14–10:29)
5. The Tenth Plague and the Exodus (Chaps. 11–13)
6. In the Wilderness I: The Deliverance at the Sea (14:1–15:21)
7. In the Wilderness II: Early Experiences (15:22–18:27)
8. Covenant at Sinai (Chaps. 19–20)
9. The Terms (Laws) and Conclusion of the Covenant (Chaps. 21–24)
10. Details of the Tabernacle (Chaps. 25–27)
11. Details of the Cult (Chaps. 28–31)
12. Rebellion and Reconciliation (Chaps. 32–34)
13. The Building of the Tabernacle, Priestly Vestments (Chaps. 35–39)
14. Conclusion (Chap. 40)

Such a measured shifting of focus helps to maintain the flow of the text and our interest in it.

A glance through this list will also lead to the positing of larger structures. The traditions collected in Exodus fall naturally into both geographical and thematic divisions. The first part of the book takes place in Egypt (1:1–15:21), the second in the wilderness (15:22–40:38); this could alternatively be viewed as the events preceding Mount Sinai (Chaps. 1–17/18) and those that take place there (Chaps. 18/19–40). One could also combine the geographical and thematic aspects, resulting in the structure (1) Israel in Egypt (1:1–15:21), (2) Israel in the Wilderness (15:22–24:18), and (3) Tabernacle and Calf (Chaps. 25–40).

My own preference for structuring Exodus also combines these aspects, as follows:

I. The Deliverance Narrative (1:1–15:21)
II. In the Wilderness (15:22–18:27)
III. Covenant and Law (Chaps. 19–24)
IV. The Blueprints for the Tabernacle and Its Service (Chaps. 25–31)
V. Infidelity and Reconciliation (Chaps. 32–34)
VI. The Building of the Tabernacle (Chaps. 35–40)

These divisions exhibit a great deal of overlapping. In Part I, Israel's life in Egypt (Chap. 1) paves the way for Moshe's early years (Chaps. 2–4), then the account of his mission before Pharaoh and the Plagues (Chaps. 5–13), and the final victory (Chaps. 14–15); Part II is anticipated by some of what happens after the exodus itself (Chap. 14), and leads to Sinai (Chap. 19); the covenant and laws of Part III naturally lead to other prescriptions, this time the building instructions for the Tabernacle (Chaps. 25–31); planning the sacred structure in Part IV is followed by the making of a forbidden construction, the Golden Calf (Chaps. 32–33); and the reconciliation between God and Israel (Chap. 34) restores Israel's capacity to return to the actual building of the Tabernacle, and to complete it (Chaps. 35–40). So despite the presence of what must have been several very diverse traditions behind the final text of Exodus, it has been skillfully woven together to form a coherent whole. In addition to the above structures, it can be said that the book of Exodus rests on several textual backbones, inner structures and recurring themes and motifs that help to create a unified work. These may be listed by category:

1. There are various climaxes which serve to highlight the action—the Encounter at the Bush (Chaps. 3–4), the Tenth Plague and Exodus (12:29–42), the Deliverance at the Sea (14–15:21), the Revelation at Sinai (Chaps. 19–20), the Calf Episode (Chap. 32), and Completion of the Tabernacle (Chap. 40). Anchoring these dramatic scenes, at the center of the book, is the Sinai Revelation. The Binding of Yitzhak (Isaac) in Chapter 22 of Genesis serves much the same focusing function.

2. There exist three strategically placed accounts of God's Presence accompanying the Israelites (13:21–22, 24:15–18, 40:34–38) which share a common vocabulary. Key words in these passages are "day/night," "cloud," "fire," "dwell,"

"Glory," "cover," "go up," and "in the eyes of the Children of Israel/before the people" (it should be noted that not every passage uses all of these terms). These words chart God's movement: first, following the Exodus; second, following the concluding of the covenant; and third, following the erection of the Tabernacle, at the end of the book. A variation of these Presence accounts occurs in Numbers 9:15–23, where it rounds out the picture—for it is at this point that the Israelites finally depart from Sinai (having spent about a year there), on their journey toward the Promised Land.

3. Several leading words recur throughout the book and give it a sense of unity:

serve— The Israelites pass from "servitude" to Pharaoh into the "service" of God; laws are given that warn against "serving" other gods, that specify how a "serf" is to be treated, and that detail the "service" (i.e., construction and dismantling) of a sanctuary where God is to be properly "served."

Glory—Liberated from Pharaoh's "stubbornness" (Heb. *koved lev*), the Israelites experience God's "Glory" (Heb. *kavod*) at the Sea of Reeds, and encounter it again at Sinai (Chap. 24) and when the Tabernacle is completed (Chap. 40). When Israel falters in Chapter 32, Moses begs to see God's "Glory" as a sign of reassurance. This is one of the central issues of the book, receiving its clearest formulation in Chap. 17:7—"Is YHWH in our midst, or not?" Without the accompanying Presence, the Israelites can survive neither in Egypt nor in the wilderness. That the book ends with the "Glory" taking up residence in the Tabernacle is a sign that all is well in this regard.

know—The Plagues and the liberation take place so that Egyptian and Israelite alike will acknowledge God as the true ruler (who "knows" the slaves' sufferings). The book as a whole portrays a God who is "known" by his compassion toward the oppressed.

see—God "sees" and rescues the people early in the book (Chap. 3); they "see" his deliverance at the sea (Chap. 14) and the awesome display at Sinai (Chaps. 19–20); the Tabernacle blueprint is given to Moshe to "see" (Chaps 25ff.).

4. Aside from theme words, there are also several thematic threads that run through the book. These may be listed as well:

distinction—The Israelites learn what it is to be separated out, first for oppression and later for God's service. This process occurs during the Plagues and throughout the legal sections, which are often based on the making of distinctions (the Hebrew word for "holy," *kadosh*, may originally have had this connotation). In general, Exodus is a book that abounds in polarities and distinctions: between God and Pharaoh, life and death, slavery and freedom, Egyptianness and Israeliteness, city and wilderness, visible gods/magic and an invisible God who is not conjurable, doubt and trust.

construction—The Israelites are enslaved as builders of Egyptian cities; they go on to build a society, a calf-god, and a Tabernacle.

rebellion—From the beginning, God and Moshe are often unheeded, as the Israelites seek to maintain or return to their status as dependent slaves in Egypt (Chaps. 2, 5, 14, 15–17, 32).

Sabbath—As a newly freed people, Israel is to adapt to a rhythm of work and sacred cessation, which celebrates both creation and freedom. The Sabbath is at issue immediately after liberation (Chap. 16) and is commanded three times (Chaps. 20, 31, 35); and the account of the Tabernacle's completion echoes the vocabulary of God's completed creation in Genesis 2, a passage which serves as one justification for observing the Sabbath (see Ex. 20:11).

origins—We are told of the beginnings of the new covenant (distinct from that concluded with Abraham), the law system, the cult/priesthood, and the sacred calendar, but with the significant omission of the monarchy.

covenant—God establishes a relationship with the people of Israel: if they will obey him and observe his laws, he will protect them and treat them as his "firstborn son." This form of covenant is different from the ones in Genesis, and plays a significant role in subsequent books of the Bible.

God in History—The God of Exodus actively intervenes to rescue a people, defeating their oppressors in battle; he leads them through the wilderness, meets them, and makes a covenant with them.

5. The above themes are specifically Israelite themes. There are, however, motifs in Exodus that have a more universal ring. One could term these anthropological, since they employ standard aspects of human experience to convey the overall messages of the book.

Fire is used frequently and in varied contexts (at the Burning Bush and later back at Mount Sinai, in the desert trek, in the Tabernacle service, and at the Calf incident), usually to make a statement about God. In contrast to conventional fire gods (e.g., the Norse trickster Loki), the God of Exodus is most often associated with the more positive aspects of fire: constancy, purity, and transformation. The fire at Sinai does not destroy Moshe and the people, but rather turns them into something new. At the same time it should not be forgotten that fire is used regularly to connote anger in the Bible, especially God's, and especially in the later wilderness narratives.

Water appears throughout Exodus, not as a backdrop but as an active medium which most often signifies life and death simultaneously. The Nile, into which the enslaved Hebrews' babies are thrown, gently bears the infant Moshe to safety: the Nile, the giver of life in Egypt, is changed into blood, itself a major signifier of life in the Bible but useless here because it is undrinkable; the Sea of Reeds acts as a passageway of birth for the Israelites but as a graveyard for their Egyptian pursuers. The availability of water becomes a central issue in the wilderness, as an instrument for survival and for the testing of the Israelites' faith. Finally, water creates the ritual purity necessary for the people at Sinai and their priests in the Tabernacle to approach God.

Desert/Wilderness is the scene of the crucial second part of the book. Only in the desert, away from the massive influence of age-old Egyptian culture, can the new Israelite society be forged. Moshe, like many other real-life and fictional heroes, demonstrates this in his own early life. The desert acts as a purifying agent for him, changing the Egyptian prince into a member of his own true people. Similarly, the Israelites begin the process of transformation from bondage to self-rule, a process which is taught in the harsh reality of desert life and which will take an entire generation to complete.

In point of fact, all these media—fire, water, and desert—suggest change as a major concern of the book of Exodus. Our text chronicles the start of Israel's journey as a nation, a transformative journey which takes vastly changed circumstances, a whole generation in time, and indeed several books of recounting to complete. Exodus is very concerned with topography—not for the purposes of historical recollection (as Genesis was, apparently) but as an account of an inner journey. Thus the people travel to the boundary between Egypt and the desert, through the sea, to the great fiery mountain; and we know that they cannot but be on their way to a final goal. That goal, the Promised Land, will not be realized in Exodus, because in this book we stand only at the beginning of the journey. Change does not occur quickly, and the true molding of a people, like that of an individual, requires formative experiences over time. In Exodus, then, the People of Israel begins in adolescence, as it were. It has survived infancy in Genesis, a period marked by constant threats of physical extinction, and must now begin the tortuous process of learning to cope with adulthood—that is to say, people-hood—in a hostile world.

That process will take us past the present text. Exodus stands at the beginning of a trilogy in the middle of the Torah. It takes us from slavery up to Sinai, inaugurating the law-giving process. Leviticus will concentrate almost exclusively on laws (of "holiness"), never budging geographically, while Numbers will see the conclusion of the Sinai experience and the traveling toward (and actually reaching) the land of Israel. Exodus is thus of great importance in the overall five-book pattern, introducing key elements of the wilderness books: law, institutions, rebellion, and—Moshe himself. It serves as a bridge between the great narratives of Genesis and the priestly code of Leviticus and the wanderings of Numbers (Greenberg 1972 notes how the opening of Exodus points back, to Gen. 46; and the closing points forward, to Num. 9). It in fact contains elements of all three books.

Exodus is the basis not only of what follows in the Torah, but also sets the stage for the rest of the Hebrew Bible. What Israel understood of its God, and what that God expects of them, are set forth most directly and unforgettably in the memories enshrined in the book of Exodus.

PART I

THE DELIVERANCE NARRATIVE

(1–15:21)

THE FIRST PART OF THE BOOK OF EXODUS IS PRESENTED AS A CONTINUATION OF THE
Genesis narratives, by abbreviating the genealogy of the immigrant Yaakov from
Gen. 46:8–25. We find here the same centrality of God, the same kind of sparse
but powerful biographical sketch of the human hero, and a narrative style similar
to that of the previous book.

And yet Exodus introduces a new and decisive element into the Hebrew Bible,
which becomes paradigmatic for future generations of biblical writers. The book
speaks of a God who acts directly in history, blow by blow—a God who promises,
liberates, guides, and gives laws to a people. This is, to be sure, an outgrowth of a
God who brings the Flood and disperses the Babel generation, but it is also a decisive step forward from a God who works his will in the background, through intrafamily conflicts (which comprise most of Genesis). This deity frees his people,
not by subterfuge, but by directly taking on Egypt and its gods. Pharaoh and the
Nile, both of which were considered divine in Egypt, are in the end forced to yield
to superior power. Surely it is no accident that the ending of Part I—the Song of
Moshe at the Sea—hails YHWH as Israel's true king, a king whose acts of "leading," "redeeming," and "planting" his people are exultingly affirmed in the body
of the Song.

Part I receives its structural coherence in a number of ways. For one, it encompasses a straight chronological narrative, moving from Israel's enslavement
to its liberation and triumph over its oppressors. The ending, Chapter 15, is rhetorically and stylistically fitting (see Gaster 1969), celebrating as it does the mighty
deeds of God. For another, Part I carefully paces its climaxes, building up from the
Burning Bush to various stages of Plagues, to the Tenth Plague/exodus and finally the great scene at the sea. There are also a number of key words that help to
tie together various sections of the narratives: "know," "serve," and "see." All of
these go through interesting changes in meaning, through which one can trace
the movement of central ideas (see the Commentary).

In the area of vocabulary, David Daube (1963) has made the interesting observation that the Deliverance Narrative uses a number of verbs that occur regularly
in biblical law regarding the formal release of a slave: "send free" (Heb. *shale'ah*),
"drive out" (*garesh*), and "go out" (*yatzo'*). In addition, the motif of the Israelites'

"stripping" the Egyptians (3:22, 12:36) links up with the regulation of release in Deut. 15:13. "... you are not to send him free empty-handed." Daube sees our text as bearing the stamp of Israelite social custom: Pharaoh is made to flout "established social regulations."

Finally, several scholars (Kikawada, Ackerman 1974, Fishbane 1979, and Isbell) have pointed out that the vocabulary of the first few chapters of the book foreshadows the whole of Part I. This use of sound and idea helps to create unity in these narratives (despite their possibly diverse origins), and is also of importance in viewing the biographical material in the first four chapters.

THE EARLY LIFE OF MOSHE AND RELIGIOUS BIOGRAPHY

Dominating the early chapters of Exodus, more than the description of bondage itself, is the figure of the reluctant liberator, Moshe. The portrayal of his beginnings contrasts strongly with the classic hero stories of the ancient world.

This is not immediately apparent. Moshe's birth narrative parallels that of King Sargon of Akkad; his flight from Egypt and return as leader are reminiscent of Jephthah and David in the Bible, and of the Syrian king Idrimi (as recounted in Akkadian texts) as well. In addition, half a century ago Lord Raglan attempted to demonstrate common elements in hero biographies by compiling a list of up to thirty key motifs. Those relevant to Moshe include: the father a relative of the mother, an attempt made to kill him at birth, his escape through the action of others, being raised by foster parents, little information about his childhood, his traveling to his "future kingdom" upon reaching adulthood, promulgating laws, losing favor with the deity, dying on the top of a hill, not being succeeded by his children, and a hazy death/burial. Moshe therefore shares with Oedipus, Hercules, Siegfried, and Robin Hood, among others, a host of common elements; his point total according to Raglan's scheme puts him toward the top of the list as an archetypal traditional hero. It must be concluded that, far from being a factual account, his biography is composed largely of literary constructs.

When one looks closer at the biblical portrayal of Moshe, however, the purpose and particularly Israelite thrust of these constructs becomes clear. Almost every key element in Moshe's early life—e.g., rescue from death by royal decree, rescue from death by water, flight into the desert, meeting with God on the sacred mountain—foreshadows Israel's experience in the book of Exodus. The key theme of the distinction between Israel and Egypt, so central to the Plague Narrative and to Israelite religion as a whole, is brought out beautifully in the depiction of Moshe's development from Egyptian prince to would-be liberator to shepherd in the wilderness, the latter an ancestral calling (cf. Nohrnberg, who also discusses Yosef as developing in exactly the opposite direction—from Israelite shepherd boy to Egyptian viceroy, complete with Egyptian appearance, wife, and name). What is important in these early chapters of Exodus, then, is not the customary focus on the young hero's deeds (e.g., Hercules strangling serpents in the cradle) or his fatal flaw (although there is a hint of this too!), but on what he shares with his people, or, more precisely, how he prefigures them.

Another aspect of these stories removes them from the usual realm of heroic biography. Elsewhere in the Bible, individual hero types are at least partially overshadowed by the true central "character": God. This appears to be true in Exodus as well. Moshe develops only so far; he recedes as a full-blown personality during the Plague Narrative, to emerge sporadically in later encounters with the people (e.g., Chaps. 16 and 32–33; the portrait expands in the narratives of the book of Numbers). No wonder that later Jewish legend (and further, Christian and Muslim stories as well) found it necessary to fill in the tantalizing hints left by the biblical biographer, with sometimes fantastic tales. But in the Exodus text, it is God who holds sway. In this context, one is reminded that Israelite thinking had room neither for worship of human heroes nor interest in the biography of God (i.e., divine birth and marriage) on the model of surrounding cultures. The biblical portrayal of both God and Moshe has been reduced in our book to only such facts as will illuminate the relationship between Israel and its God. Thus we learn from the Moshe of Exodus much about the people themselves, and about prophecy (cf. Chaps. 3–4); from the God of Exodus, how he acts in history and what he demands of the people. More than that is not easily forthcoming from our text (interestingly, the Passover Haggadah picked up on the Bible's direction and all but omitted Moshe's name in the celebration of the holiday).

As we have suggested, later Jewish legend—some of which may actually be of great antiquity—sought to fill in various aspects of Moshe's life that are missing from the Exodus text. A perusal of Ginzberg will uncover rich legendary material, dealing with Moshe's childhood, family identity, experience in Midyan and elsewhere as a hero. While this material does not always illuminate the biblical story, it does demonstrate how folk belief includes a need for heroes in the classic Raglan mold; the Midrashic portrait of Moshe corresponds nicely to what we find in other cultures.

Turning to stylistic characteristics of these early chapters, we may note that a good deal of repetition occurs, as if further to highlight the themes. Baby Moshe is saved from death twice; three times he attempts acts of opposing oppression; twice (Chaps. 2 and 5) he fails in his attempts to help his enslaved brothers; and twice (Chaps. 3 and 6) God reassures him with long speeches that center around the Divine Name. This kind of continuity is artfully literary, but it is also an echo of real life, where people often live out certain themes in patterns.

Finally there is the matter of recurring words. Most important is the telling use of "see," from the loving gaze of Moshe's mother (2:2), through to the auspicious glance of Pharaoh's daughter (2:6), then to Moshe's sympathetic observing of his brothers' plight (2:11); all this seems to be linked to the episode at the Burning Bush, where God "is seen" by the future leader (3:2), and where the climax of this whole development takes place: God affirms that he has "seen, yes, seen the affliction of my people that is in Egypt. . . . and I have also seen the oppression with which the Egyptians oppress them" (3:7, 9). Thus Moshe's biography leads to, and is an outgrowth of, the people's own situation.

In sum, Moshe's early biography leads us to ponder the "growing up" process through which the people of Israel must pass on their way out of Egypt. The narratives that deal with his leadership of the people in the wilderness period, from Ex. 16 on, will help to round out our picture of him as a real personality, with the tragedies and triumphs that are a part of human life but magnified in the case of great individuals.

ON THE JOURNEY MOTIF

World literature is dominated by stories involving a journey. More often than not, these tales are framed as quests for holy or magical objects (e.g., the Holy Grail), or for eternal youth/immortality (Gilgamesh). The classic pattern, as Joseph Campbell has described it, calls for the hero to make a kind of round trip, crossing dangerous thresholds (monsters, giants, unfriendly supernatural beings) both on the way toward the goal and on the way home. Either at the middle or at the end of the journey stands the goal, which often entails meeting with the divine and/or obtaining a magical or life-giving object (e.g., the Golden Fleece).

Such stories mirror our own longings for accomplishment and acceptance, as well as our universal desire to overcome the ultimate enemy, Death. In the hero's triumphs, we triumph; his vanquishing of death cathartically becomes our own.

This mythic substructure has penetrated the biblical tales, but it has been toned down for human protagonists, to suppress the idea of the mortal hero in favor of the divine one. Thus all the Patriarchs except Yitzhak (Isaac) go on fateful long journeys (his is reserved for the three-day trip to Moriah in Gen. 22), yet there is none of the color and adventure that we find, for example, in Greek mythology. Outside of Yaakov's encounter with the mysterious wrestler in Gen. 32, there is little in Genesis to suggest hero tales on the classic mold. In Exodus, too, Moshe makes a significant journey—to Midyan—one might say, within himself, to find his true identity and calling, but it is highly muted, containing virtually no details. The round trip contains two thresholds of death, with Moshe first threatened by Pharaoh's justice (2:15) and, on the way back to Egypt, by God himself (4:24–26). The initial goal is attained at the "mountain of God" "behind the wilderness," where, meeting with divinity amid fire, he is finally able to integrate his own past, present, and future (as he will return to this mountain with the entire people in Chaps. 19ff). At the Burning Bush, the Egyptian prince, the Israelite shepherd, and the Hebrew liberator coalesce, investing Moshe with unique qualifications for his task.

But it is to a larger journey framework that we must look to understand the "hero" content of Exodus, and with it, that of the Torah as a whole. The major journey undertaken is, of course, that of the people of Israel, from slavery to

Promised Land. It is also a journey from death to life, from servitude to god-king to the service of God as king; along the way, death serves to purify an entire generation. And yet even this most obvious of journey stories differs markedly from those of gods and heroes so familiar in Western culture. The people of Israel function as a collective antihero, an example of precisely how *not* to behave. They play no active role whatsoever in their own liberation, use neither brawn nor wits to survive in the wilderness, constantly grumble about wanting to return to Egypt, and at both Sinai and the threshold of the Promised Land (in the book of Numbers), their chief form of behavior is first fear and later rebellion.

Moshe's own journeys parallel those of the entire people later on. Like them, he flees from Pharaoh into the wilderness, meets God at flaming Sinai, and has trouble accepting his task but must in the end. Here is where Moshe shines as the true leader: he epitomizes his people's experience and focuses and forges it into something new.

MOSHE BEFORE PHARAOH: THE PLAGUE NARRATIVE (5–11)

The heart of the Exodus story sets out the confrontation between the visible god-king, Pharaoh, who embodies the monumental culture of Egypt, and the invisible God of Israel who fights for his ragtag people. The drama is conveyed by means of alternating conversations/confrontations and events. The narrator has built his account, bracketed by the early approach of Moshe and Aharon (Aaron) to Pharaoh, which fails (Chap. 5), and the extended construct of the Tenth Plague (11–13); in between fall the schematically arranged first nine plagues.

Three overall stages characterize this latter section. The first is indicated by the oft-repeated demand, "Send free my people, that they may serve me!"; the second is the "hardening" of Pharaoh's heart; and the third, the unleashing of each plague. Further, it can be shown that the plagues are presented via a variety of structures and substructures (see Greenberg 1969 and the chart in Sarna 1986). Some commentators divide them into five thematic groups of two apiece—1 and 2, the Nile; 3 and 4, insects; 5 and 6, disease; 7 and 8, airborne disaster; and 9 and 10, darkness/death (Plaut). Also fruitful is the following threefold division: 1, 4, and 7, God's command to confront Pharaoh in the morning; 2, 5, and 8, God says, "Come to Pharaoh"; 3, 6, and 9, no warning is given to Pharaoh. Yet another grouping of themes is possible (Bar Efrat): 1–3, God vs. the magicians of Egypt; 4–6, stress on the distinction between Israel and Egypt; 7–9, the most powerful plagues.

This utilization of order, symbolized by "perfect" numbers such as 3 and 10, finds a parallel in the creation story of Genesis 1 (where the key number, of course, is 7, 3 + 3 + 1, whereas here we have 3 + 3 + 3 + 1). Both texts display a desire to depict God as one who endows nature and history with meaning. The poetic tradition about the plagues, as represented, for instance, by Psalm 78, was content to describe the plagues in brief, within the setting of a single poem. The narrator of the Pentateuchal traditions, however, has a different point to make, and structured exposition is the best way to do it.

There is another structural tendency that one may observe in the Plague Narrative. Repeating words and motifs comprise over twenty shared and discrete elements in the story. Since the vast majority of these occur by the end of the fourth plague, this leaves the narrator free to develop plagues 7 and 8 with particular intensity, using a full palette of descriptions, with the addition of the theme that these were the worst of their kind ever to take place in Egypt. It will be useful here to list a few of the key words and phrases, and motifs, that can be found in the Plague Narrative:

Words/phrases: Go to Pharaoh; send . . . free; know; throughout the land of Egypt; plead; distinguish; tomorrow; man and beast; not one remained; heavy [i.e., severe] as YHWH had said.

Motifs: Moshe's staff; Aharon as agent; magicians; death.

It is important to note here that the structuring of the plagues is not a perfectly balanced one. The narrative varies between exact repetition of elements and phrases and nonrepetition (Licht). By thus using sounds and ideas in variation, the narrator is able to weave a tale whose message constantly reinforces itself, and which holds the audience's attention without getting tedious.

I have deliberately omitted the question of Pharaoh's heart above, as a separate issue. A host of expressions is used in the text to describe Pharaoh's stubbornness: "harden" (Heb. *hiksha*), "make heavy-with-stubbornness" (*hakhbed*), and "strengthen" (*hehezik/hazzek*), with the resultant "refused" and "did not hearken." This motif is the only one that occurs in all nine plagues, and therefore stands at the very heart of our narrative. When one notes the pattern within— that Pharaoh does the hardening at the beginning, God at the end—the intent begins to become clear. The Plague Narrative is a recounting of God's power, and Pharaoh's stubbornness, which starts out as a matter of will, eventually becomes impossible to revoke. The model is psychologically compelling: Pharaoh becomes trapped by his own refusal to accept the obvious (in biblical parlance, to "know"). Despite the prophetic idea that human beings can be forgiven, we find here another one—that evil leads to more evil, and can become petrified and unmovable.

A final note about the backdrop of these stories. Cecil B. DeMille did it differently, and in the difference lies the gap between Western culture and biblical culture. In the movie *The Ten Commandments* (a strange title, given the actual content of the film!), DeMille's own 1956 remake of his earlier silent film, great stress is put on the physical, visual trappings of Pharoah's court. Apparently no expense was spared to bring in costumes, sets, and extras, and the result causes the audience to focus on the splendor of Egyptian culture, despite the fact that it is peopled by the villains of the story. In contrast, the Bible says practically nothing about the visual backdrop of the Plague Narrative. Just as Genesis made reference to the mighty culture of Babylonia by parodying it (for instance, in the

Babel story of Chap. 11), Exodus strips down Egyptian culture by making it disappear, and by ridiculing its gods. The book saves descriptive minutiae for the Tabernacle (Chaps. 25ff.), preferring to stress the positive and simply to omit what it found as negative. This profoundly "anticultural" stance (see the intriguing analysis by Schneidau) was characteristic of Israel's worldview and was a mystery to the Greeks and Romans who centuries later conquered the land; it was to stand the people of Israel in good stead in their wanderings through the centuries.

Prologue in Egypt (1): Rather than being presented as a totally separate story, the book of Exodus opens as a continuation of the Genesis saga. This is true both specifically and generally: the first five verses echo and compress the information about the descent of Yaakov's family into Egypt that was given in Gen. 46:8–27, while "Now these are the names" (v.1) recalls the oft-repeated formula "Now these are the begettings," which forms the structural background of Genesis. At the same time one might note that the main subject matter of our chapter, life and death (or, threatened continuity), is central to the thematic content of Genesis (see my *At the Beginning*, "On the Book of Genesis and Its Structure").

Kikawada and Ackerman (1974) have shown that the opening chapters of Exodus reflect other Genesis material as well. For instance, the five verbs in v.7 mirror the language of creation (Gen. 1:28 and 9:1–2), where a similar vocabulary of fecundity signals the divine desire to "fill the earth." It is as if Israel's "becoming many" in Exodus fulfills the plan of history inaugurated at creation, at the same time reminding us of God's promise to Avraham, to make his descendants as numerous "as the stars in the heavens and [as] the sand that is on the shore of the sea" (Gen. 22:17).

This leads to the predominant issue of Chap. 1: Pharaoh's paranoid fears about Israel's growth. What for God was a sign of blessing (cf. the "swarming" of creatures in Gen. 1:20f.) is for Pharaoh a sign of disaster, a feeling of being overwhelmed by what is alien. The birth of the Israelite nation is thus placed in a vivid context, completely physical in its description. And because birth, and not the economic aspects of slavery, is central, the actual description of the oppression of the Hebrews has been reduced to a bare minimum here. Contrary to DeMille's spectacular and stereotyped portrayal of the Israelites' sufferings, the Bible limits itself to a few brief verses in the early chapters of the book. The same holds true for parallel depictions of bondage in biblical literature, such as Psalms 78 and 105. It is the experience of being a stranger in Egypt that the Bible has chosen to focus on, rather than on the horrors of slave labor.

In Exodus, the Egyptians cannot stand having aliens among them (this theme has already appeared in Genesis regarding their eating habits—see Gen. 43:32); they dread their presence and fear their increase. A natural plan of attack, to stem the human tide, is genocide. Ironically, because of his fear of war Pharaoh concentrates his worries around the males, ignoring the true source of fecundity. And it is the women in these chapters, as many commentators have pointed out (see Exum), who play the major role in beginning the liberation process. The midwives accomplish a successful coverup; Moshe's mother and sister, and Pharaoh's daughter, save the future liberator's life. "If she be a daughter, she may live" (v.16), along with four other occurrences of "live" in vv.17–22, underscore the irony and the certainty of Israelite survival. The use of women—a group that was often powerless in ancient societies—in these stories makes the eventual vic-

1:1 Now these are the names of the children of Israel coming to
     Egypt,
     with Yaakov, each-man and his household they came:
2 Re'uven, Shim'on, Levi and Yehuda,
3 Yissakhar, Zevulun and Binyamin,
4 Dan and Naftali, Gad and Asher.
5 So all the persons, those issuing from Yaakov's loins, were seventy
     persons,
     —Yosef was (already) in Egypt.

6 Now Yosef died, and all his brothers, and all that generation.
7 Yet the Children of Israel bore fruit, they swarmed, they became
     many, they grew mighty (in number)—exceedingly, yes,
     exceedingly;
     the land filled up with them.

8 Now a new king arose over Egypt, who had not known Yosef.
9 He said to his people:
     Here, (this) people, the Children of Israel, is many-more and
     mightier (in number) than we!

1:1 **children of Israel:** Or "sons," though it should be
noted that the Hebrew *b'nei* can denote members of
a group in general, not just family. In this verse,
"children" has been printed with a lowercase "c";
v.7 the whole expression comes to mean a nation,
and so a capital "C" has been utilized (Hebrew writing does not make this distinction). **Yaakov:** Trad.
English "Jacob."

2–4 **Re'uven, Shim'on, Levi, Yehuda, Yissakhar, Zevulun, Binyamin, Dan, Naftali, Gad, Asher:** Trad.
English "Reuben, Simeon, Levi, Judah, Issachar, Zebulun, Benjamin, Dan, Naphtali, Gad, Asher."

5 **issuing:** The same Hebrew verb (*yatzo'*) is later
used to describe the Israelites' "going out" of Egypt
(e.g., 12:31, 41). **loins:** A figurative expression denoting the genitals. **seventy:** A number expressing perfection or wholeness in the thought of many
ancient cultures; see Gen. 46:8–27 for the original
passage.

6 **Now Yosef died . . . :** Note the rhythmic lilt of this
verse; such devices are often used in biblical style
when a key event is portrayed. **Yosef:** Trad. English
"Joseph."

7 **Yet:** Despite the disappearance of the politically in-
fluential generation of Yosef, the Israelites' success
continues (Cassuto). **swarmed:** This verb is usually
applied to animals (see Gen. 1:20) (Greenberg 1969).
Here the term is positive, as part of God's plan;
shortly, it will carry a negative connotation for
Pharaoh. **grew mighty (in number):** This reflects
the promise of God to Avraham in Gen. 18:18 (to become "a mighty nation") (Keil and Delitzsch).

8 **a new king:** His name is not given, even though
later biblical books do refer to foreign rulers by
name. This is perhaps another example of the biblical text's playing down history in favor of stressing
the story and its lesson. **who had not known
Yosef:** Just as his successor will say "I do not know
YHWH" (5:2), and will continue the oppression
begun here.

9 **his people . . . (this) people:** Pharaoh states the
case as the conflict between one national entity and
another.

tory of the Israelites all the more striking from a traditional patriarchal point of view (see Ackerman 1982); the motif returns a number of times in Israelite literature, as with Jael and Judith.

Failing in his commissioning of special agents (midwives) to carry out his genocidal plan, Pharaoh finally must enlist "all his people" (v.22), and shift the scene to a cosmic setting, the Nile. The stage is thus set for the birth, endangering, and rescue of Moshe.

The historically minded reader may ask: Why would the ruler of a society that is (literally) built on slavery destroy his own workforce? Two answers are possible. First, the story is tied to Chap. 2, the survival of Moshe, and thus must be told to that end (a threat to males). Second, the story does not describe a rational fear, but paranoia—paralleling the situation in Nazi Germany of the 1930s and 1940s, where Jews were blamed for various economic and political catastrophes not of their own making and were eliminated from a society that could have used their resources and manpower.

◆ 10   Come-now, let us use-our-wits against it,
lest it become many-more,
and then, if war should occur,
it too be added to our enemies
and make war upon us
or go up away from the land!

11   So they set gang-captains over it, to afflict it with their burdens.
It built storage-cities for Pharaoh—Pitom and Ra'amses.

12   But as they afflicted it, so did it become many, so did it burst
forth.
And they felt dread before the Children of Israel.

13   So they, Egypt, made the Children of Israel subservient with
crushing-labor;

14   they embittered their lives with hard servitude in loam and
in bricks and with all kinds of servitude in the field—
all their service in which they made them subservient with
crushing-labor.

15   Now the king of Egypt said to the midwives of the Hebrews
—the name of the first one was Shifra, the name of the
second was Pu'a—

---

10 **use-our-wits:** Others, "We must be prudent," "Let us deal shrewdly." **it:** The shift from plural to singular to refer to a plural object is not unusual in biblical parlance. **added:** Heb. *nosaf*, like Yosef (Joseph), whose name is interpreted as "May God add . . . another son" at his birth in Gen. 30:24. **go up away:** Heb. unclear.

11 **afflict:** Or "oppress." **Pharaoh:** Heb. *Par'o*. This is an Egyptian title, "(Lord of) the Great House," and not a proper name. One could justifiably translate, as some do, *"the* Pharaoh."

12 **so . . . so:** Heb. *ken . . . ken*. Ackerman (1974) interprets this as a rhyming retort to Pharaoh's earlier *pen* ("*lest* he become many more") in 1:10. **burst forth:** The verb (Heb. *parotz*) is connected to fertility and wealth in Genesis (e.g., 28:14).

13 **crushing-labor:** A rare Hebrew word, here translated according to early rabbinic tradition, *perekh* is used rhetorically three times in Lev. 25 (vv. 43, 46, and 53), where the Israelites are given laws about how to deal with their impoverished countrymen (v.43, "you are not to oppress him with crushing-labor").

14 **in the field:** In Egyptian accounts, the phrase indicates hard labor. **all their service . . . :** The Hebrew syntax is difficult. Here the phrase is taken as the object of "they embittered."

15 **midwives of the Hebrews:** The ambiguity of this phrase raises an ancient question: were they Hebrew or Egyptian? The names seem Semitic (and hence un-Egyptian); then, too, the use of "Hebrew" in the Bible usually occurs when a foreigner is talking about Israelites. Yet the women's answer in v.19 suggests that they are in fact Egyptians. Abravanel notes that Hebrew women would not be likely to kill Hebrew babies.

Moshe's Birth and Early Life (2:1–22): Picking up from the last phrase of Chap. 1, "let every daughter live," Chap. 2 opens as a story of three daughters (the word occurs six times here), Moshe's real and foster mothers, and his sister.

It has long been maintained that the story of Moshe's birth is a classic "birth of the hero" tale, sharing many features with other heroes of antiquity. (See p. 298.) The parallel most often drawn is that of Sargon of Akkad, whose birth story is set in an era before Moshe but was written down later; similar elements include being separated from the real parents through a death threat, and being set adrift on the river. Hallo cites other parallels in Hittite and Egyptian literature, noting at the same time that "none of them includes all of the elements of the Moses birth legend."

If, as I maintained in the introduction ("On the Book of Exodus and Its Structure"), most of this material has been collected for didactic and not for historical purposes, we are entitled to ask what this story was intended to teach. It cannot simply be written off as an attempt to explain away Moshe's name and origins. Two elements seem crucial. First, the text as we have it centers around the activity of women—giving birth, hiding, watching and adopting Moshe. The female principle of life-giving triumphs over the male prerogatives of threatening and death-dealing; the Nile, source of all life in Egypt, births another child. Second, the story and its continuation to the end of the chapter set up Moshe as a man of two sides: Hebrew and Egyptian. He is at once archetypal victim (of Pharaoh's death decree) and archetypal collaborator, growing up, as he apparently does, in Pharaoh's palace. What are we to make of this two-sided fate and personality? It may well have been intended as a reflex of the people of Israel itself. Often in the Hebrew Bible the hero's life mirrors that of Israel (see Greenstein 1981), and the case of Moshe is a good example. Moshe develops into a Hebrew—that is, he eventually recovers his full identity. This is accomplished, first, through his empathy with and actions on behalf of "his brothers" (vv.11, 12), then through his exile from Egypt, and finally through the purifying life in the wilderness as a shepherd. Thus Moshe's personality changes are wrought by means of separations, and the same process will characterize the coming Plague Narrative (with its emphasis on "distinction" between Egypt and Israel) and the entire Israelite legal and ritual system, which stresses holiness and separation.

The first section of the chapter (vv.1–10) uses a number of repeating words: "take" appears four times, indicative of divine protection; "child," seven times (Greenberg 1969); and "see," which as I have mentioned, will recur meaningfully in Chap. 3. There is also a threefold motif of death threat in the chapter: at birth, on the Nile, and at the hand of the avenging Pharaoh. Isbell notes several items of vocabulary (e.g., "deliver," "feared," "amid the reeds") that return in the victory account at the Sea of Reeds (Chap. 14).

From the other two accounts here (vv.11–14 and 15–22), we learn all we need to

16 he said:
When you help the Hebrew women give birth, see the
supporting-stones:
if he be a son, put him to death,
but if she be a daughter, she may live.

17 But the midwives held God in awe,
and they did not do as the king of Egypt had spoken to them,
they let the (male) children live.

18 The king of Egypt called for the midwives and said to them:
Why have you done this thing, you have let the children live!

19 The midwives said to Pharaoh:
Indeed, not like the Egyptian (women) are the Hebrew (women),
indeed, they are lively:
before the midwife comes to them, they have given birth!

20 God dealt well with the midwives.
And the people became many and grew exceedingly mighty (in
number).

21 It was, since the midwives held God in awe, that he made them
households.

22 Now Pharaoh commanded all his people, saying:
Every son that is born, throw him into the Nile,
but let every daughter live.

2:1 Now a man from the house of Levi went and took (to wife) a
daughter of Levi.

---

16 **supporting-stones:** Some suggest that these were stools or other objects on which to support women in labor, while others see them as a reference to the testicles of the newborn males.

17 **held . . . in awe:** Trad. "feared." This may be a sound-play on "see" in v.16: *va-yire'u* (held in awe) resembles *va-yir'u* ("saw").

19 **lively:** Another form of the Hebrew would mean "animals," and so B-R combined the two ideas in rendering the word as "lively-like-animals."

20-21 **And the people . . . :** The order here seems confused. "And the people . . ." is perhaps out of place, although the thought is not inappropriate for the context.

22 **all his people:** Specialists (the midwives) are not equal to the task of checking the Israelite population explosion, and so the whole Egyptian population must now be enlisted. **Nile:** Heb. *ye'or*, Egyptian *itrw:*, "the great river" (cf. Heb. *ha-nahar ha-gadol*, with the same meaning, used for the Euphrates in Gen. 15:18 etc.).

2:1 **a man . . . a daughter:** Moshe's parents are anonymous, unlike the usual king and queen of the hero myth found in other cultures. The namelessness of all the secondary characters in this chapter—sister, Pharaoh's daughter and her maids—helps us to focus on the protagonist and on his name.

know about Moshe's early personality: he is Hebrew-identifying but Egyptian-looking; concerned with justice, but impetuous and violent in pursuit of that goal. It is also ominous that his first contacts with the Israelites end in rejection, since that will so often be his experience with them later on. The doubly unsatisfactory situation of confused identity and impetuous means must be rectified, and it is exile that accomplishes it. The Midyanite wilderness transforms Moshe into shepherd, foreigner, father, and seer—in short, into a son of the Patriarchs (see also "On the Journey Motif," above).

Incredibly, the man whose activity is to span four whole books has, it seems, half his life (or, according to the chronology of 7:7, two-thirds of his life!) described in a single chapter. Typical of biblical storytelling, much has been compressed and left out, but enough is told to establish the person who is to come.

2   The woman became pregnant and bore a son.
    When she saw him—that he was goodly, she hid him, for three
        months.
3   And when she was no longer able to hide him,
    she took for him a little-ark of papyrus,
    she loamed it with loam and with pitch,
    placed the child in it,
    and placed it in the reeds by the shore of the Nile.
4   Now his sister stationed herself far off, to know what would be
        done to him.

5   Now Pharaoh's daughter went down to bathe at the Nile,
    and her girls were walking along the Nile.
    She saw the little-ark among the reeds
    and sent her maid, and she fetched it.
6   She opened (it) and saw him, the child—
    here, a boy weeping!
    She pitied him, and she said:
    One of the Hebrews' children is this!
7   Now his sister said to Pharaoh's daughter:
    Shall I go and call a nursing woman from the Hebrews for you,
    that she may nurse the child for you?

2 **she saw him—that he was goodly:** The parallel in Genesis is "God saw the light: that it was good" (Gen. 1:4). **goodly:** Handsome (so Ibn Ezra, among others), although others interpret the Hebrew *tov* as "healthy," given the context. What is important is the Genesis connection just mentioned. **three months:** Another "perfect" number, which will recur with the Israelites' three-month trip to Mount Sinai (see 19:1).

3 **little-ark:** The term used to designate the little basket/boat, *teiva*, has clearly been chosen to reflect back to Noah's ark in Genesis. The implication is that just as God saved Noah and thus humanity from destruction by water, so will he now save Moshe and the Israelites from the same. **papyrus:** A material that floats; it was also used in biblical times for writing, including biblical texts. **in the reeds:** Another foreshadowing; when Moshe grows up, he will lead the liberated people through the Sea of Reeds. The word *suf* (reeds) appears to be a loan-word from Egyptian.

4 **to know:** Better English would be "to learn." This first occurrence of the Hebrew word *yado'a* fore-shadows the later theme of the Egyptians' and the Israelites' coming to "know" (or "acknowledge") God's power. For the moment, and in the story that follows, the issue is one of revealing information—Moshe's fate (2:4) and the discovery of his crime (2:14).

5 **Pharaoh's daughter:** Her station is important, for it enables Moshe to be saved and to be brought up in the Egyptian palace (useful both for his political future and for literary irony of situation). **girls:** Maid-servants.

6 **She opened . . . boy weeping!:** The emphatic, halt-ing syntax of the narrative brings out the visual drama of seeing, taking, opening, and identifying. **One of the Hebrews' children:** How does she know that? The simplest explanation lies in the situation itself and not in any identifying marks. Who else but a Hebrew, under the threat of losing her baby, would set such a child adrift? **is this:** Or "must this be."

8   Pharaoh's daughter said to her:
    Go!
    The maiden went and called the child's mother.
9   Pharaoh's daughter said to her:
    Have this child go with you and nurse him for me,
    and I myself will give you your wages.
    So the woman took the child and she nursed him.
10 The child grew, she brought him to Pharaoh's daughter,
    and he became her son.
    She called his name: Moshe/He-Who-Pulls-Out;
    she said: For out of the water *meshitihu*/I-pulled-him.

11 Now it was some years later, Moshe grew up;
    he went out to his brothers and saw their burdens.
    He saw an Egyptian man striking a Hebrew man, (one) of his
        brothers.
12 He turned this-way and that-way, and seeing that there was no
        man (there),
    he struck down the Egyptian
    and buried him in the sand.

---

8 **Go:** In biblical Hebrew, a verb repeated from a question is the equivalent of "Yes," for which there was no other expression.

10 **grew:** His age is not mentioned, but weaning may be inferred (cf. Gen. 21:8) as the appropriate boundary, and hence the child was probably around three (DeVaux 1965). **he became her son:** A formulaic expression for legal adoption. **Moshe/He-Who-Pulls-Out:** Trad. English "Moses." *Mss* is a well-attested name in ancient Egypt, meaning "son of" (as in Ra'amses—"son of Ra"—in Ex. 1:11). Thus it is quite appropriate that Pharaoh's daughter names her adopted son in this manner. However, there is an explicit irony here, as Buber (1988) and others have pointed out. The princess, in a Hebrew folk etymology (one based on sound rather than on the scientific derivation of words), thinks that the name Moshe recalls her act of "pulling out" the baby from the Nile. But the verb form in *moshe* is active, not passive, and thus it is Moshe himself who will one day "pull out" Israel from the life-threatening waters of both slavery and the Sea of Reeds.

11 **some years later:** Heb. *yamim*, lit. "days," can mean longer periods of time, and often years. Here the narrative skips over what it considers unimportant, and we are presented with a young man, who already has strong identity and opinions. **his brothers:** Occurring twice in this verse, this phrase can only mean that Moshe was aware of his background, and concerned with the plight of the Israelites (Heb. *r'h b-*, "see" with a specific preposition, indicates not only observation but sympathy).

12 **no man (there):** Although some have interpreted this as "no man around to help," the expression taken in context would seem to indicate that Moshe was afraid of being seen. This incident reveals Moshe's concern and early leanings toward being a liberator, but also demonstrates his youthful lack of forethought. In fact, it will take God, not Moshe's own actions, to set the liberation process in motion. **struck down:** This is the same verb (Heb. *hakkeh*) that the narrator used in v.11 to describe the fatal beating received by the Israelite slave.

13 He went out again on the next day, and here: two Hebrew men
    scuffling!
    He said to the guilty-one:
    For-what-reason do you strike your fellow?

14 He said:
    Who made you prince and judge over us?
    Do you mean to kill me
    as you killed the Egyptian?
    Moshe became afraid and said:
    Surely the matter is known!

15 Pharaoh heard of this matter and sought to kill Moshe.
    But Moshe fled from Pharaoh's face and settled in the land of
    Midyan;
    he sat down by a well.

16 Now the priest of Midyan had seven daughters;
    they came, they drew (water) and they filled the troughs,
    to give-drink to their father's sheep.

17 Shepherds came and drove them away.
    But Moshe rose up, he delivered them and gave-drink to their
    sheep.

18 When they came (home) to Re'uel their father, he said:
    Why have you come (home) so quickly today?

19 They said:
    An Egyptian man rescued us from the hand of the shepherds,

---

13 **Hebrew men scuffling:** A rhyme in Hebrew, *anashim 'ivriyyim nitzim.*

14 **Who made you prince . . . :** One hears here echoes of Moshe's later experiences with his "hard-necked" people, which commence in the book of Exodus (Greenberg 1969). **judge:** Or "ruler." I have retained "judge" here in order not to lose the connection with 5:21.

15 **Moshe fled . . . and settled:** The details about what must have been a psychologically important journey are not spelled out, as the narrative rushes toward its first great climax in Chap. 3. More important than the journey motif is that of exile, brought out tellingly in v.22. **settled . . . sat:** Adding the "settle down" of v.21, we hear a threefold use of *yashov,* perhaps to stress Moshe's new life.

16 **priest of Midyan:** This title has spawned extensive theorizing about the origins of Mosaic religion (sometimes called the "Kenite Hypothesis" after the Kenites, a tribe of smiths connected to Moshe's father-in-law and spoken of favorably at a number of points in the Bible). It has been suggested that Moshe learned the rudiments of his religious or legal system from this source. We do not have enough evidence to make a positive judgment on this theory; biographically, it does make sense for Moshe to marry into a holy family of some sort. **seven daughters:** The requisite "magic" number, as in a good folk tale.

19 **An Egyptian man:** Moshe would have been recognizable as such from his manner of dress and lack of facial hair. In addition, he is not yet fully an Israelite, spiritually speaking.

God Takes Notice (2:23–25): Chap. 2 ends on a note that looks forward and backward simultaneously. The fourfold "God" plus verb (vv.24–25) echo the same structure at Creation's first day (Gen. 1:3–5), and suggest that he puts his concern for the people of Israel on a par with his concern for creation of light (connoting "good" in folklore). In addition, the four verbs used here play a prominent role in the entire Deliverance Narrative, as Isbell has shown.

and also he drew, yes, drew for us and watered the sheep!

20 He said to his daughters:
So-where-is-he?
For-what-reason then have you left the man behind?
Call him, that he may eat bread (with us)!

21 Moshe agreed to settle down with the man,
and he gave Tzippora his daughter to Moshe.

22 She gave birth to a son,
and he called his name: Gershom/Sojourner There,
for he said: A sojourner have I become in a foreign land.

23 It was, many years later,
the king of Egypt died.
The Children of Israel groaned from the servitude,
and they cried out;
and their plea-for-help went up to God, from the servitude.

24 God hearkened to their moaning,
God called-to-mind his covenant with Avraham, with Yitzhak,
and with Yaakov,

25 God saw the Children of Israel,
God knew.

---

20 **So-where-is-he:** This is one word in the Hebrew *(ve-ayyo)*. The whole verse stands in ironic contrast to Moshe's earlier treatment (v. 14) at the hand of "his brothers" (Childs). There, he was rejected; here, his host cannot welcome him quickly enough. **For-what-reason:** Similarly this is one Hebrew word *(lamma)*. **bread:** As often in both the Bible and other cultures, "bread" is here synonymous with "food."

21 **Tzippora:** Trad. English "Zipporah." The name means "bird"; such animal names are still popular among Bedouin.

22 **Gershom/Sojourner There:** Related to the Hebrew *ger*, "sojourner" or resident alien. The name more accurately reflects the sound of the verb *garesh*, "drive out" (so Abravanel), which plays its role in the Exodus stories (and in Moshe's recent experience in the narrative). As my student Nancy Ginsberg once pointed out, this naming of sons to express the feelings about exile has already occurred in a more personally positive context—with Yosef

(see Gen. 41:50–52). **A sojourner . . . in a foreign land:** The King James Version phrase, "a stranger in a strange land," is stunning, but the Hebrew uses two different roots *(gur* and *nakhor)*.

23 **the king of Egypt died./ The Children of Israel groaned:** The change in regime does not prove beneficial to the suffering slaves, but makes it possible for Moshe to return to Egypt, thus impelling the narrative along and reestablishing the link between Moshe and his people. **cried out:** The same verb (Heb. *tza'ok*) is used to describe the "hue and cry" of Sodom and Gomorra (Gen. 18:20; see also the note to 22:22, below).

23–24 **groaned . . . cried out . . . plea-for-help . . . moaning:** As in 1:7, four phrases describe the Israelites' actions. Note also the double use of "from the servitude."

24 **Avraham, Yitzhak, Yaakov:** Trad. English "Abraham, Isaac, Jacob."

25 **knew:** Others, "took notice," but *yado'a* needs to be noticed throughout the book as a key word.

At the Bush: The Call (3:1–4:17): The great revelation scene in these two chapters, so much a classic in the literature of the West, comes as somewhat of a surprise in the close context of our story. Nothing in Exodus so far has prepared us for such a religious, inward vision on the part of Moshe; and indeed, Genesis itself contains no meeting between God and a human being of such a dramatic character. Adam and Avraham converse with God; Yaakov experiences him, to be sure, in dreams and in the guise of a wrestler; but nowhere thus far does one find a biblical hero encountering God with such intensity and purity of vision.

The shepherd, now in the service of his father-in-law, the "priest," comes upon the "mountain of God," "behind the wilderness." The results are those of an unintended or half-intended journey. Moshe, who had fled previously, finds himself at the utmost reaches of the wilderness, almost like Jonah in the bowels of the boat or of the great fish. The sight that Moshe is granted is of unclear nature, but it involves fire, with all its pregnant associations: passion, purity, light, mystery (Greenberg 1969), and here, inextinguishability.

God's initial speech (vv.6–10) contains all the elements basic to the Deliverance Narrative: it identifies him as the ancestral deity, establishes his compassion for the oppressed people, demonstrates his resolve to rescue them, and ends with the commissioning of Moshe to be his emissary. Central here is the verb *see,* whose threefold occurrence (vv.7 and 9) ties together the threads of the previous parts of Moshe's story (see above).

The entire scene is the model for the "call" of the biblical prophet, with its emphasis on God's speaking to the fledgling prophet amid a vision and the motif of refusal; of the call scenes in the Bible, this is the longest and most memorable in its starkness. A man is called by God to return to society and serve as God's spokesperson—despite any opposition he may encounter and despite his personal shortcomings. Moshe's reluctance, indeed his almost obsessive need to turn down the commission, is as much indicative of the general nature of prophecy (cf. Elijah and Jeremiah) as it is of Moshe's own personality. The prophet must be prepared "to uproot and tear down, to destroy and overthrow, to build and plant" (Jer. 1:10), and to stand tall against kings if necessary (Jer. 1:13). So it comes as no surprise that the call is met with less than enthusiasm. And this refusal also teaches something about Israel's political conceptions. With such a response as this, there can be no question of personal ambition or inner lust for power. The prophet does what he does out of compulsion: he is driven by forces that he perceives as external to him.

In our text, Moshe refuses the commission five times, and five times God counters. In four of these cases the assurance is given that God will "be-there" with him (3:12, 14; 4:12, 15), and the use of that verb carries in its essence one of the most significant motifs of the Bush Narrative: the interpretation of God's name.

When Moshe asks God for his name in 3:13, he asks for more than a title

3:1 Now Moshe was shepherding the flock of Yitro his father- in-law,
        priest of Midyan.
     He led the flock behind the wilderness—
     and he came to the mountain of God, to Horev.
2   And Y H W H's messenger was seen by him
     in the flame of a fire out of the midst of a bush.
     He saw:
     here, the bush is burning with fire,
     and the bush is not consumed!
3   Moshe said:
     Now let me turn aside
     that I may see this great sight—
     why the bush does not burn up!
4   When Y H W H saw that he had turned aside to see,
     God called to him out of the midst of the bush,
     he said:
     Moshe! Moshe!
     He said:
     Here I am.

3:1 **Now Moshe was shepherding . . . :** The Hebrew syntax indicates the beginning of an entirely new story. **shepherding:** A symbol of great power in the ancient Near East; witness the enduring image of King David, sprung from shepherding roots, and of course that of Jesus. **Yitro:** Trad. English "Jethro." It is not clear why other names (Re'uel, Hovav) are also associated with him. The name, if Semitic, means "excellence." **behind:** Others, "to the west side of," "to the far side of," or simply "into," although the word seems to convey a certain mystery. Fairy tales often portray the hero's going deep into a forest and the like. **mountain of God:** Sinai is so designated only several times subsequently in the Pentateuch, suggesting perhaps biblical religion's reluctance to make of it a shrine of permanence. **Horev:** Another name for Sinai, principally used in Deuteronomy (but also twice more in Exodus, 17:6 and 33:6). A related Hebrew root, *harev,* means "dry."

2 **Y H W H's messenger:** Traditionally "angel," but the English word stems from the Greek *angelos,* which means "messenger." In Genesis, God appears in somewhat human guise (cf. Chap. 18), and "messenger" indicates an unspecified manifestation of God, open to wide interpretation. **in the flame:** Others, "as a flame." **bush:** Jewish tradition identifies it as a thornbush, but the precise plant remains unknown. The bush, called *s'neh* in Hebrew, perhaps has the added function here of providing assonance with *Sinai.* **the bush is burning . . . the bush is not consumed:** The use of tense (plus the opening "here") conveys the immediacy of the vision. **not consumed:** The symbolism of the imperishable bush is left open for the reader; commentators suggest variously Israel and God himself.

3 **let me turn aside:** Despite Moshe's apparent retirement from intervening on behalf of his brothers in Egypt, his reaction here seems active, not passive. He does not shirk from seeking out the strange sight.

4 **Moshe! Moshe!:** The name is repeated for emphasis, as in Gen. 22:11 **Here I am:** The classic response of biblical heroes; see Gen. 22:1, 11; I Sam. 3:4.

(Buber and Rosenzweig 1994). In the context of Egyptian magic, knowing the true name of a person or a god meant that one could coerce him, or at the very least understand his true essence. Moshe foresees that the slaves will want to be able to call on this power that has promised to deliver them.

God's answer is one of the most enigmatic and widely debated statements in the Hebrew Bible (the reader will want to consult Childs for a full bibliography). What does *ehyeh asher ehyeh* mean? One's suspicions are aroused from the outset, for the answer is alliterative and hence already not easy to pin down; the poetics of the phrase indicate both importance and vagueness or mystery. There is some scholarly consensus that the name may mean "He who causes (things) to be" or perhaps "He who is." Buber and Rosenzweig, taking an entirely different tack (of which one occasionally finds echoes in the scholarly literature), interpret the verb *hayoh* as signifying presence, "being-*there,*" and hence see God's words as a real answer to the Israelites' imagined question—an assurance of his presence. The B-R interpretation has been retained here, out of a desire to follow them on at least this significant point of theology, and out of my feeling that it also fits the smaller context. For of the several times that Moshe tries to wriggle out of his mission, God answers him all but once with the same verb, in the same meaning: "I will be-there with you" (note the parallel between Moshe and the people again).

It is, however, also possible that *ehyeh asher ehyeh* is a deliberately vague phrase, whose purpose is antimagical and an attempt to evade the question (Rosenzweig speaks of this as well), as if to suggest that possession of the true name cannot be used to coerce this God. In this interpretation, it would follow that, just as God is magicless (see v. 20), he is nameless, at least in the conventional sense of religion. On the other hand, the name YHWH, however it may have been vocalized throughout the history of the text, did function as a name in ancient Israel (and possibly outside of Israel as well). It was used in oaths (e.g., Gen. 22:16, II Sam. 12:5), and later, in the Second Temple period, limited in public pronunciation to the high priest on the Day of Atonement. As happens frequently in the history of religion, if we follow a concept long enough it transforms back to the beginning, often in an opposite meaning, and so when the use of YHWH is traced through the Middle Ages one finds it turned into a magical name at the hands of Jewish mystics.

To return to the Bush Narrative as a whole: these chapters introduce a number of important words that will recur throughout the enire Liberation Narrative. These include "trust," "hearken to (my) voice," "staff," "heavy," "go out," "strong," "send," and "blood" (see Isbell). It should also be mentioned that several key words occur in multiples of 7 from 2:23 to 4:31 (Cassuto): "see" (7), "send" (7), "go" (14), "mouth" (7), "speak/word" (Heb. *dabber/davar;* 7). This vocabulary in particular focuses the story around major aspects of prophecy.

5   He said:
    Do not come near to here,
    put off your sandal from your foot,
    for the place on which you stand—it is holy ground!

6   And he said:
    I am the God of your father,
    the God of Avraham,
    the God of Yitzhak,
    and the God of Yaakov.
    Moshe concealed his face,
    for he was afraid to gaze upon God.

7   Now YHWH said:
    I have seen, yes, seen the affliction of my people that is in Egypt,
    their cry I have heard in the face of their slave-drivers;
    indeed, I have known their sufferings!

8   So I have come down
    to rescue it from the hand of Egypt,
    to bring it up from that land
    to a land, goodly and spacious,
    to a land flowing with milk and honey,
    to the place of the Canaanite and the Hittite,
    of the Amorite and the Perizzite,
    of the Hivvite and the Yevusite.

9   So now,
    here, the cry of the Children of Israel has come to me,

---

5   **put off your sandal from your foot:** A common form of respect in the ancient East, still practiced by Muslims in worship.

6   **the God of your father:** Hearkening back to the personal and family relationships with God in Genesis (see, for instance, Gen. 26:24, 31:42, 32:10). **Avraham . . . :** The text stresses the Patriarchs, reminding both Moshe and the reader of the promises made to them in Genesis.

7   **I have seen . . . heard . . . known:** Echoing the narrative above, 2:24–25. **the affliction of my people:** Heb. *'oni 'ammi.* **my people:** This fateful designation signals the beginning of the liberation process. The Golden Calf story (Chaps. 32ff.) provides a tragic variation on this phrase.

8   **I have come down:** The phrase indicates God's intervention in human affairs (as, negatively, in Gen. 11:7). **a land flowing with milk and honey:** Or with "goats' milk and date-syrup." This description of Canaan is repeated many times in the three subsequent books of the Pentateuch, but is not found in Genesis. **Canaanite** [etc.]: These names are the Bible's designation for the indigenous peoples of Canaan at the time of the Israelite conquest. Biblical lists contain varying numbers of peoples, from six to ten. **Yevusite:** The pre-Israelite inhabitants of Jerusalem.

In the end, what does Moshe have with which to return from the mount of vision? In the DeMille film version his face and personality clearly change; in the biblical text, however, he comes back with a word—the divine promise—and a staff, "with which you shall do the signs" (4:17). He had previously been a man whose lack of tolerance for injustice produced violence; now he is armed with words and a wonder-working object—not a sword or a helmet, but a shepherd's staff.

and I have also seen the oppression with which the Egyptians
oppress them.

10 So now, go,
for I send you to Pharaoh—
bring my people, the Children of Israel, out of Egypt!

11 Moshe said to God:
Who am I
that I should go to Pharaoh,
that I should bring the Children of Israel out of Egypt?

12 He said:
Indeed, I will be-there with you,
and this is the sign for you that I myself have sent you:
when you have brought the people out of Egypt,
you will (all) serve God by this mountain.

13 Moshe said to God:
Here, I will come to the Children of Israel
and I will say to them:
The God of your fathers has sent me to you,
and they will say to me: What is his name?—
what shall I say to them?

14 God said to Moshe:
EHYEH ASHER EHYEH/I will be-there howsoever I will be-there.
And he said:
Thus shall you say to the Children of Israel:
EHYEH/I-WILL-BE-THERE sends me to you.

15 And God said further to Moshe:
Thus shall you say to the Children of Israel:
YHWH,
the God of your fathers,
the God of Avraham, the God of Yitzhak, and the God of Yaakov,
sends me to you.

---

12 **this is the sign:** The thought is not entirely clear. It
may signify that liberation signals Israel's birth as a
people, and therefore Moshe's legitimacy as well.
(all): "You" is plural here. **by:** As opposed to
"upon," since the people will not be allowed to tres-
pass its sacred boundaries (see 19:12).

13 **What is his name?:** See Commentary below. B-R:
"What is behind his name?"

14 EHYEH ASHER EHYEH . . . : The syntax is difficult.
Others, "I am that I am."

That is my name for the ages,
that is my title (from) generation to generation.

16 Go,
gather the elders of Israel
and say to them:
YHWH, the God of your fathers, has been seen by me,
the God of Avraham, of Yitzhak, and of Yaakov,
saying:
I have taken account, yes, account of you and of what is being
done to you in Egypt,

17 and I have declared:
I will bring you up from the affliction of Egypt,
to the land of the Canaanite and of the Hittite,
of the Amorite and of the Perizzite,
of the Hivvite and of the Yevusite,
to a land flowing with milk and honey.

18 They will hearken to your voice,
and you will come, you and the elders of Israel, to the king of
Egypt
and say to him:
YHWH, the God of the Hebrews, has met with us—
so now, pray let us go a three days' journey into the wilderness
and let us slaughter (offerings) to YHWH our God!

19 But I, I know
that the king of Egypt will not give you leave to go,
not (even) under a strong hand.

20 So I will send forth my hand
and I will strike Egypt with all my wonders which I will do in its
midst—
after that he will send you free!

---

15 **title:** Others, "memorial."
16 **elders:** They are the holders of political power in such a tribal society. **taken account.** As per Yosef's promise in Gen. 50:24.
18 **pray let us go:** Interestingly, the initial request made of Pharaoh is not for emancipation but for permission to observe a religious festival. It eventually becomes clear that Israel cannot be Israel until it is free of Egyptian hegemony. **slaughter (offerings):** Offer animal sacrifices.

21 And I will give this people favor in the eyes of Egypt;
it will be that when you go, you shall not go empty-handed:

22 each woman shall ask of her neighbor and of the sojourner in her
house
objects of silver and objects of gold, and clothing,
you shall put (them) on your sons and on your daughters—
so shall you strip Egypt!

4:1 Moshe spoke up, he said:
But they will not trust me, and will not hearken to my voice,
indeed, they will say: YHWH has not been seen by you. . . !

2 YHWH said to him:
What is that in your hand?
He said:
A staff.

3 He said:
Throw it to the ground!
He threw it to the ground, and it became a snake,
and Moshe fled from its face.

4 YHWH said to Moshe:
Send forth your hand! Seize it by its tail!
—He sent forth his hand, took hold of it, and it became a staff in
his fist—

5 so that they may trust that YHWH, the God of their fathers,
the God of Avraham, the God of Yitzhak, and the God of
Yaakov, has been seen by you.

6 YHWH said further to him:
Pray put your hand in your bosom!

21 **you shall not go empty-handed:** The despoiling of
the Egyptians is reminiscent of obtaining booty in
war. At the same time, there is probably a legal
background to this (Daube 1961): the furnishing of a
freed slave with provisions. The follow-up to the despoiling, intended or not, is God's command that, in
Israel's future observance of religious festivals in
the Promised Land, "no one is to be seen in my presence empty-handed" (Ex. 23:15).

22 **ask of:** Others, "borrow." **strip:** Here the verb
(natzel) means "strip," perhaps punning on a different form used in v.8 which means "rescue."

4:1 **spoke up . . . said:** This coupling of verbs is common in Ugaritic and Hebrew to denote a new
thought on the speaker's part (Cassuto 1967).

4 **send forth:** Or "stretch out."

6 **bosom:** Others, "upper folds of (his) cloak."

The Journey Back (4:18–31): It is clear that something has been inserted into the normal course of our narrative. What follows v.20 should be v.27; Moshe, ready to go back to Egypt, is met by Aharon in the wilderness, and they subsequently announce their mission to the Children of Israel. However, the editor has prefaced the brothers' meeting, first with a warning to Moshe that his mission will be strongly resisted by Pharaoh, and a warning that Moshe is to deliver to Pharaoh. Then follows a bizarre episode, which, like the Name passage discussed above, has provoked centuries of comment and attempts to explain it. What are we to make of the circumcision story here, especially the last scene, which is unclear not only in import but in details such as pronouns as well?

Buber (1988) explains it as an event that sometimes occurs in hero stories: the deity appears as "divine demon" and threatens the hero's life. Perhaps this underlines the dangerous side of contact between the human and the divine. But there seem to be other reasons for the passage's inclusion at this point in the text. First, it serves as an end bracket to Moshe's sojourn in Midyan. As mentioned earlier, Moshe flees Egypt under pain of death (2:15); here, on his return, he is in mortal danger once more. Second, our passage seems to be an *inclusio* or bracketing passage for the entire Plague Narrative (Kosmala and others). This is confirmed by the use of vv.21–23 as an introduction. God, designating Israel his firstborn and alluding to the future killing of Pharaoh's/Egypt's firstborn sons, demonstrates his power as life-taker, to be pacified or turned away only by a ceremonial blood-smearing—parallel to the Israelites' smearing of blood on their doorposts when their own firstborn are threatened by the Tenth Plague (12:12–13).

Two final points should be noted here. First, it is with the act of his son's circumcision that Moshe finally becomes a true Israelite (that, after all, was the major term of God's covenant with Abraham in Gen. 17). Similarly, Yehoshua (Joshua), Moshe's successor, will circumcise the next generation of Israelites in the process of conquering the Promised Land (Josh. 5:2). And second, it is telling, again, that the person who saves Moshe's life in adulthood is a woman. In a sense, Moshe's early life is now over, having come full circle.

He put his hand in his bosom, then he took it out,
and here: his hand had *tzaraat*, like snow!

7 Now he said:
Return your hand to your bosom!
—He returned his hand to his bosom, then he took it out of his
   bosom,
and here: it had returned (to be) like his (other) flesh.

8 So it shall be, if they do not trust you, and do not hearken to the
   voice of the former sign,
that they will put their trust in the voice of the latter sign.

9 And it shall be, if they do not put their trust in even these
   two signs, and do not hearken to your voice:
then take some of the water of the Nile
and pour it out on the dry-land,
and the water that you take from the Nile will become blood on
   the dry-land.

10 Moshe said to YHWH:
Please, my Lord,
no man of words am I,
not from yesterday, not from the day-before, not (even) since you
   have spoken to your servant,
for heavy of mouth and heavy of tongue am I!

11 YHWH said to him:
Who placed a mouth in human beings
or who (is it that) makes one mute or deaf
or open-eyed or blind?
Is it not I, YHWH?

---

6 **had *tzaraat*:** Trad. "was leprous," but *tzaraat* is now understood as a kind of skin disease, not as serious as true leprosy. In the Bible, it was, however, often taken as a sign from God of wrongdoing on the part of the victim.

8 **voice:** Meaning "message," as in Ugaritic usage. **sign:** These were often required or used by prophets in the Bible (see the discussion in Deut. 13:2ff.) (Greenberg 1969).

9 **blood:** Since the Nile was regarded as divine by the Egyptians, not only would such a plague be miraculous and devastating, but it would also be a direct swipe at the Egyptian religion.

10 **no man of words am I:** Yet this is exactly the quality that Moshe's mission requires! (Greenberg 1969). Similarly, Jeremiah (1:6) seeks to evade the call, although his refusal is based more on inexperience than on lack of eloquence. **yesterday . . . the day-before:** A Hebrew idiom for "the past." **heavy of mouth and heavy of tongue:** The nature of Moshe's speech impediment is not clear. Curiously, writes Buber (1988), it is the stammerer whose task it is to bring down God's word to the human world.

12 So now, go!
I myself will be-there with your mouth
and will instruct you as to what you are to speak.
13 But he said:
Please, my Lord,
pray send by whose hand you will send!
14 YHWH's anger flared up against Moshe,
he said:
Is there not Aharon your brother, the Levite—
I know that *he* can speak, yes, speak well,
and here, he is even going out to meet you;
when he sees you, he will rejoice in his heart.
15 You shall speak to him,
you shall put the words in his mouth!
I myself will be-there with your mouth and with his mouth,
and will instruct you as to what you shall do.
16 He shall speak for you to the people,
he, he shall be for you a mouth, and you, you shall be for him a
god.
17 And this staff, take in your hand,
with which you shall do the signs.

18 Moshe went and returned to Yitro his father-in-law
and said to him:
Pray let me go and return to my brothers that are in Egypt,
that I may see whether they are still alive.

13 **pray send by whose hand you will send!:** That is,
find someone else!
14 **flared up:** Literally, burned, the normal biblical metaphor for anger. **Aharon:** Trad. English
"Aaron." This is the first mention of the brother
whom we later find out was the firstborn. **the
Levite:** Why this designation here? Some theorize
that it means "joiner," while others see it as a tracing
of Levite roots as spokespeople in Israel. The
phrase could also be translated as "Is not your
brother Aharon the Levite?"
15 **you shall put . . . :** Moshe is to Aharon as God is to

a prophet; the latter is to serve principally as a
mouthpiece.
16 **a god:** Others, "an oracle."
18 **Yitro:** Here his name appears as *Yeter* in Hebrew.
Pray let me go: B-R: "Now I will go." **my brothers:** This concern has not been heard from Moshe
during his years in Midyan, nor has he mentioned his
past at all. **whether they are still alive:** Reminiscent
of Yosef's cry in Gen. 45:3, "Is my father still alive?"
Note that Moshe says nothing to Yitro about what
happened to him on the mountain.

Yitro said to Moshe:
Go in peace!

19 Now YHWH said to Moshe in Midyan:
Go, return to Egypt,
for all the men who sought (to take) your life have died.

20 So Moshe took his wife and his sons and mounted them upon a
donkey, to return to the land of Egypt,
and Moshe took the staff of God in his hand.

21 YHWH said to Moshe:
When you go to return to Egypt,
see:
All the portents that I have put in your hand, you are to do before
Pharaoh,
but I will make his heart strong-willed, so that he will not send
the people free.

22 Then you are to say to Pharaoh:
Thus says YHWH:
My son, my firstborn, is Israel!

23 I said to you: Send free my son, that he may serve me,
but you have refused to send him free,
(so) here: I will kill your son, your firstborn!

24 Now it was on the journey, at the night-camp,
that YHWH encountered him and sought to make him die.

25 Tzippora took a flint and cut off her son's foreskin,
she touched it to his legs and said:

---

19 **all the men:** Moshe need no longer fear for his life at Pharaoh's hands, but he will shortly be threatened by God himself (see vv. 24–26).

20 **mounted them upon a donkey:** A stereotyped biblical way of describing setting out on a journey. **staff of God:** In standard hero stories, one would expect to hear a good deal more about this object, which would normally possess magical powers. Here, as usual, such a motif has been suppressed. It surfaces later in Jewish legend, in full mythical garb. The staff is mentioned in this verse, possibly, to provide a dramatic conclusion to the entire revelation account: Moshe sets out for Egypt armed, as it were, with a token from God. This was the missing piece in his activity in Egypt.

21 **portents:** Signs, wonders. **send . . . free:** Others, "let . . . go."

22 **Thus says YHWH:** A formula often used by the prophets to open their pronouncements. The context is similar as well: the prophets stand frequently against the kings of Israel and Judah, arguing for an end to oppression. **my firstborn:** The use of this image is a statement of emotional force, not actual primacy of birth or antiquity, as Israel was a comparative latecomer in the ancient Near East.

24 **to make him die:** To kill him; the means is not specified, but one could surmise that illness is meant.

25 **his:** Whose? Presumably those of Moshe, who is then "released" by God.

Before Pharaoh (5:1–6:1): Moshe and Aharon's initial efforts to free the people—even temporarily for an act of worship—are unsuccessful, as foretold in the previous chapter. But even though God had predicted failure, we are still left with a portrait of clashing human wills: the liberators', the king's, and the reluctant people's. The narrative appears to be a set-up for the second major revelation of God to Moshe (Chap. 6), which, preceded by expressions of doubt on both Moshe's part and that of the people, harks back to the concerns voiced at the Burning Bush. There is also a forward-looking figure, Pharaoh, who is a prototype for other foreign rulers and enemies in the Bible who challenge God (Greenberg 1969).

Chap. 5 contains the Bible's most extended description of the conditions of Egyptian bondage. Not surprisingly, the root "serve" occurs seven times in vv.9 to 21 (Greenberg 1969), and sound variations on the Hebrew *ra'* ("ill/evil") three times (vv.19–23).

Indeed, a bridegroom of blood are you to me!
26 Thereupon he released him.
Then she said, "a bridegroom of blood" upon the circumcision-
cuttings.

27 Now YHWH said to Aharon:
Go to meet Moshe in the wilderness!
He went, he encountered him at the mountain of God
and he kissed him.
28 And Moshe told Aharon all YHWH's words with which he had
sent him
and all the signs with which he had charged him.
29 Moshe and Aharon went,
they gathered all the elders of the Children of Israel,
30 and Aharon spoke all the words which YHWH had spoken to
Moshe,
he did the signs before the people's eyes.
31 The people trusted,
they hearkened
that YHWH had taken account of the Children of Israel,
that he had seen their affliction.
And they bowed low and did homage.

5:1 Afterward Moshe and Aharon came and said to Pharaoh:
Thus says YHWH, the God of Israel:
Send free my people, that they may hold-a-festival to me in the
wilderness!
2 Pharaoh said:
Who is YHWH, that I should hearken to his voice to send Israel
free?

---

26 **released him:** Or "relaxed (his hold upon) him."
circumcision-cuttings: Others, "on account of the
circumcision," "because of the circumcision," "referring to the circumcision."
31 **The people trusted . . . :** For the first time in the
Torah, Israel responds to God's promises in a positive manner, something which will rarely happen
again. The vocabulary and attitude form an *inclusio*
(a bracket) with the end of the Liberation Narrative, 14:30–31 (cf. the verbs "trust" and "see").

5:1 **hold-a-festival:** Or "observe a pilgrimage-festival."
The Hebrew *hag* is still echoed in the great pilgrimage of Islam, the hajj, in which worshipers make
(sometimes long) journeys to Mecca.
2 **Who is YHWH:** This attitude recalls an earlier obstacle to the liberation process, "Who am I" of Moshe
(3:11). **I do not know YHWH:** Colloquially, "I care
not a whit for YHWH!" To Pharaoh's pointed challenge, the entire narrative that follows is an answer
(cf. 14:4, 18).

I do not know YHWH,
moreover, Israel I will not send free!

3 They said:
The God of the Hebrews has met with us;
pray let us go a three days' journey into the wilderness,
and let us slaughter (offerings) to YHWH our God,
lest he confront us with the pestilence or the sword!

4 The king of Egypt said to them:
For-what-reason, Moshe and Aharon,
would you let the people loose from their tasks?
Go back to your burdens!

5 Pharaoh said:
Here, too many now are the people of the land,
and you would have them cease from their burdens!

6 So that day Pharaoh commanded the slave-drivers of the people
    and its officers, saying:

7 You are no longer to give straw to the people to make the bricks
    as yesterday and the day-before;
let it be them that go and gather straw for themselves!

8 But the (same) measure of bricks that they have been making,
    yesterday and the day-before.
you are to impose on them,
you are not to subtract from it!
For they are lax—
therefore they cry out, saying: Let us go, let us slaughter
    (offerings) to our God!

9 Let the servitude weigh-heavily on the men!
They shall have to do it, so that they pay no more regard to false
    words!

---

3 **pray let us go:** A milder phrase than the earlier "Send free my people!" **three days' journey:** Either the magical three again, or a standard biblical way of describing a journey (see Gen. 22:4). **lest he confront us:** In the ancient world the gods demanded sacrifices at specified times. "Confront" and "sword" also occur in vv.20–21, nicely balancing this section of narrative.

4 **For-what-reason:** Heb. *lamma*, as distinct from *maddu'a* ("why," with similar meaning).

5 **too many:** Echoing 1:9ff. (Fishbane 1979). **the people of the land:** This phrase occurs here in its wider usage, i.e., the common folk, as opposed to what is found in Gen. 23:7, where the term indicates the landed nobility.

6 **slave-drivers:** In several Semitic languages *nagos* denotes "pressing" or "overpowering" (Ullendorff), hence "driving" here.

9 **so that they pay:** Others, "Let them pay" (Greenberg 1969).

◆ 10 The slave-drivers of the people and its officers went out
and said to the people, saying:
Thus says Pharaoh:
I will not give you straw:
11 You go, get yourselves straw, wherever you can find (it),
indeed, not one (load) is to be subtracted from your servitude!
12 The people scattered throughout all the land of Egypt,
gathering stubble-gatherings for straw.
13 But the slave-drivers pressed them hard, saying:
Finish your tasks, each-day's work-load in its day, as when there
was straw!
14 And the officers of the Children of Israel, whom Pharaoh's slave-
drivers had set over them, were beaten,
they said (to them):
For-what-reason have you not finished baking your allocation as
yesterday and the day-before,
so yesterday, so today?
15 The officers of the Children of Israel came and cried out to
Pharaoh, saying:
Why do you do thus to your servants?
16 No straw is being given to your servants, and as for bricks—they
say to us, Make (them)!
Here, your servants are being beaten, and the fault is your
people's!
17 But he said:
Lax you are, lax,
therefore you say: Let us go, let us slaughter (offerings) to
Y HWH—
18 so now, go—serve;
no straw will be given to you,
and the full-measure in bricks you must give back!

---

10 **Thus says Pharaoh:** An ironic transformation of
the prophetic formula noted in v.1 above, "the language of redemption turned sour" (Greenberg
1969).
14 **beaten:** The same Hebrew verb as "striking" in
2:11–13.

16 **your people's:** Heb. *'ammekha,* which some read
'immakh ("with you").
18 **go—serve:** This phrase will be repeated three times
during the Plague Narratives (10:8, 24; 12:31), with a
different meaning: Go serve God! Pharaoh cannot
wait to free the Israelites! (Greenberg 1969).

The Promise Renewed (6:2–13): Greenberg (1969) and others have noted how this section in many respects recapitulates God's speeches at the Bush. Once again God assures Moshe that he has "heard" and "recalled" the Israelites and their old covenant; once again he promises to act ("bring out" resounds four times); once again the promise is linked to an interpretation of God's name; and once again Moshe expresses doubt as to whether he will be believed or listened to (v.12).

Why the repetition? Perhaps here, as elsewhere, to double is to emphasize. Also, just as Moshe initially failed as a self-appointed liberator in Chap. 2, only to be sought out by God in the wilderness, he fails as a leader here as well, followed by God's reassuring speech. There can be no question from whence the liberation comes.

19 The officers of the Children of Israel saw that they were in an ill-
plight,
having to say: Do not subtract from your bricks each-day's work-
load in its day!
20 They confronted Moshe and Aharon, stationing themselves to
meet them when they came out from Pharaoh,
21 they said to them:
May YHWH see you and judge,
for having made our smell reek in the eyes of Pharaoh and in the
eyes of his servants,
giving a sword into their hand, to kill us!
22 Moshe returned to YHWH and said:
My Lord,
for-what-reason have you dealt so ill with this people?
For-what-reason have you sent me?
23 Since I came to Pharaoh to speak in your name, he has dealt only
ill with this people,
and rescued—you have not rescued your people!
6:1 YHWH said to Moshe:
Now you will see what I will do to Pharaoh:
for with a strong hand he will send them free,
and with a strong hand he will drive them out of his land.

2 God spoke to Moshe,
he said to him:
I am YHWH.

19–21 **saw . . . see:** In these negative usages it is as if the
earlier redemptive theme of God's "seeing" has
gone awry. But all is righted below, in 6:1 ("Now you
will see . . .").

21 **having made our smell reek:** An expression meaning the causing of hatred or horror. **giving a sword
into their hand:** This scenario often occurs historically with liberators; initial attempts fail or are rejected. Here we have a replay of Moshe's earlier
efforts (note the use of "judge" there as well, in
2:14). The tension in this chapter may be said to revolve around whether God's sword (v.3) or
Pharaoh's will prevail.

22 **My Lord:** The Hebrew *Adonai* is used often in the
Bible for pleading one's case, as before a king (see
Gen. 18:27, 30, 31, 32; 19:18, and Ex. 3:10).

22–23 **this people . . . this people . . . your people:** Note
Moshe's brilliant use of psychology in dealing with
God, similar to what he will do again in 32:11–13.

23 **to speak in your name:** The issue of God's name
will become paramount in the passage following.

6:1 **out of his land:** The phrase is also used in connection with "sending free" in 6:11, 7:2, and 11:10.

2 **I am YHWH:** I am [name] is an authority formula in
the ancient Near East (as in Gen. 41:44, where it
refers to an earlier Pharaoh) (Greenberg 1969).

The Genealogy of Moshe and Aharon (6:14–27): At this tension-filled moment in the narrative, in the face of Moshe's self-doubt and the possible collapse of his mission, there is an unlikely break, at least by Western storytelling standards. Apparently the genealogy has been inserted to buttress Moshe and Aharon's claim to represent the people before the Egyptian crown, and to stress their Levite ancestry (which solidly establishes them within the priestly class in Israel). Significantly, the genealogy of Yaakov's sons ends with the third, Levi, and the rest of the list enumerates the Levite clans. More significantly, the ages mentioned are composed of patterned numbers such as 3, 7, 30, and 100. As in Genesis, this betokens a concept of order and meaning in history.

Thus legitimated, Moshe and Aharon can return to the task at hand. It would seem, then, that the passage is speaking to the Israelites, both in Egypt and in the audience of later generations.

◆ 3 I was seen by Avraham, by Yitzhak, and by Yaakov
as God Shaddai,
but (by) my name YHWH I was not known to them.

4 I also established my covenant with them,
to give them the land of Canaan,
the land of their sojournings, where they had sojourned.

5 And I have also heard the moaning of the Children of Israel,
whom Egypt is holding-in-servitude,
and I have called-to-mind my covenant.

6 Therefore,
say to the Children of Israel:
I am YHWH;
I will bring you out
from beneath the burdens of Egypt,
I will rescue you
from servitude to them,
I will redeem you
with an outstretched arm, with great (acts of) judgment;

7 I will take you
for me as a people,
and I will be for you
as a God;
and you shall know
that I am YHWH your God,
who brings you out
from beneath the burdens of Egypt.

---

3 **Shaddai:** Heb. obscure; traditionally translated "Almighty," while some understand it as "of the mountains." In Genesis the name is most often tied to promises of human fertility (see 17:12); a possibly related Hebrew word means "breasts." **was not known:** Others, "did not make known."

6ff. **I will bring . . . :** God's answer comprises verbs of action: "bring out," "rescue," "redeem," "take," and "give." The Hebrew rhymes (*ve-heveti etkhem . . . ve-hitzalti etkhem . . .*).

6-7 **beneath . . . beneath:** A more vivid image than merely rescuing them.

7 **I will take you . . . :** This covenant language recalls the vocabulary of marriage in many societies ("take you," "be for/to you"). **you shall know:** The verb "know" in the ancient Near East is often part of covenant (treaty) language, and so Moshe's task is not only to force Pharaoh to acknowledge God, but also to bring the Israelites into a special relationship with God (see Chaps. 19ff.).

◆

8 I will bring you
    into the land (over) which I lifted my hand (in an oath) to give to
        Avraham, to Yitzhak, and to Yaakov.
    I will give it to you as a possession,
    I, YHWH.
9 Moshe spoke thus to the Children of Israel.
    But they did not hearken to Moshe,
    out of shortness of spirit and out of hard servitude.

10 YHWH spoke to Moshe, saying:
11 Go in, speak to Pharaoh king of Egypt,
    that he may send free the Children of Israel from his land.
12 Moshe spoke before YHWH, saying:
    Here, (if) the Children of Israel do not hearken to me,
    how will Pharaoh hearken to me?
    —and I am of foreskinned lips!
13 YHWH spoke to Moshe and to Aharon,
    and charged them to the Children of Israel and to Pharaoh king
        of Egypt,
    to bring the Children of Israel out of the land of Egypt.

14 These are the heads of their Fathers' Houses:
    The sons of Re'uven, firstborn of Israel: Hanokh and Pallu,
        Hetzron and Karmi,
    these are the clans of Re'uven.
15 And the sons of Shim'on: Yemuel, Yamin, Ohad, Yakhin and
        Tzohar, and Sha'ul the son of the Canaanite-woman,
    these are the clans of Shim'on.
16 Now these are the names of the Sons of Levi according to their
        begettings:

---

8 **(over) which I lifted my hand . . . :** The promise of
the land forms the backbone of the book of Genesis, which ends with it as well (Gen. 50:24).
9 **shortness of spirit:** Others, "impatience" (so Ramban), "shortness of breath" (so Rashi). Also notable
is Walzer's suggestion of "dispiritedness." A parallel
Ugaritic phrase probably means "wretchedness."
12 **spoke before:** Appealed to (Orlinsky). **of foreskinned lips:** Either Moshe had some physical
defect, as legend has it, or he is alluding to his

difficulties as a public speaker (cf. 4:10). The use of
"foreskinned" may express the biblical idea that
things in their natural state require sanctifying, as
can be seen with firstborn humans and animals,
first-fruits, food, sexuality, etc.
14 **Fathers' Houses:** Family units, listed according to
the name of the ancestor. **sons:** Heb. *banim*, translated above as "children," but here clearly referring
to the males.

Gershon, Kehat and Merari.

Now the years of Levi's life were seven and thirty and a hundred
 years.

17 The sons of Gershon: Livni and Shim'i, according to their clans.

18 And the sons of Kehat: Amram, Yitzhar, Hevron and Uzziel.

Now the years of Kehat's life were three and thirty and a hundred
 years.

19 And the sons of Merari: Mahli and Mushi.

These are the Levite clans, according to their begettings.

20 Amram took himself Yokheved his aunt as a wife,

she bore him Aharon and Moshe.

Now the years of Amram's life were seven and thirty and a
 hundred years.

21 Now the sons of Yitzhar: Korah, Nefeg and Zikhri.

22 And the sons of Uzziel: Mishael, Eltzafan and Sitri.

23 Aharon took himself Elisheva daughter of Amminadav,
 Nahshon's sister, as a wife.

She bore him Nadav and Avihu, Elazar and Itamar.

24 Now the sons of Korah: Assir, Elkana and Aviasaf; these are the
 Korahite clans.

25 Elazar son of Aharon took himself one of Putiel's daughters for
 himself as a wife,

she bore him Pin'has.

These are the heads of the Levite father-groupings according to
 their clans.

26 That is (the) Aharon and Moshe to whom Yhwh said:

Bring the Children of Israel out of the land of Egypt by their
 forces;

27 those (were they) who spoke to Pharaoh king of Egypt, to bring
 the Children of Israel out of Egypt,

that Moshe and Aharon.

---

16 **seven and thirty and a hundred years:** Here, and
 in vv.18 and 20, the life spans of Moshe's family
 members are composed of "perfect" numbers in
 combinations and multiples, as if to say that heroic
 biography as well as group history has a preor-
 dained meaning.

25 **Pin'has:** Trad. English "Phinehas." He will play an
 important role in Num. 25:7 as a zealot for the new
 faith. The name is Egyptian in origin.

26 **by their forces:** The term has a military ring, and is
 used frequently in the Bible with that connotation.

The Mission Renewed (6:28–7:13): As preparation for the next meeting with Pharaoh, Moshe is once more reminded that the king will not listen to him. Taking a page from his speech at the Bush, God instructs Moshe and Aharon to use the "sign" that had previously served to convince the people: snake magic. Yet despite Aharon's one-upping the Egyptian magicians in the warm-up for the plagues, Pharaoh remains unconvinced. This episode helps to prepare for what follows, and indeed contains a virtual glossary of Exodus words. Some of these are: "speak," "send," "harden," "heart," "sign/portent," "hand," "bring out," "know," "staff," "hearken," "midst."

28 So it was on the day that Yнwн spoke to Moshe in the land of
   Egypt,
29 Yнwн spoke to Moshe, saying:
   I am Yнwн;
   speak to Pharaoh king of Egypt all that I speak to you.
30 Moshe said before Yнwн:
   If I am of foreskinned lips,
   how will Pharaoh hearken to me?
7:1 Yнwн said to Moshe:
   See, I will make you as a god for Pharaoh,
   and Aharon your brother will be your prophet.
2 You are to speak all that I command you,
   And Aharon your brother is to speak to Pharaoh
   so that he may send free the Children of Israel from his land.
3 But I,
   I will harden Pharaoh's heart,
   I will make my signs and my portents many in the land of Egypt:
4 Pharaoh will not hearken to you,
   so I will set my hand against Egypt,
   and I will bring out my forces,
   my people, the Children of Israel,
   from the land of Egypt, with great (acts of) judgment;
5 the Egyptians will know that I am Yнwн,
   when I stretch out my hand over Egypt and bring the Children of
      Israel out from their midst.
6 Moshe and Aharon did
   as Yнwн had commanded them, thus they did.
7 Now Moshe was eighty years old, and Aharon was eighty-three
   years old, when they spoke to Pharaoh.

7:1 **as a god:** Or "oracle," as mentioned in the note to 4:16.
5 **when I stretch out my hand:** In the Plague Narrative, Moshe and Aharon will do the actual stretching out of hands (see 7:19, 8:1, 12; 9:22; 10:12, 21; and the climactic passage in 14:16, 26).
6 **Moshe and Aharon did/ as Yнwн had commanded them, thus they did:** This construction can be broken up in two ways (with, for instance, the break at "them"), a syntactical usage found

fairly frequently in biblical texts (cf. 39:43). The wording recalls the Flood Narrative in Genesis, with the same emphasis: the hero obeys God without question.
7 **eighty ... eighty-three:** Another set of "perfect" numbers, this time using forty (and three) as the base. It occurs here due to the biblical practice of mentioning age to "mark ... a milestone in life's journey" (Greenberg 1969).

First Blow (7:14–25): The first plague uses elements and words common to many subsequent plagues; in addition to those just mentioned, it introduces "refuse" and "reek" and "throughout all the land of Egypt." More important is the choice of site and object for the curse: the Nile (a god in Egypt), water (source of life for the Egyptians but earlier source of death for the Hebrew babies), and blood (sign of life and death). No more effective choice could have been made for this first demonstration of the far-reaching power of the Israelite God.

As with the first six plagues, the threat is long and the actual carrying-out brief. Note the relationship, at the end of the episode, between the uncaring Pharaoh and his own people, who have to scratch for water.

8 YHWH said to Moshe and to Aharon, saying:

9 When Pharaoh speaks to you, saying: Give, you, a portent,
   then say to Aharon:
   Take your staff and throw it down before Pharaoh: Let it become
      a serpent.

10 Moshe and Aharon came to Pharaoh,
   they did thus, as YHWH had commanded,
   Aharon threw down his staff before Pharaoh and before his
      servants, and it became a serpent.

11 Pharaoh too called for the wise men and for the sorcerers,
   that they too, the magicians of Egypt, should do thus with their
      occult-arts,

12 they threw down, each-man, his staff, and these became serpents.
   But Aharon's staff swallowed up their staffs.

13 Yet Pharaoh's heart remained strong-willed, and he did not
      hearken to them,
   as YHWH had spoken.

14 YHWH said to Moshe:
   Pharaoh's heart is heavy-with-stubbornness—he refuses to send
      the people free.

15 Go to Pharaoh in the morning, here, he goes out to the Nile,
   station yourself to meet him by the shore of the Nile,
   and the staff that changed into a snake, take in your hand,

16 and say to him:
   YHWH, the God of the Hebrews, has sent me to you, saying:
   Send free my people, that they may serve me in the wilderness!
   But here, you have not hearkened thus far.

---

9 **Give, you, a portent:** That is, "Prove yourselves by working a miracle" (Hyatt). **your staff:** It is not clear whether the staff is the aforementioned one of Moshe, or part of another tradition, connected to Aharon. **serpent:** Heb. *tanin*, a word indicating a reptile, with possible mythological overtones (as in "dragon").

11 **occult arts:** Whereas Aharon needs none, since God performs the miracle (Greenberg 1969).

12 **swallowed up:** Leaving no doubt as to whether optical illusion or sleight of hand is involved.

14 **heavy-with-stubbornness:** In the Plague Narrative, the root *kaved,* "heavy," occurs ten times—five times referring to Pharaoh's heart and five referring to the plagues themselves. The latter are perhaps seen as the direct outcome of the former.

15 **he goes out to the Nile:** Many interpretations have been proposed for this action, which must have had some significance for the biblical narrator. It remains unclear whether Pharaoh is involved in a religious rite or a function of state. More charming is the suggestion by Rashi, the medieval Hebrew commentator, that Pharaoh went secretly to the river in order to relieve himself—so that the Egyptians would not see him as less than a god.

Second Blow (7:26–8:11): The second plague is linked to the first by a number of elements: the Nile, the magicians, and of course, Pharaoh's disregard of the threats after it is all over. It is also a full narrative, containing most of the formal aspects of the plagues within itself (see "The Plague Narrative," above).

The threat of this plague breaks into poetry in a striking passage (v.28) which uses repeating prepositions. The frogs are literally everywhere. Also, for the first time Pharaoh asks that God be entreated—that is, he finally acknowledges his existence (as against which, see 5:2).

17 Thus says YHWH:
By this shall you know that I am YHWH:
here, I will strike—with the staff that is in my hand—upon the
water that is in the Nile,
and it will change into blood.

18 The fish that are in the Nile will die, and the Nile will reek,
and the Egyptians will be unable to drink water from the Nile.

19 YHWH said to Moshe:
Say to Aharon:
Take your staff
and stretch out your hand over the waters of Egypt,
over their tributaries, over their Nile-canals, over their ponds
and over all their bodies of water,
and let them become blood!
There will be blood throughout all the land of Egypt—in the
wooden-containers, in the stoneware.

20 Moshe and Aharon did thus, as YHWH had commanded them.
He raised the staff and struck the water in the Nile, before the
eyes of Pharaoh and before the eyes of his servants,
and all the water that was in the Nile changed into blood.

21 The fish that were in the Nile died, and the Nile reeked,
and the Egyptians could not drink water from the Nile;
the blood was throughout all the land of Egypt.

22 But the magicians of Egypt did thus with their occult-arts,
and Pharaoh's heart remained strong-willed, and he did not
hearken to them,
as YHWH had spoken.

23 So Pharaoh turned and came into his house, neither did he pay
any mind to this.

---

17 **change:** Continuing the theme of transformation found in the scene with the snake. Overall, of course, the change from slavery to liberation and to responsible society is a major theme in Exodus.

19 **wooden-containers . . . stoneware:** It is unclear what is meant. The context seems to suggest "even in their kitchen utensils," reflected in the present translation. On the other hand, virtually everywhere in the Bible that "wood and stone" occur as a pair in the singular, they refer to idols; Cassuto

speaks of the Egyptians' bathing their idols and thus sees the passage as another example of Exodus's denigrating Egyptian religion.

20 **He raised the staff:** "He" refers to Aharon. **struck:** The first "stroke"—that is the Hebrew term *(makka)* used for what we know in English as a "plague."

21 **throughout all the land of Egypt:** One of the refrains used in this section of the book (see "On the Book of Exodus and Its Structure," p. 241).

Third Blow (8:12–15): With the third plague, the curse becomes more intimate, affecting the bodies of all living creatures in Egypt (cf. the refrain in vv.13–14, "on man and on beast"). The narrative uses the briefest plague formula here, without introduction or warning to Pharaoh. Yet it results in an Egyptian effort to end the siege, as the magicians term the plague "the finger of a god" (v.15).

Fourth Blow (8:16–28): Despite its similarity to the previous plague (insects), number four introduces a new and important element into the tale: the idea that God makes a distinction between Egypt and Israel. It also involves protracted bargaining between Moshe and Pharaoh over the issue of allowing the Israelites to worship God.

24 But all Egypt had to dig around the Nile to drink water,
    for they could not drink from the waters of the Nile.
25 Seven days were fulfilled, after YHWH had struck the Nile.

26 YHWH said to Moshe:
    Come to Pharaoh and say to him:
    Thus says YHWH:
    Send free my people, that they may serve me!
27 Now if you refuse to send them free,
    here, I will smite your entire territory with frogs.
28 The Nile will swarm with frogs;
    they will ascend, they will come
    into your house, into your bedroom, upon your couch,
    into your servants' houses, in among your people,
    into your ovens and into your dough-pans;
29 onto you, onto your people, onto all your servants will the frogs
        ascend!
8:1 YHWH said to Moshe:
    Say to Aharon:
    Stretch out your hand with your staff, over the tributaries, over
        the Nile-canals, and over the ponds,
    make the frogs ascend upon the land of Egypt!
2 Aharon stretched out his hand over the waters of Egypt,
    the frog-horde ascended
    and covered the land of Egypt.
3 Now the magicians did thus with their occult-arts—
    they made frogs ascend upon the land of Egypt.
4 Pharaoh had Moshe and Aharon called
    and said:

---

25 YHWH **had struck the Nile:** Even though Aharon
    did the "striking," it becomes clear here that the
    brothers are only agents.
27 **frogs:** A symbol of fertility in Egyptian culture (the
    goddess Heket), and so the plague might be re-
    garded as an assault on the Egyptian gods again
    (Cassuto). There may also be an ironic hint here of
    the "swarming" of the Israelites in 1:7.
28 **ovens:** A place which, because of its dryness, would
    be most unlikely to harbor them (Childs).

8:2 **frog-horde:** The Hebrew uses a collective singular
    here (likewise with "insects" in 8:17ff. and "locusts"
    in 10:4ff.); all other "frogs" in this plague receive the
    standard plural.
3 **the magicians did thus:** The theme of Israel's dis-
    tinctiveness, so prominent in these stories, is de-
    layed. Here the magicians can do the same tricks as
    their Hebrew counterparts, although, as noted
    above, they require the aid of "occult-arts."

Plead with YHWH, that he may remove the frogs from me and
from my people,
and I will send the people free, that they may slaughter
(offerings) to YHWH!
5 Moshe said to Pharaoh:
Be praised over me:
For when shall I plead for you, for your servants, for your people,
to cut off the frogs from you and from your houses,
(so that) only in the Nile will they remain?
6 He said:
For the morrow.
He said:
According to your words, (then)!
In order that you may know
that there is none like YHWH our God.
7 The frogs shall remove from you, from your houses, from your
servants, from your people,
—only in the Nile shall they remain.
8 Moshe and Aharon went out from Pharaoh,
Moshe cried out to YHWH
on account of the frogs that he had imposed upon Pharaoh.
9 And YHWH did according to Moshe's words:
the frogs died away, from the houses, from the courtyards, and
from the fields.
10 They piled them up, heaps upon heaps, and the land reeked.
11 But when Pharaoh saw that there was breathing-room,
he made his heart heavy-with-stubbornness, and did not hearken
to them,
as YHWH had spoken.

12 YHWH said to Moshe:
Say to Aharon:

---

5 **Be praised over me:** Others, "Have the advantage over me." The sense is that Pharaoh will be allowed to choose the precise time of the frogs' removal.

6 **In order that you may know:** The intent of Moshe's words in v.5 is now revealed: precise timing, even when chosen at will, demonstrates God's total power.

9 **from the houses . . . :** The threefold repetition of "from" paints a vivid picture of the end of this plague. The dead frogs recede like water drying up.

12 **gnats:** Other translations vary here. There are many traditions, but it seems clear that some kind of small insect is indicated (Hyatt).

Stretch out your staff and strike the dust of the land,
it will become gnats throughout all the land of Egypt!

13 They did thus,
Aharon stretched out his hand with his staff and struck the dust
of the ground,
and gnats were on man and on beast;
all the dust of the ground became gnats throughout all the land
of Egypt.

14 Now the magicians did thus with their occult-arts, to bring forth
the gnats, but they could not,
the gnats were on man and on beast.

15 The magicians said to Pharaoh:
This is the finger of a god!
But Pharaoh's heart remained strong-willed, and he did not
hearken to them,
as YHWH had spoken.

16 YHWH said to Moshe:
Start-early in the morning, station yourself before Pharaoh—
here, he goes out to the water,
and say to him:
Thus says YHWH:
Send free my people, that they may serve me!

17 Indeed, if you do not send my people free,
here, I will send upon you, upon your servants, upon your
people, upon your houses—
insects,
the houses of Egypt will be full of the insects,
as well as the ground upon which they are!

18 But I will make distinct, on that day, the region of Goshen, where
my people is situated,

15 **the finger of a god:** That is, God's direct intervention in human affairs. The only other occurrence of
this expression is in Exodus (31:18) and in the text
that retells that story, Deut. 9:10. In the latter cases it
refers to the divine writing on the two tablets of
Testimony.

17 **upon you . . . :** Similar to the refrain of 7:28–29,
with regard to the frogs; here, "upon" occurs four

times in one line. **insects:** As in the last plague,
there are many opinions as to what these were (e.g.,
gnats, gadflies, mosquitos); Bekhor Shor understands the "mixture" (the literal meaning of the Hebrew term used here, '*arov*) as one of wild animals.

18 **region:** Lit. "land" (see Gen. 45:10). **in the land:**
That is, as an active force.

Fifth Blow (9:1–7): Although this plague spares humans, it is nevertheless described as "heavy" (v.3). The narrative uses a play-on-words as well: the Hebrew for pestilence (*dever*) echoes that for thing (*davar*).

Sixth Blow (9:8–12): Just as in the previous "short" plague, number 3, the magicians come to the fore. No longer do they cry to Pharaoh; they cannot even take the stage!

Seventh Blow (9:13–35): Long like its corresponding predecessors (numbers 1 and 4), the seventh plague prefaces its occurrence with an emphatic introduction by God, and its warning gives God-fearing Egyptians a chance to save themselves (vv.19–21), something new. The description of the plague itself is fraught with spectacle, presaging Sinai with its use of thunder and fire. There is also the ominous note, twice in the text (vv.18, 24), that such a plague was unique in Egyptian annals. The plagues, at least for the Egyptians, now transcend the realms of normal, explainable experience, as well as of historical recollection.

so that there will be no insects there,
in order that you may know that I am YHWH in the land;
19 I will put a ransom between my people and your people—
on the morrow will this sign occur.
20 YHWH did thus,
heavy insect (swarms) came into Pharaoh's house, into the houses
of his servants, throughout all the land of Egypt,
the land was in ruins in the face of the insects.
21 Pharaoh had Moshe and Aharon called
and said:
Go, slaughter (offerings) to your god in the land!
22 Moshe said:
It would not be wise to do thuswise:
for Egypt's abomination is what we slaughter for our God;
if we were to slaughter Egypt's abomination before their eyes,
would they not stone us?
23 Let us go a three days' journey into the wilderness,
and we shall slaughter (offerings) to YHWH our God, as he has said
to us.
24 Pharaoh said:
I will send you free,
that you may slaughter (offerings) to YHWH your God in the
wilderness,
only: you are not to go far, too far!
Plead for me!
25 Moshe said:
Here, when I go out from you, I will plead with YHWH,

19 **ransom:** Heb. *pedut*, usually emended to *pelut*, "distinction," to bring the phrase into consonance with v.18 and with the entire plague section in general.
20 **in ruins:** The verb "ruin" (Heb. *shihet*) is often used in the Bible in connection with punishment for sin (see, for example, Gen. 6:11–12; 19:13, 29).
22 **wise . . . thuswise:** Heb. *nakhon . . . ken*. **Egypt's abomination:** In Cassuto's view, there are two possibilities here: either the animals in question were venerated as holy by the Egyptians, or they were ac-

tually thought of as gods, in which case the Hebrew phrase would be quite derogatory (so too Rashi). **stone:** A widely used form of execution in biblical times (e.g., 17:4; 19:13; 21:28, 29, 32 below). It was apparently used for very severe crimes, and often connected, logically, to the anger of the populace (Greenberg 1962).
24 **only: you are not to go far, too far:** Heb. *rak harhek lo tarhiku*.

and the insects will remove from Pharaoh, from his servants, and
   from his people, on the morrow,
only: let not Pharaoh continue to trifle (with us),
by not sending the people free to slaughter (offerings) to YHWH!

26 Moshe went out from before Pharaoh and pleaded with YHWH.

27 And YHWH did according to Moshe's words,
   he removed the insects from Pharaoh, from his servants and from
      his people,
   not one remained.

28 But Pharaoh made his heart heavy-with-stubbornness this time as
   well,
   and he did not send the people free.

9:1 YHWH said to Moshe:
   Come to Pharaoh and speak to him:
   Thus says YHWH, the God of the Hebrews:
   Send free my people, that they may serve me!

2 If you refuse to send (them) free, and continue to hold-on-
   strongly to them,

3 here, YHWH's hand will be on your livestock in the field,
   on the horses, on the donkeys, on the camels, on the oxen, (and)
      on the sheep—
   an exceedingly heavy pestilence!

4 And YHWH will make-a-distinction between the livestock of Israel
      and the livestock of Egypt:
   there will not die among all that belong to the Children of Israel
      a thing!

5 YHWH set an appointed-time, saying:
   On the morrow, YHWH will do this thing in the land.

6 YHWH did that thing on the morrow—
   all the livestock of Egypt died,
   but of the livestock of the Children of Israel, there died not one.

---

27 **not one remained:** Similar words will be used of the Egyptians, drowned in the Sea of Reeds (14:28).

9:2 **hold-on-strongly:** Both Pharaoh's obduracy and his stranglehold on the slaves are described with the same verbal root.

5 **an appointed-time:** As before (8:5–6), equally striking to the plague itself is its precise removal at the time promised.

7 Pharaoh sent to inquire, and here: there had not died of the
    livestock of the Children of Israel even one.
But Pharaoh's heart remained heavy-with-stubbornness, and he
    did not send the people free.

8 YHWH said to Moshe and to Aharon:
Take yourselves fistfuls of soot from a furnace
and let Moshe toss it heavenward before Pharaoh's eyes,
9 it will become fine-dust on all the land of Egypt,
and on man and on beast, it will become boils sprouting into
    blisters,
throughout all the land of Egypt!
10 They took the soot from a furnace and stood before Pharaoh, and
    Moshe tossed it heavenward,
and it became boil-blisters, sprouting on man and on beast.
11 Now the magicians could not stand before Moshe because of the
    boils,
for the boils were upon the magicians and upon all Egypt.
12 But YHWH made Pharaoh's heart strong-willed, and he did not
    hearken to them,
as YHWH had said to Moshe.
13 YHWH said to Moshe:
Start-early in the morning, station yourself before Pharaoh and
    say to him:
Thus says YHWH, the God of the Hebrews:
Send free my people, that they may serve me!
14 Indeed, this time I will send all my blows upon your heart,
    and against your servants, and against your people,
so that you may know that there is none like me throughout all
    the land;
15 indeed, by now I could have sent out my hand and struck you and
    your people with the pestilence,
 and you would have vanished from the land;

---

8 **soot:** The transformation from soot to fine-dust and then boils reflects a poetic justice, paralleling bricks baked in a kiln (Cassuto). It also reflects the biblical concept of disease as punishment. **toss:** Moshe will later "toss" the blood of the covenant on the freed Israelites (24:8).

16 however, just on account of this I have allowed you to withstand,
to make you see my power.
and in order that they might recount my name throughout all the
land.

17 (But) still you set yourself up over my people, by not sending
them free—

18 here, around this time tomorrow I will cause to rain down an
exceedingly heavy hail,
the like of which has never been in Egypt from the days of its
founding until now!

19 So now:
send (word): give refuge to your livestock and to all that is yours
in the field;
all men and beasts who are found in the field and who have not
been gathered into the house—
the hail will come down upon them, and they will die!

20 Whoever had awe for the word of YHWH among Pharaoh's
servants had his servants and his livestock flee into the houses,

21 but whoever did not pay any mind to the word of YHWH left his
servants and his livestock out in the field.

22 YHWH said to Moshe:
Stretch out your hand over the heavens:
Let there be hail throughout all the land of Egypt,
on man and on beast and on all the plants of the field,
throughout the land of Egypt!

23 Moshe stretched out his staff over the heavens,
and YHWH gave forth thunder-sounds and hail, and fire went
toward the earth,
and YHWH caused hail to rain down upon the land of Egypt.

16 **land:** Others, "earth."
20 **Whoever had awe . . . :** The focus now shifts to the Egyptians in general (at least some of them), who now suspect the real source of their troubles, whereas only the magicians recognized it previously.

24 There was hail and a fire taking-hold-of-itself amidst the hail,
     exceedingly heavy,
   the like of which had never been throughout all the land of
     Egypt since it had become a nation.
25 The hail struck, throughout all the land of Egypt, all that was in
     the field, from man to beast;
   all the plants of the field the hail struck, and all the trees of the
     field it broke down;
26 only in the region of Goshen, where the Children of Israel were,
     was there no hail.
27 Pharaoh sent and had Moshe and Aharon called
   and said to them:
   This-time I have sinned!
   YHWH is the one-in-the-right, I and my people are the ones-in-the-
     wrong!
28 Plead with YHWH!
   For enough is the God-thunder and this hail!
   Let me send you free—do not continue staying here!
29 Moshe said to him:
   As soon as I have gone out of the city, I will spread out my hands
     to YHWH,
   the thunder will stop and the hail will be no more—
   in order that you may know that the land belongs to YHWH.
30 But as for you and your servants,
   I know well that you do not yet stand-in-fear
   before the face of YHWH, God!
31 —Now the flax and the barley were stricken, for the barley was in
     ears and the flax was in buds,
32 but the wheat and the spelt were not stricken, for late (-ripening)
     are they.—

24 **fire taking-hold-of-itself:** Heb. difficult; others, "lightning flashed back and forth," "lightning flashing through it." **the like of which had never been:** The phrase here foreshadows the final plague (11:6).
27 **one-in-the-right ... ones-in-the-wrong:** The terms are drawn from the world of legal, not religious, terminology.

28 **enough is:** Or "enough of their being. . . ."
29 **spread out my hands:** In entreaty.
31 **Now the flax . . . :** An editorial comment, to explain how much harm was done (Cassuto 1967: they used it for cloth and for food).

Eighth Blow (10:1–20): Anticipating Pharaoh's eventual capitulation, the Egyptians now urge their king to release the Israelites, before Egypt is truly "lost" (v.7). The request occurs before the plague does. This longest plague is in many ways the most devastating of all, affecting as it does the very soil itself. Here the last two plagues are anticipated (v.15, "the ground became dark"; and v.17, "this death"), and the previous one is echoed (vv.6, 14, with the reference to past history). Also foreshadowed, in the locusts' removal, is the final victory at the Sea of Reeds (Chap. 14), through the mention of the location and the use of a powerful wind.

Ninth Blow (10:21–29): Little is new here; darkness foreshadows the final plague, death. Yet at the end of the brief episode, as well as in 11:8, we are given a glimpse into the human element, as Moshe and Pharaoh rage in anger against each other.

33 Moshe went from Pharaoh, outside the city, and spread out his
   hands to YHWH:
   the thunder and the hail stopped, and the rain no longer poured
   down to earth.
34 But when Pharaoh saw that the rain and the hail and the thunder
   had stopped,
   he continued to sin: he made his heart heavy-with-stubbornness,
   his and his servants'.
35 Pharaoh's heart remained strong-willed, and he did not send the
   Children of Israel free,
   as YHWH had spoken through Moshe.

10:1 YHWH said to Moshe:
   Come to Pharaoh!
   For I have made his heart and the heart of his servants heavy-
   with-stubbornness,
   in order that I may put these my signs among them
2 and in order that you may recount in the ears of your child and of
   your child's child
   how I have been capricious with Egypt,
   and my signs, which I have placed upon them—
   that you may know that I am YHWH.
3 Moshe and Aharon came to Pharaoh, they said to him:
   Thus says YHWH, the God of the Hebrews:
   How long will you refuse to humble yourself before me?
   Send free my people, that they may serve me!
4 But if you refuse to send my people free,
   here, on the morrow I will bring the locust-horde into your
   territory!
5 They will cover the aspect of the ground, so that one will not be
   able to see the ground,
   they will consume what is left of what escaped, of what remains
   for you from the hail,
   they will consume all the trees that spring up for you from the
   field,

10:2 **been capricious:** Others, "dealt harshly with,"
"made fools of."

5 **aspect:** Lit. "eye." **not be able to see:** Foreshadowing the next plague, darkness (Plaut).

6 they will fill your houses, the houses of all your servants, and the
houses of all Egypt,
as neither your fathers nor your fathers' fathers have seen
from the day of their being upon the soil until this day.
He turned and went out from Pharaoh.

7 Pharaoh's servants said to him:
How long shall this one be a snare to us?
Send the men free, that they may serve Yhwh their God!
Do you not yet know that Egypt is lost?

8 Moshe and Aharon were returned to Pharaoh,
and he said to them:
Go, serve Yhwh your God!
—Who is it, who is it that would go?

9 Moshe said:
With our young ones, with our elders we will go,
with our sons and with our daughters,
with our sheep and with our oxen we will go—
for it is Yhwh's pilgrimage-festival for us.

10 He said to them:
May Yhwh be thus with you, the same as I mean to send you free
along with your little-ones!
You see—yes, your faces are set toward ill!

11 Not thus—go now, O males, and serve Yhwh, for that is what
you (really) seek!
And they were driven out from Pharaoh's face.

12 Yhwh said to Moshe:
Stretch out your hand over the land of Egypt for the locust-
horde,
and it will ascend over the land of Egypt, consuming all the
plants of the land, all that the hail allowed to remain.

---

8 **Who is it:** Pharaoh qualifies his approval with conditions.
9 **Moshe said . . . :** The answer is rhythmical, almost
ritual. **With our young ones . . . :** The addition of
children and animals to the request of Moshe
makes Pharaoh suspect that they will not come
back.

10 **May Yhwh be thus with you:** That is to say, may he
not be with you! **your faces are set toward ill:**
You have evil intentions; "your evil intentions are
written on your faces" (Abravanel).
11 **O males:** And only the males.

13 Moshe stretched out his staff over the land of Egypt,
and YHWH led in an east wind against the land
all that day and all night;
when it was morning, the east wind had borne in the
  locust-horde.

14 The locust-horde ascended over all the land of Egypt,
it came to rest upon all the territory of Egypt,
exceedingly heavy;
before it there was no such locust-horde as it, and after it will be
  no such again.

15 It covered the aspect of all the ground, and the ground became
  dark,
it consumed all the plants of the land, and all the fruit of the trees
  that the hail had left;
nothing at all green was left of the trees and of the plants of the
  field, throughout all the land of Egypt.

16 Quickly Pharaoh had Moshe and Aharon called
and said:
I have sinned against YHWH your God, and against you!

17 So now,
pray bear my sin just this one time!
And plead with YHWH your God,
that he may only remove this death from me!

18 He went out from Pharaoh and pleaded with YHWH.

19 YHWH reversed an exceedingly strong sea wind
which bore the locusts away and dashed them into the Sea of
  Reeds,
not one locust remained throughout all the territory of Egypt.

20 But YHWH made Pharaoh's heart strong-willed, and he did not
  send the Children of Israel free.

21 YHWH said to Moshe:
Stretch out your hand over the heavens,
and let there be darkness over the land of Egypt;

---

19 **sea wind:** The story is told from the perspective of the land of Israel where such a wind means a west wind (Plaut). **wind ... not one ... remained:** Foreshadowing the incident at the Sea of Reeds (14:21,28).

The Final Warning (11:1–10): What seems to be the introduction to the last plague is made up of motifs common to several of the previous ones. It also reintroduces the idea of despoiling the Egyptians, which had been mentioned in Moshe's original commission (3:21–22)—so we know that redemption is at hand. Artfully, the specification of what "one more blow" is, is delayed until v.5. In addition, there is the motif of Moshe's greatness/fame among the Egyptians, which would appear to be a suppressed remnant of the story (in the face of the desire to glorify God as the hero). The section ends (vv.9–10) with a summary of the entire Plague Narrative—or at least of what is to be learned from it.

they will feel darkness!

22 Moshe stretched out his hand over the heavens,
and there was gloomy darkness throughout all the land of Egypt,
for three days,

23 a man could not see his brother, and a man could not arise from
his spot, for three days.
But for all the Children of Israel, there was light in their
settlements.

24 Pharaoh had Moshe called and said:
Go, serve YHWH,
only your sheep and your oxen shall be kept back,
even your little-ones may go with you!

25 Moshe said:
You must also give slaughter-offerings and offerings-up into our
hand, so that we may sacrifice them for YHWH our God!

26 Even our livestock must go with us, not a hoof may remain
behind:
for some of them we must take to serve YHWH our God;
we—we do not know how we are to serve YHWH
until we come there.

27 But YHWH made Pharaoh's heart strong-willed, so that he would
not consent to send them free.

28 Pharaoh said to him:
Go from me!
Be on your watch:
You are not to see my face again,
for on the day that you see my face, you shall die!

29 Moshe said:
You have spoken well,
I will not henceforth see your face again.

---

21 **they:** The Egyptians.

24 **only your sheep and your oxen:** Pharaoh still tries
to salvage some control of the situation.

25 **slaughter-offerings . . . offerings-up:** That is, animals for sacrifice.

28 **Go from me!:** Others, "Out of my sight!," "Leave

my presence." **on the day . . . you shall die:** The
expression is similar to the one used in reference to
Yosef in Gen. 43:3, 5. Despite the finality of the language here, the confrontation between Moshe and
Pharaoh continues in 11:4–8 and 12:31–32.

The Tenth Blow in Its Context: With Chap. 12 the narrative leaves the realm of story telling and enters that of ritual. What has so far been recounted as a story now takes on the aspect of commemorative ceremony. Instead of proceeding from warning (11:1, 4–8) to plague (12:29–30), the tenth plague account has been embedded in a setting of the lengthy description of a festival, thus shifting the time sense of the narrative. The enactment of the ceremony is important both for the characters in the story and for the participants in the audience of later generations. Likewise, the description of the actual leaving of Egypt is followed, not by a detailing of the route or what happened next, but by a series of regulations concerning who may eat the Passover meal (12:43–51) and by rules concerning the dedication of the firstborn (13:1–16).

By means of such editing, the final text was obviously meant to move the Exodus story, with all its historical aspects, into what historians of religion call "mythical time." In our text, history becomes present event; the hearer is no longer "in the audience" but actually acts out the story. That immediacy is meant is demonstrated by the threefold occurrence of the phrase "on this/that same day" (12:17, 41, 51), which also serves to unite the various parts of the text around the tenth plague and the exodus.

The mixture of law and narrative that we find in Chaps. 12 and 13 sets the stage for the Sinai scenes that will take place later in the book (Chaps. 19ff.), and indeed for the rest of the Pentateuch.

The Passover Ritual (12:1–28): The festival depicted in this chapter is, in the opinion of many scholars, a combination of two ancient holy days: a shepherds' festival, in which each spring a lamb was sacrificed to the deity in gratitude and for protection of the flock, and a celebration of the barley harvest, at which time all leaven/fermentation products were avoided (although see Ginsberg , who theorizes a shepherds' festival with *matza*). Each has numerous parallels in other cultures (see Gaster 1949). What has apparently happened here is that the two days have been fused together and imbued with historical meaning. In addition, rites that were originally protective in function have been reinterpreted in the light of the Exodus story. But whatever its origin, Passover as described in our text bespeaks a strong sense of Israelite tribal community and of distinctiveness. And it is distinctiveness, which played such an important role in Israelite religion, that is singled out here, with the striking penalty for transgressing the boundaries of the festival—being "cut off" (probably death). One also notes the repetition of the phrase "a law for the ages" (vv.14, 17, 24). Passover, then, is central both to the Exodus story and to Israelite ideas as a whole (see Sarna 1986 for a detailed discussion).

11:1 YHWH said to Moshe:
I will cause one more blow
to come upon Pharaoh and upon Egypt;
afterward he will send you free from here.
When he sends you free, it is finished—he will drive, yes, drive
you out from here.

2 Pray speak in the ears of the people:
They shall ask, each man of his neighbor, each woman of her
neighbor, objects of silver and objects of gold.

3 And YHWH gave the people favor in the eyes of Egypt,
while the man Moshe was (considered) exceedingly great in the
land of Egypt,
in the eyes of Pharaoh's servants and in the eyes of the people.

4 Moshe said:
Thus says YHWH:
In the middle of the night
I will go forth throughout the midst of Egypt,

5 and every firstborn shall die throughout the land of Egypt,
from the firstborn of Pharaoh who sits on his throne
to the firstborn of the maid who is behind the handmill,
and every firstborn of beast.

6 Then shall there be a cry throughout all the land of Egypt,
the like of which has never been, the like of which will never be
again.

7 But against all the Children of Israel, no dog shall even sharpen
its tongue, against either man or beast,
in order that you may know that YHWH makes a distinction
between Egypt and Israel.

11:3 **Moshe was (considered) exceedingly great:** Interestingly, at this point in the narrative it is Moshe and not God who is glorified (see also the note to v.8, below).

4 **the middle of the night:** As so often in folklore. The Hebrew word for "middle" (*hatzi*) is different from the one used for "midst" on the next line (*tavekh*).

6 **cry:** See also 12:30. The cry of the Egyptians echoes that of the Children of Israel in 3:7, 9.

7 **no dog:** Much less the "bringer-of-ruin" of v.13! **sharpen:** Heb. obscure.

8   Then all these your servants shall go down to me,
    they shall bow to me, saying:
    Go out, you and all the people who walk in your footsteps!
    And afterward I will go out.
    He went out from Pharaoh in flaming anger.
9   YHWH said to Moshe:
    Pharaoh will not hearken to you,
    in order that my portents may be many in the land of Egypt.
10 Now Moshe and Aharon had done all the portents in Pharaoh's
        presence,
    but YHWH had made Pharaoh's heart strong-willed, and he had
        not sent the Children of Israel free from his land.

12:1 YHWH said to Moshe and to Aharon in the land of Egypt, saying:
    2   Let this New-Moon be for you the beginning of New-Moons,
        the beginning-one let it be for you of the New-Moons of the year.
    3   Speak to the entire community of Israel, saying:
        On the tenth day after this New-Moon
        they are to take them, each-man, a lamb, according to their
            Fathers' House, a lamb per household.

---

8   **in flaming anger:** Somewhat uncharacteristically,
    the story of this last confrontation reports the emo-
    tions of both Moshe and Pharaoh. For a change we
    get a glimpse of the human side of the drama.
9–10 **Pharaoh will not hearken . . . :** These two verses
    serve as a summary of the entire Plague Narrative.
    They also help to smooth out the transition to
    Chap. 12.
10 **from his land:** The last occurrence of this phrase.
12:1 **in the land of Egypt:** The text thereby establishes
    the antiquity of the ritual.
    2   **Let this . . . be . . . let it be:** The rhetoric helps to
    focus attention on this important section. **begin-
    ning-one:** At least one form of the ancient Hebrew
    calendar began in the spring; the Torah begins its
    ritual calendar according to its ritual beginning at
    Passover. It is significant that the new year of nature

and that of the nation's birth coalesce. For extensive
discussion of Exodus and the biblical calendar, see
Sarna 1986.
3   **entire community of Israel:** This term, "commu-
    nity" (Heb. *'eda*), is used somewhat interchangeably
    with a host of others in the Torah to indicate the
    leadership (often, the elders) of the people (Wein-
    feld 1972a). **tenth:** There is a parallel important day
    in the fall, on the tenth day of the seventh month—
    Yom Kippur, the Day of Atonement (see Lev. 16:29).
    Fathers' House: See the note to 6:14.
5   **wholly-sound:** Or "hale" (Heb. *tamim*), that is,
    physically unblemished. This primary physical
    meaning often gives way to a spiritualized one, in
    reference to human beings (Job, for instance, is de-
    scribed as *tamim*, variously translated as "blame-
    less" and "perfect" in Job 1:1).

4 Now if there be too few in the house for a lamb,
  he is to take (it), he and his neighbor who is near his house, by
    the computation according to the (total number of) persons;
  each-man according to what he can eat you are to compute for
    the lamb.
5 A wholly-sound male, year-old lamb shall be yours, from the
    sheep and from the goats are you to take it.
6 It shall be for you in safekeeping, until the fourteenth day after
    this New-Moon,
  and they are to slay it—the entire assembly of the community of
    Israel—between the setting-times.
7 They are to take some of the blood and put it onto the two posts
    and onto the lintel,
  onto the houses in which they eat it.
8 They are to eat the flesh on that night, roasted in fire,
  and *matzot,*
  with bitter-herbs they are to eat it.
9 Do not eat any of it raw, or boiled, boiled in water,
  but rather roasted in fire, its head along with its legs, along with
    its innards.
10 You are not to leave any of it until morning;
  what is left of it until morning, with fire you are to burn.
11 And thus you are to eat it:
  your hips girded, your sandals on your feet, your sticks in your
    hand;

---

6 **you . . . they:** The change in the subject of the sentence, from second to third person, is not unusual in biblical Hebrew. **fourteenth day:** Close to the full moon. **between the setting-times:** At twilight. This time is mentioned elsewhere (e.g., 16:12; 29:39, 41; and several places in Numbers) in connection with the sacrifices made by the priests. This perhaps implies that we have here the unusual situation (at least in ancient Israel) of the head of the household performing a priestly function.

8 **roasted in fire:** Not raw or boiled, since what seems to be meant is an imitation of standard sacrifices. *matzot:* Sing. *matza,* flat, unleavened bread. **with**

bitter-herbs: Others, "on bitter herbs." Gaster (1949) notes the long-standing use of such cathartics as purifiers or demon-ridders (e.g., garlic) in folk cultures. Later Jewish tradition speaks of the herbs as a symbol of the bitterness of Egyptian bondage.

9 **legs . . . innards:** That is, completely consumed.

10 **You are not to leave any of it until morning:** Again, as in the removal of leaven, what is meant is complete destruction.

11 **your hips girded . . . :** Prepared for travel. Passover is still observed in this manner by some Jews originating in Arab lands.

you are to eat it in trepidation—
it is a Passover-Meal to YHWH.
12 I will proceed through the land of Egypt on this night
and strike down every firstborn in the land of Egypt, from man
to beast,
and on all the gods of Egypt I will render judgment,
I, YHWH.
13 Now the blood will be a sign for you upon the houses where you
are:
when I see the blood, I will pass over you,
the blow will not become a bringer-of-ruin to you, when I strike
down the land of Egypt.
14 This day shall be for you a memorial,
you are to celebrate it as a pilgrimage-celebration for YHWH,
throughout your generations, as a law for the ages you are to
celebrate it!
15 For seven days, *matzot* you are to eat,
already on the first day you are to get rid of leaven from your
houses,
for anyone who eats what is fermented—from the first day until
the seventh day—: that person shall be cut off from Israel!
16 And on the first day, a proclamation of holiness,
and on the seventh day, a proclamation of holiness shall there be
for you,
no kind of work is to be made on them,
only what belongs to every person to eat, that alone may be
made-ready by you.
17 And keep the (Festival of) *matzot!*
For on this same day

11 **in trepidation:** Others, "in haste," but the element of
fear is also contained in the verb (Heb. *hafoz*).
13 **pass over:** The exact meaning of Hebrew *paso'ah* is
in dispute. Some interpret it as "protect"; others, including Buber (1988), relate it to "limp," suggesting
a halting dance performed as part of the ancient festival (perhaps in imitation of the newborn spring
lambs). It is possible that there are homonyms here,
and that the text is playing on them.

15 **seven days:** Similar to the great fall festival, Sukkot,
mentioned in Lev. 23:24. **leaven . . . fermented:**
The removal of these elements is commonly found
in agricultural societies (for more, see Gaster 1949,
1969). **from the first . . . that person . . . :** The two
phrases occur in reversed order in the Hebrew.

◆ I have brought out your forces from the land of Egypt.
Keep this day throughout your generations as a law for the ages.

18 In the first (month), on the fourteenth day after the New-Moon,
at sunset, you are to eat *matzot,*
until the twenty-first day of the month, at sunset.

19 For seven days, no leaven is to be found in your houses,
for whoever eats what ferments, that person shall be cut off from
the community of Israel,
whether sojourner or native of the land.

20 Anything that ferments you are not to eat;
in all your settlements, you are to eat *matzot.*

21 Moshe had all the elders of Israel called and said to them:
Pick out, take yourselves a sheep for your clans, and slay the
Passover-animal.

22 Then take a band of hyssop, dip (it) in the blood which is in the
basin,
and touch the lintel and the two posts with some of the blood
which is in the basin.
Now you—you are not to go out, any man from the entrance to
his house, until daybreak.

23 YHWH will proceed to deal-blows to Egypt,
and when he sees the blood on the lintel and on the two posts,
YHWH will pass over the entrance,
and will not give the bringer-of-ruin (leave) to come into your
houses to deal-the-blow.

24 You are to keep this word
as a law for you and for your children, into the ages!

---

16 **a proclamation of holiness:** Others, "a holy convocation." It is not entirely clear what is meant. **proclamation . . . no kind of work:** The same rules apply to the fall festival (Lev. 23:33–43). **on them:** The first and seventh days.

17 *matzot:* This probably describes a festival separate from the one connected to the lambs, as indicated above.

20 **not to eat . . . to eat *matzot*:** The section ends with an emphatic doublet.

22 **hyssop:** The leaves are known for having a cooling effect (but some understand the Hebrew *'ezov* as meaning "marjoram"). **entrance:** Lit. "opening." This spot of entrance often serves as a figurative threshold in folklore; here, it is the separation point between life and death, Israelites and Egyptians, home and the outside world. Later, it functions as the place of revelation or contact with the holy (e.g., 33:10).

23 **pass over:** Or, following the comments on v.13, above, "skip over."

Tenth Blow and Exodus (12:29–42): The final blow falls. This most horrifying of all the plagues, and the reaction to it, are described in only two verses, whereas the rest of the narrative concerns itself with preparations for and actual description of the exodus. Note how, as above, the narrative is surrounded by ritual concerns—trying to explain the subsequent reason for eating unleavened bread (which had not been done in v.15f., above). There also returns the important motif of despoiling ("stripping") Egypt.

The section ends (vv.40–42) with a dramatic summary of Israel's sojourn in Egypt and the importance of the Passover festival, built on repetition ("thirty years and four hundred years," "a night . . . for YHWH," "keeping-watch"). Again, a past event is made immediate for the audience. The powerful religious tones of story and ceremony are established by the threefold reference to night as the setting for both (vv.29–31).

25 Now it will be,
  when you come to the land which YHWH will give you, as he has
    spoken,
  you are to keep this service!
26 And it will be,
  when your children say to you: What does this service (mean) to
    you?
27 then say:
  It is the slaughter-meal of Passover to YHWH,
  who passed over the houses of the Children of Israel in Egypt,
  when he dealt-the-blow to Egypt and our houses he rescued.
  The people did homage and bowed low.
28 And the Children of Israel went and did
  as YHWH had commanded Moshe and Aharon, thus they did.

29 Now it was in the middle of the night:
  YHWH struck down every firstborn in the land of Egypt,
  from the firstborn of Pharaoh who sits on his throne
  to the firstborn of the captive in the dungeon,
  and every firstborn of beast.
30 Pharaoh arose at night,
  he and all his servants and all Egypt,
  and there was a great cry in Egypt;
  for there is not a house in which there is not a dead man.
31 He had Moshe and Aharon called in the night
  and said:
  Arise, go out from amidst my people, even you, even the
    Children of Israel!
  Go, serve YHWH according to your words,

25 **service:** Ritual; the Israelites have begun their transformation from serfs to divine servants, under-
scored by the recurrence of "service" in 12:26 and
13:5.
26 **when your children say:** This framework is used
frequently in Deuteronomy (e.g., Deut. 6:20).
27 **when he . . . :** The chiastic structure *(A-B/B-A;* here,
a verb-noun/ noun-verb) ends the speech, a device
common in biblical style (Andersen).

29 **captive in the dungeon:** Cf. v.5, "the maid who is
behind the handmill"; both phrases express the idea
of the lowest person in the society.
30 **for there is not a house:** The omission of the perfect tense expresses the immediacy of the situation.
31 **according to your words:** Pharaoh has never thus
conceded before, and so we know that this time he
is sincere. The same change of heart is indicated in
the next verse, "And bring a blessing even on me!"

Who May Make Passover (12:43–50): Continuing the immediacy of ritual, the narrative pauses where one would expect it to talk about the Israelites' route, to specify carefully that partaking of the Passover meal, and indeed being a part of the community in general, requires circumcision on the part of the participant. In essence, it creates the new Israelite nation, on the heels of common participation in a historical event. This small passage has been inserted between two occurrences of the same phrase ("that same day"), an editorial device often used in biblical literature.

32 even your sheep, even your oxen, take, as you have spoken, and go!
  And bring-a-blessing even on me!

33 Egypt pressed the people strongly, to send them out quickly from
      the land,
  for they said: We are all dead-men!

34 So the people loaded their dough before it had fermented, their
      kneading-troughs bound in their clothing, upon their
      shoulders.

35 Now the Children of Israel had done according to Moshe's words:
  they had asked of the Egyptians objects of silver and objects of
      gold, and clothing;

36 YHWH had given the people favor in the eyes of the Egyptians,
  and they let themselves be asked of.
  So did they strip Egypt.

37 The Children of Israel moved on from Ra'amses to Sukkot,
  about six hundred thousand on foot, menfolk apart from little-
      ones,

38 and also a mixed multitude went up with them,
  along with sheep and oxen, an exceedingly heavy (amount of)
      livestock.

39 Now they baked the dough which they had brought out of Egypt
      into *matzot* cakes, for it had not fermented,
  for they had been driven out of Egypt, and were not able to
      linger,
  neither had they made provisions for themselves.

32 **even . . . :** The fourfold use of "even" here shows that Pharaoh is finally not hedging. He gives permission for *all* the Israelites to leave, without preconditions.

33 **Egypt pressed the people strongly:** Contrasting with Pharaoh's "strong-willed heart" of 10:27 and previously.

34 **their kneading-troughs bound:** To explain why only *matza* was baked; see v.39, below.

37 **moved on:** The Hebrew (*naso'a*) literally means "pulled out their tent pegs." **six hundred thousand . . . menfolk:** That is, there were over 600,000 men of military age (over twenty). Extrapolating from this several million slaves strains credibility; one might accept either the explanation put forth in

Plaut that *elef* means, not "thousand," but "troop/contingent" (of nine or ten men each), or Cassuto's designation of the number as a "perfect" or folkloric one, built on the numerical system of 6/60. For a full discussion, see Sarna (1986).

38 **mixed multitude:** This is the usual translation in English. The Hebrew is *'erev rav,* "riffraff." **heavy:** Their wealth is a counterpart to Pharaoh's previously "heavy" heart (and "heavy" plagues).

39 **were not able to linger,/ neither had they made provisions:** It comes almost as a surprise to the Israelites. Here there can be no question of military victory, as in a coup; history depends on the incursion of God.

Passover and the Firstborn (12:51–13:16): To close out the text's celebration of the exodus event, the editor includes a peroration on the firstborn. This too is a reinterpretation of earlier religious practices. Many ancient cultures selected the firstborn as an object for sacrifice to the gods—whether firstborn of fruit, of animals, or of human beings—the grounds for this being that the firstborn represents the best that nature has to offer (see Gen. 49:3, where Jacob's firstborn is "beginning of my strength"). The idea of strength is played upon in the reinterpretation of sacrifice: four times, including at the end of the passage, we are told that the firstborn is to be consecrated, "for by strength of hand YHWH brought you out of Egypt" (vv.3, 9, 14, 16).

The chapter has a few notable characteristics. For one, the eating of *matzot* has been integrated into the firstborn material; for another, the language is unmistakably reminiscent of Deuteronomy (vv.5 and 11, "it shall be [a refrain here]/when YHWH brings you to the land of the Canaanite . . ."; see Deut. 6:10, 7:1, etc.). This has led some scholars to point to a relatively late date for the material, supporting the idea that Israel in its sixth-century B.C.E. exile in Babylonia looked back to recast the past in its own image. At any rate, memory is clearly important here, with two passages stressing the continuity of commemoration through the following generations (vv.8–10 and 14–16).

40 And the settlement of the Children of Israel which they had
    settled in Egypt was thirty years and four hundred years.
41 It was at the end of thirty years and four hundred years,
    it was on that same day:
    All of YHWH's forces went out from the land of Egypt.
42 It is a night of keeping-watch for YHWH,
    to bring them out of the land of Egypt;
    that is this night for YHWH,
    a keeping-watch of all the Children of Israel, throughout their
    generations.

43 YHWH said to Moshe and Aharon:
    This is the law of the Passover-meal:
    Any foreign son is not to eat of it.
44 But any man's serf who is acquired by money—if you have
    circumcised him, then he may eat of it.
45 Settler and hired-hand are not to eat of it.
46 In one house it is to be eaten,
    you are not to bring out of the house any of the flesh, outside.
    And you are not to break a bone of it.
47 The entire community of Israel is to do it.
48 Now when a sojourner sojourns with you, and would make the
    Passover-meal to YHWH,
    every male with him must be circumcised, then he may come-
    near to make it, and will be (regarded) as a native of the land.
    But any foreskinned-man is not to eat of it.

---

40 **thirty years and four hundred years:** The numbers are patterned as usual; although this total disagrees with Gen. 15:13, for instance (which reckons it as 400 years), the differences seem to be more over which patterned numbers to use and not historical exactitude.

41 **YHWH's forces:** A term with clear military flavor; later in the Bible, Israel becomes the "armed forces of YHWH" (the same Hebrew term).

42 **keeping-watch:** Reflecting the play on words in the Hebrew *shamor*, by including ideas of both "guarding" and "observing." Cassuto (1967) sees *shamor* as a shepherd's term, appropriate here. Note again, in the tense structure, the conflation of narrative and contemporary ritual.

43 **foreign son:** Or "foreigner." The English here echoes Hebrew usage and the English idea of "native son" (Greenstein, personal communication).

46 **outside:** Into that area which has the function of being the realm of death in the story. **you are not to break a bone:** As if to violate its perfection, since the bone was identified as symbolic of the whole (viz., the same Hebrew word used for "bone" and "essence, person"). The biblical idea, found in reference to all animal sacrifices, is that only unblemished ("whole" or "hale") animals may be used for such purposes. In Gaster's (1969) view, the prohibition in this verse was originally instituted to ensure a full flock.

48 **come-near:** This verb (Heb. *karev*) is often used in connection with the priestly cult.

49 One Instruction shall there be for the native and for the sojourner
    that sojourns in your midst.

50 All the Children of Israel did
    as YHWH commanded Moshe and Aharon, thus they did.

51 It was on that same day,
    (when) YHWH brought the Children of Israel out of the land of
       Egypt by their forces,

13:1 YHWH spoke to Moshe, saying:
  2 Hallow to me every firstborn,
    breacher of every womb among the Children of Israel, of man or
       of beast,
    it is mine.

  3 Moshe said to the people:
    Remember this day,
    on which you went out from Egypt, from a house of serfs,
    for by strength of hand YHWH brought you out from here:
    no fermentation is to be eaten.
  4 Today you are going out, in the New-Moon of Ripe-Grain.
  5 And it shall be,
    when YHWH brings you to the land of the Canaanite,
    of the Hittite, of the Amorite, of the Hivvite and of the Yevusite,
    which he swore to your fathers to give you,
    a land flowing with milk and honey,
    you are to serve this service, in this New-Moon:
  6 For seven days you are to eat *matzot*,
    and on the seventh day (there is): a pilgrimage-festival to YHWH.
  7 *Matzot* are to be eaten for the seven days,
    nothing fermented is to be seen with you, no leaven is to be seen
       with you, throughout all your territory.

---

49 **Instruction:** Or "teaching," "priestly ruling." The same word later refers to Moshe's fuller "teaching," and eventually to the entire Pentateuch.
51 **that same day:** The phrase serves to bridge the two chapters here (Plaut).
13:2 **Hallow:** Make holy. **breacher:** Opener. This should not be confused with a so-called breech birth.

3 **Remember:** Here and again at 20:8, the Hebrew verbal form is an emphatic one.
4 **Ripe-Grain:** Heb. *aviv.* The month later took on a Babylonian name (Nisan), as did all the months of the Jewish calendar.

8 And you are to tell your child on that day, saying:
It is because of what YHWH did for me, when I went out of
Egypt.

9 It shall be for you for a sign on your hand and for a reminder
between your eyes,
in order that YHWH's Instruction may be in your mouth,
that by a strong hand did YHWH bring you out of Egypt.

10 You are to keep this law at its appointed-time from year-day to
year-day!

11 It shall be,
when YHWH brings you to the land of the Canaanite, as he swore
to you and to your fathers,
and gives it to you,

12 you are to transfer every breacher of a womb to YHWH,
every breacher, offspring of a beast that belongs to you,
the males (are) for YHWH.

13 Every breacher of a donkey you are to redeem with a lamb;
if you do not redeem (it), you are to break-its-neck.
And every firstborn of men, among your sons, you are to
redeem.

14 It shall be
when your child asks you on the morrow, saying: What does this
mean?
You are to say to him:
By strength of hand YHWH brought us out of Egypt, out of a
house of serfs.

9 **sign ... reminder:** This may have been figurative
originally; it became taken literally and gave rise to
the phylacteries *(tefillin)* in rabbinic Judaism. Notable in this verse is how the body is pressed into the
service of memory ("hand ... eyes ... mouth").
Rashi draws attention to the parallel idea of the
Song of Songs: "Set me as a seal upon your heart ...
upon your arm" (Song 8:6).

10 **year-day:** Heb. *yamim;* the rendering follows B-R,
which took the expression to denote both "year to
year" and specifically the holiday.

11–12 **It shall be ... every breacher:** Returning to the
subject of v.2.

12 **to ... for YHWH:** That is, for sacrifice to him.

13 **a donkey:** Not one of the "pure" animals fit for sacrifice, and hence its substitution ("redeeming") by a
lamb. **break-its-neck:** Others, "decapitate." The intent seems to be that if the animal is not redeemed,
one is not allowed to benefit economically from it
(Plaut). **firstborn of men ... redeem:** In this case
the male child is symbolically transferred to God;
child sacrifice was of course abhorrent to the Bible
(see Gen. 22). To this day religious Jews "redeem"
their firstborn sons with money given to charity,
thirty days after birth *(Pidyon Ha-Ben).*

14 **What does this mean?:** Lit. "What is this?"

The Route and the Escort (13:17–22): The initial exit from Egypt highlights an ominous fact about the Israelites: God is well aware of their weaknesses and leads them by a detour, lest they "see war" and seek to recover the familiar security of being serfs. The section also explains what they are doing out of the way of the logical route to Canaan (the place names are difficult to identify, but the general stress is clear), and sets up the great final victory of the next chapter.

Two other elements of weight enter in this brief passage. One concerns Yosef's bones, which leave Egypt with his descendants. The body of Yosef seems to anchor early Israelite history: its mummification brings the Genesis stories to a close, its journey here links up Israel's patriarchal past with the radically new deliverance from bondage, and its final interment in the land of Israel formally closes out the conquest of the land under Yehoshua (Joshua) (Josh. 24:32).

Another unifying motif is that of God's accompanying the journeying Israelites in the form of cloud and fire. This passage is the first of what I have called the "Presence Accounts" described in "On the Book of Exodus and Its Structure," above.

15 And it was
   when Pharaoh hardened (his heart) against sending us free,
   that YHWH killed every firstborn throughout the land of Egypt,
   from the firstborn of man to the firstborn of beast.
   Therefore I myself slaughter-offer to YHWH every breacher of a
      womb, the males,
   and every firstborn among my sons I redeem.
16 It shall be for a sign on your hand and for headbands between
      your eyes,
   for by strength of hand YHWH brought us out of Egypt.

17 Now it was, when Pharaoh had sent the people free,
   that God did not lead them by way of the land of the Philistines,
      which indeed is nearer,
   for God said to himself:
   Lest the people regret it, when they see war,
   and return to Egypt!
18 So God had the people swing about by way of the wilderness at
      the Sea of Reeds.
   And the Children of Israel went up armed from the land of
      Egypt.
19 Now Moshe had taken Yosef's bones with him,
   for he had made the Children of Israel swear, yes, swear, saying:
   God will take account, yes, account of you—so bring my bones
      up from here with you!
20 They moved on from Sukkot and encamped in Etam at the edge
      of the wilderness.

---

16 **headbands:** Others, "frontlets." The meaning is unclear; see the discussions in Plaut and Tigay (1982), from which the present translation is taken.
17 **lead them . . . regret:** A play on words: Heb. *naham . . . yinnahem.* **way:** Some take this to be a proper noun or name: "The Way/Road of the Land of the Philistines." **land of the Philistines:** That is, along the Mediterranean coast.
18 **Sea of Reeds:** Not "Red Sea," which came from an ancient translation. It has more recently been suggested that the term (Heb. *suf*) can be read "End

[*sof*] Sea," that is, the Sea at the End of the World. This mythological designation is attractive, given the cosmically portrayed events of the next chapter, but is not provable. The exact location, in any event, has not been established with certainty. **armed:** Heb. *(hamush)* unclear. The present rendering is supported by ancient versions; Plaut raises the possibility of "groups of five/fifty."
19 **he had made the Children of Israel swear:** See Gen. 50:25. The bones will be reburied, marking the end of the conquest of Canaan, in Josh. 24:32 .

At the Sea of Reeds (14): The liberation account ends with two literary masterpieces: the semipoetic story of Israel's miraculous passage through the Sea of Reeds along with God's smashing of the Egyptian war machine, and the song of triumph that follows in Chap. 15. Taken together, they form a natural conclusion to what has gone before and a bridge to what follows. Chap. 14 marks the Israelites' last contact with the Egyptians, and the beginning of their desert journey.

As if the actual exodus were not dramatic enough, the narrator or editor has included a battle scene at this point in the text. As before, the principal combatants are God and Pharaoh, and as before, we begin with God's hardening the monarch's heart (v.4) to teach him a final lesson ("I will be glorified"). In that vein, some of the plague motifs are repeated, making Chap. 14 a fitting conclusion to the Deliverance account stylistically and thematically (see also Isbell). At the same time the story includes a foreshadowing of Israel's behavior in the wilderness for the next two years, with a detailed account of their complaints against Moshe (and God's miraculous response).

God appears in this story in his most warlike garb, and temporarily resembles many of the gods of antiquity (Cross uses the term "the divine warrior," relating it to Northwest Semitic imagery). This is not unusual for the Bible, and seems appropriate here, given the climactic nature of the events and the general context of the Deliverance Narrative. Otherwise, the Hebrew God was conceived of as the originator of all things, good and evil, and was of course not compartmentalized into limited tasks as were other gods of neighboring cultures.

From a formal point of view, the sea narrative is among the most formulaic in the Hebrew Bible. That is, it is built entirely upon several phrases that repeat throughout the text, stressing its major themes. These include: God's "making Pharaoh's heart strong-willed" (vv.4, 8, 17); God's "being glorified" through what he does to the Egyptians (vv.4, 17, 18); Israel's going "upon dry-land" (vv.16, 22, 29); the waters' "returning" (vv.26, 27, 28); Israel's marching "through/into the midst of the sea" (vv.16, 22, 23, 27, 29); Pharaoh's "chariots and riders" (vv.17, 18, 23, 26, 28); and a description of the standing waters, "the waters a wall for them to their right and to their left" (vv.22, 29); see also the refrain, "before Pi ha-Hirot . . . before Baal-Tzefon" (v.4) and "by Pi ha-Hirot, before Baal-Tzefon" (v.9). The text is thus much more than a journalistic account of what happened: it is a rhythmic retelling of an experience, strongly conditioned by traditional (probably oral) Israelite forms of storytelling.

The ending (vv.29–31) betrays the influence of Deuteronomy. Using language that mirrors the end of the entire Torah (Deut. 34), the text speaks of seeing, fearing, hand, eyes, and the unique-to-Deuteronomy phrase "Moshe his servant" (see Deut. 34:5). Significantly, then, the final narrative of Israel's relationship to Egypt is cast as a classic ending in general.

What exactly happened at the sea? As I indicated in "On the Book of Exodus

21 Now YHWH goes before them,
by day in a column of cloud, to lead them the way,
by night in a column of fire, to give light to them,
to (be able to) go by day and by night.

22 There does not retire
the column of cloud by day
or the column of fire by night
from before the people!

14:1 YHWH spoke to Moshe, saying:

2 Speak to the Children of Israel,
that they may turn back and encamp before Pi ha-Hirot, between
Migdol and the sea,
before Baal-Tzefon, opposite it, you are to encamp by the sea.

3 Now Pharaoh will say of the Children of Israel:
They are confused in the land! The wilderness has closed them
in!

4 I will make Pharaoh's heart strong-willed, so that he pursues
them,
and I will be glorified through Pharaoh and all his army,
so that the Egyptians may know that I am YHWH.
They did thus.

5 Now the king of Egypt was told that the people fled,
and Pharaoh's heart and (that of) his servants changed regarding
the people, they said:
What is this that we have done, that we have sent free Israel from
serving us?

---

21 **YHWH goes before them:** Others, "went before them." The Hebrew idiom here means "to lead," especially in war, and is the classic biblical description of a king. **column of cloud:** Heb. *'ammud' anan.* **cloud . . . fire:** These are seen as physical manifestations of God's presence, and are brought back in the narrative at Sinai (19:16, 18).

14:2 **Pi ha-Hirot:** The location is unknown.

4 **be glorified through:** The Hebrew uses the same stem *(k-b-d)* earlier in the narrative, as if to suggest that Pharaoh's "heaviness" (stubbornness) is answered, not only by "heavy" (severe) plagues, but by God, showing his "heaviness" (glory) at the sea. I did not find a solution in English to the unified use of the one root in Hebrew—a frustrating defeat, given the principles of this translation.

5 **told that the people fled:** As if they were not expecting it; now it is obvious that the Israelites are not leaving simply to observe a religious festival (Plaut).

and Its Structure," above, such a point is unanswerable, and may not have a great bearing on the meaning of our text. Scholars have scrambled their brains for decades, trying either to reconstruct precisely what "natural" event this "really" was (e.g., tides, tidal wave), or to identify the exact location of the "Sea of Reeds." While such matters are important to the historian, the Bible itself concentrates on the theme of the story. The narrator was concerned to demonstrate God's final victory and to portray Israel's escape in terms of a birthing (through a path, out of water), and these themes had the most influence both on later biblical tradition and on the generations of inspired Jews and Christians that heeded them.

6 He had his chariot harnessed,
   his (fighting-) people he took with him,

7 and he took six hundred selected chariots and every (kind of)
      chariot of Egypt,
   teams-of-three upon them all.

8 Now YHWH made the heart of Pharaoh king of Egypt strong-
      willed, so that he pursued the Children of Israel,
   while the Children of Israel were going out with a high hand.

9 The Egyptians pursued them and overtook them encamped by
      the sea,
   all of Pharaoh's chariot-horses, his riders, and his army,
   by Pi ha-Hirot, before Baal-Tzefon.

10 As Pharaoh drew near, the Children of Israel lifted up their eyes:
   Here, Egypt marching after them!
   They were exceedingly afraid.
   And the Children of Israel cried out to YHWH,

11 they said to Moshe:
   Is it because there are no graves in Egypt
   that you have taken us out to die in the wilderness?
   What is this that you have done to us, bringing us out of Egypt?

12 Is this not the very word that we spoke to you in Egypt,
   saying: Let us alone, that we may serve Egypt!
   Indeed, better for us serving Egypt
   than our dying in the wilderness!

13 Moshe said to the people:
   Do not be afraid!
   Stand fast and see

---

6 **(fighting-) people:** This reading is supported by
Num. 31:32 and Josh. 8:1 (Childs).
7 **six hundred:** A nice counterpart of the 600,000 (or
600 units of) Israelite males mentioned previously.
teams-of-three: Others, "officers," "warriors," "a
picked team."
8 **a high hand:** Others, "defiantly," "in triumph."
11–12 **they said . . . wilderness:** The Israelites' complaint
has been shaped into a great rhetorical paragraph,
with the people's first "grumbling" against Moshe

an ominous foreshadowing of what will occur
throughout the wanderings. In this construction,
the longed-for "Egypt" is repeated five times, and
the unknown "wilderness" twice. Note also the
stress on Moshe: "you have taken us out . . . you
have done to us."
13 **Moshe said . . . :** There follow four rapid-fire verbs
of command, to quiet the complaints. **Stand fast
and see:** Heb. *hityatzevu u-re'u.*

YHWH's deliverance which he will work for you today,
for as you see Egypt today, you will never see it again for the ages!

14 YHWH will make war for you, and you—be still!

15 YHWH said to Moshe:
Why do you cry out to me?
Speak to the Children of Israel, and let-them-march-forward!

16 And you—
hold your staff high, stretch out your hand over the sea
and split it,
so that the Children of Israel may come through the midst of the
sea upon the dry-land.

17 But I,
here, I will make Egypt's heart strong-willed,
so that they come in after them,
and I will be glorified through Pharaoh and all his army,
his chariots and his riders;

18 the Egyptians shall know that I am YHWH,
when I am glorified through Pharaoh, his chariots and his riders.

19 The messenger of God that was going before the camp of Israel
moved on and went behind them,
the column of cloud moved ahead of them
and stood behind them,

20 coming between the camp of Egypt and the camp of Israel.
Here were the cloud and the darkness,
and (there) it lit up the night;
the-one did not come near the-other all night.

21 Moshe stretched out his hand over the sea,
and YHWH caused the sea to go back
with a fierce east wind all night,

---

13 **deliverance:** A word meaning "rescue," but extending to circumstances that appear miraculous to those who experience them.

15–16 **YHWH said . . . :** God echoes Moshe, issuing four commands.

15 **let-them-march-forward:** Countering the "Egypt marching after them" of v. 10.

16 **and split it:** As if that were as natural an act as stretching out one's hand!

20 **and (there) it lit up:** Heb. unclear; some read the verb as coming from a different root, meaning "cast a spell on," which, however, weakens the theme of distinction mentioned earlier.

21 **fierce east wind:** Looking back to the "east wind" that rid Egypt of the locusts in 10:13, and forward to God's "fierce-might" in 15:2, after the triumph at the sea. **firm-ground:** In the Flood Narrative, another story of deliverance (and death) by water, the same word appears as a sign that all is well. Similarly, the "dry-land" of the next verse appears in Gen. 8:14.

and made the sea into firm-ground;
thus the waters split.

22 The Children of Israel came through the midst of the sea upon
the dry-land,
the waters a wall for them on their right and on their left.

23 But the Egyptians pursued and came in after them,
all of Pharaoh's horses, his chariots and his riders,
into the midst of the sea.

24 Now it was at the daybreak-watch:
YHWH looked out against the camp of Egypt in the column of
fire and cloud,
and he panicked the camp of Egypt,

25 he loosened the wheels of his chariots and made them to drive
with heaviness.
Egypt said:
I must flee before Israel,
for YHWH makes war for them against Egypt!

26 Then YHWH said to Moshe:
Stretch out your hand over the sea,
and the waters shall return
upon Egypt—upon its chariots and upon its riders.

27 Moshe stretched out his hand over the sea,
and the sea returned, at the face of dawn, to its original-place,
as the Egyptians were fleeing toward it.
And YHWH shook the Egyptians in the midst of the sea.

28 The waters returned,
they covered the chariots and the riders of all of Pharaoh's army
that had come after them into the sea,
not even one of them remained.

---

24 **daybreak-watch:** Before sunrise; the biblical night was divided into three "watches." **panicked:** "stirred up." Others, "threw into panic." The phrase is used in the Bible to describe God's effect on his enemies (e.g., Josh. 10:10, Judg. 4:15, I Sam. 7:10) (Hyatt).

25 **heaviness:** Again, possibly a play on Pharaoh's "heaviness" (stubbornness) and God's "glory."

27 **face:** Or "turning," which, however, would have clashed with the frequent "returning" (another Hebrew verb) in these verses. **original-place:** Others, "bed," "normal depth."

The Song of God as Triumphant King (15:1–21): Moshe's famous Song at the Sea provides a natural boundary in the book of Exodus. It sets off the Egypt traditions from those of Sinai and the wilderness, and brings to a spectacular close the saga of liberation. This is borne out even in scribal tradition, still observed in the writing of Torah scrolls today, where the Song is written out with different spacing from the preceding and following narrative portions.

A poem is necessary at this point in the story, to provide emotional exultation and a needed break before the next phase of Israel's journey in the book. The Song manages to focus the Israelites' (the audience's?) intense feelings in a way that neither the ritual of Chaps. 12–13 nor even the semipoetic description of God's miraculous intervention in Chap. 14 can do. Only poetry is capable of expressing the full range of the people's emotions about what has happened. This is similar to the effect of the great poems that occur toward the end of Genesis (Chap. 49, the Blessing of Yaakov) and Deuteronomy (Chaps. 32–33, the Song and Blessing of Moshe).

A major concern of the poet is God's kingship, with which he ends the poem (a one-liner—"Let YHWH be king for the ages, eternity!"—contrasting with the doublets and triplets in the body of the poem). This is no accident, nor is it inappropriate; since Chaps. 4 and 5 the story of Exodus has revolved around just who shall be king (God or Pharaoh) and just who shall be served. By the end of Chap. 14 this is no longer an issue. The victorious YHWH can now be acclaimed as king, while we hear nothing further of Pharaoh. (Has he drowned or merely been written out of the story? Later generations of Jews enjoyed giving him a role in the world to come: he stands at the gate of Hell, admonishing evildoers as they enter; see Ginzberg.)

The attempts to recover what happened at the sea through the poem are doomed to failure, considering that the piece is constructed out of two traditional stories, the victory at the sea and the later conquest of Canaan (vv.1–12, 13–17). Further, it is set in cosmic terms. The words "Oceans" (Heb. *tehomot;* vv.5, 8) and "breath" *(ru'ah;* v.8) recall the primeval chaos at the beginning of Creation itself (Gen. 1:2). This technique is characteristic of much of ancient/religious literature: a great event is told in a way that reflects the beginnings of the gods and the world (this may include statements about the end of the world as well).

It should be noted that some scholars point out the close resemblance between God's victory here and scenes in other ancient Near Eastern literatures that portray the triumph of a storm god over a sea god. So however historical the events in Chaps. 14–15 may have been, in their biblical retelling they have been patterned after antecedents in myth.

Much has been written concerning the structure of the Song (see, e.g., Cassuto, Cross, and Lichtenstein). I will mention only a few points here. The vocabulary of the poem is extremely concentrated. Major ideas are expressed by

29 But the Children of Israel had gone upon dry-land, through the
  midst of the sea,
 the waters a wall for them on their right and on their left.

30 So YHWH delivered Israel on that day from the hand of Egypt;
 Israel saw Egypt dead by the shore of the sea,

31 and Israel saw the great hand that YHWH had wrought against
  Egypt,
 the people held YHWH in awe,
 they trusted in YHWH and in Moshe his servant.

15:1 Then sang Moshe and the Children of Israel
this song to YHWH,
 they uttered (this) utterance:

  I will sing to YHWH,
  for he has triumphed, yes, triumphed,
  the horse and its charioteer he flung into the sea!

2 My fierce-might and strength is YAH,
  he has become deliverance for me.

   This is my God—I honor him,
   the God of my father—I exalt him.

3 YHWH is a man of war,
  YHWH is his name!

4 Pharaoh's chariots and his army
  he hurled into the sea,
  his choicest teams-of-three
  sank in the Sea of Reeds.

5 Oceans covered them,
  they went down in the depths
  like a stone.

30–31 **saw . . . saw:** The key verb again, echoing back not only to v. 13 but to various narratives throughout the book.

15:1 **uttered (this) utterance:** Giving a wider range of meaning for the Hebrew *va-yomeru le'mor.* **triumphed:** A rendering based on Ugaritic.

2 **strength.** Others, "song." **YAH:** A shortened form (YH) of the name of God (YHWH), and found often in biblical names (e.g., Uriah).

3 **man of war:** Or "warrior."

clusters of key verbs. Note, for instance, the grouping of "flung," "hurled," "plunged," "shattered," "smashed," "consumed"—a veritable lexicon of military victory. A number of verbs describe divine leadership ("led," "guided," "brought"), and God's establishment of the Israelites in Canaan ("planted," "founded"). The fear of the Canaanites (of Israel and its God) is graphically expanded to "shuddered," "seized with writhing," "terrified," "seized with trembling," "melted away," ". . . dread and anguish," and "grew dumb." Finally, there are a number of nouns that express weight (cf. Heb. *kaved*, previously discussed): "stone," "dam," and "lead."

The overall effect of the poem is of fierce pride at God's victory, and exultant description of the destruction and discomfort of enemies, whether Egyptian or Canaanite. This general tone parallels many ancient war poems; what is characteristically Israelite about it is God's choosing and leading a people. Therefore the last verse goes far beyond the celebration of a single military victory. The Song constitutes the founding of a theocratic people.

Scholars have long noted the archaic style of the Song, which uses forms characteristic of early biblical Hebrew. Its tone is for this reason even more exalted than is usual in biblical poetry. An imaginative reflection of the effect can be found in Daiches, who paraphrases the Song in the style of early English epic poetry.

Two sections have been appended to the end of the poem. First there is the poetically remarkable summary of the narrative in v.19, notable for the fact that it is composed wholly from phrases used in Chap. 14. There follows a women's repetition/performance of at least part of the Song complete with dance. Some scholars see this as the "original" form of the poem. Of equal interest is the characterization of Miryam as a "prophetess." But there may be a structural reason for her appearance as well: the enterprise of deliverance from Egypt began with a little girl at the Nile, watching through the reeds to make sure her baby brother would survive; it ends with the same person, now an adult, a "prophetess" celebrating the final victory at the Sea of Reeds.

6   Your right-hand, O Yhwh,
    majestic in power,
    your right-hand, O Yhwh,
    shattered the enemy.

7   In your great triumph
    you smashed your foes,
    you sent forth your fury,
    consumed them like chaff.

8   By the breath of your nostrils
    the waters piled up,
    the gushing-streams stood up like a dam,
    the oceans congealed in the heart of the sea.

9   Uttered the enemy:
    I will pursue,
    overtake,
    and apportion the plunder,
    my greed will be filled on them,
    my sword I will draw,
    my hand—dispossess them!
10 You blew with your breath,
    the sea covered them,
    they plunged down like lead
    in majestic waters.

11 Who is like you among the gods, O Yhwh!
    who is like you, majestic among the holy-ones,
    Feared-One of praises, Doer of Wonders!

6   **right-hand:** As elsewhere in the ancient and me-
    dieval world, the right hand was symbolic of
    strength.
8   **piled up:** Heb. root *'rm,* found only here.
9   **Uttered the enemy . . . :** The Hebrew uses allitera-
    tion, as well as a concentration on "I/my," to ex-
    press the vividness and urgency of the enemy's
    greed: *'amar 'oyev/ 'erdof 'asig/ 'ahallek shallal.* I have

tried to use alliterative English words ("uttered . . .
enemy/I . . . overtake . . . and apportion") and at
least to hint at the poetic force of the Hebrew.
greed: The Hebrew *(nefesh)* means "seat of feelings,
emotions"; trad. "soul."
11 **among the gods:** The sea is the scene of Yhwh's
final triumph over the gods of Egypt, as it were.

12　You stretched out your right-hand,
　　the Underworld swallowed them.

13　　You led in your faithfulness
　　your people redeemed,
　　guided (them) in your fierce-might
　　to your holy pasture.

14　The peoples heard,
　　they shuddered;
　　writhing seized
　　Philistia's settlers,
15　and then, terrified,
　　Edom's chieftains,
　　Moav's "rams"—
　　trembling did seize them;
　　then melted away
　　all Canaan's settlers.

16　There fell upon them
　　dread and anguish;
　　before your arm's greatness
　　they grew dumb like stone.

17　　Until they crossed—your people, O YHWH,
　　until they crossed—the people you fashioned.
　　You brought them, you planted them
　　on the mount of your heritage,
　　foundation of your (royal) seat
　　which you prepared, O YHWH,
　　the Holy-Shrine, O Lord,
　　founded by your hands.

12　**Underworld:** Others, "earth."

13　**holy pasture:** A shepherd's term, which could indicate the entire land of Canaan, and hence support the background of the Conquest in the poem (Childs).

14–15　**Philistia . . . Edom . . . Moav:** Israel's later (and hostile) neighbors, to the west and east.

15　**"rams":** Perhaps, as in Ugaritic usage, a technical term for "chieftains."

17　**mount . . . foundation . . . Holy-Shrine:** Probably the Jerusalem Temple of later times, although the entire land is sometimes referred to as "mount of your inheritance" (see Deut. 3:25) (Hertz).

18   Let Y<small>HWH</small> be king for the ages, eternity!

19 For Pharaoh's horses came with (their) chariots and riders into
      the sea,
    but Y<small>HWH</small> turned back the sea's waters upon them,
    and the Children of Israel went upon the dry-land
    through the midst of the sea.

20 Now Miryam the prophetess, Aharon's sister, took a timbrel in
      her hand,
    and all the women went out after her, with timbrels and with
      dancing.
21 Miryam chanted to them:
      Sing to Y<small>HWH</small>, for he has triumphed, yes, triumphed,
      the horse and its charioteer
      he flung into the sea!

---

20 **Miryam the prophetess:** Trad. English "Miriam." This is the first time in the narrative that she is mentioned by name, and also the first appearance of a "prophetess" in the Hebrew Bible.

IN THE WILDERNESS

(15:22–18:27)

THE WILDERNESS NARRATIVES IN THE TORAH MUST HAVE BEEN EXTRAORDINARILY IM-
portant to the narrator/editor, as evidenced by their placement at this point in
Exodus. Why did he/they see fit to insert here material which, chronologically at
least, would fit better at a later point—for instance, in the book of Numbers
(which reports essentially the same sort of incidents)?

The answer comes from several quarters. The wilderness stories embody a key
process for the Torah story: Israel's passage from enslaved childhood to troubled
adolescence, with a hopeful glance toward adulthood (the Promised Land). This
process starts immediately after liberation; indeed, it is its direct result. Further,
the three "desert themes" prominent in Chapters 15–18—"grumbling" against
God and Moshe, hostile neighbors, and early self-government—are appropriate
to include before the meeting at Sinai, in that they demonstrate dramatically the
people's need for reassurance, protection, group solidarity, and institutions
(whereby they can live harmoniously). These narratives, therefore, lay out Israel's
precarious position and create the hope for a cure. It is only later on in the Torah,
in the book of Numbers, that we will discover that the growing-up process in the
wilderness could not be accomplished in a single generation.

The portrait of a people (or of an individual, as is often the case in religious literature) undergoing transformation in a place outside of normal geographic/
cultural boundaries is a well-known phenomenon in traditional stories.
Anthropologist Victor Turner speaks of the "liminal" experience, where the protagonist or initiant is separated spiritually and geographically from his origins in
order to be changed into something new (see Fredman and Cohn). This is paral-
leled by the process of pilgrimage in the world of ritual, as can still be observed
among many communities of the world to this day. The desert is the site of limi-
nality par excellence: it is a harsh place that contains none of the succoring elements of human civilization, yet at the same time it leads the wanderer into truer
communication with nature and the divine, metacultural forces of the universe.
It is a place of betwixt and between, which mirrors the experiencer's psychological state. In the case of Israel, later biblical sources speak of the wilderness period
with striking force, either as an example of the people's long-standing and deeply
ingrained rebelliousness (e.g., Psalm 95), or fondly, as a kind of honeymoon pe-

riod between God and Israel (e.g., Jer. 2:2). In both cases what is evoked is only a stage on the way, and not the final goal (see Talmon).

Transformation always involves both life and death, and so it is not surprising that a characteristic theme of the stories before us is lack of food and/or water. The opening episodes of the section (15:22–17:7) comprise three scenes of "grumbling" about the difficulties of survival (with the structure: water–food–water), with a unique biblical twist: God and the people "testing" each other. And so the transformation depends very much on God's action on the people's behalf (twice he has to "instruct" them—the very verb from which the term "Torah" is derived). The suspension of the life process, or at least its imperiling, is notable also in the fact that, in contrast to the fertility of the Israelites in Egypt, "the trek narrative does not relate a single birth" (Cohn). This is especially striking given the strong birth image of Israel at the Sea of Reeds, which is still in the reader's mind as the section opens.

Grumbling I (15:22–27): The first of the wilderness narratives is linked to what has gone before via the theme of water. Fresh from their rescue from death at the sea, the Israelites look for water in the desert and find the discovery of unpotable water intolerable. The key word, especially for the many later wilderness traditions such as we find in Numbers, is "grumbled" (Heb. *lyn*), which leads to God's nurturing of the people. Strangely, the theme of undrinkable water recalls the beginning of the plague sequence in Egypt (7:20–21).

Right away in this first desert episode we are told the purpose of Israel's journey: God is testing them, to see if they will "hearken" to what he bids them to do. The language is in the style of Deuteronomy. One should also mention the idea of "law and judgment," indicating another crucial desert theme: Israel's ability or inability to govern itself.

The account ends with an abundance of water in v.27.

Grumbling II (16): Moving now halfway (in terms of time) to their Sinai destination, the people encounter a new lack: food. This reintroduces the "testing" motif (v.4), with its built-in answer: God provides quails and *mahn* (trad. English "manna"). The story is full-blown, and its repeating vocabulary sets forth the issues clearly: "grumble" occurs seven times, and "command/commandments" four times, linked to the idea of testing. Indeed, this long story poses the question central to all the wilderness narratives: ". . . whether they will walk according to my instruction or not" (v.4).

The manna was important in early Israelite tradition as a witness to God's nurturing, as attested by the end of the chapter with its ritual prescriptions regarding it (vv.32–34; note the threefold repetition of "safekeeping"). But it also sets up an emphasis on a more permanent institution in Israelite culture: the Sabbath. One notion that this passage may convey is the antiquity and importance of the Sabbath, preceding the laws of Sinai as it does here. Also at issue is whether the Israelites can follow simple rules laid down by God.

22 Moshe had Israel move on from the Sea of Reeds,
  and they went out to the Wilderness of Shur.
  They traveled through the wilderness for three days, and found
      no water.
23 They came to Mara,
  but they could not drink water from Mara, because it was
      mar/bitter.
  Therefore they called its name Mara.
24 The people grumbled against Moshe, saying:
  What are we to drink?
25 He cried out to YHWH,
  and YHWH directed him (to some) wood
  which he threw into the water, and the water became sweet.—
  There he imposed law and judgment for them, and there he
      tested them.
26 He said:
  If you will hearken, yes, hearken to the voice of YHWH your God,
  and what is right in his eyes will do,
  giving-ear to his commandments
  and keeping all his laws:
  all the sicknesses which I have imposed upon Egypt, I will not
      impose upon you;
  for I am YHWH, your healer.

27 They came to Elim;
  there were twelve springs of water
  and seventy palms,
  and they camped there by the water.

---

22 **Shur:** Some translate as "Wall" (of Egypt)—the outer fortified boundary of the country, and hence the edge of civilization.

24 **grumbled:** Others, "murmured," which is, however, more alliterative than the Hebrew itself *(va-yilonu)*.

25 **There he imposed law and judgment:** Others, "There he made for them statute and ordinance," etc. The force is not clear, but the phrase seems to fit in with the overall section, which, as I have noted, concerns itself with the Israelites' early government.

26 **sicknesses . . . upon Egypt:** A recurring theme in the Torah; see the curse in Deut. 28:60.

27 **Elim:** Lit. "terebinths" (great trees already mentioned in Gen. 12:6 and 18:1). **twelve springs . . . seventy palms:** Once again the numbers are obviously typological.

16:1 They moved on from Elim, and they came, the entire community
          of the Children of Israel, to the Wilderness of Syn, which is
          between Elim and Sinai,
      on the fifteenth day after the second New-Moon after their going-
          out from the land of Egypt.
    2 And they grumbled, the entire community of the Children of
          Israel, against Moshe and against Aharon in the wilderness.
    3 The Children of Israel said to them:
      Would that we had died by the hand of YHWH in the land of
          Egypt,
      when we sat by the flesh pots,
      when we ate bread till (we were) satisfied!
      For you have brought us into this wilderness
      to bring death to this whole assembly by starvation!
    4 YHWH said to Moshe:
      Here, I will make rain down upon you bread from the heavens,
      the people shall go out and glean, each day's amount in its day,
      in order that I may test them, whether they will walk according
          to my Instruction or not.
    5 But it shall be on the sixth day:
      when they prepare what they have brought in,
      it shall be a double-portion compared to what they glean day
          after day.
    6 Moshe and Aharon said to all the Children of Israel:
      At sunset
      you will know that it is YHWH who brought you out of the land
          of Egypt;
    7 at daybreak
      you will see the Glory of YHWH:
      when he hearkens to your grumblings against YHWH—
      what are we, that you grumble against us?

16:1 **entire community:** See the note to 12:3. **Syn:** Pronounced "seen." The present spelling has been
adopted to avoid the unfortunate associations of the
sound "sin" in English.
  3 **Egypt ... flesh pots ... :** Notice the endings of
each line, which can be grouped into two clusters:
"Egypt ... flesh pots ... satisfied" versus "wilderness ... starvation."

  4 **YHWH said:** Notice how God's answer is totally devoid of anger, for the dissatisfaction of the people is
to provide them with a "test." **them . . . they:** The
pronouns are collective singular in Hebrew.
  5 **a double-portion:** For the Sabbath, when no glean-
ing is permitted.
  7 **what are we:** The issue is not between Israel and its
human leaders, but really between them and God.

◆ 8 Moshe said:
Since YHWH gives you
flesh to eat at sunset,
and at daybreak, bread to satisfy (yourselves);
since YHWH hearkens to your grumblings which you grumble
against him—
what are we:
not against us are your grumblings, but against YHWH!
9 Moshe said to Aharon:
Say to the entire community of the Children of Israel:
Come-near, in the presence of YHWH,
for he has hearkened to your grumblings!
10 Now it was, when Aharon spoke to the entire community of the
Children of Israel,
they faced the wilderness,
and here:
the Glory of YHWH could be seen in the cloud.
11 YHWH spoke to Moshe, saying:
12 I have hearkened to the grumblings of the Children of Israel—
speak to them, and say:
Between the setting-times you shall eat flesh,
and at daybreak you shall be satisfied with bread,
and you shall know
that I am YHWH your God.
13 Now it was at sunset
a horde-of-quail came up and covered the camp.
And at daybreak
there was a layer of dew around the camp;
14 and when the layer of dew went up,
here, upon the surface of the wilderness,
something fine,

---

8 **bread:** See the note to 2:20.
9 **Come-near:** See the note to 12:48.
14 **something fine:** The *mahn* (trad. English "manna"), described again in v.31, below, possibly refers to insect secretions found on the branches of certain Sinai plants. The question has been asked, however, whether the amount so produced would under normal circumstances be sufficient to feed a large population—hence the text itself stresses the divine element, and any attempt to explain it scientifically misses the point of the biblical story.

scaly,
fine as hoar-frost upon the land.

15 When the Children of Israel saw it
they said each-man to his brother:
Mahn hu/what is it?
For they did not know what it was.
Moshe said to them:
It is the bread that YHWH has given you for eating.

16 This is the word that YHWH has commanded:
Glean from it, each-man according to what he can eat,
an *omer* per capita, according to the number of your persons,
each-man, for those in his tent, you are to take.

17 The Children of Israel did thus,
they gleaned, the-one-more and the-one-less,

18 but when they measured by the *omer,*
no surplus had the-one-more, and the-one-less had no shortage;
each-man had gleaned according to what he could eat.

19 Moshe said to them:
No man shall leave any of it until morning.

20 But they did not hearken to Moshe,
and (several) men left some of it until morning;
it became wormy with maggots and reeked.
And Moshe became furious with them.

21 They gleaned it in the morning, (every) morning, each-man in
accordance with what he could eat,
but when the sun heated up, it melted.

22 Now it was on the sixth day
that they gleaned a double-portion of bread, two *omers* for (each)
one.

---

15 *Mahn hu:* A folk etymological corruption of the Hebrew *mah hu,* although there is some support for
this form in other Semitic languages. A playful rendering might be "whaddayacallit" or "what's-its-
name."

16 *omer:* A dry measure, approximately 2⅓ liters or 2
dry quarts.

17 **the-one:** Or "some of them."

18 **no surplus . . . no shortage:** In the tradition of mir-

acle stories, exactly the right amount is found for
each person.

19 **No man shall leave any of it until morning:** Like
the Passover sacrifice in 12:10 and 34:25, or the festi-
val-offering in 23:18. The idea may be not to disturb
the perfection of the offering by risking putrefac-
tion.

22 **exalted-leaders:** Or "princes."

All the exalted-leaders of the community came and told it to
    Moshe.

23 He said to them:

It is what Yʜwʜ spoke about:

tomorrow is a Sabbath/Ceasing, a Sabbath of Holiness for
    Yʜwʜ.

Whatever you wish to bake—bake, and whatever you wish to
    boil—boil;

and all the surplus, put aside for yourselves in safekeeping until
    morning.

24 They put it aside until morning, as Moshe had commanded,

and it did not reek, neither were there any maggots in it.

25 Moshe said:

Eat it today,

for today is a Sabbath for Yʜwʜ,

today you will not find it in the field.

26 For six days you are to glean,

but on the seventh day is Sabbath, there will not be (any) on it.

27 But it was on the seventh day

that some of the people went out to glean, and they did not find.

28 Yʜwʜ said to Moshe:

Until when will you refuse to keep my commandments and my
    instructions?

29 (You) see

that Yʜwʜ has given you the Sabbath,

therefore on the sixth day, he gives you bread for two days.

Stay, each-man, in his spot;

no man shall go out from his place on the seventh day!

30 So the people ceased on the seventh day.

31 Now the House of Israel called its name: *Mahn.*

—It is like coriander seed, whitish,

and its taste is like (that of) a wafer with honey.—

---

23 **It is what Yʜwʜ spoke about:** Although this speech is not mentioned in a previous text. This may support the position that the story was originally placed after Chap. 20 (which contains the command to observe the Sabbath). **Ceasing:** The root meaning of the Hebrew *shabbat,* "Sabbath."

24 **it did not reek:** Since this time they followed God's orders.

28 **you:** Plural, referring to the people.

31 **Now . . . honey:** A parenthetical comment. For another biblical description of the manna, see Num. 11:8.

Grumbling III (17:1–7): With the third wilderness story we return to the water theme. This time the element of "quarreling" with Moshe is added, in addition to the portrayal of Moshe's eroding patience (v.4). Otherwise it is a variation on the basic theme (notice, for instance, the similarities between 16:3 and 17:3). The ending is ominous, reversing the previously held idea of God's testing Israel.

32 Moshe said:
This is the word that YHWH has commanded:
An *omer* of it for safekeeping throughout your generations,
in order that they may see the bread that I had you eat in the
    wilderness
when I brought you out of the land of Egypt.

33 Moshe said to Aharon:
Take a vat and put an *omer* of *mahn* in it,
and put it aside in the presence of YHWH, in safekeeping
    throughout your generations.

34 As YHWH had commanded Moshe, Aharon put it aside before the
    Testimony, in safekeeping.

35 And the Children of Israel ate the *mahn* for the forty years, until
    they came to settled land,
the *mahn* they ate, until they came to the edge of the land of
    Canaan.

36 Now an *omer*—it is a tenth of an *efa*.

17:1 They moved on, the whole community of the Children of Israel,
    from the Wilderness of Syn,
by their moving-stages, at YHWH's bidding.
They encamped at Refidim,
and there is no water for the people to drink!

2 The people quarreled with Moshe, they said:
Give us water, that we may drink!
Moshe said to them:
For-what do you quarrel with me?
For-what do you test YHWH?

3 The people thirsted for water there,
    and the people grumbled against Moshe, and said:
For-what-reason then did you bring us up from Egypt,

34 **Testimony:** The tablets of the covenant mentioned
in 25:21 and 31:18; their citing seems out of place
here, but it should be borne in mind that the Torah
is not always chronological, as was already recognized
by medieval commentators.

17:2 **For-what:** Why. Notice how the text equates quarreling with Moshe and testing YHWH. **quarrel:** A
verb that often denotes a legal case in biblical texts.

War with Amalek (17:8–16): In addition to testing/grumbling, conflict with foreigners is a significant wilderness theme (see Num. 20–24). It is perhaps for this reason that it has been included in the pre-Sinai traditions. Its placement here may depend on its use of Moshe's staff; the previous narrative ended with the use of that object, and such linkage was a known form of composition in ancient literature.

The tradition about Israel's relationship with Amalek, however brief, persists as an important one in the Bible. Saul, Israel's first king, is commanded by God to wipe out the Amalekites, as punishment for their opposition of Israel in our passage (I Sam. 15), and centuries later, Haman, the evil Persian councillor who proposes to exterminate the Jews of his country, is portrayed as a descendant of the Amalekite king (Esther 3:1).

Our story, however, is no mere military report, but also a tradition about the power of the "staff of God." In another culture, indeed in later Midrashic literature, such a theme would receive Excalibur-like treatment, but the Bible suppresses the magical side and simply uses it as a tool, expressing God's continuing deliverance of Israel.

to bring death to me, to my children and to my livestock by
 thirst?

4 Moshe cried out to YHWH, saying:
What shall I do with this people?
A little more and they will stone me!

5 YHWH said to Moshe:
Proceed before the people,
take some of the elders of Israel with you,
and your staff with which you struck the Nile, take in your hand,
 and go!

6 Here, I stand before you there on the rock at Horev,
you are to strike the rock, and water shall come out of it, and the
 people shall drink.
Moshe did thus, before the eyes of the elders of Israel.

7 And he called the name of the place: *Massa*/Testing, and
 Meriva/Quarreling,
because of the quarreling of the Children of Israel,
and because of their testing of YHWH, saying:
Is YHWH among us, or not?

8 Now Amalek came and made-war upon Israel in Refidim.

9 Moshe said to Yehoshua:
Choose us men,
and go out, make-war upon Amalek!
On the morrow I will station myself on top of the hill, with the
 staff of God in my hand.

10 Yehoshua did as Moshe had said to him,
to make-war against Amalek.
Now Moshe, Aharon and Hur went up to the top of the hill.

11 And it was, whenever Moshe raised his hand, Israel prevailed, and
 whenever he set down his hand, Amalek prevailed.

12 Now Moshe's hands are heavy;

---

3 **me:** Personalizing the complaint.

6 **you are to strike the rock:** See Num. 20:2–13 for the famous variation on this story that proves to be Moshe's undoing.

7 **saying:** Meaning or signifying.

9 **Yehoshua.** Trad. English "Joshua." He appears subsequently as Moshe's personal attendant, but it is significant that the first mention of him is in a military context, since he will ultimately command the invasion of Canaan.

10 **Hur:** He is mentioned again in 24:4 as Aharon's assistant in the governing of the people during Moshe's absence.

The New Society: Yitro's Visit (18): Israel finally reaches the "mountain of God," but this, remarkably, is subordinated to the fact that Moshe and the people meet up with Yitro, whom we recall from Chaps. 2–4. The designation "father-in-law" recurs throughout this chapter (thirteen times), perhaps playing up the importance of the relationship in Israelite society. The real concern of the story, however, is Moshe's early attempt to set up a functioning judicial system in Israel (hence the key word *davar*, ten times, translated here as "matter" in the sense of "legal matter"). The chapter thus serves as a good prelude to Sinai, which will include far-ranging legal material (despite the fact that some scholars see it as an insertion from a later period—cf. v.16, "God's laws and his instructions").

It has been noted (Cohn) that the "trek narratives" in Exodus and Numbers have been laid out evenly, with six "stations" between Egypt and Sinai and another six between Sinai and the land of Israel. Thus here, Israel has come to the midpoint of its journey. In another perspective, Moshe himself has come full circle, returning to both the spot and the man in whose presence the mature adult phase of his life had begun.

so they took a stone and placed it under him, and he sat down
   on it,
while Aharon and Hur supported his hands, one on this-side and
   one on that-side.
So his hands remained steadfast, until the sun came in.

13 And Yehoshua weakened Amalek and his people, with the edge of
   the sword.

14 YHWH said to Moshe:
Write this as a memorial in an account
and put it in Yehoshua's hearing:
Yes, I will wipe out, wipe out the memory of Amalek from under
   the heavens!

15 Moshe built a slaughter-site
and called its name: YHWH My Banner.

16 He said:
Yes,
Hand on YAH's throne!
War for YHWH against Amalek
generation after generation!

18:1 Now Yitro, the priest of Midyan, Moshe's father-in-law, heard
about all that God had done for Moshe and for Israel his people,
that YHWH had brought Israel out of Egypt.

2 Yitro, Moshe's father-in-law,
took Tzippora, Moshe's wife—after she had been sent home—

3 and her two sons,
of whom the first-one's name was Gershom / Sojourner There,
   for he had said: I have become a sojourner in a foreign land,

---

12 **sun came in:** Set.
13 **weakened:** Disabled or defeated.
14 **account:** Or "document." **wipe out the memory:** The command demonstrates the depth of Israel's animosity toward Amalek.
16 **Hand on:** Cassuto suggests "monument to," fol-

lowing the meaning of *yad* in I Sam. 15:12,
II Sam. 18:18, and other instances. **throne:** Heb. *kes*,
either a corruption of the more standard *kisse* or,
most probably, a scribal error for *nes*, "banner," as in
V.15.
18:3 **he:** Moshe, in 2:22, above.

4 and the name of the other was Eliezer/God's-Help, for: the God
of my father is my help, he rescued me from Pharaoh's sword;

5 Yitro, Moshe's father-in-law, came with his sons and his wife to
Moshe, to the wilderness, where he was encamped,
at the mountain of God.

6 He (had it) said to Moshe:
I, your father-in-law Yitro, am coming to you, and your wife and
her two sons with her.

7 Moshe went out to meet his father-in-law,
he bowed and kissed him, and each-man asked after the other's
welfare;
then they came into the tent.

8 Moshe related to his father-in-law
all that YHWH had done to Pharaoh and to Egypt on Israel's
account,
all the hardships that had befallen them on the journey,
and how YHWH had rescued them.

9 And Yitro was jubilant because of all the good that YHWH had
done for Israel, that he had rescued him from the land of
Egypt.

10 Yitro said:
Blessed be YHWH,
who has rescued you from the hand of Egypt and from the hand
of Pharaoh,
who has rescued the people from under the hand of Egypt!

---

4 **Eliezer:** This is the first and only time we hear of this son. **he rescued me from Pharaoh's sword:** Here, as sometimes occurs in the biblical text, we learn of earlier events or emotions. Moshe's emotional makeup while he was in Midyan (Chaps. 2–4) thus becomes a little clearer.

5 **at the mountain of God:** Another important fact has been casually slipped in at this point, again probably from a narrative taking place later. In the next chapter Israel's arrival at Sinai will be more dramatically heralded.

8 **YHWH had rescued them:** The verb was used above

in relation to Moshe, and is a key repeating word in this chapter. Thus the experience of leader and people unite again, and the narrative of deliverance comes full circle. Moshe had begun his mission at Sinai, as a member of Yitro's household, and now the latter meets him in Sinai, on the brink of the confirmation of 3:12 ("you will serve God on this mountain").

9 **jubilant:** Heb. *va-yihd,* from *hdy,* a rare verb.

10 **who has rescued the people:** There is obviously a redundancy in this verse, based perhaps on a scribal error.

11 (So) now I know:
yes, YHWH is greater than all gods—
yes, in just that matter in which they were presumptuous against
them!

12 Yitro, Moshe's father-in-law, took an offering-up and slaughter-
animals for God,
and Aharon and all the elders of Israel came to eat bread with
Moshe's father-in-law, before the presence of God.

13 Now it was on the morrow:
Moshe sat to judge the people,
and the people stood before Moshe from daybreak until sunset.

14 When Moshe's father-in-law saw all that he had to do for the
people,
he said:
What kind of matter is this that you do for the people—
why do you sit alone, while the entire people stations itself
around you
from daybreak until sunset?

15 Moshe said to his father-in-law:
When the people comes to me to inquire of God,

16 —when it has some legal-matter, it comes to me—
I judge between a man and his fellow
and make known God's laws and his instructions.

17 Then Moshe's father-in-law said to him:
Not good is this matter, as you do it!

18 You will become worn out, yes, worn out, so you, so this people
that are with you,
for this matter is too heavy for you,
you cannot do it alone.

11 **in just that matter:** Heb. difficult; others either omit this phrase altogether, or use complex English constructions to reproduce it (e.g., "for he did this to those who treated Israel arrogantly," "for he has routed the mighty foes of his folk"). **they were presumptuous:** The Egyptians.

12 **before presence of God:** An expression that usually carries a cultic meaning (Levine 1974).

14 **all that he had to do:** Compare vv.8 and 9, where the great "doing" of God is accomplished with ease. Perhaps a contrast is being drawn between divine and human deeds; Moshe cannot do the "all" that God can.

18 **heavy:** Again the key word that was mentioned earlier (see the note to 14:4); it aids in linking up stories, as it has occurred in 17:12.

19 So now, hearken to my voice,
   I will advise you, so that God may be-there with you:
   Be-there, yourself, for the people in relation to God.
   You yourself should have the matters come to God;
20 You should make clear to them the laws and the instructions,
   you should make known to them the way they should go, and the
      deeds that they should do;
21 but you—you are to have the vision (to select) from all the people
      men of caliber, holding God in awe,
   men of truth, hating gain,
   you should set (them) over them
   as chiefs of thousands, chiefs of hundreds, chiefs of fifties, and
      chiefs of tens,
22 so that they may judge the people at all times.
   So shall it be:
   every great matter they shall bring before you,
   but every small matter they shall judge by themselves.
   Make (it) light upon you, and let them bear (it) with you.
23 If you do (thus in) this matter
   when God commands you (further), you will be able to stand,
   and also this people will come to its place in peace.
24 Moshe hearkened to the voice of his father-in-law,
   he did it all as he had said:
25 Moshe chose men of caliber from all Israel,
   he placed them as heads over the people,
   as chiefs of thousands, chiefs of hundreds, chiefs of fifties, and
      chiefs of tens.
26 They would judge the people at all times:
   the difficult matters they would bring before Moshe,
   but every small matter they would judge by themselves.
27 Moshe sent his father-in-law off,
   and he went home to his land.

---

21 **the vision (to select):** The verb "see" in Hebrew (*ra'oh*) also has the connotation of "select" (cf. Gen. 22:8). **caliber:** A term often used in a military context (see Judg. 11:1, 18:2).

22 **at all times:** That is, in minor matters—as we would say, "everyday affairs."

23 **stand:** Endure.

27 **sent . . . off/ . . . went . . . to his land:** A stock biblical farewell passage (see Num. 24:25, for instance).

PART III

THE MEETING AND COVENANT AT SINAI

(19–24)

THE NARRATIVE HAS RETURNED TO ITS SOURCE. AT SINAI IT HAD BEEN FORETOLD THAT when Pharaoh "sends you free, you will serve God on this mountain," and it is at Sinai that Moshe and the people now arrive. The fateful public meeting between the deity and the amassed human community will betoken the formal change of masters: the people, no longer enslaved by the Egyptian crown, now swear fealty to their divine Lord, who imposes rules of conduct upon them in return for his protection and their well-being.

The settings for these events of covenant-making and law-giving are appropriately impressive. The mountain naturally functions as a bridge between heaven and earth (with only Moshe allowed to ascend!), but it is additionally accompanied on this occasion by the powerful manifestations of smoke, fire, cloud, thunder, lightning, and trumpet blasts. To try and pin down exactly to what natural phenomena the story alludes, be they volcano, earthquake, or the like, is somewhat beside the point; what speaks through the text is the voice of an overwhelming experience. Indeed, as Greenberg (1972) points out, the account in Chapter 19 may have been deliberately left ambiguous and contradictory, showing that the editor wished to include all the received traditions about the event.

At the same time, it should be noted that the Sinai revelation resembles the appearance of the storm-god Baal in Canaanite texts, especially in the combining of thunder/lightning and earthquake. Psalm 18:8 portrays a similar scene. So as varied as the phenomena accompanying God's appearance here are, they conform to a known literary pattern (Greenstein 1984c).

As mentioned previously, Sinai stands geographically at the center of the Israelite wanderings. As the textual center of the book of Exodus as well, it anchors the people of Israel on their journey toward the fulfillment of their destiny. But that function is purely a mythic one. Sinai never became an important biblical cult site, and the only later story to take place there, that of Elijah in I Kings 20, clearly stems from the desire to draw a parallel between Elijah and Moshe. The Hebrews apparently could not conceive of God's abiding place's being located outside the land of Israel. On the other hand, it was necessary to demonstrate that Israel's laws and institutions arose, not out of normal settled political and economic circumstances, but rather as the direct gift and stipulation of God himself (see Cohn), and hence the choice of a site wholly removed from the great culture centers of the ancient Near East: the monolithic culture of Egypt, the ancestral heritage of Mesopotamia, and the fertility-based society the people were to encounter in Canaan. Sinai, the originating point of Israel as a self-defined community, had to start everything anew, on a stage in which all other considerations had been stripped away.

Early in the history of biblical exegesis (the Midrash) it was noted that the events on Sinai resemble the conclusion of a marriage ceremony. Such an idea may even have been in the minds of the transmitters of the Exodus traditions. Indeed, the entire book is remarkably reminiscent of a pattern of rescue—courting—wedding with stipulations—home planning—infidelity—reconciliation—and final "moving in" (these stages fit into the general Part divisions I have used throughout the book). Lest this appear to be too Western a model, let it be noted that such analogies occur in the writings of the prophets, where the relationship between God and Israel is likened to that between husband and wife. This constitutes Israel's version of what Joseph Campbell has termed "sacred marriage" in hero stories—not, as classically, the hero's successful wooing of a goddess or semidivine creature, but an intimate relationship established between God and his people. As such, it is unique in the ancient world.

On Covenant

Marriage may be one imaginative model for the Sinai experience, but it was covenant that the writers wished to stress above all in these chapters. Here we observe a fascinating phenomenon that occurs again and again in biblical religion: an institution well known in the secular world is given a religious emphasis in the Bible. For covenant (others, "pact") was a widespread form of political bonding in the ancient Near East. Kings and vassals, from Anatolia to Assyria, regularly aligned themselves in treaties involving either freewill granting of privileges or an agreement of mutual obligations between parties. A number of texts laying out the stipulations and ceremonies particular to covenant-making in the ancient Near East have been recovered, and study of them is helpful for an understanding of what we have in Ex. 19–24. Three things are clear. First, the stylistic pattern in our chapters resembles what is found in Hittite treaty texts (Mendenhall 1954); second, the Exodus passages use narrative to express these events, not merely a list of conditions; third, and most important, no other ancient society, so far as we know, conceived of the possibility that a *god* could "cut a covenant" with a people. This last fact leads to the observation that, for Israel, the true king was not earthly but divine—despite the later establishment of a monarchy (Weinfeld 1972b). Hence the narrator's concentration on these chapters, especially considering the dramatic nature of what had gone before (Chaps. 1–15).

The covenant found in Exodus and subsequently in the Torah differs substantively from the two described in Genesis. Noah (Gen. 9) and all living creatures had been promised no further universal destruction, with the stipulation that human beings were not to eat meat with blood or commit willful murder. Avraham, too (Gen. 15, 17), was the recipient of a covenant: God would give him land and descendants, and Avraham was to attend to the circumcision of all his males (yet this is more sign than stipulation). What these early events have in common is the aspect of bestowal—God acts and promises, and human beings are the passive recipients. Exodus introduces the notes of mutuality and conditionality. Both parties are now to have a stake in the agreement, and it can be broken by either (as in Chap. 32; contrast this with the promise to Noah in Gen. 8:21–22, "I will never doom the soil again . . . never shall [natural processes] cease," and Gen. 9:11, "Never again shall there be Deluge. . . ."). From the Creator God we have moved to the God of History, who enters into a fateful relationship with the people of Israel (for more on this, see Sarna 1986).

ON BIBLICAL LAW

A century of modern Bible scholarship has led to far-reaching changes in the perceptions of biblical law. Initial archeological findings, which often included legal documents, had led comparativists to see in the biblical material a pale reflection of its Mesopotamian antecedents. The Code of Hammurabi, for instance, was deemed the source of some of the Exodus material. These early judgments have given way to a view that places more emphasis on what is distinctive about the biblical laws.

For our purposes here, several brief points should be made, drawn from recent research; the reader may find them explored at greater depth in the essays by Greenberg (1970), Greenstein (1984), Paul, and Sarna (1986), and the work of Sonsino. Expressions of law in the ancient Near East, especially in documents from Mesopotamia, reveal a strong economic underpinning, tied to class structure. They also have at times a personal or political function. Hammurabi, for instance, presents his code with the express purpose that the gods and men may see what a just king he is. The laws are listed by category, with religion occupying its own sphere. Finally, the king acts as the enforcer of the laws, having received them from a god— who is nevertheless not their ultimate source. Law exists in the Mesopotamian texts as an abstract value, designed for the smooth functioning of society.

By way of contrast, Hebrew law, as typified by our chapters, displays very different concepts and concerns. Class is hardly alluded to, reflecting a totally different kind of society economically but also expressing an ideal that began in the Genesis creation story with the common ancestor of the human race. The laws are presented as the terms of the covenant (our section is often termed the "Book of the Covenant"), and the motivation behind them is portrayed as historical/psychological ("... for you were sojourners in the land of Egypt"). Strikingly, the biblical regulations, not only here but in the other major collections as well (in Leviticus and Deuteronomy), blur the distinctions between religious and secular, and treat all law as a matter directly related to God. He is perceived as the source of laws; they are the expression of his will; and breaking them is a direct affront to and act of rebellion against him (contrast, for example, the modern American view).

The key concept behind much of biblical law seems to be that of Ex. 19:6, to make of the people of Israel "a holy nation." This expression, which appears nowhere else in the Bible, combines a secular notion (the Hebrew *goy*, meaning a political body, a state) with a sacral one: this people is to transform all of its life into service of God. There is, therefore, no subject in the code before us—slavery, social relations, torts, cult, or diet—that is not of immediate concern to the biblical God. The first part of 19:6, "a kingdom of priests" (Buber: "a king's-retinue of priests"), would seem to suggest that despite the clear existence of a priestly group in ancient Israel, the ideal approached a more democratic form of religious expression.

This leads us to posit a final question: Are the materials in Ex. 21–24 (and other texts in the Torah that enumerate laws) to be taken as actual regulations or cases, or as something else, rather more didactic? We have little evidence for the former view, and in fact other ancient Near Eastern legal documents such as the Hammurabi Code seem to point in the other (didactic) direction. Given the nature of Torah literature, where narrative has a teaching function rather than a purely historical one, it seems plausible that the legal texts as well were intended to elucidate principles of Israelite belief—to present, as it were, a worldview. The other possibility, more in keeping with the history of law, is Daube's (1947) view that "many ancient codes regulate only matters as to which the law is dubious or in need of reform or both." In other words, law in day-to-day Israel was regulated by established precedents, and certainly not by Ex. 21–23, in the main. But in this case, too, our text would be instructive of the biblical mentality. For a fuller treatment of biblical law and its context in the ancient Near East, see Sarna (1986).

Any attempt to describe this section structurally is bound to run into a roadblock; perhaps precisely because of the Bible's desire *not* to distinguish between various categories of life, we do not have a watertight structure. Suffice it to say that, overall, most sections in these chapters begin with the general proposition "When . . ." (Heb. *ki*), and break down the issue under discussion into subsections beginning with "If . . ." (Heb. *'im*), a pattern found commonly in other legal systems as well. Beyond this, and the observation that there are some general categories and logical connections (for which, see the Commentary), one striking stylistic device in the Hebrew should be pointed out. From 21:5 through 23:24 a double verb form appears (the infinitive absolute followed by the imperfect) fully twenty-seven times. The effect of this device, which is rhetorically emphatic, is to give a sense of coherence to what are otherwise quite diverse laws.

The Meeting and the Covenant (19): The account of God's revelation at Sinai, like the narrative of the tenth plague and exodus, is embedded in a wider setting. After the covenant has been elucidated, the people assent; preparations are made to meet God; and the brief initial meeting is followed by more preparations, including stern warnings against trespassing on the mountain's sanctity. When one takes Chap. 20 into account, the effect of all this is anything but smooth, from a narrator's point of view, and I would agree with Greenberg (1969) that this may be deliberate—stemming from a desire either to include every tradition about this key event that was available to the editor(s), or else to suggest that such things are impossible to describe in normal language and logical sequence (Buber [1981], in another context, once referred to the Creation story of Gen. 1 as a "stammering account"). In any event, the entire description of the fateful meeting between God and the Israelites at Sinai is confined to a mere four verses (19:16–19). This stands in blatant contrast to other ancient Near Eastern traditions, which would have treated such an event with epic length and poetic diction (see, for instance, Deut. 32, or Psalm 78). So here, as in the opening chapter of Genesis, all has been stripped down, focusing attention on the covenant rather than on the mysterious nature of God.

In that vein, it must be observed that the narrative centers around speaking, words, and sounds, keeping the visual to a minimum (in line with the warning in Deut. 4:12: "The sound of words you heard/a form you did not see/only a voice"). It also abounds in terms connoting warning and boundaries/separateness—the text contains three sets of warnings: vv.10–13, 21–22 (introducing the phrase "burst out," which refers to God's potential destructiveness if the boundaries are violated), and 24. This recalls Moshe's own experience at Sinai earlier (cf. 3:5). And the number 3 gives the story the same touch of meaning provided by the numbers in Genesis; Israel arrives at the mountain three months after the exodus and meets God on the third day after their preparations.

As Cassuto points out, the chapter does not begin with "Now it was. . ." (Heb. *va-yehi*), a normal marker for continuing a previous narrative. The Sinai material thus presents itself in utter newness. To use the previously cited wedding analogy: this text betokens a new relationship between God and Israel, however well they have known one another previously.

Also notable in Chap. 19 is the emphasis on movement: going up (Heb. *'aloh*) and down *(yarod)* (see also 24:15–18). This movement serves to bridge the gap, usually great, between heaven and earth; but note that it is Moshe, and not the people, who does the ascending and descending.

Structurally, vv.20–25 appear to have been added, to emphasize the warning theme. They also delay the pronouncement of the "Ten Commandments," creating thereby a more dramatic effect with the appearance of the latter. But it seems clear that considerable editing has taken place.

19:1 On the third New-Moon after the going-out of the Children of
     Israel from the land of Egypt,
  on that (very) day
  they came to the Wilderness of Sinai.
2 They moved on from Refidim and came to the Wilderness of
     Sinai,
  and encamped in the wilderness.
  There Israel encamped, opposite the mountain.
3 Now Moshe went up to God,
  and Y H W H called out to him from the mountain,
  saying:
  Say thus to the House of Yaakov,
  (yes,) tell the Children of Israel:
4 You yourselves have seen
  what I did to Egypt,
  how I bore you on eagles' wings and brought you to me.
5 So now,
  if you will hearken, yes, hearken to my voice
  and keep my covenant,
  you shall be to me a special-treasure from among all peoples.
  Indeed, all the earth is mine,
6 but you, you shall be to me
  a kingdom of priests,
  a holy nation.
  These are the words that you are to speak to the Children of
     Israel.

19:1 **On the third:** The Hebrew omits the usual connecting *vav* ("now," "and," or "but"), and thus signals the start of a new narrative.

2 **There Israel encamped:** The repetition, as in 14:2,
suggests poetry, perhaps a remnant of what Cassuto
terms an epic literature here. The rhetorical force
alerts the reader that something important is about
to follow.

2–3 **the mountain:** It is not necessary to mention its
name.

3 **Say thus . . . /(yes,) tell . . . :** A formulaic opening
of a speech, highlighting this important address.

4 **eagles' wings:** Most commonly in Western culture,
be it ancient Rome, Imperial Europe, the United
States, or even Nazi Germany, the eagle is the symbol of strength, independence, and loftiness. Yet
here in the Bible it functions primarily as a symbol
of God's loving protection—see the nurturing eagle
image in Deut. 32:11.

6 **but you:** Or "and you." **kingdom of priests:** Buber
(1949) interprets the phrase as meaning a "royal-
retinue" around the king, based on the usage in I
Chron. 18:17 and II Sam. 8:18.

7 Moshe came, and had the elders of the people called,
  and set before them these words, with which YHWH had
     commanded him.
8 And all the people answered together, they said:
  All that YHWH has spoken, we will do.
  And Moshe reported the words of the people to YHWH.
9 YHWH said to Moshe:
  Here, I am coming to you in a thick cloud,
  so that the people may hear when I speak with you,
  and also that they may have trust in you for ever.
  And Moshe told the words of the people to YHWH.
10 YHWH said to Moshe:
  Go to the people,
  make them holy, today and tomorrow,
  let them scrub their clothes,
11 that they may be ready for the third day,
  for on the third day
  YHWH will come down before the eyes of all the people, upon
     Mount Sinai.
12 Fix-boundaries for the people round about, saying:
  Be on your watch against going up the mountain or against
     touching its border!
  Whoever touches the mountain—he is to be put-to-death, yes,
     death;
13 no hand is to touch him,
  but he is to be stoned, yes, stoned, or shot, yes, shot,
  whether beast or man, he is not to live!

8 **All . . . we will do:** This phrase, with variations, is repeated in 24:4 and 24:7 to frame the entire covenant and law-giving account.

9 **thick cloud:** Some interpret the cloud as a massive aura, others as a shield to protect mortals from the brilliant divine "Glory" (Heb. *kavod*). **so that the people may hear:** Or "hearken" (i.e., obey). One would expect "so that the people may see," following upon the last phrase, but the narrator apparently wants to make clear that "you saw no form" (Deut. 4:12).

10 **scrub:** The Hebrew verb (*kabbes*) is used for the washing of objects, not of people (which is expressed by *rahotz*).

13 **no hand is to touch him:** As if his contact with holiness would somehow contaminate him—a common idea in much of ancient society, and put forth with particular force throughout Leviticus. **shot:** With bow and arrows.

When the (sound of the) ram's-horn is drawn out, they may go
    up on the mountain.

14 Moshe went down from the mountain to the people,
    he made the people holy, and they washed their clothes,

15 then he said to the people:
    Be ready for three days; do not approach a woman!

16 Now it was on the third day, when it was daybreak:
    There were thunder-sounds, and lightning,
    a heavy cloud on the mountain
    and an exceedingly strong *shofar* sound.
    And all of the people that were in the camp trembled.

17 Moshe brought the people out toward God, from the camp,
    and they stationed themselves beneath the mountain.

18 Now Mount Sinai smoked all over,
    since YHWH had come down upon it in fire;
    its smoke went up like the smoke of a furnace,
    and all of the mountain trembled exceedingly.

19 Now the *shofar* sound was growing exceedingly stronger
    —Moshe kept speaking,
    and God kept answering him in the sound (of a voice)—

20 and YHWH came down upon Mount Sinai, to the top of the
    mountain.
    YHWH called Moshe to the top of the mountain,
    and Moshe went up.

21 YHWH said to Moshe:
    Go down, warn the people
    lest they break through to YHWH to see, and many of them fall;

---

15 **do not approach a woman:** The need for the people to be in a state of ritual purity precludes sexual contact.

16 **daybreak:** Perhaps to convey that there was nothing deceptive or dreamlike about this event, which was to be seen as a large-scale group experience (and hence a large-scale group commitment). **shofar:** The horn of a ram or cow. Perhaps, as part of an ancient Near Eastern convention, heralding the approach of YHWH as a warring storm-god (see the Commentary, above). **trembled:** Note how both people and mountain (v.18) seem to be in synchrony with one another (yet some scholars emend the text!).

18 **like the smoke of a furnace:** A standard biblical way of describing extensive smoke (see Gen. 19:28, which uses "dense-smoke").

19 **sound (of a voice):** Some interpret as "thunder," which is often described biblically as the "voice of God" (in Ps. 18:14 and in Ugaritic literature as well). But the emphasis in the revelation of these chapters seems to be on God's voice and the clarity of his words.

21 **fall:** That is, die, because of too-close contact with the divine.

The Ten Words (The Decalogue) (20:1–14): This section, among the most famous and important in all of religious literature, is set in dramatic tone. Its rhetoric could hardly be more striking. In a form relatively rare in ancient Near Eastern legal documents, a god sets forth demands, with no punishments listed. This "apodictic" form seems to indicate that the Ten Words function as a preamble to the actual laws of Chaps. 21–23, by laying forth the major principles on which Israel's relationship to God is to be based (as is to be expected, the secondary literature on Chap. 20 is enormous; see Childs for a bibliography).

The numbering of the ten differs slightly in the Jewish and Christian traditions, with the main divergences coming in the split of vv.2–3 (or 3–4, as here); see Cassuto. There are also different opinions on the overall structure of the "Commandments." Jewish tradition separates out those that treat the relationship between God and human beings (vv.2–11, numbers 1–5) and those that involve human society alone (vv.12–14, numbers 6–10), although it should be kept in mind that all offenses in ancient Israel were seen as affronts to God. This division might be borne out by stylistic considerations, for the last five, of course, begin "You are not to . . ." and numbers 2–4 all use the Hebrew word *ki* ("for") to express reasons or results of the initial stipulations (vv.5, 7, 11, with the substitution of "in order that" in verse 12).

Other notable stylistic aspects here include the fact that "you" is always singular, and that numbers 2–4 and 6–10 are all put in the negative.

Several other features of the "Decalogue" are unique: the prohibition against worshiping images, which would have had a strange ring in the ancient world; the Sabbath as a holy day on which not even servants, farm animals, or noncitizens are to work, equally unprecedented in its time and place; and, strangest of all, the final prohibition against desiring (another person's property).

The language and the content of the Decalogue, then, cooperate to create a lofty and challenging ethical code, which both the people of Israel and the Western world in general have struggled with ever since. The reader may wish to consult Buber's stimulating essays (1982, 1963) "The Words on the Tablets" and "What Are We to Do about the Ten Commandments?", as well as the essays in Segal.

22 even the priests who approach YHWH must make themselves holy,
   lest YHWH burst out against them.

23 But Moshe said to YHWH:
   The people are not able to go up to Mount Sinai,
   for you yourself warned us, saying: Fix boundaries for the
      mountain and make it holy!

24 YHWH said to him:
   Go, get down,
   and then come up, you and Aharon with you,
   but the priests and the people must not break through to go up to
      YHWH, lest he burst out against them.

25 Moshe went down to the people and said to them

20:1 God spoke all these words,
   saying:
2 I am YHWH your God,
   who brought you out
   from the land of Egypt, from a house of serfs.

3 You are not to have
   any other gods
   before my presence.
4 You are not to make yourself a carved-image
   or any figure
   that is in the heavens above, that is on the earth beneath, that is in
      the waters beneath the earth;
5 you are not to bow down to them,
   you are not to serve them,
   for I, YHWH your God,
   am a jealous God,

22 **lest YHWH burst out:** Lest God slay them with fire or plague. One recalls the demonic character of God portrayed in 4:24ff. The phrase is repeated in v. 24 for emphasis.

25 **and said to them:** The Hebrew is ambiguous; did Moshe report God's previous speech to them, or the following (Decalogue)? I have left this verse without final punctuation to express the unresolved nature of the question.

20:4 **figure . . . :** A representation of an animal or person.

5 **jealous:** The Hebrew word (*kanna*) has a cognate meaning in Arabic, "red (with dye)," so an interesting English analogy, expressing facial color changes, would be "livid" (from the Latin "color of lead")

Aftermath (20:15–23): The verses that follow the Decalogue highlight an important aspect of the Sinai tradition: its occurrence in a public setting. Vv.15–18 could fit nicely after 19:20a; the Decalogue would then follow 20:18. Yet it seems to have been important for the narrator to stress (v.19) that God spoke to the people as a whole, not merely secretly in a revelation to a visionary or priest. To emphasize this point, the verb *ra'oh*, "see/perceive," occurs seven times in vv.15–19. V.19 also serves as a framework for the entire Revelation episode, recalling as it does the language of 19:4. Israel now has two reasons for obeying God: he brought them out of Egyptian bondage and he talked to them "from the heavens" (v.19).

The rest of the chapter functions as an introduction to the general body of the legislation that begins in the next chapter. Like Israel's other law collections in Leviticus and Deuteronomy, it starts with rules pertaining to worship.

On the Laws: The reader should bear in mind again that the section headings used in the Commentary are for reference only. This is especially true for Chaps. 21–24, where the final form of the Hebrew text discourages distinguishing between different types of offenses (see p. 361, "On Biblical Law").

Laws Regarding Israelite Serfdom (21:1–11): Given the importance of the root "serve" in the book of Exodus, it is fitting that the Covenant Code open with this theme. In vv.1–6 the text considers the case of the native serf, a status rather like that of the indentured servant in early American history. Immediately, the act of releasing such an individual— providing for his "going out"—is stipulated. "For they are my servants, whom I brought forth out of the land of Egypt" (Lev. 25:42). While the institution of serfdom existed of necessity in ancient Israel, it could not be tolerated as a permanent and fully dehumanizing one (on the other hand, these regulations deal with natives, not with foreigners). Note the use of seven here, as the number of perfection and limit—the servant goes free after seven years, just as the land rests every seven years (23:10–11).

The second case (vv.7–11) deals with a woman whose poverty-stricken father sells her as a servant. Here, too, there is an attempt to soften the conditions and to humanize what appears as essentially a property situation in the ancient world.

calling-to-account the iniquity of the fathers upon the sons, to the
    third and the fourth (generation)
of those that hate me,
6 but showing loyalty to the thousandth
of those that love me,
of those that keep my commandments.

7 You are not to take up
the name of YHWH your God for emptiness,
for YHWH will not clear him
that takes up his name for emptiness.

8 Remember
the Sabbath day, to hallow it.
9 For six days, you are to serve, and are to make all your work,
10 but the seventh day
is Sabbath for YHWH your God:
you are not to make any kind of work,
(not) you, nor your son, nor your daughter,
(not) your servant, nor your maid, nor your beast,
nor your sojourner that is within your gates.
11 For in six days
YHWH made
the heavens and the earth,
the sea and all that is in it,
and he rested on the seventh day;
therefore YHWH gave the Sabbath day his blessing, and he
    hallowed it.

5 **the third and the fourth (generation):** A long time (Plaut)

6 **the thousandth:** That is, forever (Plaut).

7 **take up . . . for emptiness:** Use for a false purpose.

The traditional translation, "take in vain," limits its scope unnecessarily. **clear:** To acquit or hold innocent.

12 Honor
your father and your mother,
in order that your days may be prolonged
on the soil that YHWH your God is giving you.

13 You are not to murder.

You are not to adulter.

You are not to steal.

You are not to testify
against your fellow as a false witness.

14 You are not to desire
the house of your neighbor,
you are not to desire the wife of your neighbor,
or his servant, or his maid, or his ox, or his donkey,
or anything that is your neighbor's.

15 Now all of the people were seeing
the thunder-sounds,
the flashing-torches,
the *shofar* sound,
and the mountain smoking;
when the people saw,
they faltered
and stood far off.

16 They said to Moshe:
You speak with us, and we will hearken,
but let not God speak with us, lest we die!

13 **You are not to . . . :** Closer to the Hebrew rhythmi-
cally would be a sequence like "No murder! / No
adultery!" etc., or "Murder not! / Adulter not!" etc.
murder: Some interpreters view this as "killing" in
general, while others restrict it, as I have done here.
adulter: The English has been tailored to fit the Hebrew rhythm of the last five "commandments," all
of which begin with *lo* ("no") and a two-syllable
command. **steal:** Ancient Jewish tradition understood this as a reference to kidnapping (see Lauterbach).

14 **desire:** Trad. "covet." Another possibility is "yearn
for."

15 **were seeing:** Others, "perceived." The use of the
Hebrew participle again emphasizes immediacy.
flashing-torches: Perhaps a poetic description of
lightning.

17 Moshe said to the people:
Do not be afraid!
For it is to test you that God has come,
to have awe of him be upon you,
so that you do not sin.
18 The people stood far off,
and Moshe approached the fog where God was.

19 YHWH said to Moshe:
Say thus to the Children of Israel:
You yourselves have seen
that it was from the heavens that I spoke with you.
20 You are not to make beside me
gods of silver, gods of gold you are not to make for yourselves!
21 A slaughter-site of soil, you are to make for me,
you are to slaughter upon it
your offerings-up, your sacrifices of *shalom,*
your sheep and your oxen!
At every place
where I cause my name to be recalled
I will come to you
and bless you.
22 But if a slaughter-site of stones you make for me,
you are not to build it smooth-hewn,
for if you hold-high your iron-tool over it, you will have profaned
it.
23 And you are not to ascend my slaughter-site by ascending-steps,
that your nakedness not be laid-bare upon it.

21:1 Now these are the regulations that you are to set before them:

---

18 **fog:** Heb. *'arafel,* frequently used in conjunction with *anan,* "cloud."

21 **of soil:** Cf. v. 22. The altar was to be made of natural materials. **sacrifices of *shalom:*** Others, "peace-offerings"; but see Orlinsky. **you:** Here, second personal singular, as well as through v. 23.

22 **profaned:** In folklore, iron was said to drive out the soul of the stone—that is, rob it of its essence (Driver 1911).

23 **that your nakedness:** To make sure that the priests' genitals not be uncovered during the rites; the Egyptians wore rather short skirts (Plaut). Note again the desexualizing of religion.

21:1 **regulations:** Others, "judicial decisions," "judgments." See Daube (1947).

Capital Crimes of Violence (21:12–17): Four situations involving grave crimes are cited in this section, each ending with the pronouncement of the death penalty in rhetorical form (Heb. *mot yumat,* "He is to be put-to-death, yes, death"): murder, striking one's parents, kidnapping, and denigrating one's parents. Our society has in general supported the first and third of these; but the regulations concerning father and mother do not accord with twentieth-century Western practice, and point up well the enormous importance of the parent–child relationship in ancient Israel (already suggested by "Honor your father and your mother" in the Ten Words). That relationship was often used to describe the one between God and Israel, and thus obedience is an important theme in the covenant as a whole.

Injuries (21:18–32): The vocabulary of verbs in these verses outlines the subject at hand: "quarrel," "strike," "contend," "harm," "strike," "break-off," "give." The text treats a number of extenuating circumstances, imposing penalties of varying degrees. The case of an accidentally caused abortion is especially highlighted (vv.22–25), and in a famous verse (25), the lawgiver breaks into rhetoric in order to stress that punishments be scrupulously fair. Also notable is the regulation concerning the goring ox (vv.28–32), where an *animal* is made to pay the death penalty, since it has destroyed the most sacred thing of all—life itself. Both of the latter cases have received exhaustive treatment in the scholarly literature (see Sarna 1986).

2 When you acquire a Hebrew serf,
he is to serve for six years,
but in the seventh he is to go out at liberty, for nothing.

3 If he came by himself, he is to go out by himself;
if he was the spouse of a wife, his wife is to go out with him.

4 If his lord gives him a wife, and she bore him sons or daughters,
the wife and those she bore are to remain her lord's, and he is to
go out by himself.

5 But if the serf should say, yes, say:
I love my lord, my wife and my children, I will not go out at
liberty!,

6 his lord is to have him approach God's-oracle,
and then he is to have him approach the door or the post;
his lord is to pierce his ear with a piercer,
and he is to serve him forever.

7 When a man sells his daughter as a handmaid,
she is not to go out as serfs go out.

8 If she is displeasing in the eyes of her lord, who designated her
for himself,
he is to have her redeemed;
to a foreign people he has not the power to sell her,
since he has betrayed her.

9 But if it is for his son that he designates her,
according to the just-rights of women he is to deal with her.

10 If another he takes for himself,
(then) her board, her clothing, or her oil he is not to diminish.

---

2 **you:** Singular, to stress the perspective of the buyer. **Hebrew:** Cassuto suggests that the term here has a wide meaning: a member of a bondman class (Akkadian *Hapiru*) found all over the ancient Near East. **for nothing:** Without paying redemption money (Cassuto).

3 **by himself:** I.e., as an unmarried man.

4 **and she bore him ...:** The birth of children changes the situation, and the wife must now remain behind, in bondage, with the children.

5 **say, yes, say:** Or "declare."

6 **God's-oracle:** Others, "God," "the judges." **door ...post:** It is not clear whether the sanctuary or the master's house is meant. **pierce his ear:** The sym-

bolism of this act is not clear. Gaster (1969) theorizes that it establishes the serf's permanent bond to his master's house, through the blood on the doorpost.

7 **handmaid:** In this instance, a free woman is bound over to be a slave. **as serfs go out:** As we saw above. In Cassuto's view, now that she has a new status (that of wife), she may not be so easily disposed of.

8 **he has betrayed her:** He has not married her off, as was intended in the sale.

10 **her board:** "Her" refers to the first woman, mentioned in v.8. **her oil:** So Paul, on the basis of Mesopotamian parallels. Others, "marital-relations."

11 If these three (things) he does not do for her,
   she is to go out for nothing, with no money.

12 He that strikes a man, so that he dies,
   is to be put-to-death, yes, death.

13 Now should he not have lain in wait (for him), but should God
      have brought him opportunely into his hand:
   I will set aside for you a place where he may flee.

14 But when a man schemes against his neighbor, to kill him with
      cunning,
   from my very slaughter-site you are to take him away, to die!

15 And he that strikes his father or his mother,
   is to be put-to-death, yes, death.

16 And he that steals a man,
   whether he sells him or whether he is found in his hand,
   is to be put-to-death, yes, death.

17 And he that insults his father or his mother,
   is to be put-to-death, yes, death.

18 When men quarrel, and a man strikes his neighbor with a stone
      or with (his) fist, yet he does not die, but rather takes to his
      bed:

19 If he can rise and walk about outside upon his crutch,
      he that struck (him) is to go clear,
      only: he is to make good for his resting-time, and provide-that-he-
      be-healed, yes, healed.

11 **with no money:** Again, without having to pay redemption money.
12 **put-to-death:** Stronger than simply saying "die."
13 **opportunely:** Accidentally. **a place where he may
   flee:** The so-called cities of refuge (see Num.
   35:9–34, Deut. 19:1–12).
14 **from my very slaughter-site:** Even the traditional
   concept of sanctuary will not aid such a man.
15 **strikes:** Some interpret this as "strikes dead." But

the wording does not warrant this here (cf. 21:12),
and such a society would in any case be supportive
of this kind of severe penalty in reference to not
"honoring" (see 20:12) parents. This is further supported by v.17, below.
18 **fist:** Some ancient versions read "club" or
   "spade."
19 **to make good . . . healed:** But he is not liable for
   criminal action.

20 When a man strikes his serf or his handmaid with a rod, so that
   he dies under his hand,
   it is to be avenged, yes, avenged;
21 nonetheless, if for a day or two-days he endures,
   it is not to be avenged, for he is his own "money."

22 When two men scuffle and deal a blow to a pregnant woman, so
   that her children abort-forth, but (other) harm does not
   occur,
   he is to be fined, yes, fined, as the woman's spouse imposes for
   him,
   but he is to give it (only) according to assessment.
23 But if harm should occur,
   then you are to give life in place of life—
24 eye in place of eye, tooth in place of tooth, hand in place of
25 hand, foot in place of foot, / burnt-scar in place of burnt-scar,
   wound in place of wound, bruise in place of bruise.

26 When a man strikes the eye of his serf or the eye of his
   handmaid, and ruins it,
   he is to send him free at liberty for (the sake of) his eye;
27 if the tooth of his serf or the tooth of his handmaid he breaks off,
   he is to send him free at liberty for (the sake of) his tooth.

28 When an ox gores a man or a woman, so that one dies,
   the ox is to be stoned, yes, stoned, and its flesh is not to be eaten,
   and the owner of the ox is to be clear.
29 But if the ox was (known as) a gorer from yesterday and the day-
   before, and it was so designated to its owner,

20 **avenged:** The exact punishment is not specified, but it sounds like death.
21 **it is not . . . "money":** "He has human rights, but not those of a free man" (Plaut). Alternatively, Cassuto suggests that the master has lost his own money thereby.
22 **assessment:** As agreed by the judges.
23 **you:** Singular. **life in place of life:** This has historically been taken to indicate a kind of strict Hebrew vengeance, as in the current expression "an eye for an eye." But the passage (note, by the way, its length) may have been meant as a contrast to the

Babylonian system, where the rich could in essence pay to get out of such situations. In Israel this could not be done, and thus we are dealing not with "strict justice" but with strict fairness.
28 **When an ox gores . . . :** The ox may be taken here as the paradigm of the domestic animal. The secondary literature on this law and its parallels is enormous. **its flesh is not to be eaten:** Since the ox has not been properly slaughtered for eating or sacrificial purposes, and possibly also because it is connected with the taking of another life (carnivores are forbidden food in the Bible).

Property (21:33–22:14): These regulations cover various damages to property, commonly through negligence. The key word here is "pay" (Heb. *shallem,* denoting restitution); also repeated are "fellow" and "God's-oracle."

Laws Concerning Social Relations and Religious Matters (22:15–23:19): A great variety of offenses is covered in this section: rape, oppression, talebearing, unjust sentencing, and bribery, among others. Yet the category is not so neatly drawn; interspersed with these are laws concerning what we would consider religious affairs: sorcery, idolatry, blasphemy, and the sacred calendar. Once again the implication seems to be that all of these areas are of immediate concern to God, regardless of how they are labeled or pigeonholed.

Stylistically there is also great variety, as categorical prohibitions (22:18) alternate with pleas (23:5–6) and positive commands (23:10–12). A number of times the justification for the law is given in the text itself (e.g. 22:20, 26; 23:7, 8, 9, 11, 12), with the operative word being "for." (Such a verse is called a "motive clause," and is characteristically although not exclusively biblical; see Sonsino.)

Most notable about this section is the full use that it makes of rhetoric. Several key laws are accompanied by an emotional appeal—e.g., "Oh, if you afflict, afflict them . . . !" (22:22); "for it is his only clothing . . . in what (else) shall he lie down?" (v.26); "for a Compassionate-One am I" (v.26); and "you yourselves know (well) the feelings of the sojourner" (23:9).

No passage in these chapters, and indeed throughout the entire Torah, can easily surpass vv.21–23 (as I have mentioned above), with their appeal to language and emotions alike. So at the core of the legal concerns here is the protection of the powerless.

Toward the end (23:10–19), emphasis shifts to the festivals of Israel, with a special focus on the agricultural setting. As a result the general scholarly consensus is that these laws could not be wilderness regulations, but refer instead to life after the conquest of Canaan. Be that as it may, the fact that this section ends with ritual concerns provides a rounding-out of the entire body of Exodus legislation, which, as I noted above, began with worship as its subject (20:20ff.).

Finally, this ending passage is notable for its numerical layout—two sets of seven (years and days) and one of three (times a year).

and he did not guard it,
and it causes the death of a man or of a woman,
the ox is to be stoned, and its owner as well is to be put-to-death.

30 If a ransom is established for him,
he is to give it as a redemption for his life, all that is imposed for
    him.

31 Whether it is a son it gores or a daughter it gores,
according to this (same) judgment it is to be done to him.

32 If (it is) a serf the ox gores, or a handmaid,
silver—thirty *shekels*—he is to give to his lord, and the ox is to be
    stoned.

33 When a man opens up a pit, or when a man digs a pit, and does
    not cover it up, and an ox or a donkey falls into it,

34 the owner of the pit is to pay, the worth-in-silver he is to restore
    to its owner, and the dead-animal is to remain his.

35 When a man's ox deals-a-blow to his neighbor's ox, so that it dies,
they are to sell the live ox and split its worth-in-silver, and the
    dead-animal they are also to split.

36 Yet if it was known that it was a goring ox from yesterday and the
    day-before, and its owner did not guard it,
he is to pay, yes, pay, an ox in place of the ox, and the dead-animal
    is to remain his.

37 (Now) when a man steals an ox or a lamb, and slaughters it or sells
    it,
five cattle he is to pay in place of the ox, and four sheep in place
    of the lamb;

22:1 if in (the act of) digging through, the stealer is caught and is
    struck down, so that he dies,
there is to be on his account no bloodguilt;

---

30 **ransom:** Others, "expiation payment." This functions as a way out of his being put to death (as in the
case of the firstborn son, in Chap. 12)

37 **(Now) . . . lamb:** In most English translations, this
verse is labeled 22:1, and hence 22:1 here appears as
22:2 elsewhere. **five cattle . . . four sheep:** In contradistinction to the case of a stolen animal that is
found alive (v.3, above), where the payment is only
twofold.

22:1 **digging through:** Secretly, at night; the owner presumably has neither the time nor the light to examine the situation rationally. This issue is still a matter
of considerable debate in many state legislatures in
America. **no bloodguilt:** He is not considered a
murderer.

2 (but) if the sun rose upon him,
bloodguilt there is on his account;
he is to pay, yes, pay—if he has nothing, he is to be sold because
of his stealing.
3 (Now) if what was stolen is found, yes, found in his hand,
whether ox, or donkey, or lamb, (still) alive,
twofold he is to pay.

4 When a man has a field or a vineyard grazed in,
and sends his grazing-flock free, so that it grazes in another's
field,
the best-part of his field, the best-part of his vineyard he is to pay.

5 When fire breaks out and reaches thorn-hedges, and a sheaf-stack
or the standing-grain or the (entire) field is consumed,
he is to pay, yes, pay, he that caused the blaze to blaze up.

6 When a man gives silver or goods to his fellow for safekeeping,
and it is stolen from the man's house;
if the stealer is caught, he is to pay twofold;
7 if the stealer is not caught, the owner of the house is to come-
near God's-oracle,
(to inquire) if he did not stretch out his hand against his
neighbor's property.
8 Regarding every matter of transgression,
regarding oxen, regarding donkeys, regarding sheep, regarding
garments, regarding any kind of loss about which one can say:
That is it!—
before God's-oracle is the matter of the two of them to come;
whomever God's-oracle declares guilty, is to pay twofold to his
neighbor.

---

2 **If the sun rose:** Then the owner could have restrained himself from killing the man.
4–5 **grazed . . . blaze:** The Hebrew is perhaps a pun on
b'r, which is used for both verbs. Some take the entire case to refer to burning.
5 **pay:** Yet not necessarily the "best-part," as in v.4.

6 **stealer:** The Hebrew form (*gannav*) indicates a pro-
fessional thief, not a casual one.
7 **the owner of the house:** That is, the temporary
guardian of the goods.
8 **say:** Others, "allege."

◆

9   When a man gives his neighbor a donkey or an ox or a lamb, or
      any kind of beast, for safekeeping,
    and it dies, or is crippled or captured, no one seeing (it happen),

10 the oath of YHWH is to be between the two of them,
    (to inquire) if he did not send out his hand against his neighbor's
      property;
    the owner is to accept it, and he does not have to pay.

11 But if it was stolen, yes, stolen away from him,
    he is to pay it back to its owner.

12 If it was torn, torn-to-pieces,
    he is to bring it as evidence; what was torn, he does not have to
      pay back.

13 When a man borrows it from his neighbor, and it is crippled or it
      dies:
    (if) its owner was not with it, he is to pay, yes, pay;

14 if its owner was with it, he does not have to pay.
    If it was hired, its hiring-price is received.

15 When a man seduces a virgin who has not been spoken-for and
      lies with her,
    (for) the marrying-price he is to marry her, as his wife.

16 If her father refuses, yes, refuses to give her to him,
    silver he is to weigh out, according to the marriage-price of
      virgins.

17 A sorceress you are not to let live!

---

9 **crippled or captured:** Heb. *nishbar o nishbe.*
10 **oath of YHWH:** It functions like a lie-detector test.
    he does not: The guardian, as above.
12 **torn-to-pieces:** A technical term for "devoured by a
    wild animal" (Daube 1947); cf. Gen. 37:33. **he does
    not have to pay:** Since this could happen to anyone.
14 **he does not have to pay:** It is assumed that he did
    his best to protect his charge. **its hiring-price is re-
    ceived:** The rental price covers the loss.
15 **spoken-for:** Lit. "paid for." Others, "betrothed,"
    but it is not clear that there was such an institution
    as betrothal in biblical Israel (Orlinsky).

16 **marriage-price of virgins:** As in many cultures,
    biblical society prized a virgin as a bride.
17 **sorceress:** The specifying of women here seems to
    indicate their involvement in this practice in ancient
    Israel. Magic as such was forbidden (see the famous
    story of the "witch of Endor" in I Sam. 28) all over
    the Bible, as an attempt to manipulate God's world
    behind his back, as it were. **you:** Singular, and so ba-
    sically through v.29. The exceptions, v.21 and the
    end of v.24, may simply be stylistic variations. **not
    to let live:** An unusual Hebrew phrase, perhaps for
    emphasis.

◆ 18 Anyone who lies with a beast
is to be put-to-death, yes, death!

19 He that slaughters (offerings) to (other) gods is to be devoted-to-
destruction.
Only to YHWH alone!

20 Now a sojourner you are not to maltreat, you are not to oppress
him,
for sojourners were you in the land of Egypt.

21 Any widow or orphan you are not to afflict.
22 Oh, if you afflict, afflict them . . . !
For (then) they will cry, cry out to me,
and I will hearken, hearken to their cry,
23 my anger will flare up
and I will kill you with the sword,
so that your wives become widows, and your children, orphans!

24 If you lend money to my people, to the afflicted-one (who lives)
beside you,
you are not to be to him like a creditor,
you are not to place on him excessive-interest.

25 If you take-in-pledge, yes, pledge, the cloak of your neighbor,
before the sun comes in, return it to him,
26 for it is his only clothing,
it is the cloak for his skin,
in what (else) shall he lie down?
Now it will be that when he cries out to me,
I will hearken,
for a Compassionate-One am I!

27 God you are not to curse,
an exalted-leader among your people you are not to damn.

18 **lies with a beast:** Interestingly, Hittite law distin-
guishes between some animals in this regard, while
Israelite law does not. Just as the Bible has essentially excised mythology concerning half-gods and
half-humans, or half-humans/animals such as the
Sphinx, so the spheres are not to mix in real life.

19 **devoted-to-destruction:** Set aside for God; confiscated if an object, killed if a person.
27 **God . . . one exalted:** Here God and ruler are
equated, as later in the story of Naboth's vineyard in
I Kings 21:10 ("You cursed God and the king").

◆ 28 Your full fruit of your trickling-grapes, you are not to delay.

The firstborn of your sons, give to me.

29 Do thus with your ox, with your sheep:
for seven days let it be with its mother, (and) on the eighth day,
give it to me!

30 Men of holiness are you to be to me!
Flesh that is torn-to-pieces in the field, you are not to eat;
to the dogs you are to throw it.

23:1 You are not to take up an empty rumor.
Do not put your hand (in) with a guilty person, to become a
witness for wrongdoing.

2 You are not to go after many (people) to do evil.

And you are not to testify in a quarrel so as to turn aside toward
many—(and thus) turn away.

3 Even a poor-man you are not to respect as regards his quarrel.

4 (Now) when you encounter your enemy's ox or his donkey
straying, return it, return it to him.

5 (And) when you see the donkey of one who hates you crouching
under its burden, restrain from abandoning it to him—
unbind, yes, unbind it together with him.

6 You are not to turn aside the rights of your needy as regards his
quarrel.

---

28 **Your full fruit . . . :** Heb. difficult. Cassuto cites a parallel Hittite law. **give to me:** Paralleling 13:13 (Cassuto).

29 **eighth day:** Circumcision also takes place on the eighth day, reflecting either a belief that the young are more viable by then, or a symbolic number (7 + 1). Others suggest that it takes seven days for the impurity of birth to be expunged (cf. Lev. 12:2).

30 **Men of holiness:** The idea is continued in Leviticus, where Chapters 19ff. have come to be known as the "Holiness Code," a collection of varied laws dealing with different aspects of human conduct. **Flesh that is torn-to-pieces:** Lev. 17:15 and 22:8 forbid the eating of an animal that has been slain by another. **to the dogs:** The force of the idea is similar in both Hebrew and English.

23:1 **You:** Singular through v. 12, except for the second and third lines of v.9. **empty:** Insubstantial, not based on fact. **Do not put your hand (in):** That is, do not throw your weight toward, side with.

2 **quarrel:** Legal dispute. **many:** Or "the majority." **turn away:** Referring to either turning the judgment in favor of the wicked, or else the "turning" of justice itself.

3 **respect:** Others, "prefer." Contrast this idea with v.6.

5 **abandoning . . . unbind:** That same Hebrew root, *'azov,* is used for both. It is also possible that the text is the result of a scribal error, and some read the second verb as *'azor,* "help."

Epilogue. The Future Conquest (23:20–33): It would not be suitable, given the grave nature of the covenant, to end the legal passages merely with a particular law, and so our narrator appends a long speech, in the style of Deuteronomy, warning the Israelites, first, to follow God's messenger, and second, not to assimilate with the nations they are about to conquer. The Deuteronomic themes are classic: "taking care," smashing Canaanite idols, God's removing disease from the faithful Israelites, and the spelling-out of Israel's future borders.

Also to be remarked are the sevenfold repetition of "before you" as a stylistic unifying device, and the ending theme of serving YHWH as opposed to "their gods."

7 From a false matter, you are to keep far!
And (one) clear and innocent, do not kill,
for I do not acquit a guilty-person.

8 A bribe you are not to take,
for a bribe blinds the open-eyed,
and twists the words of the righteous.

9 A sojourner, you are not to oppress:
you yourselves know (well) the feelings of the sojourner,
for sojourners were you in the land of Egypt.

10 For six years you are to sow your land and to gather in its
produce,
11 but in the seventh, you are to let it go and to let it be,
that the needy of your people may eat,
and what they (allow to) remain, the wildlife of the field may eat.
Do thus with your vineyard, with your olive-grove.

12 For six days you are to make your labor,
but on the seventh day, you are to cease,
in order that your ox and your donkey may rest
and the son of your handmaid and the sojourner may pause-for-
breath.

13 In all that I say to you, take care!
The name of other gods, you are not to mention,
it is not to be heard in your mouth.

14 Three times you are to hold pilgrimage for me, every year.
15 The Pilgrimage-Festival of *matzot* you are to keep:
for seven days you are to eat *matzot,* as I commanded you,
at the appointed-time of the New-Moon of Ripe-Grain—
for in it you went out of Egypt,
and no one is to be seen before my presence empty-handed;

8 **open-eyed:** Here, the equivalent of "wise."
9 **oppress:** Recalling the oppression suffered at the hands of the Egyptians in 3:9.
12 **pause-for-breath:** Later (31:17), God himself is portrayed as having needed to rest after his work of creation.

13 **you:** Plural. **name . . . it:** Understood as plural.
14 **you:** Singular.
15 **before my presence empty-handed:** No one is to make a religious pilgrimage on these occasions without bringing "gifts" (sacrifices).

16 and the Pilgrimage-Festival of the Cutting, of the firstlings of
    your labor, of what you sow in the field;
  and the Pilgrimage-Festival of Ingathering, at the going-out of
    the year,
  when you gather in your labor's (harvest) from the field.

17 At three points in the year
  are all your males to be seen
  before the presence of the Lord, YHWH.

18 You are not to slaughter my blood offering with anything
    fermented.

  The fat of my festive-offering is not to remain overnight, until
    morning.

19 The choicest firstlings of your soil, you are to bring to the house
    of YHWH your God.

  You are not to boil a kid in the milk of its mother.

20 Here, I am sending a messenger before you
  to care for you on the way,
  to bring you to the place that I have prepared.

16 **Pilgrimage-Festival of the Cutting:** The wheat harvest and that of first-fruits, occurring in the third month, usually in early June (also known as Shavu'ot, "Weeks"). **Pilgrimage-Festival of In-gathering:** The final (grape) harvest, in the seventh month in late September or early October (also known as Sukkot, "Huts").

17 **be seen before the presence of . . . YHWH:** A technical expression for one's appearing at the sanctuary (Plaut). **the Lord, YHWH:** Some see this title as a polemic against the Canaanite Baal, whose name means "master" or "lord."

18 **with anything fermented:** Excluding bread and honey (cf. Lev. 2:11) from the offering, possibly since these were included by the Canaanites (Cassuto), or because the sacrifice was to be kept as "natural" as possible.

19 **You are not to boil . . . :** This law occurs three times in the Torah, and so must have been of particular importance. Despite this, interpreters disagree as to its origins and meaning. Some see it as directly opposing a Canaanite practice; others, as parallel to the law in Deuteronomy (22:6–7) against taking the mother bird along with her young. It also keeps the separation between milk (life-giving) and death; it was thus understood in Jewish mystical tradition of the Middle Ages. The phrase is also cited by Talmudic sages as a basis for the separation of milk and meat in postbiblical Jewish dietary laws (*kashrut*).

20 **a messenger:** As sometimes occurs with this word, it is not entirely clear what the distinction is between God and messenger. Here, however, the context seems to require a separate being, whether an angel or Moshe himself.

21 Take-you-care in his presence,
and hearken to his voice,
do not be rebellious against him,
for he is not able to bear your transgressing,
for my name is with him.

22 So then, hearken, hearken to his voice,
and do all that I speak,
and I will be-an-enemy to your enemies,
and I will be-an-adversary to your adversaries.

23 When my messenger goes before you
and brings you
to the Amorite, the Hittite, the Perizzite, and the Canaanite, the
Hivvite and the Yevusite,
and I cause them to perish:

24 you are not to bow down to their gods,
you are not to serve them,
you are not to do according to what they do,
but: you are to tear, yes, tear them down,
and are to smash, yes, smash their standing-stones.

25 You are to serve YHWH your God!
and he will give-blessing to your food and your water;
I will remove sickness from amongst you,

26 there will be no miscarrier or barren-one in your land,
(and) the number of your days I will make full.

27 My terror I will send on before you,
I will panic all the peoples among whom you come,
I will give all your enemies to you by the neck.

---

21 **my name is with him:** Or "in him"; "my authority rests with him" (Clements).

22 **be-an-enemy:** The Hebrew expresses this idea with one verb, without auxiliary.

23 **to the Amorite . . . :** To their land, Canaan.

24 **standing-stones:** Possibly, phallic representations of Canaanite gods.

26 **no miscarrier:** No distinction is made here be-

tween human and animal, and presumably both would share in the blessing.

27 **terror . . . panic:** Heb. *'emati . . . hammati.* **panic:** As in 14:24, above, describing God's routing of the Egyptians. **give all your enemies to you by the neck:** I.e., they will be routed by you, their backs turned.

Sealing the Covenant (24:1–11): To close out the account of covenant-making which began back in Chap. 19, the text recounts a formalized ceremony which has many points of contact with what was generally done throughout the ancient Near East when a covenant was "cut." Twice Moshe reads God's words to the people, and twice (vv.3, 7) they give their assent. This is no imposing of laws by a dictator, but a freely accepted, "signed, sealed, and delivered" agreement cemented by blood, the signifier of life itself.

As representatives of the people, Moshe, Aharon, Aharon's sons, and seventy elders ascend Mount Sinai, and, most remarkably, "see" God in some sort of vision—without, as one might expect, their being destroyed. They also eat and drink, as was customary in the sealing of the agreement (and often done in business to this day; see Gen. 31:44–54).

28 I will send Despair on before you
   so that it drives out the Hivvite, the Canaanite and the Hittite
      from before you.
29 I will not drive them out from before you in one year,
   lest the land become desolate
   and the wildlife of the field become-many against you.
30 Little by little will I drive them out from before you,
   until you have borne-fruit and possessed the land.
31 And I will make your territory
   from the Sea of Reeds to the Sea of the Philistines,
   from the Wilderness to the River.
   For I give into your hand the settled-folk of the land, that you
      may drive them out from before you.
32 You are not to cut with them or with their gods any covenant,
33 they are not to stay in your land, lest they cause you to sin against
      me,
   indeed, you would serve their gods—
   indeed, that would be a snare to you.

24:1 Now to Moshe he said:
   Go up to YHWH,
   you and Aharon, Nadav and Avihu, and seventy of the elders of
      Israel,
   and bow down from afar;
2 Moshe alone is to approach YHWH,
   but they, they are not to approach,
   and as for the people—they (too) are not to go up with him.

---

28 **Despair:** Others, "hornet"; the Hebrew implies both.

29 **I will not drive them out . . . in one year:** This is the situation at the beginning of the book of Judges (after the Conquest); apparently Yehoshua did not finish the job, and so various (later) biblical texts attempt to explain the reason for this.

31 **Sea of the Philistines:** The Mediterranean. **Wilderness:** The southland or Negev. **the River:** The Euphrates, in the north. **drive them out:** Heb. *gerashtemo* is an archaic form (such as we find in 15:17—

tevi'emo ve-titta'emo), used perhaps for reasons of rhythm.

32 **cut . . . any covenant:** A common Semitic idiom for concluding a treaty (see Gen. 15), perhaps stemming from a ritual. The parties would pass between the halves of sacrificed animals, perhaps implying that such would be the penalty for any party that would break the agreement.

24:1 **Nadav and Avihu:** Aharon's first two sons. **seventy:** The "perfect" number with which the book of Exodus began.

Moshe Ascends Alone (24:12–18): Finally, Moshe leaves the people, in order to receive the laws in permanent (stone) form. He "goes up" the mountain four times (or, most likely, is on his way up). In order to give his absence the weight it needs—so that the people will grow restless, setting up the situation that produces the Golden Calf in Chap. 32—the text will now turn to a completely different matter for fully seven chapters.

The ending of this section anticipates the ending of the book of Exodus, with its mention of God's "glory," "dwelling," "fire," and "day/night."

3 So Moshe came
  and recounted to the people all the words of YHWH and all the
    regulations.
  And all the people answered in one voice, and said:
  All the words that YHWH has spoken, we will do.
4 Now Moshe wrote down all the words of YHWH.
  He started-early in the morning,
  building a slaughter-site beneath the mountain
  and twelve standing-stones for the twelve tribes of Israel.
5 Then he sent the (serving-) lads of the Children of Israel,
  that they should offer-up offerings-up, slaughter slaughter-
    offerings of *shalom* for YHWH—bulls.
6 Moshe took half of the blood and put it in basins,
  and half of the blood he tossed against the slaughter-site.
7 Then he took the account of the covenant
  and read it in the ears of the people.
  They said:
  All that YHWH has spoken, we will do and we will hearken!
8 Moshe took the blood, he tossed it on the people
  and said:
  Here is the blood of the covenant
  that YHWH has cut with you
  by means of all these words.

9 Then went up
  Moshe and Aharon, Nadav and Avihu, and seventy of the elders
    of Israel.
10 And they saw
  the God of Israel: beneath his feet
  (something) like work of sapphire tiles,
  (something) like the substance of the heavens in purity.

---

4 **standing-stones:** As distinct from the phallic stones mentioned in 23:24, these functioned as boundary markers and memorials.
5 **lads:** Or "youths"; the Hebrew term *(na'ar)* is analogous to "apprentice."
7 **and we will hearken:** This is an addition to the "we will do" of 19:8. In Deuteronomy "hearken" is often found connoting "obey."

10 **work of sapphire tiles:** Others, "pavement." Childs notes parallel Ugaritic texts to this description. **purity:** In Ugaritic, this word has an association of clarity or brightness, especially as regards precious stones (see "pure gold" in the Tabernacle account: 24:11, 17, 24, 31, 39, below).

11　Yet against the Pillars of the Children of Israel, he did not send
　　　forth his hand—
　　they beheld Godhood
　　and ate and drank.

12　Now Yнwн said to Moshe:
　　Go up to me on the mountain
　　and remain there,
　　that I may give you tablets of stone:
　　the Instruction and the Command
　　that I have written down, to instruct them.

13　Moshe arose, and Yehoshua his attendant,
　　and Moshe went up to the mountain of God.

14　Now to the elders he said:
　　Stay here for us, until we return to you;
　　here, Aharon and Hur are with you—
　　whoever has a legal-matter is to approach them.

15　So Moshe went up the mountain,
　　and the cloud covered the mountain;

16　the Glory of Yнwн took up dwelling on Mount Sinai.
　　The cloud covered it for six days,
　　and he called to Moshe on the seventh day from amidst the cloud.

17　And the sight of the Glory of Yнwн
　　(was) like a consuming fire
　　on top of the mountain
　　in the eyes of the Children of Israel.

18　Moshe came into the midst of the cloud
　　when he went up the mountain.
　　And Moshe was on the mountain
　　for forty days and forty nights.

11　**Pillars:** Apparently a technical term for the representatives of the people (Buber 1988: "corner-joints"). **send forth his hand:** Kill them. **beheld:** Heb. *hazoh*, often used in connection with prophetic vision (see Isa. 1:1).

12　**them:** The Children of Israel.

17　**like a consuming fire:** In contrast to Moshe's striking positive experience of God in Chap. 3, where the bush burned but was not consumed, the Israelites experience him through fear.

18　**forty:** Another meaningful number, reminiscent of the Flood. It is echoed in Elijah's later experience on the same summit (I Kings 19:8).

PART IV

THE INSTRUCTIONS FOR THE DWELLING AND THE CULT

(25–31)

DESPITE THE IMPORTANCE OF ALL THAT HAS PRECEDED, THE SECTION OF EXODUS WE now encounter occupies a significant amount of text, and therefore commands our attention, in the overall scheme of the book. It may seem puzzling to modern readers that a book that purports to be about a people's origins should choose to fill a third of its pages with a detailed description of a sanctuary, down to the last piece of tapestry and the last ritual vessel. Yet it is an indication of the "Tabernacle's" centrality in Israel's idea system that the story of its construction dominates the last half of Exodus.

Several factors may help to explain. First, the system of animal and grain sacrifices, or cult, was as important in ancient Israel as it was elsewhere in antiquity, as the chief means of formally expressing religious feeling. Indeed, the Bible traces this institution back to the beginning of human history, to Cain and Abel (Gen. 4:3–4). The cult's centrality survived the railings of the Prophets and the destruction of Solomon's Temple, and was still strong enough in late antiquity to provoke a severe crisis when its chief site, the Second Temple, fell to the Romans in the year 70 C.E. The latter event was a crux upon which the creation of classical Judaism took place, and the process was a painful one. So the opinion that many moderns have, that animal sacrifice was a barbaric custom, is quite beside the point as far as ancient Israel was concerned.

Second, there is the great theme of the book of Exodus, "Is YHWH in our midst or not?" (17:7), to which our account gives a resounding positive answer. The book of Exodus traces not only the journey of the people of Israel from Egypt to Sinai, but also the journey of God to rescue the people and to dwell ("tabernacle") among them (Greenberg 1972). A detailed presentation of God's "residence," as it were, is meant to convey the assurance that the people are led by God himself. This further supports the biblical image of the divine king, who dwells among his subjects and "goes before" them.

Third, the Israelites shared with their neighbors the idea that a victorious God, following his triumph, was to be honored by his enthronement in a human-built structure (see Hallo). Thus the last half of Exodus, far from trailing off into obscure priestly details, fits a well-known mold in its contemporary environment.

A final explanation of the prominence of the Tabernacle sections may be found in their intimate connection with the idea of the Sabbath. The "blueprint" chapters, 25–31, end with an extended passage on observing the Sabbath; the construction chapters, 35–40, begin with a brief passage on the prohibition of work on the holy day. These structural aspects suggest (as the ancient rabbis also saw) that cessation from work here means precisely from the tasks of construction, and that once a week human beings must step back from their own creating to acknowledge the true "work" of creation. Chapters 25–40, including the Golden Calf narrative, bring out these ideas through their use of refrainlike phrases, especially the repetition of one key word: "make" (Heb. 'asoh). The entire section is an object lesson in what the Bible deems it proper for human beings to make, and is a vehicle of contrast between God's creation and human attempts to reach the divine. Israel is engaged in the making of the Tabernacle (notice how "build," which would make more sense, is not used); when the time comes for the work to be put aside temporarily, they are to "make" the Sabbath. To these observations may be added the long-observed fact that the vocabulary of the Tabernacle's completion ("finished," "work," "blessed") recalls the completion of Creation in Gen. 2:1–4. Thus we are taught that Israel, through its religious life as typified by Sabbath and cult, becomes a partner in the process of Creation, either by imitating the divine act or by celebrating it.

Other peoples, to be sure, recall the beginning of the world in ritual and story, so it is important to make an anthropological observation. The purpose of all sanctuaries is to build a bridge to the divine, to link up with the forces that transcend human beings. It is perceived that certain places are particularly appropriate for this (folklore terms such places "the navel of the earth"), and, by extension, sanctuaries firmly anchor that inherent holiness. What the Tabernacle account initially accomplishes, most notably in its closing chapter (40), is to transfer a topographic "bridge" to a human-made and portable one. With the completion of this Dwelling, we find God resident neither on Sinai nor in the later Jerusalem, but rather accompanying the people "upon all their marches" (40:38). The sacred center here thus moves; it is a portable anchor that establishes stability wherever it goes. The vitality that surrounded this idea is still to be seen in the successors of the Hebrew Bible, classical Judaism and Christianity, for whom, respectively, Torah and Cross provide a center that is at once movable and stabilizing.

But the sacred center, for biblical religion, finds equal expression in *time*. While the Dwelling account seems obsessed with matters of space, its setting among the Sabbath passages stresses more the concept of time. Such an aspect already begins to make itself felt in 24:16, where Moshe, on Sinai to receive the laws, waits for six days while the "cloud" covers the mountain, and is able to ascend only on the seventh day, at God's summons. We are thus left, paradoxically, with a structure (Dwelling) which at first glance uses many well-known art forms and religious motifs common to the ancient Near East, but which is a total departure from them via its connection with the Sabbath—an institution with no known equivalent in the ancient world. The Dwelling account presents us with a people for whom sacred time takes precedence over sacred space (for more on these themes, see Sarna 1986).

There have been many attempts, textually and artistically, to reconstruct the Tabernacle on the basis of our text here, the rationale being that surely so much detail as we find here will serve as the guidelines for an actual structure. Rabbinic and medieval Jewish commentators, as well as modern scholars, have expended considerable energy to that end. But in fact none of the reconstructions has succeeded, for, as with narrative, the text is as much message as description. The text's main concern, it seems, is for the Dwelling to reflect holiness, in its choice of measurements and materials (see Haran 1985). The layout of the Dwelling expresses aesthetic ideas of perfection, through various symmetrical proportions (see Appendix); the materials are graded such that the closer one gets to God (in the "Holiest Holy-Shrine"), the more precious the metal. In addition, both the colors used and the types of workmanship employed are similarly graded. In a general way, the intent of the narrator seems to have been close to the intent of the great cathedral builders of the Middle Ages: to reflect divine perfection and order in the perfection and order of a sacred structure.

The Dwelling, as described in Exodus, resembles other ancient Near Eastern sanctuaries in many particulars (for which, see the Commentary below), as well as strongly reflecting aspects of the later Temple of Solomon (I Kings 6–7). Some scholars have also likened it to a Bedouin tent (Heb. *shakhen* seems to be an archaic verb for "to tent"), appropriate to desert conditions. It is perhaps all three, a coalescing of Israel's ideas of the cult from a variety of historical and religious settings. That the Dwelling was viewed as historical is clear from biblical tradition itself (see II Sam. 7:6, for instance). But one should keep in mind that it is also a paradigmatic model, that helps to round out the overall scheme of Exodus. The book traces the progress of the people of Israel from servitude (to Pharaoh) to service (of God), and uses the human activity of building to do so. Thus, as Exodus opens, the Israelites are forcibly made to build royal storage cities; as the book ends, the people complete a structure through which they may serve the divine king.

Finally, there is the sequence of description in these chapters: the text begins with the blueprint for the holiest object, the "coffer" (ark), and proceeds through the structure in descending order of holiness. After the building instructions themselves are given, a number of related matters are treated, chief among them the attire of the priests and the ceremony consecrating the priests. The establishment of the cult, like that of the system of justice, is thus viewed as the command of God rather than the result of the need or request of human beings (contrast this with the "requested" monarchy in I Sam. 8).

The "Contribution" (25:1–9): In the first seven verses of this opening section dealing with the Dwelling, the Israelites' contribution toward the structure is described in detail; but only in v.8 is the purpose of this activity made clear. Despite the concreteness of the description, however, the actual blueprints, as it were, are shown to Moshe by God, and are not recorded in the text. Architects in the creative sense are superfluous here.

Moderns want to know where the Israelites procured such materials as gold and silver in quantity (see Chap. 38), or how they acquired the skills necessary for the fine artisanry involved (e.g., weaving, dyeing, manufacture of incense, and the setting of jewels). These questions, while logical in a historical setting, do not take the Bible on its own terms. The text appears to present the awed report of the Dwelling and its construction without leaving room for totally practical issues (just as Gen. 4 deals with Cain and his descendants without being concerned with the origins of Cain's wife).

The Coffer (25:10–16): The coffer or ark was a cult object of major importance in premonarchic and early monarchic Israel. In our text it contains the "Testimony" (i.e., the tablets with the Ten Words); in Josh. 3:14–15 it precedes the people into the Promised Land; in I Sam. 4:11–5:12 it is captured in battle but mysteriously wreaks havoc among the enemy (hence its cinematic offspring *Raiders of the Lost Ark*). Finally, David's transporting of it to Jerusalem (II Sam. 6) marks the formal establishment of that city as a holy one and as the capital of Israel.

In Exodus the coffer literally plays a central role. It stands in the innermost recesses of the Tabernacle, at the sacred center. Considering what the coffer contained—tablets with God's words on them rather than statues of gods—it addresses the primacy of divine word over divine representation in ancient Israelite thought.

◆ 25:1 Now YHWH spoke to Moshe, saying:

 2 Speak to the Children of Israel,
   that they may take me a raised-contribution;
   from every man whose heart makes-him-willing, you are to take
     my contribution.

 3 And this is the contribution that you are to take from them:
   gold, silver, and bronze,

 4 blue-violet, purple, and worm-scarlet (yarn), byssus, and goats'-
     hair,

 5 rams' skins dyed-red, tanned-leather skins,
   acacia wood,

 6 oil for lighting,
   spices for oil of anointing and for fragrant smoking-incense,

 7 onyx stones, stones for setting
   for the *efod* and for the breastpiece.

 8 Let them make me a Holy-Shrine
   that I may dwell amidst them.

 9 According to all that I grant you to see,
   the building-pattern of the Dwelling and the building-pattern of
     all its implements,
   thus are you to make it.

 10 They are to make

25:2 **raised-contribution:** A collective noun (Plaut). The image is a common one, as in English "raise money."

4 **blue-violet:** The exact color is not certain; others, "blue." What does seem clear is that this was precious, probably because the dye was difficult to extract from its natural setting, and was the color of royalty (viz., "royal purple") (Milgrom 1983). The same color was used on the fringes commanded as a memorial garment in Num. 15:37–38. **worm-scarlet:** Others, "crimson." The dye was produced by crushing the shell of a certain insect, and hence the two-word Hebrew name. **byssus:** Fine linen (Heb. *shesh,* a loan-word from Egyptian), as opposed to the plain *bad* (linen) of 28:42.

5 **tanned-leather:** Previous translations, going back to antiquity, have theorized "dolphin" or "dugong"; current scholarship understands Heb. *tahash* as either the color orange-yellow or the leather that has that shade. **acacia:** This particular tree, well suited

for construction, is found most often in the Bible in reference to the Tabernacle.

6 **anointing:** For consecrating priests (e.g., 29:7) and kings (e.g., I Sam. 10:1). **fragrant smoking-incense:** See 30:34–38, below.

7 **for setting:** In the high priest's breastpiece (see 28:17–21, below). **efod:** An important garment of the high priest (see 28:6ff., below). **breastpiece:** Hung on the *efod* (see 28:15ff., below).

8 **Holy-Shrine:** Others, "sanctuary."

10 **coffer:** Others, "ark." The Hebrew word *aron,* like "ark," means a chest or box, and is also used of Yosef's "coffin" in Gen. 50:20. I have used a different word here so as not to confuse it with Noah's ark (Heb. *teiva*). **cubits:** The cubit was a common measure in the ancient world, conceived of as the length of a man's forearm. The biblical cubit existed in two versions, measuring between 17½ and 20½ inches. **two cubits and a half . . . :** Thus the proportions of the coffer are 5:3:3.

The Purgation-Cover (25:17–22): *Kapporet* here could indicate simply "cover," yet its function goes beyond mere protection. The name of this central part of the above-cited central cult object may be a play on words. The Hebrew verb *kapper,* which occurs again later in these texts (see 29:33–37), often means "purge" or "purify"; earlier translators rendered it as "expiate" or even "propitiate," and the *kapporet* as "mercy-seat" or "propitiatory." The *kapporet* was apparently the holiest spot in the Israelite cult system, and it was there that God was said to speak his will to the people. This idea represents a remarkable shrinking and intimatizing process: the God who spoke to the assembled people, amid thunder, fire, and trembling earth at Sinai, now communicates with them from an area roughly the size of a small desk or table. In addition, there is a shift from a one-time event (Sinai) to the permanent fact of a sanctuary—a development which will later be repeated in Solomon's Temple.

a coffer of acacia wood,
two cubits and a half its length,
a cubit and a half its width,
and a cubit and a half its height.

11 You are to overlay it with pure gold,
inside and outside you are to overlay it,
and are to make upon it a rim of gold all around.

12 You are to cast for it four rings of gold
and are to put them upon its four feet,
with two rings on its one flank
and two rings on its second flank.

13 You are to make poles of acacia wood
and are to overlay them with gold

14 and are to bring the poles into the rings on the flanks of the
coffer,
to carry the coffer by (means of) them.

15 In the rings of the coffer are the poles to remain,
they are not to be removed from it.

16 And you are to put in the coffer
the Testimony that I give you.

17 You are to make a purgation-cover of pure gold,
two cubits and a half its length
and a cubit and a half its width.

18 You are to make two winged-sphinxes of gold,
of hammered-work are you to make them,

11 **a rim of gold all around:** Heb. *zer zahav saviv.*

16 **Testimony:** B-R, seeking to connect *'edut* ("Testimony") with the sound of *mo'ed* ("appointment"), translate these two terms as "representation" and "presence." The tablets bear the name "Testimony" because they "testify" or bear witness to God's relationship with the Israelites. It should also be noted that Akkadian *'adu,* cognate with our *'edut,* means "treaty," somewhat like the Hebrew *berit* ("covenant"), which is often found parallel to *'edut* in the Bible (DeVaux 1965).

17 **purgation-cover:** Heb. *kapporet.* There are two long-held traditions of translating this word: "expiation" or "mercy-seat" and plain "cover." I have kept both ideas in the present rendering. The *kapporet* was used for the purpose of obtaining forgiveness from God (see Lev. 16:13-15), and also served symbolically as God's "footstool" to the throne represented by the coffer. Such symbolism is in line with ancient Near Eastern practice, as is the keeping of the covenant documents within the footstool.

18 **winged-sphinxes:** Others, "cherubim," which, however, is too reminiscent of chubby-cheeked baby angels in Western art. In Mesopotamian temples, these mythical figures in sculpture served as guardians; so too at the end of the Garden of Eden story in Gen. 3:24. See Albright.

The Table (25:23–30): The table and its implements, like some of the other features of the Tabernacle, are holdovers from a more blatantly pagan model, where the gods were seen to be in need of nourishment. By thus using conventions of worship common throughout the ancient Near East, Israel expressed its desire to serve God, even while it was aware that he was not the sort of deity who requires food and drink. It might also be mentioned that another common object found in ancient sanctuaries, a bed, has intentionally been omitted from our structure.

at the two ends of the purgation-cover.

19 Make one sphinx at the end here
and one sphinx at the end there;
from the purgation-cover are you to make the two sphinxes,
at its two ends.

20 And the sphinxes are to be spreading (their) wings upward
with their wings sheltering the purgation-cover,
their faces, each-one toward the other;
toward the purgation-cover are the sphinxes' faces to be.

21 You are to put the purgation-cover on the coffer, above it,
and in the coffer you are to put
the Testimony that I give you.

22 I will appoint-meeting with you there
and I will speak with you
from above the purgation-cover,
from between the sphinxes that are on the coffer of Testimony—
all that I command you
concerning the Children of Israel.

23 You are to make a table of acacia wood,
two cubits its length,
a cubit its width,
and a cubit and a half its height;

24 you are to overlay it with pure gold.
You are to make a rim of gold for it, all around,

25 you are to make for it a border, a handbreadth all around,
thus you are to make a rim of gold for its border, all around.

26 You are to make for it four rings of gold
and are to put the rings at the four edges, where its four legs (are).

27 Parallel to the border are the rings to be,

---

19 **here . . . there:** Or "on one side . . . on the other side"; at either end. **from:** Or "out of"; others, "of one piece with." This one-piece construction is a frequent feature of the objects associated with the Tabernacle.

20 **toward the purgation-cover:** Facing downward, as if to avoid the direct presence of God.

22 **appoint-meeting:** The Hebrew verb refers to fixing a time, and is not the same as the earlier "meeting"

(5:3). Exodus speaks of the "Tent of Appointment" from Chap. 27 on; it is unclear as to whether the Tabernacle itself or a separate structure is meant. **from above the purgation-cover,/from between the sphinxes:** So this was seen as the precise spot of God's presence in the Tabernacle.

27 **as holders for the poles:** Heb. *le-vatim le-vaddim. Batim* are literally "housings."

The Lampstand (25:31–40): Despite the wealth of detail lavished on this striking symbol, its exact construction, like that of the Dwelling in general, remains unclear. The vocabulary used for its constituent parts comes from the realm of plants: shaft, stems, blossoms, almond shapes, etc. Indeed, the major latent symbol behind the lampstand is the tree—which appears in many forms and in almost all religions (Meyers). The tree as a symbol is to be found throughout human culture, in such diverse settings as Native American stories and Norse myths; in the ancient Near East it specifically connoted permanence, growth, and majesty—in other words, a reflection of the divine. If one adds to this range of meanings the function of the lampstand—illumination (which often implies not only the giving of physical light but also, as the English phrase has it, enlightenment)—the lampstand will be seen to emerge as an object with considerable evocative power. All these meanings may not have been immediately obvious and conscious to the ancient pilgrim or worshiper, but they periodically surfaced; the lampstand was ancient Judaism's symbol of preference (judging from synagogue ruins) and not the "Star of David," which, as Gershom Scholem has shown, was a medieval mystical addition.

The importance of the lampstand in our text is indicated by v.40, where the motif of God's revealing the structure of a sacred object on the mountain is resumed. Its significance is also attested by its major material of construction: pure gold.

as holders for the poles, to carry the table.

28 You are to make the poles of acacia wood, and are to overlay
   them with gold,
   that the table may be carried by (means of) them.

29 You are to make its plates and its ladles,
   its jars and its jugs, from which (offerings) are poured;
   of pure gold are you to make them.

30 And you are to put on the table
   the Bread of the Presence, before my presence, regularly.

31 You are to make a lampstand of pure gold;
   of hammered-work is the lampstand to be made, its shaft and its
       stem;
   its goblets, its knobs and its blossoms are to be from it.

32 Six stems issue from its sides,
   three lamp-stems from the one side,
   and three lamp-stems from the second side:

33 three almond-shaped goblets on the one stem, with knobs and
       blossoms,
   and three almond-shaped goblets on the other stem, with knobs
       and blossoms—
   thus for the six stems that issue from the lampstand;

34 and on the lampstand (itself) four almond-shaped goblets, with
       their knobs and their blossoms,

35 a knob beneath two stems, from it,
   a knob beneath two stems, from it,
   and a knob beneath two stems, from it,
   for the six stems that issue from the lampstand.

36 Their knobs and their stems are to be from it,
   all of it hammered-work, of pure gold.

29 **plates . . . cups . . . jars . . . jugs:** Translations vary considerably on these terms. Haran (1985) cites several (e.g., "plates, bowls, dishes, cups," "ladles, jars, saucers, beakers").

30 **Bread of the Presence:** Trad. English "shew-bread." **regularly:** Not "perpetually," as earlier interpreters understood.

31 **shaft . . . stem:** Meyers (1976) interprets this as a hendiadys (two Hebrew words that yield a composite meaning), "thickened shaft." **knobs . . . blossoms:** Others, "calyxes . . . petals."

33 **almond-shaped:** Like the shape of the almond flower.

35 **from it:** See the note to v.19, above.

The Dwelling Proper (26:1–14): The text describes the network of tapestries or curtains that comprise the structure itself, in two layers (vv.1–6 and 7–12), with two additional layers mentioned (v.14). The outer layers function to protect the inner ones from the elements, while the inner ones, true to the gradations of holiness previously mentioned, are more elaborate.

The Framework (26:15–30): The rigid part of the Tabernacle structure, while described in some detail, leaves room for many questions about specifics (e.g., how exactly did the boards fit together? was there one corner board or two? is the text perhaps describing planks or frames?). What is most important, as mentioned above, is the sense of proportion and approach to the divine implied by symmetrical numbers.

37 You are to make its lamps, seven (of them),
  you are to draw up its lampwicks so that they light up (the space)
    across from it.

38 And its tongs and its trays (shall be) of pure gold.

39 (From) an ingot of pure gold they are to make it, together with
    all these implements.

40 Now see
  and make,
  according to their building-pattern which you are granted to see
    upon the mountain.

26:1 Now the dwelling you are to make
  from ten tapestries
  of twisted byssus, blue-violet, purple and worm-scarlet (yarn),
  with sphinxes, of designer's making, you are to make it.

2 The length of each one tapestry (shall be) twenty-eight by the
    cubit,
  and the width, four by the cubit
  of each one tapestry,
  one measure for all of the tapestries.

3 Five of the tapestries are to be joined, each-one to the other,
  and five tapestries joined, each-one to the other.

4 You are to make loops of blue-violet
  on the edge of one tapestry, at the end of the one joint;
  and thus you are to make at the edge of the end tapestry, at the
    second joint.

5 Fifty loops are you to make on the first tapestry,
  and fifty loops are you to make at the end of the tapestry that is
    at the second joint,
  the loops opposite, each-one from the other.

6 You are to make fifty clasps of gold
  and you are to join the tapestries, each-one to the other, with the
    clasps,
  so that the dwelling may be one-piece.

---

38 **tongs:** Others, "snuffers."
26:1 **the dwelling:** In this context it signifies the inside por-
    tion of the Tabernacle; lowercase is used here to dis-

tinguish it from the entire structure. **tapestries:**
Others, "curtains," "cloths." **designer's making:**
According to the designer's craft.

7 You are to make the tapestries of goats'-hair for a tent over the
        dwelling,
    eleven tapestries you are to make them.
8 The length of each one tapestry (shall be) thirty by the cubit,
    and the width, four by the cubit,
    for each one tapestry,
    one measure for the eleven tapestries.
9 You are to join five of the tapestries separately
    and six of the tapestries separately,
    but you are to double over the sixth tapestry, facing the tent.
10 You are to make fifty loops at the edge of the one tapestry, the
        end-one, at the joint,
    and fifty loops at the end of the second joining tapestry.
11 You are to make clasps of bronze, fifty,
    and you are to bring the clasps into the loops, so that you join the
        tent together,
    that it may become one-piece.
12 And as for the extension that overlaps in the tapestries of the tent,
    half of the overlapping tapestry you are to extend over the back
        of the dwelling.
13 The cubit over here and the cubit over there of the overlap, in the
        long-part of the tapestries of the tent,
    is to be extended over the sides of the tent over here and over
        there, in order to cover it.
14 You are to make a covering for the tent of rams' skins dyed-red,
    and a covering of tanned-leather skins, above it.

15 You are to make boards for the Dwelling
    of acacia wood, standing-upright;
16 ten cubits, the length of a board,
    and a cubit and a half, the width of each one board;

---

9 **double over:** Since it overlaps (see vv.12–13).
14 **covering:** A different Hebrew verb (*kasse*) from the
   one translated by "purgation-cover" (*kapper*).

15 **boards:** Some interpret as "beams" or "frames." See
   the discussion of the possibilities in Haran (1965).

17 with two pegs for each one board, parallel one to the other,
   thus are you to make for all the boards of the Dwelling.
18 And you are to make the boards for the Dwelling:
   twenty as boardwork on the Negev border, southward,
19 and forty sockets of silver are you to make beneath twenty of the
     boards,
   two sockets beneath each one board for its two pegs
   and two sockets beneath each other board for its two pegs;
20 and for the second flank of the Dwelling, on the northern border,
     twenty as boardwork,
21 with their forty sockets of silver,
   two sockets beneath each one board,
   and two sockets beneath each other board.
22 And for the rear of the Dwelling, toward the sea, you are to make
     six boards,
23 and two boards you are to make for the corners of the Dwelling,
     at the rear,
24 so that they may be of twin-use, (seen) from the lower-end,
   and together may be a whole-piece, at the top, toward the first
     ring;
   thus shall it be for the two of them,
   for the two corners shall they be.
25 Then there are to be eight boards with their sockets of silver,
     sixteen sockets,
   two sockets beneath each one board,
   and two sockets beneath each other board.
26 You are to make running-bars of acacia wood,
   five for the boards of Dwelling's one flank
27 and five bars for the boards of the Dwelling's second flank,
   and five bars for the Dwelling's flank at the rear, toward the sea.

---

17 **pegs:** Others, "tenons," a more technical architectural term. **parallel:** Heb. obscure.
18 **Negev:** The desert southland of Israel.
22 **the sea:** The Mediterranean, and hence the west,
from the perspective of one living in the land of
Israel.
24 **of twin-use:** Used for two purposes? The exact

meaning here has been long debated, with many
sketches as to what the corners of the Tabernacle
might have looked like. **toward the first ring:** Heb.
obscure.
26 **running-bars:** Horizontal bars designed to hold the
structure together.

The Curtain and the Screen (26:31–37): Two hangings separate different parts of the Tabernacle: the curtain, which closes off the inner sanctum; and the screen, which separates tent and courtyard.

The Altar (27:1–8): As Cassuto points out, Israelite worship, like that in surrounding cultures, would have been unthinkable without an altar for animal sacrifices. The one described here is a compromise between permanence and portability: it was hollow for transporting, to be filled in with earth at each encampment.

As with the lampstand, the exact construction of the object is to proceed along lines given to Moshe by God at Sinai.

The Courtyard (27:9–19): Returning to the Tabernacle structure, the outer courtyard is laid out, composed of hangings and columns. Again, the numbers fit meaningfully together. Since we are dealing with the extremity of the Dwelling, the material used is the least precious: bronze.

◆ 28 And the middle bar (shall be) in the midst of the boards, running
        from end to end.
29 Now the boards you are to overlay with gold,
        their rings you are to make of gold, as holders for the bars,
        and are to overlay the bars with gold.
30 So erect the Dwelling, according to its plan,
        as you have been granted to see upon the mountain.

31 You are to make a curtain
        of blue-violet, purple, worm-scarlet and twisted byssus;
        of designer's making they are to make it, with winged-sphinxes.
32 You are to put it on four columns of acacia,
        overlaid with gold, their hooks of gold,
        upon four sockets of silver;
33 and you are to put the curtain beneath the clasps.
        You are to bring there, inside the curtain,
        the coffer of Testimony;
        the curtain shall separate for you
        the Holy-Shrine from the Holiest Holy-Shrine.
34 You are to put the purgation-cover
        on the coffer of Testimony;
        in the Holiest Holy-Shrine.
35 You are to place the table outside the curtain,
        and the lampstand opposite the table on the south flank of the
            Dwelling,
        but the table you are to put on the north flank.
36 You are to make a screen for the entrance to the tent,
        of blue-violet, purple, worm-scarlet and twisted byssus,
        of embroiderer's making;
37 you are to make for the screen five columns of acacia,
        you are to overlay them with gold, their hooks of gold,
        and are to cast for them five sockets of bronze.

33 **Holiest Holy-Shrine:** Trad. "Holy of Holies."

27:1 You are to make the slaughter-site of acacia wood,
    five cubits in length
    and five cubits in width;
    square is the slaughter-site to be,
    and three cubits its height.
2 You are to make its horns on its four points,
    from it are its horns to be;
    and you are to overlay it with bronze.
3 You are to make its pails for removing-its-ashes,
    its scrapers, its bowls, its flesh-hooks and its pans—
    all of its implements, you are to make of bronze.
4 You are to make for it a lattice,
    as a netting of bronze is made,
    and are to make on the netting four rings of bronze
    on its four ends;
5 you are to put it beneath the ledge of the slaughter-site, below,
    so that the netting (reaches) to the halfway-point of the slaughter-
       site,
6 You are to make poles for the slaughter-site,
    poles of acacia wood,
    and are to overlay them with bronze.
7 Its poles are to be brought through the rings,
    so that the poles are on the two flanks of the slaughter-site when
       they carry it.
8 Hollow, of planks, are you to make it;
    as he has granted you to see it on the mountain, thus are they to
       make it.

27:2 **horns:** Many altars have been dug up in the area, both Israelite and non-Israelite in origin, fitting this description. The origin and purpose of the "horns" is not clear. We do know that when an Israelite wanted to be granted asylum, for instance, he could grasp the horns of the altar (see I Kings 1:50ff.).

3 **scrapers . . . bowls . . . flesh-hooks . . . pans:** As in 25:29, above, the exact identification of these objects is not known.

4 **lattice . . . netting:** To let air through and facilitate burning (Cassuto).

7 **poles:** In contrast to those of the coffer, these were apparently removable. The altar was of lesser sanctity than the coffer, and it was not deemed as crucial that no human hand touch it.

8 **Hollow:** And thus easily transportable, to be filled with dirt every time it was set up.

9 You are to make the courtyard of the Dwelling:
on the Negev border, southward,
hangings for the courtyard, of twisted byssus,
a hundred by the cubit, the length on one border;

10 with its columns, twenty, their sockets, twenty, of bronze,
the hooks of the columns and their binders, of silver.

11 And thus on the northern border, lengthwise,
hangings a hundred (cubits) in length,
with its columns, twenty, their sockets, twenty, of bronze,
the hooks of the columns and their binders, of silver.

12 And (along) the width of the courtyard on the sea border
hangings of fifty cubits,
with its columns, ten, their sockets, ten.

13 And (along) the width of the courtyard on the eastern border,
toward sunrise,
fifty cubits,

14 namely: fifteen cubits of hangings for the shoulder-piece,
their columns, three, their sockets, three,

15 and for the second shoulder-piece, fifteen (cubits) of hangings,
their columns, three, their sockets, three,

16 and for the gate of the courtyard, a screen of twenty cubits,
of blue-violet, purple, worm-scarlet and twisted byssus, of
embroiderer's making,
their columns, four, their sockets, four.

17 All the columns of the courtyard all around are attached with
silver, their hooks of silver,
their sockets of bronze,

18 —the length of the courtyard, a hundred by the cubit, the width,
fifty by fifty, the height, five cubits of twisted byssus,
their sockets of bronze.

---

9 **twisted byssus:** Heb. *shesh moshzar.*
10 **binders:** Others, "rods."

14 **shoulder-piece:** That is the literal Hebrew; "side"
would be acceptable idiomatically.

The Oil (27:20–21): The transition from structure to human institution (the priesthood) is accomplished by both the opening formula here, "Now you . . . ," and by the oil itself, which is here used for light but which will soon be spoken of (Chap. 29) as a major agent in the anointing of the priests.

The Priestly Garments (28:1–5): As in the opening section on the Tabernacle itself (25:1–9), we are now given a listing of what is to come, the clothing in which the priests will perform their sacred functions. The purpose of the objects is mentioned again, this time at both the beginning and the end of the section.

In virtually all traditional religions such garments are of great importance, often signaling the status of the wearer as representative of the community (hence Aharon's breastpiece in this chapter). An additional function, stressed in our account, is that the garments somehow reflect God himself, through the use of certain colors and/or materials. That the term "glory" is used to indicate their function—a key term in the book, and always applied to God, never to Moshe, for instance—signals what is at stake.

The Efod (28:6–12, 13–14): This garment, which here seems to be a kind of apron worn only by the high priest, is mentioned elsewhere in the Bible in connection with worship (e.g., Judg. 8:27), but with unclear meaning. Even here, the exact nature of the *efod* is not entirely certain; but what is cited is its function as the setting for the stones that symbolize the twelve tribes of Israel in God's presence. This is followed by a description of chains, whose use is mentioned immediately thereafter.

The Breastpiece (28:15–30): The central garment in this section is the breastpiece, which seems to be some sort of woven pouch or bag. On the outside it displays precious stones, each one engraved with the name of an Israelite tribe; inside, it holds the oracular objects known as *Urim* and *Tummin* (see the note to v.30, below). In this passage, which is cast in poetic form, the narrator appears to be drawing our attention to the specific function of the garments. Vv.29 and 30 repeat the phrase "over his/Aharon's heart" (three times), "in the presence of YHWH" (three times), and "regularly" (twice) to make clear their importance: Aharon represents the people whenever he officiates in the sanctuary, and bears the emblem of this office upon his very heart.

412

19 All the implements of the Dwelling for all its service (of
     construction),
and all its pins, and all the pins of the courtyard,
—bronze.

20 Now you,
command the Children of Israel,
that they may fetch you
oil of olives, clear, beaten,
for the light,
to draw up a lampwick, regularly.
21 In the Tent of Appointment,
outside the curtain that is over the Testimony,
Aharon and his sons are to arrange it,
from sunset until daybreak
before the presence of YHWH—
a law for the ages, throughout your generations,
on the part of the Children of Israel.

28:1 Now you, have come-near to you
Aharon your brother and his sons with him,
from amidst the Children of Israel,
to be-priests for me;
Aharon,
Nadav and Avihu, Elazar and Itamar, the sons of Aharon.
2 You are to make garments of holiness for Aharon your brother,
for glory and for splendor.

---

19 **service (of construction):** Not worship (divine
service), but rather a term referring to the Levites'
setting up and dismantling of the Tabernacle
(Milgrom 1983). **pins:** Others, "pegs."
20 **beaten:** Crushed until the substance is pure.
21 **Tent of Appointment:** See the note to 25:22, above.
DeVaux (1965) translates as "Tent of Rendezvous,"
and Moffatt (in his 1926 Bible translation) as "Tryst-
ing Tent," but these are too romantic in English,

even in view of what I have said about the relationship between God and Israel. **arrange:** Or "set up."
28:1 **be-priests:** One translation possibility was to coin
an English verb, "to priest."
2 **glory ... splendor:** Others, "dignity and magnifi-
cence," but retaining "glory" for *kavod* enables one
to see in the priest's garb a reflection of the divine
splendor.

3 So you, speak to each who is wise of mind
whom I have filled with the spirit of practical-wisdom,
that they may make Aharon's garments,
to hallow him, to be-priest for me.

4 And these are the garments that they are to make:
breastpiece and *efod* and tunic,
braided coat,
wound-turban and sash.
So they are to make garments of holiness
for Aharon your brother and for his sons,
to be-priests for me.

5 And they, they are to take gold, blue-violet, purple, worm-scarlet
and byssus.

6 They are to make the *efod*
of gold, of blue-violet and of purple, of worm-scarlet and of
twisted byssus,
of designer's making.

7 Two shoulder-pieces, joined, it is to have, at its two ends,
and it is to be joined.

8 The designed-band of its *efod*, which is on it,
according to its making, is to be from it,
of gold, of blue-violet, of purple, of worm-scarlet and of twisted
byssus.

9 You are to take two onyx stones
and are to engrave on them the names of the Children of Israel,

10 six of their names on the one stone,
and the names of the six remaining-ones on the second stone,
corresponding to their begettings.

11 Of stone-cutter's making, with seal engravings,
you are to engrave the two stones,
with the names of the Children of Israel;
surrounded by braids of gold are you to make them.

---

3 **wise of mind:** Idiomatically, "skilled" or "talented." **practical-wisdom:** Wisdom in biblical literature most often denotes worldly wisdom or artisanry, not abstract intellectual prowess.

8 **designed-band:** Perhaps resembling a belt.
10 **begettings:** Birth order.
11 **braids:** Others, "mesh," "checkered-work."

12 You are to place the two stones on the shoulder-pieces of the *efod*,
as stones of remembrance for the Children of Israel.
Aharon is to bear their names before the presence of Yhwh
on his two shoulders,
for remembrance.

13 You are to make braids of gold
14 and two chains of pure gold,
(like) lacings are you to make them, of rope-making,
and are to put the rope chains on the braids.

15 You are to make the breastpiece of Judgment
of designer's making,
like the making of the *efod* are you to make it,
of gold, of blue-violet, of purple, of worm-scarlet and of twisted
byssus are you to make it.
16 Square it is to be, doubled-over,
a span its length and a span its width.
17 You are to set-it-full with a setting of stones,
four rows of stones—
a row of carnelian, topaz and sparkling-emerald, the first row,
18 the second row: ruby, sapphire, and hard-onyx,
19 the third row: jacinth, agate, and amethyst,
20 the fourth row: beryl, onyx, and jasper.
Braided with gold are they to be in their settings.
21 And the stones are to be with the names of the Children of Israel,
twelve with their names,
(with) signet engravings, each-one with its name, are they to be,
for the twelve tribes.
22 You are to make, on the breastpiece, laced chains, of rope
making, of pure gold;

12 **for remembrance:** For a visible symbol.
16 **a span:** A measure taken to be the distance between
the outstretched thumb and the little finger, half a
cubit or about nine inches.

17–20 **carnelian . . . jasper:** The exact identification of
many of these stones is uncertain. The reader will
find a different list in virtually every Bible translation.

The Tunic (28:31–35): Aharon's tunic or shirt is notable for its design of bells and pomegranates, but even more for its protective function, supplied by actual bells, of maintaining the proper distance between Aharon and God in the sanctuary.

The Head-Plate (28:36–38): Foremost among the symbols on Aharon's garments is what he bears on his brow: a band with the words "Holiness for YHWH." It serves as a symbol of his efforts to obtain forgiveness on behalf of the Israelite people, one of his primary functions as priest. This function extends to cover even unintentional transgressions, such as accidents in the handling of sacred cultic objects.

Other Priestly Garments (28:39–43): These include remaining vestments for Aharon and his sons, to the end that "they do not bear iniquity and die" (v.43)—a major concern of the priesthood, which viewed all impurities as ritually dangerous before God. Note the solemn ending of this passage: "—a law for the ages, for him and for his seed after him."

23 and you are to make, on the breastpiece, two rings of gold;
you are to put the two rings on the two ends of the breastpiece.

24 And you are to put the two ropes of gold on the two rings
at the ends of the breastpiece;

25 and the two ends of the two ropes, you are to put on the two
braids
and you are to put them on the shoulder-piece of the *efod,* facing
frontward.

26 You are to make two rings of gold,
and are to place them on the two ends of the breastpiece, on its
edge, which is across from the *efod,* inward,

27 and you are to make two rings of gold,
and are to put them on the two shoulder-pieces of the *efod,*
below, facing frontward, parallel to its joint, above the
designed-band of the *efod.*

28 They are to tie the breastpiece from its rings to the rings of the
efod
with a thread of blue-violet,
to be (fixed) on the designed-band of the *efod;*
the breastpiece is not to slip from the *efod.*

29 So Aharon is to bear
the names of the Children of Israel
on the breastpiece of Judgment
over his heart,
whenever he comes into the Holy-Shrine
for remembrance, before the presence of Yhwh,
regularly.

29 **over his heart:** Or "upon his heart," three times
here. A similar idea occurs in later Judaism, which
interpreted Deut. 6:8 ("you shall bind them as a sign
upon your hand, and they shall serve as bands between your eyes") literally. The resulting *tefillin*
("phylacteries"), leather straps with small boxes
containing the relevant Deuteronomy passages
worn during weekday morning prayers, include a
text that is worn on the arm in such a way as to
point to the heart.

30 And you are to put
   in the breastpiece of Judgment
   the *Urim* and the *Tummim,*
   that they may be over Aharon's heart,
   whenever he comes before the presence of Yhwh.
   So Aharon is to bear
   the breastpiece of Judgment for the Children of Israel
   over his heart
   before the presence of Yhwh,
   regularly.

31 You are to make the tunic for the *efod*
   all of blue-violet.

32 Its head-opening is to be in its middle;
   there shall be a seam for its opening, all around, of weaver's
      making,
   like the opening for armor is it to be for him, it is not to be split.

33 You are to make on its skirts
   pomegranates of blue-violet, purple, and worm-scarlet,
   on its skirts, all around,
   and bells of gold amidst them, all around:

34 bell of gold and pomegranate,
   bell of gold and pomegranate,
   on the skirts of the tunic, all around.

35 It is to be (put) on Aharon, for attending,
   that its sound may be heard

---

30 **Urim . . . Tummim:** Oracular objects, used for divining God's plans (e.g. learning if it was the right time to go into battle). Their exact shape and mode of operation are the subject of much scholarly debate (see Cassuto, for instance). In I Sam. 28:6, *Urim* are equated with dreams and prophets as a means of answering human queries. B-R, following Luther, translate the terms as *Lichtende und Schlichtende* ("lights and perfections"), a possible literal but unclear translation. It is also worth noting that *Urim* begins with the first letter of the Hebrew alphabet, and *Tummim* the last, giving rise to the possibility that the names themselves are symbolic.

31 **tunic:** Others, "robe."
32 **armor:** Or "coat of mail." **split:** Or "splittable."
33 **pomegranates:** Cassuto notes that these were a common ornamental device in the ancient world, and a symbol of fertility (as in Song 6:7, 11; 8:2). **bells:** Their use is explained in v. 35, "so that he [Aharon] does not die." Bells serve to drive away demons or to warn of human approach in many cultures; see Gaster (1969) for parallels.
34 **bell of gold and pomegranate:** In alternating design.

whenever he comes into the Holy-Shrine before the presence of
YHWH, and whenever he goes out,
so that he does not die.

36 You are to make a plate of pure gold
and are to engrave on it signet engravings:
Holiness for YHWH.
37 You are to place it on a thread of blue-violet,
that it may be on the turban;
on the forefront of the turban is it to be.
38 It is to be on Aharon's brow.
So Aharon is to bear
the iniquity of the holy-offerings that the Children of Israel offer-
as-holy,
all their gifts of holiness;
it is to be on his brow
regularly,
for (receiving) favor for them, before the presence of YHWH.

39 You are to braid the coat with byssus;
you are to make a turban of byssus,
and a sash you are to make, of embroiderer's making.
40 And for the sons of Aharon, you are to make coats,
you are to make them sashes
and caps you are to make for them,
for glory and for splendor.
41 You are to clothe in them Aharon your brother, and his sons with
him,
you are to anoint them,
you are to give-mandate to them,

36 **plate:** Lit. "flower" or "gleamer," perhaps alluding to its shining quality, or to its shape of some kind.
38 **to bear/the iniquity of the holy-offerings:** To atone for accidental violations of purity concerning sacrifices brought by the people. This is a classic concern of priests.
40 **caps:** Of less splendor than Aharon's turban, but constructed along the same lines (wound cloth).

41 **give-mandate:** Lit. "fill the hand." The term indicates induction into office; possibly something was put into the inductee's hand symbolizing their new status. *Mandatus* in Roman law is similar, and hence the present translation. Plaut also points out that this expression in Akkadian means "to appoint." **anoint . . . give-mandate . . . hallow:** "A rising trilogy of near synonyms" (Plaut).

The Investiture Ceremony (29:1–46): Although the text still has a number of Tabernacle items to discuss, viz., the incense and its altar, other objects, and the commissioning of the artisans for the construction work, it naturally moves from describing the priestly garb to the ritual through which the priests are installed in their sacred office. First, sacrificial animals and bread are brought and prepared; then the priests are systematically clothed in their sacred vestments. After the first animal is slaughtered, its blood is dashed against the altar and the innards are burned as an offering; then the second ram is slain, and its blood is placed on the priests' extremities, to purify them. Blood is sprinkled on the priests' garments; then they hold up the fat-parts and breast of the ram, and follow by offering it up. Then the priests eat the cooked flesh of a special ram, the remains of which are to be burnt. Finally, the altar is purified.

After the regular sacrifice is specified (vv.38–41), the section ends with a powerful meditation on the purpose of the Tabernacle: "hallow" occurs three times, and "dwell" twice. In a word: by "meeting" with the Children of Israel at the Tent, God's glory makes tent, altar, priests, and most important, the people of Israel, holy. Indeed, the root *kaddesh,* "holy," occurs numerous times in the chapter, presaging its multiple use in the next book, Leviticus.

and you are to hallow them,
that they may be-priests for me.

42 You are to make them breeches of linen
to cover the flesh of nakedness;
from the hips to the thighs are they to extend.

43 They are to be on Aharon and on his sons,
whenever they come into the Tent of Appointment
or whenever they approach the slaughter-site
to attend at the Holy-Shrine,
that they do not bear iniquity and die
—a law for the ages, for him and for his seed after him.

29:1 Now this is the ceremony
that you are to make for them
to hallow them, to be-priests for me:
Take a bull, a young-one of the herd, and rams, two, wholly-
sound,

2 and bread of *matza* and flat cakes of *matza*, mixed with oil, and
wafers of *matza*, dipped in oil,
of wheat flour are you to make them.

3 You are to put them in one basket
and are to bring-them-near in the basket,
along with the bull and along with the two rams.

4 And Aharon and his two sons
you are to bring-near to the entrance of the Tent of Appointment
and are to wash them with water.

5 You are to take the garments
and are to clothe Aharon—
in the coat, in the tunic of the *efod*, in the *efod* and in the
breastpiece;
you are to invest him in the designed-band of the *efod*,

42 **breeches...to cover...nakedness:** As previously
(20:23), any hint of sexuality is separated from the
cult.
29:1 **ceremony:** Lit. "matter." The actual implementa-

tion of the ceremony is recounted in Lev. 8:13ff. So
unlike the rest of the Tabernacle material (Chaps.
35–40), this ritual is delayed.

2 *matza:* See 12:8 and the accompanying note.

6   you are to place the turban on his head,
    and are to put the sacred-diadem of holiness on the turban.

7   You are to take the oil for anointing
    and are to pour it on his head, anointing him.

8   And his sons, you are to bring-near
    and are to clothe them in coats;

9   you are to gird them with a sash, Aharon and his sons,
    and are to wind caps for them.
    It shall be for them as priestly-right,
    a law for the ages.
    So you are to give-mandate to Aharon and to his sons:

10 You are to bring-near the bull, before the Tent of Appointment,
    and Aharon and his sons are to lean their hands on the head of
        the bull.

11 You are to slay the bull in the presence of YHWH,
    at the entrance of the Tent of Appointment,

12 and are to take some of the blood of the bull
    and are to put it on the horns of the slaughter-site with your
        finger,
    but all the (rest of the) blood, you are to throw against the
        foundation of the slaughter-site.

13 You are to take all the fat that covers the innards,
    with the extension on the liver, the two kidneys and the fat that is
        on them,
    and turn-them-into-smoke on the slaughter-site.

14 And the flesh of the bull, its skin and its dung,
    you are to burn with fire, outside the camp;
    it is a *hattat*/decontamination-offering.

15 And the first ram, you are to take,
    and Aharon and his sons are to lean their hands on the head of
        the ram.

---

6 **sacred-diadem:** See 28:36 above; the diadem was apparently in the shape of a flower, and was a "sign of consecration" (DeVaux 1965).

9 **to wind caps:** Like small turbans: see the note to 28:40, above.

14 *hattat*/**decontamination-offering:** Or "purification-offering," which purges the sanctuary of ritual pollution (cf. Lev. 4 and 6). Pronounced *hah-táht*.

16 You are to slay the ram,
 you are to take its blood
 and you are to toss it on the slaughter-site, all around.

17 And the ram you are to section into sections,
 you are to wash its innards and its legs
 and you are to put (them) on its sections and on its head

18 and are to turn-into-smoke the entire ram, on the slaughter-site;
 it is an offering-up for YHWH,
 a soothing savor,
 it is a fire-offering for YHWH.

19 And you are to take the second ram
 and Aharon and his sons are to lean their hands on the head of
  the ram.

20 You are to slay the ram,
 you are to take (some) of its blood
 and you are to put (it)
 on the ridge of Aharon's ear and on the ridge of the right ear of
  Aharon's sons,
 and on the thumb of their right hands and on the thumb-toe of
  their right feet,
 then you are to toss the blood on the slaughter-site, all around.

21 You are to take some of the blood that is on the slaughter-site,
  and some of the oil for anointing,
 and you are to toss it on Aharon and on his garments, on his sons
  and on his sons' garments with him,
 that he and his garments may be hallowed, and his sons and his
  sons' garments with him.

22 You are to take the fat from the ram,
 the tail, the fat that covers the innards and the extension on the
  liver, the two kidneys and the fat that is on them,

---

18 **soothing savor:** Heb. *re'ah niho'ah.* The original signification of this concept must have been the common ancient one of feeding the gods, and hence the idea of an attractive smell. Already in Gen. 9:21 (after the Flood), however, it has been severed from that context, and the smell only pleases God and induces him to be more merciful with human beings.

20 **ridge . . . thumb . . . thumb-toe:** These comprise the extremities of the body, and thus are a way of including the entire body symbolically.

and the right thigh,
for it is the ram for giving-mandate;

23 and one loaf of bread and one cake of oil-bread and one wafer
from the basket of *matza* that is in the presence of YHWH;

24 you are to place them all
on the palms of Aharon and on the palms of his sons,
and you are to elevate them as an elevation-offering, in the
presence of YHWH.

25 You are to take them from their hand
and you are to turn-them-into-smoke on the slaughter-site, beside
the offering-up,
for a soothing savor in the presence of YHWH,
it is a fire-offering for YHWH.

26 You are to take the breast from the ram of giving-mandate that is
Aharon's,
and you are to elevate it as an elevation-offering, in the presence
of YHWH,
that it may be an allotment for you.

27 So you are to hallow the breast for the elevation-offering, and the
thigh of the raised-contribution,
that is elevated, that is raised
from the ram of giving-mandate,
from what is Aharon's and from what is his sons'.

28 It is to be Aharon's and his sons',
a fixed-allocation for the ages, on the part of the Children of
Israel,
for it is a contribution,
and a contribution is it to be on the part of the Children of Israel,
from their slaughter-offerings of *shalom*,
their raised-contribution for YHWH.

29 Now the garments of holiness that are Aharon's
are to belong to his sons after him,
to anoint them in them and to give-them-mandate in them.

---

24 **elevation-offering:** The earlier translation of "wave-offering" has been shown to be incorrect by Milgrom (1983).

26 **allotment:** For the priests.

27 **that is elevated, that is raised:** Heb. *asher hunaf va-asher huram.* Both denote "presenting."

30 For seven days is the one of his sons that acts-as-priest in his stead
    to be clothed in them,
  the one who comes into the Tent of Appointment to attend at
    the Holy-Shrine.

31 And the ram for giving-mandate you are to take
  and are to boil its flesh in the Holy-Shrine.

32 Aharon and his sons are to eat the flesh of the ram, along with
    the bread that is in the basket,
  at the entrance of the Tent of Appointment.

33 They are to eat them—those who are purged by them,
  to give-them-mandate, to hallow them;
  an outsider is not to eat (them), for they are holiness.

34 Now if there be anything left over of the flesh of giving-mandate
    or of the bread in the morning,
  you are to burn what is left by fire,
  it is not to be eaten, for it is holiness.

35 You are to make (thus) for Aharon and for his sons,
  according to all that I have commanded you,
  for seven days, you are to give-them-mandate.

36 A bull for the *hattat*-offering, you are to make-ready for each day,
    concerning the purging,
  that you may decontaminate the slaughter-site, by your
    purging it,
  and you are to anoint it, to hallow it.

37 For seven days you are to purge the slaughter-site, that you may
    hallow it.
  Thus the slaughter-site will become
  holiest holiness;
  whatever touches the slaughter-site shall become-holy.

---

31 **boil:** This clearly indicates that the food in question is meant for the priests' consumption, since sacrifices were normally completely burned.
33 **purged:** Purified. **outsider:** Not in the sense of "foreigner," but of "one unauthorized" for the purpose, a layman (Clements).
36 **purging it:** Or "purging in regard to it."

37 **whatever:** Others, "whoever." **become-holy:** When an object came in contact with holy objects, it became removed from the everyday, in a state resembling what we, in a sense more negative than the Bible means it, would call contamination (as in radioactivity).

The Incense Altar (30:1–10): This altar, which is not mentioned again, is seen by some as a later interpolation (DeVaux 1965): here it links up with what has gone before through the theme of purging (purification), in v. 10. For more on the incense itself, see vv. 22ff., below.

Census and Ransom (30:11–16): Continuing the theme of purgation, divine command provides for a ransom to be given to the priests, in order to remove ("purge away") sin incurred by census-taking.

The idea that numbering the people could bring down the wrath of God is portrayed in most striking fashion in II Sam. 24:1–9, where David usurps God's prerogative in numbering the men for military purposes, leading to a plague among the people. It seems that a census was viewed as a dangerous undertaking, perhaps analogous to the taking of photographs among certain peoples (which is felt to be threatening to one's essence). One who can number, can control (Gaster 1969).

38 And this is what you are to sacrifice on the slaughter-site:
   year-old lambs, two for each day, regularly.

39 The first lamb you are to sacrifice at daybreak,
   and the second lamb you are to sacrifice between the setting-
      times.

40 A tenth-measure of fine-meal, mixed with beaten oil, a quarter of
      a *hin,*
   and (as) poured-offering, a quarter of a *hin* of wine—for the first
      lamb.

41 And the second lamb you are to sacrifice between the setting-
      times,
   like the grain-gift of morning, and like its poured-offering, (that)
      you make-ready for it,
   for a soothing savor,
   a fire-offering for YHWH;

42 a regular offering-up, throughout your generations,
   at the entrance to the Tent of Appointment, before the presence
      of YHWH;
   for I will appoint-meeting with you there,
   to speak to you there.

43 So I will appoint-meeting there
   with the Children of Israel,
   and it will be hallowed
   by my Glory.

44 I will hallow the Tent of Appointment and the altar,
   and Aharon and his sons I will hallow,
   to be-priests for me.

45 And I will dwell amidst the Children of Israel
   and I will be a God for them,

46 that they may know
   that I am YHWH their God
   who brought them out of the land of Egypt

38 **year-old:** That is, newly mature and hence in a state of perfection.
40 ***hin:*** About a gallon.
46 **that they may know:** This pervasive theme of Exodus finds its true resolution through the Tabernacle texts—not only will the Israelites experience ("know") God through the "wonders" wrought on their behalf in Egypt, but also through their communication with him in ritual.

to dwell, myself, in their midst,
I am Yhwh their God.

30:1 You are to make a site, a smoking (site) for smoking-incense,
of acacia wood are you to make it,

2 a cubit its length and a cubit its width;
square is it to be, and two cubits its height,
its horns from it.

3 You are to overlay it with pure gold—
its roof, its walls all around, and its horns,
and you are to make a rim of gold all around.

4 And two rings of gold you are to make for it, beneath its rim,
on its two flanks, you are to make (them) on its two sides,
that they may be for holders for poles, to carry it by (means of)
them.

5 You are to make the poles of acacia wood
and you are to overlay them with gold.

6 And you are to put it in front of the curtain that is over the coffer
of Testimony,
in front of the purgation-cover that is over the Testimony,
where I will appoint-meeting with you.

7 And Aharon is to send-up-in-smoke, fragrant smoking-incense on
it,
in the morning, (every) morning;
when he polishes the lamps, he is to send-it-up-in-smoke.

8 And when Aharon draws up the lampwicks,
between the setting-times,
he is to send-it-up-in-smoke,
a regular smoke-offering before the presence of Yhwh,
throughout your generations.

9 You are not to offer-up upon it any outsider's smoking-incense,
either as offering-up or as grain-gift,
nor are you to pour out any poured-offering upon it.

30:6 **in front of . . . :** Some ancient versions and manuscripts omit this entire line as a redundancy.

7 **when he polishes:** Others, "when he dresses" or
"trims."

9 **outsider's smoking-incense:** This prohibition is
violated by Aharon's sons in Lev. 10:1 ("offering outsider's fire"), resulting in their death by "fire from
before Yhwh."

10 Aharon is to do-the-purging upon its horns,
once a year,
with the decontaminating blood of purgation;
once a year
he is to do-the-purging upon it,
throughout your generations,
holiest holiness it is for YHWH.

11 Now YHWH spoke to Moshe, saying:

12 When you take up the head-count of the Children of Israel, in
counting them,
they are to give, each-man, a ransom for his life, for YHWH,
when they count them,
that there be no plague on them, when they count them.

13 This (is what) they are to give, everyone that goes through the
counting:
half a *shekel* of the Holy-Shrine *shekel*—twenty grains to the
shekel—
half a *shekel*, a contribution for YHWH.

14 Everyone that goes through the counting, from the age of twenty
years and upward,
is to give the contribution of YHWH.

15 The rich are not to pay-more and the poor are not to pay-less
than half a *shekel*
when giving the contribution of YHWH,
to effect-ransom for your lives.

16 You are to take the silver for ransoming
from the Children of Israel
and are to give it over for the construction-service of the Tent of
Appointment,
that it may be for the Children of Israel

10 **do-the-purging:** On the day of Yom Kippur, when the ancient sanctuary was, as it were, detoxified (of sins).
13 *shekel:* Lit. a "weight" of silver. Coins as such are not documented in the land of Israel until centuries

after the events documented in Exodus took place. For a full discussion of biblical currency, see Sellers.
14 **twenty years:** The age for military service (and so referring to males).

The Basin (30:17–21): Returning to the familiar stylistic pattern of the Tabernacle account, "You are to make . . . ," we are told of the basin in which the priests washed. Yet this brief aside links up with the motif of protection from death that was encountered earlier (see 28:35).

The Anointing Oil (30:22–33): "Holy" is once again heard as a key word, both in the sense of making something sacred and in the sense of being reserved for special use only. Oil was used in many ancient cultures for positive purposes; elsewhere in the Bible, of course, it played its role in the anointing of kings and prophets, as well as the courteous treatment of guests and after bathing. Oil, then, carried with it connotations of brightness (see Ps. 104:15) and life itself.

The Incense (30:34–38): This particular incense, warns the text, was to be used only for the sanctuary and not for everyday purposes.

The offering-up of incense was a feature common to worship all over the ancient Near East. At least two reasons have been advanced for its use: purification, and a fragrance pleasing to the deity. It is also curious how our text speaks of God's being with the Israelites as a column of cloud and of fire; the incense smoke might also then be reminiscent of this divine manifestation.

Craftsmen (31:1–11): As the Tabernacle account opened with a summary description of what was to be constructed, so it ends, with some names added. The craftsmen for the task, Betzalel and Oholiav, are depicted as "wise" (Heb. *hakham*), that is, skilled; they will make what Moshe has been given to see.

as a remembrance before the presence of YHWH,
to effect-ransom for your lives.

17 Now YHWH spoke to Moshe, saying:
18 You are to make a basin of bronze,
its pedestal of bronze,
for washing,
and you are to put it between the Tent of Appointment and the
slaughter-site;
you are to put water therein,
19 that Aharon and his sons may wash with it
their hands and their feet.
20 When they come into the Tent of Appointment
they are to wash with water
so that they do not die,
or when they approach the slaughter-site, to be-in-attendance,
to send up fire-offerings in smoke for YHWH,
21 they are to wash their hands and their feet,
so that they do not die.
It is to be for them a law for the ages,
for him and for his sons, throughout their generations.

22 Now YHWH spoke to Moshe, saying:
23 And as for you, take you fragrant-spices, essence,
streaming-myrrh, five hundred,
cinnamon-spice, half as much—fifty and two hundred,
fragrant-cane, fifty and two hundred,
24 and cassia, five hundred
by the Holy-Shrine *shekel*,
as well as olive oil, a *hin*,
25 and you are to make (from) it anointing oil of holiness,
perfume from the perfume-mixture, of perfumer's making;
anointing oil of holiness is it to be.

18 **basin:** Others, "laver." The Hebrew denotes something round.
20 **so that they do not die:** Twice here, underscoring the power of water to do away with ritual impurity.
23 **essence:** Lit. "head." **five hundred:** The measure here is "by the *shekel*-weight," as clarified in the next verse.
25 **perfume . . . perfume-mixture . . . perfumer's:** Heb. *rokah mirkhahat . . . roke'ah.* The verb seems to mean "to mix."

26 You are to anoint with it
the Tent of Appointment
and the coffer of Testimony

27 and the table and all its implements,
and the lampstand and all its implements
and the site for smoke-offerings

28 and the site for offering-up and all its implements
and the basin and its pedestal.

29 You are to hallow them
that they may become holiest holiness,
whatever touches them shall become-holy.

30 And Aharon and his sons you are to anoint,
you are to hallow them to be-priests for me.

31 And to the Children of Israel you are to speak, saying:
Anointing oil of holiness
this is to be for me
throughout your generations.

32 On any (other) human body it is not to be poured out;
in its (exact) proportion, you are not to make any like it—
holiness is it,
holiness it shall remain for you.

33 Any man who mixes-perfumes like it
or who puts any of it on an outsider
is to be cut off from his kinspeople!

34 Now Yhwh said to Moshe:
Take you fragrant-spices,
drop-gum, onycha, and galbanum,
(these) fragrances and clear incense;
part equaling part are they to be.

26 **to anoint with it/the Tent . . . :** Oil is thus used to anoint not only people but also objects.

32 **in its (exact) proportion:** That is, according to an exact "recipe."

33 **cut off:** The exact meaning of this is not clarified anywhere, but it seems to indicate the death penalty. It is often mentioned in connection with violations of the cult (see 12:15, for example).

34 **drop-gum . . . :** The identification of some of these substances is debated.

35 You are to make (with) it smoking-incense,
   perfume, of perfumer's making,
   salted, pure—holy.
36 You are to beat some of it into fine-powder
   and are to put some of it
   in front of the Testimony
   in the Tent of Appointment,
   where I will appoint-meeting with you;
   holiest holiness it is to be for you.
37 As for the smoking-incense that you make,
   you are not to make any for yourselves in its (exact) proportion;
   holiness shall it be for you, for YHWH.
38 Any man that makes any like it
   to savor it
   is to be cut off from his kinspeople!

31:1 Now YHWH spoke to Moshe, saying:
  2 See,
    I have called by name
    Betzalel son of Uri, son of Hur, of the tribe of Yehuda.
  3 I have filled him with the spirit of God
    in practical-wisdom, discernment and knowledge
    in all kinds of workmanship,
  4 to design designs,
    to make them in gold, in silver and in bronze,
  5 in the cutting of stones for setting and in the cutting of wood,
    to make them through all kinds of workmanship.

---

35 **salted:** Salt was employed in sacrifices perhaps originally to ward off demons; it has taken on importance in both worship and folklore (viz., the practice of throwing salt over one's shoulder). Some suggest that salt was used simply to improve the taste of the food, or to absorb the blood.

31:2 **called by name:** Or "chosen/singled out."
   3 **spirit of God:** Or "breath of God," the transfer of which to human beings in the Bible results in great strength, leadership qualities, or, especially, prophetic inspiration.

The Sabbath (31:12–17): *The Tablets* (31:18): As a reminder of the Sabbath's importance amid all the anticipated construction activity, the Israelites are now commanded to observe the holy day. The section is also a prelude to the Golden Calf
story, which will be concerned with improper "making"; and "make" appears in a
variety of different contexts.

A second prelude draws the initial Tabernacle section to a close. Moshe receives God's word engraved in stone, by God himself; this will presumably be deposited in the "coffer" of which the text spoke in its opening chapter (25). But the
section is forward-looking as well, in that the tablets will play a dramatic role in
the story immediately following this passage.

6 And I, here I give (to be) with him
Oholiav son of Ahisamakh, of the tribe of Dan;
in the mind of all those wise of mind I place wisdom,
that they may make all that I have commanded you:

7 the Tent of Appointment
and the coffer of Testimony
and the purgation-cover that is over it
and all the implements of the Tent

8 and the table and all its implements
and the pure lampstand and all its implements
and the site for smoke-offering

9 and the site for offering-up and all its implements
and the basin and its pedestal,

10 and the officiating garments
and the garments of holiness for Aharon the priest and the
garments of his sons for being-priests

11 and oil for anointing
and fragrant smoke for the holy-offerings—
according to all that I have commanded you, they are to make.

12 Now YHWH said to Moshe:

13 And you, speak to the Children of Israel, saying:
However: my Sabbaths you are to keep!
For it is a sign
between me and you, throughout your generations,
to know that I, YHWH, hallow you.

14 You are to keep the Sabbath,
for it is holiness for you,
whoever profanes it is to be put-to-death, yes, death!
For whoever makes work on it—
that person is to be cut off from among his kinspeople.

---

6 **Oholiav:** Trad. English "Oholiab"; the name means "Tent of Father / God," rather appropriate here.

10 **officiating:** The Hebrew (*serad*) is not entirely clear, but may be related to *sharet,* "attending" (in the sanctuary).

13 **However:** In contrast to all the previous activity, the Israelites are not to forget about the Sabbath, the "ceasing" from work (so too Rashi). *Akh* may also be taken as a positive term, "above all."

15 For six days is work to be made,
    but on the seventh day
    (is) Sabbath, Sabbath-Ceasing, holiness for YHWH,
    whoever makes work on the Sabbath day is to be put-to-death,
        yes, death!
16 The Children of Israel are to keep the Sabbath,
    to make the Sabbath-observance throughout their generations
    as a covenant for the ages;
17 between me and the Children of Israel
    a sign it is, for the ages,
    for in six days
    YHWH made the heavens and the earth,
    but on the seventh day
    he ceased and paused-for-breath.

18 Now he gave to Moshe
    when he had finished speaking with him on Mount Sinai
    the two tablets of Testimony,
    tablets of stone,
    written by the finger of God.

---

17 **paused-for-breath:** A rather daring anthropomorphism which, by describing God's resting, encourages humans and animals to do the same (see 23:12).

18 **he gave:** God gave. **the finger of God:** Just as in Egypt (8:15), God intervenes in human affairs here as well.

PART V

THE COVENANT BROKEN AND RESTORED

(32–34)

WITHOUT THE STORY THAT FOLLOWS, THE BOOK OF EXODUS WOULD BE INCOMPLETE OR at least hopelessly idealistic and idealized. Thanks to the inclusion of the Golden Calf episode, we recognize the people of Israel so familiar from the bulk of the wilderness narrative—stubborn, untrusting, and utterly unable to comprehend what has just occurred at Sinai (note the parallel between this section and 15:22ff.: after witnessing the awesome displays of God, the people fall prey to typical human anxieties about their own survival). We are also given a classic biblical description of God in this story—that he is demanding but also compassionate.

There is no doubt that the narrative wishes to portray the breaking of the recently made covenant, and also to focus once again on the anxiety about God's presence that pervades the whole book. Some see it as a political polemic, given that a similar story is found in I Kings 12:28ff., about Jeroboam's split from the Solomonic monarchy; according to this theory, the Exodus account is a projection backward of the sin of the Northern Kingdom. Jeroboam, leading a secessionist movement, intended to set up a sanctuary to rival Jerusalem. At the same time, the Exodus story does appear first, and thereby helps to explain why Jeroboam's deed was considered so terrible by later generations.

But surely the Golden Calf story plays such an important role in the present book of Exodus as to sidestep the question of which version came first. It puts into sharp relief the nature of the people, its leader, and its God, and provides some insights into the complex relationships between these parties; it focuses particular aspects of the Tabernacle idea (see above); and it makes clear the difficulties of the emerging faith community.

The story also contributes some welcome dramatic scenes at this point. It is as if the reader has awakened from a dream: major characters, including God himself, reemerge as real personalities, while secondary characters (Aharon and Yehoshua) are fleshed out. Everywhere there are fierce emotions: doubt, anger, panic, pleading for mercy, courage, fear. And, indeed, the entire enterprise of Exodus hangs in the balance, as God wishes only to destroy the faithless people (a rough parallel exists in Gen. 22, where all that has previously been promised to Avraham is threatened). Only after the stark emotions just mentioned have been cathartically absorbed, and the covenant restored, can there be a return to the task at hand—the building of an abode for the divine amid the very human community of Israel. As to the stylistic aspects of the story, we should note the repeated use of the verbs "see" and "know," among others. Their transformation at different points of the story signals a return to these earlier Exodus themes, this time with a new urgency and a new enterprise at stake: the continuity of the fledgling people.

The Sin of the Molten Calf (32:1–6): We have spent twelve chapters—a major portion of the book of Exodus—dwelling on the heights of Sinai; we have witnessed revelation, law-giving, the command to build a shelter for the presence of God, and the establishment of a priestly cult. But now, as Moshe prepares to descend from the mountain, we are reminded of the other side of the coin: the real world of human frailty. This has occurred before, at the very same site: in Chaps. 19 and 20 we observed a fearfulness on the part of the people toward getting too close to the divine, as a power too awesome to deal with. Now the fear goes the other way, and, with the disappearance of Moshe, the intermediary, turns to despair. The very thing that had been warned against in the Decalogue (and hence, the first of the terms of the covenant)—the making of a "carved-image/or any figure/that is . . . on the earth beneath" (20:4), and bowing down to it (20:5)—takes place here, requested by the people in their hour of need. It is abetted by, of all people, their divine spokesman and priest, Aharon.

Some scholars have sought to soften the sin of the calf by claiming that the Israelites did not view it as an idol but rather merely as a representation of the divine. This does not seem to be borne out by the text, either in the Decalogue or later in the Jeroboam incident, which is often equated with the most heinous crimes (see I Kings 16:26).

Response: God's Anger (32:7–14): Now that the people have committed what amounts to a capital crime, the issue at stake is what the punishment shall be. After informing the unsuspecting Moshe of what has taken place down below, with the words *"your* people [italics mine] . . . has wrought ruin" (v.7), God indicates his intent to destroy Israel, and to found a new nation beginning with Moshe. However, early Jewish tradition already sensed that something deeper might be happening here. The phrase "let me be" (Heb. *hanniha li*), it has been observed, suggests that God actually wishes Moshe to argue with him, and this is supported by his acquiescence in record time (v.14). Indeed, the text never says "God's anger flared up," reserving that key verb for Moshe (v.19). What we learn from this section is not only God's forgiving nature but something significant about Moshe: faced with a dictator's dream—the cloning of an entire nation from himself—he opts for staunchly defending the very people who have already caused him grief through their rebelling, and who will continually do so in the ensuing wanderings. And he does not even eschew blackmail to attain his goal. His argument in v.12, that the Egyptians will jeer at this God who liberated a people only to kill them in the wilderness, rings truer in a pagan context than in the Bible. But the next verse reveals Moshe's vision: he knows that his task is to continue the foundation established by the Patriarchs and to assure the continuity that has been imperiled so many times before.

32:1 Now when the people saw that Moshe was shamefully-late in
coming down from the mountain,
the people assembled against Aharon
and said to him:
Arise, make us a god who will go before us,
for this Moshe, the man who brought us up from the land of
Egypt,
we do not know what has become of him!

2 Aharon said to them:
Break off the gold rings that are in the ears of your wives, your
sons and your daughters,
and bring (them) to me.

3 All the people broke off the gold rings that were in their ears,
and brought (them) to Aharon.

4 He took (them) from their hand,
fashioned it with a graving-tool,
and made it into a molten calf.
Then they said:
This is your God, O Israel,
who brought you up from the land of Egypt!

5 When Aharon saw (this), he built a slaughter-site before it,
and Aharon called out and said:
Tomorrow is a festival to YHWH!

6 They (started) early on the morrow,
offered offerings-up
and brought *shalom*-offerings;
the people sat down to eat and drink
and proceeded to revel.

32:1 **saw:** Ironically, after all the "seeing" of revelation in
Chaps. 19–24, what now impresses the people most
is Moshe's absence, leading to a need to make a god
that can be "seen." **was shamefully-late:** Others,
"delayed," but the Hebrew verb *(boshesh)* carries the
connotation of "causing-shame/embarrassment."
a god: Others, "gods"; but there is one calf and one
god that it represents. **go before us:** As in 23:23 the
meaning is to lead, especially in battle.

2 **Break off:** Or simply "remove."

4 **fashioned it with a graving-tool:** Others, "cast it in

a mold" or even "tied it in a bag" (see Plaut). **calf:**
Or young bull, symbol of fertility in Canaan. **This is
your God . . . :** Cf. 20:2 above, "I am YHWH your
God, who brought you out . . . ."

5 **called out:** Or "proclaimed."

6 **proceeded:** Or the Hebrew *kum* can be understood
as "arose," as opposed to "sat down" in the phrase
to follow. **revel:** There seems to be a sexual connotation here (as in Gen. 26:8; 39:14, 17) which would
support the use of the calf as the divine symbol.

Response: Moshe's Anger (32:15–29): In a sense, the text backtracks chronologically here, to focus solely on Moshe. The first four verses are prefatory but important. Possibly to set the drama of the scene to follow, Moshe is described as carrying the "tablets of the Testimony," which are dubbed the work of God. Yet another point is being made: the work of God is contrasted with the imperfect work of human beings, the law with its hope versus the idol with its underlying despair.

Sounds of revelry, implied as being worse than sounds of war, reach Moshe, and upon his descent into the Israelite camp he loses control. But smashing the tablets has implications beyond the emotional: it is a legal voiding of the covenant (as in the English "breaking an agreement"). Moshe deals with all concerned in swift succession: the calf is destroyed, Aharon is confronted, and the people are brutally purged.

It is possible that there are historical considerations behind this section. Some see the portrayal of Aharon, who certainly comes across as weak, as part of a strain in the political thinking of a later period. According to this view, the later decline of Aharon's priestly line is reflected in his behavior here. Others see the "mandating" of the Levites (v.29) as a reflection of a later power struggle among the priestly classes in Israel. Childs finds Aharon's role in the story to be a literary one: he is a foil for Moshe. Aharon is willing to capitulate to the people, seeing them (perhaps realistically) as "set-on-evil" (v.22). Moshe holds fast to his dream of a "kingdom of priests" (19:6) and thus demands of himself a type of leadership that cannot compromise. The Calf story, then, focuses not only on the great crime of idolatry but also on the nature of Moshe as leader. It is the resumption of the biblical portrait of Moshe, which will return again with greatest force throughout the book of Numbers.

7 YHWH said to Moshe:
Go, down!
for your people
whom you brought up from the land of Egypt
has wrought ruin!

8 They have been quick to turn aside from the way that I
commanded them,
they have made themselves a molten calf,
they have bowed to it, they have slaughtered-offerings to it,
and they have said: This is your God, O Israel, who brought you
up from the land of Egypt!

9 And YHWH said to Moshe:
I see this people—
and here, it is a hard-necked people!

10 So now,
let me be, that my anger may flare against them
and I may destroy them—
but you I will make into a great nation!

11 Moshe soothed the face of YHWH his God,
he said:
For-what-reason,
O YHWH,
should your anger flare against your people
whom you brought out of the land of Egypt
with great power,
with a strong hand?

12 For-what-reason
should the Egyptians (be able to) say, yes, say:
With evil intent he brought them out,
to kill them in the mountains,

---

7 **your people:** God not so subtly renounces his king-ship of Israel. **wrought ruin:** The verb *shahet* is often used to describe moral decay (see Gen. 6:11–12).

8 **turn aside from the way:** In the Bible, as in many religious systems, the correct mode of behavior is often called "the way" or "path." Here it is probably elliptical for "the way of God." Postbiblical Judaism calls its system of laws *Halakhah*, from the Hebrew *halokh*, "to go/walk."

9 **hard-necked:** Others, "stiff-necked." The usage of "hard" ironically recalls the earlier hard-hearted character, Pharaoh.

11 **soothed:** Lit. "softened."

to destroy them from the face of the soil?
Turn away from your flaming anger,
be sorry for the evil (intended) against your people!

13 Recall Avraham, Yitzhak and Yisrael your servants,
to whom you swore by yourself
when you spoke to them:
I will make your seed many
as the stars of the heavens,
and all this land which I have promised,
I will give to your seed,
that they may inherit (it) for the ages!

14 And YHWH let himself be sorry concerning the evil
that he had spoken of doing to his people.

15 Now Moshe faced about to come down from the mountain,
the two tablets of the Testimony in his hand,
tablets written on both their sides,
on this-one, on that-one they were written;

16 and the tablets were God's making,
and the writing was God's writing,
engraved upon the tablets.

17 Now when Yehoshua heard the sound of the people as it shouted,
he said to Moshe:
The sound of war is in the camp!

18 But he said:
Not the sound of the song of prevailing,
not the sound of the song of failing,
sound of choral-song is what I hear!

---

12 **be sorry:** Others, "repent" or "change your mind." **the evil:** Destruction. The biblical use of "evil" *(ra')* corresponds more closely to our idea of "ill" as in "ill-fortune"; it includes not only immorality but also disasters that befall people.

13 **Recall:** This particular form of the verb *zakhor* (with the preposition *le-*) means "to remember to one's credit" (Childs). **I will make . . . :** Recalling the promise to Avraham and Yitzhak in Gen. 15:5 and 22:17, also 26:4.

16 **God's making . . . God's writing:** In contrast to the "making" of the Calf.

17 **as it shouted:** Heb. *be-re'o*, possibly a pun on *ve-ra* ("set-on-evil") in v.22.

18 **song:** Heb. *'anot*, as distinct from *shira* in 15:1. **prevailing . . . failing:** Heb. *gevura . . . halusha*, meaning "victory" and "defeat." **choral-song:** Or "antiphonal (alternating) song." The Hebrew is *'annot* as opposed to *'anot*. But some interpreters view it as identical to the two previous uses, and find something missing here (as in "the sound of —— is what I hear.").

444

19 And it was,
   when he neared the camp
   and saw the calf and the dancing,
   Moshe's anger flared up,
   he threw the tablets from his hands
   and smashed them beneath the mountain.

20 He took the calf that they had made,
   burned it with fire,
   ground it up until it was thin-powder,
   strewed it on the surface of the water
   and made the Children of Israel drink it.

21 Then Moshe said to Aharon:
   What did this people do to you
   that you have brought upon it (such) a great sin!

22 Aharon said:
   Let not my lord's anger flare up!
   You yourself know this people, how set-on-evil it is.

23 They said to me: Make us a god who will go before us,
   for this Moshe, the man who brought us up from the land of
      Egypt,
   we do not know what has become of him!

24 So I said to them: Who has gold?
   They broke it off and gave it to me,
   I threw it into the fire, and out came this calf.

25 Now when Moshe saw the people: that it had gotten-loose,
   for Aharon had let-it-loose for whispering among their foes,

19 **the calf and the dancing:** Apparently both angered Moshe. **beneath the mountain:** The very same place where the covenant was concluded! (Cassuto).

20 **burned . . . ground . . . strewed . . . made . . . drink:** The first three of these verbs also occur together in a Canaanite (Ugaritic) text, describing the goddess Anat's destruction of the god Mot; our text perhaps plays off that literature (Childs). At any rate, Moshe's action is the equivalent of making the Israelites "eat their words." As has long been noted, this echoes the treatment of the suspected adulter-

ess in Num. 5:11–31; the connection appears intentional, in light of the constant "marriage" imagery used of God and Israel in the Bible (Sarna 1986 discusses the parallels at length).

24 **out came this calf:** Aharon's reply sounds like that of a child who has been caught in the act.

25 **gotten-loose:** The same verb (*paro'a*) was used in 5:4, where Pharaoh complained about the Israelites. **for whispering:** A derisive kind of whispering.

After the Purge (32:30–33:6): Although blood has been spilled to punish the guilty, Moshe must still expiate Israel's sin. In this vein, he offers to be erased from God's "record" if the people are not forgiven. Then commences God's reply, couched in terms of who will lead the people to the Promised Land. He will not do it himself, as previously (see the glorious image of 13:21–22), but through the agency of a "messenger." He will fulfill his promise to the Patriarchs, but not himself among his "hard-necked" people. Their "sin" (the word occurs eight times in vv.30–34) has destroyed that possibility.

An interesting chord is struck at the end. Israel must strip themselves of their ornaments, the spoils of battle, as it were, from the Egyptians. Those ornaments had been used to build the Calf. The final note is ominous: God is yet to decide "what to do with you," reminiscent perhaps of another scene with identical wording—2:4, where Moshe's sister had followed the little-ark downstream, "to know what would be done to him." In both cases, the people of Israel stand on the brink of disaster, saved only by divine intervention.

Moshe at the Tent (33:7–11): This brief digression seems to function as support for Moshe's role, so important in the book as a whole and in this story in particular. Only one who is accustomed to speaking to God face to face can effect forgiveness for Israel's crime.

26 Moshe took-up-a-stand at the gate of the camp
and said:
Whoever is for YHWH—to me!
And there gathered to him all the Sons of Levi.
27 He said to them:
Thus says YHWH, the God of Israel:
Put every-man his sword on his thigh,
proceed and go back-and-forth from gate to gate in the camp,
and kill
every-man his brother, every-man his neighbor, every-man his
relative!
28 The Sons of Levi did according to Moshe's words.
And there fell of the people on that day some three thousand
men.
29 Moshe said:
Be-mandated to YHWH today,
even though it be every-man at the cost of his son, at the cost of
his brother,
to bestow blessing upon you today.

30 It was on the morrow,
Moshe said to the people:
You, you have sinned a great sin!
So now, I will go up to YHWH,
perhaps I may be able to purge away your sin.
31 Moshe returned to YHWH and said:
Ah now,
this people has sinned a great sin,
they have made themselves gods of gold!
32 So now,
if you would only bear their sin—!
But if not,
pray blot me out of the record that you have written!

27 **every-man . . . :** The repetition stresses the horror
of the situation.
28 **three thousand:** Another stereotyped number
(e.g., Samson kills 3,000 Philistines in Judg. 16:27).

32 **blot . . . out:** Erase, as in writing. **record:** Heb.
sefer, earlier (17:14) rendered as "account."

33 YHWH said to Moshe:
    Whoever sins against me,
    I blot him (alone) out of my record.

34 So now,
    go,
    lead the people to where I have spoken to you.
    Here, my messenger will go before you,
    but on the day of my calling-to-account,
    I will call-them-to-account for their sin!

35 And YHWH plagued the people
    because they made the calf that Aharon made.

33:1 YHWH said to Moshe:
    Go, up from here,
    you and the people that you brought up from the land of Egypt,
    to the land of which I swore to Avraham, to Yitzhak and to
        Yaakov, saying:
    I will give it to your seed.

2 I will send a messenger before you
    and will drive out the Canaanite, the Amorite and the Hittite and
        the Perizzite, the Hivvite and the Yevusite—,

3 to a land flowing with milk and honey.
    But: I will not go up in your midst,
    for a hard-necked people are you,
    lest I destroy you on the way!

4 When the people heard this evil word
    they mourned,
    no man put on his ornaments (again).

5 Now YHWH said to Moshe:
    Say to the Children of Israel:
    You are a hard-necked people—

---

34 **my messenger will go before you:** Apparently restoring the state of affairs promised in 23:20ff. **calling-to-account:** In Gen. 50:24, *pakod* meant "taking account of," that is, remembering the Israelites in their Egyptian bondage.

35 **they made . . . Aharon made:** Heb. ambiguous; possibly a scribal error. Or the ambiguity may serve to shift the blame from the perpetrator to the act itself (Greenstein, personal communication).

33:1 **the people that you brought up:** The use of "you" (Moshe) suggests that God still has not fully reaccepted them.

3 **I will not:** Myself, in person, as it were.

if for one moment I were to go up in your midst,
I would destroy you!
So now, take down your ornaments from yourselves,
that I may know what I am to do with you.
6 So the Children of Israel stripped themselves of their ornaments
from Mount Sinai on.

7 Now Moshe would take the Tent
and pitch it for himself outside the camp, going-far from the
camp.
He called it the Tent of Appointment.
And it was,
whoever besought YHWH
would go out to the Tent of Appointment that was outside the
camp.
8 And it was:
whenever Moshe would go out to the Tent,
all the people would rise,
they would station themselves, each-man, at the entrance to his
tent,
and would gaze after Moshe
until he had come into the Tent.
9 And it was:
whenever Moshe would come into the Tent,
the column of cloud would come down
and stand at the entrance to the Tent,
and he would speak with Moshe.
10 And all the people would see
the column of cloud
standing at the entrance to the Tent,
and all the people would rise,

---

6 **stripped themselves:** This feels analogous to having one's battle ribbons stripped off, or having one's spoils taken away.
7 **outside the camp:** Already in early Jewish tradition it was pointed out that this phrase often has negative connotations (that is, one was sent outside the camp because of ritual impurity), and it has been suggested that our passage shows Moshe separating himself from the sinning people. On the other hand, it is usually the carrier/causer of impurity who goes outside!
9 **he:** God.

Moshe's Plea and God's Answer (33:12–34:3): Continuing the dialogue with God from 32:34f., Moshe now pleads that what is necessary is nothing less than the personal assurance that God will lead the people. Six times the verb "know" echoes, along with repetitions of "pray" and "favor"—and so the issue at hand is intimacy and the bonded relationship of covenant. Significantly, also, Moshe refers to Israel three times as "your people," trying to force God to acknowledge them as his own once more. Answering Moshe's request for intimacy, God agrees to let him get close, but with limits, and we are reminded of Sinai once more (see the boundary-setting in 19:12–13, 21ff.). The earlier revelation scene is about to be replayed, in altered form—most notably, without the people themselves present.

God Reveals Himself (34:4–9): This passage is another one of the climaxes of the book, of which I spoke in "On the Book of Exodus and Its Structure," above. In contrast to the scenes given in other ancient literatures, where, for instance, the texts speak of a physical brightness too great to bear, or of epic descriptions of the gods, our passage is remarkably brief and devoid of physical description. All that is ventured here is a statement of God's essence, or, more precisely, of his essence for human beings: merciful but just. This image, which had such a great influence on the development of Christianity and Islam as well as Judaism, is of the highest importance in the understanding of the biblical God; it is almost as if the text is saying "This is all that can be known, intimately, of this God, and this is all one needs to know." There is no shape, no natural manifestation (in contrast to the thunder and lightning approach at Sinai—but one should bear in mind what has just happened with the Calf): only words, which describe God's relationship to human beings.

Moshe hastens, at the climactic moment, to plead on behalf of the people. Most curious is the fact that God does not seem to agree to "go in their midst," nor does he ever give in and reinstate Israel with the term "my people" (see v.10). Nevertheless, it appears that the rift between deity and people has been satisfactorily repaired, given what comes next.

they would bow down,
each-man at the entrance to his tent.
11 And YHWH would speak to Moshe
face to face,
as a man speaks to his neighbor.
Now when he would return to the camp,
his attendant, the lad Yehoshua,
would not depart from within the Tent.

12 Moshe said to YHWH:
See,
you,
you say to me:
Bring this people up!
But you,
you have not let us know
whom you will send with me!
And you,
you said:
I have known you by name,
and you have found favor in my eyes!
13 So now—
if I have, pray, found favor in your eyes,
pray let me know your ways,
that I may (truly) know you,
in order that I may find favor in your eyes:
See,
this nation is indeed your people!

11 **face to face:** See Gen. 32:31, where Jacob is amazed at still being alive after an encounter with a manifestation of God. In the ancient world in general, direct contact with the gods is often portrayed as leading to madness or death (see the Greek story of Semele, the mortal mother of the god Dionysus). Cf. v.20, below. **Yehoshua,/would not depart:** Once again, he appears in a fragmentary way, but importantly, as Moshe's attendant (and so he will be not only a military leader, as in 17:9ff., but also a spiritual one).

13 **know:** Intimately. **indeed your people:** And not only Moshe's, as God suggests in v. 1.

14 He said:
   If my presence were to go (with you), would I cause you to rest-
      easy?
15 He said to him:
   If your presence does not go,
   do not bring us up from here!
16 For wherein, after all, is it to be known
   that I have found favor in your eyes,
   I and your people?
   Is it not (precisely) in that you go with us,
   and that we are distinct,
   I and your people,
   from every people that is on the face of the soil?
17 Yhwh said to Moshe:
   Also this word that you have spoken, I will do,
   for you have found favor in my eyes,
   and I have known you by name.
18 Then he said:
   Pray let me see your Glory!
19 He said:
   I myself will cause all my Goodliness to pass
   in front of your face,
   I will call out the name of Yhwh
   before your face:
   that I show-favor to whom I show-favor,
   that I show-mercy to whom I show-mercy.
20 But he said:
   You cannot see my face,
   for no human can see me and live!

16 **that we are distinct:** The text returns to a motif important in the Plague Narrative.
18 **your Glory:** In the Greek story, Semele desires to see Zeus in full battle dress; the Hebrew narrative is understandably more vague.

19 **that I show-favor . . . :** Recalling the earlier answer to Moshe in 4:13. The meaning here is "I choose to whom to reveal myself."

21 YHWH said:
Here is a place
next to me;
station yourself on the rock,

22 and it shall be:
when my Glory passes by,
I will place you in the cleft of the rock
and screen you with my hand
until I have passed by.

23 Then I will remove my hand;
you shall see my back,
but my face shall not be seen.

34:1 Then YHWH said to Moshe:
Carve yourself two tablets of stone
like the first-ones,
and I will write on the tablets the words
that were on the first tablets
which you smashed.

2 And be ready by the morning:
go up in the morning to Mount Sinai,
station yourself for me there, on top of the mountain.

3 No man is to go up with you,
neither is any man to be seen on all the mountain,
neither are sheep or oxen to graze in front of this mountain.

4 So he carved two tablets of stone like the first-ones.
Moshe (started) early in the morning
and went up to Mount Sinai,
as YHWH had commanded him,
and he took in his hand the two tablets of stone.

5 YHWH came down in the cloud,
he stationed himself beside him there
and called out the name of YHWH.

---

23 **my back:** That is, hiding the actual appearance of God.

34:2 **in the morning**: As at Sinai, there is no question of a night vision/illusion.

The New Covenant (34:10–28): A preamble (vv.10–16) promises God's continued "wonders" and warns emphatically against Israel's mixing with the Canaanites upon its future possession of the land. Once the actual legislative content of the passage begins in v.17, one notes the continuation of the stylistic pattern which began with v.10: Deuteronomic language. The laws bespeak an agricultural society, not a nomadic one, and suggest that the warning against blending with Canaanite society may be from the perspective of a later period—an Israel long settled in the land. Although some scholars see Egypt as the origin of the Calf symbol, it also has a well-known existence in Canaanite mythology, as a symbol of Baal, god of fertility. Therefore the connection between our text and that of Kings may be close indeed, and the Calf story may have had a very contemporary ring to later audiences.

As is typical of the Calf narrative, our passage concludes, not only with wider issues—the formal writing-down of the covenant—but also with Moshe: that he neither ate nor drank during the encounter with God. We see the story both from its inception and its end concerned with the man whose task it must be to bring the divine word to the Israelite people.

◆

6 And Yhwh passed before his face
and called out:
Yhwh Yhwh
God,
showing-mercy, showing-favor,
long-suffering in anger,
abundant in loyalty and faithfulness,

7 keeping loyalty to the thousandth (generation),
bearing iniquity, rebellion and sin,
yet not clearing, clearing (the guilty),
calling-to-account the iniquity of the fathers upon the sons and
upon sons' sons, to the third and fourth (generation)!

8 Quickly Moshe did-homage, on the ground, bowing low,

9 and said:
Pray if I have found favor in your eyes,
O my Lord,
pray let my Lord go among us!
Indeed, it is a hard-necked people—
so forgive our iniquity and our sin,
and make-us-your-inheritance!

10 He said:
Here,
I cut a covenant:
before all your people I will do wonders
such as have not been created
in all the earth, among all the nations.
Then shall all the people among whom you are, see
the work of Yhwh, how awe-inspiring it is,
which I do with you.

6–7 **Yhwh Yhwh . . . :** These two verses became an important part of later Jewish liturgy, and are known as the "Thirteen Attributes of God." **showing-mercy, showing-favor:** Heb. *rahum ve-hanun.*

7 **third and fourth (generation):** This may mean an entire household, that is, generally the largest number of generations alive at one time (Clements).

8 **Quickly:** This, as perhaps the greatest moment of divine–human intimacy in the Bible, is the one most ripe for forgiveness, and Moshe seizes the opportunity.

10 **Here . . . :** Does God ever really answer Moshe's request to "let my Lord go among us!"? We can only tell by the ending of the entire book, when all seems right again (40:34–38). **Then shall all . . . see:** The Hebrew word order is "Then shall see . . . ."

11 Take care for yourself
regarding what I command you today!
Here, I am driving out before you
the Amorite, the Canaanite, the Hittite, the Perizzite, the Hivvite
and the Yevusite,—

12 take-you-care,
lest you cut a covenant
with the settled-folk of the land against which you are coming,
lest they become a snare among you.

13 Rather:
their slaughter-sites you are to pull down,
their standing-pillars you are to smash,
their tree-poles you are to cut down.

14 For: You are not to bow down to any other god!
For YHWH—
Jealous-One is his name,
a jealous God is he!

15 —Lest you cut a covenant with the settled-folk of the land:
when they go whoring after their gods
and slaughter-offer to their gods,
they will call to you to eat of their slaughter-offerings;

16 should you take of their women (in marriage) for your sons,
their women will go whoring after their gods,
and they will cause your sons to go whoring after their gods.

17 Molten gods you are not to make for yourselves!

18 The Pilgrimage-Festival of *Matzot* you are to keep;
for seven days you are to eat *matzot,* as I commanded you,
at the appointed-time, in the New-Moon of Ripe-Grain,
for in the New-Moon of Ripe-Grain you went out of Egypt.

---

13 **standing-pillars:** These stood near Canaanite altars
(Plaut). **tree-poles:** Phallic idols.

14 **jealous:** Cf. 20:5, above.

15 **whoring:** A common biblical metaphor for faith-
lessness to God.

16 **their women:** They are singled out as the ones en-
ticing the Israelite men into idolatry, perhaps based
on the prominence of goddesses and sacred prostitutes in Canaanite worship.

19 Every breacher of a womb is mine,
    and every one that your herd drops-as-male, breacher among
        oxen and sheep;
20 the breacher among donkeys you are to redeem with a sheep,
    and if you do not redeem it, you are to break-its-neck.
    Every firstborn among your sons you are to redeem.
    No one is to be seen before my presence empty-handed.

21 For six days you are to serve,
    but on the seventh day, you are to cease,
    at plowing, at grain-cutting, you are to cease.
22 The Pilgrimage-Festival of Weeks you are to make for yourselves,
    of the first-fruits of the wheat cutting,
    as well as the Pilgrimage-Festival of Ingathering
    at the turning of the year.
23 At three points in the year
    are all your male-folk to be seen
    before the presence of the Lord, YHWH,
    the God of Israel.
24 For I will dispossess nations before you, and widen your territory,
    so that no man will desire your land,
    when you go up to be seen before the presence of YHWH your
        God,
    at three points in the year.

25 You are not to slay my blood offering with anything fermented.

    You are not to leave-overnight, until morning, the pilgrimage-
        offering of Passover.

26 The premier of the firstfruits of your soil you are to bring into
    the house of YHWH your God.

    You are not to boil a kid in the milk of its mother.

---

19 **drops-as-male:** Others, "every male."
21 **serve:** Here perhaps connoting farm work, as in Gen. 2:5, 4:12. See also Ex. 20:9.
21 **plowing . . . grain-cutting:** For once, the Bible specifies the work that is not to be done on the Sabbath.

22 **turning of the year:** When the last harvest occurs (September–October), and hence connected to a solar calendar model.
23 **points:** Lit. "beats." **Lord:** Cf. the note to 23:17.
24 **no man will desire your land:** Not even desire it, much less take it away.

457

Moshe Radiant (34:29–35): As if to underscore the point just made, and like the Tent section in Chap. 33, the Calf account ends with a focus on Moshe's leadership. Gone is any reference to the molten image; the central concern is the effect of God's communication upon Moshe. Indeed, "speak" occurs seven times here, and the formula "the skin of Moshe's face was radiating" three times. Putting this section at the end of the narrative leaves the reader with the sense that Moshe's prayer for God's closeness in Chap. 33 has at last been answered, and that his very body now bears the sign of divine favor (note the use of the rich symbol of light). Communication between God and Moshe, with Israel witnessing and therefore involved again (in contrast to its removal from this activity at the beginning of Chap. 32), may now proceed again without interruption, and it will now be possible and appropriate to resume construction of the structure whose purpose it is to embody God's presence in the world of human beings.

27 YHWH said to Moshe:
Write you down these words,
for in accordance with these words
I cut with you a covenant, and with Israel.

28 Now he was there beside YHWH
for forty days and forty nights;
bread he did not eat
and water he did not drink,
but he wrote down on the tablets the words of the covenant,
the Ten Words.

29 Now it was
when Moshe came down from Mount Sinai
with the two tablets of Testimony in Moshe's hand,
when he came down from the mountain
—(now) Moshe did not know that the skin of his face was
   radiating because of his having-spoken with him,—
30 Aharon and all the Children of Israel saw Moshe:
and here, the skin of his face was radiating!
So they were afraid to approach him.
31 Moshe called to them,
and then Aharon and all those exalted in the community came
   back to him,
and Moshe spoke to them.
32 Afterward all the Children of Israel approached,
and he commanded them
all that YHWH had spoken with him on Mount Sinai.
33 Now when Moshe had finished speaking with them,
he put a veil upon his face.

---

28 **Ten Words:** These are known in the Bible as such, not as the "Ten Commandments."

29 **radiating:** Or "radiant." As is well known, Michelangelo created his famous horned statue of Moses (in the Roman church of San Pietro in Vincoli) on the basis of the Latin translation of the Bible, the Vulgate, which rendered the Hebrew *karan* as "horned." There have now been found other ancient Near Eastern texts that support this reading, although the present context and comparative religion seem also to throw weight to "radiating."

34 Now whenever Moshe would come before the presence of
YHWH, to speak with him,
he would remove the veil, until he had gone out;
and whenever he would come out and speak to the children of
Israel that which he had been commanded,
35 the Children of Israel would see Moshe's face,
that the skin of Moshe's face was radiating;
but then Moshe would put back the veil on his face,
until he came in to speak with him.

PART VI

THE BUILDING OF THE DWELLING

(35–40)

As if nothing had gone awry, the narrative now returns to describe how the Dwelling was built. This time, as was noted by the sages of the Talmud, the order follows the natural logic of construction (i.e., dwelling, tapestries, covering, boards, sockets, bars, etc., and then the ritual objects), rather than the earlier one of sanctity (i.e., coffer, purgation-cover, table, lampstand, etc., and then the structure itself). The most notable omission is the carrying out of priestly ordination; that is reserved for Lev. 8, perhaps so as not to interfere with the narrative momentum of the construction process, or else to focus more on the Dwelling itself and its divine resident. The only major interruption in this part is 38:21–31, which fits in with one of the important themes of these chapters: the extent of the Israelites' contribution to the sanctuary.

As there is no need to repeat what was said about each part of the Tabernacle in the commentary to Chaps. 25–31, the commentary here will be limited to brief remarks on the differences between the two long Tabernacle sections (Parts IV and VI); here Cassuto has provided most of the necessary material.

The Sabbath Restated (35:1–3): Bracketing the Calf Narrative, we return to the regulations concerning the Sabbath, which receive here a different explanation from what was given in 31:12–17. There the stress was on the symbolic nature of the Sabbath day, but in the present context no reason for observance is given. Cassuto understands this as a clarification of the rules of "making" as the Dwelling is about to be constructed.

The Contribution Restated (35:4–19): The theme returns to that of the opening of the Tabernacle account in Chap. 25, with a list of what was to be brought for the "work of the Dwelling."

Preparations for the Construction (35:20–36:7): The account of what the Israelites brought as contributions for the work, and the description of those who were to carry it out, is long and repetitive. This factor, with the addition of a refrainlike pattern of key words (e.g., "mind," "willing," "service," "work," "wise," "design," "brought"), strongly portrays the people's enthusiasm for and participation in the sacred task. Note also the fourteenfold occurrence of "every/all/entire" (Heb. *kol*) in vv.20–29. Vv.3–7 push the narrative to a crescendo, with the people actually bringing much more than is needed (and may also be a contrast to their briefly stated surrendering of jewels in the Calf episode, 32:3).

35:1   Now Moshe assembled the entire community of the Children of
      Israel
    and said to them:
    These are the words that YHWH has commanded, to do them:

2   For six days is work to be made,
    but on the seventh day,
    there is to be holiness for you,
    Sabbath, Sabbath-Ceasing for YHWH;
    whoever makes work on it is to be put-to-death!
3   You are not to let fire burn throughout all your settlements on
    the Sabbath day.

4   Now Moshe spoke to the entire community of the Children of
    Israel,
    saying:
    This is the matter that YHWH has commanded, saying:
5   Take, from yourselves, a raised-contribution for YHWH,
    whoever is of willing mind is to bring it,
    YHWH's contribution:
    gold, silver, and bronze,
6   blue-violet, purple, worm-scarlet, byssus and goats'-hair,
7   rams' skins dyed-red, tanned-leather skins,
    acacia wood,
8   oil for lighting,
    spices for oil of anointing and for fragrant smoking-incense,
9   onyx stones and stones for setting,
    for the *efod* and for the breastpiece.
10   And everyone wise of mind among you
    is to come and is to make all that YHWH has commanded:
11   The Dwelling, its tent and its cover,
    its clasps and its boards,
    its running bars, its columns and its sockets;

35:3 **You are not to let fire burn:** This prohibition perhaps reflects the anthropological use of fire as a
transforming force in culture (see Fredman). Since
the Shabbat was apparently to be static in nature,
or at least transformative of time alone, fire (which
by its nature causes chemical changes) could not
be employed. **throughout all your settlements:**
And not only in the area of building the Dwelling
(Cassuto).

◆ 12 the coffer and its poles,
  the purgation-cover and the curtain for the screen;

13 the table and its poles and all its implements,
  and the Bread of the Presence;

14 and the lampstand for lighting and its implements and its lamps,
  and the oil for lighting;

15 and the site for smoke-offering and its poles, and the oil for
    anointing,
  and the fragrant smoking-incense;
  and the entrance screen for the entrance of the Dwelling;

16 the site for offering-up and the bronze lattice that (belongs) to it,
    its poles and all its implements;
  the basin and its pedestal;

17 the hangings of the courtyard, its columns and its sockets, and
    the screen for the gate of the courtyard;

18 the pins of the Dwelling and the pins of the courtyard, and their
    cords,

19 the officiating garments for attending at the Holy-Shrine;
  the garments of holiness for Aharon the priest
  and the garments of his sons for acting-as-priest.

20 So the entire community of the Children of Israel
  went out from Moshe's presence,

21 and then they came, every man whose mind uplifted him,
  and everyone whose spirit made-him-willing brought YHWH's
    contribution
  for the skilled-work on the Tent of Appointment, for all its
    service (of construction), and for the garments of holiness.

22 Then came men and women alike, everyone of willing mind,
  they brought
  brooch and nose-ring and signet-ring and necklace, every kind of
    gold object,
  every man that wished to elevate an elevation-offering of gold to
    YHWH;

---

22 **necklace:** This is a conjecture, as the meaning of
  the Hebrew *kumaz* is uncertain.

23 and everyone with whom could be found
   blue-violet, purple, worm-scarlet, byssus and goats'-hair, rams'
       skins dyed-red and tanned-leather skins,
   brought it.
24 Everyone that raised a raised-contribution of silver and bronze
   brought YHWH's contribution,
   and everyone with whom could be found
   acacia wood for all the work of the service (of construction),
       brought it.
25 And every woman wise of mind,
   with their hands they spun
   and brought their spinning—
   the blue-violet, the purple, the worm-scarlet and the byssus,
26 and every one of the women whose mind uplifted them in
       practical-wisdom
   spun the goats'-hair.
27 And the exalted-ones brought
   the onyx stones and the stones for setting,
   for the *efod* and for the breastpiece,
28 and the fragrant-spice and the oil
   for lighting, for oil of anointing, for fragrant smoking-incense.
29 Every man and woman
   whose mind made-them-willing to bring (anything) for all the
       workmanship
   that YHWH had commanded (them) to make through Moshe, the
       Children of Israel brought it,
   freewill-offering for YHWH.

30 Now Moshe said to the Children of Israel:
   See,
   YHWH has called by name
   Betzalel son of Uri, son of Hur, of the tribe of Yehuda,

---

25 **spun:** The Hebrew verb *tavoh* occurs only here in
the Bible.

465

Dwelling II (36:8–19): Missing here (cf. 26:1–14) is the description of how the tapestries were to be joined to the boards; the section pertains to the actual making of the tapestries.

Boards II (36:20–34): In reference to 26:15–30, the present text has omitted the command to erect the entire structure. The passage is limited in a manner similar to the previous section.

31 he has filled him with the spirit of God
in practical-wisdom, in discernment and in knowledge,
and in all kinds of workmanship

32 to design designs,
to make (them) in gold, in silver and in bronze,

33 in the carving of stones for setting and in the carving of wood,
to make all kinds of designed workmanship,

34 and (the ability) to instruct he has put in his mind,
he and Oholiav son of Ahisamakh, of the tribe of Dan;

35 he has filled them with wisdom of mind
to make all kinds of workmanship
of the jewel-cutter, the designer and the embroiderer,
in blue-violet, in purple, in worm-scarlet and in byssus,
and of the weaver—
makers of all kinds of workmanship
and designers of designs.

36:1 So are Betzalel and Oholiav to make,
and every man wise of mind
in whom YHWH has put wisdom and discernment,
to know (how) to make all the work for the service of
(constructing) the Holy-Shrine
for all that YHWH has commanded.

2 So Moshe called
for Betzalel, for Oholiav,
and for all men wise of mind into whose mind YHWH had put
wisdom,
all those whose mind uplifted them to come-near for the work,
to make it.

3 And they took from Moshe all the contributions
that the Children of Israel had brought for the work of the
service of (constructing) the Holy-Shrine,
to make it.
Now they brought him further, freewill-offerings in the morning,
(every) morning;

34 **(the ability) to instruct:** Now that the actual construction is about to take place, it is crucial that the head craftsman be not only skilled himself, but a master instructor as well.

4 and came, all the wise-ones who were making all the skilled-work
     for the Holy-Shrine,
   man after man, from their skilled-work that they were making,
5 and said to Moshe, saying:
   The people are bringing much more
   than enough for the service of (doing) the work
   that YHWH has commanded, to make it!
6 So Moshe commanded and they had a call go throughout the
     camp, saying:
   Man and woman—let them not make-ready any further work-
     material for the contribution of the Holy-Shrine!
   So the people were stopped from bringing;
7 the work-material was enough for them, for all the work, to
     make it, and more.

8 Then made all those wise of mind among the makers of the
     work,
   the dwelling, of ten tapestries
   of twisted byssus, blue-violet, purple and worm-scarlet;
   with winged-sphinxes, of designer's making, was it made.
9 The length of each one tapestry, twenty-eight by the cubit,
   and the width—four by the cubit,
   of each one tapestry,
   one measure for all of the tapestries.
10 Then were joined five of the tapestries, each-one to each-one,
   and five tapestries were joined, each-one to each-one.
11 Then were made loops of blue-violet
   on the edge of the one tapestry, at the end of the one joint;
   thus were made in the edge of the end tapestry at the second
     joint.

36:10 **each-one to each-one:** In 26:3, the parallel passage, the text reads "each one to the other." This is one example of the changes that occur between Chaps. 25–31 and 35–40; the reader should consult the parallel accounts for the differences in wording.

12 Fifty loops were made on the one tapestry,
   and fifty loops were made at the end of the tapestry that is at the
      second joint,
   opposite the loops, this-one to that-one.
13 Then were made fifty clasps of gold
   and then were joined the tapestries, this-one to that-one, with the
      clasps,
   so that the dwelling became one-piece.
14 Then were made the tapestries of goats'-hair for a tent over the
      dwelling,
   eleven tapestries were they made.
15 The length of each one tapestry (was) thirty by the cubit,
   and four cubits, the width of each one tapestry,
   one measure for the eleven tapestries.
16 Then were joined five of the tapestries separately
   and six of the tapestries separately.
17 Then were made loops, fifty (of them), at the edge of the end
      tapestry, at the joint,
   and fifty loops were made at the edge of the second joining
      tapestry.
18 Then were made clasps of bronze, fifty (of them),
   to join the tent together,
   to become one-piece.
19 Then was made a covering for the tent, of rams' skins dyed-red,
   and a covering of tanned-leather skins, above it.
20 Then were made the boards for the Dwelling,
   of acacia wood, standing-upright;
21 ten cubits the length of the board
   and a cubit and a half the width of each one board,
22 with two pegs for each one board, parallel this-one to that-one,
   thus were made for all the boards of the Dwelling.
23 And then were made the boards for the Dwelling:
   twenty as boardwork on the Negev border, southward,
24 and forty sockets of silver were made beneath twenty of the
      boards,
   two sockets beneath each one board for its two pegs
   and two sockets beneath each other board for its two pegs;

Curtain and Screen II (36:35–38): Again (cf. 26:31–37), only the making of the objects themselves is described, not their positioning within the Tabernacle.

Coffer and Purgation-Cover II (37:1–9): Parallel to 25:10–22, this account specifies Betzalel as the artist, otherwise behaving like the other passages in this chapter.

Table II (37:10–16): This corresponds to 25:23–30, with the omission of the Bread of the Presence.

Lampstand II (37:17–24): The parallel account is 25:31–40, except for details there regarding its placement in the overall structure.

Incense Altar II (37:25–28): This is a case similar to that of the lampstand (cf. 30:1–5).

25 and for the second flank of the Dwelling, on the northern border,
       were made twenty as boardwork,
26 with their forty sockets of silver,
    two sockets beneath each one board
    and two sockets beneath each other board.
27 And for the rear of the Dwelling, toward the sea, were made six
       boards,
28 and two boards were made for the corners of the Dwelling, at the
       rear,
29 so that they were of twin-use, (seen) from the lower-end,
    and together formed a whole-piece, toward the top, toward the
       first ring;
    thus were made for the two of them, for the two corners.
30 So there were eight boards with their bases of silver, sixteen bases,
    two bases each, two bases beneath each one board.
31 Then were made running-bars of acacia wood,
    five bars for the boards of the Dwelling's one flank
32 and five bars for the boards of the Dwelling's second flank,
    and five bars for the boards of the Dwelling at the rear, toward
       the sea.
33 Then was made the middle running-bar, to run amidst the
       boards,
    from (this) end to (that) end.
34 And the boards were overlaid with gold,
    and their rings were made of gold, as holders for the bars,
    and the bars were overlaid with gold.
35 Then was made the curtain
    of blue-violet, purple, worm-scarlet and twisted byssus;
    of designer's making was it made, with winged-sphinxes.
36 Then were made for it four columns of acacia
    and were overlaid with gold, their hooks of gold,
    and four bases of silver were cast for them.
37 Then was made a screen for the entrance to the Tent
    of blue-violet, purple, worm-scarlet and twisted byssus,
    of embroiderer's making,
38 and their columns, five (of them), and their hooks,
    and their tops and their binders were overlaid with gold—
    and their bases, five, of bronze.

37:1 Then Betzalel made
the coffer, of acacia wood,
two cubits and a half its length,
a cubit and a half its width,
and a cubit and a half its height.

2 He overlaid it with pure gold, inside and outside,
and made for it a rim of gold all around.

3 He cast for it four rings of gold
(to be) upon its four feet,
with two rings on its one flank
and two rings on its second flank.

4 He made poles of acacia wood
and overlaid them with gold,

5 he brought the poles into the rings on the flanks of the coffer, to
carry the coffer.

6 He made a purgation-cover of pure gold,
two cubits and a half its length
and a cubit and a half its width.

7 He made two winged-sphinxes of gold,
of hammered-work did he make them,
at the two ends of the purgation-cover.

8 One sphinx at the end here
and one sphinx at the end there,
from the purgation-cover did he make the sphinxes, at its two
ends.

9 And the sphinxes were spreading (their) wings upward,
with their wings sheltering the purgation-cover,
their faces, each toward the other;
toward the purgation-cover were the sphinxes' faces.

10 He made the table of acacia wood,
two cubits its length,
a cubit its width,
and a cubit and a half its height.

11 He overlaid it with pure gold.
And he made a rim of gold for it, all around,

12 and made a border for it, a handbreadth all around,
thus he made a rim of gold for its border, all around.

13 He cast for it four rings of gold
   and put the rings at the four edges, where its four legs (are).
14 Parallel to the border were the rings,
   holders for the poles, to carry the table.
15 He made the poles of acacia wood, and overlaid them with gold,
   to carry the table.
16 He made the implements that are on the table:
   its dishes and its ladles,
   its jugs and jars, from which (offerings) are poured,
   of pure gold.

17 He made the lampstand of pure gold,
   of hammered-work did he make the lampstand, its shaft and its
      stem,
   its goblets, its knobs and its blossoms were from it;
18 six stems issuing from its sides,
   three lamp-stems on the one side,
   three lamp-stems on the second side:
19 three almond-shaped goblets on the one stem, with knobs and
      blossoms,
   and three almond-shaped goblets on the other stem, with knobs
      and blossoms—
   thus for the six stems that were issuing from the lampstand.
20 And on the lampstand (itself) four almond-shaped goblets, with
      their knobs and their blossoms,
21 a knob beneath two stems, from it,
   a knob beneath two stems, from it,
   and a knob beneath two stems, from it,
   for the six stems that were issuing from it.
22 Their knobs and their stems were from it,
   all of it one-piece of hammered-work, of pure gold.
23 He made its lamps, seven (of them),
   and its tongs and its trays, of pure gold.
24 From an ingot of pure gold did he make it, with all its implements.

25 He made the site for smoking-incense, of acacia wood,
   a cubit its length and a cubit its width,
   squared, and two cubits its height,
   from it were its two horns.

Anointing Oil and Incense II (37:29): To round out the description of the incense altar, the text adds mention of these ingredients (cf. 30:25, 35).

Altar II (38:1–7): Parallel to 27:1–8, the major omission is "to receive its ashes" (27:3), which does not relate to the actual construction.

Basin and Pedestal II (38:8): Only one line is used to record the making of the basin; the parallel account in 30:17–21 says much more about its function. There is a brief allusion in this verse about the "mirrors" which were the raw material for the basin; Cassuto (1967) sees this as a contemporary citing of what must have been a well-known tradition about the special contribution of the Israelite women, above and beyond the official contributions listed in Chap. 35.

26 He overlaid it with pure gold—
   its roof, its walls all around, and its horns,
   and he made a rim of gold for it, all around.
27 Two rings of gold did he make for it, beneath its rim,
   on its two flanks, on its two sides,
   as holders for poles, to carry it by (means of) them.
28 He made the poles of acacia wood,
   and overlaid them with gold.

29 And he made the anointing oil of holiness
   and the fragrant smoking-incense, pure, of perfumer's making.

38:1 Then he made the slaughter-site of offering-up, of acacia wood,
   five cubits its length, five cubits its width, square,
   and three cubits its height.
2 He made its horns on its four points,
   from it were its horns.
   He overlaid it with bronze.
3 He made all the implements for the slaughter-site,
   the pails, the scrapers, the bowls, the flesh-hooks, and the pans;
   all its implements, he made of bronze.
4 He made for the slaughter-site a lattice, as a netting of bronze is made,
   beneath its ledge, below, (reaching) to its halfway-point.
5 He cast four rings on the four edges of the netting of bronze,
   as holders for the poles.
6 He made the poles of acacia wood
   and overlaid them with bronze.
7 He brought the poles through the rings on the flanks of the altar,
   to carry it by (means of) them;
   hollow, of planks, did he make it.

8 He made the basin of bronze, its pedestal of bronze,
   with the mirrors of the women's working-force that was doing-
      the-work at the entrance of the Tent of Appointment.

9 And he made the courtyard:
   on the Negev border, southward,
   the hangings of the courtyard, of twisted byssus, a hundred by
      the cubit,

Courtyard II (38:9–20): Corresponding to 27:9–19, there are a number of wording divergencies from the earlier passage, but none of these is particularly significant.

Accountings (38:21–31): A new section enters here, continuing to achieve the effect of impressing the audience. Previously the reader was to be struck by the Israelites' zeal in piling up contributions for the new sanctuary (36:3–7); now, toward the end of the actual construction work, there is a full accounting of the considerable material that went into it. The list follows the standard order of value: gold, silver, and bronze.

10 with their columns, twenty, their sockets, twenty, of bronze,
   the hooks of the columns and their binders, of silver.

11 And on the northern border, a hundred by the cubit,
   their columns, twenty, their sockets, twenty, of bronze,
   the hooks of the columns and their binders, of silver.

12 And on the sea border, hangings, fifty by the cubit,
   their columns, ten, their sockets, ten,
   the hooks of the columns and their binders, of silver.

13 And on the eastern border, toward sunrise, fifty by the cubit,

14 (namely:) hangings of fifteen cubits to the shoulder-piece,
   their columns, three, their sockets, three,

15 and for the second shoulder-piece—(over) here and (over) there
      for the gate of the courtyard—
   hangings of fifteen cubits,
   their columns, three, their sockets, three.

16 All the hangings of the courtyard all around, of twisted byssus,

17 and the sockets for the columns, of bronze,
   the hooks of the columns and their binders, of silver,
   and the overlay for their tops, of silver, they themselves bound
      with silver,
   all the columns of the courtyard.

18 The screen of the courtyard gate, of embroiderer's making,
   of blue-violet, purple, worm-scarlet and twisted byssus,
   twenty cubits in length,
   their height along the width, five cubits,
   corresponding to the hangings of the courtyard,

19 their columns, four, their sockets, four, of bronze,
   their hooks, of silver,
   and the overlay for their tops and their binders, of silver,

20 and all the pins for the Dwelling and for the courtyard all around,
      of bronze.

21 These are the accountings of the Dwelling,
   the Dwelling of Testimony,

38:21 **the accountings:** I.e., the inventory of materials
used to construct the Dwelling.

Garments II (39:1): Although in scribal tradition this verse is connected to the previous section, it makes sense as the start of a new one, as it concludes with what will now be in one form or another the refrain to the end of the book: "as YHWH had commanded Moshe" (see also vv.5, 21, 26, 29, 31, 32, 42, 43; then 40:16, 19, 21, 23, 25, 27, 29, and 32).

Efod and Breastpiece II (39:2–21): Corresponding to 28:6–30, the account of how these garments were constructed conforms to the previous pattern: their function "for remembrance" and more, so movingly laid out in Chap. 28, is not mentioned.

that were accounted by Moshe
for the service of the Levites,
under Itamar, son of Aharon the priest:

22 So Betzalel son of Uri, son of Hur, of the tribe of Yehuda
had made
all that YHWH had commanded Moshe,

23 and with him, Oholiav son of Ahisamakh, of the tribe of Dan,
carver, designer, embroiderer in the blue-violet, purple and
worm-scarlet and byssus.

24 All the gold that was made-use-of in the work, in all the work of
(building) the Holy-Shrine
all the gold from the elevation-offering (was)
twenty-nine ingots and seven hundred thirty *shekels*, by the Holy-
Shrine *shekel*.

25 And the silver accounted for by the community (was) a hundred
ingots,
and a thousand and seven hundred and seventy-five *shekels* by the
Holy-Shrine *shekel*,

26 a *beka*/split-piece per capita, the half of a *shekel* by the Holy-
Shrine *shekel*,
for every one who went through the counting,
from the age of twenty years and upward,
for the six hundred thousand and three thousand and five
hundred and fifty.

27 There were a hundred ingots of silver for the casting of the
sockets of the Holy-Shrine and of the sockets of the curtain
a hundred bases per hundred ingots, an ingot per socket.

28 And the thousand, seven hundred and seventy-five they made into
hooks for the columns,
and overlaid their tops and bound them.

29 And the bronze from the elevation-offering (was) seventy ingots,
and two thousand and four hundred *shekels*.

---

21 **Itamar:** Previously mentioned only in the genealogical list of 6:23 and the enumeration in 28:1.
24 **ingots:** Others, "talents." These were of fairly large
weight, perhaps 75 pounds.
26 **603,550:** A more specific number than the "about
600,000" mentioned in 12:37; it has been shown by

Cassuto to conform to a patterned scheme (600,000
+ 7,000/2 + 100/2), and hence may be a number designed more for didactic than for reporting purposes.

30 They made with it the sockets for the entrance of the Tent of
Appointment,
the slaughter-site of bronze, the netting of bronze that belonged
to it, all the implements of the slaughter-site,
31 the sockets of the courtyard all around and the sockets of the
courtyard gate
and all the pins of the Dwelling and the pins of the courtyard, all
around.

39:1 Now from the blue-violet and the purple and the worm-scarlet
they made the officiating garments for attending at the Holy-
Shrine
and they made the garments of holiness that are for Aharon,
as YHWH had commanded Moshe.

2 Then was made the *efod*
of gold, blue-violet, purple, worm-scarlet and twisted byssus.
3 Then were beat out sheets of gold
and they were split into threads,
to make-use-of-them amid the blue-violet, amid the purple, amid
the worm-scarlet and amid the twisted byssus,
(all) of designer's making.
4 Shoulder-pieces they made for it, (to be) joined together,
on its two ends joined.
5 The designed-band of its *efod* that was on it, was from it, of like
making,
of gold, blue-violet, purple, worm-scarlet and twisted byssus,
as YHWH had commanded Moshe.

6 They made the onyx stones,
surrounded by braids of gold,
engraved with seal engravings, with the names of the Children of
Israel.

39:3 **to make-use-of them amidst:** Or "to work them   6 **surrounded by braids:** Heb. *meshubbot mishbetzot.*
into."

7 They placed them on the shoulder-pieces of the *efod,*
as stones of remembrance for the Children of Israel,
as YHWH had commanded Moshe.

8 Then was made the breastpiece
of designer's making, like the making of an *efod,*
of gold, blue-violet, purple, worm-scarlet and twisted byssus.

9 Square it was, doubled they made the breastpiece,
a span its length and a span its width, doubled.

10 They set-it-full with four rows of stones—
a row of carnelian, topaz, and sparkling-emerald, the first row,

11 the second row: ruby, sapphire and hard-onyx,

12 the third row: jacinth, agate, and amethyst,

13 the fourth row: beryl, onyx and jasper;
surrounded, braided with gold in their settings.

14 And the stones were with the names of the Children of Israel,
twelve with their names,
signet engravings, each-one with its name,
for the twelve tribes.

15 They made, on the breastpiece, laced chains, of rope-making, of
pure gold:

16 They made two braids of gold and two rings of gold,
and put the two rings on the two ends of the breastpiece,

17 and put the two ropes of gold on the two rings on the ends of the
breastpiece,

18 and the two ends of the two ropes they put on the two braids,
and put them on the shoulder-pieces of the *efod,* on its forefront.

19 They made two rings of gold,
and placed them on the two ends of the breastpiece, on its edge
that is across from the *efod,* inward,

20 and they made two rings of gold and put them on the two
shoulder-pieces of the *efod,* below, facing frontward, parallel to
its joint, above the designed-band of the *efod.*

21 They tied the breastpiece from its rings to the rings of the *efod,*
with a thread of blue-violet,

8 **an *efod*:** Some ancient versions read "the *efod.*"

Tunic II (39:22–26): Parallel to 28:31–35, this account leaves out the protective function of the tunic cited in 28:35.

Other Priestly Garments II (39:27–29): The parallel text is 28:39–43. This passage should come after the section on the head-plate, as was the case in the earlier passages; Cassuto (1967) explains the inversion as characteristic of the construction texts—all the weaving is to take place together.

Head-Plate II (39:30–31): Characteristically, the function of the plate is omitted (cf. 28:36–38).

to be (fixed) on the designed-band of the *efod;*
the breastpiece was not to be dislodged from the *efod,*
as Y<small>HWH</small> had commanded Moshe.

22 Then was made the tunic of the *efod,*
of weaver's making, all of blue-violet.
23 The head-opening of the tunic (was) in its middle, like the
opening for armor,
a seam-edge for its opening, all around—it was not to be split.
24 They made, on the skirts of the tunic, pomegranates,
of blue-violet, purple, worm-scarlet and twisted byssus.
25 They made bells of pure gold
and they put the bells amidst the pomegranates
on the skirts of the tunic, all around,
amidst the pomegranates:
26 bell and pomegranate, bell and pomegranate,
on the skirts of the tunic, all around,
for attending,
as Y<small>HWH</small> had commanded Moshe.

27 They made the coat of byssus, of weaver's making,
for Aharon and for his sons,
28 and the turban of byssus,
the splendid caps of byssus,
the breeches of linen, of twisted byssus,
29 and the sash of twisted byssus, blue-violet, purple, and worm-
scarlet, of embroiderer's making,
as Y<small>HWH</small> had commanded Moshe.

30 They made the plate (for) the sacred-diadem of holiness, of pure
gold,
and wrote upon it writing of signet engravings:
Holiness for Y<small>HWH</small>.
31 They put on it a thread of blue-violet, to put on the turban from
above,
as Y<small>HWH</small> had commanded Moshe.

The Completion of the Parts: Bringing Them to Moshe (39:32–43): The listing of all the elements of the Dwelling fittingly closes the account of their construction, with a certain grandeur, and, because of the pace, even a certain excitement. The key term "service (of construction)" occurs three times.

More significant is what has long been noted: the literal parallels between our section and the initial creation story in Genesis (see, for instance, Leibowitz and Sarna 1986). The phrases "Thus was finished . . ." (v.32), "And Moshe saw all the work: and here, they had made it" (v.43), and "Then Moshe blessed them" (v.43), echo "Thus were finished . . ." (Gen. 2:1), "Now God saw all that he had made, / and here: it was exceedingly good" (Gen. 1:31), and "God gave the seventh day his blessing" (Gen. 2:3). At the end of the passage describing the erection of the Tabernacle, there is an additional parallel: "So Moshe finished the work" (40:33); cf. Gen. 2:2: "God had finished . . . his work." The close parallels suggest what we find in the case of many cultures: human building, especially (but not exclusively) of sanctuaries, is to be viewed as an act of imitating God. The Israelites, at the close of the book chronicling their founding as a people, link up with God's scheme in creating the world. The Dwelling is therefore a reflection of the perfection of the world and the divine hand that oversees it. Yet neither the people nor Moshe pronounces the Genesis words "it was (exceedingly) good" over the sanctuary; that would be human *hubris*.

Final Instructions: Setting Up (40:1–16): Most prominent in God's commands to erect the Tabernacle are two related verbs: "hallow" and "anoint," each of which occurs in one form or another eight times here. So the major theme here is not the actual building, but dedication for a purpose. Included in this section, as it was in Part IV, is the appointment of Aharon and his sons to "be-priests."

The completion of the sanctuary takes place, appropriately, on the first day of what was the month of the exodus a year earlier; it is also ten months after the people reached Sinai. The dedication thus combines the ideas of sacred space and sacred time.

The Implementation (40:17–33): Meaningfully, the formula "as YHWH had commanded Moshe" ends each of the seven paragraphs that describe the erection of the Dwelling.

32 Thus was finished all the service (of construction) for the
　　Dwelling, the Tent of Appointment.
　The Children of Israel made (it)
　according to all that YHWH had commanded Moshe,
　thus they made.

33 And they brought the Dwelling to Moshe:
　the tent and all its implements,
　its clasps, its beams, its bars and its columns and its sockets,

34 the covering of rams' skins dyed-red and the covering of tanned-
　　leather skins,
　the curtain for the screen,

35 the coffer of Testimony and its poles
　and the purgation-cover,

36 the table, all its implements and the Bread of the Presence,

37 the pure lampstand, its lamps—lamps for arranging, and all its
　　implements,
　and the oil for lighting,

38 the site of gold,
　and anointing oil and the fragant smoking-incense
　and the screen for the entrance of the Tent;

39 the slaughter-site of bronze and the netting of bronze that
　　belongs to it, its poles and all its implements,
　the basin and its pedestal;

40 the hangings of the courtyard,
　its columns and its sockets,
　and the screen for the courtyard gate,
　its cords and its pegs
　and all the implements for the service (of constructing) the
　　Dwelling, the Tent of Appointment;

41 the officiating garments for attending at the Holy-Shrine, the
　　garments of holiness for Aharon the priest and the garments
　　for his sons, to be-priests—

---

32 **made:** More idiomatically, "did" (similarly in 39:42, 43 and 40:16). See Gen. 6:22, where Noah also follows God's instructions to the letter.

37 **lamps for arranging:** Others, "lamps in due order." **implements:** Others, "fittings."

42 according to all that YHWH had commanded Moshe,
   thus had made the Children of Israel,
   all the service (of construction).
43 Now Moshe saw all the work, and here: they had made it
   as YHWH had commanded,
   thus had they made.
   Then Moshe blessed them.

40:1 Now YHWH spoke to Moshe, saying:
2 On the day of the first New-Moon, on the first (day) of the New-
   Moon,
   you are to erect the Dwelling, the Tent of Appointment.
3 You are to place there the coffer of Testimony
   and you are to screen the coffer with the curtain.
4 You are to bring in the table and arrange its arrangement,
   you are to bring in the lampstand and are to draw up its
   lampwicks,
5 you are to put the site of gold (there), for smoking-incense,
   before the coffer of Testimony,
   and you are to place the screen of the entrance for the Dwelling,
6 you are to put the slaughter-site for offering-up before the
   entrance of the Dwelling, the Tent of Appointment,
7 you are to put the basin between the Tent of Appointment and
   the slaughter-site,
   and you are to put water therein.
8 You are to place the courtyard all around, and you are to put the
   screen for the gate of the courtyard (there).
9 Then you are to take the anointing oil
   and you are to anoint the Dwelling and all that is in it,
   you are (thus) to hallow it and all its implements, that they may
   become holiness;
10 you are to anoint the slaughter-site for offering-up and all its
   implements,
   you are (thus) to hallow the slaughter-site, that the slaughter-site
   may become holiest holiness;

40:2 **the first New-Moon . . . the first (day):** The date is almost a year after Israel's departure from Egypt. The completion of the sanctuary takes place on the first day of the month (new moon), whereas the exodus had occurred on the fifteenth (full moon), also considered a sacred time.

11 you are to anoint the basin and its pedestal,
you are (thus) to hallow it.
12 You are to bring-near Aharon and his sons to the entrance of the
Tent of Appointment,
you are to wash them with water,
13 and you are to clothe Aharon in the garments of holiness;
you are to anoint him,
you are (thus) to hallow him, to be-priest to me,
14 and his sons you are to bring-near,
you are to clothe them in coats,
15 and are to anoint them as you anointed their father, that they
may be-priests for me;
that shall become for them—their being-anointed—priesthood
for the ages, throughout their generations.
16 Moshe made (it)
according to all that Yhwh had commanded him,
thus he made.

17 And so it was on the first New-Moon in the second year, on the
first (day) of the New-Moon,
the Dwelling was erected.
18 Moshe erected the Dwelling:
he put up its sockets,
he placed its boards,
he put up its bars,
he erected its columns,
19 he spread out the tent over the Dwelling,
he placed the cover of the tent over it, above,
as Yhwh had commanded Moshe.

20 He took and put the Testimony in the coffer,
he placed the poles of the coffer,
he put the purgation-cover of the coffer, above,
21 he brought the coffer into the Dwelling,
he placed (there) the curtain of the screen and screened the coffer
of Testimony,
as Yhwh had commanded Moshe.

22 He put the table in the Tent of Appointment,
on the flank of the Dwelling, northward, outside the curtain,

The End: God's Glory (40:34–38): The book ends, not with a paean to the completed structure or its builders, but with a description of how its purpose was fulfilled. Central is the "cloud," basically synonymous with God's "Glory," which now dwells among the people of Israel. At the end of the book of Exodus, which began with a people in servitude to an earthly god-king, we find a people that has completed one aspect of service to a divine king, ready to set forth on their journey to a Promised Land in the company of the king's inextinguishable presence.

23 he arranged on it the arrangement of the Bread of the Presence,
  before the presence of YHWH,
  as YHWH had commanded Moshe.

24 He placed the lampstand in the Tent of Appointment,
  opposite the table, on the flank of the Dwelling, southward,
25 he set up the lamps before the presence of YHWH,
  as YHWH had commanded Moshe.

26 He placed the site of gold in the Tent of Appointment, before the
  curtain,
27 and sent-up-in-smoke on it fragrant smoking-incense,
  as YHWH had commanded Moshe.

28 He placed (there) the screen for the entrance of the Dwelling,
29 the slaughter-site for offering-up he placed at the entrance of the
  Dwelling, of the Tent of Appointment,
  and offered-up on it the offerings-up and the grain-gifts,
  as YHWH had commanded Moshe.

30 He placed the basin between the Tent of Appointment and the
  slaughter-site,
  and put water therein, for washing,
31 that Moshe and Aharon and his sons might wash from it their
  hands and their feet,
32 (that) whenever they came into the Tent of Appointment and
  whenever they came-near the slaughter-site, they might wash,
  as YHWH had commanded Moshe.

33 He erected the courtyard all around the Dwelling and the
  slaughter-site,
  and put up the screen for the courtyard gate.

  So Moshe finished the work.

34 Now the cloud covered the Tent of Appointment,
  and the Glory of YHWH filled the Dwelling.
35 Moshe was not able to come into the Tent of Appointment,
  for the cloud took-up-dwelling on it, and the Glory of YHWH
  filled the Dwelling.
36 Whenever the cloud goes up from the Dwelling,
  the Children of Israel march on, upon all their marches;

37 if the cloud does not go up,
   they do not march on, until such time as it does go up.
38 For the cloud of YHWH (is) over the Dwelling by day,
   and fire is by night in it,
   before the eyes of all the House of Israel
   upon all their marches.

APPENDIX:
SCHEMATIC FLOOR PLAN
OF THE DWELLING

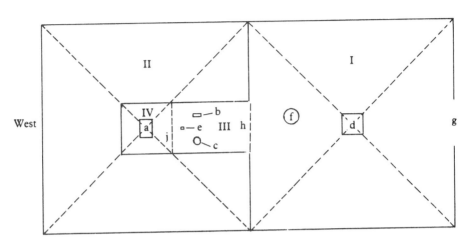

I	Outer Court	a Coffer	e Site for Incense
II	Inner Court	b Table	f Basin
III	Holy-Shrine	c Lampstand	g Entrance
IV	Holiest Holy-Shrine	d Slaughter-site	h Screen
			j Curtain

According to the measurements given in Chaps. 25–30, the proportions are as follows:

Perfect Squares (1:1) are the Outer Court, the Inner Court, the Holiest Holy-Shrine, the Slaughter-site, and the Site for Incense.

Perfect Rectangles (2:1) are the whole structure, the Holy-Shrine, and the Table.

The relationship of the whole structure to each court is 2:1, as is that of the Holy-Shrine to the Holiest Holy-Shrine.

The relationship of the entrances (Entrance, Screen, and Curtain) is 2:1:1.

The Coffer and the Slaughter-site appear to stand at the exact centers of their respective squares. They share proportions different from those above: their length/width/height ratios are 5:3:3 (Coffer) and 5:5:3 (Slaughter-site). The departure from the standard 2:1 ratio may be an attempt to draw attention to these two holy objects, which functioned as the spiritual as well as geographical centers of the Israelite encampment in the wilderness.

To Aid the Reader of Leviticus-Numbers-Deuteronomy

In the Preface, I pointed out that much has changed in biblical scholarship since the inception of Buber and Rosenzweig's work. Nowhere is this as true as in reference to the last three books of the Torah. In the case of Leviticus, although the Israelite cult was of intense interest to nineteenth-century Protestant scholars such as Wellhausen, and Jewish scholars such as David Hoffmann, there has been a flowering of new work on this book in the last few decades. The opening up of ancient Near Eastern material on sacrifice and ritual, made possible by the scholarship of philologists, archaeologists, and comparativists in this century, and recent insights of anthropology, now bring to Leviticus a new level of comprehension and appreciation.

Most outstanding in this regard is the work of Milgrom and Levine, who have also greatly advanced the understanding of the book of Numbers. The contributions of these scholars properly constitute in each case a lifework, and one cannot study Leviticus or Numbers without a close reading of what they have done. If as translator I have accepted only a percentage of what they have suggested, that is due to the constraints imposed by my method, and also to the unenviable task of deciding between them in areas where they disagree. Any reader serious about studying the Torah must consult their work. In line with these developments, I should note that I have relied less on B-R in translating the last three books than I did with the first two.

A similar situation obtains in the case of Deuteronomy, with the many years of research done by Weinfeld. But the work of the three scholars mentioned here should not exclude the many fine commentaries that have appeared since the turn of the century, whether in such series as the International Critical Commentary or in individual volumes or studies of Israelite cult and law, by Jews and Christians alike. Then, too, the reader may turn to the *Anchor Bible Dictionary,* or the shorter *Harper's Bible Dictionary,* for instance, for an in-depth look at many issues. Finally, I would like to single out the helpful introductions by Hallo in the Plaut commentary; these are now reprinted with additional material in Hallo 1991.

I have therefore approached the last three books of the Torah with some trepidation and caution, knowing that to present them for the general reader in translation, and through brief notes and commentary, is an undertaking full of potential pitfalls. But these books, no less than the more famous and accessible first two, constitute the "instruction" or "teaching" found in the Five Books of Moses, and are well worth the effort required to experience them. The reader is directed to the works mentioned in "Suggestions for Further Reading" for the opportunity to digest the great wealth of material now available.

For the sake of simplification, in the Commentary and Notes to these books, citations from the major commentaries of Levine, Milgrom, Weinfeld, and now Tigay (appearing variously in *The Anchor Bible* and *The New JPS Commentary*) are not followed by their publication dates; these appear in the "Suggestions" section just mentioned. The same holds for the Leviticus commentaries of Bamberger (in Plaut) and Wenham.

ויקרא

LEVITICUS

NOW HE CALLED

ON TRANSLATING LEVITICUS

THE BOOK OF LEVITICUS, ALONG WITH OTHER PARTS OF THE TORAH THAT DEAL WITH cultic and legal matters, presents particular problems for a translator who chooses to work in the Buber-Rosenzweig mode. There are a number of technical terms which, in addition to their constant repetition in the text, inviting overemphasis on strangeness, are difficult to render accurately into English. For their part, Buber and Rosenzweig translated what they understood as the meaning of these terms, even if it meant creating new words in German that made little sense to someone not familiar with the Hebrew concepts. Some examples are found below.

My initial inclination was to leave the names of sacrifices, etc., in Hebrew transcription, but I have come to feel that this places an undue burden on the English reader. With some reservations I have therefore opted for a mix of transcription and translation.

Buber saw the names of several sacrifices as suggesting movement between the human and the divine. Thus the names of the two most common sacrifices, *korban* and *ola,* were rendered "Nearbringing" and "Highbringing" in B-R. I have utilized "near-offering" and "offering-up"; in the case of the former, the intent of the text may simply have been to indicate what the worshiper "brings-near" to the altar, although the effect was certainly understood to bring humans closer to God. A third type of sacrifice, the *minha,* which B-R rendered as "leading-gift," always indicates a "grain-gift" in cultic texts. My German predecessors would undoubtedly not have approved of my less radical approach to these terms; I have, however, followed them in retaining "bringing-near" as a verb, denoting variously "to bring," "to sacrifice," and "to officiate" (in the sanctuary), which I have indicated in the Notes.

As for *hattat* and *asham,* these two key sacrifices have a number of meanings in the text. I have chosen to retain them in transcription, providing occasional translations on location or explanations in the notes.

A most important term in the priestly material is the adjective *tamei* (along with its noun, *tum'a*). The word refers to a ritual state, the existence of which was understood in ancient Israel as a grave danger to the "purity" of the sanctuary. It is not, however, "uncleanness" in the physical sense, but a state akin perhaps to radioactivity: in this case, it drives away the divine presence from Israel (cf. Greenstein 1984a for another analogy). B-R used "stained/tainted" in their translation; most recent scholars use "polluted" and "pollution" to describe the phenomenon. I have accepted the latter in my discussions below but have chosen to stay with Hebrew transcription in the text itself, allowing for a wider and less overtly negative form of the term. Were I in a flippant mood brought on by political correctness, I might suggest "ritually challenged" for *tamei*.

One more problem in translating Leviticus is worthy of mention. A Buber-Rosenzweig type of rendition is fairly adaptable for narrative and even poetry; but in legal and cultic passages, such as we find in abundance in Leviticus, it imposes huge constraints on the translator. Recent English translations such as JPS and the New Revised Standard Version have conveyed the basic meaning of these passages in reasonably clear language. I, on the other hand, have not found it possible to avoid awkward English in this material. I hope nevertheless that, despite the difficulties involved for the reader, the rhetoric and structure—and sometimes the obscurity—of the Hebrew, which left the text open to later disagreement and interpretation, will still be visible and instructive.

A final note on translation practices. Buber and Rosenzweig did not always hold to the principle of one Hebrew root, one corresponding German root, if this was unimportant or simply an impossibility. I have similarly on occasion deviated from full consistency in translating certain words. So, for instance, I found that the many different uses of Heb. *shamor*—"guard," "keep," "take-care"—simply could not be standardized in translation. In the main, when I have found it possible to connect passages via their standardized language in the Hebrew, I have done so in English.

ON THE BOOK OF LEVITICUS AND ITS STRUCTURE

FOR MOST LAY READERS, THE THIRD OF THE FIVE BOOKS OF MOSES PRESENTS FORMIDAble obstacles. Many people find it difficult to relate to the description of ritual slaughter of animals and the disposal of their blood and flesh in the opening section of the book, or to the detailed prescriptions regarding bodily functions, skin disease, and mold in Chapters 12–15. Others experience Leviticus as obscure: Why exactly do Aaron's sons die in Chapter 10? How can one explain the ritual of the scapegoat in Chapter 16? A frequently encountered reaction to the book is the desire to get on to the book of Numbers—which at least has some intriguing narratives such as Moses' sin and punishment, the faint-heartedness of the spies, and Balaam's reversed prophecies.

Yet Leviticus, as it has been placed in the Torah, signals that something of singular importance is at work. The book, after all, occurs at the center of the overall five-book structure. Unlike the other four, it is set entirely around Mount Sinai, and so it forms, geographically as well as structurally, the heart of the Torah document. In addition, the priestly interests so clearly presented in Leviticus appear throughout the Torah: as genealogical lists (Genesis, Exodus, Numbers), descriptions of rituals (Exodus, Numbers, Deuteronomy), and details about the building of the desert "Dwelling" of God (Exodus). Indeed, the opening chapter of it all,

Gen. I (the Creation story), has strong links in both its themes and terminology with the priestly law.

Leviticus in fact presents a significant strain, conventionally termed the "priestly" view, in biblical thought. Anthropologically considered, it sheds important light on the outlook of some of those who compiled and read the Hebrew Bible. And the process did not stop there. Many of the categories found in Leviticus were continued and expanded by later Judaism: regulations concerning sexuality and diet, concepts of separation and holiness, and how to deal with one's fellow human beings in a variety of economic and social settings. These found expression in different but still recognizable form simultaneously in the development of Christianity.

In late antiquity Leviticus was known as *Torat Kohanim,* the Priestly Instruction (or simultaneously understood, as Levine suggests, as the Instruction of the Priests). Given both the concerns of the priestly writers and the wording they use to express those concerns, I see Leviticus as the Book of Separations, the book in which are set forth distinctions between a whole range of aspects of ancient Israelite experience and practice: holy and profane; ritual purity and pollution; permitted and forbidden in sexuality and diet; Israelites and others; and priests, Levites, and common folk among the Israelites. This near-obsession with drawing lines (or, as Douglas has presented it, concentric circles) may in some sense reflect the position of Israel in the ancient Near East as a small, beleaguered newcomer in a region of hoary empires, situated on land that was constantly invaded by both great powers and local foes. It may also be an echo of the larger Bronze Age and Iron Age process of change from the former, well-nigh universal worship of the Mother Goddess, to the later patriarchal societies with which the Western world still deals through its three monotheistic religions and their cultural outgrowths.

Overarching the theme of separations or distinctions, through much of the book, is the polarity of order/disorder, represented best in Leviticus by the problem of life and death. As many scholars have noted, regulations regarding sacrifice here connect up with symbolically offering up human life—through the substitution of an animal—to the deity; blood is avoided at all costs, due to its connoting life. Animals that may be used for food (as well as for sacrifice) are in the main those which do not consume other living creatures. Pollutants which endanger the purity of the sanctuary ("Dwelling") include bodily emissions which the Israelites connected with death (e.g., menstrual blood and "wasted" semen). Finally, the complex system of purification from some kind of skin disease may well originate in the similarity between disease and death. In sum, then, it is no surprise that, two books later, the Deuteronomic Moses implores the people to "choose life" rather than the "death" engendered by improper behavior by both priests and commoners.

Interestingly, the strong urge to make order (ritual laws) out of disorder (the chaotic processes of human life, from killing animals for food to sexual relations) is reflected in other aspects of the Torah—most notably in the narrative portrayal of the descent lines from father Abraham. Here, the discontinuity represented by sibling rivalries and other threats to survival is countered by God's establishing a kind of continuity through the choosing of younger brothers. In this case, the strong hand of ritual control is replaced by the somewhat hazardous element of surprise and close calls. But it does manage to provide for family continuity and, ultimately, the survival of the people. Whether this points to early or later experiences historically is the subject of ongoing and unresolved debate among biblical scholars. A widely accepted possibility is that the Torah as we have it was edited by priestly editors living in or shortly after the Babylonian Exile (6th–5th centuries B.C.E.), and that those editors took earlier material (which itself was already multilayered) and adapted it into an overall scheme expressing promise, disobedience, destruction, and survival/hope (cf. Fox 1993).

In point of fact, Leviticus is best viewed as only a part, albeit the major one as a bloc, of a major thrust of the Torah. According to most biblical scholars, the "priestly" worldview, and the texts that may be attributed to it, makes its appearance with the very chapter with which the entire Torah begins, Gen. 1. Here distinctions and ordering are at the very heart of the text. God, immediately after his first creation-by-word (light), "separates" between light and darkness, then goes on to perform the same operation between heavenly waters (the storehouses of rain) and earthly ones. His remaining acts of creation involve putting heavenly bodies, vegetation, and animal life in order—each "according to its kind," on specific days of creation. Animals are distinguished from plants through their receiving vocal divine blessing; humans from animals through the addition to the blessing of the phrase "have dominion over" the rest of living things. At the same time, humans are told that they may eat only what grows from the ground, implying that to do otherwise would be a violation of the order of things. Crowning the whole account is the poem (Gen. 2:1–4a) about God's "finishing" of the "work" of creation, symbolized by his "hallowing" (making holy or separate-for-God) the seventh day. In Gen. 1, then, we are presented with a brief but complete vision of the cosmos as ordered in space, time, and life-forms, under the aegis of a metasexual, nonviolent, and benevolent deity.

As Genesis unfolds under priestly influence, humans are presented with basic rules and warned of the consequences if those rules are broken. The paradisical situation of Adam and Eve (no labor, vegetarianism, no danger from animals, and sexual innocence) is disrupted by human disobedience, resulting in banishment from Eden—a shattering of the previous wholeness and order. Cain's murder of his brother leads to the same punishment: uprootedness and hard labor. The mixing of divine and human beings in Gen. 6:1–2 results in a clear distinction being established by God, that humans will henceforth be limited in age. Finally, the account of the universal flood in Chapters 6–9 presents a picture that uses a number of Leviticus motifs. The earth is to be destroyed because human wrongdoing has "ruined" it (or, in Levitical language, "polluted" it). Animal life is rescued by means of taking pairs of animals aboard the ark—with Leviticus's distinctions of "pure" and impure dutifully mentioned. Noah's three sons, who also come onto the ark, later become the forefathers of three great divisions of humanity, as laid out in detail in the genealogical lists of Chapters 10–11. Finally, the new beginning of the cosmos, with Noah as a second Adam (cf. the latter's blessing in 1:28 with that of the former in 9:1–2), is accompanied by both animal sacrifices and dietary restrictions (the introduction of meat is new, accompanied by the caveat—as in Lev. 17—that blood is not to be consumed).

A major part of the priestly scheme emerges with the detailed instructions concerning the construction of the Tabernacle (God's place of "Dwelling" on earth) and the priestly vestments that are to be worn there, in Ex. 25–31 (with much of this material repeated in narrative form in Chapters 35–40). The details make sense as part of a larger picture, in which the closer one gets to the "Holiest Holy-Shrine" where God takes up dwelling, the more central the measurements of space and the more precious the materials used. This concentric sense of order is reflected also in the layout of the wilderness camp of the Israelites in Num. 2. Thus the Tabernacle functions as a minicosmos, a visible and ritual representation of the creation itself. Through the layout of curtains within and tribal encampments without, space is ordered; through the festivals (enumerated in Leviticus and Deuteronomy, with some mention in Exodus as well), time is ordered. And, thanks to the provisions laid out in Leviticus, through priest/lay hierarchy, dietary rules, and sacrificial regulations, life-forms are ordered. The result is an almost utopian scheme. It is a world in which everything and everyone are to take their place under the perfect worship of a perfect God, banishing or avoiding death, defect, and disorder. In the priestly view, the world is to be an echo of the divine order that is portrayed in the Creation story.

Viewed in the perspective of priestly concerns (only part of which we have just outlined), Leviticus is largely concerned with the potential disruption of this utopia. If Genesis chronicles threats to the fulfillment of God's promises to Abraham, if Numbers recounts threats to his descendants' survival on their march through the wilderness, then Leviticus concentrates on threats to Israel's life with God. It presents a whole system of rules designed, first, to provide for purification and reconciliation with God through the sacrificial cult; second, to protect sanctuary, priests, land, and people from estrangement from God (via "pollution" of various kinds); and, finally, to establish a code of behavior that will ensure the perpetual enjoyment of God's blessings on the land promised to Israel's ancestors. From this it can readily be seen how Leviticus, far from being of interest to specialists and historians only, is in fact a crucial part of the Torah—perhaps its most crucial part, in that it supplies the ideological center of gravity for the whole. Once Leviticus is added to the narratives, poems, laws, and lists that comprise the rest of the Torah, a picture emerges that is more than literature and more than history. The five books become the multilayered and multifaceted monument that has been studied, puzzled over, and built upon for over two millennia.

In sum, the world of the priestly strain in the Torah is a realm of desired order and perfection, a realm in which wholeness is to reign, in which anomaly and undesired mixture are not permitted, and in which boundaries are zealously guarded. The human body becomes symbolic of the cosmos: its life/death boundary is marked, and troublesome flows from it are carefully regulated. The land of Israel becomes symbolic of the cosmos: too much evildoing pollutes it, to the point where it can do naught else but "vomit out" its settlers (as it vomited out the previous ones). The animal kingdom, from which humans are allowed to take life under carefully prescribed circumstances, becomes symbolic of cosmic values, through heightening awareness of predator and victim, and careful avoidance of blood, the symbol of life. Indeed, in the system of Leviticus, it is no wonder that death is the major pollutant, and that blood of acceptable animal sacrifice is the agent through which human beings find atonement for minor pollutants.

The book as it is presently laid out falls into three major sections, with a number of chapters that function either as connectors or appendices to various sections. Linkages and connecting theme words will be spelled out in more detail in the commentary; for the moment, the following outline may suffice:

> I The Sacrificial Cult
> 1–7 Sacrificial Offerings: Their Ritual and Disposal
> 8–9 The Installation of the Priests
> 10 Systems Failure
>
> II Ritual Pollution and Purification
> 11 Forbidden and Permitted Foods: Transition
> 12–15 Pollution from Bodily Fluids and Skin Disease
> 16 Purifying the Sanctuary and the High Priest
> Appendix: 17 On the Shedding of Animal Blood
>
> III Holiness
> 18 Pollution from Forbidden Unions: Transition
> 19:3–4 Frame at Beginning
> 19–20 Holiness in Public/Private Behavior
> 21–22 Holiness in Priestly Behavior
> 23 Holiness in the Calendar
> 24 Miscellaneous
> 25 Regulations Concerning Land and Slaves
> 26:1–2 Frame at End
> 26:3–46 Holiness Confirmed or Denied: The Blessing and the Curse
> Appendix: 27 Assessments for the Priests

Other commentators have of course seen it differently. Most follow the traditional scholarly approach of starting the "Holiness Code" with Chapter 17; Levine rightly parallels it to the beginnings of other law collections in the Torah (Ex. 20:19–23 and Deut. 12; the ending here in Chapter 26 also parallels the endings in the other two codes). Hallo understands the structure as 1–11: Rites of Consumption; 12–16: Rites of Purification; and 17–26: Holiness.

Overshadowing the clear three-part structure, however one wants to divide it up, is the complex issue of two apparent documents or schools of thought. Biblical scholarship terms these P ("Priestly") and H ("Holiness"), and roughly attributes the first part of the book (through Chap. 16) to P, with the rest to H. There has been detailed, ongoing debate about the approaches and dating of these sources. As of this writing, it is generally accepted that H is later than P, but there seem to be numerous interpolations of one source into the other, and it is difficult to place them historically with certainty. Here, as elsewhere in biblical literature, we have a layering effect rather than a clear-cut delineation of "authors." As usual, that appears to have been intentional.

A word should be said about the relationship between law and narrative in the Torah. As Damrosch has noted, the legal and cultic texts in the five books might be seen by modern readers as intrusive. On the surface, they certainly seem to interrupt a good story. Genesis is largely unencumbered by nonaction (except for the genealogical lists—attributed to P!), but the gripping account of the redemption from Egypt in Exodus, and the drama of revelation on and apostasy beneath Mount Sinai, give way to the sober architectural details of the Tabernacle's construction. Similarly, the narratives of the book of Numbers, which are among the most striking in the literature, are set off against a background of censuses, laws about suspected adultery and the taking of vows, Levitical duties in the Dwelling, and an enumeration of sacrificial gifts brought by the tribes, among other things.

The bulk of material in Leviticus, and its placement in the Torah, make it clear that the five books that we have convey their point precisely through the medium of narrative *plus* cult/law. In the Israelite worldview, these two rather distinct forms, which intermingle past, present, and future (Damrosch), fruitfully enrich and explain one another. It is as if a history of the American Revolution contained all of the debates on and drafts of the Declaration of Independence and the Constitution, as well as accounts of battles and biographies of key personalities. That such an approach parallels neither Homeric epic nor ritual texts in their purity of form is exactly the point: we have here a new genre of great complexity and richness, in which narratives exemplify laws and laws follow narratives. The result is truly a torah, a "teaching" or "instruction."

Finally, we might mention the issue of priests and laypeople. Scholars have often seen Leviticus as originating as a manual for priests. What is most fascinating, and perhaps most important (for later history), about this book is the way in which it takes priestly rules and transmutes at least some of them for use in the general populace of ancient Israel. This can be seen most dramatically in the dietary laws, which in other cultures often serve exclusively for priests, and in the area of sexual taboos, which do likewise. In postbiblical Judaism this shift becomes particularly evident: the Jew's dinner table is termed a "sanctuary in miniature" (complete with loaves of bread and the use of salt—two elements found in the ancient sacrificial cult); dietary laws are expanded for the general population to provide for separation of milk and meat; and separation of husband and wife during menstruation, among Orthodox Jews, leaves the context of Sanctuary pollution and finds a home in the context of a philosophy of marriage. Many other examples could be brought of the widening of priestly laws to an entire people. Perhaps most dramatic—and most significant—is the eventual shift of the learning and interpretation of sacred texts away from the priests, who in most cultures served as the guardians of the text (and often the culture's only literate body; cf. medieval Christian Europe). In Judaism of late antiquity, this monopoly was decisively broken; first the scribe and then the rabbi ("master") took over, with learning extended at last to all those who might make the effort to acquire it. The great exception, at least in antiquity, was women—who, it will be noted, were also excluded from priestly functions in the Bible.

Three relatively recent developments make it possible to approach Leviticus as a significant, powerful, and interesting biblical text. The first is the explosion of both full-length and shorter studies of the book and its concerns that have appeared in recent years. The work of Milgrom (1991), Levine (1989), Wenham (1979), Eilberg-Schwartz (1990), and Bamberger (1981), to cite just a few of the English-language studies on aspects of Leviticus, now makes it possible to have a serious entry into the book based largely on advances in understanding the cultures of the ancient Near East. It also, admittedly, puts the translator and commentator in a bind: is it possible to add anything new, or will it suffice simply to summarize? My approach in this volume has been largely the latter, along with suggesting to the reader some fruitful directions for further study.

The second development helpful for approaching Leviticus, which also informs many of the studies just mentioned, is the using of anthropological insights to understand concepts and rituals found in the book. Such an approach places Leviticus in a broader human context, indicating what it does and does not share with other cultural and religious systems. For Leviticus is concerned with the same issues that plague all human societies: how to deal with the boundaries of life and death, how to comprehend and approach the transcendent in life, how to understand one's (or one's nation's) place in the cosmic order, how to make for a just society. Viewed in this light, the book is a "Small Code" (cf. Northrop Frye's designation of the Bible as "the Great Code"). That is, Leviticus need not remain a total mystery to us, to be unraveled only through detailed analysis and even change (Judaism) or substitution (Christianity), but can be understood on its own terms, if approached with care and in the spirit of seeking the larger picture in the details.

Finally, we should mention the aesthetic dimension. Like the other books of the Torah, Leviticus uses its own rhetoric to convey its message. Far from employing flat "priestly" style (whatever that may be), it uses formulas, refrains, and other rhythmical forms to impress its teaching (Heb. *tora*) upon its hearers. This aspect of the book has been the subject of recent study (cf. Paran), but was already echoed in the Buber-Rosenzweig translation. It is my hope that the present volume will contribute to an appreciation of the style of Leviticus.

PART I

THE CULT
AND THE PRIESTHOOD

(1–10)

THE SECOND HALF OF THE BOOK OF EXODUS CONCERNED ITSELF WITH SETTING UP THE sacrificial cult of Israel. It therefore set forth the prescriptions for and construction of a sanctuary and the priestly garments, and laid out a ceremony for the investiture of priests. But the description of how sacrifices were to be offered, and for what purpose, is not part of the book, which as edited seems more interested in contrasting the building of a sanctuary with building cities for the Pharaohs, as part of its portrayal of the victory of the biblical God over the gods of Egypt. Although at the end of the book the "Dwelling" is completed, we do not get to see the various sacral rites performed there.

Leviticus also delays the ordination of the priests, until Chapter 8, preferring instead to begin with a kind of manual on the offering and disposal of sacrifices. It then moves us from the details of sacrifice into the narrative of the sanctuary's dedication and opening rites, providing a natural bridge for Part II, in which ritual pollution and purity, the province of priests, is dealt with.

The function of the sacrificial cult in ancient Israel will be discussed in "On Animal Sacrifice" below. In general it should be noted that the existence of a class or profession whose job it is to mediate between the divine and human realms is widespread in most older cultures, and the Israelite priesthood, whatever its origins and development, was but one of many such groups in the ancient Near East. It existed, to use the language of Exodus, to "serve" God, maintaining his holiness through ritual and helping to maintain the order of sacred culture which was supposed to mirror God's ordering of the cosmos. Accordingly, as we will learn later in Leviticus, priests were to be set apart from the general population in a number of areas. There were strict rules about whom they could and could not marry, and they were barred from coming into any contact with the dead, for instance. Their functions extended beyond sacrifice; they could provide oracular advice in times of need, and taught the people "instructions" (Heb. *torot*) regarding various ritual matters.

As part of an overall scheme, there was a conscious parallel between priests as part of a select circle and sacrificial animals—as well as the people of Israel. That is, all three stood at the center of concentric circles dedicated to God; and as one moved out (toward Levite and commoner, animals permitted for eating and those forbidden, and neighbors and foreigners), one got further and further away from the divine. The hierarchy regarding the cult thus reinforced the theme of separation which we have noted above.

In the view of Milgrom, Israel's cult was distinguished from those of its neighbors by its purposefully ignoring the complex web of rituals regarding demons. The sanctuary was to be purged of ritual pollution, not only by semimagical means (the sprinkling of sacrificial blood) but also and primarily by the confession of wrongdoing and the sincere desire to repent. Then, too, the sanctuary, while in most respects resembling shrines elsewhere in the ancient Near East, omitted certain crucial items, most notably statuary representing the gods and a bed for them to rest on. Finally, certain religious rituals were forbidden, such as mutilation of the priests' bodies. In all these cases, Israel introduced something new into the area of worship.

For many decades there has been major and heated debate by scholars in favor of one or the other scheme for following the history of the priesthood and the cult. There are those who view these institutions as stretching back to Israel's earliest history, while others see strong evidence of a late, possibly even exilic, reworking of the priestly material. Similar arguments dot the landscape of literary criticism of the Torah, in which scholars have tried to divine at what point priestly editors might have put their distinctive stamp on the literature. From Wellhausen in the nineteenth century to Knohl, Milgrom, and Levine in the late twentieth, there has been no lack of theorizing on these issues—and no definitive answers. For the moment we are left to read Leviticus as it is placed in the Torah, with an awareness that a variety of historical and ideological influences are imbedded, if not hidden, in our text.

ON ANIMAL SACRIFICE

ALTHOUGH IT APPEARS EARLIER IN THE TORAH, ANIMAL SACRIFICE RECEIVES ITS FULLest treatment in Leviticus. Besides the opening seven chapters, which are devoted to a relatively brief description of how sacrifices are to be offered and disposed of, many other chapters in the book talk about sacrificial rituals: the installation of the priests (8–9), rules about disposing of the *hattat* sacrifice (10), purification offerings brought in the event of such "polluting" states as childbirth and skin diseases (12–15), and finally the "scapegoat" ceremony of Chapter 16. They appear in most of the later chapters as well.

What function did sacrifice, particularly of animals, play in the religion of ancient Israel? How could a God who proscribed the murder of human beings (Ex. 20:13, 21:12) countenance the taking of animal life for ritual purposes? To answer these questions, we must turn briefly to some of the commonly proposed theories surrounding sacrifice.

The idea of offering up living creatures to the gods is one of hoary antiquity. Walter Burkert, on the basis of the study of Greek religion, suggests that sacrifice is a means of dealing with guilt over the taking of life. That is, the switch from gathering to hunting society, made possible by technology (the invention of tools), while it raised human accomplishment and consciousness to a new level, also brought with it the acute sense of having violated something essential in the cosmic order. Such guilt is not mitigated by the fact that early people hunted for food and not for pleasure. The way of dealing with the guilt, giving life back to the gods, is in a true sense restoration; life is given back for life taken, so that it may ultimately be renewed (contrast this to the profoundly unecological use of living and inorganic resources over the past "civilized" centuries). And it must be done via ritual. In Burkert's view, ritual deals with human anxiety by "raising the ante"—by means of increasing anxiety, it is controlled. So guilt over life-taking is assuaged by making a ritual out of the killing, and the shared experience of trauma helps to create solidarity within the group. Despite the subsequent rise of agriculture, says Burkert, the hunting ritual played out in sacrifice could not be done away with, so ingrained had it become, and the rationale behind sacrifices was therefore transformed. Now domesticated animals could be used, giving greater control over the process.

In another approach, De Vaux (1965) postulates three motives for sacrifice. In the first model, that of "gift," the worshiper brings something of value to the deity. The animal is killed, setting it apart for sacred use; it is burned, turning it into an invisible substance which can rise to the gods. The gift may be for thanksgiving or, more likely, may be to assuage the demonic powers that many societies (especially Mesopotamia, Abraham's homeland) felt controlled everyday life. Giving establishes reciprocal movement; altruism has no place here (Burkert). One is reminded of the elaborate giving ceremonies among many peoples on occasions such as weddings; giving establishes relationship and maintains the social order.

In addition to gifts, another mode of sacrifice involves communion, as nineteenth-century scholars such as Robertson Smith observed. Here the model of the meal is crucial: humans and gods share a great repast, thereby cementing kinship as surely as the closing of business deals is celebrated by drinks and dinner. Passover, both in the Bible and subsequently (even when the sacrifice per se was no longer involved), may serve as a striking example of the effectiveness of such a paradigm.

A final type or function of sacrifice is atonement or expiation. Here a sin, communal or individual, is purged away by the act of sacrifice; the gods receive life as a substitute for the sinner's own, which is symbolized by the victim's blood. The fact that the animals permitted in the Bible for sacrifice are pastoral and hence frequently used metaphorically for the Israelites themselves, is significant in this regard. This approach is further illustrated in the Bible by the end of the Flood story, where God accepts Noah's sacrifice, implying that he accepts animal life (which now, simultaneous with properly offered sacrifice, is permissible for food) in place of that of humans (Eilberg-Schwartz). It should be noted that, in the Bible, sacrifice for the sake of atonement is almost always in reference to unintentional sins, whereas deliberate wrongdoing may not be atoned for through this system.

Which of these rationales is truly at work in Levitical sacrifice? Actually, at various times one can find all of them—the texts present a variety of motives and occasions for sacrifice in biblical Israel, from thanksgiving to purification and reparation. But in general one may say of Israelite sacrifice, as one may say of much of the ritual in Leviticus, that it is designed primarily to maintain or repair the relationship between God and Israel. Such an understanding helps to explain the unity of the book, as we will see in our discussion of pollution: sacrifice was a crucial element in keeping the covenant, and hence God's beneficent presence among the Israelites, intact.

The fact that this reconciliation, as it were, takes place against a background of slaughter should not be as upsetting to moderns as it is usually felt to be. In ironic contrast to our mechanized and mass-produced society, where the killing of animals for food takes place at a remove from our consciousness and from our direct participation, the sacrificial system in fact involved worshiper and priest alike, and the symbolic value of the operation, whatever it may have been in specific cases, lay in its directness, in its consciousness of the taking of life. Some would even maintain that in societies where the practice and rationale for sacrifice has broken down, there is inevitably an increase in intrahuman violence (Girard).

Varied Sacrificial Offerings I (1): The first chapter begins with a description of the *ola,* the "offering-up," which appears throughout the Bible as a standard sacrifice, frequently preceding others. It is characterized by being totally burned on the altar, and functions essentially to bring human beings to the attention of God and to win his acceptance. So the offering-up does not deal with sin, as later sacrifices do (Wenham).

This opening chapter of the book sets the standard pattern for the first seven chapters concerned with sacrifices. It lays out general rules about the preparation and presentation of the offerings; from 7:38 on and throughout the rest of the Torah, specific applications and how they work will be explained (Anderson). Enumerated are the kind of animal to be sacrificed (in order of value, and hence indicating that rich and poor alike have access to the system); the personal participation of the worshiper; and the tasks of the priests. Many of the phrases recur throughout the opening chapters of the book, but the main refrain is the concluding "fire-offering of soothing savor for YHWH." Three kinds of animals appear here; they are, again, all domesticated.

Varied Sacrificial Offerings II (2): The *minha,* understood earlier in the Bible as simply "tribute" or "gift" (cf. Gen. 4:3 and 32:14), comes in the priestly texts to indicate specifically an offering of grain. Using a three-part structure of grain cooked in an oven / griddle / pan, paralleling Chap. 1's cattle / sheep / birds, the description of the *minha* focuses on the type of grain offered, what is added to it, the strictures against fermenting, and the "covenant of salt." The chapter ends with the usual refrain, "a fire-offering for YHWH."

1:1 Now he called to Moshe—
YHWH spoke to him from the Tent of Appointment, saying:

2 Speak to the Children of Israel and say to them:
Anyone—when (one) among you brings-near a near-offering for
YHWH
from domestic-animals: from the herd or from the flock you may
bring-near your near-offering.

3 If an offering-up is his near-offering, from the herd,
(then) male, wholly-sound, let him bring-it-near,
to the entrance of the Tent of Appointment let him bring-it-near,
as acceptance for him, before the presence of YHWH.

4 He is to lean his hand on the head of the offering-up,
that there may be acceptance on his behalf, to effect-ransom for
him.

5 He is to slay the herd-animal (for sacrifice) before the presence of
YHWH,
and the Sons of Aharon, the priests, are to bring-near the blood
and are to dash the blood against the slaughter-site, all around,
that is at the entrance of the Tent of Appointment.

1:1 **Now he called . . . YHWH spoke:** The unusual syntax here links the opening of Leviticus with the revelation at Mount Sinai in Ex. 24:16, the only other passage in the Torah where God "called to Moshe" (in these exact words). Indeed, as Milgrom points out, from the end of Ex. 40 to Num. 9, the Torah contains the bulk of its laws given at Sinai after Ex. 20–23. Leviticus thus verbally returns to the revelation of law.

2 **Anyone:** Including both men and women. As these texts unfold, I will be using "he," as the Hebrew does, but both Hebrew and English should be understood as including both sexes in these contexts. **near-offering:** For this and the rendering of other technical terms, cf. "On Translating Leviticus," above.

3 **offering-up:** Or "ascent-offering." Others, "holocaust," to show that this sacrifice is to be wholly consumed by fire. **wholly-sound:** Perfect, unblemished—that is, fit for sacrifice. The adjective is used of humans as well (cf. Gen. 6:9, referring to Noah,

and 17:1, referring to Avraham), in the sense of "wholehearted, perfect, full of integrity." **before the presence of YHWH:** A refrain in these texts, usually indicating a location at the sanctuary.

4 **lean his hand:** The meaning of this act has puzzled commentators. It may symbolize ownership, a statement of the reason for the sacrifice, or perhaps identification with the animal (as a substitute for the life of the worshiper). **to effect-ransom:** Heb. root *k-p-r* (again, see "On Translating Leviticus"). The aspect of "ransoming" mentioned here does not recur with the other sacrifices; some have postulated an original nonpriestly venue for this type of offering.

5 **He is to slay . . . (for sacrifice):** Technically, slitting the animal's throat. This is apparently done by the worshiper himself. As in similar cases, I have left the text ambiguous here regarding the principal actor. **dash the blood:** For Milgrom, this action prevents murder being imputed to the sacrificer—he has returned the "life" (namely, the blood) to God.

6 Then he is to flay the offering-up, and is to section it into its
sections.

7 Now the Sons of Aharon the priest are to put fire upon the
slaughter-site
and are to arrange wood upon the fire.

8 The Sons of Aharon, the priests, are to arrange the sections, the
head and the suet,
upon the wood that is upon the fire, that is upon the slaughter-
site,

9 its innards and its shins he is to wash in water;
and the priest is to turn all-of-it into smoke upon the slaughter-
site,
for an offering-up, a fire-offering of soothing savor for YHWH.

10 Now if from the flock is his near-offering,
from the sheep or from the goats, for an offering-up,
(then) male, wholly-sound, let him bring-it-near.

11 He is to slay it on the flank of the slaughter-site, northward,
before the presence of YHWH,
and the Sons of Aharon, the priests, are to dash its blood against
the slaughter-site, all around.

12 Then he is to section it into its sections, with its head and with its
suet,
and the priest is to arrange them upon the wood that is upon the
fire, that is upon the slaughter-site,

13 the innards and the shins he is to wash in water;
and the priest is to bring all-of-it near and turn it into smoke upon
the slaughter-site:
it is an offering-up,
a fire-offering of soothing savor for YHWH.

---

6 **flay:** Or "strip the skin." The hide (which goes to the
priests) is the only part of the offering-up not
burned.
7 **Sons of Aharon:** The priests, not only Aaron's own
sons but those from the tribe of Levi, who were
seen as descending from him.
9 **fire-offering:** B-R render Heb. *ishe* with "fire-pre-
sent"; some scholars link the word with Ugaritic

itht, "gift." Wenham notes the parallel with "food"
in a number of passages. **soothing savor:** Or "scent
of assent" (L. Rosenwald). It first appears in Gen.
8:21, where Noah offers sacrifices after the Flood,
and the pleasing smell leads God to vow never again
to annihilate the earth. So the function of the sacrifice in this chapter, at least, is to gain God's favor and
compassion.

14 Now if from fowl is his offered-up near-offering for YHWH,
    he is to bring-near from turtledoves or from young pigeons as his
        near-offering.
15 The priest is to bring-it-near upon the slaughter-site
    and pinch off its head,
    he is to turn it into smoke upon the slaughter-site,
    and its blood is to be drained out against the side-wall of the
        slaughter-site.
16 He is to remove its crissum by means of its plumage
    and is to fling it next to the slaughter-site, eastward,
    into the place of the ashes.
17 He is to tear it open by its wings—he is not to divide (it)!—
    and the priest is to turn it into smoke upon the slaughter-site,
        upon the wood that is upon the fire:
    it is an offering-up,
    a fire-offering of soothing savor for YHWH.

2:1 A person—when he brings-near a near-offering of a grain-gift for
        YHWH,
    of (proper) flour shall his near-offering be.
    He is to pour oil upon it and is to put frankincense upon it,
2   then he is to bring it to the Sons of Aharon, the priests.
    He is to scoop from there a scoopful from its flour and from its
        oil, along with all its frankincense;
    the priest is to turn its reminder-portion into smoke upon the
        slaughter-site,
    a fire-offering of soothing savor for YHWH.
3 Now what is left of the grain-gift (is) Aharon's and his sons',
    a holiest holy-portion from the fire-offerings of YHWH.

---

15 **its blood is to be drained out:** Not dashed against the altar; a bird does not contain much blood, compared to a grazing animal.
16 **crissum:** The anal area (Milgrom); others, "crop," the throat pocket where food stays during digestion.
2:1 **flour:** As opposed to "meal," this was made from the hard kernels of the wheat that remain after the removal of bran. Others, "choice flour," "fine meal," "semolina."

2 **frankincense:** Perhaps an indicator of the festive nature of this sacrifice. **reminder-portion:** Others "token portion." It apparently functions to remind God of the whole offering, most of which is eaten by the priests.
3 **holiest holy-portion:** The phrase *kodesh kodashim* recurs in connection with the cult, indicating, variously, the inner sanctum of the Tabernacle ("Dwelling"), objects, and sacrifices. The food here is to be eaten by the priests in a holy area.

Varied Sacrificial Offerings III (3): The purpose of the so-called *shalom* sacrifice has been debated. Levine, for one, sees it as a "sacred gift of greeting," intended to address God in the fellowship of other laypeople and priests at a sacred meal. This communal, lay aspect of the sacrifice is signifcant. Some scholars have understood animal sacrifice to be essentially humanity's way of bonding with the gods (as well as with dead ancestors), and would thus see in the present form, with its emphasis on the meat, an example of this idea.

Unlike the obligatory sacrifices, the shalom sacrifice accepts a variety of animals, and the rules regarding them are not as stringent. Some theorize that originally all meat-eating in ancient Israel was of this type.

Once again, we have the division into larger and smaller domestic animals. Notable is the descriptive refrain regarding the disposal of the animals' innards.

4 When you bring-near a near-offering of a grain-gift baked in an
    oven,
  (it is to be) of flour: *matza*/unleavened cakes mixed with oil,
    matza wafers spread with oil.
5 And if a grain-gift on a griddle is your near-offering,
  flour mixed with oil—unleavened shall it be.
6 Crumble it into crumbled-bits, and pour oil upon it,
  it is a grain-gift.
7 And if a grain-gift in a frying-pan is your near-offering,
  of flour in oil shall it be made.
8 Should you bring a grain-gift that is made in (any of) these ways
    to YHWH,
  it is to be brought-near to the priest, and he is to bring-it-close to
    the slaughter-site.
9 The priest is to set-aside from the grain-gift its reminder-portion
  and is to turn it into smoke upon the slaughter-site;
  a fire-offering of soothing savor for YHWH.
10 And what is left of the grain-gift is Aharon's and his sons',
  a holiest holy-portion from the fire-offerings of YHWH.
11 Every grain-gift that you bring-near to YHWH, it is not to be made
    leavened,
  for any fermentation and any date-honey—you may not turn
    (any) of it into smoke as a fire-offering to YHWH;
12 as a near-offering of premier-fruits you may bring them near to
    YHWH,
  but upon the slaughter-site they are not to offer them up as a
    soothing savor.

---

4 *matza*/**unleavened:** This is typical of Israelite practice; grain connected to the cult is not to be suscep-
tible to rotting—because its imperfection would
denigrate divine worship. Cf. v.11 below.
5 **griddle:** Resulting in a crisp wafer-type food.

7 **pan:** A frying pan; the result was a breadlike product.
11 **date-honey:** Heb. *devash* may well have this meaning generally, even including the oft-used phrase "a
land flowing with milk and honey."

13 All your near-offerings of a grain-gift you are to salt with salt,
    you are not to omit the salt of your God's covenant from atop
        your grain-gift,
    atop all your near-offerings you are to bring-near salt.

14 Now if you bring-near a grain-gift of firstfruits to Yʜᴡʜ,
    budding-grain, parched with fire, grits of fresh-grain you are to
        bring-near as your grain-gift of firstfruits.

15 You are to put on it oil,
    you are to place on it frankincense,
    it is a grain-gift.

16 The priest is to turn the reminder-portion into smoke, from its
        grits and from its oil, along with all its frankincense,
    a fire-offering for Yʜᴡʜ.

3:1 Now if a slaughter-offering of *shalom* is his near-offering:
    if it is from the herd that he brings-it-near,
    whether male or whether female, wholly-sound he is to bring-it-
        near, before the presence of Yʜᴡʜ.

2 He is to lean his hand on the head of his near-offering,
    and he is to slay it at the entrance of the Tent of Appointment,
    and the Sons of Aharon, the priests, are to dash the blood against
        the slaughter-site, all around.

3 Then he is to bring-near from the slaughter-offering of *shalom*, a
        fire-offering to Yʜᴡʜ:
    the fat that covers the innards and all the fat that is about the
        innards,

---

13 **with salt:** In a number of Middle Eastern cultures, continuing down to the present day, salt is used in the sealing of an agreement, hence the term "salt of the covenant" (others, "binding agreement"). Wenham points out that salt was considered indestructible in the ancient world, hence its use as a symbol of permanence here. Or it may simply be that the expensive and tasty nature of salt is the crucial factor here.

14 **firstfruits:** Not literally "fruit," but figuratively, the first-processed (= best) of the grain.

3:1 **slaughter-offering of *shalom*:** Or "slaughter-meal of *shalom*." Earlier translations use "peace offering," which is now felt less likely to be accurate than the widely accepted "sacred gift of greeting" (*shalom* connotes well-being, wholeness, and also greeting). **whether male or whether female:** Interestingly, female animals, usually excluded from sacrifice because of their reproductive value, are included here.

3 **the fat** etc.: Perhaps symbolizing the choicest part of the animal, it denotes here the removable fat around internal organs. The kidneys may be stressed here because of the belief that they were, in humans, the seat of the emotions (Wenham).

4 the two kidneys and the fat that is about them, that is on the
tendons,
and the extension on the liver—along with the kidneys he is to
remove it.
5 And the Sons of Aharon are to turn it (all) into smoke upon the
slaughter-site,
along with the offering-up that is upon the wood, that is upon
the fire,
—a fire-offering of soothing savor for YHWH.

6 Now if from the flock is his near-offering,
as a slaughtered-offering of *shalom* for YHWH,
male or female, wholly-sound he is to bring-it-near.
7 If it is a sheep that he brings-near as a near-offering,
he is to bring-it-near before the presence of YHWH.
8 He is to lean his hand on the head of his near-offering,
and he is to slay it in front of the Tent of Appointment,
and the Sons of Aharon are to dash its blood against the
slaughter-site, all around.
9 Then he is to bring-near, from the slaughtered-offering of
shalom—as a fire-offering for YHWH—
its fat:
the whole thick tail, close to the backbone he is to remove it,
the fat that covers the innards and all the fat that is about the
innards,
10 the two kidneys and the fat that is on them, that is on the
tendons,
and the extension on the liver—along with the kidneys he is to
remove it.
11 Then the priest is to turn it into smoke upon the slaughter-site
as food, a fire-offering for YHWH.

4 **extension on the liver:** A protrusion at the lower
part.
9 **the whole thick tail:** This kind of sheep has a long,
thick, bushy tail. It was highly valued, and hence appropriately offered to God.

11 **food:** Heb. *lehem,* which in narrower contexts
means simply "bread."

517

Obligatory Sacrificial Offerings I (4): The first of these, the *hattat*, is the subject of voluminous recent debate among scholars. Formerly translated as "sin-offering," it is now (thanks to Milgrom) understood more accurately as a purification offering in a variety of settings. The *hattat* decontaminates the sanctuary, and apparently individuals as well, and so is extraordinarily important in Israelite cultic thinking and practice. B-R rendered it (as have others) as a "de-sin offering," which, while inelegant, preserves the biblical connection between sin (moral pollution) and ritual pollution. Again the sacrifice involves a multiple structure, dealing with the different components of the community: priests, community as a whole, leaders, and individuals. The High Priest's ritual is more elaborate than those that follow, as befits the representative of the community. Once his ritual is complete, we encounter for the other parties the refrain "and he/they shall be granted-pardon."

Central to the *hattat*-offering is the use of its blood as a detergent to absorb and purify the pollution that has accrued in the sanctuary. As a prime signifier of life, it will have this function a number of times in the Torah.

12 Now if it is a goat that is his near-offering:
   he is to bring-it-near, before the presence of YHWH.

13 He is to lean his hand on its head
   and he is to slay it in front of the Tent of Appointment;
   and the Sons of Aharon are to dash its blood against the
      slaughter-site, all around.

14 Then he is to bring-near from it his near-offering—a fire-offering
      for YHWH:
   the fat that covers the innards and all the fat that is about the
      innards,

15 the two kidneys and the fat that is on them, that is on the
      tendons,
   and the extension on the liver—along with the kidneys he is to
      remove it.

16 The priest is to turn them into smoke upon the slaughter-site
   as food, a fire-offering of soothing savor,
   —all the fat is for YHWH,

17 a law for the ages, into your generations, throughout all your
      settlements:
   any fat, any blood, you are not to eat!

4:1 Now YHWH spoke to Moshe, saying:

2 Speak to the Children of Israel, saying:
   (Any) person—when one sins in error
   regarding any of YHWH's commandments that should not be
      done,
   by doing any one of them:

3 if the Anointed Priest should sin, bringing-guilt upon the people,
   he is to bring-near, for the sin that he has sinned,

---

16 **all the fat is for YHWH:** This phrase extends beyond
the usual ending pattern in these chapters of "a fire-
offering for YHWH"; the change is a rhetorical device
meant to emphasize a point.

17 **throughout all your settlements:** And thus beyond
the holy places! (Levine)

4:2 **sins:** Heb. *teheta'*; more properly, it means "fails"
(B-R) or "misses" (as with an arrow). The word connotes giving offense to or wronging God (or another person).   **in error:** That is, unintentionally.

3 **Anointed Priest:** The High Priest.   **bringing-guilt:**
Or "blame." He is responsible not only for his own
actions, but his misdeeds potentially pollute the
whole community, for whom he is the representative.   *hattat:* Cf. "On Translating Leviticus," above.
It should be pronounced "hah*taht.*"

a bull, a young of the herd, wholly-sound, for Yhwh as a
     hattat/decontamination-offering.

4   He is to bring the bull to the entrance of the Tent of
          Appointment, before the presence of Yhwh,
     he is to lean his hand on the head of the bull
     and he is to slay the bull before the presence of Yhwh.

5   Then the Anointed Priest is to take some of the blood of the bull
     and is to bring it into the Tent of Appointment,

6   the priest is to dip his finger in the blood
     and is to sprinkle some of the blood seven times, before the
          presence of Yhwh,
     in front of the curtain of the Holy-Shrine.

7   Then the priest is to put some of the blood on the horns of the
          site of fragrant smoking-incense, before the presence of
          Yhwh,
     that is in the Tent of Appointment;
     as for all the (rest of the) blood of the bull, he is to pour it out at
          the foundation of the slaughter-site of offering-up
     that is (at) the entrance of the Tent of Appointment.

8   As for all of the fat of the bull of the *hattat*-offering, he is to set it
          (all) aside from it:
     the fat that covers the innards and all the fat that is about the
          innards,

9   the two kidneys and the fat that is about them, that is on the
          tendons,
     and the extension on the liver—along with the kidneys he is to
          remove it

10 just as it is set-aside from the ox of the slaughter-offering of
          shalom.
     And the priest is to turn them into smoke on the slaughter-site of
          offering-up.

6   **in front of the curtain:** Separating the Holy Area
     from the "Holiest Holy-Shrine"; thus, sprinkling
     the blood near the curtain was as close as one could
     normally get to God (Milgrom).

7   **horns of the site:** The purpose of these four corner
     "horns," found in archaeological remains all over

ancient Israel, is unknown. Milgrom theorizes that
daubing blood on them symbolically purified the
whole altar, by means of the extremities symbolizing the whole.

8   **set . . . aside:** Lit. "lift off."

11 As for the skin of the bull, and all its flesh,
     along with its head, along with its shins, and its innards and its
       dung:
12 he is to take out all (the rest of) the bull, outside the camp,
     to a (ritually) pure place, to the ash dump,
     and he is to burn it upon pieces-of-wood, in fire;
     upon the ash dump it is to be burned.

13 Now if the entire community of Israel errs,
     and the matter is hidden from the eyes of the assembly
     so that they do one of any of the things (regarding) YHWH's
       commandments that should not be done,
     and so incur-guilt:
14 when it becomes-known, the sin that they sinned,
     the assembly are to bring-near a bull, a young of the herd, as a
       hattat-offering;
     they are to bring it before the Tent of Appointment.
15 The elders of the community are to lean their hands on the head
       of the bull, before the presence of YHWH,
     and one is to slay the bull before the presence of YHWH.
16 Then the Anointed Priest is to bring some of the blood of the
       bull into the Tent of Appointment;
17 the priest is to dip his finger in some of the blood
     and is to sprinkle (it) seven times before the presence of YHWH,
     in front of the curtain.
18 And some of the blood he is to put on the horns of the slaughter-
       site that is before the presence of YHWH
     that is in the Tent of Appointment;
     as for all the (rest of the) blood, he is to pour it out at the
       foundation of the slaughter-site of offering-up
     that is (at) the entrance of the Tent of Appointment.

11-12 **As for the skin** etc.: The High Priest cannot eat from his own *hattat*-offering in the same way that he eats from others', as that would be in a sense profiting from his wrongdoing.

13 **the entire community:** Here *eda* indicates the whole people, not just the leaders (as often elsewhere in the Torah) (Milgrom). The passage rein-forces the idea of group responsibility, a concept well illustrated in Deut. 21:1-9, where a town must atone for an unsolved murder committed within its borders. **they do:** The community. **incur-guilt:** Whether or not they are cognizant of what they have done wrong (Levine).

19 As for all its fat, he is to set it (all) aside from it
and turn it into smoke on the slaughter-site.

20 He is to do with the bull just as he did with the bull of the *hattat*-
offering, thus is he to do with it;
the priest shall effect-purgation on their behalf, and they shall be
granted-pardon.

21 He is to take the bull outside the camp,
and he is to burn it just as one burned the first bull;
it is a *hattat*-offering for the assembly!

22 Where a leader sins,
by doing any one of (the things) regarding the commandments of
YHWH his God that should not be done, in error,
and so incurs-guilt,

23 or it is made known to him his sin that he has sinned:
he is to bring (as) his near-offering: a hairy-one of goats, male,
wholly-sound.

24 He is to lean his hand on the head of the hairy-one
and it is to be slain at the place where the offering-up is slain,
before the presence of YHWH;
it is a *hattat*-offering.

25 The priest is to take some of the blood of the *hattat* with his
finger
and is to put (it) on the horns of the slaughter-site of offering-up;
its blood he is to pour out at the foundation of the slaughter-site
of offering-up.

26 All its fat he is to turn into smoke on the slaughter-site,
like the fat of the slaughter-offering of *shalom,*
thus the priest is to effect-purgation for him from his sin,
and he shall be granted-pardon.

---

20 **effect-purgation:** Or "effect-ransom." **granted-pardon:** The verb is not used of humans in the Bible; so perhaps the idea is not forgiveness in the usual sense of "forgive and forget"—there is reconciliation, but punishment still occurs (Milgrom).

22 **leader:** Of a tribe (Wenham).

27 Now if any person sins in error, from among the people of the
   land,
   by doing one (thing) regarding the commandments of YHWH that
      should not be done,
   and incurs-guilt,

28 or it is made known to him the sin that he sinned:
   he is to bring as his near-offering a hairy-one of goats, wholly-
      sound, female, for the sin whereby he sinned.

29 He is to lean his hand on the head of the *hattat*-offering
   and is to slay the *hattat*-offering, at the place of the offering-up.

30 The priest is to take some of the blood of the *hattat*-offering with
      his finger
   and is to put (it) on the horns of the slaughter-site of offering-up;
   all (the rest of) its blood he is to pour out at the foundation of the
      slaughter-site of offering-up.

31 All of its fat, he is to remove, as was removed the fat from upon
      the slaughter-offering of *shalom*,
   and the priest is to turn it into smoke on the slaughter-site,
   as a soothing savor for YHWH;
   thus the priest is to effect-purgation for him,
   and he shall be granted-pardon.

32 If (it is) a sheep he brings as his near-offering for a *hattat*-offering,
   a female, wholly-sound, he is to bring.

33 He is to lean his hand on the head of the *hattat*-offering,
   and it is to be slain as a *hattat*-offering in the place where the
      offering-up is slain.

34 The priest is to take some of the blood of the *hattat*-offering with
      his finger
   and is to put (it) on the horns of the slaughter-site of offering-up;
   all (the rest) of its blood he is to pour out at the foundation of the
      slaughter-site of offering-up.

27 **the people of the land:** JPS "populace." In early biblical texts, this term usually denotes nobility, the "landed people." In postbiblical Judaism, *am ha-aretz* came to indicate the "common folk," often with the connotation of "the unlearned."

Obligatory Sacrificial Offerings II (5): The last sacrifice described in these opening chapters is the *asham,* variously translated as "guilt-offering" and (more recently) "reparation-offering." Its use varies, but can involve financial restitution for wrong-doing. There is disagreement about whether the verb means "to feel guilt" (Milgrom) or "to realize guilt"; in any event, the sacrifice deals with the realm of blame/liability, especially in cases of unintentional wrongdoing. Notable in this chapter are several refrains: "and the priest is to effect-purgation for him from his sin," "it is a *hattat*-offering" (which returns here), and "he shall be granted-pardon."

35 All of its fat he is to remove, as he removed the fat of the sheep
  from the slaughter-offering of *shalom,*
and the priest is to turn them into smoke on the slaughter-site,
  along with the fire-offerings of YHWH.
Thus the priest is to effect-purgation for him from his sin
  whereby he sinned;
and he shall be granted-pardon.

5:1 Now a person—when he sins:
should he hear the public-voice (carrying) a threat
and though he was a witness, either seeing or knowing,
he does not tell,
he is to bear his iniquity;
  2 or a person that touches anything *tamei,*
either the carcass of a *tamei* wild-animal or the carcass of a *tamei*
  domestic-animal or the carcass of a *tamei* swarming-creature,
and though (the fact) is hidden from him,
he has become-*tamei,* and so has incurred-guilt;
  3 or when he touches human *tum'a,* including any *tum'a* whereby
  one can become-*tamei*—
and though (the fact) is hidden from him,
he (later) comes-to-know that he incurred-guilt;
  4 or a person—when he swears rashly with his lips, to-do-ill or to-
  do-good, including whatever a human might say-rashly in
  swearing—

5:1 **the public-voice (carrying) a threat:** That is, testimony has been called for, but the person with
knowledge has not come forward; the threat is one
of a curse on that person. Levine reminds us that
testimony, then as frequently still, took place under
oath and thus was connected with the name of
God. So the offense described here was a most serious one.   **tell:** Or "report"; it bears the technical
meaning "testify."   **bear his iniquity:** This phrase,
which recurs frequently in Leviticus, is now understood not as suffering punishment but as in a sense
carrying sin around, as liability; it implies that the
sin can at some point be taken away (Schwartz 1994).
  2 *tamei:* As stated above, the term is not well served
by negative translations such as "impure" or "un-

clean"; the Hebrew signifies that something is in a
charged state and must not come in contact with
the sanctuary. In Milgrom's analogy with *The Picture of Dorian Gray,* accumulated moral and ritual
pollution eventually contaminates the sanctuary,
potentially beyond repair—hence the original importance of the ritual in Chap. 16, where the Holy-
Shrine was "decontaminated" every year. *tamei*
wild-animal: As found in the list starting in 11:29
below.
  2, 3, 4 **hidden from him:** Or "escapes his notice."
  3 **human *tum'a:*** Indicating pollution from bodily
flows (cf. Chap. 12), certain skin diseases (cf. Chaps.
13–14), and especially death (cf. Num. 19).

and though (the fact) is hidden from him,
he comes-to-know that he incurred-guilt in (any) one of these
matters:
5 it shall be, when he incurs-guilt in (any) one of these,
and confesses how he has sinned thereby,
6 then he is to bring his *asham*/guilt-offering to YHWH, for the sin
whereby he has sinned:
a female from the flock, a she-lamb or a hairy she-goat, as a
hattat-offering,
and the priest is to effect-purgation for him from his sin.
7 Now if his hand cannot reach enough (means) for a sheep,
he is to bring as his *asham*-offering (for) what he sinned:
two turtledoves or two young pigeons, to YHWH,
one for a *hattat*-offering and one for an offering-up;
8 he is to bring them to the priest,
and he is to bring-near the one for the *hattat*-offering first,
pinching off its head opposite the back-of-the-neck—he is not to
divide (it)!
9 He is to sprinkle some of the blood of the *hattat*-offering against
the side-wall of the slaughter-site;
what remains of the blood is to be drained out at the foundation
of the slaughter-site,
it is a *hattat*-offering.
10 And the second-one he is to sacrifice as an offering-up, according
to regulation,
the priest is to effect-purgation on his behalf from the sin
whereby he has sinned,
and he shall be granted-pardon.
11 Now if his hand cannot reach two turtledoves or two young
pigeons,

---

6 **guilt-offering:** Or "penalty-offering, reparation-offering." The Hebrew term is pronounced "ah-shahm."
7 **cannot reach enough (means):** That is, he cannot afford it. The birds were regarded as the most inexpensive alternative.
8 **divide:** That is, sever.

11 **efa:** A dry measure, equaling perhaps 20 liters (the "tenth" spoken of here might equal two *omers* or sheaves, an amount thought of as daily rations [Ibn Ezra]). **for it is a *hattat*-offering:** And therefore does not take the festive additions of oil and frankincense (Bamberger).

he is to bring as his near-offering (for) what he sinned
a tenth of an *efa* of flour, for a *hattat*-offering;
he is not to put on it (any) oil, he is not to place on it (any)
    frankincense,
for it is a *hattat*-offering.

12 He is to bring it to the priest,
the priest is to scoop out with his fist a fistful of some of it, as a
    reminder-portion,
and is to turn it into smoke on the slaughter-site, along with the
    fire-offerings of YHWH,
it is a *hattat*-offering.

13 So the priest is to effect-purgation for him for his sin whereby he
    sinned, in (any) one of these,
and he shall be granted-pardon.
And it shall be for the priest, like the grain-gift.

14 YHWH spoke to Moshe, saying:

15 A person—when he breaks-faith, yes, faith, sinning in error
    regarding any of the holy-things of YHWH,
he is to bring as his *asham*/penalty to YHWH: a ram, wholly-
    sound, from the flock,
by your assessment in silver *shekels* by the Holy-Shrine *shekel,* as
    an *asham.*

16 For that whereby he sinned regarding the holy-things, he is to
    pay, and its fifth he is to add to it, giving it to the priest;
then the priest is to effect-purgation on his behalf with the ram
    of *asham,*
and he shall be granted-pardon.

17 But if a person—when he sins,
by doing any one of the commandments of YHWH that are not to
    be done,

---

15 **breaks-faith:** Or "commits a breach of trust." Milgrom understands this as "sacrilege" against the sacred vessels. **by your assessment:** More comfortably in English, "by assessment." **the Holy-Shrine shekel:** The standard of currency in this and many other cases. Biblical money consisted in the main of metal weights (lit. *"shekels"*) and not of coins.

16 **its fifth:** Twenty percent additional, the standard fee for the priests (Levine).

Instructions on Disposing of Sacrifices I (6): What happened to the sacrifices after their being offered belongs to the category of what Hallo calls "consumption"—that is, a complex system of either nonuse (burning), "payment" for the priests (eating), or permission for the worshiper to eat. Here again we encounter a three-fold structure corresponding to groups of three sacrifices. This time, however, the order adopted depends on the frequency of the sacrifice, from daily to voluntary (Wenham). The chapter also introduces the important word *tora* (conventionally spelled *Torah*), "instruction," which will recur at key points throughout the first half of Leviticus. It apparently originally meant "[priestly] rules/instructions," but later came to connote portions of Moses' teachings (especially Deuteronomy) and eventually the Five Books of Moses as a whole.

(even) if he did not know that he incurred-guilt,
he must bear his iniquity;

18 he is to bring a ram, wholly-sound, from the flock,
by your assessment, as an *asham*-offering, to the priest;
the priest is to effect-purgation on his behalf for the error
whereby he erred, (even) if he did not know,
and he shall be granted-pardon.

19 It is an *asham*/guilt-offering—he incurred-guilt, yes, guilt before
YHWH.

20 YHWH spoke to Moshe, saying:

21 A person—when one sins, breaking-faith, yes, faith against YHWH
by denying his fellow's (charges) regarding a deposit, or what is
placed in one's hand (for safekeeping), or robbery,
or by withholding (property) from his fellow;

22 or by finding a lost-object and denying it,
or by swearing falsely regarding one of anything that a human
may do, to sin by the aforementioned—

23 it shall be, when he has sinned and realized-his-guilt,
he is to return the robbed-object that he robbed
or the withheld (property) that he withheld
or the deposit that was deposited with him
or the lost-object that he found,

24 or anything (else) about which he swore falsely;
he is to repay it in its capital-amount, and its fifth he is to add to
it.
To the one whose it is, he is to give it at the time of his being-
proven-guilty.

25 And as his *asham*-offering he is to bring to YHWH:
a ram, wholly-sound, from the flock, by your assessment, for an
asham-offering, to the priest,

---

21 **withholding:** Either "restraint" of wages or "dis-
traint" (seizure) of property when a loan has not
been repaid; in either case, it involves withholding
what a person is due.
23 **he is to return:** That is, first must come restitution,

and only then can the *hattat* act to remove the
wrongdoing (Sforno). **the robbed-object that he
robbed . . . :** Note the almost poetic structuring of
object and verb in this verse, which is a legal text!
24 **capital-amount:** Lit. "head"; the principal.

26   the priest is to effect-purgation for him, before the presence of
      Y<small>HWH</small>,
    and he shall be granted-pardon,
      for (whichever) one of all (the things) that he may have done to
        incur-guilt thereby.

6:1   Y<small>HWH</small> spoke to Moshe, saying:
2   Command Aharon and his sons, saying:
    This is the Instruction for the offering-up—
      that is what goes-up on the blazing-hearth on the slaughter-site
        all night, until daybreak,
      while the fire of the slaughter-site is kept-blazing on it:
3   The priest is to clothe himself in his wide-raiment of linen,
    with breeches of linen he is to clothe himself, over his "flesh";
    he is to set-aside the ashes from which the fire has consumed the
      offering-up on the slaughter-site,
    and is to put them beside the slaughter-site.
4   Then he is to strip off his garments and clothe himself in other
      garments,
    and he is to bring the ashes outside the camp, to a ritually-pure
      place.
5   Now the fire on the slaughter-site is to be kept-blazing upon it—it
      must not go out!—
    and the priest is to stoke on it (pieces-of-)wood, in the morning,
      (every) morning,
    and he is to arrange on it the offering-up,
    and is to turn into smoke on it the fat-parts of the *shalom-*
      offering.
6   A regular fire is to be kept-blazing upon the slaughter-site—it is
      not to go out!

6:2 **for:** Or "concerning." **until daybreak:** Since everything of the offering-up had to be burned (Bamberger).

  3 **breeches of linen:** To prevent the exposure of the

lower body while ascending to the altar. Ex. 20:23
tries to accomplish the same thing by providing for
a ramp up the altar instead of steps. **"flesh":** Most
probably a euphemism for "genitals."

7 Now this is the Instruction for the grain-gift:
Aharon's sons must bring-it-near, before the presence of YHWH,
in front of the slaughter-site.

8 There shall be set-aside from it, by the handful, some of the flour
of the grain-gift and some of its oil, with all the frankincense
that is upon the grain-gift,
and it is to be turned into smoke on the slaughter-site, as a
soothing savor, as its reminder-portion to YHWH.

9 What is left of it, Aharon and his sons are to eat,
unleavened it is to be eaten, in a holy place,
in the courtyard of the Tent of Appointment they are to eat it.

10 It is not to be baked with leaven;
as their portion I have given it from my fire-offerings
—it is a holiest holy-portion, like the *hattat*-offering, like the
asham-offering.

11 Any male among the Children of Aharon may eat it,
(as) an allotment for the ages, throughout your generations, from
the fire-offerings of YHWH;
whatever touches it becomes holy (property).

12 YHWH spoke to Moshe, saying:

13 This is the near-offering of Aharon and his sons that they are to
bring-near to YHWH at the time of his being-anointed:
a tenth-measure of an *efa* of flour as a regular grain-gift, half of it
in the morning and half of it in the evening.

14 On a griddle, with oil, it is to be made,
well-stirred are you to bring it,
as baked crumbled-bits of grain you are to bring-it-near,
a soothing savor for YHWH.

15 Thus shall the priest anointed in his stead, from (among) his sons,
sacrifice it,

---

10 **holiest holy-portion:** And hence only priests may
eat it (Wenham).

11 **becomes holy (property):** Levine ("must be in a
holy [state]") and Wenham ("Whoever . . . becomes
holy") understand this phrase as referring to persons, but Milgrom argues for its meaning objects,

and the "contracting" of holiness as a kind of con-
tagion—hence the objects must be isolated.

14 **well-stirred:** Many commentators render "well-
baked." **as baked crumbled-bits of grain:** Heb. unclear; JPS: "a meal-offering of baked slices."

15 **sacrifice:** Lit. "do, make."

Instructions on Disposal of Sacrifices II (7): The first part of the chapter concerns the eating of three more categories of sacrifice. Vv.16–27 demonstrate the extreme caution regarding lay consumption, including (vv.20–22) what happens when blood is accidentally spilled on something, with the punishment refrain "cut off shall that person be from his kinspeople." The ending (vv.37–38) provides a summary (which mentions a "mandate-offering" not described in this chapter!) and phraseology that usually occurs at the end of a book or major section in the Torah: "which YHWH commanded Moshe at Mount Sinai . . . in the wilderness of Sinai."

a law for the ages, for YHWH:
completely it is to be turned into smoke.

16 And every grain-gift of a priest, completely-offered shall it be;
it is not to be eaten.

17 YHWH spoke to Moshe, saying:
18 Speak to Aharon and to his sons, saying:
This is the Instruction for the *hattat*-offering:
in the place where the offering-up is slain, the *hattat* is to be slain,
before the presence of YHWH;
it is a holiest holy-portion.

19 The priest who sacrifices-the-*hattat*-offering is to eat of it,
in a holy place it is to be eaten, in the courtyard of the Tent of
Appointment.

20 Whatever touches its flesh becomes holy (property).
And if some of its blood is spattered on a garment,
(the spot) on which it is spattered is to be scrubbed in a holy
place.

21 Now a vessel of earthenware in which it was boiled is to be
broken;
if (it was) in a copper vessel that it was boiled, it is to be scoured
and rinsed with water.

22 Any male among the priests may eat it,
it is a holiest holy-portion.

23 But any *hattat*-offering from whose blood is brought to the Tent
of Appointment, to effect-purgation in the Holy-Shrine, shall
not be eaten,
in fire it is to be burned.

7:1 Now this is the Instruction for the *asham*-offering:
it is a holiest holy-portion.

2 In the place where they slay the offering-up, they are to slay the
asham-offering,
and its blood is to be dashed against the slaughter-site, all around.

---

20 **is to be scrubbed:** Reading *tekhubbas* for *tekhabbes*.   21 **broken:** Earthenware was considered porous, and
therefore could not be washed/purified.

3 Now from all its fat is to be brought-near:
the thick tail and the fat that covers the innards,

4 the two kidneys and the fat that is about them (and) that is on the
tendons,
and the extension on the liver, along with the kidneys is to be
removed.

5 The priest is to turn them into smoke on the slaughter-site, a fire-
offering to YHWH,
it is an *asham*-offering.

6 Any male among the priests may eat it,
in a holy place it is to be eaten,
it is a holiest holy-portion!

7 Like the *hattat*-offering, so the *asham*-offering—
one Instruction for them;
the priest who effects-purgation through it, his shall it be.

8 And the priest who brings-near the offering-up of a (lay)man,
the skin of the offering-up that he brings-near is for the priest—
his shall it be.

9 And any grain-gift that is baked in an oven, and any that is
prepared in a frying pan or on a griddle,
(it is) for the priest that brings-it-near—his shall it be.

10 But any grain-gift mixed with oil, or dry,
for any of the Sons of Aharon shall it be, each-man like his
brother.

11 Now this is the Instruction for the slaughter-offering of *shalom*
that is brought-near for YHWH:

12 if (it is) on account of thanksgiving that he brings-it-near,
he is to bring-near along with the slaughter-offering of
thanksgiving:
matza cakes, mixed with oil, *matza* wafers smeared with oil,
and flour well-stirred into cakes, mixed with oil.

7:12 **thanksgiving:** Rashi understands this as gratitude for having survived a difficult journey, illness, or imprisonment. Such concerns persist in later Judaism, in the form of a public blessing said in synagogue by the survivor.

13 Along with cakes of leavened bread he is to bring-near his near-
offering,
along with his slaughter-offering of thanksgiving of *shalom.*
14 He is to bring-near from it one of each (kind of) near-offering as
a contribution for YHWH,
(it is) for the priest that dashes the blood of the *shalom*-offering—
his shall it be.
15 As for the flesh of his slaughter-offering of thanksgiving of *shalom,*
on the day of his bringing-it-near it is to be eaten,
he may not leave (any) of it until morning.

16 Now if a vow-offering or a freewill-offering is his slaughtered
near-offering,
on the day of his bringing-near his slaughter-offering it is to be
eaten,
on the morrow, what is left of it may be eaten.
17 And what is left of the flesh of the slaughter-offering—
on the third day, in fire it is to be burned.
18 Now should there be eaten, yes, eaten any of the flesh of his
slaughter-offering of *shalom* on the third day, it is not
acceptable (for) him that brings-it-near, it will not be reckoned
to him.
Tainted-meat shall it be (considered),
and the person who eats of it—his iniquity he shall bear!
19 Flesh that touches anything *tamei* is not to be eaten, in fire it is to
be burned.
As for (other) flesh: anyone ritually-pure may eat the flesh.
20 But the person that eats flesh from the slaughter-offering of
shalom that is YHWH's
while his *tum'a* is upon him,
cut-off shall that person be from his kinspeople!

14 **contribution:** Or "raised-contribution." The purpose of this was "to transfer the object from its
owner to the deity" (Milgrom).
18 **reckoned to him:** That is, "credited" to him. Since
the sacrifice has not been disposed of properly, its efficacy is void (Bamberger). **Tainted-meat:** Or "des-

ecrated meat" (Wright, cited by Milgrom). Here the
penalty for eating from the sacrifices is being "cut-
off" from the community, probably meaning death.
As elsewhere in Leviticus, the crossing of sacred
boundaries threatens the sacred whole of the community.

21 And a person—when he touches anything *tamei*, human *tum'a* or
a *tamei* animal or any *tamei* detestable-creature,
and eats from the flesh of the slaughter-offering of *shalom* that is
YHWH's,
cut-off shall that person be from his kinspeople!

22 YHWH spoke to Moshe, saying:
23 Speak to the Children of Israel, saying:
Any fat of an ox or a lamb or a goat, you are not to eat.
24 Now fat from a carcass, fat from a torn-animal may be used for
any work-purpose,
but eating—you are not to eat it!
25 For whoever eats fat from an animal from which a fire-offering
may be brought-near for YHWH,
cut-off shall the person be that eats (thus), from his kinspeople!

26 And any blood you are not to eat throughout all your
settlements, (either) of fowl or of a domestic-animal.
27 Any person that eats any blood—
cut-off shall that person be from his kinspeople!

28 YHWH spoke to Moshe, saying:
29 Speak to the Children of Israel, saying:
He who brings-near his slaughter-offering of *shalom* for YHWH
is to bring his near-offering (himself) to YHWH, from his
slaughter-offering of *shalom;*
30 his (own) hands are to bring the fire-offerings for YHWH.
The fat—along with the breast he is to bring it,
the breast for elevating it as an elevation-offering, before the
presence of YHWH.

21 **detestable-creature:** Heb. *sheketz;* emendation to
sheretz, "swarming-creature," also makes sense, and
indeed appears in some of the ancient versions.
23 **fat:** Prohibited to humans, since these "choice-
parts" were exclusively sacrificed to God.
29 **(himself):** Milgrom, quoting Saadiah Gaon.

30 **elevating . . . elevation-offering:** Trad. "waving
. . . a wave-offering" has been shown incorrect by
Milgrom; the act consists of raising the offering in
dedication to God, to indicate transfer of ownership.

31 And the priest is to turn the fat into smoke on the slaughter-site.
And the breast is to be Aharon's and his sons'.

32 Now the right thigh you are to give as a contribution to the
priest, from your slaughter-offerings of *shalom.*

33 He who brings-near the blood of the *shalom*-offerings and the fat,
from among the Sons of Aharon—his shall it be,
the right thigh as a portion.

34 For the breast of the elevation-offering and the thigh of the
contribution, I take from the Children of Israel, from their
slaughter-offerings of *shalom,*
and I give them to Aharon the priest and to his sons, as an
allotment for the ages, from the Children of Israel.

35 This is the anointed-share of Aharon and the anointed-share of
his sons from the fire-offerings of YHWH,
from the time he brought-them-near to be-priests for YHWH,

36 which YHWH commanded to be given them from the time of his
anointing them, from the Children of Israel—
as a law for the ages, throughout their generations.

37 This is the Instruction
concerning the offering-up, concerning the grain-gift,
concerning the *hattat*-offering and concerning the *asham*-offering,
concerning the mandate-offering and concerning the slaughter-
offering of *shalom*

38 that YHWH commanded Moshe at Mount Sinai
at the time of his commanding the Children of Israel to bring-
near their near-offerings to YHWH,
in the wilderness of Sinai.

---

35 **anointed-share:** The Heb. root *m-sh-h* indicates either "anointing" or "measuring"; I have attempted
to keep both senses.

36 **from the time:** Others, "at the time."

37 **mandate-offering:** Sacrificed in connection with

the installation of Aharon's sons as priests; cf. the
following chapter.

38 **in the wilderness of Sinai:** This phrase ties Chaps.
6–7 to the first five chapters, as an editorial device
(Milgrom).

Installing the Priests (8): This chapter and the next, which might easily have followed the instructions for it in Ex. 29, has instead been placed here, perhaps as the
logical conclusion to material about offering sacrifices. (Placing it at the end of
Exodus might also have detracted from the impressive scene with which that
book ends. For a discussion of the complex relationship between the Exodus and
Leviticus texts, see Milgrom.) We now shift from a prescriptive mode to a descriptive, narrative one, which will prepare us for the brief but disastrous story of
Aharon's sons in Chap. 10.

A refrain here is various forms of "as Yнwн had commanded Moshe," also a
key phrase in the Exodus texts. In addition, one hears the constant use of the verb
"make-holy," appropriate in this context. Finally, one might point to the balance
between Moshe's sequence of action in Chap. 8 and Aharon's parallel actions in
Chap. 9.

There is much in this chapter that is rhythmic. The description of Aharon's
being clothed in the holy vestments in vv.7–9 has the ring of ritual to it, as conveyed through its steady alternation of verb and garment.

◆ 8:1 YHWH spoke to Moshe, saying:

2 Take Aharon and his sons with him,
   the garments and the oil for anointing,
   the bull for the *hattat*-offering, the two rams and the basket of
      matzot;

3 and the entire community, assemble at the entrance to the Tent
   of Appointment.

4 Moshe did as YHWH had commanded him.
   The community assembled at the entrance to the Tent of
   Appointment.

5 Then Moshe said to the community:
   This is the thing that God has commanded to be done.

6 Moshe brought-near Aharon and his sons
   and washed them with water;

7 he put on him the tunic,
   he girded him with the sash,
   he clothed him in the coat,
   he put on him the *efod*-vest,
   he girded him with the designed-band of the *efod*, investing him
      in it,

8 he placed on him the breastpiece,
   he put into the breastpiece the *Urim* and the *Tummim*,

9 he placed the turban on his head,
   he placed on the turban, in front of his face, the plate of gold, the
      sacred-diadem of holiness,
   as YHWH had commanded Moshe.

8:2 **the garments:** For Aharon and his sons, enumerated in some detail in Ex. 29.

3 **at the entrance to the Tent:** Not necessarily *at* the entrance, but opposite it (Levine).

7 *efod*-**vest:** A kind of embroidered apron on the High Priest's garment. To it was attached the breastpiece.

8 **the *Urim* and the *Tummim*:** Objects of unknown form contained in the breastpiece; they might mean "lights and perfections" or, alternatively, "A to Z," but were in any event used in various parts of the Bible for the prediction of the future. The *efod* too is difficult to reconstruct from the Bible's description. Levine sees it as a holdover from paganism, where statues of the gods were clothed in special garments (cf. Judg. 8:17 and 18:18, which refer to the worship of Gideon's *efod*).

10 Then Moshe took the oil for anointing and anointed the dwelling
　　and all that was in it,
　　making-them-holy.

11 He sprinkled some of it on the slaughter-site, seven times,
　　anointing the slaughter-site, all its vessels, the basin and its
　　　pedestal,
　　to make-them-holy.

12 He poured some of the oil for anointing on the head of Aharon,
　　anointing him,
　　to make-him-holy.

13 Then Moshe brought-near the sons of Aharon,
　　he clothed them in coats,
　　he girded them with sash(es),
　　and wound them caps,
　　as YHWH had commanded Moshe.

14 He brought forward the bull of the *hattat*-offering,
　　and Aharon and his sons leaned their hands upon the head of the
　　　bull of the *hattat*-offering,

15 and he slew (it).
　　Moshe took the blood
　　and put it on the horns of the slaughter-site, all around, with his
　　　finger, (thus) decontaminating the slaughter-site;
　　and the blood he poured out at the foundation of the slaughter-
　　　site.
　　So he made-it-holy, for effecting-purgation upon it.

16 Then he took all the fat that is about the innards,
　　the extension of the liver, the two kidneys and their fat,
　　and Moshe turned (them) into smoke on the slaughter-site.

17 The (rest of the) bull, its skin, its flesh and its dung,
　　he burned in fire, outside the camp,
　　as YHWH had commanded Moshe.

---

10 **the dwelling:** With a lowercase *d* in English, this indicates, not the Tabernacle itself, but the holy area,
which contained the altars, the lampstand, and the
table.

14 **the bull of the *hattat*-offering:** Offered first here
because the sanctuary must be purified before any-

thing else can happen; and Moshe officiates since as
yet there are no consecrated priests (Wenham).

15 **decontaminating:** Or "removing-sin-from." The
two ideas are virtually identical here, creating an
unsolvable translator's problem.

18 Then he brought-near the ram for the offering-up;
Aharon and his sons leaned their hands upon the head of the
ram,

19 and he slew (it).
Moshe dashed the blood against the slaughter-site, all around.

20 Then the ram he sectioned into its sections,
and Moshe turned into smoke the head, the sections and the suet.

21 Now the innards and the shins he washed in water,
and Moshe turned the entire ram into smoke upon the slaughter-
site.
It (was) an offering-up, for a soothing savor,
it (was) a fire-offering for YHWH,
as YHWH had commanded Moshe.

22 Then he brought-near the second ram, the ram for giving-
mandate.
Aharon and his sons leaned their hands on the head of the ram.

23 and he slew (it).
Moshe took some of its blood and put it on the ridge of the right
ear of Aharon, and on the thumb of his right hand, and on the
thumb-toe of his right foot.

24 Then he brought-near the sons of Aharon,
and Moshe put some of the blood on the ridge of their right ear,
on the thumb of their right hand, and on the thumb-toe of
their right foot;
then Moshe dashed the blood on the slaughter-site, all around.

25 He took the fat—the broad-tail and all the fat that is about the
innards,
the extension of the liver, the two kidneys and their fat, and the
right thigh;

26 and from the basket of *matzot* that was before the presence of
YHWH

22 **giving-mandate:** Lit. "filling the hand," i.e., installing the priests. Cf. note to Ex. 28:41.

23 **ridge of the right ear . . . thumb . . . thumb-toe:**
Probably, this use of the extremities symbolically includes the whole person, and it was the whole person that needed to be purified.

24 **brought-near:** Playing on the frequent use of this
verb, which usually means "sacrifice," but here connotes "consecrate" or "initiate." **dashed:** Parallel to
the dashing of blood that signifies the making of a
covenant in Ex. 24:6–8 (Levine).

Installation Continued: The System in Operation (9): Until now, the description of sacrifices has been largely from the viewpoint of the worshiper. Now the perspective changes to narrative, and is from the viewpoint of the priests—with the recognition at the same time that it is a public ceremony. Again, as Milgrom has noted, there is no verbal component to the ceremony (although some have argued that it is inconceivable that sacrifices could have been offered in silence). The sacrifice of the *hattat*-offering, along with other types of offerings, once again suggests the importance of a purified, perfect system in the worship of God.

The refrain in vv.4 and 6 concerns God's "being-seen" by the Israelites; what is in fact seen is his "Glory" or "aura," reminiscent of Mount Sinai and the completion of the Dwelling in the book of Exodus. The ending of the chapter also recalls the ending of Exodus, with the leaders blessing the people and fire proceeding from God.

he took one cake of *matza* and one cake of oil bread, and one wafer

and put (them) on the fat-parts and on the right thigh.

27 He placed all (of them) on the palms of Aharon and on the palms of his sons,

and they elevated them as an elevation-offering, before the presence of YHWH.

28 Then Moshe took them from their palms

and turned them into smoke on the slaughter-site, along with the offering-up.

They are mandate-offerings, for a soothing savor,

it is a fire-offering for YHWH.

29 Then Moshe took the breast and elevated it as an elevation-offering, before the presence of YHWH,

from the ram of mandating—for Moshe it was a portion,

as YHWH had commanded Moshe.

30 Now Moshe took some of the oil for anointing and some of the blood that was upon the slaughter-site

and sprinkled (it) on Aharon, on his garments, on his sons and on the garments of his sons with him;

(thus) he made-holy Aharon, his garments, his sons and the garments of his sons with him.

31 Moshe said to Aharon and to his sons:

Boil the flesh at the entrance to the Tent of Appointment,

there you are to eat it, along with the bread that is in the basket of mandating,

as I have commanded, saying: Aharon and his sons are to eat it!

32 What is left of the flesh and of the bread, in fire you are to burn (it).

33 Now from the entrance to the Tent of Appointment you are not to go out, for seven days,

33 **the entrance:** Once again meaning the courtyard area in front of the "dwelling." **for seven days:** A common period of sanctification in biblical Israel, found in reference to childbirth, holiday periods, etc. Seven was of course a number that pointed to perfection in the ancient world; it is emphasized in the sacred calendar outlined in Chap. 23 below.

◆ until the time of fulfilling the days of full-mandating.
For seven days (it takes) to fill your hands (in mandating).

34 As has been done this day, YHWH commanded to be done, to
effect-purgation for you.

35 At the entrance to the Tent of Appointment you are to stay, day
and night, for seven days;
you are to keep the charge of YHWH, so that you do not die,
for thus I have been commanded.

36 And Aharon and his sons did all the things that YHWH had
commanded by the hand of Moshe.

9:1 Now it was on the eighth day,
(that) Moshe called Aharon and his sons and the elders of Israel,

2 and he said to Aharon:
Take yourself a calf, a young of the herd, as a *hattat*-offerings, and
a ram as an offering-up, wholly-sound,
and bring-them-near, before the presence of YHWH.

3 And to the Children of Israel you are to speak, saying:
Take a hairy-one of goats as a *hattat*-offering
and a calf and a lamb, year-old ones, wholly-sound, as an offering-
up,

4 and an ox and a ram as a *shalom*-offering,
to slaughter before the presence of YHWH,
and a grain-gift mixed with oil;
for today, YHWH will make-himself-seen by you!

5 So they took what Moshe had commanded, to the front of the
Tent of Appointment,
and there came-near the entire community, standing before the
presence of YHWH.

6 And Moshe said:
This is the word that YHWH has commanded (that) you do,
that the Glory of YHWH may be seen by you!

---

35 **so that you do not die:** The penalty for not taking extreme care with the priestly rules around the sanctuary. Cf. Chap. 10 below for a narrative example.

9:4 **make-himself-seen by:** Others, "appear to."

7 And Moshe said to Aharon:
Come-near to the slaughter-site and sacrifice your *hattat*-offering
and your offering-up,
effecting-atonement on behalf of yourself and on behalf of the
people,
and sacrifice the near-offering of the people, effecting-atonement
on their behalf,
as YHWH has commanded.

8 So Aharon came-near to the slaughter-site
and slew the calf for the *hattat*-offering that was his.

9 Then the sons of Aharon brought-near the blood to him,
he dipped his finger in the blood and placed (it) on the horns of
the slaughter-site.
The (remaining) blood he poured out at the foundation of the
slaughter-site.

10 Now the fat and the kidneys and the extension from the liver,
from the *hattat*-offering,
he turned into smoke on the slaughter-site,
as YHWH had commanded Moshe;

11 the flesh and the skin he burned in fire, outside the camp.

12 Then he slew the offering-up,
and the sons of Aharon handed the blood to him, and he dashed
it against the slaughter-site, all around.

13 The offering-up they handed to him in its sections, as well as the
head,
and he turned (them) into smoke upon the slaughter-site.

14 He washed the innards and the shins,
and turned (them) into smoke, along with the offering-up, upon
the slaughter-site.

15 Then he brought-near the near-offering of the people.
He took the hairy-goat for the *hattat*-offering that was the
people's,
he slew it, and he sacrificed-the-*hattat*-offering, like the first-one.

16 Then he brought-near the offering-up, sacrificing it according to
regulation.

Systems Failure (10): As so often in the Torah, a brief narrative breaks in at this point, apparently to illustrate the dangers associated with the priests' tasks that we have just celebrated in the previous chapter. Just as the sin of the Golden Calf followed scenes of revelation at Sinai, so here too we are taken from the pomp of the priests' installation and set face to face with human failure. Alternatively, the story could be explained as a lead-in to the laws on priestly behavior in vv.9–11, just as the Golden Calf story precedes a remade covenant in Ex. 34.

What exactly was Nadav and Avihu's capital crime? Commentators over the ages have argued back and forth. Some see it as accidental: Nadav and Avihu somehow misconstrued what they were supposed to do—but divine service can brook no errors on the part of the people's representatives. Other interpreters, taking their clue from v.9, feel that Nadav and Avihu were drunk and so not in full control of their ritual duties. Milgrom's suggestion, that the story serves to warn the Israelite audience to stay away from offering their own incense (which often was connected to idolatry), makes historical sense; but the context of the tale here, after what has gone before, makes the specific crime less important than the idea that the priests must in general "get it right."

The chapter has a three-part structure: crime/ punishment/mourning; laws on drunkenness of priests and the proper disposal of the sacrifices; and a confrontation between Moshe and Aharon over ritual procedure, which is resolved, not by death but by reasoned discussion.

17 Then he brought-near the grain-gift, filling his palm with some of
    it;
    and he turned it into smoke upon the slaughter-site—aside from
    the morning offering-up.
18 Then he slew the ox and the ram of the slaughter-offering of
    shalom that was the people's;
    the sons of Aharon handed the blood to him,
    and he dashed it against the slaughter-site, all around,
19 along with the fat-parts of the ox and of the ram:
    the broad-tail and what covers the kidneys, and the extension of
    the liver.
20 They put the fat-parts over the breasts
    and he turned the fat-parts into smoke on the slaughter-site;
21 the breasts and the right thigh, Aharon elevated as an elevation-
    offering, before the presence of YHWH,
    as he had commanded Moshe.
22 Now Aharon lifted his hands toward the people, and he blessed
    them,
    then he came-down from sacrificing the *hattat*-offering, the
    offering-up and the *shalom*-offering.
23 Now Moshe and Aharon had entered the Tent of Appointment;
    when they came out, they blessed the people,
    and the Glory of YHWH was seen by the entire people.
24 And fire went out from the presence of YHWH
    and consumed, upon the slaughter-site, the offering-up and the
    fat-parts;
    when all the people saw, they shouted and flung themselves on
    their faces.

17 **aside from the morning offering-up:** Which still
must be offered (Ramban).
22 **and he blessed them:** We do not know the wording
of the blessing. The medieval commentators make
various proposals based on other biblical passages.

24 **fire went out from the presence of YHWH:** As in
the famous Elijah incident on Mount Carmel, in I
Kings 18. There it functions to impress and convince
the people of God's power.

◆ 10:1 Now Aharon's sons, Nadav and Avihu, took each-man his pan,
and, placing fire in them, put smoking-incense on it,
and brought-near, before the presence of YHWH, outside fire,
such as he had not commanded them.

2 And fire went out from the presence of YHWH
and consumed them, so that they died, before the presence of
YHWH.

3 Moshe said to Aharon:
It is what YHWH spoke (about), saying:
Through those permitted-near to me, I will be-proven-holy,
before all the people, I will be-accorded-honor!
Aharon was silent.

4 Now Moshe called Mishael and Eltzafan, the sons of Uzziel uncle
of Aharon,
and said to them:
Come-near, carry your brothers from in front of the Holy-Shrine
to beyond the camp.

5 They came-near and carried them, by their tunics, beyond the
camp,
as Moshe had spoken.

6 Now Moshe said to Aharon and to Elazar and Itamar his sons:
Your heads, do not bare,
your garments, you are not to tear,

10:1 **them ... it:** The pronoun shift occurs at times in biblical Hebrew. **outside fire:** Either coals from a place outside the prescribed altar, or incense. Cf. Ex. 30:9, about the prohibition of offering incorrect or unauthorized incense. **such as he had not commanded them:** Priestly institutions and practices in all cultures are essentially conservative, not innovative (Bamberger). The phrase itself is a pointed countering of the refrain constantly sounded in Chaps. 8 and 9, "as YHWH commanded Moshe" (Wenham).

2 **fire went out:** An ironic echo of the positive divine fire that came down and completed the sanctifying of the sanctuary/priesthood, just two verses previously.

3 **Through those permitted-near:** The priests. God seems to be saying that he is only so holy/honored as the behavior of the priests permits. Therefore the

death of Aharon's sons is a way of demonstrating that God's holiness is established through correct performance of his commands, and the penalty for its abuse is death (cf. in this connection Num. 20, where Moshe is promised punishment by death outside the promised land for not having "proven God holy" in the performance of his duties).

6 **do not bare:** Lit. "do not let-loose (your hair)." The loosening of the hair and the tearing of the garments were common ways of expressing mourning in ancient Israel. The priests are forbidden to mourn here as part of the general prohibition against their coming in contact with the dead (since death is seen in priestly texts as the major source of *tum'a*). **he be furious:** God. The verb is often used in connection with plagues (Levine). **are to weep:** Or, "may weep," that is, you may grieve over the punishment, but not over the deaths of Nadav and Avihu.

so that you do not die

and he be furious with the entire community!

Your brothers, the entire House of Israel, are to weep over the

burning that YHWH caused-to-burn.

7   And from the entrance to the Tent of Appointment, do not go

out, lest you die,

for the oil of anointing of YHWH (is) upon you!

They did according to the word of Moshe.

8   Now YHWH spoke to Aharon, saying:

9   Wine and intoxicant, do not drink, you and your sons with you,

when you enter the Tent of Appointment,

so that you do not die—

a law for the ages, throughout your generations:

10   and so that there be-separation between the holy and the profane,

between the *tamei* and the pure,

11   and so that (you) might instruct the Children of Israel in all the

laws that YHWH spoke to them through the hand of Moshe.

12   Now Moshe spoke to Aharon and to Elazar and to Itamar, his

sons that were left:

Take the grain-gift that is left of the fire-offerings of YHWH

and eat it unleavened next to the slaughter-site,

for it is a holiest holy-portion.

13   You are to eat it in a holy place,

for it is for your allotment and your sons' allotment, from the

fire-offerings of YHWH,

for thus have I been commanded.

14   But the breast of the elevation-offering and the thigh of the

contribution, you may eat in (any) pure place, you and your

sons and your daughters with you,

---

7   **do not go out:** Remain in your priestly function.

8   **Now YHWH spoke to Aharon:** This reassurance is the only time in Leviticus that God speaks directly to Aharon alone (Wenham).

9   **Wine and intoxicant, do not drink:** Does this suggest that such was Nadav and Avihu's crime? Or is it merely one on a list of prohibitions designed to guard against improper functioning of the priests in general?

10   **so that there be separation:** As the following chapters provide (Ibn Ezra).

12   **and eat it:** Even though you are in mourning (Rashi).

14   **children's:** The Hebrew can be read as "sons'," but surely both sons and daughters are meant here, as earlier in the verse (and several versions add "daughters").

for as your allotment and your children's allotment they have
been given (you), from the slaughter-offerings of *shalom* of the
Children of Israel.

15 The thigh of the contribution and the breast of the elevation-
offering, along with the gifts of the fat-parts, they are to bring
to elevate as an elevation-offering before the presence of
YHWH;
it is to be for you and for your sons with you as an allotment for
the ages,
as YHWH has commanded.

16 Now about the hairy-goat of *hattat* Moshe inquired, yes,
inquired, and here: it had (already) been burned!
And he became furious at Elazar and Itamar, the sons of Aharon
that were left, saying:

17 Why did you not eat the *hattat*-offering in the place of the Holy-
Shrine?
For it is a holiest holy-portion,
and he has given it to you to bear the iniquity of the community,
to effect-purgation for them, before the presence of YHWH.

18 Here, its blood was not brought into the Holy-Shrine, inside;
you should have eaten, eaten it in the Holy-Shrine, as I
commanded!

19 But Aharon said to Moshe:
Here, today they brought-near their *hattat*-offering and their
offering-up, before the presence of YHWH,

---

15 **allotment:** Heb. *hok* can be understood either this way or as "law" (this is true of many similar passages in Leviticus).

16 **Moshe inquired . . . became furious:** Fishbane (1988) points out that Aharon's failure to eat of the sacrifices is in line with Lev.9:15, but against the earlier and perhaps more authoritative law in 6:17–23. The text resolves the contradiction, and deals with the new situation of death as a factor, via divine oracle here.

17 **bear the iniquity:** Eating the remains of the *hattat*

is one of the two ways in which the sanctuary is purified (the other is the sprinkling of the blood) (Milgrom, Levine). **effect-purgation:** or "effect-atonement."

18 **its blood was not brought:** "As is done in the case of most solemn offerings" (Bamberger).

19 **such (things) as these:** The death of his two sons. Given that event, Aharon is justifiably cautious about the correct performance of his priestly duties.

and such (things) as these have happened to me!

Had I eaten the *hattat*-offering today, would it have been good in
   the eyes of YHWH?

20 Moshe hearkened, and it was good in his eyes.

PART II

RITUAL POLLUTION
AND PURIFICATION

(11–17)

As I have previously noted, Leviticus is largely about how to keep God's earthly realm, and hence his relationship with the people of Israel, viable and "pure" (cf. Greenstein 1985a). Once the book of Exodus ends, with the erection of the Tabernacle—a symbolic reflection of the cosmos in which God "takes up dwelling" among the Israelites—we are left with a structure that must be carefully guarded and its ritual purity maintained. To this end, Leviticus now turns to the issue of pollutants, largely of the body, that arise from what we might call territorial problems: the border of what goes into the body, expressed through animals permitted and forbidden for food; the border between life and death, as expressed through sexual functions and discharges; and the border of outer surfaces, as expressed through skin disease (*tzaraat*), mildew on clothing, and mold on houses. The system of avoidance and purification that is presented in Chapters 11–15 ensures that the "Holy-Area" will either not become polluted or, should that prove to be unavoidable, will be properly decontaminated, for such contamination has the potential of leading to God's withdrawal from dwelling "in the midst" of the people of Israel.

The pollutants discussed in these chapters do not by and large carry with them punishments per se; that is, they are not regarded as violations of the moral order (although *tzaraat* in biblical stories often did carry the implication that the victim had in fact done something to deserve his or her condition). Nor do they pose an actual danger to the person—unless he or she comes in contact with holy objects, people, or space. Then it becomes clear that biblical pollution was considered contagious; hence the need for rituals. What was generally required was that the polluted person observe a period of separation from the sanctuary (or, in more extreme cases, from the camp), to be reintegrated after either time alone or with the addition of laundering their clothes and / or washing themselves. In the latter cases, water was seen as acting as a purifying agent, not as cleanser in the detergent sense (and so the word "unclean," so often used in translating Heb. *tamei*, is misleading). As before, these processes applied to priests (cf. Chap. 22) and to laypeople alike (Chaps. 12–15). The major pollutant, death, was seen as so virulent that it received treatment in a separate setting, Num. 19.

A different category of pollution existed alongside the one we have just mentioned. It included human wrongdoing, which we might call immoral or unjust actions (e.g., incest, oppression of the poor), and also transgression of boundaries (e.g., between holy and profane, or breaching the fairly rigid system of classification in nature among animals, textiles, etc.). These types of pollution, then, involved behavior which can be seen to be disruptive or worse to the established social order. As a rule they could not be atoned for through sacrifice or other ritual forms, but lead to exile or death. They are dealt with mainly in the final section of Leviticus, Chapters 18–26.

For a full discussion of the issue of pollution in biblical Israel, see Frymer-Kensky (1983) and Greenstein (1984a).

On the Dietary Rules

The subject of countless interpretations over the ages, the system of dietary laws laid down in Lev. 11 is best understood in the broader context of both the structure of the book and of the Levitical worldview. For the former, see the commentary to Chapter 11; for the latter, the following may be helpful.

It has long been recognized that seeing the dietary laws as resulting from consciousness of hygiene is a deeply inadequate way of understanding them. Nor can some of the later explanations adduced by Jewish tradition, however noble (for instance, that adhering to such a system teaches self-discipline), provide a satisfactory explanation for the rules in the context of Leviticus. What is more to the point is that the priestly worldview stressed boundaries and order. A hierarchy reigns in virtually every aspect of Israelite life as conceived in the Torah: people, land, animals, eligibility for the priesthood, the Tabernacle, and the calendar. There is a complex system of "graded holiness" (Jenson) informing Israelite life, with two basic messages: (1) God is to be approached in stages, and (2) the world is set up in a tight, ordered structure which reflects the distinctions between God and humans, Israel and the other peoples.

It is especially the latter that is at work in the dietary laws. The animals are discussed in categories that are reminiscent of the (priestly) creation story of Genesis 1; note the refrain in both passages of (each animal) "according to its kind." Lev. 11 makes distinctions, and scholars have sought to understand them according to a number of possible criteria: ease/clarity of classification (anomalies, especially as regards locomotion, tend to be prohibited), whether or not the animal is carnivorous (those that are, are prohibited), and the wild or domestic status of the animal (the former are frequently prohibited). The message that emerges from the scheme is multifaceted. It would appear to hold that:

1. Human activity is to reflect the inherent orderliness of creation, a kind of imitation of God (namely, as he kept things clear at the beginning, you should do the same with what enters your body).

2.   The ideal state, already portrayed in the Garden of Eden story, is vegetarianism—where no animal life need be taken by humans (this despite God's command to Adam to "dominate [the earth]" in Gen. 1:28).

3.   Animals permitted for consumption, among them those fit for sacrifice, are by and large those which are familiar to the Israelites in daily life through domestication. They tend to be animals often used by the Bible to symbolize humans. Eilberg-Schwartz calls this phenomenon "Israel in the mirror of nature," and gives numerous examples extending throughout Israelite culture. He concludes that "the dietary restrictions carve up the animal world along the same lines as Israelite thought . . . [they] specify what kinds of animals are 'food for thought.'"

It should be mentioned that Mary Douglas, who pioneered an anthropological approach to these laws three decades ago, has recently given them another go (1993b). In earlier studies, Douglas (1966) saw the system in Lev. 11 as we have indicated above—as a "cognitive ordering of the universe"; she also spoke of it as symbolizing the protection of boundaries in Israelite society. Her latest understanding focuses on the animals as reflective of the idea that (Israelite) culture is aimed at demonstrating God's righteousness/ justice in all areas of life, through laws regarding the body. Thus, priests, sacrificial animals, and food animals may not have any "blemish" (below, "defect") in them; and animals prohibited for eating are either the perpetrators or victims of predation (symbolizing the human perpetrators or victims of injustice).

A final point relates to a major theme in Leviticus and indeed in many of the priestly texts of the Torah: separateness. We have seen how a major function in God's creation of the world—with which the Bible opens!—is "separating" aspects of the natural world. A parallel verb was used in the plague narratives of Exodus, "making a distinction" (between Israelites and Egyptians). With the dietary regulations, "separating" returns. Given these thematics, one can say that Chapter 11 is a linchpin of priestly thinking. Like sexual relations, the other area of intimacy in human affairs, eating in the Bible goes far beyond the confines of one's home and comes to symbolize an entire approach to life.

ON THE RITUAL POLLUTION
OF THE BODY

OF SPECIAL CONCERN TO THE COMPILERS OF LEVITICUS WAS RITUAL POLLUTION ARISing from certain physical conditions. To many people, this section is even less interesting than the opening chapters of the book, and seems impossibly bogged down in primitive conceptions of disease and hygiene. But despite the fact that they undoubtedly reflect some ancient conceptions in these areas, these conditions and the role of the priest in making rulings on them have less to do with hygiene and medicine than they do with maintaining the borders between life and death, and symbolically affirming life.

It seems that the polluting discharges are primarily sexual in nature, and this is probably not accidental. The biblical priests, in their extreme concern with both procreation/genealogy (especially of men, since the priesthood was male-hereditary) and purity (in approaching the sanctuary), were presented with a major problem. God, who was to be served in purity, was also the One in whose image human beings were made (Gen. 1:26), yet as a being beyond sexuality, who had neither relationships with other deities nor even a body. He left it ambiguous as to just how humans were to work out their sexual relations. The answer to the dilemma is at least partly solved by the Torah's regulations regarding pollution and purity, incest and marriage. It is here that the issue of control is most significant. Eilberg-Schwartz points out that control and boundaries apply not only to Israel and the nations, but also and especially to male and female. As a male hierarchy, the priests viewed women, with their closer connections to the life process (and maybe also to previous forms of paganism in the form of goddess worship), as potentially dangerous, or at least problematic, to their system of purity. The seeming "disorder" of women's discharges (perhaps representing "nature") threatened the imposition of order ("culture") that is so central to priestly thinking. But as a group concerned with the perpetuation of both the priestly class and the people of Israel, the priestly class could not do without women altogether, and the inescapable conclusion was strict regulation (cf. also Wegner 1992). Such regulation—labeling certain states or acts "polluting"—had the added benefit of controlling private morality in a way that could not be done otherwise (Douglas 1966).

It is important to note that in classical Judaism after the year 70 (the date of the destruction of the Second Temple), the "purity" laws, while still assiduously studied, by and large ceased to operate except within the sphere of marriage. Thus, to this day, religious Jewish couples temporarily separate sexually during the wife's period, but this by itself does not legally affect her participation in traditional ritual.

The disease here termed *tzaraat,* translated for millennia as "leprosy," is now recognized to be something different, perhaps several forms of skin disease involving scaling or flaking. These have nowhere near the frightening and fatal implications of classic leprosy (Hansen's Disease). Leviticus nevertheless treats *tzaraat* at great length and in close detail. Here, perhaps more than anywhere else in the book, it is clear that at least parts of Leviticus were originally intended as manuals for priestly "instruction" (note, by the way, the sevenfold occurrence of the term in the pollution chapters, 11–15). It has been theorized that *tzaraat* is of such concern here because it was felt to resemble death/decay in a clear, outward fashion, and hence fits into these chapters, which deal so much with boundaries.

An unexpected addition, from a contemporary point of view, to the *tzaraat* of the body is that which appears on textiles and on house walls (a fungus or mold or "dry rot"). The fact that the same word is used to apply to all these situations indicates that a wide concept is being applied here: how visible imperfection damages the utopia of the sacred society.

Finally, the role of the priest in these chapters should be noted. He does not function to remove demons or perform magical rites, but rather to examine the one suspected of having the disease (note the repetition of "look" in the chapter). He is more teacher and guardian of purity than healer or intermediary.

The Dietary Rules (11): After ten chapters devoted mainly to cultic rules, we move from the priestly altar to everyone's table—a fine example of the dual concerns of Leviticus (later Judaism was in fact to dub the table an "altar in miniature," taking literally the injunction in Exodus for Israel to become a "kingdom of priests"). The chapter, as mentioned in "On the Book of Leviticus and Its Structure," functions as a bridge between the first two parts of the book. As Hallo notes, it rounds out the question of consuming food, a major issue in sacrifices; it also introduces the motif of pollution in a systematic way (there were references to it in regard to sacrifices, but not in as full a manner). The use of "Instruction" in v.46 echoes the summaries of sacrifices in Chap. 7, while "you are to separate" in v.47 links the chapter with the previous one. Looking forward, "Instruction" is also used in the pollution chapters that follow, and the fivefold repetition of "hallow/holy" in vv.44–45 even points us toward the major section on Holiness in the third part of the book.

It should be noted that, from vv.24–40, eating is not the issue, but rather coming into contact with the carcass of a *tamei* animal. The two areas are joined with the introduction of "swarming" creatures in vv.41–44, and the whole chapter concludes with a call to "separation."

Refrains are many, giving the chapter a more poetic structure than one would expect from such a list: "it is *tamei* for you," "it is a detestable-thing for you," "it is an abominable-thing," "according to its kind," "*tamei* until sunset." The overwhelmingly negative character of the refrains serves to drum in caution and promote avoidance.

Many of the animals on the lists of Lev. 11 are familiar, but it must be stressed that, as with plant and place-names in the Bible, a number of the precise identifications have been lost to us, and educated guesses are in order.

11:1 YHWH spoke to Moshe and to Aharon, saying to them:

2 Speak to the Children of Israel, saying to them:
These are the living-creatures that you may eat, from all the
domestic-animals that are upon the earth:

3 any one having a hoof, cleaving a cleft in (its) hooves,
bringing-up the cud, among the animals—
that-one you may eat.

4 However, these you are not to eat
from those bringing-up the cud, or from those having a hoof:
the camel, for it brings-up the cud, but a hoof it does not have,
it is *tamei* for you;

5 the hyrax, for it brings-up the cud, but a hoof it does not have,
it is *tamei* for you;

6 the hare, for it brings-up the cud, but a hoof it does not have,
it is *tamei* for you;

7 the pig, for it has a hoof and cleaves a cleft in the hoof, but (as
for) it—the cud it does not chew up,
it is *tamei* for you.

8 From their flesh you are not to eat, their carcasses you are not to
touch,
they are *tamei* for you!

9 These you may eat from all that are in the water:
any one that has fins and scales in the water, (whether) in the seas
or in the streams,
them you may eat.

10 But any one that does not have fins and scales,
(whether) in the seas or in the streams,
from all swarming-things in the water, from all living beings that
are in the water—
they are detestable-things for you!

11:2 **domestic-animals:** Heb. *behema*, as distinct from *hayya*, wild animals.

3 **cleaving:** Creating the effect of a two-part foot, to make clear that the animal does not walk on its "hands" (which would be unnatural, in the biblical view) (Levine). **bringing-up:** Descriptive of the digestive process of these animals: they have multiple stomachs, and so after food is first chewed and swallowed, it is brought up, rechewed, and reswallowed.

5 **hyrax:** A brown rodentlike mammal with short ears which is actually not part of the rodent family (also called the coney or rock-rabbit).

7 **pig:** Still avoided by many Jews and Moslems today, it was also used in cults worshiping gods of the underworld.

11   And they shall remain detestable-things for you:
  from their flesh you are not to eat, their (very) carcasses you are
      to detest.
12   Any one that does not have fins and scales in the water—
  it is a detestable-thing for you!

13   Now these you are to hold-detestable from fowl
  —they are not to be eaten, they are detestable-things:
  the eagle, the bearded-vulture and the black-vulture,
14   the kite and the falcon according to its kind,
15   every raven according to its kind;
16   the desert owl, the screech owl and the sea gull,
  and the hawk according to its kind;
17   the little-owl, the cormorant, and the great owl;
18   the barn-owl, the pelican, and the Egyptian-vulture;
19   the stork, the heron according to its kind,
  the hoopoe and the bat.
20   Any flying swarming-creature that goes about on all fours—
  it is a detestable-thing for you!
21   However, these you may eat from any flying swarming-creature
      that goes about on all fours:
  (those) that have jointed-legs above their feet, with which to leap
      on the earth;
22   as for these, from them you may eat:
  the locust according to its kind, the bald-locust according to its
      kind;
  the cricket according to its kind, the grasshopper according to its
      kind.
23   But every (other) flying swarming-creature that has four legs,
  it is a detestable-thing for you!

---

11 **detestable-things:** They are not merely prohibited, but are labeled as abhorrent. Milgrom, in defining the difference between "detestable" and "polluted" (*tamei*) creatures, finds that the former, unlike the latter, do not convey impurity, perhaps because they live in the water, which usually serves as a purifying agent.

21 **on all fours:** What is meant here is unclear, since insects with wings always have six legs (Bamberger). Perhaps it connotes "the opposite of upright" (Douglas 1993a).

24 Now from these you can become *tamei*
——whoever touches their carcass shall be *tamei* until sunset,

25 whoever carries (any part) of their carcass is to scrub his
garments, and remain-*tamei* until sunset:

26 every animal that divides a divided-hoof, but cleaving does not
cleave it through, and its cud does not bring up;
they are *tamei* for you,
whoever touches them is *tamei!*

27 And any one that goes about on its paws, among all animals that
go about on all fours,
they are *tamei* for you,
whoever touches their carcass is *tamei* until sunset;

28 one who carries their carcass is to scrub one's garments and be
tamei until sunset,
they are *tamei* for you.

29 Now these are for you (the) ones *tamei*
among the swarming-creatures that swarm on the earth:
the weasel, the mouse, and the great-lizard according to its kind;

30 the gecko, the monitor and the lizard,
the sand-lizard and the chameleon.

31 These are (the) ones *tamei* for you among all the swarming-
creatures;
whoever touches them when they are dead shall be *tamei* until
sunset,

32 anything upon which one of them should fall when they are dead
shall be *tamei*,
whether any vessel of wood or cloth or skin or sackcloth
——any vessel that can be used in work——
it is to be put through water;

24 **from these:** Despite the fact that some animals are prohibited for eating, one cannot become polluted through them by mere touch; only dead animals convey pollution.

27 **paws:** Lit. "soles/palms."

29 **swarming:** Their mode of locomotion is unusual (the Bible would characterize it as abnormal), since they dart to and fro. The special rules concerning them may stem from their tendency to get into houses and hence to be in regular contact with humans and vessels (Wenham, both comments).

32 **put through water:** Or "dipped in water." This is done for purification purposes, as in other cases.

Pollution from Childbirth (12): This chapter, which is in chiastic relation to Chap. 15, designates a new mother as *tamei*, most likely due to her intimate contact with the life/death boundary during childbirth. Her separation from and reintegration into the community echo similar customs in many societies (see Bamberger); as often happens with life-cycle events, ritual here reflects what is happening psychologically. The doubling of the separation period when it is a girl that is born is best explained by the concept that a girl potentially doubles the "life-leak" that has taken place (Greenstein 1984a), since she will one day be a childbearing woman who will herself confront the life-death continuum.

While men obviously do not contract ritual pollution through childbirth, the concept of pollution from bodily discharges applies to them as well, as in the case of an involuntary emission of semen (cf. Chap. 15).

Pollution from Tzaraat (13): Notable in this chapter is the role of the priest, who functions neither as medicine man nor as doctor, but simply as a religious official whose duty it is to check the afflicted person for signs of what is considered ritually polluting, and to act accordingly.

Like other sections of Leviticus, this chapter and the next show signs of editing (for instance, the material in 13:47–59). Nevertheless, there is a clear structural pattern characterized by variations of "when . . . if . . . if" (Wenham).

The chapter's character as "instruction manual" is brought out, according to Fishbane (1974), by its chiastic structure. It is built on three word-groups: (1) "swelling," (2) "scab/spread," (3) "shiny-spot" that recur in vv.4–38 (in the form: 3,2,1; 1,2,3; 3,2,1; 2,3). This "unexpected structure" (especially in a nonliterary text), he maintains, may have had the function of easing memorization for the priests, who needed to know this material for their "fieldwork."

it remains-*tamei* until sunset,
    then it is pure.
33 And (regarding) any earthen vessel into which one of them falls,
        within it,
    everything within it shall be *tamei*,
    and it—you are to break (it)!
34 As for any food that might be eaten,
    should water come in (contact with) it, it shall be *tamei*;
    and any beverage that might be drunk,
    (if) in any vessel, it shall be *tamei*.
35 Anything (else) on which their carcass falls shall be *tamei*;
    an oven or a two-pot-stove is to be demolished—
    they are *tamei*,
    they shall remain *tamei* for you.
36 However, a spring or a cistern (for) gathering water shall remain
        pure,
    but one who touches their carcass shall be *tamei*.
37 Now if (part) of their carcass falls upon any sowing seed that is to
        be sown,
    it remains-pure.
38 But if water is put on the seed and (part) of their carcass falls on
        it,
    it is *tamei* for you.
39 If there should die one of the animals that are (permitted) to you
        for eating,
    one who touches its carcass shall remain-*tamei* until sunset.
40 One who eats from its carcass is to scrub his garments,
        remaining-*tamei* until sunset,
    one who carries its carcass is to scrub his garments, remaining-
        tamei until sunset.

33 **you are to break (it)**: Earthenware was considered
porous, and hence could not lose its pollution;
stone, in contrast, was perceived as incapable of
contracting pollution.
34 **water . . . beverage**: In a vessel; running water (as in
a stream) neutralizes pollution (Bamberger).

35 **two-pot-stove**: A kind of stove top.
36 **cistern**: A kind of underground tank for storing
rainwater or dry goods; examples can still be seen in
Israel. Into such a "pit" Joseph was thrown by his
brothers (Gen. 37).

41 Any swarming-creature that swarms upon the earth:
it is a detestable-thing, it is not to be eaten.

42 Anything going about on its belly, anything going about on all
fours, up to anything with many legs, among all swarming-
creatures that swarm upon the earth:
you are not to eat them,
for they are detestable-things!

43 Do not make yourselves detestable through any swarming-thing
that swarms;
you are not to make yourselves *tamei* through them, becoming
tamei through them!

44 For I YHWH am your God:
you are to hallow yourselves and be holy,
for holy am I;
you are not to make yourselves *tamei* through any swarming-
creature that crawls about upon the earth.

45 For I am YHWH, the one bringing you up from the land of Egypt,
to be God to you;
you are to be holy, for holy am I!

46 This is the Instruction for animals, fowl and all living beings that
stir in the water, all beings that swarm upon the earth,

47 that there may be-separation between the *tamei* and the pure,
between the living-creatures that may be eaten and the living-
creatures that you are not to eat.

12:1 YHWH spoke to Moshe, saying:

2 Speak to the Children of Israel, saying:
A woman—when she produces-seed and bears a male,
she remains-*tamei* for seven days,

---

42 **detestable-things:** Continuing the sense of abhorrence noted above.

43 **yourselves:** Milgrom points out that *nefesh*, which
usually means "person, emotions, life," can also
have the narrower meaning of "throat," which
makes sense here as well.

45 **bringing you up:** Instead of the usual "taking you
out." It might be a purely verbal balance to the
"bringing up" of the cud with which the chapter
opens.

47 **be-separation:** As we had in 10:10, regarding the
priests' duties.

12:2 **produces-seed:** According to ancient belief,
women "produce-seed" which is fertilized by the
male "seed." **being-apart:** Traditionally rendered
"impurity," this refers to menstruation. The present
rendering follows B-R, Greenstein, and others. The
word may, alternatively, derive from the verb "to
spatter."

like the days of her infirmity of being-apart she shall remain-
tamei;
3 and on the eighth day, the flesh of his foreskin is to be
circumcised.
4 For thirty days and three days she is to stay in her period of blood
purification;
any holy-thing she is not to touch, the Holy-Area she is not to enter,
until the fulfilling of the days of her purification.
5 Now if (it is) a female (that) she bears,
she remains-tamei for two-weeks, like her time of being-apart;
and for sixty days and six days she is to stay for (a period of) blood
purification.
6 And at the fulfilling of the days of her purification, for a son or
for a daughter,
she is to bring a lamb, in its (first) year, as an offering-up,
and a young pigeon or a turtledove, as a hattat-offering,
to the entrance of the Tent of Appointment, to the priest.
7 He is to bring-it-near, before the presence of YHWH, and is to
effect-purgation for her,
then she will be purified from her source of blood.
This is the Instruction for one giving-birth, (whether) to a male
or to a female.
8 But if her hand does not find enough (means) for a sheep,
she is to take two turtledoves or two young pigeons,
one for an offering-up and one for a hattat-offering;
when the priest effects-purgation for her,
then she is pure.

13:1 YHWH spoke to Moshe and to Aharon, saying:
2 (Any) human being—when there is on the skin of his body a
swelling or a scab or a shiny-spot

---

4 **blood purification:** That is, being "decontaminated" from the state of danger between life and
death that childbirth represents.
7 **source of blood:** Her state in childbirth.
13:2 **swelling . . . scab . . . shiny-spot:** The exact identification of these marks is not certain. **affliction:**
Heb. *nega*, which could also be rendered "mark" or

even "plague." The word connotes being touched
or stricken (cf. the word for the plagues in the exodus story, *makka*, from the verb "to strike"). The use
of "affliction" in these passages is not connected to
the Heb. verb *'-n-h*, which I have also rendered "afflict," and which the Torah frequently uses to depict
oppression or maltreatment.

and it becomes on the skin of his body an affliction of *tzaraat*,
he is to be brought to Aharon the priest or to one of his sons the
priests.

3 The priest is to look at the affliction on the skin of the flesh;
should hair in the afflicted-area have turned white, and the look
of the affliction is deeper than the skin of his flesh,
it is an affliction of *tzaraat*;
when the priest looks at it, he is to declare-him-*tamei*.

4 Now if it is a white spot on the skin of his flesh, and deeper its
look is not than the skin,
and the hair has not turned white,
the priest is to shut up the afflicted-one for seven days.

5 When the priest looks at him on the seventh day,
and here: the affliction is at a standstill in his eyes,
—the affliction has not spread on the skin—
the priest is to shut him up for seven days a second time.

6 When the priest looks at him on the seventh day a second time,
and here: the affliction has faded, and the affliction has not spread
on the skin,
the priest is to declare-him-pure
—it is (only) a scab—
when he scrubs his garments, he is pure.

7 But if the scab has spread, yes, spread on the skin
after he has had the priest look at him, for declaring-him-pure,
he is to have the priest look at him a second time.

8 When the priest looks, and here: the scab has spread on the skin,
the priest is to declare-him-*tamei*,
it is *tzaraat*!

9 An affliction of *tzaraat*—when it shows on a person, and he is
brought to the priest,

---

3 **look:** Or "appearance." **deeper:** According to one
view, lower; to another, deeper in color.
5 **at a standstill:** Or "retained its appearance"
(Levine).
6 **spread:** Heb. *pasah* (alternatively rendered

"grown"); **scab:** Heb. *mispahat;* the two terms are
considered similar sounding enough by Fishbane
(1988) to make his point above.
9 **he:** Or she.

10   when the priest looks, and here: a white swelling is on the skin,
      and it has turned into white hair,
  with a live-patch of "live" flesh in the swelling:
11   it is mature *tzaraat* in the skin of his body,
  and the priest is to declare-him-*tamei;*
  he is not to shut him up, for he is *tamei.*
12   Now if the *tzaraat* sprouts, yes, sprouts on the skin
  so that the *tzaraat* covers all the skin of the afflicted-one, from his
      head to his feet,
  wherever the priest's eyes look:
13   if the priest looks, and here: the *tzaraat* has covered all his flesh,
  he is to declare the afflicted-one pure
  —all of it has turned white,
  then he is pure!
14   But at the time of there reappearing on him live flesh, he is to be
      considered-*tamei.*
15   When the priest looks at the live flesh, he is to declare-him-*tamei;*
  the live flesh—it is *tamei,* it is *tzaraat.*
16   Or when the live flesh recurs and turns back to white,
  he is to come to the priest;
17   when the priest looks, and here: the affliction has turned back to
      white,
  the priest is to declare the afflicted-one pure,
  he is pure.

18   Now flesh—when there is in its skin a boil, and it heals,
19   but there is in place of the boil a white swelling or a white (and)
      reddish shiny-spot:
  he is to have the priest look at him.
20   When the priest looks, and here: its look is lower than the skin,
  and its hair has turned white,
  the priest is to declare-him-*tamei,*
  it is an affliction of *tzaraat,* in the boil it has sprouted.
21   But should the priest look at it, and here: there is not in it any
      white hair,

---

10 **"live" flesh:** Others, "raw," skin that is exposed.   11 **mature:** Or "prior" (Levine).

and it is not lower than the skin, but it has faded,
the priest is to shut him up for seven days.
22 Now if it should spread, yes, spread on the skin,
the priest is to declare-him-*tamei*—
it is an affliction.
23 But if, under it, the affliction is at-a-standstill, not having spread,
it is the inflammation of the boil;
the priest is to declare-him-pure.

24 Or flesh—when there is on the skin a burn by fire
and on the live-patch of the burn is a shiny-spot, white (and)
reddish, or white,
25 when the priest looks at it, and here: hair has turned white in the
shiny-spot,
and its look is deeper than the skin,
it is *tzaraat*, in the burn it has sprouted;
the priest is to declare-him-*tamei*—
it is an affliction of *tzaraat!*
26 But if the priest looks at it, and here: there is not in the bright-
spot any white hair, and lower it is not than the skin, and it has
faded,
the priest is to shut him up for seven days.
27 When the priest looks at him on the seventh day:
if it has spread, yes, spread on the skin, the priest is to declare-
him-*tamei*—
it is an affliction of *tzaraat.*
28 But if, under it, the shiny-spot is at-a-standstill, not having spread
on the skin, and it has faded,
it is a swelling from the burn,
the priest is to declare-him-pure,
for it is an inflammation from the burn.

29 Now a man or a woman—when they have an affliction on the
head or on the (site of the) beard:

30 when the priest looks at the affliction, and here: its look is deeper
   than the skin,
   and in it there is thin yellow hair,
   the priest is to declare-him-*tamei*—
   it is a scall, it is *tzaraat* of the head or of the beard.

31 But when the priest looks at the affliction of the scall, and here:
   its look is not deeper than the skin,
   and black hair there is none on it,
   the priest is to shut up the one afflicted with the scall for seven
   days.

32 When the priest looks at the affliction on the seventh day, and
   here: the scall has not spread, and there is not in it (any) yellow
   hair,
   and the look of the scall is not deeper than the skin,

33 he is to shave himself,
   but the scall he is not to shave,
   and the priest is to shut up the scall-bearer for seven days a
   second time.

34 When the priest looks at the scall on the seventh day, and here:
   the scall has not spread on the skin,
   and its look is not deeper than the skin,
   the priest is to declare-him-pure;
   when he scrubs his garments, then he is pure.

35 But if the scall has spread, yes, spread on the skin, after his being-
   purified,

36 when the priest looks at him, and here: the scall has spread on the
   skin,
   the priest need not examine (him) for the yellow hair,
   he is *tamei*.

37 Now if in his eyes the scall is at-a-standstill, and black hair has
   sprouted in it,
   the scall has healed,
   he is pure,
   and the priest is to declare-him-pure.

30 **scall:** From a root that means "torn apart," here referring to follicles of hair ripped after splitting.

38 Now a man or a woman—
   when there is in the skin of their flesh shiny-spots, white shiny-
      spots,

39 when the priest looks, and here: in the skin of their flesh (are)
      shiny-spots, faded (or) white,
   it is a rash, it has sprouted on the skin,
   he is pure.

40 Now a man—when his head becomes smooth, he is bald,
   he is pure.

41 And if on the edge of his face his head becomes smooth, he is
      forehead-bald,
   he is (still) pure.

42 But when there is on the bald spot or on the forehead an
      affliction, white (and) reddish,
   it is sprouting *tzaraat*, on his bald spot or on his forehead.

43 When the priest looks at him, and here: the swelling of the
      affliction is white (and) reddish, on his bald spot or on his
      forehead,
   like the look of *tzaraat* on the skin of flesh:

44 he is a man with *tzaraat*, he is *tamei*,
   (yes), *tamei*, *tamei* shall the priest (declare) him, on his head is his
      affliction.

45 Now the one with *tzaraat* that has the affliction,
   his garments are to be torn,
   his head is to be made-bare,
   and his upper-lip is to be covered;
   Tamei! Tamei! he is to cry out.

46 All the days that the affliction is on him, he shall remain-*tamei*,
   tamei is he,
   alone shall he stay, outside of the camp is his staying-place.

39 **rash:** And not a ritually polluting condition.
41 **becomes smooth:** The verb means "to pluck out" or "to shine." **forehead-bald:** As opposed to baldness that goes toward the back of the head (Rashi).
44 **on his head is his affliction:** Some scholars understand the wording as reversed, hence "on account of the infection on his head" (Levine).

45 *Tamei! Tamei!:* Only at this point does the text turn to the procedure for dealing with the polluted person.
46 **alone:** The quarantine is as much visual as it is hygienic.

47 Now a cloth:
  when there is on it an affliction of *tzaraat,*
  on a cloth of wool or a cloth of linen,

48 or in the woof or in the warp of the linen or of the wool,
  or in an animal-skin or in anything worked of skin:

49 if the affliction is greenish or reddish on the cloth or the skin, or
    on the woof or on the warp, or in any vessel of skin,
  it is an affliction of *tzaraat,*
  he is to have the priest look at it.

50 When the priest looks at the affliction,
  he is to shut up the afflicted-item for seven days;

51 when he looks at the affliction on the seventh day,
  if the affliction has spread on the cloth or on the woof or on the
    warp or on the skin,
  for whatever might be done with the skin for work:
  the affliction is acute *tzaraat,*
  it is *tamei.*

52 It is to be burned, the cloth, or the woof or the warp in the wool
    or in the linen, or in any vessel of skin that has in it any
    affliction,
  for it is acute *tzaraat,* in fire it is to be burned.

53 But if the priest looks, and here: the affliction has not spread in
    the cloth
  —whether in the woof or in the warp, or in any vessel of skin—

54 the priest is to command that they scrub that which contains the
    affliction,
  and he is to shut it up for seven days a second time.

55 When the priest looks, after the afflicted-thing has been scrubbed,
    and here:
  the affliction has not changed its aspect, the affliction has not
    spread—

---

47 **cloth** etc.: The text moves on to another form of imperfection: mold or fungus.
49 **greenish:** Others, "yellowish."
51 **acute:** Or "persistent serious" (Wenham), "menacing, maleficent" (Greenstein, personal communication).

55 **decay:** From a verb meaning "to dig out." **"bald-spot" . . . "forehead":** These physiological terms describe the inside and outside of a piece of cloth, again highlighting the parallels and sense of order in priestly thinking.

Purification from Tzaraat (14): In 13:44–45 we were informed about the diseased person's isolation from the camp. We now turn to the ceremony attending his purification and, from v.33 on, that of a house. In a complex ritual that foreshadows the great Purgation ceremony of Chap. 16 (with some connections to the ritual of purging the impurity of death in Num. 19), *tzaraat* is removed from its dangerous position in the camp. Many aspects seem to be archaic and even tinged with magic; in Milgrom's view, these characteristics survive only symbolically, and ancient Israel has rid itself of dependence on magic—in his words, it has "eviscerated" demonism.

The substances used for purification—cedar, scarlet, hyssop—seem to connote life (and hence remove the death symbolism of *tzaraat*): they all bear the red color of blood, which itself was the great biblical indicator of life (cf. 17:11 below). Notable is the adjective "living," applied to both the birds and the water utilized in the ceremony.

The purification ritual itself, interestingly, parallels the consecration of the priests in Chap. 8. This is particularly evident in the fourfold dabbing of blood on the right extremities of the diseased person (cf. 8:23, 24 for the corresponding action). In Chap. 8, movement took place from the everyday sphere into that of the holy; here, the person with *tzaraat* moves from isolation to eventual reintegration into society (i.e., the camp).

it is *tamei,* in fire you are to burn it,
it is decay, on its "bald-spot" or on its "forehead."

56 But if the priest looks, and here: the affliction has faded, after it
has been scrubbed,
he is to tear it from the cloth or from the skin or from the woof
or from the warp,

57 and if it is seen again on the cloth—whether in the woof or in the
warp, or in any vessel of skin,
it is a sprouting-thing, in fire you are to burn it, anything in which
there is the affliction.

58 But the cloth or the woof or the warp or any vessel of skin that
you have scrubbed, so that the affliction disappears from them,
when it is scrubbed a second time,
then it is pure.

59 This is the Instruction for the affliction of *tzaraat* in cloth of wool
or linen, or the warp or the woof, or any vessel of skin,
for declaring-it-purified or for declaring-it-*tamei.*

14:1 YHWH spoke to Moshe, saying:

2 This is to be the Instruction for the one-with-*tzaraat,* on the day
of his being-purified:
he is to be brought to the priest.

3 The priest is to go outside the camp;
when the priest looks, and here: the affliction of *tzaraat* has
healed on the one-with-*tzaraat,*

4 the priest is to command that they take for the one-to-be-purified
two birds, live, pure,
and wood of cedar and scarlet of the worm and hyssop.

5 Then the priest is to command that they slay the one bird
in an earthen vessel, (held) above living water,

14:2 **Instruction:** Here as elsewhere, the meaning of this
key structural term in Leviticus is not far from "ritual."

4 **live:** One bird will be killed, the other set free. **scarlet of the worm:** As in Ex. 25:4, obtained from
crushing a small insect. **hyssop:** A bush known for
its use in ceremonies as a kind of brush (cf. Ex. 12:22,

where it is used to smear the blood on the Israelites'
doorposts in Egypt).

5 **slay:** Unlike the ritual killing of birds in 1:15, which
is accomplished by the pinching of the creature's
neck. Hence this is not technically a sacrifice (Sifra,
quoted by Bamberger).

◆ 6 and the live bird—he is to take it, and the cedar wood, the scarlet
of the worm and the hyssop,
and is to dip them and the live bird in the blood of the slain bird,
(held) above living water.

7 Then he is to sprinkle (it) over the one-to-be-purified of *tzaraat*
seven times, declaring-him-pure,
and is to send-out the live bird into the open field.

8 When the one-being-purified scrubs his garments, shaves his
entire (head of) hair and washes in water,
then he is pure,
afterward he may enter the camp,
staying outside his tent for seven days.

9 And it shall be on the seventh day: when he shaves all his hair—
his head, his beard and his eyebrows,
all his body-hair he shaves—
and scrubs his garments and washes his flesh in water,
then he is pure.

10 On the eighth day he is to take two lambs, wholly-sound, and one
lamb in its (first) year, wholly-sound,
and three tenth-measures of flour as a grain-gift, mixed with oil,
and one *log* of oil.

11 The priest making-purification is to stand the man to-be-purified
and them
before the presence of YHWH, at the entrance to the Tent of
Appointment;

12 the priest is to take the one lamb and is to bring-it-near as an
asham-offering, with the *log* of oil,
and is to elevate them as an elevation-offering, before the
presence of YHWH.

6 **living water:** I.e., running water, also required for
purification in v.50 and in the next chapter.

7 **send-out:** The liberation of the live bird, into the
open field (the countryside), sounds like a scapegoat
ritual, whereby sins or noxious influences are driven
into uninhabited space and hence disposed of.

9 **shaves . . . his head, his beard:** Normally forbid-

den, but permitted here for purposes of purification
(Levine).

10 **On the eighth day:** Paralleling circumcision, another ritual of integration into the community (Cal-
vin, quoted by Wenham). **log:** A liquid measure,
perhaps equivalent to a pint. Its equivalent is found
in Ugaritic texts (Cohen).

13 Then he is to slay the lamb in the place where one slays the
     hattat-offering and the offering-up,
   in a holy place,
   for like the *hattat*-offering, the *asham*-offering is the priest's,
   it is a holiest holy-portion.
14 Then the priest is to take some of the blood of the *asham*
   and the priest is to place it on the ridge of the right ear of the
     one-being-purified, and on the thumb of his right hand, and on
     the thumb-toe of his right foot.
15 And the priest is to take some of the *log* of oil and is to pour it on
     the left palm of the priest.
16 Then the priest is to dip his right finger in some of the oil that is
     on his left palm
   and is to sprinkle some of the oil with his finger, seven times,
     before the presence of YHWH.
17 From the remainder of oil that is on his palm, the priest is to
     place some on the ridge of the right ear of the one-being-
     purified, and on the thumb of his right hand, and on the
     thumb-toe of his right foot,
   on top of the blood of the *asham*-offering.
18 And what remains of the oil that is on the palm of the priest
   he is to place upon the head of the one-being-purified;
   then the priest is to effect-purgation for him, before the presence
     of YHWH.
19 Then the priest is to sacrifice the *hattat*-offering and is to effect-
     purgation for the one-being-purified from his *tum'a*,
   afterward he is to slay the offering-up.
20 And the priest is to offer-up the offering-up and the grain-gift on
     the slaughter-site,
   and when the priest effects-purgation for him,
   then he is pure.

17 **oil:** The oil serves to cover and protect the blood, so
   that the latter may do its purifying work (Greenstein 1984a); likewise in v.28.

21 But if he is poor and his hand does not reach (far),
   he is to take one lamb as an *asham,* for elevating, for effecting-
      purgation for him,
   and one tenth-measure of flour, mixed with oil, as a grain-gift,
      and a *log* of oil,

22 and two turtledoves or two young pigeons, (as far as) his hand
      can reach,
   the one shall be the *hattat*-offering and the other, the offering-up.

23 He is to bring them on the eighth day of his being-purified, to the
      priest,
   to the entrance of the Tent of Appointment, before the presence
      of YHWH.

24 Then the priest is to take the lamb of *asham*-offering and the *log*
      of oil,
   and the priest is to elevate them as an elevation-offering, before
      the presence of YHWH;

25 he is to slay the lamb of *asham*-offering,
   then the priest is to take some of the blood of the *asham*-offering
   and is to place (it) on the ridge of the right ear of the one-being-
      purified, and on the thumb of his right hand, and on the
      thumb-toe of his right foot,

26 and some of the oil the priest is to pour out on the left palm of
      the priest;

27 the priest is to sprinkle with his right finger some of the oil that is
      on his left palm, seven times, before the presence of YHWH.

28 Then the priest is to place some of the oil that is on his palm
   on the ridge of the right ear of the one-being-purified, and on the
      thumb of his right hand, and on the thumb-toe of his right
      foot,
   on the place above the blood of the *asham*-offering;

29 what-is-left of the oil that is on the palm of the priest he is to
      place on the head of the-one-being-purified,
   to effect-purgation for him, before the presence of YHWH.

30 Then he is to sacrifice one of the turtledoves or the young
      pigeons, from (within) what his hand can reach

31 —whatever his hand can reach—
   the one as a *hattat*-offering and the other as an offering-up, along
      with a grain-gift,

and the priest is to effect-purgation for the one-being-purified,
 before the presence of YHWH.

32 This is the Instruction for the one who has an affliction of *tzaraat,*
 whose hand cannot reach (means) for his purification.

33 YHWH spoke to Moshe and to Aharon, saying:

34 When you enter the land of Canaan, that I am giving you as a
 holding,
 and I place an affliction of *tzaraat* on a house in the land of your
 holding,

35 there shall come the one whose house it is
 and report to the priest, saying:
 (Something) like an affliction has been seen by me on the house!

36 Then the priest is to command that the house be cleaned before
 the priest enters to look at the affliction,
 so that nothing that is in the house becomes-*tamei;*
 after that the priest may enter to look at the house.

37 When he looks at the affliction, and here: the affliction (is) on the
 walls of the house (as) greenish or reddish eruptions,
 their look lower than the wall:

38 the priest is to go out of the house, to the entrance of the house,
 and is to have the house shut up for seven days.

39 When the priest returns on the seventh day,
 and he looks, and here: the affliction has spread on the walls of
 the house,

40 the priest is to command that they pull out the stones on which
 the affliction is
 and throw them outside the city, into a *tamei* place;

41 the house someone shall scrape inside, all around,
 and they are to pour the dried-mud that was scraped off outside
 the city, into a *tamei* place.

42 Then they are to take other stones and bring them in place of the
 (original) stones,
 other dried-mud they are to take, and are to replaster the house.

---

34 **Canaan:** As in Chap. 25, the law here reflects the
later period of settlement and not the one of wandering in the wilderness.

Polluting Discharges (15): This chapter concerns genital discharges—both those that arise from disease and those that are normal but involuntary. As Levine notes, sexual purity was crucial for approaching the Israelite sanctuary, as opposed to ancient Near Eastern rituals in general, where sexuality was frequently part and parcel of the worship of the gods.

Such pollution was considered much more contagious than that we have encountered previously, which is not surprising, given the area in which it falls. Wenham has noted the chiastic structure here, with male and female interchanging with short-term and long-term events. The core (vv.16–24)—the normal flows of seminal emissions for men and menstrual discharge from women—contrasts with discharges resulting from disease (vv.2–12, 25–27). The former merely pollute until sunset (except for the case of a couple having intercourse during the wife's period), and thus demonstrate the modesty and restraint in matters of divine worship more than pointing to some kind of stigma per se.

43 Now if the affliction returns and sprouts in the house
after one has pulled out the stones,
and after the house's being-scraped, and after its having-been-
plastered,

44 the priest is to enter,
and when he looks, and here: the affliction has spread in the
house,
it is acute *tzaraat* in the house, it is *tamei*.

45 Then one is to demolish the house—its stones, its wood and all
the dried-mud on the house,
and one is to take (it) outside the town, to a *tamei* place.

46 One entering the house (during) all the days of its being shut up
is to remain-*tamei* until sunset;

47 one lying in the house is to scrub his garments;
one eating in the house is to scrub his garments.

48 Now if the priest should enter, yes, enter
and look, and here: the affliction has not spread through the
house
after the replastering of the house,
the priest is to declare the house pure, since the affliction has
healed.

49 He is to take, to decontaminate the house, two birds,
and cedar wood, scarlet of the worm, and hyssop,

50 and he is to slay the one bird in an earthen vessel, over living
water,

51 then he is to take the cedar wood and the hyssop and the scarlet
of the worm, and the live bird,
and is to dip them in the blood of the slaughtered bird, and in the
living water,
and is to sprinkle (it) on the house seven times.

52 So he is to decontaminate the house with the blood of the bird
and with the living water,
with the live bird, with the cedar wood, with the hyssop and with
the scarlet of the worm;

48 **healed:** The language is figurative; it is as if the
mold/mildew were a disease.

53 then he is to send-free the live bird, outside the town, toward the
    open field.
   When he effects-purgation for the house,
    then it is pure.

54 This is the Instruction for any affliction of *tzaraat,* for scalls,
55 for *tzaraat* of cloth or of a house,
56 for swelling, for scabs or for shiny-spots,
57 to provide-instruction, at the time of the *tamei* and at the time of
    the pure.
   This is the Instruction for *tzaraat.*

15:1 YHWH spoke to Moshe and to Aharon, saying:
   2 Speak to the Children of Israel and say to them:
    Any-man, any-man, when he becomes one-with-a-flow from his
     "flesh,"
    his flow—it is *tamei.*
   3 And this is his *tum'a* during his flow,
    (whether) his "flesh" oozes with his flow or his "flesh" is sealed
     up by his flow,
    it is his *tum'a:*
   4 any place-of-lying that the one-with-a-flow lies on becomes *tamei,*
    and any vessel that he sits on becomes *tamei.*
   5 A man that touches his place-of-lying is to scrub his garments and
     wash in water,
    and will remain-*tamei* until sunset.
   6 One who sits on the vessel on which the one-with-the-flow sits
    is to scrub his garments and wash in water,
    and will remain-*tamei* until sunset.
   7 One who touches the flesh of the one-with-the-flow
    is to scrub his garments and wash in water,
    and will remain-*tamei* until sunset.

15:2 **a-flow from his "flesh":** A discharge from his genitals.
 4 **place-of-lying:** Either a bed, or, more likely, some
 padding on the floor.

7 **flesh:** Here the meaning of the word probably re-
 verts to any part of the body.

580

8 Now if one-with-a-flow spits on one (who is) pure,
(that one) is to scrub his garments and wash in water,
and will remain-*tamei* until sunset.

9 Any saddle-mounting that one-with-a-flow mounts, becomes-
tamei.

10 Anyone who touches anything that is under him
will remain-*tamei* until sunset,
one-who-carries them is to scrub his garments and wash in water,
and will remain-*tamei* until sunset.

11 Anyone whom the one-with-the-flow touches, not having rinsed
his hands in water,
is to scrub his garments and wash in water,
and will remain-*tamei* until sunset.

12 And an earthen vessel that the one-with-a-flow touches is to be
broken,
and any wooden vessel is to be rinsed in water.

13 Now when the one-with-a-flow is purified from his flow,
he is to number himself seven days of being pure;
when he scrubs his garments and washes his flesh in living water,
then he is pure.

14 On the eighth day he is to take himself two turtledoves or two
young pigeons
and is to come before the presence of YHWH, at the entrance to
the Tent of Appointment,
and is to give them to the priest.

15 The priest is to sacrifice them, the one as a *hattat*-offering and the
other as an offering-up,
thus will the priest effect-purgation for him before the presence of
YHWH, from his flow.

16 Now a man, when there goes out from him an emission of seed,
he is to wash in water all of his flesh,
and will remain-*tamei* until sunset.

11 **rinsed his hands:** That is, the polluted person. The nineteenth-century commentator S. D. Luzzatto understands "hands" as euphemistic for genitals—so the whole body needed to be immersed.

14 **before the presence of YHWH:** This formula, which occurs frequently in priestly texts, is omitted in v.29 below; biblical women are not allowed the same cultic access to the divine as men (Wegner 1988).

17   Any garment or any animal-skin on which there is an emission of
seed

     is to be scrubbed in water,

     and will remain-*tamei* until sunset.

18   And (also) a woman with whom a man lies, (with) an emission of
seed:

     they are to wash in water,

     and will remain-*tamei* until sunset.

19   A woman—when she is one-with-a-flow, her flow being of blood
from her "flesh,"

     seven days shall she remain in her (state of) being-apart.

     Anyone who touches her is to remain-*tamei* until sunset.

20   Anything that she lies upon in her (state of) being-apart becomes
tamei,

     anything that she sits upon becomes *tamei.*

21   Anyone who touches her lying-place is to scrub his garments and
wash in water,

     and will remain-*tamei* until sunset.

22   Anyone who touches any vessel that she sat upon is to scrub his
garments and wash in water,

     and will remain-*tamei* until sunset.

23   Whether it is upon the lying-place or upon the vessel that she has
sat upon,

     on touching it he will remain-*tamei* until sunset.

24   And if a man lies, yes, lies with her, so that her (state of) being-
apart is upon him,

     he will remain-*tamei* for seven days,

     any place-of-lying upon which he lies becomes *tamei.*

25   Now a woman—when the flow of her blood flows for many
days, when it is not the time of her being-apart,

     or when it flows out over-and-above her being-apart,

---

18 **emission:** Lit. "laying" or "layer."   19 **(state of) being-apart:** Cf. note to 12:2.

all the days of her *tamei* flow she shall be like (during) the days of
her being-apart,

she is *tamei*.

26 Any lying-place upon which she lies, all the days of her flow, shall
be for her like the lying-place (during) her being-apart,

and any vessel that she sits upon shall be *tamei,* like the *tum'a* of
her being-apart.

27 Whoever touches them becomes *tamei;*

he is to scrub his garments and wash in water,

and will remain-*tamei* until sunset.

28 Now when she is purified from her flow,

she is to number seven days,

and afterward, she becomes pure.

29 And on the eighth day she is to take herself two turtledoves or
two young pigeons

and is to bring them to the priest, to the entrance of the Tent of
Appointment.

30 The priest is to sacrifice the one as a *hattat*-offering and the other
as an offering-up,

the priest is to effect-purgation for her before the presence of
Y<small>HWH</small>, from her *tamei* flow.

31 You are to have the Children of Israel avoid their *tum'a,*

that they not die from their *tum'a*

when they make my Dwelling *tamei* that is in their midst.

32 This is the Instruction for the one-with-a-flow

and for (one) from whom goes out an emission of seed,
becoming *tamei* thereby,

33 and for one infirm in her (state of) being-apart, for one who has-
a-flow with his flow, male or female,

and for a man that lies with a *tamei*-woman.

31 **have . . . avoid:** A form of the verb rendered "consecrate" in Num. 6. **that they not die:** Death would
result, not from the pollution itself, but from carrying it into the sacred areas, and thus polluting them.

The Day of Purgation/Atonement (16): This chapter forms the climax of the section that began in Chap. 11. It is, along with Num. 19, the purification ritual par excellence, and has received much attention throughout the ages. As modern commentators have pointed out, two things are happening here: first, the sanctuary is being purged of the ritual pollution that has accumulated from both priests and laypeople; and second, the accumulated sins of the community are receiving atonement. It is not surprising, therefore, that the chapter is built on different uses of the verb *kipper*, which can denote covering, purging, atonement (expiation), or ransom; here the two meanings "purging" and "atoning" seem to fit the double context best. Probably the "purging" part is the earlier one, as many ancient Near Eastern cults utilized purification ceremonies for their sanctuaries.

Appropriately, the ritual includes two processes, outlined by Levine: riddance, which involves transferring sin to a living creature and driving it outside the community into the uninhabited wilderness, and purification, which utilizes the blood of a sacrifice (rather like the *hattat* encountered previously in the book). Both rituals are conducted largely by Aharon, who as High Priest acts on behalf of the entire community.

Later Judaism was fascinated by these rites; a detailed account of how they were to be conducted in postbiblical times has survived in the Mishnah (ed. c. 200), and a narrative version is still verbally reenacted by traditional Jews once a year on the Day of Atonement.

The chapter opens with direct mention of the deaths of Nadav and Avihu (Chap. 10). This serves at least two purposes: first, it creates a bracket into which the Leviticus texts on pollution occur; and second, it reminds the audience of the pressing need to purify the sanctuary, whose very first recorded defilement came about as a result of the illegitimate act of Aharon's sons.

◆ 16:1   Now YHWH spoke to Moshe
      after the death of the two sons of Aharon,
      when they came-near before the presence of YHWH and died;
  2   YHWH said to Moshe:
      Speak to Aharon your brother,
      (so) that he (does) not enter, at (just) any time, the Holy-Shrine,
          inside the curtain, facing the Purgation-Cover that is on top of
          the Coffer,
      that he (does) not die;
      for in a cloud I make-myself seen, over the Purgation-Cover.
  3   In this (manner) is Aharon to enter the Holy-Shrine:
      with a bull, a young-one of the herd, for a *hattat*-offering, and a
          ram for an offering-up.
  4   In a holy tunic of linen he is to dress,
      linen breeches are to be upon his (naked) body,
      with a sash of linen he is to gird himself,
      with a turban of linen he is to turban himself;
      they are garments for the Holy-Shrine.
      When he has washed his body in water, he may dress in them.
  5   From the community of the Children of Israel he is to take two
          hairy goats for a *hattat*-offering, and one ram for an offering-
          up.
  6   And Aharon is to bring-near the bull for the *hattat*-offering that is
          his,
      so that he may effect-atonement on behalf of himself and on
          behalf of his household.
  7   He is to take the two hairy (goats) and is to stand them before the
          presence of YHWH,
      at the entrance to the Tent of Appointment.

16:1 **the two sons of Aharon:** Nadav and Avihu, whose death was detailed in Chap. 10.

2 **at (just) any time:** Indiscriminately. The end of the chapter restricts Aharon's entry to just once a year. **Purgation-Cover:** Heb. *kapporet;* as described in Ex. 25:17–22; the part of the Coffer or Ark which served as God's "footstool," and the holiest object in the cult. **in a cloud:** In which dwells the "Glory" of God.

3 **for a *hattat*-offering:** Aharon cannot approach God without undergoing purification.

8   Aharon is to place upon the two hairy (goats) lots,
     one lot for Yhwh and one lot for Azazel.

9   Aharon is to bring-near the hairy-one for which the lot for Yhwh
     came up,
     and is to designate it as a *hattat*-offering;

10   and the hairy-one for which the lot of Azazel came up is to be left
     standing-alive, before the presence of Yhwh,
     to effect-atonement upon it,
     to send it away to Azazel into the wilderness.

11   Then Aharon is to bring-near the bull of the *hattat*-offering that is
     his,
     effecting-atonement on behalf of himself and on behalf of his
     household;
     he is to slay the bull of the *hattat*-offering that is his,

12   and is to take a panful of fiery coals from atop the slaughter-site,
     from before the presence of Yhwh,
     and (two) fistfuls of fragrant-incense, finely-ground,
     and is to bring (it) inside the curtain.

13   Then he is to place the incense on the fire, before the presence of
     Yhwh,
     so that the cloud (from) the incense covers the Purgation-Cover
     that is over the Testimony,
     so that he does not die.

14   Then he is to take (some) of the blood of the bull
     and sprinkle (it) with his finger on the front of the Purgation-
     Cover, eastward,
     and before the Purgation-Cover he is to sprinkle, seven times,
     some of the blood with his finger.

15   Then he is to slay the hairy-goat of the *hattat*-offering that is the
     people's,

---

8 **Azazel:** The identification of this name has been a subject of debate for centuries. Proposals include *ez azal*, meaning "a goat that escapes" (hence English "scapegoat"), and another reading signifying "a fierce region." Many recent commentators, however, agree in seeing Azazel as the name of a wilderness demon, and hence the rite is taken as a vestige of an old pagan practice. Appropriately, in modern Hebrew *lekh la-azazel* is the equivalent of English "go to hell" or "get lost." Regardless of the precise meaning of Azazel, that is, in fact, what the community wants to happen to its sins.

13 **Testimony:** That is, the "Coffer of Testimony."

and bring its blood inside the curtain,
doing with its blood as he did with the blood of the bull:
he is to sprinkle it on the Purgation-Cover, and before the
Purgation-Cover.

16 So he is to effect-purgation for the Holy-Shrine
from the *tum'ot* of the Children of Israel, from their
transgressions, for all of their sins,
and thus he is to do with the Tent of Appointment, which dwells
with them in the midst of their *tum'ot*.

17 No human is to be in the Tent of Appointment when he enters it
to effect-atonement in the Holy-Shrine, until he goes out.
He is to effect-atonement on behalf of himself and on behalf of
his household, and on behalf of the entire assembly of Israel.

18 Then he is to go out to the slaughter-site that is before the
presence of YHWH, and effect-purgation on it,
he is to take some of the blood of the bull and some of the blood
of the hairy-goat
and is to place (it) on the horns of the slaughter-site, all around;

19 he is to sprinkle on it from (the rest of) the blood with his finger
seven times;
he is to purify it and he is to hallow it
from the *tum'ot* of the Children of Israel.

20 When he has finished purging the Holy-Shrine and the Tent of
Appointment and the slaughter-site,
he is to bring-near the live hairy (goat),

21 Aharon is to lean his two hands on the head of the live hairy
(goat)
and is to confess over it
all the iniquities of the Children of Israel, all their transgressions,
for all of their sins;
he is to place them upon the head of the hairy (goat)

16 **for:** Milgrom: "including," JPS: "whatever." ***tum'ot:***
Plural of *tum'a*, so here, "pollutings." The idea is
that God is with the Israelites even in the presence
of *tum'a* (up to a point, of course).

17 **No human:** Even regular priests are excluded on
this occasion.

21 **confess:** In Levine's view, sins were originally listed
one by one and thus wiped away.

On the Shedding of Animal Blood (17): This chapter appears to be either an appendix to the first two parts of the book (sacrifices and purity) or a transition between them and the chapters on "holiness." It must be said, however, that it does not use the standard wording of the holiness chapters. The text deals with the Israelites' slaughtering of animals for food outside the sanctuary ("Dwelling"), insisting instead that such killing take place "at the entrance to the Tent of Appointment." In contrast, Deut. 12:20ff. permits the slaughtering of animals for meat without bringing them to the sanctuary—provided that their blood is poured out (since the consumption of blood is universally prohibited in the Torah). Scholars disagree about which practice came first; some (e.g., Wenham) argue for a wilderness setting here, while others see the chapter as reflecting the antipagan feelings of postexilic Israel (Bamberger; cf. v.7). Whatever the provenance, our chapter is clear about the extraordinary power of blood in Israelite thinking. As the life, which belongs to God, it must be returned to him, either actually, at the altar, or symbolically, on the ground (Greenstein 1984a). Here it is seen as effecting ransom; the life of the sacrificial animal substitutes for that of the sacrificer (cf. "On Sacrifice," above). The upshot is that the taking of animal life is done with extreme awareness and care.

The chapter is built at least partially on repeating sound patterns. A threefold refrain is "that man is to be cut off from his kinspeople," stressing the seriousness of the prohibition. Four times we hear "any-man, any-man" (Heb. *ish ish*), reinforcing the unusually broad scope of the command indicated by the beginning of the chapter ("to Aharon and to his sons and to all the Children of Israel"). Finally, in v.10 through 15, the word *nefesh* occurs nine times, with the alternating meanings of "person" and "life" (the pattern is 1–3–1–3–1 in these meanings).

and is to send it free by the hand of a man for the occasion, into
the wilderness.

22 The hairy (goat) is to bear upon itself all their iniquities, to a land
cut off;
he is to send-free the hairy (goat) in the wilderness.

23 Then Aharon is to enter the Tent of Appointment and is to strip
off his linen garments in which he dressed when he entered
the Holy-Shrine,
and is to leave them there;

24 then he is to wash his flesh in water, in a holy place, and is to
dress in his garments,
he is to go out and sacrifice his offering-up and the offering-up of
the people;
so shall he effect-atonement on behalf of himself and on behalf
of the people.

25 And the fat of the *hattat*-offering he is to turn-into-smoke upon
the slaughter-site.

26 Now the one who sent free the hairy (goat) for Azazel is to scrub
his garments and wash his flesh in water;
after that he may reenter the camp.

27 And the bull of *hattat* and the hairy (goat) of *hattat* whose blood
was brought in to effect-purgation in the Holy-Shrine are to be
taken outside the camp,
and in fire are to be burned their skins, their flesh, and their
dung.

28 And (each) one who burns them is to scrub his garments and
wash his flesh in water;
after that he may reenter the camp.

29 And it shall be for you a law for the ages:
in the seventh New-Moon, on the tenth after the New-Moon
you are to afflict your selves;

---

22 **bear upon itself . . . iniquities:** To carry them off; a
play on the common phrase "bear one's iniquity." **a
land cut off:** That is, remote from human experience.
27 **and their dung:** Completely!
29 **seventh New-Moon:** Today, Yom Kippur occurs in

the first month of the Jewish calendar, in the fall; an
earlier calendar viewed the spring as the beginning
of the year (cf. Ex. 12:1). **afflict your selves:** Virtually all commentators (and Jewish tradition) interpret this as a reference to fasting.

any-kind of work you are not to do—
(both) the native and the sojourner that sojourns in your midst.

30 For on this day atonement is to be effected for you,
to purify you from all your sins;
before the presence of YHWH, you will become-pure.

31 It is a Sabbath of Sabbath-Ceasing for you,
you are to afflict your selves,
a law for the ages.

32 The priest shall effect-purgation who has been anointed and
whose hand has been filled to act-as-priest in place of his
father.
He is to dress in garments of linen, garments of the Holy-Area;

33 he is to effect-purgation for the Holiest of Holy-Shrines,
for the Tent of Appointment and the slaughter-site he is to effect-
purgation,
and for the priests and for all the people of the assembly he is to
effect-atonement.

34 This shall be for you a law for the ages,
to effect-atonement for the Children of Israel from all their sins,
once a year.
And he did as YHWH commanded Moshe.

17:1 YHWH spoke to Moshe, saying:

2 Speak to Aharon and to his sons and to all the Children of Israel,
and say to them:
This is the word that YHWH has commanded, saying:

3 Any-man, any-man of the House of Israel who slays an ox or a
sheep or a goat in the camp
or who slays (it) outside the camp,

---

31 **a Sabbath of Sabbath-Ceasing:** A kind of Super-Sabbath, a total cessation of the everyday for the sake of concentrating on atonement.

33 **Holiest of Holy-Shrines:** Pointing to the inner sanctum, "inside the curtain" (Ibn Ezra).

17:3 **House of Israel:** Levine views this phrase, which is found in the Prophets, as possibly a late one.

4   and to the entrance of the Tent of Appointment does not bring
      it,
    to bring-it-near as a near-offering to Y<small>HWH</small> before the Dwelling of
      Y<small>HWH</small>:
    bloodguilt is to be reckoned to that man, blood has he shed,
    that man is to be cut off from amid his kinspeople—

5   in order that the Children of Israel may bring their slaughter-
      offerings that they are slaughtering in the open field,
    that they may bring them to Y<small>HWH</small>, to the entrance of the Tent
      of Appointment, to the priest,
    and slaughter them as slaughter-offerings of *shalom* to Y<small>HWH</small>.

6   The priest is to dash their blood against the slaughter-site of
      Y<small>HWH</small>, at the entrance of the Tent of Appointment,
    and is to turn the fat into smoke as a soothing savor to Y<small>HWH</small>—

7   that they may slaughter no longer their slaughter-offerings
    to the hairy (goat-demons) after whom they go whoring.
    A law for the ages shall this be for them, throughout their
      generations.

8   And to them you are (also) to say:
    Any-man, any-man of the House of Israel or of the sojourners
      that sojourn in their midst
    who offers-up an offering-up or a slaughter-offering

9   and to the Tent of Appointment does not bring it, to perform-as-
      sacrifice to Y<small>HWH</small>:
    cut off shall that man be from his kinspeople!

10 And any-man, any-man of the House of Israel or of the
      sojourners that sojourn in their midst
    that eats any blood:

---

4 **bloodguilt:** Such slaughtering seems to be equated with the murder of a human being. **cut off from amid his kinspeople:** Schwartz (1987) understands this as premature death (dying before one's normally allotted time); Frymer-Kensky (1983) as dying without heirs. Greenstein, on the other hand, shows that it indicates execution, not by human beings, but by some kind of divine agency—perhaps as punishment "for transgressions that escape human detection" (personal communication).

7 **goat-demons:** Heb. *se'irim,* a common word for "hairy (goats)," but here with a clearly pagan ring.

8 **an offering-up or a slaughter-offering:** Probably a merism indicating "any sacrifice" (Schwartz 1987).

10 **eats any blood:** The prohibition against eating blood was unique to Israel in the ancient Near East (Bamberger). It has survived throughout the ages among Jews; those who keep the kosher laws still drain blood out of meat before cooking it (cf. v.13).

I set my face against the person who eats the blood;
I will cut him off from amid his kinspeople!

11 For the life of the flesh—it is in the blood;
I (myself) have given it to you upon the slaughter-site, to effect-
ransom for your lives,
for the blood—it effects-ransom for life!

12 Therefore I say to the Children of Israel:
Every person among you is not to eat blood,
and the sojourner that sojourns in your midst is not to eat blood.

13 And any-man, any-man of the Children of Israel or of the
sojourner that sojourns in your midst
who hunts any hunted wild-animal or a bird that may be eaten
is to pour out its blood and cover it with the dust.

14 For the life of all flesh—its blood is its life!
So I say to the Children of Israel:
The blood of all flesh you are not to eat,
for the life of all flesh—it is its blood,
everyone eating it shall be cut off!

15 And any person that eats a carcass, or an animal-torn-to-pieces,
among the native-born or among the sojourners,
when he scrubs his garments and washes in water,
and remains-*tamei* until sunset—
then he is pure.

16 But if he does not scrub (them), and his flesh he does not wash,
he continues-to-bear his iniquity!

11 **it effects-ransom:** Or perhaps "effects-atonement" for taking a life. We have already seen that blood "effects-purgation" for holy objects that have been ritually contaminated (cf. Chap. 16).

14 **its blood is its life:** Heb. difficult.

HOLINESS

(18–26)

THE ADDITION OF CHAPTERS 18–26 CHANGES THE NATURE OF THE BOOK BEFORE US. IT accomplishes this, not by introducing something entirely new into biblical thinking, but by broadening the base of God's words to Moshe in Leviticus. In this book we have already encountered the "Holy-Shrine," "holy-things," "holy donations," and the like; we have seen that Israel is to be "separate" from the nations around it in a variety of life areas. But now we move toward expansion of what was called for at the first moments at Sinai: for Israel to be a "[kingdom of priests and a] holy nation" (Ex. 19:6).

While the exact structure and setting of the Holiness Code, as these chapters were designated a century ago, are subject to scholarly debate, its thrust seems clear enough. Beginning with sexual relations, Israel is to be "holy," "separate" from other nations. Holiness here has a connotation of wholeness and perfection; Wright (1992) has defined it as "that which is consistent with God and his character."

Imitatio dei, the human urge to be godlike, is an ancient, undoubtedly prehistoric one. We long to be linked with the primal powers of existence, whose rush we feel at heightened moments of *perception,* but whose perfection is always out of reach in the flesh and blood world of human beings. The Torah, in contrast, presents the longing for perfection and wholeness as properly expressed through a discipline of *behavior* in all areas of life, personal and communal. The central lines "Holy are you to be, / for holy am I, YHWH your God" (19:2) are followed by line after line calling for holiness in worship, agriculture, interpersonal relations, business, the treatment of the disabled and the elderly, court procedure, and sexuality, to list some of the areas covered.

Many communities of the "elect," from Qumran at the Dead Sea to medieval monasteries, and many individuals, from biblical Nazirites (Num. 6) to Sufi mystics and St. Francis, have sought to create lives suffused with holiness; one could easily maintain that many of the mainstream forms and ideas in Judaism, Christianity, and Islam have remained wedded to this approach. They all owe a debt, one way or the other, to Lev. 18–26, especially in the communal sphere. Rarely has the drive toward holiness found as full expression in a vision of "real life" society, grounded in the everyday world of people and institutions, as it does in the texts to be found in the following chapters.

For many decades, debate has raged within the scholarly community as to the date and setting of H, the putative stratum of literature to which these chapters belong. As of this writing there is still not full agreement on (a) whether H was indeed a separate document or school, and (b) whether its origin and influence can be easily traced (cf., for instance, Knohl, and Milgrom 1993). These disagreements, however, should not and must not detract from the importance of what we have in these chapters: a significant statement of the ethical code of ancient Israel which continues to speak to contemporary problems.

Pollution from Forbidden Unions (18): Now begin, thematically and stylistically, the chapters on holiness. Like much of this final section of the book, Chap. 18 is distinguished by its powerful use of rhetoric (cf. vv.3–5, similar in tone to much of Deuteronomy). Separation returns as a major theme, this time stressing the divide between Israel and the nations around (vv.3 and 27–30). The emphasis on sexuality mirrors that on food in Chap. 11; the two often reflect each other in culture, both in practice and in imagery. Thus the wording here ("it is insidiousness," "it is perversion") parallels the rhetoric of Chap. 11 ("it is abomination," "it is a detestable-thing"). Structurally, just as the laws on pollution began with categories of and distinctions between animals for the purpose of eating, so the holiness laws begin with categories of and distinctions between partners for the purposes of sexual relations (Eilberg-Schwartz, Goodman). The confusing of boundaries again becomes a grave matter.

In Schwartz's (1987) view, the list of forbidden women goes through a sequence from close relatives, to indirect ones, to women related to each other, and finally to other cases of "abomination." In general, the list deals with women whose sexuality and reproductivity are controlled by males (Wegner 1992)—in other words, it reflects a highly patriarchal society.

An odd omission of sexual prohibitions is the one between a man and his daughter; perhaps it was universally understood as the primary one, and hence did not require mentioning.

Refrains in the chapter, which create its backbone, include "I am YHWH your God" and the constant "the nakedness of X you are not to expose." Late in the chapter, the words "abomination" and "*tum'a*" frequently recur.

◆ 18:1 YHWH spoke to Moshe, saying:

2   Speak to the Children of Israel and say to them:
    I am YHWH your God!

3   What is done in the land of Egypt, wherein you were settled, you
      are not to do;
    what is done in the land of Canaan, to which I am bringing you,
      you are not to do;
    by their laws you are not to walk.

4   My regulations you are to do, my laws you are to keep, walking
      by them,
    I am YHWH your God!

5   You are to keep my laws and my regulations,
    which when a human does them, he lives by (means of) them,
    I am YHWH!

6   Any-man, any-man—to any kin of one's (own) flesh you are not
      to come-near, exposing their "nakedness"!
    I am YHWH!

7   The nakedness of your father, and the nakedness of your mother,
      you are not to expose!
    She is your mother—you are not to expose her nakedness!

8   The nakedness of your father's wife, you are not to expose!
    She is the nakedness of your father.

9   The nakedness of your sister, the daughter of your father or the
      daughter of your mother,
    born in the house or born outside—
    you are not to expose their nakedness!

10   The nakedness of your son's daughter or of your daughter's
      daughter,
    you are not to expose their nakedness!
    Indeed, they are your nakedness.

18:4 **do:** Elsewhere (especially in Deuteronomy) I translate Heb. *'-s-h* as "observe"; here, I have retained "do" as a theme word in v. 3–5.

6 **kin:** Heb. *she'er,* "flesh, meat," synonymous with *basar,* which, however, does not bear the additional meaning of "kin." Note again the connection between food and sexuality. **exposing their "naked-** **ness":** To have sexual contact with them; "nakedness" is probably a euphemism for "genitals."

7 **The nakedness of your father, and the nakedness of your mother:** Perhaps better understood as "the nakedness (reserved for) your father, the nakedness of your mother" (Levine). See Ehrlich's earlier comments on Deut. 23:1.

11 The nakedness of the daughter of your father's wife, (as one)
　　born to your father—
she is your sister.
You are not to expose her nakedness!

12 The nakedness of your father's sister, you are not to expose!
She is the kin of your father.

13 The nakedness of your mother's sister, you are not to expose!
Indeed, she is the kin of your mother.

14 The nakedness of your father's brother, you are not to expose!
To his wife you are not to come-near—
she is your aunt!

15 The nakedness of your daughter-in-law, you are not to expose!
She is your son's wife.
You are not to expose her nakedness!

16 The nakedness of your brother's wife, you are not to expose!
She is the nakedness of your brother.

17 The nakedness of a woman and her daughter (together), you are
　　not to expose!
Her son's daughter or her daughter's daughter you are not to
　　take-in-marriage, exposing their nakedness!
They are kin, it is insidiousness!

18 And a woman along with her sister, you are not to take-in-
　　marriage, producing-rivalry, exposing her nakedness in
　　addition to her, during her lifetime!

19 To a woman during her *tum'a* of being-apart you are not to
　　come-near, exposing her nakedness!

20 To the wife of your fellow you are not to give your emission of
　　seed, becoming-*tamei* through her!

---

11 **the daughter of your father's wife** etc.: It is not entirely clear what is meant by this case.

14 **your father's brother:** His "nakedness" is exposed
by your sleeping with his wife.

17 **insidiousness:** Heb. *zimma,* from a verb meaning
"to scheme"; the word is sometimes translated as
"wickedness, lewdness."

18 **And a woman** etc.: As in the story of Leah and
Rahel, Yaakov's wives (Gen. 29–31).

19 **during her *tum'a* of being-apart:** Here, unlike in

15:24, the man is not merely ritually polluted until
sunset, but sleeping with the woman during her period is regarded as a grave offense that cannot be expiated. This section of Leviticus evidently considers
such an act on a par with bestiality and adultery;
perhaps it too falls under the category of "forbidden
mixtures" (in this case, semen and menstrual blood)
that are mentioned in 19:19, or else the mixture is another instance of the life-death boundary being violated (Greenstein 1984a).

21 Your seed-offspring you are not to give-over for bringing-across to
    the Molekh,
    that you not profane the name of your God,
    I am YHWH!
22 With a male you are not to lie (after the manner of) lying with a
    woman,
    it is an abomination!
23 With any animal you are not to give your emission of seed,
    becoming-*tamei* through it;
    a woman is not to stand before an animal, mating with it,
    it is perversion!
24 You are not to make-yourselves-*tamei* through any of these,
    for through all these, they make-themselves-*tamei*, the nations
    that I am sending out before you.
25 Thus the land became-*tamei,* and I called it to account for its
    iniquity,
    so that the land vomited out its inhabitants.
26 But you are to keep, yourselves, my laws and my regulations,
    not doing any of these abominations,
    the native and the sojourner that sojourns in your midst,
27 for all these abominations did the men of the land do that were
    before you,
    and the land became-*tamei*—
28 that the land not vomit you out for your making it *tamei*
    as it vomited out the nation that was before you.
29 For whoever does any of these abominable-things—
    cut off shall be those persons that do (them) from amid their
    kinspeople!

---

21 **... the Molekh:** While there is disagreement on the meaning here, it can be shown that this probably does refer to child sacrifice to a deity (Levine). A crucial question is why it intrudes on the list of sexual prohibitions. The answer may lie in the observation that to the Israelite mind, paganism (of which Molekh-worship was likely seen as the most egregious kind) was synonymous with sexual immorality.

22 **With a male:** The text here directly condemns homosexuality, which was a feature of many ancient societies. This prohibition may reflect the central issue of separation once again.

23 **perversion:** Or "confusion, mingling" (Frymer-Kensky 1983), adding to the strong vocabulary of condemnation in this chapter.

25 **vomited out:** Once again, a food metaphor!

General Regulations on Holiness I (19): As the key chapter of this part of Leviticus, Chap. 19 is wide-ranging and rhetorically powerful. It extends holiness to virtually all areas of life—family, calendar, cult, business, civil and criminal law, social relations, and sexuality. Most (but not all) of the laws deal with what we would term ethics, that is, relations between people (Wenham notes the alternation of the terms "fellow [citizen]," "kinsman," and "neighbor"). As such, they have become an exemplar and a cornerstone, at least in idealized form, in Western thinking about these issues.

Structurally speaking, the chapter is not systematic. As Schwartz (1987)has noted, this is probably intentional, reflecting the desire to avoid categorization or compartmentalization of life before God. He lays out the structure of the core part of the chapter, vv.3–32, as discrete subsections, each ending with "I am YHWH [your God]," with vv.33–36 as two appendices, and a summary in v.37.

The opening (v.2) is crucial, even though the word-root "holy" does not recur in the chapter (it does, however, reverberate within the next four chapters). The style is predominantly apodictic—"You are not to . . . ," as was Chap. 18, and concentrates mostly on the negating of certain kinds of behavior. At the same time, the chapter makes a moving positive plea for proper treatment of the elderly, the poor, and, in general, one's "neighbor" (which is extended to the foreigner ["sojourner"] in vv.33–34).

Modern commentators have noted the similarity between certain passages in the chapter and the Ten Commandments, but do not see our chapter as directly derivative. Similar parallels may also be found in the Naboth story from the Elijah cycle (I Kings 21).

30 You are to keep my charge by not doing (any of) the abominable
     practices that were done before you,
   that you not become-*tamei* through them,
   I am YHWH your God!

19:1 YHWH spoke to Moshe, saying:
   2 Speak to the entire community of the Children of Israel, and say
       to them:
     Holy are you to be,
     for holy am I, YHWH your God!

   3 Each-man—his mother and his father you are to hold-in-awe,
     and my Sabbaths you are to keep:
     I am YHWH your God!

   4 Do not turn-your-faces to no-gods,
     and molten gods you are not to make yourselves,
     I am YHWH your God!

   5 Now when you slaughter a slaughter-offering of *shalom* to YHWH,
     for your being-accepted you are to slaughter it.
   6 At the time of your slaughtering it, it is to be eaten, and on the
       morrow (as well),
     but what remains by the third day is to be burned in fire.
   7 Should it be eaten, yes, eaten on the third day,
     it is tainted-meat, it will not be accepted;
   8 those who eat it—his iniquity must he bear,
     for the holy-offering of YHWH he has profaned,
     cut off shall that person be from his kinspeople!

   9 Now when you harvest the harvest of your land,
     you are not to finish (to the) edge of your field in harvesting,
     the full-gathering of your harvest you are not to gather;
  10 your vineyard you are not to glean,
     the break-off of your vineyard you are not to gather—

19:3 **mother and father . . . Sabbaths:** The two are cou-
    pled elsewhere (e.g., 19:30, 26:2).
   4 **no-gods:** Heb. *elilim*, a popular play on *el/elohim*

("God, gods") and *al,* "nothing." Greenstein (personal communication) suggests "little-gods" as another possibility.

rather, for the afflicted and for the sojourner you are to leave
    them,
I am YHWH your God!

11 You are not to steal,
    you are not to lie,
    you are not to deal-falsely, each-man with his fellow!
12 You are not to swear by my name falsely,
    thus profaning the name of your God—
    I am YHWH!

13 You are not to withhold (property from) your neighbor,
    you are not to commit-robbery.
    You are not to keep-overnight the working-wages of a hired-hand
        with you until morning.
14 You are not to insult the deaf,
    before the blind you are not to place a stumbling-block:
    rather, you are to hold your God in awe;
    I am YHWH!

15 You are not to commit corruption in justice;
    you are not to lift-up-in-favor the face of the poor,
    you are not to overly-honor the face of the great;
    with equity you are to judge your fellow!
16 You are not to traffic in slander among your kinspeople.
    You are not to stand by the blood of your neighbor,
    I am YHWH!

17 You are not to hate your brother in your heart;
    rebuke, yes, rebuke your fellow,
    that you not bear sin because of him!

---

10 **afflicted:** Or "wretched." **leave:** In the sense of "relinquish."
13 **commit-robbery:** Possibly an evaluation or explanation of the previous line.
15 **equity:** Heb. *tzedek,* often translated "righteous-

ness," but here, as often, it has the meaning of even-handedness in judgment.
17 **rebuke:** The emotions are to come into the open, not to lie festering. **that you not bear sin:** Because you did not alert him to the consequences of his behavior.

18 You are not to take-vengeance, you are not to retain-anger against
    the sons of your kinspeople—
but be-loving to your neighbor (as one) like yourself,
I am YHWH!

19 My laws, you are to keep:
Your animal, you are not to (allow to) mate (in) two-kinds;
your field, you are not to sow with two-kinds;
a garment of two-kinds, of *shaatnez,* is not to go on you.

20 A man—when he lies with a woman, (with) an emission of seed,
and she is a handmaid destined for (another) man,
and redeemed, she has not been redeemed, or freedom has not
    been given her:
compensation shall there be;
they are not to be put-to-death, for she has not been freed.

21 But he is to bring as his *asham-*offering to YHWH, to the entrance
    of the Tent of Appointment, a ram of *asham-*offering.

22 The priest is to effect-atonement for him with the ram of *asham-*
    offering, before the presence of YHWH,
for the sin that he has sinned,
and he shall be granted-pardon for the sin that he has sinned.

23 Now when you enter the land, and plant any-kind of tree for
    eating,
you are to regard its fruit (like) a foreskin, a foreskin.
For three years it is to be considered-foreskinned for you,
you are not to eat (it).

24 And in the fourth year shall all its fruit be a holy-portion, (for)
    jubilation for YHWH;

---

18 **be-loving to your neighbor:** The meaning of this
phrase, and the concept, have been widely debated
throughout the ages. The translation follows B-R,
which emphasizes the personhood of one's neighbor—and of the sojourner in v.34.

19 **two-kinds:** That is, a mixture. The prohibition regarding the field entails avoiding mixing different
crops on a single field. Mixtures in the Bible seem to
be reserved for the divine sphere alone. **shaatnez:**
Of uncertain origin, this word probably means "of

mixed-stuff"; it breaks the rhythm of the law, and so
was probably a later addition meant to explain
"two-kinds" in reference to clothing (Fishbane
1988).

20 **destined . . . redeemed:** Cf. Ex. 21:7–11 (Levine).
This does not qualify as biblical adultery.

23 **(like) a foreskin:** Because it is incomplete or
"unfit," in the biblical view. Here culture is to overcome nature.

General Regulations on Holiness II (20): We move now into laws dealing with some of the more serious offenses against God in the biblical view: idolatry (including worship of the "Molekh" and consulting spirits), insulting parents, adultery, and sexual crimes. These are distinguished from the previous chapter by the inclusion of punishments; their seriousness is indicated by their capital nature. The reiteration of sexual laws forms a bracket with Chap. 18, thus highlighting the central position and rhetoric of 19. Another bracket, this time within the chapter, involves the chiasm of necromancy and the exhortation to be holy (vv.6–7 and 26–27). Finally, while the motifs of the Israelites avoiding pagan practices, and the land "vomiting out" its wrongdoers, return from Chap. 18, there is a further throwback (vv.24–26): to Chap. 11, where "separation" from the nations was a major issue in terms of diet.

25 in the fifth year may you eat its fruit, to add for you its produce,
I am YHWH your God!

26 You are not to eat (anything together) with blood.
You are not to practice-divination, you are not to practice-
soothsaying.

27 You are not to round off the edge-growth of your head, you are
not to diminish the edge-growth of your beard;

28 an incision for a (dead) person you are not to make in your flesh,
writing of skin-etching you are not to place on yourselves,
I am YHWH!

29 You are not to profane your daughter by making her a whore,
that the land not go whoring
and the land be filled with insidiousness.

30 My Sabbaths you are to keep, my Holy-Shrine you are to hold-
in-awe,
I am YHWH!

31 Do not turn-your-faces to ghosts, of favorable-spirits do not
inquire, to become-*tamei* through them,
I am YHWH your God!

32 In the face of the gray-hair, you are to rise,
you are to honor the face of the elderly, thus holding your God
in awe,
I am YHWH!

33 Now when there sojourns with you a sojourner in your land,
you are not to maltreat him;

34 like the native-born among you shall he be to you, the sojourner
that sojourns with you;

26 **You are not to eat** etc.: Vv.26 through 28 deal with "practices associated with idolatry" (Schwartz 1987). **divination:** This act of predicting the future typically involved reading the shapes of nonmixing liquids in goblets; cf. Gen. 44:5.
27 **round off ... diminish:** These prohibitions are likely related to what immediately follows: they were acts appearing in Canaanite funeral practices.

As has often been noted, Leviticus is practically silent about cultic practices concerning the dead—which it wishes to avoid (perhaps out of a desire to avoid worshiping the dead).
31 **favorable-spirits:** others, "familiar spirits."
33 **maltreat:** Schwartz (1987) understands this as "unfair commerce."

◆ be-loving to him (as one) like yourself,
for sojourners were you in the land of Egypt.
I am YHWH your God!

35 You are not to commit corruption in justice,
in measure, weight, or capacity;

36 scales of equity, weighing-stones of equity, an *efa* of equity and a
hin of equity you shall have.
I am YHWH your God, who brought you out of the land of
Egypt!

37 You are to keep all my laws and all my regulations, and observe
them,
I am YHWH!

20:1 YHWH spoke to Moshe, saying:

2 And to the Children of Israel you are to say:
Any-man, any-man of the Children of Israel and of the
sojourners that sojourn in Israel
that gives of his seed-offspring to the Molekh
is to be put-to-death, yes, death;
the People of the Land are to pelt him with stones.

3 As for me, I will direct my face against that man
and will cut him off from amid his kinspeople,
since of his seed he has given to the Molekh
with the result that he makes my Holy-Shrine *tamei* and profanes
my holy name.

4 Now if the People of the Land should hide, yes, hide their eyes
from that man
when he gives of his seed to the Molekh, by not putting him to
death,

5 I myself will set my face against that man and against his clan,
and will cut off him and all who go whoring along with him, to
whore after the Molekh,
from amid their kinspeople.

---

36 **weighing-stones:** Weights used in calculating amounts of goods.
20:2 **the Molekh:** that is, "the [divine] King," the designation of this particular god.

4 **hide their eyes:** Choose to ignore.

6 And the person who turns-his-face to ghosts or to familiar-spirits,
to whore after them,
I will direct my face against that person
and will cut him off from amid his kinspeople!

7 So you are to hallow-yourselves, you are to be holy,
for I YHWH am your God!

8 You are to keep my laws, and observe them,
I YHWH am the one-who-hallows you!

9 Indeed, any-man, any-man that insults his father or his mother
is to be put-to-death, yes, death,
his father and his mother he has insulted, his bloodguilt is upon
him!

10 A man who adulters with the wife of (another) man, who
adulters with the wife of his neighbor,
is to be put-to-death, yes, death,
the adulterer and the adulteress.

11 A man who lies with the wife of his father—
the nakedness of his father he has exposed,
the two of them are to be put-to-death, yes, death, their
bloodguilt is upon them!

12 A man who lies with his daughter-in-law—
the two of them are to be put-to-death, yes, death,
they have done perversion, their bloodguilt is upon them!

13 A man who lies with a male (as one) lies with a woman—
abomination have the two of them done,
they are to be put-to-death, yes, death, their bloodguilt is upon
them!

14 A man who takes-in-marriage a woman and her mother—
it is insidiousness,
in fire they are to be burned, he and they,
that there be no such insidiousness in your midst!

15 A man who gives his emission to an animal

---

11 **the nakedness of his father:** For an explanation of
this phrase, cf. note to 18:7 above.

Regulations Concerning Holiness: Priests I (21): This chapter, and the one that follows, relate holiness to the suitability of priests to serve in the sanctuary. The laws are in the main negative ones, that is, they outline ways in which a priest may be disqualified. The first part of the chapter concentrates on how contact with death disqualifies a priest; in Levine's view, this avoidance of the dead reflects the Bible's abhorrence of pagan cults centered around death. The laws concerning soundness of body and sexuality confirm earlier passages on holiness as wholeness.

The central word-root is again "holy"; six times in Chaps. 21–22 we hear the refrain "I am YHWH the one-who-hallows you / them."

is to be put-to-death, yes, death,
and the animal you are to kill!

16 A woman who comes-near any animal to mate with it—
you are to kill the woman and the animal,
they are to be put-to-death, yes, death, their bloodguilt is upon
them!

17 A man who takes-in-marriage his sister, the daughter of his father
or the daughter of his mother,
so that he sees her nakedness and she sees his nakedness—
it is a disgraceful-thing,
they are to be cut off before the eyes of their kinspeople,
the nakedness of his sister he has exposed,
his iniquity he shall bear!

18 A man who lies with a woman (in her) infirmity, exposing her
nakedness—
her source he has laid-naked, and as for her, she has exposed her
source of blood;
the two of them are to be cut off from amid their kinspeople!

19 The nakedness of your mother's sister or your father's sister, you
are not to expose!
For his (own) kin he has laid-naked,
their iniquity they are to bear!

20 A man who lies with his aunt—
the nakedness of his uncle he has exposed,
their sin they are to bear, accursed will they die!

21 A man that takes-in-marriage the wife of his brother:
she is one-set-apart,
the nakedness of his brother he has exposed, accursed they will
be!

22 You are to keep all my laws and all my regulations, and observe
them,

---

18 **the two of them are to be cut off:** Once again, the
serious punishment here exceeds what was mentioned in the earlier context of 15:24, and echoes the
treatment in 18:19.

20 **accursed:** Or "in shame" (Ehrlich); sometimes
translated "childless" (Buber: "naked-of-children").

that the land not vomit you out into which I am bringing you to
    settle.

23 You are not to walk by the laws of the nations that I am sending-
    out before you,
    for all these they did, and (so) I abhorred them,

24 so I say to you: It is you who will possess their soil,
    I myself will give it to you, to take-possession of it,
    a land flowing with milk and honey.
    I am YHWH your God, who has separated you from the (other)
    peoples!

25 So you are to separate between the pure animals and the *tamei*-
    ones, and between the *tamei* fowl and the pure ones,
    that you not make your selves detestable through animal or fowl
    or anything with which the soil stirs,
    that I have separated for you to treat-as-*tamei*.

26 You are to be holy to me,
    for holy am I, YHWH;
    I have separated you from the (other) peoples
    to be mine!

27 A man or a woman with whom is a ghost or a favorable-spirit—
    they are to be put-to-death, yes, death,
    with stones you are to pelt them, their bloodguilt is upon them!

21:1 YHWH said to Moshe:
    Say to the priests, the Sons of Aharon, say to them:
    For a (dead-)person among his people, one is not to make oneself
    tamei,

2 except for his kin, one near to him:
    for his mother or for his father, or for his son, or for his daughter
    or for his brother,

3 or for his virgin sister, near to him, who has never belonged to a
    man,
    for her he may make himself *tamei*.

---

23 **sending-out:** or "driving out" (JPS).
21:1 **For a (dead-)person:** That is, the priests are not supposed to come in contact with the dead. Vestiges of
this prohibition still survive among religious Jews:
the descendant of a priestly family is not supposed
to enter a cemetery.

◆ 4 He is not to make himself *tamei* (as) a husband among his people
    (does), to profane himself.
5 They are not to make-bald a bald-spot on their head,
    the edge of their beard they are not to shave off,
    in their flesh they are not to incise an incision.
6 Holy are they to be to their God,
    they are not to profane the name of their God—
    for the fire-offerings of Yhwh, the food-offerings of their God
        they bring-near,
    so they are to be holy!
7 A woman (who is a) whore, a profaned-one, they are not to take-
        in-marriage,
    a woman divorced from her husband they are not to take-in-
        marriage,
    for holy is he to his God
8 and you are to treat-him-as-holy—
    for the food-offerings of your God he brings-near;
    holy shall he be for you,
    for holy am I, Yhwh, the one-who-hallows you!
9 And the daughter of a man (who is a) priest—
    when she profanes herself by whoring,
    it is her father that she profanes,
    in fire she is to be burned!
10 Now the priest that is greater than his brothers,
    who has had poured on his head the oil of anointing
    and has been mandated to dress in the garments:
    his head he is not to bare,
    his garments he is not to tear;
11 (the presence of) any dead persons he is not to enter,
    for (even) his father or his mother he is not to make himself
        tamei,
12 from the Holy-Shrine he is not to go out—
    that he not profane the Holy-Shrine of his God,

---

10 **the priest that is greater:** The "Great Priest," i.e.,
the High Priest.

Regulations Concerning Holiness: Priests II (22): The priestly rules on holiness continue, with special attention given to the priest's proper state when he eats of the
"holy donations." The second part of the chapter, from v.17 on, turns to the state
of the sacrificial animals. They are to be without blemish, just as the priests must
be (cf. Chap. 21). This correspondence between human and animal has been noted
before; it is part of Leviticus's general scheme of a perfect God requiring perfection in worship.

for the sacred oil of anointing is upon him,
I am Yhwh!

13 And he—(only) a woman in her virginity may he take-in-
marriage;

14 a widow or a divorcée, or one profaned (by) whoring,
these he is not to take-in-marriage;
rather, a virgin from his people he is to take as a wife,

15 that he not profane his seed among his people,
for I am Yhwh, the one-who-hallows him!

16 Yhwh spoke to Moshe, saying:

17 Speak to Aharon, saying:
A man of your seed, throughout their generations, who has in
him a defect
is not to come-near to bring-near the food of his God.

18 Indeed, any man who has in him a defect is not to come-near:
a man (who is) blind or lame or mutilated or too long-limbed,

19 or a man that has in him a broken leg or a broken arm,

20 or a hunchback or a dwarf, or one spotted in his eye,
or (with) a scab or (with) eruptions, or (with) crushed testicles.

21 Any man that has in him a defect, from the seed of Aharon the
priest,
is not to approach to bring-near the fire-offerings of Yhwh,
a defect is in him,
with the food of Yhwh he is not to approach, to bring-it-near.

22 The food-offerings of his God from the holiest holy-portions, or
from the holy-portions, he may eat;

23 however, the curtain he is not to enter, the slaughter-site he is not
to approach,
for a defect is in him,
he is not to profane my holy-shrines;
for I am Yhwh, the one-who-hallows them.

24 So spoke Moshe to Aharon and to his sons
and to all the Children of Israel.

17 **a defect:** Some physical blemish, as enumerated in
v.18ff. **come-near . . . bring-near:** Here with the
meanings "officiate . . . sacrifice."

◆ 22:1 YHWH spoke to Moshe, saying:

2 Speak to Aharon and to his sons,
that they may be-careful (in handling) the holy-donations of the
    Children of Israel
—that they not profane my holy name—
which they hallow to me,
I am YHWH!

3 Say (further) to them:
Throughout your generations, any man that comes-near—of all
    of your seed—
to the holy-donations that the Children of Israel hallow to YHWH,
    with his *tum'a* upon him:
that person will be cut off from my presence,
I am YHWH!

4 Any-man, any-man of the seed of Aharon, if he has-*tzaraat* or
    has-a-flow:
of the holy-donations he is not to eat, until he is pure;
whoever touches anything *tamei* by a (dead) person,
or a man from whom an emission of seed goes out,

5 or a man that touches any swarming-thing through which he
    becomes-*tamei,* or a human through which he becomes-*tamei,*
whatever his *tum'a*—

6 the person who touches it is to remain-*tamei* until sunset,
he is not to eat of the holy-donations
unless he washes his flesh in water;

7 when the sun comes in, (then) he is pure,
afterward he may eat of the holy-donations, for they are his food.

8 A carcass or a torn-animal he is not to eat, to become-*tamei* by
    means of them,
I am YHWH!

9 So they shall keep my charge,
that they not bear sin thereby and die on account of it
when they profane it,
I am YHWH, the one-who-hallows them!

10 Any outsider is not to eat the holy-donation;
a settler (belonging) to a priest, or a hired-hand, is not to eat the
    holy-donation;

11   but a priest, when he purchases a person through his purchase of
        silver—he may eat of it,
       and one born into his household may eat of his food.

12   The daughter of a priest—when she belongs (in marriage) to a
        man, an outsider,
       she—of the raised holy-donations she is not to eat.

13   And the daughter of a priest—if she is a widow or a divorcée, and
        seed-offspring she has none,
       when she returns to her father's house, as in her youth, from her
        father's food she may eat,
       any outsider may not eat of it;

14   but a (lay)man—if he eats a holy-donation in error, he is to add its
        fifth to it, giving to the priest the holy-donation.

15   They are not to profane the holy-donations of the Children of
        Israel, that they set aside for YHWH,

16   by causing them to bear iniquity (requiring an) *asham*-offering by
        eating their holy-donations,
       for I am YHWH, the one-who-hallows you!

17   YHWH spoke to Moshe, saying:

18   Speak to Aharon and to his sons and to all the Children of Israel,
       and say to them:
       Any-Man, any-man of the House of Israel or of the sojourners in
        Israel
       that brings-near his near-offering—including any of their vow-
        offerings or including any of their freewill-offerings that they
        bring-near to YHWH, as an offering-up—

19   for your acceptance
       (they must be): wholly-sound, male among the cattle, among the
        sheep or among goats;

20   any-one in whom is a defect, you are not to bring-near,
       for not for acceptance will it be-considered on your behalf.

21   A man—when he brings-near a slaughter-offering of *shalom* to
        YHWH—

22:11 **he may eat:** That is, the slave "person."   20 **any-one:** Among the animals brought for sacrifice.

Holy Days (23): Having dealt with holiness in such areas as worship, family life, ethics, priestly qualifications and behavior, and sacrificial animals and objects, the text now turns to holiness in time: the sacred calendar. While all ancient societies marked sacred time, in Judaism as it evolved out of the Bible the calendar took on particular significance, especially in the situation of exile. The centrality of time in Judaism has been articulately portrayed by Heschel; here we will limit discussion to the fullest of the biblical sacred calendars (others occur in Ex. 23 and 34, and Deut. 16), the one set forth in the present chapter.

The scheme is characteristically Levitical—it focuses on order and perfection, expressing these qualities by the use of the number 7, which was used thus in a number of ancient Near Eastern cultures. A partial list in this regard would include: 7 days from sabbath to sabbath; 7 days of two major festivals, spring and fall; 7 weeks between the two pilgrimage festivals in the spring; and all the holy days falling within the first 7 months of the year, with a major cluster occurring in the seventh month. To this could be added material from other passages in the Torah: 7 years to every sabbatical year (Ex. 23:10–11, Lev. 25:2–7, Deut. 15:1–3); and 7-times-7 years (plus one) till each Jubilee year (Lev. 25:8–17). One could go further (cf. the discussion and lists in Jenson), but the thrust should be clear: time, as well as space and behavior, is to be ordered in a way that again reflects divine perfection. One might also mention the continuation of this kind of thinking in both later Judaism and Christianity, which looked upon history itself in a schematic way.

As laid out in Leviticus, the sacred days of the seventh month follow a conventional ancient pattern described by Gaster (1961): the dying of the old year ("mortification" and "purgation," as expressed in Rosh Ha-Shanah and Yom Kippur), followed by the birth of the new year ("invigoration" and "jubilation," as expressed in Sukkot). The biblical calendar, then, evolved along dual tracks—lunar-solar (lunar months of 29 or 30 days, with an extra month added in late winter, 7 times every 19 years); and spring/fall new year (Passover falls in the "first month," but the full new year pattern, as we have mentioned, is played out in the fall).

A final indication of a late provenance for Chap. 23's calendar lies in the long treatment (vv.9–22, a third of the chapter) of Shavuot, the "Feast of Weeks." The emphasis seems to be on land here, suggesting a resettlement motif that would be particularly appropriate after the exile in Babylonia.

Theme words in the chapter include: "appointed-times," "proclamation of holiness," "throughout all your settlements," "a fire-offering to YHWH," and "anykind of servile work you are not to do." V.39–43, on the practice of and rationale behind Sukkot, seem to be another addition to the text, as they disrupt its natural flow.

for making a vow-offering or for a freewill-offering—among the
    herd or among the flock:
wholly-sound must it be, for acceptance,
any defect there must not be in it.

22 (One that is) blind or broken, or mutilated or (with) spotted-eye
    or scab or eruptions,
you are not to bring-near (any of) these to YHWH;
a fire-offering you may not place from (any of) them, on the
    slaughter-site to YHWH.

23 But an ox or a sheep, (too) long-limbed or stunted,
you may sacrifice it as a freewill-offering,
but for a vow-offering it will not be accepted.

24 (One that is) bruised or smashed or torn-up or cut out (in the
    testicles)
you are not to bring-near to YHWH,
in your land these may not be sacrificed.

25 And from the hand of a foreigner you are not to bring-near the
    food of your God from any of these,
for their ruin is in them, a defect is in them,
they will not be accepted on your behalf!

26 YHWH spoke to Moshe, saying:

27 An ox or a sheep or a goat, when it is born,
shall remain seven days under its mother,
and from the eighth day and forward it will be accepted as a near-
    offering, as a fire-offering to YHWH.

28 And an ox or a sheep—it and its young you are not to slay on one
    day.

29 When you slaughter a slaughter-offering of thanksgiving to YHWH,
for acceptance for you, you are to slaughter it:

30 on that (very) day it is to be eaten,
you are not to let (any) of it remain until morning,
I am YHWH!

---

23 **You may sacrifice:** The exception to the rule here concerns a voluntary offering; a defective animal would of course not be acceptable in the case of a *hattat*, for example (Wenham). The rabbis under-stood that this animal was not even placed on the altar, but merely sold, with the proceeds going to the sanctuary (Sifra, quoted in Bamberger).

25 **ruin:** Others, "mutilation" (Levine).

31 You are to keep my commandments, and observe them,
I am YHWH!

32 You are not to profane my holy name,
that I may be hallowed amid the Children of Israel;
I am YHWH, the one-who-hallows you,

33 who is bringing you out of the land of Egypt, to be for you a
God,
I am YHWH!

23:1 YHWH spoke to Moshe, saying:

2 Speak to the Children of Israel and say to them:
The appointed-times of YHWH, which you are to proclaim to
them (as) proclamations of holiness—
these are they, my appointed-times:

3 For six days may work be done,
but on the seventh day (is) Sabbath, Sabbath-Ceasing, a
proclamation of holiness,
any-kind of work you are not to do.
It is Sabbath to YHWH, throughout all your settlements.

4 These are the appointed-times of YHWH, proclamations of
holiness, which you are to proclaim at their appointed-times:

5 on the first New-Moon, on the fourteenth after the New-Moon,
between the setting-times
(is) Passover to YHWH.

6 On the fifteenth day after this New-Moon
(is) the pilgrimage-festival of *matzot* to YHWH:
for seven days, *matzot* you are to eat!

7 On the first day
a proclamation of holiness shall there be for you,
any-kind of servile work you are not to do.

23:2 **appointed-times:** Festivals. **proclamations of ho-**
liness: Heb. *mikra'ei kodesh;* an alternative rendering is "holy convocations," that is, sacred
gatherings.

3 **you are not to do:** I have translated this as "make"
(work) in Ex. 31ff., to underscore a major theme of
the book; here, such awkwardness may be avoided.

5 **between the setting-times:** Between the time that
the sun is below the horizon, no longer visible, and
total darkness. An idiomatic rendition would be "at
twilight."

8   You are to bring-near a fire-offering to YHWH, for seven days,
    on the seventh day (is) a proclamation of holiness,
    any-kind of servile work you are not to do.

9   YHWH spoke to Moshe, saying:

10 Speak to the Children of Israel and say to them:
    When you enter the land that I am giving you,
    and you harvest its harvest,
    you are to bring the premier sheaf of your harvest to the priest.

11 He is to elevate the sheaf before the presence of YHWH, for
        acceptance for you;
    on the morrow of the Sabbath the priest is to elevate it.

12 You are to perform-a-sacrifice on the day of your elevating the
        sheaf:
    a sheep, wholly-sound, in its (first) year, as an offering-up to
        YHWH,

13 and its grain-gift: two tenth-measures of flour mixed with oil, a
        fire-offering to YHWH, of soothing savor;
    and its poured-offering of wine: a fourth of a *hin*.

14 Now bread or parched-grain or groats, you are not to eat, until
        that same day,
    until you have brought the near-offering of your God—
    (it is) a law for the ages, into your generations, throughout all
        your settlements.

15 Now you are to number for yourselves, from the morrow of the
        Sabbath, from the day that you bring the elevated sheaf,
    seven Sabbaths-of-days,
    whole (weeks) are they to be;

8   **servile work:** What appears to be meant is heavy labor.
10 **and you harvest its harvest:** The wheat harvest, in the late spring.
11 **the morrow of the Sabbath:** The precise meaning of this phrase was the subject of lengthy debate among the ancient rabbis. Traditionally in Judaism, seven weeks are counted until this Festival of Weeks (Shavuot), beginning on the day after the start of Passover. Another old interpretation understands the phrase to mean the Sunday after Passover. Fish-

bane (1988) proposes that an older meaning of *shabbat,* namely "full moon," may be operative here, and that it solves the problems inherent in this passage.
13 **poured-offering:** Conventionally called a "libation," this involved the pouring out of wine on the altar, and was common in ancient religions.
14 **groats:** Or "fresh ears" (JPS).

16 until the morrow of the seventh Sabbath you are to number—
   fifty days,
   then you are to bring-near a grain-gift of new-crops to YHWH.

17 From your settlements you are to bring bread as an elevation-
   offering,
   two (loaves of) two tenth-measures of flour are they to be,
   leavened you are to bake them,
   as firstfruits to YHWH.

18 And you are to bring-near along with the bread seven sheep,
   wholly-sound, a year old,
   and one bull, a young of the herd, and rams, two,
   they shall be an offering-up for YHWH,
   with their grain-gift and their poured-offerings,
   a fire-offering of soothing savor to YHWH.

19 And you are to perform-as-sacrifice: one hairy goat for a *hattat,*
   and two sheep, a year old, for a slaughter-offering of *shalom.*

20 The priest is to elevate them, together with the bread of the
   firstfruits
   as an elevation-offering before the presence of YHWH,
   together with the two sheep;
   they shall be a holy-portion for YHWH, for the priest.

21 And you are to make-proclamation on that same day,
   a proclamation of holiness shall there be for you,
   any-kind of servile work you are not to do—
   a law for the ages, throughout your settlements, into your
   generations.

22 Now when you harvest the harvest of your land,
   you are not to finish-off the edge of your field when you harvest
   (it),
   the full-gleaning of your harvest you are not to glean;
   for the afflicted and for the sojourner you are to leave them,
   I am YHWH your God!

23 YHWH spoke to Moshe, saying:
24 Speak to the Children of Israel, saying:
On the seventh New-Moon, on (day) one of the New-Moon,
you are to have Sabbath-ceasing,
a reminder by (horn-)blasting, a proclamation of holiness.
25 Any-kind of servile work you are not to do;
you are to bring-near a fire-offering to YHWH.

26 YHWH spoke to Moshe, saying:
27 Mark, on the tenth after this seventh New-Moon,
it is the Day of Atonement,
a proclamation of holiness shall there be for you.
You are to afflict your selves,
and you are to bring-near a fire-offering to YHWH;
28 any-kind of work you are not to do on that same day,
for it is the Day of Atonement, to effect-atonement for you
before the presence of YHWH your God.
29 Indeed, if any person does not afflict-himself on that same day,
he is to be cut-off from his kinspeople,
30 and if any person does any-kind of work on that same day—
I will cause that person to perish from amid his kinspeople!
31 Any-kind of work you are not to do—
a law for the ages, into your generations, throughout all your
settlements.
32 It is Sabbath, a Sabbath-ceasing for you,
you are to afflict your selves;
on the ninth (day) after the New-Moon, at sunset,
from sunset to sunset, you are to make-a-ceasing of your ceasing!

---

24 **a reminder by (horn-)blasting:** This became the Jewish festival of Rosh Ha-Shanah, the "head of the (New) Year," at which a *shofar* (ram's horn) is still blown in synagogue. The reason here is probably a combination of proclamation (as before a king) and driving out demons (who, it should be noted, do not like loud noises).

27 **Mark:** Following JPS. **selves:** Heb. *nefesh,* variously rendered "soul," "emotions," and even "gullet" (Milgrom). The *nefesh* was one's personhood, one's essence.

Miscellany (24): Two issues, unrelated to what has gone before, are treated here: certain ritual objects in the Dwelling (oil/lamps and "showbread"), and the story of a man who insulted God and therefore had to be executed (along with further rules about capital crimes). The function of this chapter is not clear; perhaps it serves as a breather between the important sections on sacred days (23) and land tenure (25). It is also possible (as Levine notes) that chapters such as this one and Num. 15 serve as a repository for various cultic laws that needed a location. There are two other places in the Torah where a brief passage on the lights in the sanctuary may originally have served to separate sections: the end of Ex. 27 and the beginning of Num. 8. If so, that function no longer is as major as it once might have been.

The first two parts (2–4 and 5–9) are linked by their common vocabulary: "take," "arrange," "regularly," and "before the presence of YHWH" (Wenham). The second section (vv.10–23) is united by its chiastic structure (cf. Wenham here as well). It has points of contact with material in the Exodus laws, but here with the characteristic addition (v.22) of "I, YHWH, am your God."

33 YHWH spoke to Moshe, saying:

34 Speak to the Children of Israel, saying:
On the fifteenth day after this seventh New-Moon:
the pilgrimage-festival of Huts, for seven days, to YHWH.

35 On the first day (is) a proclamation of holiness,
any-kind of servile work you are not to do.

36 For seven days you are to bring-near a fire-offering to YHWH;
on the eighth day, a proclamation of holiness shall there be for
you,
you are to bring-near a fire-offering to YHWH
—it is (a day of) Restraint—
any-kind of servile work you are not to do.

37 These are the appointed-times of YHWH, which you are to
proclaim as proclamations of holiness,
to bring-near fire-offerings to YHWH—offering-up, grain-gift,
slaughter-offering and pour-offerings,
each-day's protocol in its day,

38 aside from the Sabbaths of YHWH, aside from your presents,
aside from all your vow-offerings and aside from all your freewill-
offerings that you give to YHWH.

39 Mark, on the fifteenth day after the seventh New-Moon,
when you have gathered-in the produce of the land,
you are to celebrate-as-pilgrimage the pilgrimage-festival of
YHWH, for seven days:
on the first day (is) a Sabbath-ceasing and on the eighth day is a
Sabbath-ceasing.

40 You are to take yourselves, on the first day, the fruit of beautiful
trees, branches of palms,
and boughs of thick tree-foliage, and willows of the brook.

34 **Huts:** Heb. *sukkot,* the name of the festival. Others, "booths."

36 **Restraint:** Heb. *atzeret,* understood by some as "solemn assembly."

37 **each-day's protocol . . . :** Each sacrifice appropriate for the particular holy day.

39 **celebrate-as-pilgrimage . . . pilgrimage-festival:** Heb. *tahoggu . . . hag;* cf. the Moslem *hajj* to Mecca.

B-R use "do-a-circle-dance," which is from another (although similar-sounding) root.

40 **fruit . . . branches . . . boughs . . . willows:** This was understood as the "Four Species" (*etrog* and three-bound *lulav*) that are used to this day in the Jewish festival of Sukkot.

And you are to rejoice before the presence of Yhwh your God for
    seven days,
41 you are to celebrate-it-as pilgrimage, a pilgrimage-festival to
    Yhwh, for seven days a year—
a law for the ages, throughout your generations:
in the seventh New-Moon you are to celebrate-it-as-pilgrimage
42 —in huts you are to stay for seven days,
every native in Israel is to stay in huts—
43 in order that your generations may know that in huts I had the
    Children of Israel stay
when I brought them out of the land of Egypt,
I am Yhwh your God!

44 So Moshe declared the appointed-times of Yhwh to the Children
    of Israel.

24:1 Yhwh spoke to Moshe, saying:
2 Command the Children of Israel,
that they take you oil of olives, clear, beaten, for lighting,
to draw up lampwicks, regularly.
3 Outside the Curtain of the Testimony, in the Tent of
    Appointment, Aharon is to arrange it,
from sunset to daybreak, before the presence of Yhwh,
    regularly—
a law for the ages, throughout your generations.
4 On the pure lampstand he is to arrange the lampwicks, before the
    presence of Yhwh, regularly.

5 You are to take flour and are to bake it (into) twelve loaves,
two tenth-measures shall be the one loaf;
6 you are to put them (into) two arranged-rows, six per row,
on the pure table, before the presence of Yhwh.
7 And you are to place on (each) row clear frankincense,
it shall be for the bread as a reminder-portion, a fire-offering to
    Yhwh.

---

40 **you are to rejoice:** That the festival was known as
the celebration is seen from the emphasis here on
joy.
42 **stay:** Or "dwell."

24:4 **the pure lampstand:** Detailed in Ex. 25:31–40.
5 **two tenth-measures:** Of an *efa.*
6 **the pure table:** Described in Ex. 25:23–30.

8 Sabbath day (by) Sabbath day he is to arrange it before the
    presence of YHWH, regularly,
from the Children of Israel as a covenant for the ages.

9 They are to be Aharon's and his sons',
they are to eat them in a holy place,
for they are a holiest holy-portion for him, from the fire-offerings
    of YHWH—an allotment for the ages.

10 Now the son of an Israelite woman went out
—he was (also) the son of an Egyptian man—
amid the Children of Israel;
and they scuffled in the camp,
the son of the Israelite-woman and a (fully) Israelite man.

11 Now the son of the Israelite woman reviled the Name, and
    insulted (it),
so they brought him to Moshe
—now the name of his mother (was) Shelomit daughter of Divri,
    of the tribe of Dan—

12 and they put him under guard, to clarify it for them by order of
    YHWH.

13 And YHWH spoke to Moshe, saying:

14 Take-out the insulter, outside the camp,
let all those who heard (the curse) lean their hands on his head
and let the entire community pelt him!

15 And to the Children of Israel you are to speak, saying:
Any-man, any-man that insults his god—
he shall bear his sin!

16 But whoever reviles the name of YHWH
is to be put-to-death, yes, death,
the entire community is to pelt, yes, pelt him;
as the sojourner, so the native,
when he reviles the Name, he is to be put-to-death!

8 **Sabbath day (by) Sabbath day:** Jewish tradition reflects this practice by mandating two loaves of bread at every sabbath meal.
11 **the Name:** Of God. **Divri:** From the root meaning "to speak."
12 **clarify:** This is one of four Torah passages where

something must be "clarified" by God during the case itself. The other three, which all occur in Numbers (9:6ff., 15:32ff., and 27:1ff.), fit logically in with their surroundings; this text, less so (Bamberger).
14 **the entire community:** Not only the witnesses (Greenstein, personal communication).

625

Regulations Concerning Land and Slavery (25): A final area of holiness that Leviticus discusses is that of ownership. The rules set forth in this chapter are based on the assumption that land, a most precious commodity in the ancient (and modern) Near East, and human beings, equally precious in the Bible, are not in fact the property of other human beings. The phrases "the land is not to be sold in-harness, / for the land is mine" (v.23) and "For my servants are they . . . they are not to be sold as the sale of serfs" (v.42) express the main corollary: God is the sole owner of land and people. The chapter, then, sets out regulations that make perpetual human ownership of these impossible. In the case of land, not only is the soil to rest every seven years, but every fifty years ($7 \times 7 + 1$), the land is to be "released" back to its original owner (who "redeems" it). Similarly, indentured servants—those who are forced into working for someone because of debts—are redeemable, if not by kin then by the occurrence of the Jubilee year.

Several things about the chapter suggest a late date to Levine. Redemption focuses on the individual rather than on the clan; "at Mount Sinai" might indicate an editorial hand; and the passages here, unlike their counterparts in Ex. 21 and Deut. 15, concentrate less on eradicating poverty than on ensuring that property stays in the family over generations. Indeed, some of the conditions presupposed by the chapter suggest the situation portrayed in Neh. 5, after the Babylonian Exile.

17 Now a man—when he strikes-down any human life,
   he is to be put-to-death, yes, death!
18 One who strikes the life of an animal is to pay for it, life in place
   of life.
19 And a man—when he renders a defect in his fellow:
   as he has done, thus is to be done to him—
20 break in place of break, eye in place of eye, tooth in place of
   tooth;
   as he has rendered a defect in (another) human, thus is to be
   rendered in him.
21 Whoever strikes-down an animal is to pay for it,
   but one who strikes-down a human is to be put-to-death.
22 One standard-of-judgment shall there be for you;
   as the sojourner, so shall the native be,
   for I, Yhwh, am your God!
23 Thus spoke Moshe to the Children of Israel.
   They took out the insulter, outside the camp
   and they pelted him with stones;
   so the Children of Israel did as Yhwh had commanded Moshe.

25:1 Yhwh spoke to Moshe at Mount Sinai, saying:
   2 Speak to the Children of Israel, and say to them:
     When you enter the land that I am giving you,
     the land is to cease, a Sabbath-ceasing to Yhwh.
   3 For six years you are to sow your field,
     for six years you are to prune your vineyard,
     then you are to gather in its produce,
   4 but in the seventh year
     there shall be a Sabbath of Sabbath-ceasing for the land,
     a Sabbath to Yhwh:
     your field you are not to sow,
     your vineyard you are not to prune,

20 **break in place of break** etc.: Cf. Ex. 22:23–25 for a
parallel passage.

5 the aftergrowth of your harvest you are not to harvest,
　 the grapes of your consecrated-vines you are not to amass;
　 a Sabbath of Sabbath-ceasing shall there be for the land!

6 Now the Sabbath-yield of the land (is) for you, for eating,
　 for you, for your servant and for your handmaid,
　 for your hired-hand and for your resident-settler who sojourn
　　 with you;

7 and for your domestic-animal and the wild-beast that (are) in
　　 your land
　 shall be all its produce, to eat.

8 Now you are to number yourselves seven Sabbath-cycles of years
　 —seven years, seven times—
　 so the time of the seven Sabbath-cycles of years will be for you (a
　　 total of) nine and forty years.

9 Then you are to give-forth (on the) *shofar* a blast,
　 in the seventh New-Moon, on the tenth after the New-Moon, on
　　 the Day of Atonement,
　 you are to give(-blast on the) *shofar* throughout all your land.

10 You are to hallow the year, the fiftieth year,
　 proclaiming freedom throughout the land and to all its
　　 inhabitants;
　 it shall be Homebringing for you,
　 you are to return, each-man to his holding,
　 each-man to his clan you are to return.

11 It is Homebringing, the fiftieth year—it shall be for you,
　 you are not to sow,
　 you are not to harvest its aftergrowth,
　 you are not to gather its consecrated-grapes,

25:5 **consecrated-vines:** JPS "untrimmed vines."
6 **Sabbath-yield:** What the land produces on its own in the sabbatical year.
8 **Sabbath-cycles:** Others, "weeks," as understood in Deut. 16:9. **seven years, seven times:** Probably a gloss inserted to explain the word "sabbath[-cycles]" in the previous phrase (Fishbane 1988).
9 *shofar:* A curved horn, from a ram or other animal.
10 **proclaiming freedom . . . inhabitants:** These words were used on the Liberty Bell in Philadelphia, in the form: "Proclaim liberty. . . ." **holding:** An-

cestral or "granted" land. **Homebringing:** So B-R and cognates in Akkadian and Ugaritic. Most interpreters understand the word *yovel* as "ram," and by extension its horn, but the root seems to indicate "bringing in" of the sheep through horn blowing (cf. Josh. 6:5 for the full term "horn of homebringing"). It usually appears in English as "Jubilee," a transcription of the Hebrew word. The Septuagint and several medieval commentators interpret it as "release," which would make it parallel to the meaning of *shemitta* in Deut. 15.

12   for it is Homebringing, holy shall it be for you,
      (only) from the field may you eat its produce;
13   in this Year of Homebringing you are to return, each-man to his
      holding.

14   Now when you sell property-for-sale to your fellow
      or purchase (it) from the hand of your fellow,
      do not maltreat any-man his brother!
15   By the number of years after the Homebringing
      you are to purchase (it) from your fellow,
      by the number of years of produce (left) he is to sell it to you:
16   according to the many years (left), you may charge-him-much for
      his purchase,
      according to the few years (left), you may charge-him-little for his
      purchase,
      since a (certain) number of harvests is what he is selling to you.
17   So you are not to maltreat any-man his fellow,
      rather, you are to hold your God in awe,
      for I YHWH am your God!
18   You are to observe my laws,
      my regulations you are to keep, and observe them,
      that you may be settled on the land in security,
19   that the land may give forth its fruit
      and that you may eat to being-satisfied,
      and be settled in security upon it.
20   Now if you should say (to yourselves):
      What are we to eat in the seventh year?
      —(for) here, we may not sow, we may not gather our produce!
21   Then I will dispatch my blessing for you during the sixth year
      so that it yields produce for three years;

---

12 **(only) from the field:** Only what grows by itself.
14 **maltreat:** By playing with the time-frame of the Homebringing Year (Jubilee).
16 **according to the many-years (left):** "The more the [remaining] years, the higher you may fix its purchase price" (Levine).
18 **in security:** A phrase common in reference to covenant making (Levine).

19 **to being-satisfied:** Or "your fill."
20 **Now if you should say:** Fishbane (1988) sees this as an answer to the practical problems posed by the sabbatical year. **(for) here:** Or, "if [we may not sow . . .]."
21 **dispatch:** Following Levine.

22 you may sow the eighth year('s yield), but you must eat of the
old produce until the ninth year;
until its produce comes in, you must eat what-is-old.

23 But the land is not to be sold in-harness, for the land is mine;
for you are sojourners and resident-settlers with me,

24 throughout all the land of your holdings, you are to allow for
redemption of the land.

25 When your brother sinks down (in poverty) and has to sell (some
of) his holding,
his redeemer nearest-in-kin to him is to come
and redeem the sold-property of his brother.

26 Now a man—if he has no redeemer,
but his hand reaches (means) and finds enough to redeem with,

27 he is to reckon the years since its sale,
returning the surplus to the man to whom he sold it,
and it is to return to his holding.

28 But if his hand does not find enough (means) for returning it,
what he sold is to remain in the hand of the one purchasing it,
until the Year of Homebringing,
it is to go-free in the Homebringing-Year, and it is to return to his
holding.

29 A man—if he sells a residential house in a walled town,
its redemption-period (is) until the end of the year of its sale,
a year-of-days shall be its redemption-period.

30 If it is not redeemed before a whole year of it has been fulfilled,
the house that is in the town that has a wall shall be-established,
in-harness, for him who purchases it, throughout his
generations,
it is not to go-free in the Homebringing-Year.

---

23 **sold in-harness:** A permanent state of ownership.
24 **redemption:** Retrieval of the land, so that it stays within the family.
25 **redeemer:** A close relative who fulfills various obligations to the family (another example, from Deut.19:6, is avenging the murder of a family member).
28 **go-free:** JPS "released." Literally it means "depart," a legal term also applying to the release of inden-

tured servants (cf. Ex. 21, where it was rendered "go out").
29 **a walled town:** A different case than the above. Land was the primary value in these texts; a walled town contained artisans' shops but not farmland.
30 **be-established:** Cf. Gen. 23, where the cave of Makhpela is similarly "established" for Abraham—that is, it becomes his property.

31 But houses in villages that do not have a wall around them,
as open-fields of the land are they to be reckoned,
there may be redemption for them,
and in the Homebringing-Year they may go-free.

32 Now (as for) the towns of the Levites, the houses in the towns of
their holding—
redemption-right for the ages is to belong to the Levites.

33 (That) which is redeemed from the Levites:
it is to go-free, the house sold in the town of their holding, in the
Homebringing-Year,
for houses of Levitical towns, they are their holding amid the
Children of Israel.

34 But pasture-land of the field (near) their towns is not to be sold,
for it is a holding for the ages for them.

35 Now when your brother sinks down (in poverty)
and his hand falters beside you,
then shall you strengthen him
as (though) a sojourner and resident-settler,
and he is to live beside you.

36 Do not take from him biting-interest or profit,
but hold your God in awe,
so that your brother may live beside you!

37 Your silver you are not to give him at interest,
for profit you are not to give (him) your food;

38 I Yhwh am your God
who brought you out of the land of Egypt
to give you the land of Canaan,
to be for you a God!

39 And when your brother sinks down (in poverty) beside you, and
sells himself to you,
you are not to make him serve the servitude of a serf;

---

31 **open-fields of the land:** Levine: "arable land."
35 **his hand falters:** The same "hand" that "reached far enough" (i.e., had enough financial means) in v.26.
36 **biting-interest:** The Hebrew word *neshekh* is highly descriptive; we still use "taking a bite out of the bud-

get" in English. **profit:** Interest added to the principal at the time of payment (Bamberger).
39 **serve the servitude of a serf:** The emphatic repetition warns against putting fellow Israelites into indentured servitude.

Conclusion: Blessings and Curses (26:3–45): The initial ending of Leviticus (Chap. 27 was added later) follows a pattern common to treaties in the ancient Near East: it provides blessings for remaining loyal to God (the suzerain) and curses for spurning him. A similar pattern, with greater rhetoric and emotional force, occurs in Deut. 28–30, with briefer examples in Ex. 23:25ff. and Josh. 24:20. The blessings center around peace and its attendant benefit, agricultural abundance; the curses detail, in increasing force, the calamities brought on by war: famine, defeat, and ultimately exile. That the curses take up much more room than the blessings is not surprising, given the didactic nature of the chapter; this is also characteristic of ancient Near Eastern suzerain-vassal treaty literature, where the major emphasis is placed on what will happen if the pact is violated. Later Jewish tradition dealt with the devastating tone and content of the curses by prescribing that, when read publicly as part of the weekly Torah cycle, they be chanted in an undertone.

The structure of the chapter gives strong indication that there has been considerable editorial work here, and that may explain some of the difficulties in the later parts of the chapter. The confusion may well reflect the passage of time during and after the fall of Jerusalem to the Babylonians in 587 B.C.E., and thus an evolving response to the catastrophe. The pattern (suggested by H. L. Ginsberg, who is quoted by Levine) moves from doom to hope, and then to an explanation of why restoration has been delayed. In any event, it should be noted (as Levine does) that the curses are not all doom; they do, at various points, leave the door open for Israel's "turning," a point much emphasized by the Prophets.

Lev. 26 is the first great monotheistic response to catastrophe, built on the idea that human beings have the capacity to influence their own fate by obeying or disobeying God. In Judaism, which was to experience numerous such catastrophes over the course of its history, literary response became an important mode of coping. Christianity took its own characteristic path in answering some of the same issues on a personal level.

40 as a hired-hand, as a resident-settler is he to be beside you,
  (only) until the Year of Homebringing is he to serve beside you.

41 Then he is to go-free from beside you,
  he and his children beside him;
  he may return to his clan,
  to the holding of his fathers he may return.

42 For my servants are they
  whom I brought out of the land of Egypt,
  they are not to be sold as the sale of serfs.

43 You are not to have-dominion over him with crushing-labor,
  rather, you are to hold your God in awe!

44 Your servant and your maid that belong to you from the nations
    surrounding you, from them you may purchase serf and maid;

45 also from the sons of the residents who sojourn beside you, from
    them you may purchase (slaves),
  or from their clans that are beside you, that they beget in your
    land,
  and they shall become your holdings.

46 You may keep-them-as-an-inheritance for your children after you,
  for (them to) possess as holdings;
  for the ages you may make them serve you.
  But as for your brothers, the Children of Israel, each-man toward
    his brother,
  you are not to have-dominion over him with crushing-labor!

47 Now if the hand of a resident sojourner reaches (means) beside
    you,
  and your brother sinks down (in poverty) beside him,
  so that he sells himself to the resident sojourner beside you, or to
    an offshoot of the sojourner's clan,

---

43 **crushing-labor:** A powerful allusion to the way the Egyptians oppressed their Israelite slaves in Ex. 1:13–14 (the word is used in the Torah only in these two passages).

46 **over him:** That is, over "his brother" of the previous line.

48 (even) after he has sold himself, redemption may be his;
one of his brothers may redeem him,

49 or his uncle or the son of his uncle may redeem him,
or (some) kin of his flesh, from his clan, may redeem him,
or, should his hand reach (means), he may redeem-himself.

50 He is to reckon with his purchaser from the year that he was sold
to him until the Year of Homebringing;
the silver from his sale shall be by the number of years—
like the time-period of a hired-hand is he to be beside him.

51 If there are still many years (left),
according to them he is to return-payment for his redemption
from the silver of his purchase;

52 and if few remain in years until the Year of Homebringing,
he is to reckon it to him,
according to its years he is to return-payment for his redemption.

53 As a hired-hand, year by year, he is to be beside him,
he is not to have-dominion over him with crushing-labor before
your eyes.

54 And if he has not been redeemed in (any of) these (ways),
he is to go-free in the Year of Homebringing, he and his children
beside him.

55 For it is to me that the Children of Israel are servants,
my servants are they,
whom I brought out of the land of Egypt,
I am Yhwh your God!

26:1 You are not to make for yourselves no-gods,
a carved-image or a standing-pillar you are not to establish for
yourselves,
a decorated stone you are not to place in your land, to prostrate
yourselves to it,
for I Yhwh am your God!

---

53 **year by year:** Hired by the year, not as a slave in per-
petuity.

2   My Sabbaths you are to keep, my Holy-Shrine you are to hold-in-
       awe,
    I am YHWH!

3   If by my laws you walk, and my commands you keep, and
       observe them,
4   then I will give-forth your rains in their set-time,
    so that the earth gives-forth its yield
    and the trees of the field give-forth their fruit.
5   Threshing will overtake vintage for you, and vintage will
       overtake sowing;
    you shall eat your food to being-satisfied, and be settled in
       security in your land.
6   I will give peace throughout the land, so that you will lie down
       with none to make you tremble,
    I will cause-to-cease wild beasts from the land, and a sword shall
       not cross through your land.
7   You shall pursue your enemies, and they will fall before you to
       the sword;
8   five of you will pursue a hundred, and a hundred of you, a
       myriad pursue,
    your enemies falling before you to the sword.
9   I will turn-my-face toward you, making-you-fruitful and making-
       you-many,
    and I will establish my covenant with you.
10 You will eat old-grain, the oldest-stored,
    and the old for the new you will have to clear out.
11 I will place my Dwelling in your midst,
    and I will not repel you.
12 I will walk about in your midst,
    I will be for you as a God, and you yourselves will be for me as a
       people.

26:1–2: The combination of laws about worship, together
    with "Sabbaths" and "hold-in-awe," makes this pas-
    sage a structural bracket to 19:3–4, and hence func-
    tions to close out the Holiness section begun there.

3 **If . . . :** One would have expected "Now if . . . ."
10 **the old for the new:** There will be so much old
    grain that it will still be there when the new is har-
    vested.

13　I Yhwh am your God
who brought you out of the land of Egypt,
from your being serfs to them;
I broke the bars of your yoke, enabling you to walk upright!

14　But if you do not hearken to me, by not observing all these
commandments,

15　if my laws you spurn, and my regulations you repel
by not observing all my commandments, by your violating my
covenant,

16　I in turn will do this to you:
I will mete out to you
shock, consumption, and fever,
wearing out the eyes and exhausting the breath,
you will sow your seed for naught, for your enemies will eat it.

17　And I will set my face against you, you will be hit-by-plague in
the face of your enemies;
those who hate you will have-dominion over you,
you will flee, with no one pursuing you!

18　Now if, after all that, you do not hearken to me,
I will continue to discipline you, sevenfold, for your sins—

19　I will break your fierce pride!
I will give your heavens to be like iron, and your earth like
bronze,

20　so that your power will be spent for naught;
your land will not give-forth its yield,
the trees of the land will not give-forth their fruit.

21　Now if you walk with me (in) opposition, and do not consent to
hearken to me,
I will continue against you blows, sevenfold, according to your
sins—

13　**from your being-serfs:** An echo of the formula in
Ex. 20:2, "from a house of serfs." **upright:** Heb.
komamiyyut, related to the root producing "established" in vv.1 and 9.

21　**opposition:** Heb. *keri,* perhaps from *kara,* "to encounter" or "come up against." Ancient translations
suggest "in obstinacy."

22 I will send-loose against you the wild-beasts of the field,
so that they bereave you,
so that they (utterly) cut off your animals,
so that they make you few, and your roads become desolate.

23 Now if, after these-things, you do not accept-discipline from me,
but (continue to) walk with me (in) opposition,
24 I will walk with you, I myself, with opposition;
I will strike you, yes, I myself, sevenfold for your sins.
25 I will bring against you an avenging sword, taking-vengeance for
the covenant.
Should you gather yourselves into your cities,
I will send-free pestilence in your midst,
and you will be given into the hand of your enemies.
26 When I break the "staff of bread" for you, ten women shall bake
your bread in one oven;
they will return your bread by weight,
and you will eat, but you will not be satisfied.

27 And if after this you will not hearken to me,
but (still) walk with me with opposition,
28 I will walk with you in the heat of opposition;
I will discipline you, even I myself, sevenfold for your sins!
29 You will eat the flesh of your sons,
the flesh of your daughters, you will eat!
30 I will destroy your high-places, I will cut down your cult-stands,
I will place your corpses atop the corpses of your idol-clods;
I will repel you.
31 I will make your cities a wasteland,
I will make-desolate your holy-shrines,
and I will not savor your soothing savors!

25 **the covenant:** The breaking of the covenant.
26 **the "staff of bread":** Understanding bread as the
substance that "supports" life. Parallel passages
occur in ancient Near Eastern treaties.

30 **high-places . . . cult-stands:** Pagan shrines. **idol-clods:** A derogatory term for local idols.

32   And I will make-desolate, I myself, the land,
     so that your enemies that settle in it will be appalled-at-the-
         desolation in it.
33   And you I will scatter among the nations;
     I will unsheath the sword against you,
     so that your land becomes a desolation and your cities become a
         wasteland.
34   Then the land will find-acceptance regarding its Sabbaths,
     all the days of desolation—when you are in the land of your
         enemies—
     then the land will enjoy-cessation, and find-acceptance regarding
         its Sabbaths.
35   All the days of desolation it will enjoy-cessation,
     since it did not enjoy-cessation during its Sabbaths when you
         were settled on it.
36   Now those that remain among you—I will bring faintness into
         their hearts, in the lands of their enemies,
     they will be set-in-pursuit by the sound of a leaf blown-about,
     they will flee as if in flight from a sword and will fall, though
         there is no pursuer!
37   They will stumble, each-man over his brother, as before the
         sword, though pursuer there is none.
     And you will not be able to stand-your-ground before your
         enemies;
38   rather, you will perish among the nations—
     it will devour you, the land of your enemies.
39   Those that remain among you will rot away in their iniquity, in
         the lands of their enemies,
     yes, because of the iniquities of their fathers, with them they
         shall rot away.

---

34 **find-acceptance regarding:** Levine: "atone for" or
    "make up for."

◆ 40 Now should they confess their iniquity and the iniquity of their
fathers, in their breaking-faith by which they broke-faith with
me
—yes, since they have walked with me in opposition,
41 yes, I myself will walk with them in opposition,
and will bring them into the land of their enemies—
if then their foreskinned heart should humble itself,
if then they should find-acceptance regarding their iniquity,
42 I will bear-in-mind my Yaakov covenant,
and yes, my Yitzhak covenant, and yes, my Avraham covenant
I will bear-in-mind, and the land I will bear-in-mind.
43 —The land will have to be left-behind by them, attaining-
acceptance through its Sabbaths by being-desolate-of them,
and they will have to find-acceptance regarding their iniquity,
because, because my regulations they spurned, and my laws they
repelled.—
44 And yes, even then, when they are in the land of their enemies,
I will not spurn them, I will not repel them, to finish them off, to
abrogate my covenant with them,
for I YHWH am their God!
45 I will bear-in-mind to their (benefit) the covenant of the former-
ones
whom I brought out of the land of Egypt, before the eyes of the
nations,
to be for them a God,
I am YHWH!

46 These are the laws, the regulations, and the instructions
that YHWH gave between himself and the Children of Israel at
Mount Sinai, by the hand of Moshe.

39–40 **yes:** Here, the repeated word affirms the punishment; in vv.42 and 44, in reply, as it were, it affirms
God's mercy toward Israel.
41 **bring them:** The Septuagint reads *ve-heveti* ("I will
bring them") as *ve-he'evadti* ("I will cause them to
perish"). **foreskinned heart:** A strong metaphor for

a stubborn heart—a heart with a thick layer that
needs removing. **find-acceptance regarding their
iniquity:** Their punishment will be deemed fair
payment.
46 **These are the laws:** The fitting end to Leviticus,
which this once undoubtedly was.

Appendix: Support for the Sanctuary (27): Clearly a later addition to Leviticus, Chap. 27 provides for the upkeep of the sanctuary through a variety of means: donations of silver; pledging animals or property which is later redeemed for silver; confiscated property; and tithes. The nature of the text as appendix is obvious, given the finality of tone in the previous chapter, but it could also be said that 27 provides an appropriate ending to Leviticus, since it talks about dedication of property to God, as the book does in regard to all areas of life.

27:1   YHWH spoke to Moshe, saying:

2   Speak to the Children of Israel and say to them:
Any-man—when he would make a vow-offering
in your assessed-equivalent of persons to YHWH,

3   your assessment shall be:
(if) a male, from the age of twenty years up to the age of sixty
years,
your assessment shall be fifty silver *shekels* by the Holy-Shrine
shekel.

4   And if it is a female, your assessment shall be thirty *shekels.*

5   If the age (is) from five years up to the age of twenty years,
your assessment for a male is twenty *shekels,* and for a female, ten
shekels.

6   If from the age of a month up to the age of five years,
your assessment is for a male, five silver *shekels,* and for a female,
your assessment, three silver *shekels.*

7   If from the age of sixty years and upward,
if it is a male, your assessment shall be fifteen *shekels,* and for a
female, ten *shekels.*

8   If he sinks down (in poverty), lower than the assessment,
he is to be stood before the priest,
and the priest is to assess (the amount) for him,
according to what the hand of the one-making-the-vow can
reach, the priest is to assess him.

9   If it concerns an animal from which they bring-near a near-
offering for YHWH,
all of what he gives from it to YHWH is to be a holy-portion.

10   He is not to substitute for it and he is not to exchange it, good for
ill or ill for good,
if they exchange, yes, exchange animal for animal,
it will be that it and its exchanged-one will be a holy-portion.

27:2 **in your assessed-equivalent of persons:** Lit. "in
the your-assessment"; this is a grammatically
"frozen" form, meaning simply "the assessed-
equivalent."

11 If it (concerns) any *tamei* animal from which there may not be
        brought-near a near-offering for YHWH,
    the animal is to be stood before the priest,

12 and the priest is to make-assessment for it, between good and ill,
    according to your assessment by the priest, thus shall it be.

13 And if he (wants to) redeem, yes, redeem it,
    he is to add its fifth-part to your assessment.

14 Now a man—when he hallows his house as holy-property to
        YHWH,
    the priest is to assess it, between good and ill;
    as the priest assesses it, thus shall (its cost) be-established.

15 And if the one-who-hallows-it would redeem his house,
    he is to add a fifth-part (to the) silver of your assessment,
    and it shall remain his.

16 If from the field of his holding any-man hallows (part) to YHWH,
    your assessment shall be according to its seed-requirement:
    the seed-requirement of a *homer* of barley, fifty silver *shekels*.

17 If as of the year of Homebringing he hallows his field, as your
        assessment (its cost) will be-established.

18 but if it is after the Homebringing that he hallows his field,
    the priest is to reckon for him the silver according to the years left
        until the Year of Homebringing,
    and it is to be subtracted from your (first) assessment.

19 If he wants to redeem, yes, redeem the field, the one hallowing it,
    he is to add a fifth-part of the silver of your assessment of it, and
        (its cost) is to be-established for him.

20 But if he does not want to redeem the field,
    or if he has sold the land to another man,
    it cannot be redeemed again—

21 the field shall be, when it goes-free in the Homebringing, a holy-
        portion for YHWH,
    like a field specially-devoted;
    for the priest it shall be, for his holding.

22 And if his purchased field that is not a field of his holding (is
        what) he hallows to YHWH,

23 the priest is to reckon for him the value of your assessment, until
   the Year of Homebringing,
   he is to give your assessment (in payment) at that time,
   as a holy-portion for YHWH.
24 In the Year of Homebringing the field shall return to the one
   from whom it was purchased,
   the one whose holding of land it is.

25 All your assessments are to be according to the Holy-Shrine
   shekel,
   twenty grains being the (one) *shekel.*
26 However, a firstborn that is assigned-as-firstborn to YHWH,
   among animals—
   no man may hallow it;
   whether ox or sheep, it is YHWH's.
27 Now if (it is) of a *tamei* animal, he is to redeem it at your
   assessment,
   adding its fifth-part to it,
   and if it is not redeemed, it is to be sold at your assessment.
28 However, everything specially-devoted that a man devotes for
   YHWH from all that is his,
   whether of man or of beast or of field of his holding,
   is not to be sold and not to be redeemed,
   everything specially-devoted—it is a holiest holy-portion for
   YHWH.
29 Anyone specially-devoted that has been devoted-to-destruction,
   among humans, is not to be ransomed;
   he is to be put-to-death, yes, death.
30 And every tithe of the land, (whether) from the seed of the land
   or from the fruit of the tree:
   for YHWH it is, a holy-portion for YHWH.

---

26 **assigned-as-firstborn:** Following Levine.
29 **Anyone specially-devoted . . . devoted-to-destruction:** Heb. *kol herem asher yohoram.* The institution of *herem* involved setting people or property apart for the divine; property was confiscated, and people usually killed (for a full study of the concept, see Stern).

30 **tithe:** Cf. the description of this 10 percent tax in Deut. 14:22ff. In our passage, the disposition of tithes is adapted to the thrust of the chapter (Levine).

31 If a man wants to redeem, yes, redeem (any) of his tithes,
   its fifth-part he is to add to it;
32 and every tithe of herd or flock, from all that passes under the
   (shepherd's) rod,
   (each) tenth-one, is to be a holy-portion for YHWH.
33 He is not to search between good and ill, he is not to make-
   exchange for it;
   but if he makes-exchange, yes, exchange for it,
   then it and its exchange are a holy-portion, they cannot be
   redeemed.

34 These are the commandments
   that YHWH commanded Moshe for the Children of Israel at
   Mount Sinai.

---

33 **not to search:** The condition of the animal does not matter.
34 **These are the commandments:** Another, briefer attempt at an ending. The phrase "at Mount Sinai" echoes the beginning of Chap. 25, and thus forms a bracketed ending section for the book.

במדבר

NUMBERS

IN THE WILDERNESS

On the Book of Numbers and Its Structure

THE READER WHO APPROACHES THE BOOK OF NUMBERS UNDER THE INFLUENCE OF ITS common Hebrew name, *Bemidbar,* "In the Wilderness," will logically expect a narrative account of the wanderings of the Israelites before they reach the Promised Land. But the book in its present form is a great deal more than that. To be sure, it contains stories of the long trek from Egypt to Canaan, with moments of triumph and difficulty, obedience and rebellion. Some of the great narratives of the Pentateuch are here, from the account of Korah's revolt (Chap. 16) to Moshe's sin (20) to Bil'am's recalcitrant donkey (22). But the book also features census and sacrificial donation lists; details of the setup of Israel's camp; the duties of the Levites in the traveling sanctuary; laws regarding wives suspected of adultery and those who take on extraordinary vows; a complicated and mysterious ritual for removing the extreme ritual pollution carried by death; a doubled tale about daughters inheriting land; and a host of other rules and regulations.

It is this composite character and apparent lack of easily definable structure that imbue the book with fascination for scholars and with frustration for lay readers. While the four other books of the Torah also mix narrative, law, poetry, and cultic regulations, none of them has combined and alternated these genres with such abandon. There are a number of possible explanations for this. First, it is conceivable that Numbers as we have it reflects the desire to preserve as many traditions about the wilderness wanderings as possible; as Greenberg (1972) has demonstrated with the traditions about the revelation on Mount Sinai, it may have been more important to collect everything relevant than to create a smooth or seamless text. Second, here as elsewhere in the Torah, narrative may serve to introduce law or to provide the preceding background for it. Third, there is an aesthetic consideration: the great rebellion stories in the center of the book, to give an example, are separated from one another by prescriptive legal passages. Earlier books in the Torah similarly utilize breaks of varying lengths (e.g., the genealogical lists in Genesis, the Tabernacle texts of Exodus). The result is to highlight both narrative and law, and also to provide a large-scale rhythm to the book (Milgrom comments on the consistent alternating pattern).

The kind of literary mixture that we find in Numbers goes beyond that rabbinic dictum that "the Torah speaks in human language." It suggests that, far from betraying human frailties in the composition or transmission of the traditions presented in Numbers, a purposeful and powerful hand has been at work. More than any other book in the Torah, this one gives evidence of an editorial process. While the finished product may not be able to help us unravel the detailed history of that process, we may at least observe that much has been added to the wilderness narratives, in a way that transforms them into a patterned view of Israel's early history.

Recent commentaries see a two- or three-part structure to Numbers, based either on geography—the Sinai Wilderness, Kadesh, the plains of Moab—or chronology. Since the book as we have it is not entirely clear about either area—there seems to be internal disagreement about where the spies (Chap. 13) left from and went, and also about when the forty-year punishment began—I am in general agreement with Olson's scheme of seeing the book as "The Death of the Old and the Birth of the New," that is, the slave generation and that of their children, which are set apart by the two census lists in Chapters 1 and 26. But the differences between Chapters 1–10 and 11–25 must also be taken into account. I propose the following theoretical structure:

I   In the Wilderness of Sinai: The Camp
- 1   The Census (Musterings) of the Israelites; the Duties of the Levites
- 2   The Ordering of the Camp
- 3   The Census of the Levites According to Their Duties
- 4   The Tasks of the Levites
- 5   Threats to the Ritual Integrity of the Camp
- 6   Procedure Regarding a Nazirite; the Priestly Blessing
- 7   Gifts of the Tribes to the Tabernacle
- 8   The Tabernacle Lamps; Purification of the Levites
- 9   Passover in the Wilderness; God's Presence with the Tabernacle
- 10   The Journey to Canaan Commences

II   The Rebellious Folk: Narratives of Challenge
    A   Sealing the Fate of the First Generation
- 11   First Rebellion: Food
- 12   Second Rebellion: Siblings
- 13   The Spies' Mission
- 14   Third Rebellion: Panic
- 15   Interlude: Rules on Sacrifices, Sabbath, and Tassels

    B   The Crisis of Leadership
- 16   Fourth Rebellion: Korah and the Levites
- 17   Fifth Rebellion: After the Purge
- 18   The Levites as Guardians
- 19   Pollution by Death and Its Removal
- 20   Sixth Rebellion: The Sin of Moshe and Aharon

    C   Encountering the Other
- 21   Encounters with Various Neighbors; Seventh Rebellion: Food and Water

In this scheme, not only does the otherwise haphazard subject matter of the book fit roughly into the three divisions, but the divisions themselves seem to correspond to narrative mood swings. This might be characterized as a movement from order to chaos, and back to order again. The wilderness camp is still connected to the ordering—nation-founding—experience of Sinai; God speaks to Moshe from the Tabernacle, both here and in Leviticus, and the structure serves as a surrogate Mount Sinai. The concerns of Part I, therefore, are expressed in lists, and the section is filled with them.

With the rebellion narratives of Part II, which not coincidentally take place as soon as Israel sets out on its journey through the wilderness, the idealistic order of Sinai is broken, and the people (and Moshe) must deal with the harsh reality of life in the desert. It becomes clear that nation-founding involves not only the giving of laws and the arranging of societal roles, but also the developing of the ability to cope with physical and spiritual challenges to survival.

The slave generation is unable to successfully meet the challenge, and Part II chronicles their failures and their punishment. They had been born into the rigidly ordered situation of slavery—an order with underlying spiritual chaos—and only their children, born into the chaotic but free air of the wilderness, can be readied for the orderly transition into conquest and societal life on their own soil. This readying process is portrayed in Part III, through a series of lists once again: another military census, clear inheritance laws, a sacred calendar tied to the growing cycles of the land, a tracing of the Israelites' travels through the wilderness, and a laying out of future borders. By the end of the book, Israel is fully prepared to enter the land, with a new generation, new leadership in the wings, a full set of societal rules, an operative cult, and, above all, a collective memory of experiences that serve to instruct and warn future generations. These issues will be fully and memorably summarized in the great final speeches of Moshe that comprise the last book of the Torah, Deuteronomy.

Of special note in the book of Numbers is the emphasis on the Levites and their tasks. The text introduces this group, which may have originated as a guild rather than as a tribe, already in Chapter 1 (v.47). Thereafter, they play a major role in the book—the portrayal of their purification for service (Chap. 8), the great rebellion fomented by some of them (16), their important function as guardians against encroachment on the sanctuary (18), and their distribution in certain towns that serve also as places of refuge for accidental manslayers (35) is spread throughout the book, as if to form a distinctive thread amid the other themes of wandering, rebellion, and preparation for conquest. This interest in the Levites, in the eyes of some scholars, signals a particularly late development in the history of Israelite religion, and perhaps a late editing for our book as well. It also indicates how thoroughly the wilderness traditions have been reworked, to establish a hoary history for the central Israelite institutions connected with divine worship. While it is next to impossible to trace the internal struggles of the Israelite priesthood over the centuries with historical precision, it seems clear that such strife was part of history, and may be reflected in the portrayals of Aharon, Korah, and Pin'has, to mention just a few of the priestly/Levitical figures that populate the wilderness stories. At any rate, the combining of clearly priestly material into the varied narrative and poetic stuff of Numbers has created a book different than what might have been, had the editors sought a story and only a story. The same, of course, might be said for the entire five books of which Numbers is a part.

As I noted in the introduction to Volume II of this work, *Now These Are the Names* (Exodus), the hero's journey through the unknown is, of course, a central theme in Western literature. From Homer's *Odyssey* to Sinbad's journeys in *A Thousand and One Nights* to the many twentieth-century works on the theme, the protagonist's unfamiliar terrain has become the familiar metaphor for our own inner journeys. Such accounts normally concentrate on obstacles in the way: opponents divine and human, harsh landscapes, wild beasts, lack of water, lack of people and succor. Heroes are left to their own devices, and if they are successful in completing their journey, the audience experiences the vicarious triumph of conquering the impossible. Indeed, the operating principle seems to be: the greater the obstacles, the more stunning the triumph.

The wilderness trek recounted in the heart of the book of Numbers has a wholly different feel. To be sure, there are obstacles, some of them standard, such as the dearth of food and water and the opposition of hostile nations along the way. But the main emphasis in these texts is on internal obstacles—the people's lack of trust, faith, and courage. And as so often happens in the Torah, physical background, as important as it obviously is in Numbers, what with a myriad of geographical locations noted, is overshadowed by the dominant issue of the relationship between Israel and God. The God of the wilderness journey is initially a provider and protector (cf. Ex. 15–18); when he turns lawgiver, Israel's situation seems secure despite the harsh ecological setting. But Numbers has chosen to remember the people's moments of doubt and rebellion above all, and so the orderly leaving of Sinai which closes the first part of the book, along with the orderly preparations for conquest that mark its third part, fade in the reader's consciousness before the memorable narratives in Chapters 11–25.

It has been pointed out (Tunyogi) that these stories serve as "foundation accounts," as stories that tell about "the archetypes to be repeated in all coming generations." As such, they are significant in later Israel's understanding of itself. Through the book of Numbers, later generations were warned not to repeat the sins of the wilderness; and Moshe himself came to be looked upon as the quintessential prophet. For the era of the literary prophets (ninth-sixth centuries B.C.E.), concerned as they were with Israel's forgetfulness and backsliding, and the era of Babylonian Exile (sixth century B.C.E.), in which the exiles also found themselves outside the Promised Land, there could have been no stronger warning or cause for hope than the stories and laws set down in the Torah, and especially the traditions recorded in the book of Numbers.

THE WILDERNESS CAMP

(1–10)

TO LIST IS TO DEMONSTRATE A SENSE OF ORDER AND CONTROL. THE BOOK OF Numbers commences with several lists that serve to arrange and catalog the Israelite camp in the wilderness: first, the "accountings" of the Israelites fit for battle; then, the symmetrical arrangement of the camp itself, around the Tabernacle; and finally, the special listing of the Levite population, accompanied by an enumeration of its special tasks in the camp. The first part of Numbers thus takes place as it were in the shadow of Mount Sinai—that is, under the aegis of the priestly school of thinking, in which order is everything.

There is a strong military bent to the arrangement. The census of Chapter 1 is not a head count of the entire Israelite population, but rather of those "twenty years of age and upward," those eligible to serve in the army. The setup of the camp resembles that in ancient Egypt, with the sanctuary and ark (here "Dwelling" and "coffer") in the center (in the Egypt of Raamses II—thought by some to have been the Pharaoh of the Exodus—it was the king's throne). The Levites, whom we have not encountered previously as a group with tasks distinct from those of the priests, emerge in this part of the book as caretakers and perhaps guardians of the sanctuary, in addition to their tasks of dismantling and transport of the "Holy-Shrine." This military aspect reflects an ancient concept of Israel as the "forces of YHWH," surely a conquest image, which later becomes standardized in language in the phrase usually rendered "the LORD of Hosts."

Some of the material in this section might well have been put elsewhere. Chapters 5–7 would have fit nicely in Leviticus; Chapter 7, the listing of the tribal gifts brought to the sanctuary upon its dedication, could even have followed Ex. 40, where Moshe completes the erection of the structure. That these chapters are here therefore must be the result of a conscious decision, either to include material that did not find its way into the other books, or out of a feeling that they were appropriately placed in the book about Israel's wanderings in the wilderness.

The Mustering of Israel (1): For the opening of the book about the Israelites' wanderings in the wilderness, the editor has chosen a logical point of departure: a tally of males prepared for war, listed by tribe. It is in fact a double list—first, the names of the tribal representatives who are to assist Moshe, and second, the count itself. The chapter is the epitome of orderliness, proceeding from the date of the census to who is to be counted, on to the counters and the census itself, and finally a treatment of the special case of the Levites (who, as noncombatants, are not mustered). It utilizes a number of repeating phrases, especially in the central census section. In this sense, the opening chapters of the book are a fitting companion to Leviticus—which likewise opens with God speaking from the Tent of Appointment, still in the Wilderness of Sinai.

The large numbers that appear here have been a major source of debate in modern as well as earlier interpretation. After all, extrapolating from 600,000 adult males (excluding the elderly), one certainly winds up with a population in the millions—a theoretically possible but extremely unlikely scenario. Some alternatives are: (a) to understand Hebrew *elef* as not "thousand," but rather as "unit" or "division," which would especially make sense in a military setting; and (b) to regard the numbers as simply exaggerated. One might also, following Olson, see the statistics here as an attempt to impress the audience with the size of Israel, and/or to demonstrate how God has blessed them (as in the promises to Avraham in Genesis and the account in Ex. 1). There may, finally, be a "numbers game" occurring here, that is, some kind of symbolism of figures that eludes us (cf. Sarna 1986).

1:1 Now YHWH spoke to Moshe in the Wilderness of Sinai, in the
 Tent of Appointment,
 on the first (day) after the second New-Moon, in the second year
 after their going-out from the land of Egypt,
 saying:
2 Take up the head-count of the entire community of the Children
 of Israel,
 by their clans, by their Fathers' Houses,
 according to the number of names,
 every male per capita;
3 from the age of twenty years and upward,
 everyone going out to the armed-forces in Israel:
 you are to count them (for battle) according to their forces,
 you and Aharon.
4 And with you let there be
 a man, a man per tribe,
 (the) man (who is) head of his Fathers' House he is (to be).
5 Now these are the names of the men who are to stand with you:
 for Re'uven: Elitzur son of Shedei'ur;
6 for Shim'on: Shelumi'el son of Tzurishaddai;
7 for Yehuda: Nahshon son of Amminadav;
8 for Yissakhar: Netan'el son of Tzu'ar;
9 for Zevulun: Eliav son of Heilon;
10 for the Sons of Yosef: for Efrayim: Elishama son of Ammihud; for
 Menashe: Gamliel son of Pedahtzur;
11 for Binyamin: Avidan son of Gid'oni;

1:1 **the Wilderness of Sinai:** Until the departure of the Israelites in Chap. 10, they are still in the vicinity of Mount Sinai, the setting of revelation. **in the second year:** Since the exodus from Egypt (Ex. 12), only thirteen months have passed! By the end of Numbers, the text reaches year forty—yet this will occur over a relatively short stretch of text. Thus, typically, the time frame of the Torah operates.

2 **Take up the head-count:** Others, "Take a census," "calculate the total." Although "count" is a theme word in this chapter, the Hebrew for "head-count" here is simply "head," and is not meant to reflect use of the Hebrew verb *pakod*. **community:** Alterna-

tively, "assembly." The term *eda* can mean either the ruling council or the entire people (with a focus on the males, in both cases). **clans . . . Fathers' Houses:** Units of social organization in ancient Israel. **per capita:** The English/Latin expression for "by the head"; Heb. "by their skulls."

3 **going out to the armed-forces:** The force of this expression seems to be "eligible for military service." **count them (for battle):** Or "muster" or "array"; more than mere counting is meant.

4 **let there be:** To assist in the counting. **a man, a man:** One man (for each).

12 for Dan: Ahi'ezer son of Ammishaddai;

13 for Asher: Pag'iel son of Okhran;

14 for Gad: Elyasaf son of De'uel;

15 for Naftali: Ahira' son of Einan.

16 These are the (ones) called-by the community,
the exalted-leaders of the tribes of their fathers,
heads of the divisions of Israel are they.

17 Now Moshe and Aharon took these men, who were indicated by
name,

18 and the entire community they assembled,
on the first (day) of the second New-Moon;
they declared-their-lineage according to their clans, by their
Fathers' Houses,
as numbered by name, from the age of twenty years and upward,
per capita,

19 as YHWH had commanded Moshe;
thus he counted them (for battle) in the Wilderness of Sinai.

20 Thus they were: the Sons of Re'uven, firstborn of Israel,
their begettings by their clans, by their Fathers' House,
as numbered by name, per capita,
every male from the age of twenty years and upward,
everyone going out to the armed-forces:

21 their count, of the tribe of Re'uven: six and forty thousand, and
five hundred.

22 For the Sons of Shim'on:
their begettings by their clans, by their Fathers' House,
those of his count, as numbered by name, per capita,
every male from the age of twenty years and upward,
everyone going out to the armed-forces:

23 their count, of the tribe of Shim'on: nine and fifty thousand, and
three hundred.

---

16 **called-by the community:** The "elect." **divisions:** Heb. *elef* may have that alternative meaning (mentioned above) here. **exalted-leaders:** The Hebrew term for "leader" comes from the verb (*naso'*) meaning "to lift up."

24 For the Sons of Gad:
   their begettings by their clans, by their Fathers' House,
   as numbered by name,
   from the age of twenty years and upward,
   everyone going out to the armed-forces:
25 their count, of the tribe of Gad: five and forty thousand, and six
   hundred and fifty.

26 For the Sons of Yehuda:
   their begettings by their clans, by their Fathers' House,
   as numbered by name,
   from the age of twenty years and upward,
   everyone going out to the armed-forces:
27 their count, of the tribe of Yehuda: four and seventy thousand,
   and six hundred.

28 For the Sons of Yissakhar:
   their begettings by their clans, by their Fathers' House,
   as numbered by name,
   from the age of twenty years and upward,
   everyone going out to the armed-forces:
29 their count, of the tribe of Yissakhar: four and fifty thousand, and
   four hundred.

30 For the Sons of Zevulun:
   their begettings by their clans, by their Fathers' House,
   as numbered by name,
   from the age of twenty years and upward,
   everyone going out to the armed-forces:
31 their count, of the tribe of Zevulun: seven and fifty thousand,
   and four hundred.

32 For the Sons of Yosef:
   For the Sons of Efrayim:

24 **Gad:** Why does Gad break into the genealogical list at this point? He is not Jacob's third son. Milgrom points out that the order of this list depends on the physical arrangement of the tribes around the Tabernacle (cf. Chap. 2), not birth order.

their begettings by their clans, by their Fathers' House,
as numbered by name,
from the age of twenty years and upward,
everyone going out to the armed-forces:

33   their count, of the tribe of Efrayim: forty thousand and five
hundred.

34   For the Sons of Menashe:
their begettings by their clans, by their Fathers' House,
as numbered by name,
from the age of twenty years and upward,
everyone going out to the armed-forces:

35   their count, of the tribe of Menashe: two and thirty thousand,
and two hundred.

36   For the Sons of Binyamin:
their begettings by their clans, by their Fathers' House,
as numbered by name,
from the age of twenty years and upward,
everyone going out to the armed-forces:

37   their count, of the tribe of Binyamin: five and thirty thousand,
and four hundred.

38   For the Sons of Dan:
their begettings by their clans, by their Fathers' House,
as numbered by name,
from the age of twenty years and upward,
everyone going out to the armed-forces:

39   their count, of the tribe of Dan: two and sixty thousand, and
seven hundred.

40   For the Sons of Asher:
their begettings by their clans, by their Fathers' House,
as numbered by name,
from the age of twenty years and upward,
everyone going out to the armed-forces:

41   their count, of the tribe of Asher: one and forty thousand, and
five hundred.

42   For the Sons of Naftali:
their begettings by their clans, by their Fathers' House,

as numbered by name,
from the age of twenty years and upward,
everyone going out to the armed-forces:

43 their count, of the tribe of Naftali: three and fifty thousand, and
four hundred.

44 These are the accountings which Moshe and Aharon and the
leaders of Israel counted,
(the) twelve men—one man per Fathers' House were they—

45 they were, all those accounted for of the Children of Israel by
their Fathers' House,
from the age of twenty and upward,
everyone going out to the armed-forces in Israel,

46 thus they were, all those accounted for:
six hundred thousand and three thousand and five hundred and
fifty.

47 But the Levites, by the tribe of their fathers, were not counted in
the midst of them.

48 YHWH spoke to Moshe, saying:

49 Mark, the tribe of Levi you are not to count,
their head-count you are not to take up in the midst of the
Children of Israel.

50 But you, make the Levites accountable for the Dwelling of
Testimony, for all its implements and for all that belongs to it:
they are to carry the Dwelling and all its implements,
they are to attend to it,
and around the Dwelling they are to camp.

---

46 **603,550:** The round number 600,000 is the biblically agreed-upon total of military-age adult Israelite males that left Egypt. Cassuto (1967) sees it as an indicator of the centrality of a numbering system based on sixty, as was common in Mesopotamia; others (Greenstein and Marcus 1976) cite the importance of five in Assyrian texts, and thus 600,000 would derive from 5 × 10,000 × 12.

50 **accountable:** Playing on "counted," the theme of the chapter. Others, "in charge of." **Dwelling:** Trad. "Tabernacle," the portable sanctuary in the wilderness. Its design is described in detail in Ex. 25ff. **around the Dwelling:** The precise order of the camp is spelled out in the next chapter.

The Layout of the Camp (2): Chap. 2 lays out a schematic diagram of the Israelite camp prepared for the desert march. The "Dwelling" naturally stands at the center, with four groups of three tribes each surrounding the structure on the outside, and three groupings of Levite clans guarding the inside of the rectangular sanctuary. Geographical pride of place, the eastern side, goes to the tribe of Yehuda (Judah) and two other tribes tracing their ancestry to sons of Lea (outside track), while Moshe and Aharon and their sons occupy the inside track.

51 When the Dwelling moves on, the Levites are to take it down,
and when the Dwelling is encamped, the Levites are to set it up;
the outsider who comes-near is to be put-to-death!

52 The Children of Israel are to camp,
each-one according to his encampment, each-one according to
his banner-contingent, by their forces.

53 But the Levites are to camp around the Dwelling of Testimony—
that there be no fury against the community of the Children of
Israel—
and the Levites are to keep the charge of the Dwelling of
Testimony.

54 The Children of Israel did
according to all that YHWH commanded Moshe, thus they did.

2:1 YHWH spoke to Moshe and to Aharon, saying:

2 Each-one by its contingent, under the insignias of their Fathers'
House, shall the Children of Israel encamp,
at-a-distance, around the Tent of Appointment, shall they
encamp.

3 Those encamping eastward, toward-sunrise: the contingent of
the Camp of Yehuda, according to their forces.
Now the leader of the Sons of Yehuda: Nahshon son of
Amminadav;

4 his force and their count: four and seventy thousand, and six
hundred.

5 Those encamping alongside them, the tribe of Yissakhar.
The leader of Yissakhar: Netan'el son of Tzu'ar;

6 his force and their count: four and fifty thousand, and four
hundred.

---

51 **comes-near . . . put-to-death:** This is the first mention of a central problem in priestly texts: getting too close to the sphere of the holy (Milgrom terms it "encroachment"). Cf. 2:3 below, with the Israelites camping around the Dwelling "at a distance," and the story of Korah (Chaps. 16f.), where it is a central issue.

52 **banner-contingent:** The word *degel* originally signifies "banner," but comes to mean also the military grouping that stands under it.

53 **keep the charge:** Or "discharge the charge." Levine understands *shamor mishmeret* as doing the general maintenance duties of the sanctuary. Milgrom, on the other hand, argues strongly for the narrower meaning in Numbers of strictly "guarding the guard duty," citing ancient Near Eastern parallels for temple guardians.

54 **. . . thus they did:** A standard way of reporting the carrying out of God's command in priestly texts.

7 The tribe of Zevulun—
the leader of the Sons of Zevulun: Eliav son of Heilon;

8 his force and their count: seven and fifty thousand, and four
hundred.

9 All the accountings of the Camp of Yehuda: a hundred thousand
and eighty thousand and six thousand, and four hundred, by
their forces;
first are they to march.

10 The contingent of the camp of Re'uven, southward, according to
their forces—
the leader of the Sons of Re'uven: Elitzur son of Shedei'ur;

11 his force and their count: six and forty thousand, and five
hundred.

12 And those encamping beside them: the tribe of Shim'on—
the leader of the Sons of Shim'on: Shelumi'el son of
Tzurishaddai;

13 his force and their count: nine and fifty thousand, and three
hundred.

14 And the tribe of Gad—
the leader of the Sons of Gad: Elyasaf son of Re'uel;

15 his force and their count: five and forty thousand and six hundred
and fifty.

16 All the accountings of the camp of Re'uven: a hundred thousand
and one and fifty thousand, and four hundred and fifty,
according to their forces;
second are they to march.

17 Then shall march the Tent of Appointment, (in) the camp of the
Levites, in the midst of the camps;
as they encamp, so are they to march,
each-one by his position, by their contingents.

2:9 **to march:** The Hebrew *naso'a* means literally "to
pull up stakes" (i.e., tent pegs) and hence "to move
on"; but the moving in Numbers frequently has a
military nuance.

10 **southward:** Lit. "on the right hand."

18 The contingent of the Camp of Efrayim, according to their
        forces, seaward—
    the leader of Efrayim: Elishama son of Ammihud;
19 his force and their count: forty thousand and five hundred.
20 And beside them, the tribe of Menashe—
    the leader of the Sons of Menashe: Gamliel son of Pedahtzur;
21 his force and their count: two and thirty thousand, and two
        hundred.
22 And the tribe of Binyamin—
    the leader of the Sons of Binyamin: Avidan son of Gid'oni;
23 his force and their count: five and thirty thousand, and four
        hundred.
24 All the accountings of the Camp of Efrayim: a hundred thousand
        and eight thousand and a hundred, according to their forces;
    third are they to march.

25 The contingent of the Camp of Dan, northward, according to
        their forces—
    Now the leader of the Sons of Dan: Ahi'ezer son of
        Ammishaddai;
26 his force and their count: two and sixty thousand, and seven
        hundred.
27 And those encamping beside them, the tribe of Asher—
    the leader of Asher: Pag'iel son of Okhran;
28 his force and their count: one and forty thousand, and five
        hundred.
29 And the tribe of Naftali—
    the leader of the Sons of Naftali: Ahira' son of Einan;
30 his force and their count: three and fifty thousand, and four
        hundred.
31 All the accountings of the Camp of Dan: a hundred thousand,
        and seven and fifty thousand, and six hundred;
    as the last are they to march, by their contingents.

32 These (are) the accountings of the Children of Israel by their
        Fathers' Houses,
    all the accountings of the camps, by their forces:
    six hundred thousand and three thousand and five hundred and
        fifty.

Levites I (3): Already introduced in 1:47–53, the issue of the Levites' status and their tasks is an important subtheme in Numbers, and makes its central appearance in Chaps. 3 and 4. The present chapter opens with the genealogy of Moshe and Aharon (similarly, Chap. 6 of Exodus, which is a prologue to the Plague cycle, contains a genealogy of the two leaders).

Notable is the concept that the Levites symbolically replace all the firstborn sons among the Israelites. In a more manageable way, then, the entire community participates in the sacred task of ministering in the sanctuary.

Theme words in the chapter, not surprisingly, are "charge," "count/accountable," and "serve/serving-tasks." Milgrom has also noted the sevenfold "by order of YHWH" that permeates this chapter and the next.

33 But the Levites were not counted (for battle) in the midst of the
        Children of Israel,
    as Yhwh had commanded Moshe.
34 And the Children of Israel did
    according to all that Yhwh had commanded Moshe:
    thus they encamped, by their contingents,
    thus they marched, each-man by his clans, alongside his Fathers'
        House.

3:1 Now these are the begettings of Aharon and Moshe
    at the time Yhwh spoke with Moshe on Mount Sinai:
2 These are the names of the sons of Aharon: the firstborn—
        Nadav,
    and Avihu,
    El'azar and Itamar;
3 these are the names of the sons of Aharon, the anointed priests,
    whom he had mandated to act-as-priests.
4 Now Nadav and Avihu died before the presence of Yhwh,
    when they brought-near outside fire before the presence of
        Yhwh
    in the Wilderness of Sinai;
    sons they did not have,
    so El'azar and Itamar were made-priest in the living-presence of
        Aharon their father.

5 Yhwh spoke to Moshe, saying:
6 Bring-near the tribe of Levi,
    and have-it-stand (regularly) in the presence of Aharon the priest,
    that they may attend upon him.
7 They are to keep his charge and the charge of the entire
        community,

3:1 **these are the begettings:** The same formula with
which begin a number of genealogical lists in Genesis. Outside of the royal (Davidic) genealogy that
appears in Ruth 4:18, the phrase occurs only here beyond Genesis—as if to suggest that Moshe and
Aharon are continuers of the Patriarchal traditions.
For a detailed discussion of the issue, cf. Olson.
3 **anointed priests:** This designation occurs only here

in the Torah. **mandated:** Inducted into office; cf.
note to Ex. 28:41.
4 **Nadav and Avihu died:** Cf. Lev. 10. **in the living-
presence:** That is, in the lifetime (of their father); cf.
Gen. 11:28 for another example.
6 **Bring-near:** Meaning "qualify" in this context (Milgrom). **have-it-stand:** Denoting official status. **attend upon:** Or "assist," "minister to," "serve."

◆

in front of the Tent of Appointment,
to serve the serving-tasks of the Dwelling.

8 They are to be-in-charge of the implements of the Tent of
Appointment
and the charge of the Children of Israel,
to serve the serving-tasks of the Dwelling.

9 You are to give-over the Levites to Aharon and to his sons,
formally-given, given-over are they to him, from among the
Children of Israel.

10 And Aharon and his sons, you are to make-accountable,
that they may keep-the-charge of their priesthood;
the outsider who comes-near is to be put-to-death!

11 YHWH spoke to Moshe, saying:

12 As for me, I hereby take the Levites from the midst of the
Children of Israel,
in place of every firstborn, breacher of womb from the Children
of Israel;
they shall be mine, the Levites.

13 For mine is every firstborn;
at the time that I struck-down every firstborn in the land of
Egypt,
I hallowed to me every firstborn in Israel,
from man to beast.
Mine shall they be—
I am YHWH!

14 Now YHWH spoke to Moshe in the Wilderness of Sinai,
saying:

15 Count the Sons of Levi, by their Fathers' House, by their clans,
every male from the age of a month and upward, you are to
count them.

---

8 **serving-tasks:** Heb. *'avoda* denotes physical labor in these texts (Milgrom).
9 **formally-given, given-over:** Commissioned.
12 **breacher:** Or "loosener."

13 **at the time:** Heb. "on the day" frequently has this connotation. **I hallowed . . . every firstborn:** Cf. Ex. 13.

16 So Moshe counted them by order of YHWH, as he was
    commanded.

17 Now these were the Sons of Levi according to their names:
    Gershon, Kehat and Merari.

18 And these the names of the sons of Gershon, by their clans:
    Livni and Shim'i.

19 And the sons of Kehat, by their clans:
    Amram and Yitzhar, Hevron and Uzziel.

20 And the sons of Merari, by their clans:
    Mahli and Mushi.
    These are they, the Levite clans, by their Fathers' House.

21 For Gershon, the Livnite clan and the Shim'ite clan,
    these are they, the Gershonite clans:

22 those counted of them, according to the number of every male
    from the age of a month and upward,
    those counted of them: seven thousand and five hundred.

23 The Gershonite clans—behind the Dwelling they are to camp,
    seaward.

24 Now the leader of the Father's House for the Gershonites:
    Elyasaf son of Lael.

25 The charge of the Sons of Gershon at the Tent of Appointment
    (was)
    the Dwelling and the Tent,
    its covering, the screen of the entrance to the Tent of
    Appointment,

26 the hangings of the courtyard,
    the screen of the entrance to the courtyard which is about the
    Dwelling
    and about the slaughter-site, all around,
    and its cords—including all their serving tasks.

---

16 **by order of YHWH:** Or "direct order"; lit. "at the
mouth of YHWH," frequently indicating an oracle.

16–17 **commanded. / Now these were:** An ancient version reads "commanded YHWH. / These (are)."

26 **serving-tasks:** Heb. *'avoda* here specifically includes packing, carrying, and setting up.

27 To Kehat, the Amramite clan, the Yitzharite clan, the Hevronite
    clan, and the Uzzi'elite clan,
    these (are) they, the Kehatite clans,

28 numbering every male, from the age of a month and upward:
    eight thousand and six hundred,
    keepers of the charge of the holy-things.

29 The clans of the Sons of Kehat are to encamp along the flank of
    the Dwelling, southward.

30 Now the leader of the Father's House for the Kehatite clans:
    Elitzafan son of Uzziel.

31 Their charge: the coffer, the table, the lampstand and the
    slaughter-sites,
    and the implements of holiness that are used in conjunction with
    them,
    and the screen—and all their serving-tasks.

32 Now the leader of the Levite leaders: El'azar son of Aharon the
    priest,
    accountable for the keepers of the charge of the holy-things.

33 To Merari—the Mahlite clan and the Mushite clan,
    these (are they), the Merarite clans.

34 Now those counted of them, numbering every male from the age
    of a month and upward:
    six thousand and two hundred.

35 And the leader of the Father's House of the Merarite clans:
    Tzuriel son of Avihayil.
    On the flank of the Dwelling they are to camp, northward.

36 Accountable for the (following) charge (are) the Sons of Merari:
    the boards of the Dwelling and its bars,
    its columns, its sockets, and all its implements,
    with all its service-of-packing;

37 the columns of the courtyard, all around, and their bases,
    their posts and their cords.

---

28 **six hundred:** The probable reading is "three hundred," with Hebrew *shalosh* having been miscopied as *shesh;* this squares with the Septuagint reading and gives the correct total in v.39.

31 **coffer:** Trad. "Ark [of the Covenant]." "Ark" in English derives from Latin *arcus,* meaning a chest or box, as does the Hebrew *aron.*

38 Now those encamping in front of the Dwelling, eastward, in
          front of the Tent of Appointment, toward-sunrise,
     (are): Moshe and Aharon and his sons,
     keepers of the charge of the Holy-Area,
     for the charge of the Children of Israel;
     the outsider who comes-near is to be put-to-death!

39 All those counted of the Levites, whom Moshe and Aharon
          counted by order of YHWH, by their clans,
     every male, from the age of a month and upward:
     two and twenty thousand.

40 YHWH said to Moshe:
     Count every firstborn male of the Children of Israel,
     from the age of a month and upward,
     take-up the enumeration of their names.

41 Take the Levites aside for me
     —I am YHWH!—
     in place of every firstborn among the Children of Israel;
     along with the animals of the Levites,
     in place of every firstborn animal among the Children of Israel.

42 Moshe made an accounting, as YHWH had commanded him,
     of every firstborn among the Children of Israel.

43 And it was, every firstborn male by the number of names,
     from the age of a month and upward, by their count:
     two and twenty thousand, three and seventy and two hundred.

44 And YHWH spoke to Moshe, saying:

45 Take aside the Levites,
     in place of every firstborn among the Children of Israel,
     along with the animals of the Levites, in place of their animals;
     mine shall be the Levites
     —I am YHWH!

39 **Moshe and Aharon:** The traditional Hebrew text has dots placed above Aharon's name here, perhaps the equivalent of an asterisk. This denotes some scribal concerns about the text—maybe the incon-sistency with 3:14–15, where only Moshe is com-manded to count the Levites.
41 **animals:** Milgrom has "cattle."

Levites II (4): Here the tasks of the Levites are presented in great detail and listed according to clan. The jobs involve the guarding, dismantling, and transport of the "sancta" (holy objects). We are subsequently given a census of the Levites from ages 30 to 50, which fits here better than in Chap. 1. This age of service implies, perhaps, the physical strain associated with Levite tasks.

46 And as the redemption-price for the three and seventy and two
    hundred,
those-in-excess beyond the Levites from the firstborn of the
    Children of Israel,

47 you are to take five—five *shekels* per capita,
by the Holy-Shrine *shekel* you are to take,
twenty grains to the *shekel*.

48 You are to give the silver to Aharon and to his sons,
as a redemption-price for those-in-excess among them.

49 So Moshe took the silver for redemption from those-in-excess
    beyond those redeemed by the Levites,

50 from the firstborn of the Children of Israel he took the silver:
five and sixty and three hundred and a thousand, by the Holy-
    Shrine *shekel;*

51 Moshe gave the silver for redemption to Aharon and to his sons,
    by order of YHWH,
as YHWH had commanded Moshe.

4:1 YHWH spoke to Moshe and to Aharon, saying:

2 Take up the head-count of the Sons of Kehat from the midst of
    the Sons of Levi,
by their clans, by their Fathers' House,

3 from the age of thirty years and upward, until the age of fifty
    years,
all who enter the working-force
to do skilled-work in the Tent of Appointment.

4 This is the serving-task of the Sons of Kehat in the Tent of
    Appointment: the holiest holy-things.

5 Aharon and his sons are to come, when the camp marches
    forward,
and are to take down the curtain of the screen,
and are to cover with it the coffer of Testimony.

---

46 **redemption-price:** This idea survives in a Jewish ceremony, the "Redemption of the Firstborn": thirty days after the birth of a firstborn male (not in a family descended from priests or Levites), symbolic money is handed over to a person descended from priests, and the money is given to charity.

4:3 **thirty . . . fifty:** It is twenty-five to fifty in 8:24. **working-force:** The same word, *tzava,* means "armed-forces" in Chap. 1.

6   They are to put over it a covering of tanned-leather skin,
and are to spread a cloth entirely of blue-violet on top,
putting its poles (in place).

7   On the Table of the Presence they are to spread a cloth of blue-
violet,
and are to place on it the bowls, the ladles, the jars and the jugs
for pouring (offerings),
and the regular bread is to remain on it.

8   They are to spread over these a cloth of worm-scarlet,
and are to cover it with a covering of tanned-leather skin,
putting its poles (in place).

9   They are to take a cloth of blue-violet
and are to cover the lampstand for the lighting,
its lamps, its tongs and its fire-pans,
and all the implements for its oil which they use in conjunction
with them.

10   They are to place it and all its implements in a covering of
tanned-leather skin,
placing (them) on a frame.

11   Over the slaughter-site of gold they are to spread a cloth of blue-
violet,
and are to cover it with a covering of tanned-leather skin,
putting its poles (in place).

12   They are to take all the implements of attending with which they
tend in the Holy-Shrine
and are to put them into a cloth of blue-violet,
and are to cover them with a covering of tanned-leather skin,
placing (them) on a frame.

13   They are to de-ash the slaughter-site,
and are to spread on it a cloth of purple;

6 **blue-violet:** A royal color, made from a dye ob-tained from a certain mollusk. It is used in various places in the Tabernacle (cf. Ex. 25:6–9, 13–14) and in the ritual tassels (15:37ff., below). The precise shade is open to debate.

7 **regular bread:** Also known as the "Bread of the Presence," to be displayed on the table of the Taber-nacle regularly. The concept that God requires food was probably an early aspect of Israelite practice that has been retained in the cultic paraphernalia but no longer in actual biblical thinking about God.

14 they are to place on it all its implements that they use in
conjunction with them:
the fire-pans, the flesh-hooks, the scrapers and the bowls,
all the implements of the slaughter-site,
and they are to spread over it a covering of tanned-leather skin,
putting its poles (in place).

15 When Aharon and his sons have finished covering the holy-things
and all the holy implements, when the camp marches on,
(only) after that may the Sons of Kehat enter, to carry,
so that they do not touch the holy-things and die.
These are the carrying-chores of the Sons of Kehat in the Tent of
Appointment.

16 Accountable is El'azar son of Aharon the priest for:
the oil for the light, the fragrant smoking-incense, the regular
grain-gift, and the oil for anointing—
accountable for all the Dwelling and all that is in it,
whether the holy-things or its implements.

17 YHWH spoke to Moshe and to Aharon, saying:

18 Do not cut off the tribe of the clans of Kehat from the midst of
the Levites;

19 do this with them,
that they may live and not die
when they encroach upon the holiest holy-things:
Aharon and his sons are to enter and assign them,
each-man, each-man to his service, his carrying-chores.

20 But they are not to enter and see (even) for-a-moment (the
dismantling of) the Holy-Shrine, lest they die.

21 YHWH spoke to Moshe, saying:

22 Take up the head-count of the Sons of Gershon, they too,
by their Fathers' House, by their clans,

16 **implements:** Or "utensils."
18 **tribe:** Heb. *shevet*, like the other word for "tribe,"
matte (cf. 1:4), derives from a word meaning "staff"—
so the pun could be accommodated by "stick" and
"stock."
20 **see:** Beyond touching, even the unauthorized see-

ing of the sancta could be fatal. These were disman-
tled and covered only by Aharon and his sons
(vv.5–14). **for-a-moment:** Lit. "as long as it takes to
swallow." Similarly, in German, "moment" is *Augen-
blick,* lit. "the blinking of an eye."

23 from the age of thirty years and upward;
   to the age of fifty years you are to count them,
   all who enter to join-forces with the working-force, to serve the
      serving-tasks in the Tent of Appointment.
24 This is the serving-task of the Gershonite clans, for the service-of-
      packing and for carrying:
25 they are to carry
   the curtains of the Dwelling, and the Tent of Appointment,
   its covering, the covering of tanned-leather that is over it, on top,
   and the screen for the entrance of the Tent of Appointment,
26 the hangings of the courtyard
   and the screen for the entrance to the gate of the courtyard that
      is over the Dwelling and over the slaughter-site, all around,
   as well as their cords,
   and all their serving implements;
   whatever is to be done with regard to them, they are to do-the-
      serving-task.
27 By order of Aharon and his sons shall it be (done):
   all the serving-tasks of the Sons of the Gershonites,
   including all their carrying-chores, including all their service.
   You are to make them accountable for discharging all their
      carrying-chores.
28 This is the serving-task of the clans of the Sons of the
      Gershonites at the Tent of Appointment
   and their charge under the hand of Itamar son of Aharon the
      priest.

29 The Sons of Merari: by their clans, by their Fathers' House you
      are to count them,
30 from the age of thirty years and upward until the age of fifty
      years you are to count them,
   every one that may enter the working-force,
   to serve the serving-tasks of the Tent of Appointment.
31 This is their charge of carrying, including all their service-of-
      packing in the Tent of Appointment:
   the boards of the Dwelling,
   its bars, its columns and its sockets;

32 the columns of the courtyard, all around, their sockets, their pegs
and their cords—including all their implements, including all
their serving-tasks;
by name you are to account for the implements of their carrying
duties.

33 That is the service-of-packing of the clans of the Sons of Merari,
including all their serving-tasks in the Tent of Appointment
under the hand of Itamar son of Aharon the priest.

34 So Moshe, Aharon and the leaders of the community counted all
the Sons of Kehat,
by their clans, by their Fathers' House,

35 from the age of thirty years and upward until the age of fifty
years,
everyone that entered the working-force, for the serving-tasks in
the Tent of Appointment.

36 Now those counted of them were, by their clans: two thousand,
seven hundred and fifty.

37 These are the accountings of the Kehatite clans,
everyone that was serving in the Tent of Appointment,
whom Moshe and Aharon counted by order of YHWH, by the
hand of Moshe.

38 Now those counted of the Sons of Gershon,
by their clans, by their Fathers' House,

39 from the age of thirty and upward until the age of fifty years,
everyone who entered the work-force, for the serving-tasks in the
Tent of Appointment:

40 those counted of them were, by their clans, by their Fathers'
House:
two thousand, six hundred and thirty.

41 These are the accountings of the clans of the Sons of Gershon,
everyone that did-service in the Tent of Appointment,
whom Moshe and Aharon counted by order of YHWH.

42 And those counted of the Sons of Merari,
by their clans, by their Fathers' House,

43 from the age of thirty years and upward until the age of fifty
years,

Priestly Matters; The Wife Under Suspicion (5): Chaps. 5 and 6 are texts that seem most appropriate in a priestly setting. In both cases, the priest plays a central role in the ceremony described, administering the test and oath to the suspected adulteress and purifying the Nazirite (Milgrom).

Here, as in several other cases in the book of Numbers, texts that one might have expected to find in Leviticus seem to have been deferred. The reasons are not difficult to fathom. Leviticus as it has been edited deals with three broad areas: the sacrificial cult, ritual pollution and purification, and holiness in communal and priestly behavior. Chaps. 5 and 6 of Numbers do not easily fit into these categories, although some connections can be found. These chapters are also long, detailed cases, and it is possible that they might have deflected the central thrust of Leviticus.

Having said this, Chap. 5 opens, appropriately, with concern for the purity of the sacred camp that has just been described in Chap. 2. It continues with an innovation (vv.5–10): some sins that were intentional can now apparently be expiated via confession and an *asham*-offering (cf. Lev. 5)—unlike the situation that obtains in Lev. 4–5, where it is only sins committed "in error" that are forgivable by means of the sacrificial system (with the addition of confession and restitution). This little section has been placed here perhaps because of its verbal link with the next, larger section—which addresses the issue of "breaking faith" (vv.6 and 12).

Beginning with v.11, we encounter a strange ceremony such as is found nowhere else in the Torah. Its odd aspects are not surprising, though, given the gravity of the accusation. Adultery in ancient Israel was a capital crime, while in the rest of the ancient Near East (Mesopotamia, for instance) it could sometimes be expiated through payment to the wronged husband. And significantly, it is the husband who is in total control here, and the mere "breath of suspicion" (a possible rendering of the text's "rush of jealousy" in v.14) on his part results in a grave psychological ordeal for his wife. This is consistent with the male control over the sexuality of wives (and daughters) often observed in biblical texts (cf. Wegner 1988); there was of course no such procedure in regard to husbands. The last verse is telling; it presumes guilt on the part of the wife.

Frymer-Kensky (1984) sees the chapter as a manual for priests, and as a ritual that addresses "a crisis in the legal system"—for the crime is not provable by human agency (Milgrom points out that the word for "adultery" does not appear at all). She views the structure of the central parts of the ritual as revolving around pairs of verbs: the priest is to have the woman "stand before the presence of Yhwh" (vv.16–18); "swear" (vv.19, 21); and "drink" (vv.24, 27). The combination of drink, oath-taking, and declaration of innocence is found elsewhere in the ancient Near East (Fishbane 1974).

everyone who entered the working-force, for serving-tasks in the
Tent of Appointment:

44 those counted of them were, by their clans, by their Fathers'
House:
three thousand and two hundred.

45 These are the accountings of the clans of the Sons of Merari,
whom Moshe and Aharon counted by order of YHWH, by the
hand of Moshe.

46 All those counted, whom Moshe and Aharon and all the leaders
of Israel counted, the Levites,
by their clans, by their Fathers' House,

47 from the age of thirty years and upward until the age of fifty
years,
everyone that entered to serve the serving-tasks of the service-of-
packing and the serving-tasks of carrying, in the Tent of
Appointment,

48 those of them counted were: eight thousand, five hundred and
eighty.

49 By order of YHWH they were counted, by the hand of Moshe,
each-man, each-man according to his service-of-packing and to
his carrying-tasks, (with) his accountability,
as YHWH had commanded Moshe.

5:1 YHWH spoke to Moshe, saying:

2 Command the Children of Israel,
that they may send-away from the camp
anyone (with) *tzaraat*, anyone (with) a flow, and anyone *tamei* by
a (dead) person.

3 Male and female (alike), you are to send-him-away,
outside the camp you are to send-them-away,
so that they do not make their camp *tamei*
in which I keep-a-dwelling in their midst.

5:2 *tzaraat:* Pronounced "tzah-*rah*-aht." Apparently a
category of skin disease, which rendered a person
temporarily "polluted." Such a person was a danger
to the sanctuary (too much pollution would drive
God away, as it were), and had to withdraw from the
camp boundaries for a time, like the others mentioned in this chapter (cf. Lev. 13–14 for details).
flow: Such as semen or menstrual blood. **by a
(dead) person:** Physical contact with a corpse.

Fishbane (1980) notes how the chapter ends with two summaries (vv.29 and 30) relating back to the descriptions in vv.12–14. The phrase found at the end of the chapter, "This is the Instruction," often concludes ritual sections in the Torah (cf. Lev. 11–15), and indeed is found in 6:21 below; it may indicate the former existence of these laws in separate scrolls.

4 Thus did the Children of Israel, sending-them-away outside the
   camp,
   as YHWH had spoken to Moshe,
   thus did the Children of Israel.

5 YHWH spoke to Moshe, saying:
6 Speak to the Children of Israel:
   A man or a woman—when they do any sin (committed by)
   humans
   by breaking-faith, yes, faith with YHWH,
   and that person realizes his guilt:
7 they are to confess their sin that they have done,
   and (each one) is to make-restitution for one's guilt in its capital-
   amount,
   adding its fifth to it,
   and is to give it to the one toward whom one incurred-guilt.
8 Now if the man has no redeemer, to make-restitution of guilt-
   payment to him,
   the guilt-payment is to be restored to YHWH, (it is) the priest's,
   besides the ram of purgation with which purgation is effected for
   him.
9 And any contribution, including any of the holy-offerings of the
   Children of Israel that they bring-near for the priest,
   shall be his.
10 So every-man, his holy-offerings shall be his,
   every-man, what he gives to the priest, shall be his.

11 YHWH spoke to Moshe, saying:
12 Speak to the Children of Israel and say to them:
   Any-man, any-man whose wife goes-astray,
   breaking-faith, yes, faith with him,

---

6 **breaking-faith:** So JPS. In Lev. 5:15ff. the term refers to sacrilege against holy objects in the sanctuary. Here it encompasses wrongdoing against persons, which is seen as rebellion against God. Cf. also v.12 below.

7 **its fifth:** A 20 percent penalty.

8 **no redeemer:** No relative who can pay the fine.
ram of purgation: The first step in restitution is to provide for the ritual purification of the sinner via sacrifice.

9–10 **shall be his:** The priest's.

13 in that a man lay with her, (with) an emission of seed,
    and it was hidden from the eyes of her husband,
    —she concealed herself, since she had made-herself-*tamei*—
    and since there was no witness against her, she was not
        apprehended—
14 and the rush of jealousy comes over him,
    and he is jealous toward his wife, she having made-herself-*tamei;*
    or the rush of jealousy comes over him
15 and he is jealous toward his wife, though she did not make-
        herself-*tamei*—
    the man is to bring his wife to the priest.
    He is to bring a near-offering for her:
    a tenth of an *efa* of barley meal;
    there is not to be poured on it any oil, there is not to be put on it
        any frankincense,
    for it is a grain-gift of jealousy,
    grain-gift of reminding that reminds of iniquity.
16 The priest is to bring-her-near
    and have-her-stand before the presence of YHWH;
17 then the priest is to take holy water in an earthenware vessel,
    and from the dirt that will be on the floor of the Dwelling
    the priest is to take (some) and place (it) in the water.
18 When the priest has had the woman stand before the presence of
        YHWH,
    he is to loosen (the hair of) the woman's head
    and is to place on her palms the grain-gift of reminding
    —it is a grain-gift of jealousy!—
    and in the hand of the priest is to be the Water of Bitterness
        Bringing the Bane.

---

14 **rush:** Others, "fit." **jealousy:** Or "suspicion," "zealous indignation" (Fishbane 1974).

15 **near-offering:** Cf. Lev. 1–5 for a description of this and other sacrifices (grain-gift in this verse, *hattat*-offering and offering-up in 6:11, and *asham*-offering in 6:12). **barley:** The cheapest grain, and hence available even to the poor. **reminding:** God.

18 **Water of Bitterness Bringing the Bane:** Hebrew difficult. Nevertheless, it is clear (and significant) that the formula is alliterative and thus has a ritual, almost magical ring: *mei ha-marim ha-me'arrarim.* Another possible rendering, after an interpretation of Frymer-Kensky (1984) and others, is "Waters of Instruction, of Spell-Induction."

19 The priest is to have her swear, saying to the woman:
   If a man did not lie with you,
   and if you did not stray to make-yourself-*tamei* under your
       husband('s authority),
   be-clear from this Water of Bitterness Bringing the Bane!
20 But you, if you strayed under your husband('s authority),
   if you made-yourself-*tamei*,
   and a man gave you his emission, other than your husband:
21 the priest is to have the woman swear the oath curse,
   and the priest is to say to the woman:
   may YHWH make you a curse and a cause-for-oath in the midst of
       your kinspeople,
   when YHWH makes your thigh fall and your belly flood;
22 may this Water of Bitterness enter your innards,
   to cause the belly to flood and the thigh to fall!
   And the woman is to say: Amen! Amen!
23 Then the priest is to write these curses in a document
   and is to blot (them) into the Water of Bitterness,
24 he is to make the woman drink the Water of Bitterness Bringing
       the Bane,
   so that the Water Bringing the Bane may enter her, for
       "bitterness."
25 Then the priest is to take from the hand of the woman the grain-
       gift of jealousy,
   he is to elevate the grain-gift before the presence of YHWH,
   and is to bring-it-near, to the slaughter-site.
26 The priest is to scoop out of the grain-gift its reminder-portion,
   and is to turn it into smoke upon the slaughter-site;
   after that he is to make the woman drink the water.

---

21 **oath curse:** or "threat," the part of the oath threat-ening punishment. **thigh fall . . . belly flood:** While the precise biological process is not clear (the suggestions vary from miscarriage to a prolapsed uterus), sterility is one possible meaning. "Thigh" in the Bible is often a euphemism for genitals (e.g., Gen. 24:2). It is also possible that the woman is preg-nant and that the intention is to abort the fetus, since if the husband's suspicions of adultery are founded, the child will be illegitimate and hence a threat to the purity of Israel (Levine).
22 **Amen!:** Lit. "established," "firm" (i.e., true).
23 **blot:** Following Haran; others, "rub."

The Nazirite (6:1–21): A "consecrated" or "separate" person, traditionally transcribed as "Nazirite" after the Hebrew *nazir,* was one who took upon himself or herself a special vow, exceeding the normal demands of the religious life. The urge to such behavior appears throughout the ages in many religious traditions, and doubtless reflects a deep-seated human desire. The motivation may stem from a joyous or tragic event, or simply from the need to serve God in what is felt to be a fuller way.

Three prohibitions characterize the Nazirite: no drinking anything made from grapes (note the Bible's early sense that cultivation of the vine is problematic— the story of Noah's drunkenness in Gen. 9:20ff.); no shaving the hair (hair was understood by the ancients as possessing almost magical characteristics); and no contact with the dead (including relatives; death was considered the major pollutant in Israelite thinking). Given that the Nazirite's vow has a finite period, Milgrom theorizes that our chapter represents a priestly attempt to control ascetic urges.

The ritual (vv.12ff.) that ends the Nazirite's "state of consecration" involves a variety of sacrifices, most notably a *hattat*-offering (cf. Lev. 4). This purification offering suggested to later interpreters that the Nazirite vow was to be viewed in at least a somewhat negative light. Certainly by Rabbinic times, formative Judaism came to look askance at undue asceticism; on the other hand, religious vows and abstentions were to survive and even flourish in medieval and later Judaism, Christianity, and Islam.

In light of the fact that a Nazirite could be either a man or a woman, the translation of this chapter uses "one" regularly instead of the text's "he"—which in any event indicates both genders in this chapter.

27 When he has had her drink the water, it shall be:
if she made-herself-*tamei*
and broke-faith, yes, faith with her husband,
the Water Bringing the Bane shall enter her, for "bitterness,"
her belly shall flood and her thigh shall fall,
and the woman shall become an object-of-curse among her
    kinsfolk.

28 But if the woman did not make-herself-*tamei*
and she is pure,
she is to be cleared and she may-bear-seed, yes, seed.

29 This is the Instruction for cases-of-jealousy,
when a woman strays under her husband('s authority)
and makes-herself-*tamei,*

30 or when there comes over a man a rush of jealousy, so that he is
    jealous toward his wife:
he is to have the woman stand before the presence of Yhwh,
and the priest is to perform regarding her (according to) all this
    Instruction.

31 The man shall be clear of iniquity,
but that woman shall bear her iniquity.

6:1 Yhwh spoke to Moshe, saying:

2 Speak to the Children of Israel and say to them:
A man or a woman—when one sets oneself apart, by vowing the
    vow of a Nazirite / Consecrated-One, to consecrate-oneself for
    Yhwh:

3 from wine and from intoxicant one is to consecrate-oneself;
fermentation of wine and fermentation of intoxicant one is not
    to drink,
any liquid of grapes one is not to drink,
and grapes, moist or dried, one is not to eat.

---

29 **Instruction:** Heb. *Tora* (Torah), meaning "priestly regulation." From such *torot* evolved the name for longer sections, and eventually for the Five Books of Moses.

31 **bear her iniquity:** So the punishment, or the removal of iniquity, is left up to God (cf. Schwartz 1994).

6:2 **Consecrated-One:** Or "Separate-One," "Dedicated-One."

3 **any liquid of grapes:** So strict is the prohibition of alcohol here that no chances are taken.

4   All the days of one's being-consecrated,
anything that is made from the vine of wine, from seeds to skin,
    one is not to eat.

5   All the days of one's vow of being-consecrated
a razor is not to go-across one's head;
until the fulfilling of days that one is consecrated for YHWH,
holy shall one remain;
one is to grow loose the hair on one's head.

6   All the days that one consecrates-oneself for YHWH,
near a dead person one is not to come—

7   (even) for one's father or one's mother, one's brother or one's
    sister;
one is not to make-oneself-*tamei* by them when they die,
for (hair) consecrated for one's God is upon one's head.

8   All the days of one's being-consecrated,
one is holy to YHWH.

9   Now if a dead-man has died near one
suddenly, all-of-a-sudden,
so that one makes-*tamei* the consecrated (hair of one's) head,
one is to shave one's head on the day of one's becoming-pure;
on the seventh day one is to shave it.

10   Now on the eighth day
one is to bring two turtledoves or two young pigeons to the
    priest,
to the entrance of the Tent of Appointment.

11   The priest is to sacrifice one as a *hattat*/decontamination-offering,
    and one as an offering-up;
he is to effect-purgation for one,
in that one became-contaminated by the (dead) person.
One is to make one's head holy (again) on that day,

12   and is to reconsecrate to YHWH the days of one's being-
consecrated, bringing a lamb in its (first) year as an
asham/compensation-offering.

---

7 **make-oneself-*tamei*:** Others, "render himself impure."
11 **sacrifice:** Lit. "do," "perform" (as sacrifice). **became-**

contaminated: Alternatively (or simultaneously),
"incurred-sin."
12 **fallen-away:** Null and void.

The former days are to be (considered) fallen-away,
since *tamei* became one's state-of-consecration.

13 Now this is the Ritual-Instruction for the Consecrated-One:
On the day that one's days of being-consecrated are fulfilled,
one is to be brought to the entrance of the Tent of Appointment;

14 one is to bring-near as one's near-offering to Yhwh:
a lamb in its (first) year, wholly-sound, one, as an offering-up,
and one ewe-lamb in its (first) year, wholly-sound, as a *hattat*-
    offering, and one ram, wholly-sound, as a *shalom*-offering;

15 a basket of *matzot* of flour, round-loaves mixed with oil,
wafers of *matzot* spread with oil,
(as well as) their grain-gift and their poured-offerings.

16 The priest is to come-near before the presence of Yhwh,
and is to sacrifice his *hattat*-offering and his offering-up,

17 and the ram he is to sacrifice as a slaughter-offering of *shalom* to
    Yhwh,
together with the basket of *matzot;*
then the priest is to sacrifice his grain-gift and his poured-offering.

18 The Consecrated-One is then to shave, at the entrance of the
    Tent of Appointment, one's consecrated head,
and is to take the hair of one's consecrated head
and put (it) on the fire that is under the slaughter-offering of
    shalom.

19 The priest is to take the shoulder of the ram, boiled,
and one loaf of *matza* from the basket,
and one wafer of *matza,*
and is to put (them) upon the palms of the Consecrated-One,
    after one's shaving of one's consecrated (hair).

20 The priest is to elevate them as an elevation-offering, before the
    presence of Yhwh—
it is a holy-offering for the priest—

14 **wholly-sound:** Unblemished and hence fit for sacrifice to God. **shalom-offering:** Cf. Lev. 3.

15 *matzot:* Plural of *matza,* unleavened bread.

The Priestly Blessing (6:22–27) with which the chapter ends is striking and sufficiently beloved by Jews to have survived to this day in the synagogue liturgy. But why is it here? Perhaps the blessing of the people is yet another example of a priestly function that has not been preserved in Leviticus, since it relates neither to sacrifice nor to purification (although it should be pointed out that Moshe and Aharon give an unquoted blessing to the people in Lev. 9:23).

The blessing itself makes wonderful use of ancient Hebrew rhythm, with a threefold structure of progressively longer lines that is reminiscent of a magical formula. The varied verbs give comfort and reassurance, as does the last word of the blessing: *shalom* ("well-being"). The benevolent "lifting" of God's face is a known image in the ancient Near East (cf. the references in Fishbane 1988). Its devastating opposite, the "hiding" of his face, is found in the Psalms, and also in Deut. 31.

That this section was popular already in biblical times is indicated by its occurrence in a two-part version in Ps. 67:2, as well as its appearance, in various forms, on ancient Israelite amulets.

The Gifts to the Sanctuary (7): Chaps. 7–9 constitute a threefold conclusion to the Tabernacle texts that began in Ex. 25. The contribution of each chapter will be explained in sequence.

The longest chapter in the Torah in number of verses, and another one of the many lists in the book, Chap. 7 parallels what Levine calls "temple accounts" in the ancient Near East. These are inventory lists that were frequently written in columns. At the same time, it is a ritual text that focuses on description and not prescription, which is more usual. The chapter ends in v.89 with the first of our Tabernacle endings: a description of precisely where God would communicate with Moshe within the "Holiest Holy-Shrine." The implication is that with the dedication of the structure, its purpose can now be fulfilled.

The length of the chapter reinforces the importance and grandeur of the ceremony, and makes of the "Dwelling" an institution in which all participate, not only priests and Levites (Levine).

on top of the breast of the elevation-offering and on top of the
thigh of the contribution,
and after (that) the Consecrated-One may drink wine.

21 This is the Instruction for the Consecrated-One
who vows a near-offering to YHWH in addition to one's
(requirement of) consecration,
aside from what one's hand can reach:
according to the vow that one has vowed, thus is one to perform,
in addition to the instructed-requirements of one's
consecration.

22 YHWH spoke to Moshe, saying:
23 Speak to Aharon and to his sons, saying:
Thus are you to bless the Children of Israel;
say to them:

24   May YHWH bless you and keep you!
25   May YHWH shine his face upon you and favor you!
26   May YHWH lift up his face toward you and grant you *shalom*!

27 So are they to put my name upon the Children of Israel,
that I myself may bless them.

7:1 Now it was, at the time that Moshe finished setting up the
Dwelling,
he anointed it and hallowed it, with all its implements,
and the slaughter-site, with all its implements,
he anointed them and he hallowed them.
2 Then brought-near the exalted-leaders of Israel, the heads of
their Fathers' House—
3 they are the leaders of the tribes, they are those who stand over
the counting—
they brought their near-offering before the presence of YHWH:
six litter wagons and twelve cattle,
a wagon for (every) two leaders and an ox for (each) one.

---

21 **in addition to:** Or "in excess of."
27 **put my name:** The meaning is unclear; is it abstract
or concrete, in which case an amulet might have
been meant?

7:1 **finished:** Or "Had finished."

♦

When they had brought-them-near to the Dwelling,

4 Yhwh said to Moshe, saying:

5 Take (these) from them,

that they may serve for the service-of-transport of the Tent of
Appointment,

and give them to the Levites, each-man according to his serving-
tasks.

6 Moshe took the wagons and the cattle

and gave them to the Levites.

7 Two wagons and four cattle he gave to the Sons of Gershon,
according to their serving-orders,

8 four wagons and eight cattle he gave to the Sons of Merari,
according to their serving-orders,

under the hand of Itamar son of Aharon the priest,

9 but to the Sons of Kehat he did not give (any),

for the service-of-transport of the holy-things is theirs,

by shoulder they are to carry (them).

10 The leaders brought-near the initiation-offering of the slaughter-
site,

at the time of its being-anointed.

Now when the leaders brought-near their near-offering before
the slaughter-site,

11 Yhwh said to Moshe:

One leader per day, one leader per day, let them bring-near their
near-offering,

for the initiation of the slaughter-site.

12 So he who brought-near his near-offering on the first day was:
Nahshon son of Amminadav, of the tribe of Yehuda.

13 His near-offering:

one dish of silver, thirty and a hundred its *shekel*-weight,

one bowl of silver, seventy *shekels* according to the Holy-Shrine
shekel,

both of them filled with flour mixed with oil, for a grain-gift,

14 one ladle (of) ten (*shekels*) of gold, filled with smoking-incense,

---

12 **Nahshon:** The brother-in-law of Aharon (cf. Ex.
6:23).

13 **bowl:** Heb. *mizrak;* used for holding blood that was
to be dashed (*zarok*) against the altar.

15   one bull, a young of the herd, one ram, one lamb in its (first)
      year, as an offering-up;

16   one hairy goat as a *hattat*-offering;

17   and as a slaughter-offering of *shalom:*
      oxen two, rams five, he-goats five, and lambs in the (first) year
        five.
      That (was) the near-offering of Nahshon son of Amminadav.

18   On the second day, Netan'el son of Tzu'ar, leader of Yissakhar,
      brought-(it)-near;

19   he brought-near his near-offering:
      one dish of silver, thirty and a hundred its *shekel*-weight,
      one bowl of silver, seventy *shekels* according to the Holy-Shrine
       shekel,
      both of them filled with flour mixed with oil, for a grain-gift,

20   one ladle (of) ten (*shekels*) of gold, filled with smoking-incense,

21   one bull, a young of the herd, one ram, one lamb in its (first)
      year, as an offering-up;

22   one hairy goat as a *hattat*-offering;

23   and as a slaughter-offering of *shalom:*
      oxen two, rams five, he-goats five, and lambs in the (first) year
       five.
      That (was) the near-offering of Netan'el son of Tzu'ar.

24   On the third day, the leader of the Sons of Zevulun,
      Eliav son of Heilon—

25   his near-offering:
      one dish of silver, thirty and a hundred its *shekel*-weight,
      one bowl of silver, seventy *shekels* according to the Holy-Shrine
       shekel,
      both of them filled with flour mixed with oil, for a grain-gift,

26   one ladle (of) ten (*shekels*) of gold, filled with smoking-incense,

27   one bull, a young of the herd, one ram, one lamb in its (first)
      year, as an offering-up;

28   one hairy goat as a *hattat*-offering;

29   and as a slaughter-offering of *shalom:*
      oxen two, rams five, he-goats five, and lambs in the (first) year
       five.
      That (was) the near-offering of Eliav son of Heilon.

30 On the fourth day, the leader of the Sons of Re'uven,
    Elitzur son of Shedei'ur—

31 his near-offering:
    one dish of silver, thirty and a hundred its *shekel*-weight,
    one bowl of silver, seventy *shekels* according to the Holy-Shrine
        shekel,
    both of them filled with flour mixed with oil, for a grain-gift,

32 one ladle (of) ten (*shekels*) of gold, filled with smoking-incense,

33 one bull, a young of the herd, one ram, one lamb in its (first)
        year, as an offering-up;

34 one hairy goat as a *hattat*-offering;

35 and as a slaughter-offering of *shalom:*
    oxen two, rams five, he-goats five, and lambs in the (first) year
        five.
    That (was) the near-offering of Elitzur son of Shedei'ur.

36 On the fifth day, the leader of the Sons of Shim'on,
    Shelumi'el son of Tzurishaddai—

37 his near-offering:
    one dish of silver, thirty and a hundred its *shekel*-weight,
    one bowl of silver, seventy *shekels* according to the Holy-Shrine
        shekel,
    both of them filled with flour mixed with oil, for a grain-gift,

38 one ladle (of) ten (*shekels*) of gold, filled with smoking-incense,

39 one bull, a young of the herd, one ram, one lamb in its (first)
        year, as an offering-up;

40 one hairy goat as a *hattat*-offering;

41 and as a slaughter-offering of *shalom:*
    oxen two, rams five, he-goats five, and lambs in the (first) year
        five.
    That (was) the near-offering of Shelumi'el son of Tzurishaddai.

42 On the sixth day, the leader of the Sons of Gad,
    Elyasaf son of De'uel—

43 his near-offering:
    one dish of silver, thirty and a hundred its *shekel*-weight,

---

42 **De'uel:** Spelled *Re'uel* in 2:14.

one bowl of silver, seventy *shekels* according to the Holy-Shrine
shekel,
both of them filled with flour mixed with oil, for a grain-gift,

44 one ladle (of) ten (*shekels*) of gold, filled with smoking-incense,

45 one bull, a young of the herd, one ram, one lamb in its (first)
year, as an offering-up;

46 one hairy goat as a *hattat*-offering;

47 and as a slaughter-offering of *shalom:*
oxen two, rams five, he-goats five, and lambs in the (first) year
five.
That (was) the near-offering of Elyasaf son of De'uel.

48 On the seventh day, the leader of the Sons of Efrayim,
Elishama son of Ammihud—

49 his near-offering:
one dish of silver, thirty and a hundred its *shekel*-weight,
one bowl of silver, seventy *shekels* according to the Holy-Shrine
shekel,
both of them filled with flour mixed with oil, for a grain-gift,

50 one ladle (of) ten (*shekels*) of gold, filled with smoking-incense,

51 one bull, a young of the herd, one ram, one lamb in its (first)
year, as an offering-up;

52 one hairy goat as a *hattat*-offering;

53 and as a slaughter-offering of *shalom:*
oxen two, rams five, he-goats five, and lambs in the (first) year
five.
That (was) the near-offering of Elishama son of Ammihud.

54 On the eighth day, the leader of the Sons of Menashe,
Gamliel son of Pedahtzur—

55 his near-offering:
one dish of silver, thirty and a hundred its *shekel*-weight,
one bowl of silver, seventy *shekels* according to the Holy-Shrine
shekel,
both of them filled with flour mixed with oil, for a grain-gift,

56 one ladle (of) ten (*shekels*) of gold, filled with smoking-incense,

57 one bull, a young of the herd, one ram, one lamb in its (first)
year, as an offering-up;

58 one hairy goat as a *hattat*-offering;
59 and as a slaughter-offering of *shalom:*
oxen two, rams five, he-goats five, and lambs in the (first) year
five.
That (was) the near-offering of Gamliel son of Pedahtzur.

60 On the ninth day, the leader of the Sons of Binyamin,
Avidan son of Gid'oni—
61 his near-offering:
one dish of silver, thirty and a hundred its *shekel*-weight,
one bowl of silver, seventy *shekels* according to the Holy-Shrine
shekel,
both of them filled with flour mixed with oil, for a grain-gift,
62 one ladle (of) ten (*shekels*) of gold, filled with smoking-incense,
63 one bull, a young of the herd, one ram, one lamb in its (first)
year, as an offering-up;
64 one hairy goat as a *hattat*-offering;
65 and as a slaughter-offering of *shalom:*
oxen two, rams five, he-goats five, and lambs in the (first) year
five.
That (was) the near-offering of Avidan son of Gid'oni.

66 On the tenth day, the leader of the Sons of Dan,
Ahi'ezer son of Ammishaddai—
67 his near-offering:
one dish of silver, thirty and a hundred its *shekel*-weight,
one bowl of silver, seventy *shekels* according to the Holy-Shrine
shekel,
both of them filled with flour mixed with oil, for a grain-gift,
68 one ladle (of) ten (*shekels*) of gold, filled with smoking-incense,
69 one bull, a young of the herd, one ram, one lamb in its (first)
year, as an offering-up;
70 one hairy goat as a *hattat*-offering;
71 and as a slaughter-offering of *shalom:*
oxen two, rams five, he-goats five, and lambs in the (first) year
five.
That (was) the near-offering of Ahi'ezer son of Ammishaddai.

72 On the day of the eleventh day, the leader of the Sons of Asher,

◆

Pag'iel son of Okhran—

73 his near-offering:
one dish of silver, thirty and a hundred its *shekel*-weight,
one bowl of silver, seventy *shekels* according to the Holy-Shrine
shekel,
both of them filled with flour mixed with oil, for a grain-gift,
74 one ladle (of) ten (*shekels*) of gold, filled with smoking-incense,
75 one bull, a young of the herd, one ram, one lamb in its (first)
year, as an offering-up;
76 one hairy goat as a *hattat*-offering;
77 and as a slaughter-offering of *shalom:*
oxen two, rams five, he-goats five, and lambs in the (first) year
five.
That (was) the near-offering of Pag'iel son of Okhran.

78 On the day of the twelfth day, the leader of the Sons of Naftali,
Ahira' son of Einan—
79 his near-offering:
one dish of silver, thirty and a hundred its *shekel*-weight,
one bowl of silver, seventy *shekels* according to the Holy-Shrine
shekel,
both of them filled with flour mixed with oil, for a grain-gift,
80 one ladle (of) ten (*shekels*) of gold, filled with smoking-incense,
81 one bull, a young of the herd, one ram, one lamb in its (first)
year, as an offering-up;
82 one hairy goat as a *hattat*-offering;
83 and as a slaughter-offering of *shalom:*
oxen two, rams five, he-goats five, and lambs in the (first) year
five.
That (was) the near-offering of Ahira' son of Einan.

84 This (was) the initiation-offering for the slaughter-site, at the time
of its being-anointed,
from the leaders of Israel:
dishes of silver twelve,
bowls of silver twelve,
ladles of gold twelve;
85 thirty and a hundred (weight) per one dish, of silver,
seventy per one bowl;

Purifying the Levites (8): A parallel to Lev. 8–9, where the dedication of the priests is the last act before the cult goes into operation, this chapter concludes the Levitical portions of Part I of Numbers—a distinctive contribution, as we have noted. Many scholars see the Levitical sections as reflections of later power struggles within the Israelite priesthood. In Levine's view, this evolution (perhaps from family-based guilds into a full-fledged tribe) is an indication of a relatively late provenance for our text here.

Milgrom rightly makes the distinction between the "purification" of the Levites and the higher-level "hallowing" (i.e., sanctification) of the priests. It is also interesting to note the cultic rites used here: the offering of a *hattat* (the standard purificatory sacrifice), and mention of the Levites themselves being considered an "elevation-offering" (v.11).

all the silver of the implements: two thousand, four hundred, by
the Holy-Shrine *shekel.*

86 Twelve ladles of gold filled with incense:
ten, ten (weight) per ladle, by the Holy-Shrine *shekel;*
all the gold of the ladles: twenty and a hundred.

87 All the oxen for the offering-up: twelve bulls,
rams twelve, lambs in the (first) year twelve, with their grain-gift;
hairy goats twelve, for the *hattat*-offering.

88 And all the oxen for the slaughter-offerings of *shalom:* four and
twenty bulls,
rams sixty, he-goats sixty, lambs in the (first) year sixty.
This (was) the initiation-offering of the slaughter-site, after they
had anointed it.

89 Now when Moshe would come in the Tent of Appointment to
speak with him,
he would hear the voice continually-speaking to him
from above the Purgation-Cover that is atop the coffer of
Testimony,
from between the two winged-sphinxes;
and he would he speak to him.

8:1 YHWH spoke to Moshe, saying:

2 Speak to Aharon and say to him:
When you draw up the lampwicks,
toward the front of the lampstand let the seven lampwicks give
light.

3 Aharon did thus;
toward the front of the lampstand he drew up the lampwicks,
as YHWH had commanded Moshe.

4 Now this (was) the constructed-pattern of the lampstand:
hammered-work of gold,

---

89 **Purgation-Cover:** The cover of the Coffer (Ark), which was seen as the "footstool" of God in the manner of ancient Near Eastern kings. **winged-sphinxes:** Golden images of mythical creatures that served to flank God's throne, and especially, as our text indicates, as the locus for divine communication with Moshe.

8:2 **draw up:** Others, "kindle." **toward the front:** More specifically, toward the area in front.

(even) up to its stem, up to its petals, it was hammered-work.
According to the vision that YHWH had Moshe see,
thus the lampstand was made.

5 Now YHWH spoke to Moshe, saying:
6 Take the Levites from the midst of the Children of Israel,
and purify them.
7 Thus you are to do to them, in order to purify them:
sprinkle on them Water of *Hattat*/decontamination;
they are to pass a razor across their whole body,
and are to scrub their garments—
then they will have purified themselves.
8 They are to take a bull, a young of the herd, and its grain-gift,
flour mixed with oil,
and a second bull, a young of the herd, you are to take for the
hattat-offering.
9 You are to have the Levites come-near before the Tent of
Appointment;
then you are to assemble the entire community of the Children
of Israel.
10 You are to have the Levites come-near, before the presence of
YHWH,
and the Children of Israel are to lean their hands upon the
Levites.
11 Aharon is to elevate the Levites as an elevation-offering, before
the presence of YHWH,
on behalf of the Children of Israel,
that they may serve the serving-tasks of YHWH.
12 Then the Levites are to lean their hands
on the head of the bulls;
they are to assign the one as a *hattat*-offering and the other as an
offering-up to YHWH,

---

4 **stem . . . petals:** In keeping with the nature of the
lampstand's probable origin as a symbolic tree; cf.
Ex. 25:31–35.
11 **elevate . . . elevation-offering:** An act of dedicating an offering to God. Also possible in this context

is "present . . . presentation-offering." Trad. "wave-
offering," which, as Milgrom shows, is probably incorrect. The usage of the expression to refer to the
Levites is not, of course, meant literally as a sacrificial offering.

to effect-ransom for the Levites.

13 Thus you are to have the Levites stand before Aharon and before
his sons
and are to elevate them as an elevation-offering to Yhwh.

14 Now you are to separate the Levites from the midst of the
Children of Israel,
mine are the Levites to be!

15 After that the Levites may enter into the service of the Tent of
Appointment,
when you have purified them and elevated them as an elevation-
offering.

16 For given-over, given-over are they to me from the midst of the
Children of Israel,
in place of the breacher of every womb, the firstborn of every
one of the Children of Israel;
I have taken them for myself.

17 For mine is every firstborn among the Children of Israel,
of man and of beast;
at the time that I struck down every firstborn in the land of
Egypt,
I declared-them-holy for myself.

18 Now I take the Levites
in place of every firstborn from the Children of Israel,

19 and I give-over the Levites, (to be) given-over to Aharon and to
his sons
from the midst of the Children of Israel,
to serve the serving-tasks of the Children of Israel in the Tent of
Appointment,
and to effect-ransom for the Children of Israel,
that there not be among the Children of Israel (any) plague
when the Children of Israel encroach on the holy-things.

20 Moshe, Aharon, and the entire community of Israel did regarding
the Levites

19 **effect-ransom:** For the lives of Israelite firstborn.

The Second Passover; Cloud and Dwelling (9): It has been noted by Milgrom that, a number of times in the Bible, ceremonies dedicating a House of God are followed by the observance of one of the three pilgrimage festivals: Passover, Shavuot (Weeks), and Sukkot (Huts). Under Solomon, Hezekiah, Josiah, and Ezra/Nehemiah, respectively, we find a major celebration of Sukkot, Passover, Passover, and Sukkot. This linking of sacred space with sacred time is only natural. The account here echoes the first Passover as well, which similarly inaugurated a wilderness march (Milgrom). In contrast to the Exodus account, however, something new has been added with the inauguration of the Tabernacle/Dwelling. In Exodus (12:43–49), the major laws concerning Passover had to do with excluding non-Israelites and not breaking the bones of the sacrificial lamb; here, the bone motif returns, but the existence of the sanctuary raises the issue of ritual pollution.

The second part of the chapter (vv.15–23) parallels the ending of the book of Exodus (40:36–38), where, once the Tabernacle has been dedicated, the "Cloud" takes up residence there, to guide Israel "on all their marches." Our passage here is longer and rather redundant, perhaps in order to set the chronological framework of the narrative straight.

◆ according to all that YHWH had commanded Moshe regarding the
Levites,
thus they did regarding them, the Children of Israel.

21 The Levites decontaminated-themselves and scrubbed their
garments;
Aharon elevated them as an elevation-offering before the
presence of YHWH,
and Aharon effected-purgation for them, to purify them.

22 After that the Levites entered to serve their serving-tasks in the
Tent of Appointment,
in the presence of Aharon and in the presence of his sons:
as YHWH had commanded Moshe regarding the Levites, thus they
did regarding them.

23 YHWH spoke to Moshe, saying:

24 This is what (is to be done) regarding the Levites:
from the age of five and twenty years and upward,
they are to enter the working-force, to join-the-force in the
serving-tasks of the Tent of Appointment;

25 and from the age of fifty years,
they are to retire from being-on-the-force for the serving-tasks,
and shall not serve anymore.

26 They may attend upon their brothers in the Tent of
Appointment,
to keep the maintenance-duty,
but serving-tasks they are not to serve.
Thus are you to do regarding the Levites in reference to their
duties.

9:1 YHWH spoke to Moshe in the Wilderness of Sinai,
in the second year of their going-out of the land of Egypt,
at the first New-Moon,
saying:

---

26 **keep the maintenance-duty:** As opposed to heavy
physical labor.
9:1 **spoke:** Milgrom reads as "had spoken," given that
this chapter is set in time before the opening of the

book. But the chronology here betrays an editorial
hand; this chapter could not be the opening of the
book for structural reasons (the census is the backbone of the book, as Olson has suggested).

2 The Children of Israel are to sacrifice the Passover-offering at its
    appointed-time:

3 on the fourteenth day after this New-Moon,
    between the setting-times,
    you are to sacrifice it at its appointed-time;
    according to all its laws, according to all its regulations, you are to
        sacrifice it.

4 So Moshe spoke (instructions) to the Children of Israel, to
    sacrifice the Passover-offering.

5 And they sacrificed the Passover-offering
    in the first (New-Moon), on the fourteenth day after the New-
        Moon,
    between the setting-times,
    in the Wilderness of Sinai.
    According to all that YHWH had commanded Moshe,
    thus did the Children of Israel.

6 But there were some men who were *tamei* by reason of a (dead)
    human person,
    and so were not able to sacrifice the Passover-offering on that day;
    coming-near before Moshe and before Aharon on that day,

7 those men said to him:
    We are *tamei* by reason of a (dead) human person;
    (but) why should we have (a privilege) taken-away,
    by not (being allowed) to bring-near the near-offering of YHWH in
        its appointed-time in the midst of the Children of Israel?

8 Moshe said to them:
    Stand by, and let me hear
    what YHWH shall command regarding you.

9 YHWH spoke to Moshe, saying:

10 Speak to the Children of Israel, saying:
    A man, (any) man when he is *tamei* by reason of a (dead) person
    or is on a long journey,
    among you or among your generations,
    and sacrifices a Passover-offering to YHWH:

---

3 **between the setting-times:** Between sunset and total darkness; twilight. **according to all its laws...regulations:** This phrase, adapted in a short medieval poem, is still recited by Jews at the end of the Passover meal.

11 in the second New-Moon, on the fourteenth day, between the
     setting-times,
  he is to sacrifice it;
  together with *matza* (and) bitter-herbs they are to eat it.
12 They are not to leave (any) of it until morning,
  a bone is not to be broken from it,
  according to all the law of the Passover-offering, they are to
     sacrifice it.
13 But a man who is (ritually) pure, or who has not been on a
     journey,
  and holds back from sacrificing the Passover-offering:
  cut off will that person be from his kinspeople,
  for the near-offering of Passover for YHWH he has not brought-
     near at its appointed-time;
  his sin he is to bear, that man.
14 Now when a sojourner sojourns with you
  and sacrifices a Passover-offering to YHWH,
  according to the law of the Passover-offering and according to its
     regulation,
  thus he is to sacrifice (it).
  One law (alone) is there to be for you, for the sojourner and for
     the native of the land.

15 Now at the time that the Dwelling was set up,
  the cloud covered the Dwelling over the Tent of Testimony,
  and after sunset it remained over the Dwelling,
  as the appearance of fire, until daybreak.
16 Thus it was regularly:
  the cloud would cover it,
  an appearance of fire at night.
17 According as the cloud was lifted up from the tent,
  after that the Children of Israel would march on,
  and in the place that the cloud would take-up-dwelling,
  there the Children of Israel would encamp.

---

12 **a bone is not to be broken:** So as not to mar its perfection; cf. Ex. 12:26.

14 **sojourner:** A foreigner temporarily resident in Israel.

Setting Out (10): Once trumpets for signaling the march have been made, the Israelites at last begin their trek from Sinai to Canaan—nineteen days after the opening events and commandments of the book. True to the orderly character of Part I, which here draws to a close, the exact progression of the march is laid out, tribe by tribe and Levite subgroup by subgroup.

A few other brief traditions have been included here: first, a renewed mention of Moshe's father-in-law (cf. Ex. 18), who is exhorted to accompany the Israelites to Canaan. This text most likely continues the tradition recorded in the Bible of friendship between Israelites and Kenites, Hovav's group.

The departure sequence ends, as sections in the Bible sometimes do, with a poem—in this case, the battle cry (similar to the one in Ps. 68:2) associated with the coffer (vv.35–36). These verses, now completely stripped of their military connotations, are universally used by Jews when Torah scrolls are taken out and put back in the synagogue ark on Sabbaths and holidays.

◆ 18 By order of Y<small>HWH</small>, the Children of Israel would march,
and by order of Y<small>HWH</small>, they would encamp;
all the days that the cloud dwelt above the Dwelling, they would
  remain-in-camp.
19 Now when the cloud lingered over the Dwelling for many days,
the Children of Israel would keep the charge of Y<small>HWH</small>,
and would not march on.
20 At such (times) as the cloud remained for a number of days over
  the Dwelling,
by order of Y<small>HWH</small> they would remain-in-camp,
and by order of Y<small>HWH</small> they would march on.
21 At such (times) as the cloud remained from sunset until daybreak,
when the cloud lifted at daybreak, they would march on.
Whether by day or by night,
when the cloud lifted, they would march on.
22 Whether two days or a New-Moon or a year-of-days,
when the cloud lingered over the Dwelling, dwelling over it,
the Children of Israel would remain-in-camp, and would not
  march on;
at its lifting-up, they would march on.
23 By order of Y<small>HWH</small> they would encamp,
and by order of Y<small>HWH</small> they would march;
the charge of Y<small>HWH</small>, they would keep,
by order of Y<small>HWH</small>, through the hand of Moshe.

10:1 Y<small>HWH</small> spoke to Moshe, saying:
2 Make yourself two trumpets of silver,
of hammered-work you are to make them;
they are to be for you for calling-together the community
and for (signaling) the marching of the camps.
3 When you sound-a-blast on them,
there shall come-together before you the entire community,
at the entrance of the Tent of Appointment.

---

19 **keep the charge:** Milgrom, "guard the guard duty."

4 Now if (but) one blast-is-blown,
   there shall come-together before you the leaders, the heads of the
      divisions of Israel;
5 but if you give a trilling blast,
   then shall march forward the camps encamped on the east.
6 If you should give a second trilling blast,
   then shall march forward the camps encamped on the south.
   Trilling blasts are to be given for their marching forward,
7 but to assemble the assembly, you are to (blow) short-blasts, you
      are not to (blow) trilling-sounds.
8 So the Sons of Aharon, the priests, are (the ones) to sound-blasts
      on the trumpets;
   they shall be for you as a law for the ages, throughout your
      generations.
9 And when you enter into war in your land against an attacker
      who attacks you,
   blow-a-trilling-blast on the trumpets,
   so that you may be brought-to-mind before YHWH your God
   and delivered from your enemies.
10 And on the day(s) of your rejoicing, your appointed-times, and
      the heads of your New-Moons,
   you are to blow-a-blast on the trumpets
   together with your offerings-up and together with your slaughter-
      offerings of *shalom;*
   they shall be of you a reminder, before your God—
   I am YHWH your God!

11 Now it was, in the second year, in the second New-Moon, on the
      twentieth after the New-Moon,
   that the cloud went up from above the Dwelling of Testimony,
12 and the Children of Israel marched-forth on their marches, from
      the Wilderness of Sinai.
   The cloud came-to-dwell in the Wilderness of Paran.

10:8 **a law:** That is, the Levites will function as an institution in their capacity as trumpet-blowers.

◆ 13 They marched first, by order of YHWH, through the hand of
Moshe:

14 the contingent of the camp of Yehuda marched-forward first, by
their forces; over its forces (was) Nahshon son of Amminadav.

15 And over the forces of the tribe of the Sons of Yissakhar (was)
Netan'el son of Tzu'ar.

16 And over the forces of the tribe of the Sons of Zevulun (was)
Eliav son of Heilon.

17 Once the Dwelling was taken down,
there marched the Sons of Gershon and the Sons of Merari,
carriers of the Dwelling.

18 There marched the contingent of the camp of Re'uven, by their
forces;
over its forces (was) Elitzur son of Shedei'ur.

19 And over the forces of the tribe of the Sons of Shim'on (was)
Shelumiel son of Tzurishaddai.

20 And over the forces of the tribe of the Sons of Gad (was) Elyasaf
son of De'uel.

21 There marched the Kehatites, carriers of the holy-things;
they set up the Dwelling by (the time) they came.

22 There marched the contingent of the camp of the Sons of
Efrayim, by their forces;
over its forces (was) Elishama son of Ammihud.

23 And over the forces of the tribe of the Sons of Menashe (was)
Gamliel son of Pedahtzur.

24 And over the forces of the tribe of the Sons of Binyamin (was)
Avidan son of Gid'oni.

25 There marched the contingent of the camp of the Sons of Dan,
rear-guard of all the camps, by their forces;
over their forces (was) Ahi'ezer son of Ammishaddai.

26 And over the forces of the tribe of the Sons of Asher (was) Pag'iel
son of Okhran.

14 **first:** This and other number designations in this
passage refer to position, not time.

27 And over the forces of the tribe of the Sons of Naftali (was)
Ahira' son of Einan.

28 These (were) the marching-groups of the Children of Israel by
their deployed-forces;
thus did they march.

29 Now Moshe said to Hovav son of Re'uel the Midyanite, Moshe's
father-in-law:
We are marching to the place about which YHWH promised:
that-one I will give to you;
go with us and we will do-good for you,
for YHWH has promised good-things for Israel.

30 He said to him:
I will not go,
but rather to my land and to my kindred I will go.

31 He said:
Pray do not leave us,
for after all, you know our (best place to) encamp in the
wilderness,
you shall be for us as eyes!

32 So it will be, if you go with us,
so it will be:
(from) that goodness with which YHWH will do-good for us, we
will do-good for you!

33 They marched from the mountain of YHWH a journey of three
days,
the coffer of YHWH's covenant marching before them,
a journey of three days,
to scout out for them a resting-place.

---

29 **Hovav:** There is some confusion about the name. One tradition holds that he is identical to Yitro in Ex. 2:18f.; yet there, Re'uel is Moshe's father-in-law, while here he is a generation removed.

31 **you shall be for us as eyes:** More idiomatically, "you shall serve as our eyes."

34 Now the cloud of YHWH is over them by day,
   as they march from the camp.

35 Now it was, whenever the coffer was to march on, Moshe would
       say:

   Arise (to attack), O YHWH,
   that your enemies may scatter,
   that those who hate you may flee before you!

36 And when it would rest, he would say:

   Return, O YHWH,
   (you of) the myriad divisions of Israel!

34 **the cloud of YHWH is over them by day:** The phraseology is almost identical to the ending of the book of Exodus (40:38)—so everything in between, all of Leviticus and Num. 1–10, is in a sense bracketed.

35–36 In Hebrew manuscripts and published Torahs, these verses are enclosed by two inverted Hebrew letters, perhaps indicating some kind of early tradition about this poem as a separate unit that may belong somewhere else.

36 **divisions:** Or alternatively, "thousands."

THE REBELLION NARRATIVES

(11–25)

VIRTUALLY THE FIRST THING THE ISRAELITES DO AFTER SETTING OUT ON THE SECOND leg of their journey to the Promised Land is—rebel. This pattern was already seen in the book of Exodus, where, despite the climactic miracle of deliverance at the Sea of Reeds, the Israelites "grumbled against Moshe" at Mara because of lack of drinkable water. Although a strain in later biblical thinking remembered the wilderness period as a kind of honeymoon (cf. Jer. 2:2), the Torah itself chose to remember it as a severe time of testing which the ex-slaves ultimately failed to pass.

The second part of Numbers is a remarkable collection of rebellion narratives that simultaneously display striking similarities and great and colorful differences. The section details six rebellions of the people, and two of the leaders themselves. They are united by a consistent vocabulary: verbs such as "grumble" and "assemble/gather/speak against" depict complaints against Moshe and Aharon and against God. These stories also display the recurring themes of dearth of food and water, and God's anger at the rebellions, usually expressed in some form of plague (or, additionally, fire).

Rather than unfold in simple chronological order, one following another, these pieces of the text have been intensified by priestly editing, which has interspersed the stories with a number of cultic and legal passages (Chaps. 15, 18, and 19, all of which bear the theme word "law" [Heb. *hok* or *hukka*]), and which are somehow related to previous or succeeding narratives. The interruptions also allow each of the memorable rebellion narratives to "breathe," giving the audience time to digest the images and the drama presented therein. The stories possess both in abundant measure; one thinks, for instance, of the "meat between the teeth" (11:33), of the grape clusters borne on a pole by two men (13:23); and of the great confrontation with Korah in Chapter 16 (not to mention its resolution), as well as Moshe's dramatic failure in Chapter 20.

As in any great literature, repetition of story type or type scene is here accomplished via variation of the most telling kind. In this case we observe once again an alternating pattern to the rebellions, a pattern which reveals not one theme but several:

The people, over lack of food (chapter 11)
>   Moshe's siblings, over prophetic primacy (12)
The people, over the spies' false report (14)
>   Levites, over Moshe and Aharon's prerogatives (16)
The people, over the rebellious Levites' sinister fate (17)
>   Moshe himself, over the burden of leading the people (20)
The people, over the lack of food and water (21)

The pattern observable here is broken, in true biblical rhetorical style (where the last in a sequence often serves by its oddness to reinforce the whole), in a final rebellion (Chap. 25), where the people's actions involve neither the "complaining" vocabulary nor a revolt against human leadership, but rather comprise the greatest biblical crime of them all: worship of other gods. Viewed in this patterned fashion, the rebellion narratives emerge with a kind of crescendo effect.

It is also possible, as I have done in "On the Book of Numbers and Its Structure," above, to follow the scheme put forth by Mann—a three-part structure to the section, each with its internal logic and conclusions. These are treated below; for the moment, it will suffice to see in the first subsection (Chaps. 11–14) the inevitable result of wilderness rebellions: the divine decree that the slave generation must die out before entering the Promised Land; the second subsection (16–20) deals with the challenges to the leadership of Moshe and Aharon, and results in a similar decree, that they will die outside the land; and the third subsection (20–25) chronicles the encounter of the Israelites with neighboring nations, which initially goes in their favor but ends with the disastrous incident at Baal Pe'or (25).

The primary issue in these stories, to the biblical writer, is lack of trust in God. Each of the three sections mentions or implies that problem; 14:11 and 20:12 use the verb itself, and the narrative of Chapter 25 suggests it. The bottom line is that the Israelites could not keep faith with God—even after both staggering acts of divine intervention (i.e., rescue) and demonstrations of the force of divine wrath—and this lack of faith led ultimately to their dying out in the wilderness outside the Promised Land, in punishment. The stories clearly were meant to be understood as an unfortunate example for later generations, and were taken as such already in the biblical period (see, for example, the treatment in Psalm 78).

Read on another level, the rebellion narratives are largely concerned with the issue of human leadership, its qualifications, manifestations, and limitations (and even failures). Has there ever been a leader as beleaguered as Moshe? From the beginning of his career on the sands of Egypt, where he assumes the mantle of leadership in the matter of retaliating against the sadistic Egyptian taskmaster (Ex. 2:11–12), to its end at the plains of Moab, in stern address to the people he has struggled to lead (this is the setting of the entire next book, Deuteronomy), he must evoke trust in God, lead the people through an uncharted wilderness, and inspire confidence in his own leadership. His success is muted by the passing of the generation he initially leads, before it can enter Canaan; like them, he too must pass on—with merely a look beyond the Jordan, but no more. Later generations of Jewish readers wept on confronting Moshe's seemingly premature death, and created heroic tales of his pleading before God to be let into the land he had so long sought to reach. In Numbers he fully deserves this stature, alternately interceding with and cajoling God, standing up for and then almost giving up on this people with whom his life has become so enmeshed. Our stories stress his gifts of prophecy and his pathos as a deeply human leader.

A final, troubling issue is the character of God in this part of the book. It is a measure of the Bible's artistry that the rebellion accounts are so varied in content and style; but the variations in punishment—from undetailed death to skin disease to stoning and the earth opening up, just to mention a few examples—create an impression, not of artistic richness but of unremitting severity. The Bible does not seem to have a problem with this kind of divine behavior, and other ancient cultures would have felt at home here, but already in late antiquity, and continuing down to our own day, Jews and Christians most often have preferred, and prayed to, a more forgiving, nurturing, and compassionate God. Dealing with these texts, in the end, raises the question of whether to understand them as the result of "historical necessity" or "literary conceit" (that is, the old generation simply had to die out) or as they stand in the text: a harsh portrayal of what happened when the covenant people violated the covenant.

First Rebellion (11): The mood of the book, which up until now has been orderly and celebratory, abruptly shifts. We move from a God who commands, leaders who lead, and a people that obeys, to a bitter triangle of constant complaining, questioning of leadership, and divine punishment.

The chapter that introduces the rebellion narratives is long and complex. Although it resembles Ex. 16 (the manna chapter) in some general respects, it has its own distinct vocabulary and concerns. It is stylistically held together by the repeating roots "eat," "gather," and "weep"; the "grumbling" of the Exodus story does not yet appear. The chapter combines the people's complaints about the manna (and a concomitant craving for meat) with Moshe's complaints about how difficult it is to lead this people; both receive answer from God, the people in the form of quails and Moshe through the dissemination of prophetic gifts to others in the camp.

It is in this chapter that Moshe—the dramatic and at times tragic Moshe of the Golden Calf story in Exodus—reappears as a character with deep emotions. Although his fate as a leader destined never to enter the Promised Land is not sealed until Chap. 20, one has the sense already here that the strain of his mission is beginning to tell. The vividness of the portrayal of Moshe is matched by that of the Children of Israel, whose words, usually complaints, include the picturesque description of Egyptian cuisine in v.5.

11:1 Now the people were like those-who-grieve (over) ill-fortune, in
    the ears of YHWH.
  When YHWH heard, his anger flared up;
  there blazed up against them a fire of YHWH
  and ate up the edge of the camp.

2 The people cried out to Moshe
  and Moshe interceded to YHWH,
  and the fire abated.

3 So they called the name of that place Tav'era / Blaze,
  for (there) had blazed against them fire of YHWH.

4 Now the gathered-riffraff that were among them
  had a craving, hunger-craving,
  and moreover they again wept, the Children of Israel, and said:
  Who will give us meat to eat?

5 We recall the fish that we used to eat in Egypt for free,
  the cucumbers, the watermelons,
  the green-leeks, the onions, and the garlic!

6 But now, our throats are dry;
  there is nothing at all
  except for the *mahn* (in front of) our eyes!

7 —Now the *mahn* is like seed of coriander,
  its aspect like the aspect of bdellium.

8 The people would roam around and collect it,
  grind it in millstones or crush it in a crusher,
  boil it in a pot, and make it into cakes,
  so that its taste was like the taste of (something) rich (made with)
    oil.

9 And when the dew came down on the camp at night,
  the *mahn* would come down on top of it.—

11:4 **gathered-riffraff:** Heb. *asafsuf,* from the verb that means "to gather." Perhaps parallel to the ragtag "mixed multitude" (*erev rav*) of Ex. 12:38. So the rebellion over food starts among the fringes of the community.

6 *mahn:* The "manna," a substance found on plants

that God had provided for their sustenance since Ex. 16.

7 **aspect:** Or "color." **bdellium:** A certain semiclear resin or sap.

8 **crusher:** A mortar.

10 Moshe heard the people weeping by their clans,
each-man at the entrance to his tent.
Now YHWH's anger flared up exceedingly,
and in the eyes of Moshe it was ill.

11 Moshe said to YHWH:
For-what have you dealt-ill with your servant,
for-what-reason have I not found favor in your eyes,
(that you) have placed the burden of this entire people on me?

12 Did I myself conceive this entire people,
or did I myself give-birth to it,
that you should say to me,
Carry it in your bosom
like a nursing-parent carries a suckling-child,
to the soil about which you swore to their fathers?

13 Where should I (get) meat to give to this entire people,
when they weep on me, saying:
Give us meat so that we may eat!

14 I am not able, myself alone, to carry this entire people,
for it is too heavy for me!

15 If thus you deal with me,
pray kill me, yes, kill me,
if I have found favor in your eyes,
so that I do not have to see my ill-fortune!

16 Then YHWH spoke to Moshe:
Gather to me seventy men of the elders of Israel,
of whom you know that they are elders of the people and its
officers,
and take them to the Tent of Appointment,
stationing them there with you.

17 I will come down and speak with you there,
I will extend from the rushing-spirit that is upon you
and place it upon them;

10 **by their clans:** Contrasting with the sacred order of lists and censuses early in the book, this time it is the rebellious weeping of the people that is somehow orderly!

16 **seventy:** An inclusive number, indicating completeness or perfection. **stationing:** A verb often used before an appearance of God (Milgrom).

then they will carry along with you the burden of the people,
so that you will not (have to) carry it, you alone.

18 Now to the people you are to say:
Hallow yourselves for the morrow
that you may eat meat,
for you have wept in the ears of Yhwh, saying:
Who will give us meat to eat?
For it was better for us in Egypt!
Yhwh will give you meat, and you shall eat it:

19 not for (only) one day shall you eat it, and not for two days,
not for five days or for ten days or (even) for twenty days—

20 (but) for a monthful of days,
until it comes out of your nostrils
and becomes for you something-disgusting,
because you have spurned Yhwh who is among you,
by weeping before him, saying:
For-what-reason did we leave Egypt?

21 Moshe said:
Six hundred thousand on foot
(are) the (fighting-)people among whom I am,
yet you, you say:
Meat I will give them,
and they are to eat (it) for a monthful of days?!

22 Are there flocks and herds that may be slain for them,
that they would find-them-sufficient?
Or are there all the fish of the sea to be caught for them,
that they would find-them-sufficient?

23 Yhwh said to Moshe:
Is the arm of Yhwh (too) short?
Now you shall see whether my word happens to you or not.

---

18 **Hallow yourselves:** Ritually, as before Mount Sinai (Ex. 19:11, 14–15).

20 **something-disgusting:** Or "something-nauseating."

22 **Find-them-sufficient:** Lit. "overtake," "reach" them.

23 **Is the arm of Yhwh (too) short:** After all, this is the God of the "outstretched arm" (Ex. 6:6)!

Sibling Rebellion (12): A challenge to Moshe's leadership, which we had encountered both in Exodus and in the previous chapter, now comes from an unexpected source—Aharon and Miryam. Their complaint begins with some kind of objection to Moshe's wife, but its core is quickly revealed in v.2: Does not God speak through them as well as through their stuttering brother? Milgrom speculates that it is the spreading of prophetic gifts in the previous chapter that gives them the idea. God's response is to clarify Moshe's uniqueness, and to punish Miryam—yet Aharon gets off easily here, possibly owing to a later editor who was highly sympathetic to the priesthood descended from Aharon, or because the latter, as High Priest, could not be tainted by *tzaraat* without damaging his priesthood, as Lev. 22:4ff. suggests (Sakenfeld).

Chap. 12 is linked to the previous chapter by use of the words "eat" and "gather." As its own unit, it is built on the ironic use of Heb. *dabber be-*, which can mean either "speak through" or "speak against."

24 Moshe went out and spoke to the people the words of YHWH.
   He gathered seventy men from the elders of the people,
   and had-them-stand around the tent.

25 And YHWH came down in a cloud
   and spoke to him,
   and YHWH extended some of the rushing-spirit that was upon him
   and put it upon the seventy men, the elders;
   and it was,
   when the spirit rested upon them,
   that they acted-like-prophets, but did not continue.

26 Now two men remained in the camp,
   the name of the one was Eldad,
   the name of the second, Meidad,
   and the spirit rested upon them
   —they were among those-recorded,
   but they had not gone out to the Tent—
   and they acted-like-prophets in the camp.

27 A (certain) lad ran
   and told Moshe, he said:
   Eldad and Meidad are acting-like-prophets in the camp!

28 Then Yehoshua son of Nun, Moshe's attendant from his youth,
      spoke up,
   he said:
   My lord Moshe, contain them!

29 But Moshe said to him:
   Are you jealous for me?
   O who would give that all the people of YHWH were prophets,
   that YHWH would put the rush-of-his spirit upon them!

---

25 **acted-like-prophets:** The *hitpa'el* form of Heb. *n-b-'*, as opposed to the *pi'el* form, meaning "to prophesy" (speak in God's name) (Greenberg 1983). "Mantic" or "ecstatic" prophecy was known all over the ancient world. The prophet would go into a trance, or roll about, or shriek (or a combination of these); such behavior was considered inspired by the gods. While the famous prophets of the Bible, such as Isaiah and Jeremiah, are largely (but not exclusively) men of the word, who report God's mes-

sages to the people, they retain in their actions some of the characteristics of the enthusiastic kind of prophecy. **but did not continue:** But the Hebrew consonants could also be read "and did not stop!"

26 **Eldad ... Meidad:** The names are obviously intended to rhyme; they may both indicate something like "beloved of God."

28 **Yehoshua:** Trad. English "Joshua."

29 **who would give:** "Would that" or "if only."

30 Moshe took himself back to the camp,
    he and the elders of Israel;

31 and a rush-of-wind moved from YHWH
    and swept in quails from the sea,
    they spread out over the camp
    as far as a day's journey here and a day's journey there,
    all around the camp,
    and about two cubits upon the face of the ground.

32 The people arose all that day and all night, and all the morrow
        day,
    gathering the quail,
    the least gathered ten *homers.*
    They spread them, spread them out, all around the camp.

33 The meat was still between their teeth
    —(the supply) not yet exhausted,
    when the anger of YHWH flared up among the people,
    and YHWH struck down among the people an exceedingly great
        striking.

34 So they called the name of that place Kivrot Ha-Taava/Burial-
        Places of the Craving,
    for there they buried the people who had-the-craving.

35 From Kivrot Ha-Taava the people marched to Hatzeirot,
    and they remained in Hatzeirot.

12:1 Now Miryam spoke, and Aharon, against Moshe
    on account of the Cushite wife that he had taken-in-marriage,
    for a Cushite wife had he taken.

2 They said:
    Is it only, solely through Moshe that YHWH speaks?
    Is it not also through us that he speaks?
    And YHWH heard.

---

31 **rush-of-wind:** Heb. *ruah* can mean both "spirit" and "wind," as is clear from this chapter. Buber wrote extensively on this concept (1994). **two cubits:** Roughly a yard (or a meter).

32 **spread them out:** In order to dry them. One ancient version has Heb. *sh-h-t,* "slew" (them) for *sh-t-h,* which appears in standard texts. ***homers:*** A *homer* was a large measure of volume, equal to about thirty gallons in one estimate.

12:1 **Cushite:** Either an Ethiopian, which some interpretive traditions hold to, and which would be clearly a racial slur, or a Midyanite. The first would indicate another wife of Moshe; the second, the Tzippora of Ex. 2.

3 Now the man Moshe is exceedingly humble,
  more than any (other) human who is on the face of the earth.
4 And YHWH said suddenly to Moshe, to Aharon and to Miryam:
  Go out, the three of you, to the Tent of Appointment!
  The three of them went out.
5 And YHWH descended in a column of cloud
  and stood at the entrance to the Tent;
  he called out: Aharon and Miryam!
  and the two of them went out.
6 He said:
  Pray hear my words:
  If there should be among-you-a-prophet of YHWH,
  in a vision to him I make-myself-known,
  in a dream I speak with him.
7 Not so my servant Moshe:
  in all my house, trusted is he;
8 mouth to mouth I speak with him,
  in-plain-sight, not in riddles,
  and the form of YHWH (is what) he beholds.
  So why were you not too awestruck
  to speak against my servant, against Moshe?
9 The anger of YHWH flared up against them,
  and he went off.
10 When the cloud turned away from above the Tent,
   here: Miryam has *tzaraat* like snow!
   When Aharon faced Miryam,
   here: she has *tzaraat*!
11 Aharon said to Moshe:
   Please, my lord,
   do not, pray, impose on us guilt-for-a-sin
   by which we were foolish, by which we sinned!

---

3 **humble:** And not power-hungry. This description helps to prepare us for the confrontation with Korah in Chap. 16, where the rebels accuse Moshe of lording it over them. **earth:** Elsewhere rendered "soil."

6 **among-you-a-prophet:** The Hebrew is awkward, but solvable as an unusual syntactic form (Freedman 1972).

The Spies in Canaan and Back (13): Here, as at the beginning of the book, we begin with a list—this time, of the men Moshe sends out to reconnoiter the land of Canaan. Order may also be perceived in the phraseology of Moshe's questions to them (vv.18–20), and the mission goes well (witness the giant grape cluster in v.23). But everything falls apart in the middle of the report (vv.28ff.), and the ending of the chapter, in which the spies compare themselves (and, by extension, all the Israelites) to grasshoppers vis-à-vis the Canaanite natives of the land, is telling. It is a classic case of failure of nerve.

Scholars have detected a number of creative hands in this and the next chapter, based on the text's alternating use of Calev and Calev/Yehoshua as the faithful spies, as well as other factors. The final result is a tug of war between sets of spies, the people, Moshe, and God. True to the new human tone of the narrative, so mundane a form as a reconnaissance mission has been here suffused with emotion, a trend that will continue throughout this part of the book.

12 Do not, pray, let her be like a dead-child
who, when it comes out of its mother's womb,
is eaten up in half its flesh!

13 Moshe cried out to YHWH, saying:
O God, pray, heal her, pray!

14 YHWH said to Moshe:
If her father spat, yes, spat in her face,
would she not be put-to-shame for seven days (at least)?
Let her be shut up for seven days outside the camp,
afterward she may be gathered-back.

15 So Miryam was shut up outside the camp for seven days,
and the people did not march on until Miryam had been
gathered-back.

16 (Only) afterward did the people march on from Hatzeirot,
they encamped in the Wilderness of Paran.

13:1 YHWH spoke to Moshe, saying:

2 Send for yourself men,
that they may scout out the land of Canaan
that I am giving to the Children of Israel.
One man, one man per tribe of their fathers, you are to send,
each-one a leader among them.

3 So Moshe sent them from the Wilderness of Paran, by order of
YHWH,
all of them men(-of-standing)—
heads of the Children of Israel were they.

4 And these (were) their names:
for the tribe of Re'uven: Shammu'a son of Zakkur;

5 for the tribe of Shim'on: Shafat son of Hori;

6 for the tribe of Yehuda: Calev son of Yefunne;

7 for the tribe of Yissakhar: Yig'al son of Yosef;

8 for the tribe of Efrayim: Hoshe'a son of Nun;

---

13 **O God, pray, heal her, pray!:** Heb. *el na refa na la;* I could not find a way to reflect the sound of the Hebrew.

14 **If her father spat:** She cannot in any event be readmitted to the camp before seven days have passed.

be gathered-back: Be allowed back into the holy camp. "Be readmitted" would have been more palatable, but I have retained "gathered" as a theme word prominent in the chapter.

9 for the tribe of Binyamin: Palti son of Rafu;

10 for the tribe of Zevulun: Gaddiel son of Sodi;

11 for the tribe of Yosef, for the tribe of Menashe: Gaddi son of Susi;

12 for the tribe of Dan: Ammiel son of Gemalli;

13 for the tribe of Asher: Setur son of Mikhael;

14 for the tribe of Naftali: Nahbi son of Vofsi;

15 for the tribe of Gad: Ge'uel son of Makhi.

16 These the names of the men
whom Moshe sent to scout out the land
—now Moshe called Hoshe'a son of Nun: Yehoshua.

17 Now when Moshe sent them to scout out the land of Canaan,
he said to them:
Go up this (way) through the Negev/Parched-Land,
and (then) you are to go up into the hill-country.

18 And see the land—what it is (like),
and the population that is settled in it:
are they strong or weak,
are they few or many;

19 and what the land is (like), where they are settled:
is it good or ill;
and what the towns are (like), where they are settled therein:
are (they) encampments or fortified-places;

20 and what the land is (like):
is it fat or lean,
are there in it trees, or not?
Now exert yourselves,
and take (some) of the fruit of the land
—now these days (are) the days of the first ripe-grapes.

21 So they went up and scouted out the land,
from the Wilderness of Tzyn as far as Rehov, coming toward
Hamat.

13:18 **see:** Or "survey."

20 **trees, or not:** This phrase breaks the string of opposites in Moshe's instructions, thus rhetorically
ending it. **the days of the first ripe-grapes:** The
reason for this intrusion is explained in v.23.

22 They went up through the Negev
and came as far as Hevron:
there are Ahiman, Sheshai, and Talmai,
the descendants of the Anakites.
Now Hevron had been built seven years before Tzo'an of Egypt.

23 They came to the Wadi of Eshkol/Clusters
and cut down from there a branch and one cluster of grapes
—they had-to-carry it on a bar (held) by two—
and some pomegranates and some figs.

24 That place they called the Wadi of Clusters,
on account of the cluster that the Children of Israel had cut
down there.

25 Now they returned from scouting out the land
at the end of forty days.

26 They went and came before Moshe, before Aharon, and before
the entire community of the Children of Israel
in the Wilderness of Paran, at Kadesh;
they returned word to them and to the entire community,
and let them see the fruit of the land.

27 Now they recounted to him, they said:
We came to the land that you sent us to,
and yes, it is flowing with milk and honey,
and this is its fruit—

28 except that fierce are the people that are settled in the land,
the cities are fortified, exceedingly large,
and also the descendants of Anak did we see there!

29 Amalek is settled in the Negev land,
and the Hittite and the Yevusite and the Amorite are settled in the
hill-country,
the Canaanite is settled by the Sea, and hard by the Jordan!

---

22 **Anakites:** Primeval giants, from whom the tall-seeming Canaanites were reputed to be descended. **Hevron:** Trad. English "Hebron." **Tzo'an:** Tanis, the capital of Egypt at the time of the Israelite monarchy (tenth century B.C.E. and later).

23 **on a bar (held) by two:** A striking image for the richness of the land, this symbol is today the logo of the Israeli Ministry of Tourism.

24 **Wadi:** A riverbed that is usually dry in summer; a gorge.

Rebellion and Evil Decree (14): Another long and dramatic account, this chapter contains echoes of previous narratives. The "grumbling" of Ex. 16 finally returns, and God and Moshe talk to one another in a manner that recalls the Golden Calf incident of Ex. 32–34. God wishes to destroy the people and start all over again with Moshe; the prophet, for his part, reminds God of his essentially merciful nature, and basically blackmails him by pointing out what will happen to his reputation among the nations should he destroy the Israelites. Unlike the resolution in Exodus, this time the people—at least the older generation—are doomed to die out. After two years of both miraculous rescues and despair, it has become clear that the former slaves will not be able to accomplish the work of conquest—even with divine help. That is to be left to their children, whom Moshe will address in Deuteronomy.

V.26 begins a section that seems to double the earlier part of the chapter. Perhaps it stems from a separate tradition concerning the incident. It leads to the people's disastrous attempt to force the issue by invading Canaan without the Coffer and Moshe (hence, without God). Thus the spy story of 13–14, which began in orderly fashion, ends in disarray, with a crushing defeat.

30 Now Calev hushed the people before Moshe
and said:
Let us go up, yes, up, and possess it,
for we can prevail, yes, prevail against it!

31 But the men who went up with him said:
We are not able to go up against the population,
for it is stronger than we!

32 So they gave-out a (false) report of the land
that they had scouted out
to the Children of Israel, saying:
The land that we crossed through to scout it out:
it is a land that devours its inhabitants;
all the people that we saw in its midst are men of (great) stature,

33 (for) there we saw the giants—the Children of Anak (come) from
the giants—
we were in our (own) eyes like grasshoppers,
and thus were we in their eyes!

14:1 The entire community lifted up and let out their voice,
and the people wept on that night.

2 And they grumbled against Moshe and against Aharon, all the
Children of Israel,
they said to them, the entire community:
Would that we had died in the land of Egypt,
or in this wilderness, would that we had died!

3 Now why is YHWH bringing us to this land, to fall by the sword?
Our wives and our little-ones will become plunder!
Would it not be better for us to return to Egypt?

4 So they said, each-man to his brother:
Let us head back and return to Egypt!

5 Moshe and Aharon flung themselves on their faces
before the entire assembled community of the Children of Israel.

14:3 **little-ones:** From a Hebrew root that means "to
take little steps"; a direct English equivalent might
be "toddlers."

4 **Let us head back:** So Ehrlich, JPS. Others, "Let us
choose a head" (i.e., a new leader).

5 **the entire assembled community** etc.: A unique
phrase, perhaps indicating an emergency session of
the whole people (Magonet).

◆

6   Now Yehoshua son of Nun and Calev son of Yefunne,
      (alone) from among those who scouted out the land,
      ripped their garments;

7   they said to the entire community of the Children of Israel,
        saying:
      The land that we crossed through, to scout it out—
      good is that land, exceedingly, exceedingly!

8   If YHWH is pleased with us,
      he will bring us to this land and give it to us,
      a land that is flowing with milk and honey.

9   But: against YHWH, do not rebel,
      and you—
      do not be afraid of the people of the land,
      for food-for-us are they!
      Their protector has turned away from them,
      and YHWH is with us—
      do not be afraid of them!

10   But the entire community of Israel thought to pelt them with
        stones.
      Now the Glory of YHWH was seen at the Tent of Appointment
      by all the Children of Israel,

11   and YHWH said to Moshe:
      How long will this people scorn me?
      How long will they not trust in me,
      despite all the signs that I have done among them?

12   Let me strike it down with pestilence and dispossess it,
      and I will make of you a nation greater and mightier (in number)
        than it!

13   But Moshe said to YHWH:
      When they hear (about it), the Egyptians,
      that you brought up this people with your power from its midst,

14   they will tell it to the inhabitants of this land.
      They have heard that you are YHWH in the midst of this people,

---

7–8 Note the fourfold use of "land."

9 **protector:** Lit. "shade" or "shadow"; the reference is probably to pagan gods.

13 **hear (about it):** That is, about the destruction of Israel by God.

14 **eye to eye:** The equivalent of English "face to face."

that eye to eye you were seen, O Yhwh,
your cloud standing over them,
in a column of cloud going before them by day,
and in a column of fire by night—

15 should you put this people to death as one man,
then will say the nations that have heard of your fame, saying:

16 (It was) from want of Yhwh's ability
to bring this people into the land about which he swore to them,
and so he slew them in the wilderness!

17 So now,
pray let the power of my Lord (to forbear) be great,
as you have spoken, saying:

18 Yhwh,
long-suffering and of much loyalty,
bearing iniquity and transgression,
yet clearing, not clearing (the guilty),
calling-to-account the iniquity of the fathers upon the sons
to the third and to the fourth (generation)—

19 pray grant-pardon for the iniquity of this people, as your loyalty
    is great,
just as you have been bearing (iniquity) for this people
from Egypt until now!

20 Yhwh said:
I grant-pardon, according to your words;

21 however, as I live,
and as the Glory of Yhwh fills all the earth:

22 indeed, all the men who have seen my Glory and my signs
that I did in Egypt and in the wilderness,
and have tested me these ten times,
by not hearkening to my voice:

17 **as you have spoken:** Moshe cites the characterization of God in the Golden Calf story, which employs almost identical words (Ex. 34:6–7); he also argues in terms similar to the way he did there (Ex. 32:11ff.).

19 **pray grant-pardon** etc.: This verse is used in the Jewish liturgy of the Day of Atonement (Yom Kippur).

22 **ten times:** Equivalent to "many times" in biblical parlance.

23 if they should see the land
about which I swore to their fathers . . . !
All that have scorned me will not see it!

24 But as for my servant, Calev,
because there was another spirit in him, and he followed-me-fully,
so I will bring him into the land that he is about to enter,
and his seed will possess it.

25 Now the Amalekite and the Canaanite are settled in the
Lowlands;
on the morrow, face about and march into the wilderness,
by the Reed Sea Road.

26 Now YHWH spoke to Moshe and Aharon, saying:

27 Till when for this evil community,
that they stir-up-grumbling against me?
The grumblings of the Children of Israel that they grumble
against me,
I have heard!

28 Say to them:
As I live—the utterance of YHWH—
if not as you have spoken in my ears,
thus I do to you . . . !

29 In this wilderness shall your corpses fall,
all those-of-you-counted (for battle), including all your number,
from the age of twenty and upward,
(you) that have grumbled against me!

30 If (any of) you should enter the land over which I lifted my hand
(in an oath)
to have you dwell in it,
except for Calev son of Yefunne and Yehoshua son of Nun . . . !

---

23 **If they should see . . . :** Implied is an ending such as "I will destroy them."

24 **another spirit:** In this case, courage. **followed-me-fully:** As Weinfeld (1991) notes, this is semantically equivalent to Avraham's "being-whole(-hearted)" in Gen. 17:1. Both phrases are used in connection with covenant loyalty.

28 **if not . . . :** A rhetorical form meaning "I will do the following . . . ." Similarly, v.30 suggests that "none of you shall enter the land."

29 **counted (for battle) . . . number:** The census-taking at the opening of the book now turns into a census of death.

31 Your little-ones, whom you said would become plunder—
   I will let them enter,
   they shall come to know the land that you have spurned.
32 But your corpses, yours,
   shall fall in this wilderness,
33 and your children shall graze in the wilderness for forty years;
   thus shall they bear your whoring,
   until your corpses come-to-an-end in the wilderness.
34 According to the number of days that you scouted out the land,
   forty days,
   (for each) day a year, (for each) day a year,
   you are to bear your iniquities,
   forty years,
   thus you will come to know my hostility!
35 I am YHWH, I have spoken:
   If I do not do this to this whole evil community
   that has come-together against me . . . !
   In this wilderness they will come-to-an-end,
   there they will die.
36 So the men whom Moshe had sent to scout out the land
   returned and caused the entire community to grumble against
       him
   by bringing a (false) report about the land;
37 the men died,
   those bringing a report of the land, an ill one,
   in a plague, before the presence of YHWH.
38 But Yehoshua son of Nun and Calev son of Yefunne
   remained-alive from those men
   that had gone to scout out the land.
39 Now when Moshe spoke all these words to the Children of Israel,
   the people mourned, exceedingly.
40 They started-early in the morning
   and went up to the top of the hill-country, saying:
   Here we are,

---

34 **hostility:** Or "constraining/frustrating (you)."

Interlude (15): Chap. 15, which gives respite from the striking rebellion narratives of 11–14, and a breather before the Korah story in 16–17 (although Wenham notes verbal ties to 13–14, and Buber 1988 to 16–18), brings together five rather disparate pieces of material that seem wrenched out of other contexts. We can, however, make some sense of them. Vv.1–16 (on various sacrifices) and 17–21 (about a "contribution" for God) are commanded for the time "when you enter the land of your settling / that I am giving you" or "when you enter the land / that I am bringing you to," connecting them to the potential entry into Canaan of the two previous chapters and thus providing a setting that is missing in most of Leviticus. Further, vv.1–16 and 22–31, which, like Lev. 4, deal with the unintentional sins of the Israelites, both make pointed reference to the "sojourner," the resident alien who is to be treated in respect of the laws involved here exactly like a native. The final section, on the tassels (Heb. *tzitzit*), is interestingly connected to the spy narrative via the term "scout around" in v.39 (Milgrom); "scout" had occurred seven times in the earlier story. "Bear in mind" also recalls the many instances of "reminders" in the Torah—objects such as a portion of manna—that serve as a visual warning or memorial for the Israelites of later generations. This is especially important after the Israelites' losing heart in Chaps. 13–14. Stylistically, the four sections just mentioned are drawn together by the use of the phrase "throughout your generations" (vv.15, 21, 23, 38).

This leaves the incident of the Sabbath violator in vv.32–36. It has clearly been placed in Numbers because it takes place "in the wilderness" (v.32); it has found its way into this specific chapter perhaps because it is, in its own way, a miniature rebellion story. Since it is so brief, it may well have been felt that it needed to be placed in a chapter already composed of short pieces. Stylistically it might have better appeared at the end of the chapter, but that position has been reserved for the rhetorically more dramatic section on the tassels.

let us go up to (attack) the place that YHWH promised,
for we have sinned!

41 But Moshe said:
Why now do you cross the order of YHWH?
It will not succeed!

42 Do not go up, for YHWH is not in your midst—
that you not be smitten by your foes!

43 For the Amalekite and the Canaanite are there to face you,
you will fall by the sword,
for since you have turned from (following) after YHWH,
YHWH will not be-there with you!

44 But they went up recklessly to the top of the hill-country,
while the coffer of the Covenant of YHWH and Moshe did not
move from amid the camp.

45 And the Amalekite and the Canaanite who were settled in that
hill-country came down,
they struck them and crushed them, near Horma.

15:1 YHWH spoke to Moshe, saying:

2 Speak to the Children of Israel
and say to them:
When you enter the land of your settlements that I am giving
you,

3 and sacrifice a fire-offering to YHWH:
an offering-up or a slaughter-offering,
to make a vow-offering, or in free-will, or at your appointed-
times,
to sacrifice a soothing savor for YHWH,
from the herd or from the flock,

4 the one bringing-near his near-offering is to bring-near to YHWH
as grain-gift:

---

44 **went up recklessly:** Others, "stormed."

15:3 **and sacrifice a fire-offering** etc.: In Anderson's assessment, this part of the chapter returns to the
function of Lev. 1–7: a general statement about sacrificial procedure (in this case, the addition of the
grain-gift and the poured-offering). **a soothing**

savor: A description attached to many sacrifices; cf.
Lev. 1:9.

4 **bringing-near:** A verb used sometimes (especially
in Leviticus) with the technical meaning "to offer/
sacrifice."

◆

    flour, a tenth-measure,
    mixed with a fourth of a *hin* of oil,

5   and wine for a poured-offering: a fourth of a *hin;*
    you are to sacrifice it with the offering-up or the slaughter-
        offering,
    for (each) one sheep,

6   or for the ram, you are to make as a grain-gift:
    flour, two tenth-measures,
    mixed with oil, a third of a *hin,*

7   and wine for a poured-offering, a third of a *hin;*
    you are to bring-near a soothing savor for YHWH.

8   And when you sacrifice the young of the herd as an offering-up or
        as a slaughter-offering,
    to make a vow-offering or a *shalom*-offering to YHWH:

9   it is to be brought-near with the young of the herd as a grain-gift:
    flour, three tenth-measures,
    mixed with oil, half a *hin,*

10   and wine you are to bring-near as a poured-offering, half a *hin,*
    a fire-offering of soothing savor for YHWH.

11   Thus is to be sacrificed with (each) one ox or with (each) one ram
    or with (any) lamb among the sheep or among the goats,

12   according to the number that you sacrifice;
    thus are you to sacrifice for (each) one, according to their
        number.

13   Every native is to sacrifice these thus,
    to bring-near a fire-offering of soothing savor for YHWH.

14   Now when there sojourns with you a sojourner,
    or (one) that has been in your midst, throughout your
        generations,
    and he sacrifices a fire-offering of soothing savor for YHWH;
    as you sacrifice (it), thus is he to sacrifice (it).

15   Assembly!
    One law for you and for the sojourner that takes-up-sojourn,
    a law for the ages, throughout your generations:
    as (it is for) you, so will it be (for) the sojourner before the
        presence of YHWH.

16   One instruction, one regulation shall there be for you
    and for the sojourner that takes-up-sojourn with you!

17 YHWH spoke to Moshe, saying:
18 Speak to the Children of Israel
    and say to them:
    When you enter the land that I am bringing you to,
19 it shall be
    that when you eat of the bread of the land,
    you are to set-aside a contribution to YHWH:
20 premier-product of your kneading-troughs,
    round-loaves you are to set-aside as a contribution;
    like the contribution of the threshing-floor,
    so you are to set-it-aside.
21 From the premier-product of your kneading-troughs
    you are to give to YHWH a contribution,
     throughout your generations.

22 Now if you should err,
    not doing any of these commandments
    about which YHWH spoke to Moshe,
23 anything that YHWH has commanded you, through the hand of
        Moshe,
    from the day that YHWH commanded and forward, throughout
        your generations,
24 it shall be:
    if (away) from the eyes of the community it was done, by error,
    the entire community is to sacrifice
    one bull, a young of the herd, as an offering-up, as a soothing
        savor for YHWH;
    with its grain-gift and its poured-offering, according to regulation,
    and one hairy goat, as a *hattat*-offering.
25 The priest is to effect-purgation for the entire community of the
        Children of Israel,
    that there may be granting-of-pardon for them,

22 **err,/not doing:** That is, sin unwittingly. **these commandments:** Some, such as Milgrom, take this to refer to the two previous sections in the chapter; however, the wording, especially in v.23, is quite broad, and may constitute a new "teaching" about observance of the law (although not a law in and of itself) (Toeg, quoted in Fishbane 1988).

The Great Revolt (16): In the two collections of wilderness rebellion traditions we have encountered thus far in the Torah, Ex. 15:22–17:7 and Num. 11–14, the rebels are a faceless "the people" or "the entire community." An exception was Num. 12, where Aharon and Miryam complained against their brother; their personal example is now taken up by another relative, in a memorable narrative. The story of the revolt of Korah the Levite and Datan and Aviram the Reubenites, which may have stemmed from two different accounts, holds the common thread of the rebels' feeling left out—Korah, as Moshe's and Aharon's first cousin, might well have headed the priestly line (his father was older than theirs), whereas Datan and Aviram's tribe of Re'uven had lost some of its firstborn primacy, and was not even camped on the choice east side of the Dwelling. Moshe clearly sees the political motivation behind the revolt, and is indignant that anyone would impute greed (cf. v.15) or lust for power to him.

As Buber (1988) points out, however, more is at stake here. The rebels' contention that "the entire community, the entirety of them, are holy," though it sounds at first blush like the ideal expressed in Ex. 19:6 (God's offer to make of the Israelites "a kingdom of priests, / a holy nation"), is in reality a most dangerous claim. Holiness in the Bible is a trait that can be acquired, even transmitted to an extent, but it is not absolutely innate, except in the case of God; and the Torah sees as one of its major goals developing the means whereby people can, with holy intent and preparation, properly serve the Holy. The fate of the rebels therefore bespeaks the seriousness of the threat they pose, and is unique in the Bible.

The narrative hinges on a number of expressions. The conflict between Moshe and the rebels is nicely encapsulated by two pairs of identical charges and countercharges—"Too much (is) yours" (vv.3 and 7) and "Is it too little" (vv.9 and 13). The terms "community" and "assembly" are played upon, designating alternately the body of the people and the minicommunity of the rebels. More significantly, this chapter and those around it—15, 17, and 18—are meaningfully linked together by variations on the Hebrew root k-r-b (Buber 1994). The thread of meaning runs from "bringing near-offerings near," to God "declaring [Moshe and Ahron] near" to him, to the fact that he has "brought-near" the Levites in terms of their duties, to Korah and his band being asked to "bring-near" the incense, whose fire-pans later become holy because they were "brought-near," and finally, to the repeated warning to outsiders not to "come-near" the sancta. At issue is what Buber calls "authorized" and "unauthorized nearing," which is mentioned frequently in Leviticus but is used in the present text with the full artistic resources at the narrator's command. Viewed in this light, order is restored to the blurring of lines threatened by Korah.

for it was an error,
but they have brought their near-offering,
a fire-offering of soothing savor for YHWH,
and their *hattat*-offering before the presence of YHWH, on account
of their error.

26 So there shall be granting-of-pardon for the entire community of
the Children of Israel,
and for the sojourner that sojourns in their midst,
for (it was done) by the entire people in error.

27 Now if one person sins, in error,
he is to bring-near a she-goat, in its (first) year, as a *hattat*-
offering.

28 The priest is to effect-purgation for the person that errs,
in sinning, in erring, before the presence of YHWH,
to effect-purgation for him, that he may be granted-pardon.

29 The native among the Children of Israel,
and for the sojourner that sojourns in your midst:
one instruction shall there be for you,
for him that does (anything) in error.

30 But the person that does (anything) with a high hand
among the native-born or among the sojourners,
it is YHWH that he blasphemes;
cut off shall that person be from among his kinspeople,

31 for the word of YHWH he has despised, and his commandment he
has violated;
cut off, cut off shall that person be—
his iniquity is on him!

32 Now when the Children of Israel were in the wilderness,
they found a man picking wood on the Sabbath day.

33 They brought him near, those who found him picking wood,
to Moshe and to Aharon, and to the entire community;

---

26 **So there shall be** etc.: Another verse that has found
its way into the Yom Kippur prayers.
30 **with a high hand:** Defiantly.

31 **his iniquity is on him:** That is, he must carry it
around until it is "lifted off" him.

34 they put him under guard,
for it had not been clarified what should be done to him.

35 Yʜwʜ said to Moshe:
The man is to be put-to-death, yes, death,
pelt him with stones, the entire community, outside the camp!

36 So they brought him, the entire community, outside the camp;
they pelted him with stones, so that he died,
as Yʜwʜ had commanded Moshe.

37 Yʜwʜ said to Moshe, saying:

38 Speak to the Children of Israel and say to them
that they are to make themselves tassels
on the corners of their garments, throughout their generations,
and are to put on the corner tassel a thread of blue-violet.

39 It shall be for you a tassel,
that you may look at it
and keep-in-mind all the commandments of Yʜwʜ
and observe them,
that you not go scouting-around after your heart, after your eyes
which you go whoring after;

40 in order that you may keep-in-mind
and observe all my commandments,
and (so) be holy to your God!

41 I am Yʜwʜ your God,
who took you out of the land of Egypt, to be to you a God;
I am Yʜwʜ your God!

16:1 Now there betook-himself Korah son of Yitzhar son of Kehat son
of Levi,
and Datan and Aviram the sons of Eliav and On son of Pelet, the
sons of Re'uven

2 to rise up before Moshe
with men-of-stature from the Children of Israel, fifty and two
hundred,

---

34 **... clarified:** Or "there was no ruling [on how to deal with him]" (Fishbane 1988).

16:1 **there betook-himself:** This is a difficult text, since "take" in Hebrew (*lakoah*) usually requires a direct

object. Commentators have proposed that Korah "took" the men mentioned, but the phrase is still not clear. **Pelet:** The Septuagint reads "Pallu," in line with the genealogy presented in 26:5.

leaders of the community, those Called in the Appointed-
  Council, men of name.
3 They assembled against Moshe and against Aharon
  and said to them:
  Too much (is) yours!
  Indeed, the entire community, the entirety-of-them, are holy,
  and in their midst is YHWH!
  Why then do you exalt yourselves over the assembly of YHWH?
4 Now when Moshe heard, he flung himself on his face.
5 Then he spoke to Korah and to his entire community, saying:
  At daybreak
  YHWH will make-known who is his and who is holy
  and he will declare-him-near to him;
  the one that he chooses, he will declare-near to him.
6 This, do:
  Take yourselves (fire-)pans,
  Korah and his entire community,
7 and put fire in them,
  placing incense on them, before the presence of YHWH,
    tomorrow.
  And it shall be:
  the man whom YHWH chooses, he is the holy-one.
  Too much (is) yours, Sons of Levi!
8 And Moshe said to Korah:
  Pray hearken, Sons of Levi:
9 Is it too little for you
  that the God of Israel has separated you from the community of
    Israel
  to bring you near to him,
  to serve the serving-tasks of the Dwelling of YHWH,
  to stand before the community, to attend on them?

---

3 **They assembled . . . and said:** Strangely, Korah
himself is never portrayed in the text as uttering a
single word on his own—an interesting model for a
rebel. **the entirety-of-them:** All of them. **exalt
yourselves:** Or "act-as-leaders."

6 **(fire-)pans:** For offering incense—a priestly task.
7 **whom YHWH chooses:** By accepting his offering.

10 He has brought-near you and all your brothers, the Sons of Levi,
with you—
would you seek the priesthood as well?

11 Truly,
(it is) you and your entire community
that come-together against Yhwh—
as for Aharon, what is (wrong) with him that you should grumble
against him!

12 Moshe sent to call Datan and Aviram, the sons of Eliav,
but they said: We will not go up!

13 Is it too little
that you have brought us up from a land flowing with milk and
honey
to cause-our-death in the wilderness?
that you should play-the-prince over us, even the prince?

14 Then too, not to a land flowing with milk and honey have you
brought us,
(nor) have you given us an inheritance of field and vineyard.
The eyes of these men, would you gouge out?
We will not go up!

15 Then Moshe became exceedingly upset,
he said to Yhwh:
Do not turn your face toward their grain-gift—
not (even) one donkey of theirs have I carried off,
I have not done ill to (even) one of them!

16 Moshe said to Korah:
You and your entire community,
be (there) before the presence of Yhwh,
you and they and Aharon, tomorrow.

12 **We will not go up:** An ironic twist on what the entire people would not do in Chap. 13: "go up" to conquer the Promised Land.

13 **play-the-prince:** Here, near the end of Moshe's life,
an old canard returns. He had been accused at the
outset of his career (in his first attempt to save the Israelites in Ex. 2:14) of "playing-the-prince" by intervening in a quarrel.

14 **not to a land** etc.: Now the rebels blame Moshe for
the people's failure in the incident of the spies. **The
eyes . . . gouge out:** Commentators point out that
this phrase is the equivalent, albeit a grisly one, of
"pulling the wool over their eyes" or the like.

15 **turn your face toward:** Look upon favorably.

17 And take, each-man, his pan,
　　place on them smoking-incense,
　　and bring-it-near, before the presence of YHWH,
　　each-man his pan,
　　fifty and two hundred pans,
　　and (also) you and Aharon, each-man his pan.

18 So they took each-man his pan,
　　placing on them fire,
　　putting on them smoking-incense,
　　and stood at the entrance to the Tent of Appointment,
　　as (did) Moshe and Aharon.

19 And Korah and his entire community assembled against them,
　　at the entrance to the Tent of Appointment.
　　Now the Glory of YHWH was seen by the entire community;

20 and YHWH said to Moshe and to Aharon, saying:

21 Separate (yourselves) from the midst of this community,
　　that I may finish them off in an instant!

22 They flung themselves on their faces and said:
　　O God, God of the spirits of all flesh,
　　when one man sins,
　　at the entire community will you be furious?

23 YHWH spoke to Moshe, saying:

24 Speak to the community, saying:
　　Go up from around the dwelling-place of Korah, Datan and
　　　　Aviram!

25 Moshe arose and went to Datan and Aviram,
　　and there went after him the elders of Israel.

26 And he spoke to the community, saying:
　　Pray turn away from the tents of these wicked men,
　　do not touch anything that is theirs,
　　lest you be swept away for all their sins!

19 **Glory:** Or "aura," the visible manifestation of God
in the cloud accompanying the Israelites and resident upon the Dwelling.

Aftermath (17): The revolt of Korah, with its macabre ending, has made it clear that Levites must not "come-near" the priestly domains, physically or professionally. Accordingly, the incense pans of the dead rebels become plating for the altar, as a warning for the future. The "fire-pan" becomes instrumental immediately thereafter, as Aharon must obtain forgiveness for the people, who understand the deaths of Korah and his followers as a political purge by the two brothers. Aharon's action, it should be noted, cannot prevent the initial round of deaths by divine plague.

Upon hearing the "grumbling" of the Israelites (a word that did not, interestingly, appear in the Korah story), God now deems it necessary to provide another sign: proof that it is the Sons of Aharon that he has chosen (cf. 16:5)—as if the earth opening up were not enough! This is Aharon's flowering rod, a stick that, though long-severed from its original tree, still manages to produce flowers and fruit. The motif is noted in many other cultures (cf. Gaster 1969 for references); Wagner made use of it to provide the climactic moment in his opera *Tannhäuser.*

27 They went up from the dwellings of Korah, Datan and Aviram,
  all around.
  Now Datan and Aviram had come out, stationed at the entrance
    to their tents,
  with their wives, their children, and their little-ones.
28 Moshe said:
  By this you shall know
  that (it is) YHWH (who) sent me to do all these deeds,
  that (it was) not from my (own) heart:
29 if like the death of all humans these-men die,
  and the calling-to-account of all humans is accounted upon them,
  (it is) not YHWH (who) has sent me.
30 But if YHWH creates a new-creation,
  and the ground opens its mouth, and swallows up them and all
    that is theirs,
  and they go down alive into Sheol,
  then you will know
  that these men have scorned YHWH.
31 Now it was, just as he finished speaking all these words,
  there split the ground that was beneath them;
32 the earth opened its mouth
  and swallowed up them and their households,
  all the human beings that belonged to Korah
  and all the property.
33 So they went down, they and all theirs,
  alive, into Sheol;
  the earth covered them,
  and they perished from the midst of the assembly.

27 **dwellings:** The Hebrew word is, oddly, in the singular.
28 **heart:** I.e., mind.
30 **Sheol:** The underworld, which in the Bible is a nondescript, gray place, rather like the Greeks' Hades—and not the later Heaven and Hell of Judaism, Christianity, and Islam.

32 **their households:** A man's family and property were considered an extension of his personality.
33 **So they went down ... alive:** A famous later use of this motif, filtered through medieval Christian perspective, occurs in the great penultimate scene of Mozart's opera *Don Giovanni*.

34 Now all Israel that were around them
   fled at the sound-of-their-voice,
   for they said:
   Lest the earth swallow us up!
35 Now fire went out from before the presence of Yhwh
   and consumed the fifty and two hundred men,
   those who had brought-near the incense.

17:1 Yhwh spoke to Moshe, saying:
   2 Speak to El'azar son of Aharon the priest,
      that he may set-aside the pans from the burned-remains,
      and the fire-coals, scatter yonder,
      for they have become-holy;
   3 (as for) the pans of those-who-sinned, (at the cost of) their lives,
      make of them beaten plates, overlaid for the slaughter-site,
      for they were brought-near before the presence of Yhwh,
      and have become-holy.
      Let them be a sign for the Children of Israel!
   4 So El'azar the priest took
      the bronze pans that the burned-men had brought near,
      and he beat them as overlay for the slaughter-site,
   5 a reminder for the Children of Israel,
      in order that no outside man might come-near
      who is not of the seed of Aharon
      to turn smoking-incense into smoke before the presence of Yhwh,
      and so that he not become like Korah and like his community,
      as Yhwh spoke through the hand of Moshe to him.

   6 But all the Children of Israel grumbled on the morrow
      against Moshe and against Aharon, saying:
      (It is) you (who) caused-the-death of Yhwh's people!

---

35 **fire . . . consumed:** Aharon's sons Nadav and Avihu, who offered up "outside fire," were similarly punished in Lev. 10.

17:2 **become-holy:** And cannot be used for ordinary purposes.

7 Now it was, when the community assembled against Moshe and
      against Aharon,
that they turned toward the Tent of Appointment,
and here: the cloud had covered it,
and the Glory of YHWH could be seen!

8 Then Moshe and Aharon came to the front of the Tent of
      Appointment.

9 And YHWH spoke to Moshe, saying:

10 Move-aside from the midst of this community,
that I may finish them off in an instant!
They flung themselves upon their faces.

11 Moshe said to Aharon:
Take (your) pan
and place upon it fire from the slaughter-site, putting smoking-
      incense (there);
go quickly to the community and effect-appeasement for them,
for the fury is (still) going-out from the presence of YHWH,
the plague has begun!

12 Aharon took (it), as Moshe had spoken,
and he ran to the midst of the assembly:
and here, the plague had begun among the people!
So he put the smoking-incense (in it), and effected-appeasement
      for the people:

13 now he stood between the dead and the living,
and the plague was held-back.

14 Now those that died in the plague were fourteen thousand and
      seven hundred,
aside from those that died in the matter of Korah.

15 Aharon returned to Moshe, to the entrance of the Tent of
      Appointment,
since the plague was held-back.

---

11 **go quickly** etc.: Unable any more to respond to God's "that I may consume them in an instant" (v.10) as he had in 16:21—by arguing with and pacifying God—Moshe resorts to priestly measures: Aharon must use incense to attempt obtaining for-giveness for the people. **effect-appeasement:** So Milgrom, citing a parallel use of incense in an Egyptian text.

14 **14,700:** Another multiple of the "perfect" number seven.

Levite Rules (18): In order to more strictly enforce the separate roles of priest and Levite, necessitated by the rebellion of Korah, the text turns to clarification of the Levites' duties and regulations concerning them. They are to act as a buffer between the sancta and the people, but may not come into contact with the holy-things themselves; the priests, of course, may and must. The priests' reward—actually, their means of support—consists of firstborn animals and firstfruits; the Levites', of tithes.

The chief refrain in the chapter is variations on "so that they may not die"; this has occurred already in 17:25, thus linking Chaps. 17 and 18 nicely.

16 Now YHWH spoke to Moshe, saying:

17 Speak to the Children of Israel,
   take from them a staff, a staff (each) per Fathers' House
   from all their leaders, for their Father's House:
   twelve staffs,
   each-man—his name you are to write upon the staffs.

18 And the name of Aharon you are to write upon the staff of Levi,
   indeed, one staff for (each) head of their Fathers' House.

19 You are to put them in the Tent of Appointment, before the
      Testimony,
   where I appoint-meeting with you.

20 Now it shall be:
   the man whom I choose, his staff will sprout;
   thus will I still from upon me
   the grumblings of the Children of Israel that they set-grumbling
      against you (both).

21 Moshe spoke to the Children of Israel,
   and they gave him, all the leaders,
   a staff per (each) one leader, a staff per (each) one leader,
   for their Fathers' House,
   twelve staffs,
   with the staff of Aharon in the midst of their staffs.

22 Moshe laid out the staffs before the presence of YHWH,
   in the Tent of the Testimony.

23 Now it was on the morrow:
   when Moshe entered the Tent of the Testimony,
   here: it had sprouted, the staff of Aharon, of the House of Levi!
   It had put-forth a sprouting-flower, it had blossomed a blossom, it
      had ripened almonds!

24 Moshe brought out all the staffs from before the presence of
      YHWH
   to all the Children of Israel;
   they saw (them), and each-man took his staff.

---

17 **staff:** A good example of the pun inherent in Heb. *matte* (cf. note to 4:18).

19 **Testimony:** Elliptical for "Coffer of Testimony."

23 **almonds:** In Israel, almond trees are known for their dramatic blossoming in winter, before all other trees.

24 **saw:** In the sense of "found" or "selected."

25   YHWH said to Moshe:
     Return the staff of Aharon before the Testimony
     to be safeguarded as a sign for the rebellious-folk,
     that their grumblings may be finished from me,
     so that they do not die!
26   Moshe did it,
     according to all that YHWH commanded him, so he did.

27   But the Children of Israel said to Moshe, saying:
     Here, we expire, we perish, all of us perish!
28   Anyone who comes-near, comes-near (at all) to the Dwelling of
         YHWH will die;
     will there be an end to our expiring?
18:1 YHWH said to Aharon:
     You and your sons and your father's house along with you
     are to bear any iniquity (pertaining to) the Holy-Area;
     you and your sons after you
     are to bear any iniquity (pertaining to) your priesthood.
2   And also your brothers, the stock of Levi, the tribe of your father,
         bring-near with you,
     they are to be-joined to you and are to act-as-attendants for you,
     you and your sons along with you
     in front of the Tent of the Testimony.
3   They are to keep your charge and the charge of the entire Tent,
     but: to the implements of holiness and to the slaughter-site, they
         are not to come-near,
     that they not die—so they, so you!
4   They are to be-joined to you,
     that they may keep the charge of the Tent of Appointment,
     including all the serving-tasks of the Tent;
     an outsider is not to come-near with you,

18:1 **bear:** That is, upon yourselves, until it is eliminated. **iniquity (pertaining to) the Holy-Area:** That is, pollution attaching to the sanctuary, which is the burden of the priests.

2 **to be-joined:** Heb. *ve-yillavu,* a play on the name "Levi."

5 but you are to keep the charge of the Holy-Shrine and the charge
    of the slaughter-site,
that there be no further fury against the Children of Israel.

6 Now I, I hereby take your brothers, the Levites,
from the midst of the Children of Israel,
for you (they are) a gift, given-over (for the benefit) of YHWH,
for serving the serving-tasks of the Tent of Appointment.

7 And you and your sons with you
are to be-in-charge of your priesthood,
in every matter (pertaining to) the slaughter-site and (what is)
    inside the Curtain,
and you are to do-service;
serving-tasks of special-grant I give your priesthood—
any outsider who comes-near will be put-to-death!

8 YHWH spoke to Aharon:
Now I, I hereby give over to you the charge of my contributions,
including all the holy-donations (from) the Children of Israel,
to you I give them, as an anointed-share,
and to your sons, as an allotment for the ages.

9 This shall be yours from the holiest holy-offerings, from the fire:
including their every near-offering, including their every grain-
    gift, including their every *hattat*-offering
and including their every *asham*-offering that they remit to me,
it is a holiest holy-portion, for you and for your sons.

10 In the holiest state-of-holiness you are to eat it,
every male may eat it,
holy shall it be for you.

11 And this (too is) for you: their contributed gift
including every elevation-offering of the Children of Israel,
to you I give it over,
and to your sons and to your daughters along with you,
as an allotment for the ages:
everyone ritually-pure in your house may eat it.

12 All your choicest shining-oil, all your choicest new-wine and
    grain,
the premier-part that they give to YHWH,
to you I give it.

Death and the Red Cow (19): Apparently to close out the Korah story, the text turns to a mysterious and powerful ritual, one designed to remove the contaminating pollution of death. It is important to note that the revolt in Chap. 16 led, not only to the deaths of the rebels and their households, but also to the perishing of 14,700 people in the subsequent plague (17:12–14). So despite the fact that priests and Levites now have their tasks straight, thanks to Chap. 18, there remains the serious matter of purification.

Levine notes the typical priestly pattern at work: first the remedy is prescribed, and then the actual circumstances that call for it are enumerated. He also sees the chapter as essentially a protest against the widespread cult of the dead in the ancient Near East, from which the Israelites notably separated themselves.

Milgrom has illuminated a number of aspects of the Red Cow ritual, notably by characterizing it as a sort of *hattat* ceremony. That ritual, it may be recalled, enabled the priests to decontaminate the sanctuary of ritual pollution, chiefly through the sprinkling of blood against the altar. Milgrom points to the unusual nature of the ritual here, in that the purifying agent (in this case, water that has been mixed with the special cow's ashes, which came partly from burned blood) is sprinkled on persons, not objects.

13 The first-fruits of everything that is in their land, that they bring
   to YHWH,
   it is for you,
   everyone pure in your house may eat it.
14 Everything specially-devoted in Israel—
   it is for you.
15 Every breacher of a womb of all flesh
   that you bring-near for YHWH, of man and of beast,
   for you it shall be.
   However, you are to redeem, yes, redeem the firstborn of
   humans,
   and the firstborn of *tamei* animals, you are to redeem.
16 And its redemption-price, from the age of a month you are to
   redeem,
   in your assessment: silver, five *shekels* by the Holy-Shrine *shekel*,
   —twenty grains it is.
17 However, the firstborn of oxen, the firstborn of sheep, or the
   firstborn of goats
   you are not to redeem,
   (already) holy are they,
   their blood you are to dash on the slaughter-site,
   their fat you are to turn-into-smoke,
   a fire-offering as soothing savor for YHWH,
18 and their meat is to be for you,
   like the breast of the elevation-offering, like the right thigh,
   it shall be for you.
19 All the contributions of the holy-things that the Children of Israel
   set-aside for YHWH
   I give to you and to your sons and to your daughters along with
   you,
   as an allotment for the ages:
   it is a "covenant of salt" for the ages, before the presence of
   YHWH,
   for you and for your seed after you.

---

16 **in your assessment:** Lit. "in the your-assessment."
A grammatically "frozen" form, this functionally
means "by assessment."

19 **"covenant of salt":** Plaut suggests that this means
"an eternal covenant"; salt prevents decay.

20 And YHWH said to Aharon:
In their land you are not to receive-inheritance,
no portion-of-land shall be yours in their midst:
I am your portion and your inheritance
in the midst of the Children of Israel.

21 And to the Sons of Levi,
here: I give over all tithes in Israel, as an inheritance,
in exchange for their serving-tasks that they serve,
the serving-tasks of the Tent of Appointment.

22 The Children of Israel are no longer to come-near the Tent of
Appointment,
to bear sin, to die.

23 The Levite, he (alone) is to serve the serving-tasks of the Tent of
Appointment,
it is they who will bear their iniquity,
a law for the ages, throughout their generations:
but in the midst of the Children of Israel they are not to inherit a
(land-)inheritance.

24 For the tithing of the Children of Israel that they set-aside for
YHWH (as) a contribution,
I give over to the Levites as an inheritance;
therefore I have said to them:
in the midst of the Children of Israel they are not to inherit a
(land-)inheritance.

25 YHWH spoke to Moshe, saying:

26 To the Levites you are to speak, saying to them:
When you take from the Children of Israel the tithe that I am
giving you from them, as your inherited-share,
you are to set-aside from it (as) a contribution for YHWH
a tenth from the tithe;

27 it will be reckoned to you as your contribution,
like grain from the threshing-floor,
like fully-fermented (grapes) from the vat.

28 Thus you are to set-aside, on your part, the contribution of
YHWH,
from all your tithes that you take from the Children of Israel,
and are to give from them the contribution of YHWH to Aharon
the priest.

29 From all your gifts
you are to set-aside every contribution of YHWH,
from all its choice-parts,
its holy-part from it.

30 And you are to say to them:
When you set-aside the choice-part from it,
it is to be reckoned for the Levites
like the produce of the threshing-floor, like the produce of the
vat.

31 You may eat it in any place, you and your household,
for it is a wage for you,
in exchange for your serving-tasks in the Tent of Appointment.

32 You will not bear on account of it (any) sin
once you set-aside its choice-part from it,
that you not profane the holy-donations of the Children of Israel,
and you not die.

19:1 YHWH spoke to Moshe, saying:

2 This is the law of the instructed-ritual
that YHWH has commanded, saying:
Speak to the Children of Israel,
that they may take you a red cow, wholly-sound,
that has in it no defect,
that has not yet yielded to a yoke;

3 you are to give it to El'azar the priest,
it is to be brought forth, outside the camp,
and it is to be slain in his presence.

4 El'azar the priest is to take (some) of its blood with his finger
and is to sprinkle toward the face of the Tent of Appointment,
some of its blood,
seven times.

---

29 **choice-parts:** Lit. "fat"; English "cream [of the crop]" carries the same connotation.
19:2 **red:** Possibly indicating "brownish," but the sound "red" is important here as a reminder of blood, a major purifying agent in the Israelite cult (especially in the *hattat* sacrifice; cf. Lev. 4:5–7) and a neutralizer of death, given its symbolic character as the life. **not yet yielded to a yoke:** Lit. "no yoke has gone upon it" (Heb. *lo 'ala 'aleha 'ol*); but the alliteration is a characteristic feature of this text.

5 Then the cow is to be burned before his eyes;
   its hide, its flesh, and its blood
   along with its dung, are to be burned.
6 The priest is to take wood of cedar, and hyssop, and scarlet of
      worm,
   and is to throw (them) into the midst of the cow burning.
7 He is to scrub his garments, the priest, and is to wash his body in
      water,
   afterward he may enter the camp;
   but the priest will remain-*tamei* until sunset.
8 And he who burned it
   is to scrub his garments in water and is to wash his body in water,
   remaining-*tamei* until sunset.
9 And a (ritually) pure man shall collect the ashes of the cow,
   depositing them outside the camp
   in a pure place.
   It shall be for the community of the Children of Israel in
      safekeeping,
   as Waters Kept-Apart,
   it is for decontamination.
10 The collector of the cow's ashes is to scrub his garments,
   remaining-*tamei* until sunset.
   It shall be for the Children of Israel and for the sojourner that
      sojourns in their midst,
   as a law for the ages:
11 he who touches a dead-body of any human person,
   (shall be deemed) *tamei* for seven days.
12 Should he decontaminate himself with it on the third day and on
      the seventh day, then he is pure,
   if he does not decontaminate himself on the third day and on the
      seventh day, then he is not pure.

---

6 **cedar . . . hyssop . . . scarlet:** All suggesting the color (and efficacy) of blood.

7 ***tamei:*** As in previous texts, ritually impure.

12 **with it:** With the ashes.

13 Anyone who touches a dead-body of any human person that has
     died,
   and does not decontaminate himself—
   the Dwelling of YHWH has he made-*tamei,*
   cut off shall that person be from Israel,
   since the Waters Kept-Apart were not dashed on him,
   tamei shall he be, his *tum'a* (stays) within him!

14 This is the Instruction:
   A human who dies in (his) tent—
   anyone that enters the tent, and anyone that is in the tent,
   (is to be) considered-*tamei* for seven days.

15 And any open vessel that has no cover tied down on it,
   it is *tamei!*

16 And anyone who touches, on the (open) field,
   one slain by the sword or a dead man,
   or human bones or a grave,
   shall be *tamei* for seven days.

17 They are to take for the *tamei*-one (some) dust of the burned
     hattat-offering,
   they are to add to it living water, in a vessel.

18 He is to take hyssop and dip it into the water, the (ritually) pure
     man,
   he is to sprinkle (it) on the Tent and on all the implements
   and on the persons that were there,
   and on the one who touched the bones or the slain-one or the
     dead-man or the grave.

19 Then the pure-one is to sprinkle (it) on the *tamei*-one on the third
     day and on the seventh day,
   thus decontaminating him on the seventh day;
   then he is to scrub his garments and wash with water,
   and be purified after sunset.

20 Now a man who becomes-*tamei* and does not decontaminate
     himself—

15 **no cover:** Apparently, a cover would prevent the
transmission of impurity.
16 **human bones . . . a grave:** In antiquity, Jews usually buried their dead outside the city limits, to avoid
ritual pollution of the public sector.

Rebellion and the Failure of Leadership; The Edomites (20): The first part of this chapter contains a story that has deeply troubled readers for over two millennia. Its length belies its weight; in only thirteen verses, Moshe and Aharon have lost their most cherished dream—the privilege of entering the Promised Land.

The brevity here may result from the fact that, for the narrator, this story was a variant of, or constructed from, a similar one in Ex. 17, to explain more fully why the leaders shared the fate of their generation. In other words, their deaths may affect us more than the text meant it to. Nonetheless, the question of why exactly Moshe and Aharon received such a terrible punishment for a moment of indiscretion will not go away. Can it really be that the towering figure of Moshe, liberator and lawgiver, parent and prophet, is to be done away with in the blink of an eye, over a fit of justifiable temper? But it is a public moment, and there the answer may lie. The Bible consistently takes a stringent view of leadership: that leaders must be above reproach, and that they must not lose sight of the fact that it is God whom they represent. A similar impulse led to the strict standards to which the writer of Samuel-Kings, the so-called Deuteronomistic historian, held such revered personalities as David and Solomon.

From v.14 to v.21, the text gives us a moment to digest what has just happened, at the same time managing to introduce the major theme of the next several chapters: encountering other peoples and tribes as the Israelites near Canaan. First is Edom, in the territory to the east roughly between Eilat and the Dead Sea. The sequence begins tentatively, not with an Israelite victory, but not with a defeat either: they are forced to reroute their approach.

So as to keep the memory of Merivat-Kadesh close, the chapter ends with the death of Aharon, "before the eyes of the entire community" (v.27). For the first time in all the rebellion texts, the word "rebel" itself is used (v.24). On a positive note, leadership is seamlessly passed to the next generation; when Moshe returns from witnessing Aharon's death, he is accompanied by the latter's son El'azar, who is tellingly dressed in Aharon's garments.

cut off shall that person be from the midst of the assembly,
for the Holy-Area of YHWH has he made-*tamei,*
Waters Kept-Apart have not been dashed upon him,
he is *tamei!*

21 It shall be for you as a law for the ages:
the one-who-does-the-sprinkling from the Waters Kept-Apart is
to scrub his garments,
and the one-who-touches the Waters Kept-Apart shall remain-
tamei until sunset.

22 And anything that the *tamei*-man touches becomes-*tamei*—
the person that touches (it) shall remain-*tamei* until sunset.

20:1 Now they came, the Children of Israel, the entire community,
(to the) Wilderness of Tzyn,
in the first New-Moon.
The people stayed in Kadesh.
Miryam died there,
and she was buried there.

2 Now there was no water for the community,
so they assembled against Moshe and against Aharon;

3 the people quarreled with Moshe,
they said, saying:
Now would that we had expired
when our brothers expired before the presence of YHWH!

4 Now why did you bring the assembly of YHWH into this
wilderness,
to die there,
we and our cattle?

5 Now why did you make us go up from Egypt
to bring us to this evil place,
not a place of seeds and figs, vines and pomegranates
—and water (there is) none to drink!

20:1 **Wilderness of Tzyn:** In Ex. 17, the parallel story, the location is the "Wilderness of Syn" (v.1). **the first New-Moon:** Of the final year of wandering.
2 **assembled against:** This verb, which occurs two

more times in the narrative (vv.8 and 10), was also used twice in the Korah rebellion (16:3, 19).
5 **a place of seeds** etc.: Another idealized remembering of Egypt, as in 11:5.

6 Moshe and Aharon came away from the presence of the assembly
to the entrance to the Tent of Appointment,
and flung themselves upon their faces.
The Glory of YHWH was seen by them,

7 and YHWH spoke to Moshe, saying:

8 Take the staff
and assemble the community, you and Aharon your brother;
you are to speak to the boulder before their eyes
so that it gives forth its water,
thus you are to bring out for them water from the boulder,
that you may give-drink to the assembly and to their cattle.

9 So Moshe took the staff from before the presence of YHWH,
as he had commanded him.

10 And Moshe and Aharon assembled the assembly facing the
boulder.
He said to them:
Now hear, (you) rebels,
from this boulder must we bring you out water?

11 And Moshe raised his hand
and struck the boulder with his staff, twice,
so that abundant water came out;
and the community and their cattle drank.

12 Now YHWH said to Moshe and to Aharon:
Because you did not have-trust in me
to treat-me-as-holy before the eyes of the Children of Israel,
therefore:
you (two) shall not bring this assembly into the land that I am
giving them!

13 Those were the Waters of Meriva / Quarreling,
where the Children of Israel quarreled with YHWH,
and he was hallowed through them.

---

8 **boulder:** Heb. *sela';* Ex. 17:6 has *tzur,* "rock."
10 **said to them:** It is to them, rather than to the boulder, that Moshe speaks.

12–13 **treat-me-as-holy . . . hallowed:** Heb. root *k-d-sh,*
echoing the name of the place, Kadesh.

14 Now Moshe sent messengers from Kadesh to the king of Edom:
Thus says your brother Israel:
You know (about) all the hardships that have found us:

15 that our fathers went down to Egypt
and we stayed in Egypt for many years,
and Egypt ill-treated us and our fathers.

16 Now we cried out to YHWH, and he hearkened to our voice,
he sent a messenger and brought us out of Egypt.
So here we are at Kadesh, (the) town at the edge of your
     territory.

17 Pray let us cross through your land,
we will not cross through field or through orchard,
we will not drink water from wells,
(upon) the King's Road we will march,
not turning right or left,
until we have crossed through your territory.

18 But Edom said to him:
You shall not cross through me,
lest with the sword I come out to meet you!

19 The Children of Israel said to him:
On the byway we will go up;
if we drink your water, I and my livestock,
I will give (you) its selling-price—
only (let it) not be a matter-of-dispute;
on foot let me cross!

20 But he said:
You shall not cross!
And Edom went out to meet him
with a heavy (host of) fighting-people and with a strong hand.

21 So Edom refused to give (Israel) leave to cross through his
     territory,
and Israel turned away from him.

---

17 **the King's Road:** This major ancient road, paved
in later (Roman) times, went from present-day Eilat
on the Red Sea north through the part of the Rift
Valley that is east of the Dead Sea, to present-day
Amman, and then on to Damascus.

First Victory: Rebellion Again; Traveling; Sihon and Og (21): A miscellany of wilderness traditions, Chap. 21 begins with a military victory—perhaps a sign that Israel's terrible trials are coming to an end. Not insignificantly, the victory comes after the Israelites have properly vowed to allot booty to God (v.2), a far cry from their willful attempt at conquest at the end of Chap. 14. This brief account may in fact be a reworking or different account of the Horma incident in that passage.

The strange events surrounding the "viper of copper" that follow provide a reminder, even amid the progress of the march and military successes, of the Israelites' usual waywardness. As usual, the problem is food; several things, however, make this brief story unusual amid the rebellion narratives. For one, the punishment is unique; for another, the people call upon Moshe to remove the plague—in a manner that is more reminiscent of Pharaoh of Egypt, with the Plagues, than of previous Israelite behavior. Finally, there is the Bible's record of what happened to the copper object: it was preserved in the cult and worshiped by the people, until it was smashed during the large-scale religious reform under King Hezekiah of Judah (late eighth century B.C.E.). One might note that the divine punishment for sin, once accomplished, clears the way for the Israelite victories that follow immediately.

Of additional interest in this chapter is the inclusion of three ancient poems (vv. 14-15, 17-18, and 27-30), whose origins and language are both obscure. Preceded by a brief itinerary of the Israelites' travels up to Moabite territory, soon to be the scene of the Bil'am narratives (Chaps. 22–24), the chapter ends with two successful clashes against local kings, Sihon and Og. While the accounts here are brief, postbiblical Jewish tradition took delight in spinning fantastic tales about these two kings (cf. Ginzberg).

22 They marched on from Kadesh,
  and they came, the Children of Israel, the entire community, to
    Hill's Hill.
23 Now YHWH said to Moshe and to Aharon at Hill's Hill,
  by the border of the land of Edom,
  saying:
24 Let Aharon be gathered to his kinspeople,
  for he is not to enter the land that I am giving to the Children of
    Israel—
  since you (both) rebelled against my orders at the Waters of
    Meriva.
25 Take Aharon and El'azar his son,
  and bring them up on Hill's Hill;
26 strip Aharon of his garments and clothe in them El'azar his son.
  Aharon will be gathered and will die there.
27 So Moshe did as YHWH commanded him:
  they went up Hill's Hill before the eyes of the entire community;
28 Moshe stripped Aharon of his garments and clothed in them
    El'azar his son.
  So Aharon died there on top of the hill.
  When Moshe and El'azar came down from the hill,
29 the entire community saw that Aharon had expired,
  and they wept for Aharon thirty days,
  the whole House of Israel.

21:1 Now the Canaanite, the king of Arad, who sat-as-ruler in the
    Negev, heard that Israel was coming by the Atarim Road,
  so they waged war against Israel and captured from them war-
    captives.
2 Then Israel vowed a vow to YHWH
  and said:
  If you will give, yes, give this people into my hand,
  I will devote their towns (to destruction).

---

22 **Hill's Hill:** Others, "Mount Hor"; Heb. *hor ha-har*.
26 **gathered:** To his ancestors; meant literally, as the eventual remains—the bones—would be placed together with those of the ancestors in the family burial pit.

29 **thirty days:** Equal to the mourning period for Moshe, and a good indication of Aharon's stature.
21:2 **devote . . . (to destruction):** The confiscation of people or property to God; the noun is *herem* (like the Arabic-derived English word "harem").

3 Now Yhwh hearkened to the voice of Israel, he gave (them) the
Canaanites,
and they devoted-them-to-destruction along with their cities;
so they called the name of the place Horma / Destruction.

4 They marched from Hill's Hill by the Reed Sea Road,
to go-around the land of Edom,
and the people (became) short-tempered on the way.
5 The people spoke against God and against Moshe:
Why did you bring us up from Egypt to die in the wilderness?
For there is no food and no water,
and our throats loathe the despicable food!
6 So Yhwh sent upon the people vipers, burning-snakes;
they bit the people,
and there died many people of Israel.
7 The people came to Moshe
and said:
We have sinned!
For we have spoken against Yhwh and against you.
Intercede to God, so that he may remove from us the vipers!
So Moshe interceded on behalf of the people.
8 And Yhwh said to Moshe:
Make yourself a burning-snake and put it on a banner-pole;
it shall be:
whoever has been bitten and then sees it, will live.
9 So Moshe made a viper of copper, and he put it on a banner-pole,
and it was:
if a viper bit a man
and he looked upon the viper of copper, he would live.

6 **vipers:** Heb. *nehashim,* "snakes," altered here in
English because of the rhyming "viper of copper"
(*nehash nehoshet*) in v.9 below. **burning-snakes:**
Heb. obscure; perhaps linking up with the body's
reaction to the bite of this particular snake.
9 **copper:** Elsewhere translated as "bronze."

10 The Children of Israel marched on and encamped at Ovot.

11 They marched on from Ovot and encamped at Iyyei Ha-Avarim,
in the wilderness that faces Moav;
toward the rising of the sun.

12 From there they marched on and encamped at Wadi Zered.

13 From there they marched on and encamped across the Arnon
that is in the wilderness,
that goes out of the Amorite territory;
for the Arnon is the border of Moav
between Moav and the Amorites.

14 Therefore it is said in the Book of the Wars of YHWH:

> . . . Vahev in Sufa,
> the wadis, Arnon,
15 > along with its canyon wadis,
> that stretch along the settled-country of Ar,
> leaning on the territory of Moav.

16 From there to Be'er/The Well;
that is the well of which YHWH said to Moshe:
Gather the people, and I will give them water.

17 Then Israel sang this song:

> Spring up, O well, sing-in-chorus to it;
18 > —the well that was dug out by princes!
> —that was excavated by people's nobles!
> —with scepter!
> —with their rods!

Now from the wilderness—to Mattana;
19 and from Mattana—to Nahliel;
and from Nahliel—to Bamot/The Heights;
20 and from Bamot—to the valley that is at the Open-Country of
Moav,

---

14 **the Book of the Wars of YHWH:** An ancient text that has been lost to us, like a number of other works alluded to in the Bible (e.g., "The Book of Yashar" mentioned in Josh. 10:13).

20 **Pisga:** The future site of Moshe's death.

the top of Pisga/the Summit,
overlooking the face of the wasteland.

21 Now Israel sent messengers to Sihon king of the Amorites,
   saying:

22 Let me cross your land!
   We will not spread out into the fields,
   in the vineyards we will not drink well water;
   on the King's Road we will march,
   until we have crossed your territory.

23 But Sihon would not give Israel (leave) to cross through his
   territory.
   Sihon gathered all his fighting-people
   and went out to meet Israel in the wilderness,
   he came to Yahatz and waged-war against Israel.

24 But Israel struck him with the edge of the sword
   and took-possession of his land,
   from the Arnon as far as the Yabbok, as far as the Children of
   Ammon;
   for strong is the territory of the Children of Ammon.

25 Israel took all these towns
   and Israel settled in all the Amorite towns—
   in Heshbon and in all her daughter-villages;

26 for Heshbon—it was the town of Sihon king of the Amorites.
   He had made-war on a former king of Moav
   and had taken all his land from his hand, as far as the Arnon.

27 Therefore the parable-makers say:

   Come to Heshbon! be built up,
   be established, Sihon's town!

28 For fire went forth from Heshbon,
   Flame from the city of Sihon;

---

21 **Sihon:** The victories over him and Og king of
Bashan (vv.33–35) are mentioned a number of times
in later books such as Deuteronomy, Joshua, and
Judges; their proximity to the Promised Land must
have made them and their fate of great interest to
traditional poets/singers.

24 **strong:** This could also be read as a place-name, Az,
or as another location, [Y]az[er] (cf. v.32).

27 **parable-makers:** Or "bards."

devouring Ar of Moav,
    the inhabitants of the heights of Arnon.
29   Woe to you, Moav!
    You have perished, people of Kemosh!
    His sons (become) fugitives,
    His daughters, captives
    of the king of the Amorites, Sihon.
30   We shot them,
    Heshbon perished as far as Divon,
    we desolated (them) as far as Nofah,
    fire as far as Medeva!

31 Now Israel settled in the land of the Amorites.
32 And Moshe sent (men) to scout Ya'zer,
    they conquered its daughter-villages,
    dispossessing the Amorites who were there.
33 Then they faced-about and went up the Bashan Road.
    Og king of Bashan went out to meet them,
    he and all his fighting-people in war, at Edre'i.
34 YHWH said to Moshe:
    Do not be afraid of him,
    for into your hand I give him and all his people, and his land;
    you will do to him as you did to Sihon king of the Amorites who
        sat-as-ruler in Heshbon.
35 So they struck him and his sons and all his people
    until not a survivor was left to him,
    and they took-possession of his land.

22:1 And the Children of Israel marched on and encamped in the
    Plains of Moav,
    across from Jordan-Jericho.

---

29 **Kemosh:** The chief god of the Moabites (cf. I Kings 11).

30 A difficult verse that allows only tentative translation. **shot:** Or "cast down." **fire:** Reading *esh* for trad. *asher,* "which [is]."

33 **Og:** Often paired with Sihon in later retellings of the wilderness experience (e.g., Josh. 2:10, 9:10).

22:1 **Jordan-Jericho:** The sense is clearly "on the east side of the Jordan River, opposite Jericho."

ON BIL'AM

NOW EMBEDDED WITHIN THE SECOND PART OF THE BOOK OF NUMBERS, THE STORIES and exalted poetry connected with the name of the pagan prophet Bil'am (Balaam) in many ways point to the final section of the book. They provide a welcome relief from the depressing and at times exasperating narratives of rebellion. Israel in Bil'am's vision is the realization of the patriarchal dream, a sea of people (and tents) without number, upright in conduct and victorious in battle. In its focusing on the theme of reversal—curses turned to blessings, ass turned seer/prophet, and prophet turned fool—the Bil'am section suggests that, as we leave the old generation to die out in the wilderness, God's own "cursing" of the people because of their rebelliousness will somehow, ultimately, be turned into blessing. No wonder that Buber (1988) felt the hidden presence of Moses and his vision of Israel in these chapters.

Recent archaeological finds have placed Bil'am as a figure known to extrabiblical traditions located in the lands east of the Jordan. The Torah uses him (as the Bible may have used Job and other such personalities) for its own purposes, picking up a theme it has utilized earlier: the acknowledgment of God's power and Israel's glory by a wise or inspired pagan (cf., for instance, the figure of Jethro, Moses' father-in-law, in Ex. 18; or, to use later examples, Jericho's Rahab in Josh. 2 and the Queen of Sheba in I Kings 10). Just as the Pharaoh is made to acknowledge God's power and Israel's glory toward the beginning of the Exodus sequence, so the nations or tribes surrounding Israel are portrayed as coming to the same realization at its end. Bil'am, as it were, provides religious legitimacy for these ideas in the non-Israelite domain.

The narrative is built, not only on obvious theme words such as "word," "speak," and "curse/revile/doom," but also on repeating phrases. Central to them, in variation, is "only the word that I [God] speak to you, / that (alone) may speak" (22:20, 35, 38; 23:12, 36). The episode with the she-ass, one of the most unusual in the Bible, revolves around the threefold "Now the she-ass saw YHWH's messenger" (22:23, 25, 27), suggesting, of course, that Bil'am, the reputed holy man, does not see him. The story also offers an illustration of the Bible's balanced sense of justice: Balak "once again" sends emissaries, Bil'am "once again" beats the she-ass, but these actions are thwarted by the divine messenger's "once again" blocking the path (and, symbolically, the curse).

While some scholars have suggested that the she-ass section has origins independent from the main body of the story, it is verbally linked to Bil'am's speeches later in the story by a single device. The refrain of "these three times," describing Bil'am's beating of the she-ass and her refusal to continue, is matched by the threefold refusal of God to allow anything but blessing to publicly issue forth from the prophet's mouth ("[on] these three occasions," 24:10).

The poetic sections of the story are built on the basis of a stock scene: Bil'am has Balak build seven altars and prepare seven bulls and seven rams; the prophet sacrifices the animals, and has the king stand alongside the altars while he, Bil'am, goes off to encounter God. When he returns, he "takes up his parable," stressing twice how God blesses, not curses, Israel, and how he will under no circumstances revoke that blessing. The full version of the blessing, beginning in 24:3 , is distinguished by its lofty tone (clearly suggesting the infusion of the "spirit of God" [24:2]). The tripled "Utters . . ." signals an abrupt change in mood and inspiration; the word, more properly "the utterance of . . . ," is frequently used by the later Prophets to open their speeches.

A word should be said about the "oracles to the nations" that begin in 24:17 . These are reminiscent of many Prophetic passages, in which the seer turns outside Israel and addresses the neighboring peoples (e.g., Amos 1–2:3). Their inclusion in Numbers helps to link the Bil'am story with what has immediately preceded it, the account of Israel's militarily successful encounter with its historical neighbors.

Similarly, the Bil'am episode is linked to the chapter that follows it, the apostasy at Baal-Peor. A tradition reported in 31:8 informs us that Bil'am was among those killed by Pin'has in his "zeal" or "indignation" (Fishbane 1974) for YHWH.

The Hiring of Bil'am (22): Faced with overwhelming evidence of Israelite superiority, especially as evinced in the previous chapter, the Moabite king Balak tries to vanquish the invaders via a means more powerful than force of arms: a sorcerer's curse. The first part of the story is memorable in its vivid characterization, use of theme words, and comic thrust. The central personalities have suggestive names: Balak sounds like a verb that means "to destroy," Bil'am suggests "swallower" (hence destroyer), and Be'or, present only as the name of the sorcerer's father, also connotes "destroying." The text uses two different words for "curse," soon to be joined by a third. The chapter introduces key themes of the story: "honor," which Bil'am will refuse in the overwhelming face of God's truth; "once again," through which it becomes clear that, for God, "once [refusal of permission for Bil'am to go] is once-and-for-all," and God's blessing, once given, will not be rescinded (Rosenzweig 1994); and the emphatic refrain that, as noted above, in one form or another will echo throughout the story, "whatever God tells me, that (alone) must I speak/do." Most memorable, of course, is the sequence about the talking donkey, which must have been more than a little amusing to ancient audiences. For here we have a dumb animal who sees divine messengers and possesses the divine gift of speech, contrasting with a prophet—who in Israelite thinking was supposed to be distinguished by his abilities as "seer" and mouthpiece of God—who sees nothing and raises his voice only to complain.

22:2   Now Balak son of Tzippor saw
>> all that Israel had done to the Amorites,

3   and Moav was in exceeding fear before the people, since they
>>>> were so many;
>> they felt dread before the Children of Israel.

4   Moav said to the elders of Midyan:
>> Look now, this assembly will lick up everything around us like an
>>>> ox licks up the green-things of the field!
>> Now Balak son of Tzippor was king of Moav at that time.

5   He sent messengers to Bil'am son of Be'or, to Petor, which is
>>>> beside the River (in) the land of the sons of his kinspeople,
>> to call him, saying:
>> Here, a people has come up out of Egypt,
>> here, it covers the aspect of the land,
>> it has settled hard upon me!

6   Now then, pray go, damn this people for me,
>> for it is too mighty (in number) for me!
>> Perhaps I will prevail: we will strike it, so that I drive it from the
>>>> land.
>> For I know
>> that whomever you bless is blessed,
>> whomever you damn is damned!

7   The elders of Moav and the elders of Midyan went,
>> tokens-of-augury in their hand,
>> they came to Bil'am and spoke Balak's words to him.

8   He said to them:
>> Spend the night here tonight,
>> then I will bring back to you whatever word YHWH speaks
>>>> to me.
>> The nobles of Moav stayed with Bil'am.

22:2   **Tzippor:** The name means "bird."

5   **the River:** The Euphrates. **sons of his kinspeople:** Some read *ammon*, "Ammon," for *ammo*, "his kinspeople." **covers the aspect of the land:** Like locusts; the phrase was used to describe the eighth plague in Ex. 10:5.

6   **too mighty (in number) :** Identical to Pharaoh's reaction to the Israelites in Ex. 1:9.

7   **tokens-of-augury:** Either payment for the cursing, or objects used in the act.

9 Now God came to Bil'am and said:
Who are these men with you?

10 Bil'am said to God:
Balak son of Tzippor, king of Moav, has sent to me:

11 Here, the people that came out of Egypt, it covers the aspect of
the land!
Now then, pray go, revile it for me,
perhaps I will be able to make war upon it and drive it away!

12 God said to Bil'am:
You are not to go with them,
you are not to damn the people,
for it is blessed!

13 Bil'am arose at daybreak and said to Balak's nobles:
Go to your land,
for Yhwh refuses to give-me-leave to go with you.

14 The nobles from Moav arose, they came to Balak and said:
Bil'am refuses to go with us!

15 So Balak once again sent nobles,
greater and more honored than those;

16 they came to Bil'am
and said to him:
Thus says Balak son of Tzippor:
Pray do not hold back from going to me;

17 indeed, I will honor, yes, honor you exceedingly—
anything that you say to me, I will do.
Only: pray go, revile for me this people!

18 Bil'am answered,
he said to the servants of Balak:
If Balak were to give me his house's fill of silver and gold
I would not be able to cross the order of Yhwh my God
to do (anything) small or great!

19 So now,
pray stay here, you as well, tonight,

---

18 **small or great:** A merism for "anything at all."

◆
that I may know
what YHWH will once again speak with me.
20 And God came to Bil'am at night,
he said to him:
Since it is to call you that the men have come,
arise, go with them;
but—only the word that I speak to you,
that (alone) may you do.
21 Bil'am arose at daybreak,
he saddled his she-ass,
and went with the nobles of Moav.
22 But YHWH's anger flared up because he was going,
so YHWH's messenger stationed himself in the way as an
adversary to him.
Now he was riding on his she-ass, his two serving-lads with him.
23 Now the she-ass saw YHWH's messenger
stationed in the way,
his sword drawn in his hand,
so the she-ass turned aside from the way and went into the field.
And Bil'am struck the she-ass
to turn her back onto the way.
24 But YHWH's messenger stood in the furrow (between) the
vineyards,
a fence here and a fence there.
25 Now the she-ass saw YHWH's messenger,
so she pressed herself against the wall,
pressing Bil'am's foot against the wall;
and once again he struck her.
26 But YHWH's messenger once again crossed over,
standing in a narrow place
where there was no pathway to turn, right or left.

---

22 **adversary:** Heb. *satan;* in later Jewish and Christian texts, of course, it was used as a proper name (and personality) "Satan."
23 **Now the she-ass saw YHWH's messenger:** The

motif of an animal who is able to see supernatural beings is widespread in world folklore (cf. Gaster 1969).
24 **here . . . there:** On either side.

27 Now the she-ass saw Y<small>HWH</small>'s messenger,
so she crouched down beneath Bil'am.
And Bil'am's anger flared up;
he struck the she-ass with his staff.

28 Then Y<small>HWH</small> opened the mouth of the she-ass
and she said to Bil'am:
What have I done to you
that you have struck me (on) these three occasions?

29 Bil'am said:
Because you have been capricious with me!
If a sword had been in my hand,
by now I would have killed you!

30 The she-ass said to Bil'am:
Am I not your she-ass
upon whom you have ridden from your past until this day?
Have I ever been accustomed, accustomed to do thus to you?
He said:
No.

31 Then Y<small>HWH</small> uncovered Bil'am's eyes
and he saw Y<small>HWH</small>'s messenger stationed in the way,
his sword drawn in his hand;
he bowed and prostrated himself, to his brow.

32 Y<small>HWH</small>'s messenger said to him:
For what (cause) did you strike your she-ass (on) these three
occasions?
Here, I came out as an adversary,
for the way was rushed out against me.

33 Now the she-ass saw me,
so she turned aside before me (on) these three occasions.
Had she not turned aside from me,
by now, (it is) you I would have killed;
but her I would have left-alive!

---

29 **been capricious with:** As God "was capricious with" Egypt in Ex. 10:2.
31 **brow:** Lit. "nostrils."

32 **rushed out:** Heb. unclear.
33 **by now:** Echoing Bil'am's words to the she-ass in v.29.

34 Bil'am said to Yhwh's messenger:
  I have sinned,
  for I did not know that you were stationed to meet me in the
      way.
  But now, if it is ill in your eyes,
  I will head back.
35 Yhwh's messenger said to Bil'am:
  Go with the men,
  but only the word that I speak to you,
  that (alone) may you speak.
  And so Bil'am went with Balak's nobles.
36 When Balak heard that Bil'am was coming,
  he went out to meet him,
  to Ir/Town of Moav that is by the Arnon border,
  that is at the far-edge of the border.
37 And Balak said to Bil'am:
  Did I not send, yes, send to you, to call you!
  Why did you not go to me?
  Am I truly not able to honor you?
38 Bil'am said to Balak:
  Here, I have come to you;
  but now,
  am I able, able to speak anything (myself)?
  The word that God puts in my mouth,
  that (alone) may I speak.
39 Now Bil'am went with Balak;
  they came to the village of Hutzot/Streets.
40 Balak slaughtered oxen and sheep,
  and sent them out to Bil'am and to the nobles that were with
      him.

36 **Ir:** Others, "Ar."

38 **able:** As if in reply to Balak's "not able" in the previous verse.

Bil'am's First Visions (23): Having been granted permission to hire himself out to Balak, but with the caveat that he may speak only God's word, Bil'am prepares to curse Israel. But his "encounters" with God leave not the slightest doubt of the outcome; curse is turned to blessing, despite all the correct ritual preparations and previous promises of payment for services rendered. One almost has the impression of a seance gone wrong. And, professionally speaking, hired prophets are supposed to tell kings what they want to hear.

The poetry in this chapter is powerful and striking. We move from the hopeful king's lofty "mountains of Kedem," whence Bil'am was hired, to the disturbing image of the king of beasts feasting on his prey. What began as an attack from above has ended in a blood-feast by the enemy.

41 Now it was at daybreak:
Balak took Bil'am and had him go up on the Heights of Baal,
so that he could see from there the edge of the people.

23:1 Bil'am said to Balak:
Build me here seven slaughter-sites,
and prepare for me here seven bulls and seven rams.

2 Balak did as Bil'am had spoken to him;
then Bil'am and Balak offered up a bull and a ram on (each)
slaughter-site.

3 Bil'am said to Balak:
Station yourself beside your offering-up, and I will go:
perhaps YHWH will encounter me in an encounter,
the word of whatever he lets me see, I will report to you.
So he went off by-himself.

4 Now God did encounter Bil'am,
he said to him:
The seven slaughter-sites I have arranged,
and I have offered-up a bull and a ram on (each) slaughter-site.

5 YHWH put words in Bil'am's mouth
and said:
Return to Balak, and thus shall you speak.

6 So he returned to him,
and here: he was standing alongside his offering-up,
he and all the nobles of Moav.

7 He took up his parable and said:

From Aram Balak led me,
Moav's king from the hills of Kedem:
Go, damn Yaakov for me,
go, execrate Israel!

---

41 **Heights of Baal:** Perhaps a shrine, and thus an appropriate location for pronouncing the curse. **see . . . the edge:** As Milgrom notes, the one who curses must be able to see his victim in order for the curse to work.

23:1 **seven:** The use of the perfect number means that the curse should be effective.

3 **perhaps . . . encounter:** Note the chance aspect of Bil'am's contact with God. **by-himself:** Heb. *shefi*, whose meaning is not clear; others, "to the height."

5 **words:** Lit. "a [divine] word."

8 How shall I revile (him)
whom God has not reviled,
how shall I execrate (him)
whom YHWH has not execrated?

9 Indeed, from the top of crags I see him:
from hills I behold him:
here, a people, alone-in-security it dwells,
among the nations it does not need to come-to-reckoning.

10 Who can measure the dust of Yaakov,
or (find a) number (for) the dust-clouds of Israel?
May I die the death of the upright,
may my future be like his!

11 Balak said to Bil'am:
What have you done to me?
To revile my foes I took you on,
and here, you have blessed, yes, blessed (them)!

12 He answered and said:
Is it not whatever YHWH puts in my mouth,
that (alone) I must take-care to speak?

13 Balak said to him:
Pray go with me to another place from where you can see them:
only their edge will you see,
all of them you will not see
—revile them for me from there!

14 So he took him to the Field of Watchmen, to the top of the
summit.
He built seven slaughter-sites
and offered-up a bull and a ram on (each) slaughter-site.

15 Then he said to Balak:
Stand here, alongside your offering-up;
as for me, I will seek-an-encounter there.

---

10 **dust-clouds:** Heb. difficult, possibly meaning
"(even) a fourth of."

13 **to another place:** Perhaps a different approach, literally, will be successful. Such change of venue also
occurs in the nonbiblical Deir 'Alla traditions about
Bil'am (Moore).

14 **Watchmen:** Gaster (1969), on the basis of Semitic
parallels, suggests that Heb. *tzofim* here means "as-
trological observers."

16 YHWH let himself be encountered by Bil'am
and put words in his mouth,
he said:
Return to Balak, and thus shall you speak.

17 He came to him:
here, he was standing alongside his offering-up,
the nobles of Moav with him.
Balak said to him:
What did YHWH speak?

18 He took up his parable and said:

Arise, Balak, and hearken,
turn-ear toward me, O son of Tzippor:

19 No man is God, that he should lie,
or a human being, that he should retract.
He, should he say and not do,
speak and not fulfill?

20 Here, to bless I was taken on,
when he blesses, I cannot reverse it.

21 He spies no evil in Yaakov,
he sees no trouble in Israel,
YHWH their God is with them,
fanfare for the king, among them!

22 The God who brought them out of Egypt
like the horns of the wild-ox for him.

23 For there is no divination in Yaakov,
and no augury in Israel;
at once it is said to Yaakov,
to Israel, what God intends.

24 Here, a people arises like a king-of-beasts,
like a lion it lifts itself up:

19 **retract:** Or "change his mind."
21 **fanfare:** A word used to describe the "trilling" of the marching trumpets in Chap. 10.
22 **the horns of the wild-ox:** Greenstein suggests a parallel with Baal's horned helmet in Ugaritic texts (personal communication).

23 **at once:** Buber (1988) understands this as "in time," that is, in the real world, not through magic. **what God intends:** The King James Version reads "what hath God wrought"—in that form, the first message Samuel F. B. Morse sent by his new invention, the telegraph, in 1844.

Bil'am the Prophet (24): Few moments in the Torah, to my thinking, can compare with what now happens in this story. The description of Bil'am's transformation in the opening verses is matched and even surpassed by what happens to the poetry of this section. From v.3 on, we are treated to an elevation and intensification of poetic language, beginning with the rhythmic opening lines and continuing through the pregnant Middle Eastern imagery of trees and water.

With the suggestion of the blessing given to Avraham in v.9, and with Bil'am's vision of the future political triumphs of Israel vis-à-vis the surrounding nations, all that Balak can do is to "go on his way" (v.25). The king who is used to paying for what he wants, and to having enemies cursed, has no recourse left to him.

it does not lie down till it eats (its) prey,
and the blood of the slain it drinks.

25 Balak said to Bil'am:
If you just cannot revile, revile them,
just do not bless, bless them!

26 Bil'am spoke up and said to Balak:
Did I not speak to you (before), saying:
All that God speaks—
that (alone) may I do?!

27 Balak said to Bil'am:
Pray go, I will take you to another place;
perhaps it will be right in God's eyes that you will revile them for
me from there.

28 So Balak took Bil'am to the top of Pe'or that overlooks the
wasteland.

29 Bil'am said to Balak:
Build me here seven slaughter-sites
and prepare for me here seven bulls and seven rams.

30 So Balak did as Bil'am had said;
and he offered-up a bull and a ram on (each) slaughter-site.

24:1 Now Bil'am saw
that it was good in the eyes of YHWH to bless Israel,
and so he did not go forth as time and time (before) to encounter
divination-meetings;
but he set his face toward the wilderness.

2 And Bil'am lifted up his eyes
and saw Israel, dwelling by their tribes,
and there came upon him the spirit of God.

3 He took up his parable and said:

Utters Bil'am the son of Be'or,
utters the man of the open eye,

24:1 **saw:** Finally, he "sees" clearly and knows that he cannot expect to curse the people. Cf. also vv.2–4 for the theme of seeing.

2 **by their tribes:** That is, the entire camp. **spirit of God:** Thus we know that what follows is truly from God.

4   utters the hearer of Godly sayings
        who envisages a vision of Shaddai,
        bowed, but with eyes uncovered:

5   How goodly are your tents, O Yaakov,
        your dwellings, O Israel,

6   like groves stretched out,
        like gardens beside a river,
        like aloes planted by YHWH,
        like cedars beside the water;

7   dripping water from their boughs,
        their seed in many waters!
        Their king will rise above Agag,
        their kingdom be exalted.

8   The God who brought them out of Egypt
        like the horns of the wild-ox for him!
        They will consume enemy nations,
        their bones they will crush;
        their arrows they will smash!

9   They crouch, they lie down like a lion,
        like the king-of-beasts—who will (dare) rouse him?
        Those who bless you—-blessed,
        those who damn you—damned!

10 Balak's anger flared up at Bil'am,
he smacked his hands (together).
Balak said to Bil'am:
To revile my enemies I had you called,
and here: you have blessed, yes, blessed them,
these three times!

---

4 **Shaddai:** A name for God (or gods) found mainly in Genesis and Job. **bowed:** With the sense of "prostrate, humbled."

7 **Agag:** The later Amalekite king and archenemy of Israel (I Sam. 15:8).

9 **bless . . . blessed . . . damn . . . damned:** Bil'am ends his inspired speech with a blessing close to God's opening one to Avraham in Gen. 12:3.

10 **smacked his hands (together):** A gesture of contempt or mocking in the Bible.

11   So now, hasten back to your (own) place!
      I had said: I will honor, yes, honor you;
      but here: YHWH has denied you honor!

12   Bil'am said to Balak:
      Didn't I speak also to the messengers that you sent to me, saying:

13   If Balak were to give me his house's fill of silver and gold,
      I would not be able to cross the order of YHWH,
      to do good or ill from my (own) heart?
      What YHWH speaks,
      that (alone) may I speak!

14   So now,
      here, I am going (back) to my people;
      come, I will advise you
      as to what this people will do to your people in future days.

15   So he took up his parable and said:

           Utters Bil'am the son of Be'or,
           utters the man of open eye,

16   utters the hearer of Godly sayings,
           who knows the knowledge of the Most-High,
           envisaging a vision of Shaddai,
           bowed, but with eyes uncovered:

17   I see it, but not now,
           I behold it, but not soon:
           There goes forth a star from Yaakov,
           there arises a meteor from Israel,
           it smashes the pate of Moav,
           the crown of all the Children of Shet.

---

11   **honor:** Balak is referring to the bestowing of wealth.
13   **heart:** Or, in more modern parlance, "mind."
16   **the Most-High:** Another name for God, found in Gen. 14:18–20.
17   **star . . . meteor:** The verse is difficult. It could also be rendered "There marches forth an army . . . there arises a tribe," which likewise makes sense in the context. Rabbinic interpreters took the verse messianically; Rabbi Akiva understood "star," *kokhav,* as a reference to his contemporary Simon Bar Kosiba, the leader of a major Jewish rebellion against Rome (132 C.E.), renaming him Bar Kokhba, "Son of a Star." **pate . . . crown:** "Crown" (reading *kodkod* for *karkar*) in the sense of "head." An alternate translation is "borderland . . . land."

Final Rebellion: Apostasy (25): A tale ostensibly meant to establish the permanent status of the Aaronide priesthood, this chapter has another important structural function. As the last section of Part II (at least as I have laid out the book's structure), it prevents the wilderness traditions from ending on an up note. The Bil'am cycle with its exalted poetry would have made a positive conclusion, but the editor does not wish us to forget the basic facts of Israel's wilderness experience: dissatisfaction, complaint, and rebellion. Here we end with the ultimate rebellion, the moment of serious unfaithfulness in the "marriage" between God and Israel.

Like his grandfather Aharon in Chap. 17, Pin'has is able to stay the plague from God, albeit not through peaceful means. His action here recalls the killing spree of the Levites at the Golden Calf incident, another major apostasy (Wenham). The text goes out of its way to name also specific offenders; the Moabite woman who is remembered for evil is, in fact, the daughter of a chieftain.

The horrifying details of Pin'has's act remind the reader once again that, for the biblical writers, idolatry was the worst of all crimes. The books to follow, starting with Deuteronomy, will make this abundantly clear.

18   Edom becomes a possession,
      a possession becomes Se'ir of its enemies,
      but Israel does valiantly.

19   There rules (one) from Yaakov,
      destroying the remnant of Ir.

20 He saw Amalek,
    and he took up his parable and said:

         Premier of nations, Amalek,
         but its future: near to oblivion!

21 He saw the Kenites,
    and he took up his parable, and said:

         Secure (is) your settlement,
         set in the clefts (is) your nest,
22   but ablaze will be Kayin,
         when Ashur takes-you-captive.

23 And he took up his parable and said:

         Alas, who can remain-alive whom God has condemned!
24   Ships (come) from Kittite shore,
         they afflict Ashur, they afflict Ever,
         but they too: near to oblivion!

25 Then Bil'am arose and went, returning to his place;
    and also Balak went on his way.

25:1 Israel stayed in Shittim / Acacias,
      and the people began to whore with the women of Moav.
  2   They called the people for slaughter-offerings to their gods;
      the people ate

---

21 **nest:** Heb. *ken* (here *kinnekha,* "your nest"), a play on Kenites.
22 **Kayin:** Trad. "Cain." **Ashur:** The usual term for Assyria; some believe it refers to another group.

23 **Alas** etc.: A difficult verse.
25:1 **to whore:** The common biblical term not only for sexual immorality but for idolatry as well.

♦

and prostrated themselves to their gods.

3 Now Israel yoked themselves to the Baal of Pe'or,
so the anger of YHWH flared up against Israel;

4 YHWH said to Moshe:
Take all the heads of the people and impale them to YHWH,
facing the sun,
so that the flaming anger of YHWH may turn from Israel.

5 Moshe said to the officials of Israel:
Let each-man kill (those of) his men who yoked themselves to
the Baal of Pe'or!

6 Now here, a man of the Children of Israel had come
and had brought-near to his brothers a (certain) Midyanitess,
before the eyes of Moshe and before the eyes of the entire
community of the Children of Israel
while they were (all) weeping at the entrance to the Tent of
Appointment.

7 When Pin'has son of El'azar son of Aharon the priest saw (it),
he arose from the midst of the community,
taking a spear in his hand;

8 he came after the man of Israel into the private-chamber,
and he thrust through the two of them,
the man of Israel and the woman, in her private-parts,
and the plague was held-back from the Children of Israel.

9 Now those that died of the plague were four and twenty
thousand.

10 Now YHWH spoke to Moshe, saying:

11 Pin'has son of El'azar son of Aharon the priest
has turned my venomous-anger from the Children of Israel
in his being-zealous with my jealousy in their midst,

---

3 **yoked:** A strong image of attachment, in a story of strong images. **Baal:** A major Canaanite god (of thunder and fertility) the worship of whom was considered the greatest danger to the Israelite people by the Prophets (cf. the clash between Elijah and the prophets of Baal in I Kings 17f.).

6 **brought-near:** The reason is not specified; but he certainly is not hiding his deed. **before the eyes:** In broad daylight, as it were.

7 **Pin'has:** Trad. English "Phineas," a name of Egyptian origin, like Moshe and Aharon.

8 **private-chamber ... private-parts:** Suggested by Plaut; Heb. *el ha-kubba ... el kovota*. Later Jewish tradition was disturbed by the vigilante nature of Pin'has's action.

so that I did not finish off the Children of Israel in my jealousy.

12 Therefore say:
Here, I give him my covenant of *shalom;*

13 it shall be for him and for his seed after him
a covenant of everlasting priesthood—
because that he was zealous for his God
and effected-appeasement for the Children of Israel.

14 Now the name of the man of Israel, the one struck-dead,
the one struck-dead with the Midyanitess (was):
Zimri son of Salu,
leader of a Fathers' House of the Shim'onites.

15 And the name of the woman who was struck-dead, the
Midyanitess:
Kozbi daughter of Tzur;
tribal head of the Fathers' House of Midyan is he.

16 Now YHWH spoke to Moshe, saying:

17 Attack the Midyanites and strike them,

18 for they attacked you with their craftiness, with which they were
crafty with you in the matter of Pe'or,
in the matter of Kozbi daughter of the leader of Midyan, their
sister,
the one struck-dead at the time of the plague in the matter of
Pe'or.

---

12 *shalom:* Or "peace," "friendship."
15 **Kozbi:** Connoting "deceiver."
17 **Attack the Midyanites:** This will be resumed and
carried out in Chap. 31, after the intervention of a
good deal of legal material.

PART III

THE PREPARATIONS
FOR CONQUEST

(26–36)

THE LAST PART OF NUMBERS IS WHAT THE READER MIGHT HAVE EXPECTED ALL ALONG:
a collection of materials that deal directly with the upcoming conquest of Canaan. It is concerned, then, with the transfer of leadership from Moshe to
Yehoshua (Joshua); with provisions for two and a half tribes to remain on the east
bank of the Jordan River, as long as they take part in the impending invasion; with
listing the entire route of the Israelites, from Egypt to the plains of Moab; and
with the borders of the land to be conquered.

As has been the case earlier in the book, however, other material intervenes: a
theme and variation doublet on the inheritance of land in a case where a man
leaves daughters, not sons; two chapters on what sacrifices are to be brought on
holy days; a section on vows taken by women; war with Midyan and the precise
apportioning of spoils, both to warriors and to the sanctuary; and the law regarding accidental homicide, in which family vengeance is circumvented by the existence of "safe" Levite towns to which the manslayer may flee.

The inconsistent thematics may again be explained by the intrusion of an editorial hand, again by priestly interests. In Levine's view, most of Chapters 25–36
function to establish matters of importance in the priestly view, just as in
Chapters 1–10. Here law takes precedence over narrative.

Despite the varied subject matter of this section, it holds together structurally,
via the common biblical technique of word (sound) repetition. The rather common verb *tzivvah*, "command," weaves through every one of Chapters 26–36, except for 33. Sometimes it introduces what God wants the Israelites to do;
sometimes it leads to the formula of fulfillment, "as YHWH commanded the
Children of Israel, so they did"; still other times it refers to a command given by
Moshe himself. The entire section begins with the verb (26:4), and ends with it as
well (36:13). In addition, the chapters most far afield, 28–29 (taken as a unit) and 30,
begin and end with it. Whether this was a conscious technique by redactors is
hard to say, but its existence is striking.

Another structural device, that of framing, also occurs in this part of the book:
after the introductory census (Chap. 26), the rest is built between two brackets,
each involving the daughters of Tzelofhad, and each opening with the verb "to

come-near" (27:1 and 36:1). So despite the wide-ranging material, some sense of unity has been imposed upon it.

Finally, there is the key occurrence, for the book of Numbers, of more lists, from census to holiday sacrifices, from stops along the journey to the precise borders of the Promised Land. We are in the presence of order once again.

What remains lacking at the end of the book is exactly what Deuteronomy supplies: a final exhortation from Moshe, which includes reiteration and further clarification of the laws, a public covenant ceremony, Moshe's long blessing of the people, and the account of his death and burial. If added here, these topics might have tipped the scales of Numbers, which has given us almost too much to digest as it is; as the Torah has come down to us, they are more appropriately treated in the expansive and majestic rhetorical setting of Deuteronomy.

New Census (26): Out of the chaos of the wilderness, the element of order is reintroduced as we meet the new generation—which will conquer at least part of the land of Canaan. These children of slaves are now mustered, in the same tribal order as the census in Chap. 1. The purpose of the counting is set forth in vv.52–56: so that the Promised Land may be properly divided up, according to population. True to the scheme of Chap. 1, the Levites go through their own census (vv.57–62)—since they receive designated towns but not a large mass of land. The ending verses assure us that the census in this chapter does not include anyone of the Exodus generation, excluding Calev and Yehoshua. Thus we are on new ground.

◆ 26:1   Now it was after the plague

     2   that YHWH said to Moshe and to El'azar son of Aharon the priest, saying:

       Take up the head-count of the entire community of the Children of Israel,

       from the age of twenty years and upward, according to their Fathers' House,

       everyone going out to the armed-forces in Israel.

     3   Moshe spoke, and El'azar the priest, to them in the Plains of Moav,

       by Jordan-Jericho, saying:

     4   From the age of twenty years and upward . . . !

       as YHWH commanded Moshe and the Children of Israel,

       those going out of the land of Egypt:

     5   Re'uven, the firstborn of Israel:

       The Sons of Re'uven: (of) Hanokh, the Hanokhite clan,

       of Pallu, the Pallite clan,

     6   of Hetzron, the Hetzronite clan,

       of Karmi, the Karmite clan.

     7   These are the Re'uvenite clans;

       and their count was: three and forty thousand, and seven hundred and thirty.

     8   The sons of Pallu: Eliav;

     9   the sons of Eliav: Nemuel, Datan and Aviram

       —that is the Datan and Aviram, those Called by the Community,

       who struggled against Moshe and against Aharon, among the community of Korah

       when they struggled against YHWH

    10   and the earth opened its mouth and swallowed them and Korah,

       at the death of the community,

       at the consuming by fire of the fifty and two hundred men:

       they became a signal-of-warning;

26:3 **spoke:** Or "gave instructions" (JPS, following Ehrlich).

9 **struggled:** A rather physical verb, especially as applied to God on the next line!

◆ 11 but the sons of Korah did not die.

12 The Sons of Shim'on according to their clans:
of Nemuel, the Nemuelite clan,
of Yamin, the Yaminite clan,
of Yakhin, the Yakhinite clan,

13 of Zerah, the Zarhite clan,
of Sha'ul, the Sha'ulite clan.

14 These are the Shim'onite clans,
two and twenty thousand, and two hundred.

15 The Sons of Gad according to their clans:
of Tzefon, the Tzefonite clan,
of Haggi, the Haggite clan,
of Shuni, the Shunite clan,

16 of Ozni, the Oznite clan,
of Eri, the Erite clan,

17 of Arod, the Arodite clan.
of Areli, the Arelite clan.

18 These are the clans of the Sons of Gad by their accountings:
forty thousand and five hundred.

19 The sons of Yehuda: Er and Onan;
but Er and Onan died in the land of Canaan.

20 Now the Sons of Yehuda, according to their clans, were:
of Shela, the Shelanite clans,
of Peretz, the Partzite clan,
of Zerah, the Zarhite clan.

21 The Sons of Peretz:
of Hetzron, the Hetzronite clan,
of Hamul, the Hamulite clan.

22 These are the clans of Yehuda, by their accountings:
six and seventy thousand, and five hundred.

---

11 **the sons of Korah did not die:** This despite the statement in 16:32 that the earth swallowed up Korah "and all his household." The "Sons of Korah" were later renowned for their prowess as Temple singers, and fully eleven Psalms bear a superscription with their name.

17 **Arod:** Ancient versions, following Gen. 46:16, read "Arodi."

19 **Er and Onan died:** Because they did not carry on their late brother's line by fathering a son with his widow; cf. Gen. 38:6–10.

23 The Sons of Yissakhar, according to their clans:
   Tola, the Tolaite clan,
   of Puvva, the Punite clan,
24 of Yashuv, the Yashuvite clan,
   of Shimron, the Shimronite clan.
25 These are the clans of Yissakhar, by their accountings:
   four and sixty thousand, and three hundred.

26 The Sons of Zevulun, according to their clans:
   of Sered, the Sardite clan,
   of Elon, the Elonite clan,
   of Yahle'el, the Yahle'elite clan.
27 These are the clans of the Zevulunites, by their accountings:
   sixty thousand and five hundred.

28 The Sons of Yosef, according to their clans:
   Menashe and Efrayim.
29 The Sons of Menashe:
   of Makhir, the Makhirite clan,
   —now Makhir begot Gil'ad—
   of Gil'ad, the Gil'adite clan.

30 These are the Sons of Gil'ad:
   of I'ezer, the I'ezrite clan, of Helek, the Helkite clan,
31 of Asriel, the Asrielite clan,
   of Shekhem, the Shikhmite clan,
32 of Shemida, the Shemida'ite clan,
   of Hefer, the Hefrite clan;
33 now Tzelofhad son of Hefer had no sons,
   only daughters;
   the name of the daughters of Tzelofhad: Mahla and No'a, Hogla,
      Milka and Tirtza.
34 These are the clans of Menashe,
   and their accountings: two and fifty thousand, and seven
      hundred.

35 These are the Sons of Efrayim, according to their clans:
   of Shutelah, the Shutalhite clan,
   of Bekher, the Bakhrite clan,
   of Tahan, the Tahanite clan.

◆ 36 These are the Sons of Shutelah:
of Eiran the Eiranite clan.

37 These are the clans of the Sons of Efrayim, according to their
accountings:
two and thirty thousand, and five hundred;
these are the Sons of Yosef according to their clans.

38 The Sons of Binyamin, according to their clans:
of Bela, the Bal'ite clan,
of Ashbel, the Ashbelite clan,
of Ahiram, the Ahiramite clan,

39 of Shefufam, the Shufamite clan,
of Hufam, the Hufamite clan.

40 The Sons of Bela were: Ard and Naaman.
. . . , the Ardite clan,
of Naaman, the Naamite clan.

41 These are the Sons of Binyamin according to their clans,
their accountings: five and forty thousand, and six hundred.

42 These are the Sons of Dan according to their clans:
of Shuham, the Shuhamite clan.
These are the clans of Dan, according to their clans;

43 all the Shuhamite clans, according to their accountings:
four and sixty thousand, and four hundred.

44 The Sons of Asher, according to their clans:
of Yimna, the Yimna clan,
of Yishvi, the Yishvite clan,
of Beri'a, the Beri'ite clan.

45 For the Sons of Beri'a:
of Hever, the Hevrite clan,
of Malkiel, the Malkielite clan.

46 Now the name of Asher's daughter (was) Serah.

47 These are the clans of the Sons of Asher, according to their
accountings:
three and fifty thousand, and four hundred.

48 The Sons of Naftali, according to their clans:
of Yahtze'el, the Yahtze'elite clan,
of Guni, the Gunite clan,

49 of Yetzer, the Yitzrite clan,
of Shillem, the Shillemite clan.

50 These are the clans of Naftali, according to their clans,
their accountings: five and forty thousand, and four hundred.

51 These are the accountings of the Children of Israel:
six hundred thousand and a thousand, seven hundred and thirty.

52 And Yhwh spoke to Moshe, saying:

53 To these shall the land be portioned-out as an inheritance, by the
enumerated names;

54 to the many you are to give-much as their inheritance,
to the few you are to give-little as their inheritance,
each-one according to its count is to be given its inheritance.

55 However, by lot the land is to be apportioned,
by the listed-names of their ancestral tribes they are to inherit (it).

56 By means of the lot is its inheritance to be apportioned,
between the many and the few.

57 And these are the accountings of the Levites, according to their
clans:
of Gershon, the Gershonite clan,
of Kehat, the Kehatite clan,
of Merari, the Merarite clan.

58 These are the clans of Levi:
the Livnite clan, the Hevronite clan, the Mahlite clan, the
Mushite clan, the Korhite clan.
Now Kehat begot Amram;

59 the name of Amram's wife was Yokheved daughter of Levi,
who bore her to Levi in Egypt;
she bore to Amram: Aharon and Moshe,
and Miryam their sister.

60 There were born to Aharon: Nadav and Avihu, El'azar and
Itamar.

---

54 **many . . . give-much . . . few . . . give-little:** That is,
apportioned by population.

55 **However, by lot:** To determine each holding's location (Milgrom, following Abravanel).

59 **who bore her:** The Hebrew is awkward, because
the mother's name apparently has been omitted.

A Case of Inheritance: Daughters of Tzelofhad I; The Passing of Leadership (27): If the land is to be apportioned by tribe, the question of inheritance becomes a major one for the future. In that vein, the text, in almost Talmudic fashion, brings a case with some difficulties: What if a father dies without sons but does leave daughters—may they inherit the ancestral land, given the context of a patriarchal society? Moshe is unable to solve the problem, but must leave it up to God, who rules that not only daughters but other relations as well may serve to keep the land in the family (an attendant question, how to keep land within a tribe's territory, will be answered in Chap. 36). This section of the chapter is a good example of a law embedded in a narrative, or a narrative created for the sake of a law. It also has the effect of showing that the divine promise of land is about to be fulfilled, that all tribes must be included in the process, and that the growing biblical tradition allows for reinterpretation (Olson).

From v.12 on, we are reminded that Moshe is about to die. In an expansive speech (vv.18–21), God designates Yehoshua as Moshe's successor, and publicly the aging leader transfers authority to him. Given the structure of Part III of the book, which is bracketed by daughters of Tzelofhad sections, we might expect Moshe's death to parallel the passage here, and thus come at the end of Chap. 36. But that will not be the case; his death is left for the end of the entire Torah, in Deuteronomy.

◆ 61 Now Nadav and Avihu had died
when they brought-near outside fire before the presence of
YHWH.

62 And their accounting was: three and twenty thousand,
all males from the age of a month and upward,
for they had not been counted in the midst of the Children of
Israel,
for they were not given an inheritance in the midst of the
Children of Israel.

63 These are those-counted by Moshe and El'azar the priest
that they counted (of) the Children of Israel
in the Plains of Moav, by Jordan-Jericho.

64 Among these there was not a man of those counted by Moshe
and Aharon the priest
when they counted the Children of Israel in the Wilderness of
Sinai.

65 For YHWH had said to them:
They are to die, yes, die in the wilderness,
there will not be-left of them a man
except for Calev son of Yefunne and Yehoshua son of Nun.

27:1 Now there came-near the daughters of Tzelofhad
son of Hefer son of Gil'ad son of Makhir son of Menashe,
of the clan of Menashe son of Yosef,
and these are the names of his daughters:
Mahla, No'a, Hogla, Milka and Tirtza.

2 They stood before Moshe and before El'azar the priest
and before the leaders and the entire community,
at the entrance to the Tent of Appointment, saying:

3 Our father died in the wilderness.
He was not in the midst of the community that came-together
against YHWH, in the community of Korah;
rather, for his own sin he died,
and sons he did not have.

27:1 **came-near:** Here with the connotation of "came before the authorities." **Mahla** etc.: Several of these names are the names of known towns.

3 **for his own sin:** As distinct from the sin of taking part in the Korah rebellion.

4 Why should the name of our father be taken-away from the
        midst of his clan,
    (just) because he has no son?
    Give us a holding in the midst of our father's brothers!
5 Moshe brought-near their case, before the presence of YHWH.
6 And YHWH said to Moshe, saying:
7 Rightfully speak the daughters of Tzelofhad!
    You are to give, yes, give them a hereditary holding in the midst
        of their father's brothers,
    you are to transfer the inheritance of their father to them.
8 And to the Children of Israel you are to speak, saying:
    Any-man, when he dies and a son he does not have,
    you are to transfer his inheritance to his daughter.
9 And if he has no daughter,
    you are to give his inheritance to his brothers.
10 And if he has no brothers,
    you are to give his inheritance to his father's brothers.
11 And if no brothers has his father,
    you are to give his inheritance to his kin that is nearest to him
        from his clan,
    and he is to take-possession of it;
    it shall be for the Children of Israel as a law of procedure,
    as YHWH commanded Moshe.

12 YHWH said to Moshe:
    Go up these Mountains of Avarim/The-Region-Across
    and see the land that I am giving to the Children of Israel.
13 When you have seen it,
    you will be gathered to your kinspeople, even you,
    as Aharon your brother was gathered;
14 since you rebelled against my order in the Wilderness of Tzyn
    —when the community quarreled—
    to treat-me-as-holy through water before their eyes;

---

4 **holding:** An ancestral plot of land.

12 **Avarim/The-Region-Across:** The mountains beyond the Jordan to the east.

they are the waters of Merivat Kadesh/Quarreling at Kadesh, in
the Wilderness of Tzyn.

15 Then Moshe spoke to YHWH, saying:
16 Let YHWH, the God of the spirits of all flesh, designate a man
over the community
17 who will go out before them, who will come back before them,
who will lead them out, who will bring them back;
so that the community of YHWH will not be like a flock that has
no shepherd.
18 YHWH said to Moshe:
Take yourself Yehoshua son of Nun,
a man in whom the spirit is,
and lean your hand upon him.
19 You are to have him stand before El'azar the priest and before the
entire community,
and you are to commision him before their eyes.
20 You are to put of your majesty upon him,
in order that they may hearken, the entire community of the
Children of Israel.
21 Before El'azar the priest he is to stand,
he will seek judgment for him of the *Urim*, before the presence of
YHWH,
by his order he will go out and by his order he will come back,
he and all the Children of Israel with him, and the entire
community.
22 Moshe did as YHWH had commanded him;
he took Yehoshua
and had him stand before El'azar the priest, and before the entire
community.

---

15 **Then Moshe spoke to YHWH, saying:** A reversal of
the usual formula in which, typically, God commands Moshe to proclaim a new law.
17 **go out . . . come back:** These verbs are often used
to indicate military leadership. **shepherd:** A central
ancient Near Eastern metaphor for leadership, alternatively applied to Moshe, David, and later to
Jesus.

19 **commission:** The same verb normally rendered
"command."
20 **majesty:** JPS "authority." **hearken:** That is, obey.
21 *Urim:* Some kind of oracular object (usually called
Urim and *Tummim*) used to predict the future. It sits
in the *efod* worn by the High Priest (cf. Ex. 28:30).

Festival Offerings (28–29): With Chaps. 28–30 we return to a recurring phenomenon in the book of Numbers: the intrusion of priestly material. We would expect
28 and 29, which form a logical unit and enumerate the sacrifices brought on holy
days, to be properly placed in Leviticus. In fact, Lev. 23 does set out a sacred calendar. The purpose of that passage, however, was to indicate the overlay of the
holy on the cycle of the year; the material here neither creates the calendar itself
nor has anything to do with either voluntary offerings or those brought for expiation of sin. It may have been inserted at this point, in this book, because in its
drawn-out, formulaic rhetoric, it has the character of a list such as we often find
in Numbers. Part III of the book is a logical setting for it, given that it concentrates on the "pilgrimage-festivals" that fit a settled, agricultural context, and
these chapters deal with various issues arising from Israel's immanent possession
of the land.

Interesting is the addition of the New Moon festival (vv.11ff.), not mentioned
in Lev. 23. It was apparently a serious holy day, although the Bible does not forbid
work on it. The New Moon fits in the general layout of the chapter, which is, first,
according to frequency of sacrifice and then to calendar (Milgrom).

23 He leaned his hands upon him and commisioned him
as Yhwh had spoken by the hand of Moshe.

28:1 Yhwh spoke to Moshe, saying:
2 Command the Children of Israel and say to them:
Of my near-offering, my food, as my fire-offerings, my soothing
savor,
you are to be-in-charge,
bringing-it-near to me at its appointed-time.
3 And you are to say to them:
This is the fire-offering that you are to bring-near to Yhwh:
lambs a year in age, wholly-sound,
two per day,
(as) a regular offering-up.
4 The one lamb you are to sacrifice in the morning,
and the second lamb you are to sacrifice between the setting-
times;
5 and a tenth of an *efa* of flour, as a grain-gift,
mixed with oil, crushed, a fourth of a *hin*
6 —the regular offering-up
sacrificed at Mount Sinai—
as a soothing savor, a fire-offering for Yhwh.
7 And its poured-offering (is): a fourth of a *hin* for the first lamb;
in the Holy-Shrine you are to pour-it-out as a poured-offering of
intoxicant for Yhwh.
8 And the second lamb you are to sacrifice between the setting-
times;
like the morning grain-gift and like its poured-offering you are to
sacrifice it,
a fire-offering of soothing savor for Yhwh.

9 And on the day of the Sabbath:
two lambs, a year in age, wholly-sound,

28:3 **fire-offering:** Probably the plural is meant here.
9 **And on the day of the Sabbath:** This and the following passages became part of the traditional Jewish liturgy (in the *Musaf,* "Additional" Service) for
Sabbath and festivals.

and two tenth-measures of flour, for a grain-gift,
mixed with oil, and its poured-offering,

10 the Sabbath offering-up on its Sabbath,
as well as the regular offering-up, and its poured-offering.

11 And on the heads of your New-Moons,
you are to bring-near an offering-up to YHWH:
Two bulls, young of the herd, one ram,
lambs a year in age—seven, wholly-sound,

12 and three tenth-measures of flour as a grain-gift, mixed with oil,
for (each) one bull,
and two tenth-measures of flour as a grain-gift, mixed with oil,
for (each) one ram,

13 a tenth, a tenth (each) of flour, as a grain-gift, mixed with oil, for
(each) one lamb,
(as) an offering-up, a soothing savor, fire-offering for YHWH,

14 with their poured-offerings:
half a *hin* shall be for the bull and a third of a *hin* for the ram, and
a fourth of a *hin* for the lamb,
of wine.
That is the new-monthly offering-up on its New-Moon
for the New-Moons of the year.

15 And one hairy goat as a *hattat*-offering for YHWH
as well as the regular offering-up is to be sacrificed,
and its poured-offering.

16 In the first New-Moon, on the fourteenth day after the New-
Moon
is Passover to YHWH.

17 And on the fifteenth day after this New-Moon: a pilgrimage-
celebration!
For seven days, *matzot* are to be eaten:

---

10 **its Sabbath:** Probably meaning "its particular Sabbath."

11 **heads of your New-Moons:** Milgrom notes that

the number of animals sacrificed here equals that
for major festivals, indicating the biblical importance of the New Moon.

18 on the first day, a proclamation of holiness;
any-kind of servile work is not to be done.

19 You are to bring-near a fire-offering, as an offering-up for Yhwh:
bulls, young of the herd—two, and one ram,
and seven lambs a year in age,
wholly-sound are they to be for you;

20 and their grain-gift—
flour mixed with oil:
three tenth-measures for the bull and two tenth-measures for the
ram, you are to sacrifice.

21 A tenth, a tenth-measure you are to sacrifice
for (each) one lamb, for the seven lambs;

22 and one goat as a *hattat*-offering to effect-purgation for you,

23 aside from the morning offering-up that belongs to the regular
offering-up;
you are to sacrifice these.

24 Like these you are to sacrifice per day, for the seven days,
as food, a fire-offering of soothing savor for Yhwh,
along with the regular offering-up you are to sacrifice it and its
poured-offering.

25 Now on the seventh day,
a proclamation of holiness there is to be for you,
any-kind of servile work you are not to do!

26 And on the Day of the Firstfruits,
at your bringing-near a new grain-gift for Yhwh on your Feast-of-
Weeks,
a proclamation of holiness there is to be for you,
any-kind of servile work you are not to do!

27 You are to bring-near an offering-up, as a soothing savor for
Yhwh:
bulls, young of the herd—two, one ram,
seven lambs a year in age,

---

18 **a proclamation of holiness:** Others, "a holy convocation." **servile work:** Heavy labor. Later Jewish
tradition understood this to mean that certain
"work," like cooking, is in fact permitted.

28 and their grain-gift, flour mixed with oil:
   three tenth-measures for (each) one bull,
   two tenth-measures for (each) one ram,

29 a tenth, a tenth-measure for (each) one lamb,
   for the seven lambs;

30 one hairy goat to effect-purgation for you,

31 aside from the regular offering-up and its grain-gift you are to
      sacrifice;
   wholly-sound are they to be for you, with their poured-offerings.

29:1 And in the seventh New-Moon, on (day) one of the New-Moon,
   a proclamation of holiness there is to be for you,
   any-kind of servile work you are not to do.
   A day of (horn-)blasts it is to be for you.

2 You are to sacrifice an offering-up, as a soothing savor for YHWH:
   one bull, a young of the herd, one ram,
   lambs a year in age seven, wholly-sound,

3 and their grain-gift, flour mixed with oil:
   three tenth-measures per bull,
   two tenth-measures per ram,

4 one tenth-measure per (each) one lamb,
   for the seven lambs,

5 and one hairy goat for a *hattat*-offering, to effect-purgation for
      you,

6 aside from the New-Moon offering-up and its grain-gift,
   and the regular offering-up and its grain-gift
   and their poured-offerings, according to their regulation,
   as a soothing savor, fire-offering for YHWH.

7 And on the tenth after this seventh New-Moon,
   a proclamation of holiness there is to be for you,
   you are to afflict your selves,
   any-kind of work you are not to do!

29:1 **a day of (horn-)blasts:** Observed by Jews as Rosh Ha-Shanah, the "Head of the Year" (New Year) in the fall, and accompanied in synagogue by blasts on the *shofar*.

7 **afflict:** Or "oppress"; fasting is understood. **selves:** Heb. *nefesh* can occasionally also be understood as "throat" (cf. 11:6). **any-kind of work:** Not just heavy labor is prohibited.

8 You are to bring-near an offering-up for YHWH, as a soothing
   savor:
   one bull, a young of the herd, one ram,
   lambs a year in age seven,
   wholly-sound shall they be for you;
9 and their grain-gift, flour mixed with oil:
   three tenth-measures per bull,
   two tenth-measures per (each) one ram,
10 a tenth, a tenth-measure per (each) one lamb,
   for the seven lambs,
11 one hairy goat for a *hattat*-offering, aside from the *Hattat*-
   offering of Atonement,
   and the regular offering-up, its grain-gift, and their poured-
   offerings.

12 And on the fifteenth day after the seventh New-Moon,
   a proclamation of holiness there is to be for you,
   any-kind of servile work you are not to do!
   You are to celebrate-a-pilgrimage, a pilgrimage-festival to YHWH,
   for seven days.
13 You are to bring-near an offering-up, a fire-offering, soothing
   savor for YHWH:
   bulls, young of the herd thirteen, rams two,
   lambs a year in age fourteen;
   wholly-sound are they to be.
14 And their grain-gift, flour mixed with oil:
   three tenth-measures for (each) one bull of the thirteen bulls,
   two tenth-measures for (each) one ram of the two rams,
15 a tenth, a tenth-measure for (each) one lamb, for the fourteen
   lambs,
16 and one hairy goat as a *hattat*-offering,
   aside from the regular offering-up, its grain-gift, and its poured-
   offerings.

◆ 17 Now on the second day:
bulls, young of the herd twelve, rams two,
lambs a year in age fourteen, wholly-sound,
18 and their grain-gift as well as their poured-offerings
for the bulls, for the rams and for the lambs,
by their number, according to the regulation;
19 and one hairy goat as a *hattat*-offering,
aside from the regular offering-up, its grain-gift, and their poured-
offerings.

20 Now on the third day:
bulls eleven, rams two,
lambs a year in age fourteen, wholly-sound,
21 and their grain-gift as well as their poured-offerings
for the bulls, for the rams and for the lambs,
by their number, according to the regulation;
22 and one hairy goat as a *hattat*-offering,
aside from the regular offering-up, its grain-gift, and its poured-
offering.

23 Now on the fourth day:
bulls ten, rams two,
lambs a year in age fourteen, wholly-sound,
24 and their grain-gift as well as their poured-offerings
for the bulls, for the rams and for the lambs,
by their number, according to the regulation;
25 and one hairy goat as a *hattat*-offering,
aside from the regular offering-up, its grain-gift, and its poured-
offering.

26 Now on the fifth day:
bulls nine, rams two,
lambs a year in age fourteen, wholly-sound,
27 and their grain-gift as well as their poured-offerings
for the bulls, for the rams and for the lambs,
by their number, according to the regulation;
28 and one hairy goat as a *hattat*-offering,
aside from the regular offering-up, its grain-gift, and its poured-
offering.

29 Now on the sixth day:
bulls eight, rams two,
lambs a year in age fourteen, wholly-sound,

30 and their grain-gift as well as their poured-offerings
for the bulls, for the rams and for the lambs,
by their number, according to the regulation;

31 and one hairy (goat) as a *hattat*-offering,
aside from the regular offering-up, its grain-gift, and its poured-
offering.

32 Now on the seventh day:
bulls seven, rams two,
lambs a year in age fourteen, wholly-sound,

33 and their grain-gift as well as their poured-offerings
for the bulls, for the rams and for the lambs,
by their number, according to the regulation;

34 and one hairy goat as a *hattat*-offering,
aside from the regular offering-up, its grain-gift, and its poured-
offering.

35 On the eighth day:
Restraint there is to be for you,
any-kind of servile work you are not to do!

36 You are to bring-near an offering-up, a fire-offering of soothing
savor for YHWH:
one bull, one ram,
lambs a year in age seven, wholly-sound,

37 their grain-gift as well as their poured-offerings,
for (each) bull, for (each) ram, and for the lambs,
by their number, according to the regulation,

38 and one hairy-one as a *hattat*-offering,
aside from the regular offering-up, its grain-gift, and its poured-
offering.

39 These you are to sacrifice to YHWH at your appointed-times,
aside from your vow-offerings and your freewill-offerings,
whether your offerings-up or your grain-gifts,
your poured-offerings or your *shalom*-offerings.

Vows and Women (30): Taking its verbal cue from 29:39, this chapter focuses on the binding nature of vows, especially as regards women, whose legal status was typically bound up with that of their fathers or husbands (unless they were widows or otherwise adult and single; cf. Wegner 1988). In this respect it continues the priestly concern with women, who do not always fit the priestly categories as neatly as that class might have wished. The length of the chapter signals the importance, or rather the sacredness, of an oath in ancient Israel; it stood as uttered unless an annulment procedure was followed. Human words, and not only divine ones, were seen as having effects in the real world.

The chapter is built around repeating words, such as "vow," "bind," "establish," "annul," and "silent."

◆   30:1   So Moshe declared to the Children of Israel
according to all that YHWH had commanded Moshe.

2   Now Moshe spoke to the heads of the tribes of the Children of
Israel, saying:
This is the word that YHWH has commanded:

3   (Any) man who vows a vow to YHWH
or swears a sworn-oath, to bind himself by a binding-obligation:
he is not to desecrate his word,
according to all that goes out of his mouth, he is to do.

4   And a woman, when she vows a vow to YHWH
or binds (herself) by a binding-obligation in her father's house, in
her youth,

5   and her father hears her vow, or her binding-obligation by which
she has bound herself,
and her father is silent to her:
all her vows, they shall be upheld,
and all her binding-obligations by which she has bound herself
shall be upheld.

6   Now if her father constrains her at the time that he hears it,
all her vows and her binding-obligations by which she binds
herself shall not be upheld,
and YHWH will grant-her-pardon,
for her father has constrained her.

7   But if she becomes-married, becomes-married to a man
while her vows are upon her,
or the rash-statement of her lips by which she has bound herself,

8   and her husband hears,
(and) at the time that he hears he is silent to her,
her vows shall be upheld.
All her binding-obligations by which she has bound herself shall
be upheld.

9   Now if at the time that her husband hears, he constrains her,
he annuls her vow that is upon her

30:3 **desecrate:** Violate.   6 **constrains:** Or "frustrates."
5 **be upheld:** Or "be-established" (as valid), "stand."

War against Midyan (31): We return to preconquest war traditions, such as we encountered in Chap. 21. It is as if God permits Moshe a taste of conquest before he is to be "gathered to [his] kinspeople" (v.2). And it is unfinished business that he takes up here, since the Midyanites had been identified as the ones who lured the Israelites to sin at Baal Pe'or (25:16–18). Also notable in this long chapter is the detailed account of dividing the spoils (vv.25–54); this is both characteristic of Numbers, as a list, and an indication of an important issue that will need attention once the conquest proper proceeds. It also may be an indication of a later tradition; Levine sees in the allotment of spoils for sanctuary income a characteristic royal policy.

The cruel aspect of this war, while not unusual by ancient standards, feels jarring to modern Jewish and Christian readers, who perhaps expect the Bible to be more peace-oriented. It is not, although it often "seeks peace," and there are passages (e.g., Deut. 20 and 21:10–14) where an attempt is made to mute some of the harsh realities of ancient warfare.

Niditch has pointed out that this chapter presents an ideology of war slightly different from some other biblical accounts. The term "devote-to-destruction" is not used; virgin girls, who are not yet of the status of "the enemy," are spared; and war is seen as a ritually defiling activity, i.e., contact with death. In other words, the text exhibits some ambiguity about war, which must then be dealt with via purifying rituals.

as well as the rash-statement of her lips by which she has bound
 herself,
and Y<small>HWH</small> will grant-her-pardon.

10 Now the vow of a widow or a divorcée,
 anything by which she has bound herself,
 shall be upheld regarding her.

11 If in the house of her husband she made-a-vow
 or bound, bound herself by a sworn-oath,

12 and her husband heard, and was silent to her,
 not constraining her,
 all her vows, they shall be upheld,
 and all the binding-obligations by which she bound herself shall
 be upheld.

13 But if her husband annulled, yes, annulled them at the time of his
 hearing it,
 all that went out of her lips as her vows, as her binding of
 herself—
 it shall not be upheld,
 her husband has annulled them,
 and Y<small>HWH</small> will grant-her-pardon.

14 Every vow and every sworn binding, for afflicting her self:
 her husband may uphold, her husband may annul it.

15 But if her husband is silent, yes, silent to her, from (one) day to
 the (next) day,
 (then) he has upheld all her vows and all her binding-obligations
 that are upon her,
 he has them upheld,
 since he was silent to her at the time of his hearing it.

16 Now if he annuls, yes, annuls it after his hearing it,
 he shall bear her iniquity.

17 These are the laws that Y<small>HWH</small> commanded Moshe
 between a man and his wife,
 between a father and his daughter
 in her youth, (in) the house of her father.

31:1 YHWH spoke to Moshe, saying:

2 Seek-vengeance, the vengeance of the Children of Israel from the
   Midyanites;

   afterward you will be gathered to your kinspeople.

3 Moshe spoke to the people, saying:

   Draft from among you men for the attack-force,

   let them be against Midyan,

   to exact the vengeance of YHWH upon Midyan.

4 A thousand per tribe, a thousand per tribe for each of the tribes
   of Israel,

   you are to send out to the attack-force.

5 There were mustered, from the divisions of Israel, a thousand per
   tribe,

   twelve thousand (men) drafted for the attack-force.

6 Moshe sent them out, a thousand per tribe, to the attack-force,

   them and Pin'has son of El'azar, priest to the armed-forces,

   the holy implements and the trumpets for (sounding) trilling-
   blasts in his hand.

7 They arrayed-their-forces against Midyan,

   as YHWH had commanded Moshe,

   and they killed every male,

8 and the kings of Midyan they killed, along with the (other) slain:

   Evi and Rekem, Tzur, Hur and Reva,

   the five kings of Midyan;

   and Bil'am son of Be'or they killed with the sword.

9 Now the Children of Israel captured the women of Midyan, and
   their little-ones,

   and their animals and all their acquired-wealth,

   and all their goods they took-as-plunder.

10 And all their towns, among their settlements, and all their tent-
   villages, they burned with fire.

31:2 **Seek-vengeance:** This verb (Heb. *nakom*) is used to
describe the paying back of the Midyanites for the
crime of Baal-Pe'or (Chap. 25), as well as for being
coconspirators in the Bil'am incident (Chap. 22).

afterward: It sounds as though this will be Moshe's
last official act.

3 **Draft:** So the New English Bible. Others, "hand-
pick," "arm." **attack-force:** Milgrom: "campaign."

11 They took all the booty and all those-taken, among man and
among beast.

12 They brought to Moshe and to El'azar the priest, and to the
community of the Children of Israel
the captives and those-taken and the booty, to the camp,
to the Plains of Moav, that are by Jordan-Jericho.

13 Now Moshe and El'azar the priest and all the leaders of the
community, came out to meet them,
outside the camp.

14 And Moshe was furious with the commanders of the military,
the officers of thousands and the officers of hundreds,
who had come back from the armed-force in war;

15 Moshe said to them:
You have left-alive all the females!

16 Here, they were (the cause) for the Children of Israel—through
the word of Bil'am,
of turning away from YHWH, in the matter of Pe'or,
so that a plague came against the community of YHWH!

17 So now,
kill every male among the little-ones,
and every woman who has known a man by lying with a male,
kill (as well)!

18 But all the younger-ones among the women who have not known
lying with a male—
you may keep them alive for yourselves.

19 As for you: pitch-camp outside the camp, for seven days;
everyone who killed a person or everyone who touched a
corpse—
decontaminate-yourselves on the third day and on the seventh
day,
you and your captives.

16 **turning away from:** Reading *la-sur me'al* (Ehrlich)
for the traditional text's *li-msor maal,* "delivering
breaking-faith," which makes no sense.

20 And every garment and every vessel of animal-skin and
    everything made of goats'-hair and every wooden vessel,
  you are to decontaminate.
21 El'azar the priest said to the men of the armed-force who came
    back from the war:
  This is the legal Instruction that YHWH had commanded Moshe:
22 However, gold and silver,
  bronze, iron, tin and lead
23 —anything that can come through fire—
  you are to pass through fire, then it will be pure;
  however, in Waters Kept-Apart it is to be decontaminated.
  And everything that cannot come through fire, you are to pass
    through water.
24 You are to scrub your garments on the seventh day, then you will
    be purified;
  afterward you may come back into the camp.

25 YHWH said to Moshe, saying:
26 Take up the head-count of those taken captive,
  among man and among beast,
  you and El'azar the priest and the heads of the fathers of the
    community.
27 You are to halve (equally) the taken-loot
  between those wielding (swords skillfully) in war, those going-out
    to the armed-forces,
  and the entire community.
28 And you are to raise a levy for YHWH
  from the men of war, those going-out to the armed-forces,
  one life out of five hundred,
  from humans and from cattle, from donkeys and from sheep.
29 From their half-share you are to take
  and give to El'azar the priest a contribution to YHWH.

---

21 **legal Instruction:** JPS "ritual law."
22 **However:** Qualifying Chap. 19 (Milgrom). **fire . . .
   water:** Two of the great purifiers in Israelite ritual;
   the third, and most potent, is blood.

28 **one life:** JPS "one item."

30 And from the half-share of the Children of Israel you are to take
   one, withheld from the fifty,
   from humans and from cattle, from donkeys and from sheep,
   from all domestic-animals,
   and you are to give them to the Levites,
   those charged with the charge of YHWH's Dwelling.

31 Moshe and El'azar the priest did
   as YHWH had commanded Moshe.

32 Now what was taken, over-and-above the plunder that the people
   from the armed-forces plundered,
   were sheep, six hundred thousand and seventy thousand and five
   thousand,

33 and cattle, two and seventy thousand,

34 and donkeys, one and sixty thousand;

35 and human persons,
   of women who had not known lying with a male,
   all the persons: two and thirty thousand.

36 And the half-share, the portion of those going-out to the armed-
   forces,
   the number of sheep: three hundred thousand and thirty
   thousand and seven thousand and five hundred.

37 And the levy for YHWH from the sheep was
   six hundred and five and seventy,

38 and (from) the cattle, six and thirty thousand,
   and their levy for YHWH, two and seventy,

39 and (from) the donkeys, thirty thousand and five hundred,
   and their levy for YHWH, one and sixty;

40 and (from) human persons, sixteen thousand,
   and their levy for YHWH, two and thirty persons.

41 Moshe gave the levy of the contribution of YHWH to El'azar the
   priest,
   as YHWH had commanded Moshe.

42 Now from the half-share of the Children of Israel
   that Moshe had halved, from the men who served-as-armed-
   forces,

The Two and a Half Tribes (32): Although most biblical traditions place the Promised Land west of the Jordan River, Numbers includes an unusual request by the tribes of Reu'ven, Gad, and half of the tribe of Menashe: Since they are shepherds, and have heard of the fertile grazing area east of the river, they wish to remain on the east bank. Moshe accedes to their wish, provided that they assist their fellow Israelites in conquering Canaan proper. The historical result of this settlement—which gives us a taste of settlement before the larger conquest in the book of Joshua—seems to have been a checkered one, with Moabites and Ammonites reclaiming land at various subsequent periods.

Milgrom has demonstrated how the chapter is built by a select vocabulary of words repeated seven times; the whole may be summarized by the composite statement "If Gad and Reuben cross over as vanguard [Heb. *h-l-tz;* see below) before YHWH, they will receive the land holdings (they desire)." The sevenfold "before YHWH" of the chapter drums in the participation of the divine in the conquest (Milgrom also brings up the possibility that it suggests the Coffer's presence at the battle).

43 the half-share for the community, from the sheep—
    three hundred thousand and thirty thousand and seven thousand
        and five hundred;
44 and cattle six and thirty thousand;
45 and donkeys thirty thousand and five hundred;
46 and human persons sixteen thousand.
47 Moshe took from the half-share of the Children of Israel, one
        withheld out of fifty,
    among man and among beast,
    and gave them to the Levites, those charged with the duties of
        the Dwelling of YHWH,
    as YHWH had commanded Moshe.

48 Now there came-near to Moshe the commanders that belonged
        to the divisions of the armed-forces,
    officers of thousands and officers of hundreds,
49 they said to Moshe:
    Your servants have taken up the head-count of the men of war
        that are under our hand,
    there has not gone uncounted of us a (single) man!
50 And we have brought-near a near-offering for YHWH
    (from) any man who found a vessel of gold, armlets or bracelets,
    rings, earrings, or ornaments,
    to effect-ransom for our lives, before the presence of YHWH.
51 So Moshe and El'azar the priest took the gold from them,
    all kinds of implements of fine-workmanship.
52 Now all the gold of the contribution, that they set-aside for
        YHWH:
    sixteen thousand and seven hundred and fifty *shekels*,
    from the officers of thousands and from the officers of hundreds.
53 The men of the armed-forces kept-as-plunder, each-man (what)
        was his.
54 And Moshe and El'azar the priest took the gold
    from the officers of thousands and the officers of hundreds,
    and brought it to the Tent of Appointment,
    (as) a reminder for the Children of Israel, before the presence of
        YHWH.

32:1 Now many livestock had the Sons of Re'uven and the Sons of
Gad,
an exceedingly mighty (amount);
and they saw the land of Ya'zer in the land of Gil'ad:
here, the place was a place (fit) for livestock.

2 So the Sons of Re'uven and the Sons of Gad came
and said to Moshe, to El'azar the priest and to the leaders of the
community, saying:

3 Atarot and Divon, Ya'zer and Nimra,
Heshbon and El'aleh,
Sevam, Nevo and Be'on,

4 the land that YHWH has struck before the community of Israel—
it is a land for livestock,
and your servants have livestock.

5 And they said:
If we have found favor in your eyes,
let this land be given to your servants as a holding;
do not make us cross the Jordan!

6 Moshe said to the Sons of Gad and to the Sons of Re'uven:
Should your brothers go out to war,
and you, you stay here?

7 Why would you constrain the will of the Children of Israel
from crossing into the land that YHWH has given them?

8 Thus did your fathers, when I sent them out of Kadesh Barne'a
to see the land:

9 they went up as far as Wadi Eshkol and saw the land,
then they constrained the will of the Children of Israel
so they did not come into the land that YHWH had given them.

10 And the anger of YHWH flared up on that day,
and he swore, saying:

11 If they should see, the men who went up from Egypt,
—from the age of twenty and upward—

32:1 **livestock:** Lit. "that which is acquired." **Gil'ad:**
Trad. "Gilead"; the territory east and northeast of
the Dead Sea.

the soil about which I swore to Avraham, to Yitzhak and to
   Yaakov . . . !
For they did not follow-fully after me,

12 excepting Calev son of Yefunne, the Kenizzite, and Yehoshua son
   of Nun,
for they followed-fully after YHWH.

13 And the anger of YHWH flared up against Israel,
and he had them wander in the wilderness, for forty years,
until it came-to-an-end, that whole generation that was doing
   what was ill in the eyes of YHWH.

14 Now here, you have arisen in place of your fathers,
a brood of sinning men,
to add further to the flaming anger of YHWH against Israel.

15 If you turn away from him,
he will add further to leave them in the wilderness,
and you will bring-ruin-upon this whole people!

16 They came close to him and said:
Sheep fences we will build, for our livestock here,
and towns for our little-ones;

17 and as for us, we shall be drafted hastily before the Children of
   Israel,
until we have brought them to their region.
But our little-ones will stay in towns fortified against the
   inhabitants of the land.

18 We will not return to our houses
until the Children of Israel have inherited each-man his
   inheritance.

19 For we will not take-inheritance with them across the Jordan and
   further (on),
for our inheritance has become ours
across the Jordan, toward sunrise.

20 Moshe said to them:
If you do this thing,
if you are drafted before YHWH for war,

---

14 **brood:** Heb. *tarbut*, related to *rav*, "many."   17 **drafted:** Or "mobilized."

21 and you cross the Jordan, every hand-picked man, before YHWH,
until he has dispossessed his enemies from before him,

22 and the land is subdued before YHWH,
afterward you may return,
and (then) you will be clear (of obligation) before YHWH and
before Israel;
this land will be for you as a holding before YHWH.

23 But if you do not do thus:
here: you will have sinned against YHWH,
and know your sin—that (it) will overtake you!

24 Build yourselves towns for your little-ones and fences for your
flocks,
and what has gone out of your mouths, do!

25 Then said the Sons of Gad and the Sons of Re'uven to Moshe,
saying:
Your servants will do as my lord commands:

26 our little-ones, our wives, our livestock and all our animals
will stay there in the towns of Gil'ad;

27 your servants will cross over, every drafted (member) of the
armed-forces, before YHWH, in war,
as my lord has spoken.

28 So Moshe commanded El'azar the priest concerning them
and Yehoshua son of Nun
and the heads of the Fathers of the tribes of the Children of
Israel,

29 and Moshe said to them:
If the Sons of Gad and the Sons of Re'uven cross over the Jordan
with you,
everyone drafted for war, before YHWH,
and the land is subdued before you,
you may give them the land of Gil'ad as an inheritance.

30 But if the drafted (warriors) do not cross over with you,
they will receive-holdings with you in the land of Canaan.

---

24 **what has gone out of your mouths:** More idiomatically, "whatever has crossed your lips."

28 **Fathers:** Probably ellipsis for "Fathers' House" (cf.
1:4).

31 The Sons of Gad and the Sons of Re'uven answered, saying:
What YHWH has spoken to your servants, thus will we do:

32 we ourselves will cross over, as drafted men, before YHWH, into
the land of Canaan,
(remaining) with us (will be) our inherited holding, across the
Jordan.

33 So Moshe gave to them, to the Sons of Gad, the Sons of Re'uven,
and half the tribe of Menashe son of Yosef,
the kingdom of Sihon king of the Amorites,
and the kingdom of Og king of Bashan,
the land as regards its towns in the territories, the towns of the
land all around.

34 And the Sons of Gad rebuilt Divon, Atarot, and Aro'er,

35 Aterot Shofan, and Ya'zer and Yogbeha,

36 and Bet Nimra and Bet Haran,
as fortified cities and as fences for flocks.

37 And the Sons of Re'uven rebuilt Heshbon and El'alei
and Kiryatayim,

38 and Nevo and Baal Me'on—of changed name—
and Sivma;
and they called them by (other) names,
the names of the towns that they built.

39 Then went out the Sons of Makhir son of Menashe, to Gil'ad,
they conquered it
and dispossessed the Amorites that were in it.

40 And Moshe gave Gil'ad to Makhir son of Menashe,
and he settled there.

41 And Ya'ir son of Menashe marched out
and conquered their villages,
he called them Havvot-Ya'ir / Fortified-Villages of Ya'ir.

42 And Novah went out
and conquered Kenat and its daughter-towns,
and he called it Novah, after his (own) name.

38 **Baal Me'on . . . Sivma:** Note Be'on and Sevam in
v.3, which some scholars read as B[aal M]e'on and
Sivma as in our verse.

The Wilderness Marches (33): Another list in the book of Numbers traces the full journey of the Israelites from Egypt—as the Egyptians are still burying their first-born dead!—to a spot opposite Jericho by the Jordan. It would of course be ideal if we could map out the route, but the location of most of the places mentioned in the chapter has been lost over time. We are left with the rhythm of the place-names rather than a viable historical record.

Vv.50ff. introduce a new note, appropriate in view of the preconquest situation. Before Moshe lays out the future borders of Israelite Canaan in the next chapter, he must warn his charges about the dangers of leaving the conquered peoples (and their religious culture) settled in the land. This concern is typical of Deuteronomy, and figures in later history (cf. Judg. 1), where the apparent failure to do what is demanded here is understood as having led to idol-worship in Israel.

33:1 These are the marching-stages of the Children of Israel that they
    went on
from the land of Egypt, by their forces,
through the hand of Moshe and Aharon.

2 Moshe wrote down their departures, by their marching-stages, by
    order of Yhwh.
Now these are their marching-stages, by their departures:

3 They marched from Ra'mses, in the first New-Moon,
on the fifteenth day after the first New-Moon;
on the morrow of the Passover-meal
the Children of Israel departed with a high hand, before the eyes
    of all Egypt,

4 while Egypt was burying those that Yhwh had struck-dead
    among them, all the firstborn,
and on their gods, Yhwh had rendered judgment.

5 And the Children of Israel marched on from Ra'mses, and
    encamped at Sukkot;

6 they marched on from Sukkot and encamped at Eitam, which is
    at the edge of the wilderness.

7 And they marched on from Eitam and turned toward Pi-Ha-
    Hirot, that (runs) along the face of Baal Tzefon,
and encamped before Migdol.

8 They marched on from Penei Ha-Hirot and crossed in the midst
    of the Sea into the wilderness;
then they marched a journey of three days into the Wilderness of
    Eitam,
and encamped at Mara.

9 They marched on from Mara and came to Eilim;
now in Eilim (were) twelve springs of water and seventy palms,
and they encamped there.

10 They marched on from Eilim and encamped by the Sea of Reeds.

33:1 **marching-stages:** Forty-two stations, from Egypt to Sinai, from Sinai to Kadesh, and from Kadesh to the gateway to Canaan opposite Jericho. Milgrom cites the midrashic view that details have been provided to remind future generations of (a) the mira-cles God wrought for their ancestors and (b) the provocations that led God to kill off the slave gener-ation.

8 **Penei Ha-Hirot:** This location appears as "Pi Ha-Hirot" in Ex. 14:2, 9.

11 They marched on from the Sea of Reeds and encamped in the Wilderness of Syn.

12 They marched on from the Wilderness of Syn and encamped at Dofka.

13 They marched on from Dofka and encamped at Alush.

14 They marched on from Alush and encamped at Refidim, but there was no water there for the people to drink.

15 They marched on from Refidim and encamped in the Wilderness of Sinai.

16 They marched on from the Wilderness of Sinai and encamped at Kivrot Ha-Taava.

17 They marched on from Kivrot Ha-Taava and encamped at Hatzerot.

18 They marched on from Hatzerot and encamped at Ritma.

19 They marched on from Ritma and encamped at Rimmon Peretz.

20 They marched on from Rimmon Peretz and encamped at Livna.

21 They marched on from Livna and encamped at Rissa.

22 They marched on from Rissa and encamped at Kehelata.

23 They marched on from Kehelata and encamped at Mount Shefer.

24 They marched on from Mount Shefer and encamped at Harada.

25 They marched on from Harada and encamped at Mak'helot.

26 They marched on from Mak'helot and encamped at Tahat.

27 They marched on from Tahat and encamped at Terah.

28 They marched on from Terah and encamped at Mitka.

29 They marched on from Mitka and encamped at Hashmona.

30 They marched on from Hashmona and encamped at Moserot.

31 They marched on from Moserot and encamped at Benei Ya'kan.

32 They marched on from Benei Ya'kan and encamped at Hor Ha-Gidgad.

33 They marched on from Hor Ha-Gidgad and encamped at Yotvata.

34 They marched on from Yotvata and encamped at Avrona.

35 They marched on from Avrona and encamped at Etzyon Gever.

32 **Hor:** Meaning not "mountain" but "hole" or "pass"—although some ancient versions do read "mountain."

36 They marched on from Etzyon Gever and encamped in the
    Wilderness of Tzyn—that is Kadesh.

37 They marched on from Kadesh and encamped at Hill's Hill, at
    the edge of the land of Edom.

38 Now Aharon the priest went up on Hill's Hill, by order of YHWH,
    and died there,
in the fortieth year after the going-out of the Children of Israel
    from the land of Egypt,
in the fifth New-Moon, on the first of the New-Moon.

39 Aharon was three and twenty and a hundred years old
when he died at Hill's Hill.

40 Now the Canaanite, the king of Arad
—he sat-as-ruler in the Negev, in the land of Canaan—heard of
    the coming of the Children of Israel.

41 They marched on from Hill's Hill and encamped at Tzalmona.

42 They marched on from Tzalmona and encamped at Punon.

43 They marched on from Punon and encamped at Ovot.

44 They marched on from Ovot and encamped at Iyyei Ha-Avarim,
    in the territory of Moav.

45 They marched on from Iyyim and encamped at Divon Gad.

46 They marched on from Divon Gad and encamped at Almon
    Divlatayim.

47 They marched on from Almon Divlatayim and encamped in the
    hills of Avarim / The Region-Across, facing Nevo.

48 They marched on from the hills of the Avarim and encamped in
    the Plains of Moav, by Jordan-Jericho.

49 And they encamped along the Jordan, from Bet Yeshimot as far as
    Avel Shittim / Acacia Meadow,
in the Plains of Moav.

50 Now YHWH spoke to Moshe in the Plains of Moav,
by Jordan-Jericho, saying:

---

39 **three and twenty and a hundred:** The number is
"perfect," like Moshe's lifespan; it equals 3×40 (or 10×12) + 3.

40 **the king of Arad** etc.: Cf. 21:1–3 above for a fuller
version of this tradition.

45 **Iyyim:** Iyyei Ha-Avarim in the previous verse refers
to "Iyyim of the Avarim Mountains."

Parceling Out the Land (34): Again appropriate in the context, the postconquest borders of the Promised Land are laid out here. Milgrom, following Mazar, characterizes these boundaries as matching no historically verifiable Israelite territories, but rather the map of Canaan as an Egyptian province before the conquest. Be that as it may, the chapter ends with a list of representatives who will parcel out the land—another one of Numbers's leadership lists.

51 Speak to the Children of Israel, and say to them:
When you cross the Jordan into the land of Canaan,

52 you are to dispossess all the settled-folk of the land from before
you.
You are to destroy all their figured-objects,
all their molten images you are to destroy,
all their high-places you are to annihilate,

53 that you may take-possession of the land and settle in it,
for to you I have given the land, to possess it.

54 You shall arrange-inheritance of the land by lots, according to
your clans:
for the many, you are to make-much their inheritance,
for the few, you are to make-little their inheritance,
wherever the lot comes out for them there, (so) shall theirs be;
by the tribes of your fathers you are to receive-inheritance.

55 But if you do not dispossess the settled-folk of the land from
before you,
those who are left of them shall be
as barbs in your eyes, as spines in your sides;
they will assault you on the land that you are settling in,

56 and it shall be:
as I thought to do to them, so I will do to you!

34:1 YHWH spoke to Moshe, saying:

2 Command the Children of Israel and say to them:
When you enter the land, Canaan,
this is the land that will fall to you as an inheritance,
the land of Canaan by its borders:

3 the Negev limit will be for you from the Wilderness of Tzyn
alongside Edom;
the Negev border will be for you from the edge of the Sea of Salt,
on the east;

---

52 **molten:** That is, cast in metal, like the infamous
Golden Calf in Ex. 32. **high-places:** Pagan cultic
sites situated on the tops of hills.
55 **spines . . . sides . . . assault:** Heb. *tzeninim . . . tzid-
deikhem . . . tzararu.*

34:3 **Sea of Salt:** The Hebrew name, to this day, for the
Dead Sea.

4 the border will then turn for you from the Negev-side of
    Scorpions' Pass, crossing on to Tzyn;
  its outer-lines will be from the Negev-side of Kadesh Barne'a,
  (then) going out to Hatzar Addar and crossing on to Atzmon.
5 The border will then turn from Atzmon toward the Wadi of
    Egypt,
  its outer-lines will be at the Sea.
6 As the seaward border will be for you the Great Sea and (its own)
    border;
  this will be for you the seaward border.
7 And this will be for you the northern border:
  from the Great Sea you are to mark yourselves (a line) to Hill's
    Hill.
8 From Hill's Hill you are to mark going to Hamat,
  and the outer-lines of the border shall be at Tzedad.
9 Then the border will go out to Zifron,
  and its outer-lines will be Hatzar Einan;
  this will be for you the northern border.
10 And you are to mark for yourselves, for the border eastward:
  from Hatzar Einan to Shefam.
11 And the border will go down from Shefam to Rivla, on the east of
    Ayin/The Spring,
  then the border will go down and brush the shoulder of the Sea
    of Kinneret, eastward,
12 then the border will go down along the Jordan,
  its outer-lines will be the Sea of Salt.
  This will be for you the land, in all its borders round about!
13 So Moshe commanded the Children of Israel, saying:
  This is the land for which you are to arrange-inheritance by lot,
  that Yhwh commanded to be given to the nine tribes and the half
    tribe.

---

6 **the Great Sea:** The Mediterranean.
7 **Hill's Hill:** A different mountain from the one in southern Canaan where Aharon died, this is probably located in present-day Lebanon, matching an old Egyptian boundary line for the "province" of Israel (Milgrom).
11 **Sea of Kinneret:** Still the Hebrew name for the Sea of Galilee.

14 For the tribe of the Sons of the Re'uvenites, according to their
    Fathers' House,
  and the tribe of the Sons of the Gadites, according to their
    Fathers' House,
  and half of the tribe of Menashe
  have (already) taken their inheritance;

15 two tribes and the half tribe
  have taken their inheritance across from Jordan-Jericho,
  eastward, toward sunrise.

16 YHWH spoke to Moshe, saying:

17 These are the names of the men that will arrange-for-your-
    inheritance of the land:
  El'azar the priest and Yehoshua son of Nun,

18 and one leader, one leader per tribe you are to take for arranging-
    inheritance of the land.

19 And these are the names of the men:
  of the tribe of Yehuda: Calev son of Yefunne

20 Of the tribe of the Sons of Shim'on: Shemuel son of Ammihud.

21 Of the tribe of Binyamin: Elidad son of Kislon.

22 Of the tribe of the Sons of Dan, leader: Bukki son of Yogli.

23 Of the Sons of Yosef:
  of the tribe of the Sons of Menashe, leader: Hanniel son of Efod,

24 of the tribe of the Sons of Efrayim, leader: Kemiel son of Shiftan.

25 Of the tribe of the Sons of Zevulun, leader: Elitzafan son of
    Parnakh.

26 Of the tribe of the Sons of Yissakhar, leader: Paltiel son of Azzan.

27 Of the tribe of the Sons of Asher, leader: Ahihud son of Shelomi.

28 Of the tribe of the Sons of Naftali, leader: Pedah'el son of
    Ammihud.

29 These (are they) whom YHWH commanded to parcel-out-
    inheritance for the Children of Israel, in the land of Canaan.

Levitical Towns of Asylum (35): As a kind of appendix to the previous chapter, and for a last mention of the Levites in Numbers, we are given what the Torah regards as an important innovation: the institution of the Towns of Asylum (or Refuge), whereby an accidental manslayer could avoid the expected blood vengeance of the dead person's family. Greenberg (1959) has claimed that the specified towns probably were a substitute for what in other ancient Near Eastern societies was banishment; in his view, the idea of internal banishment presented here affirms the high and nonnegotiable value put on human life in the Bible—even when it is ended by accident. Be that as it may, the law in this chapter puts a brake on a reality of ancient life.

It is likely that the towns in question were previously sacred Canaanite towns, and Frick has raised the interesting possibility that from that special character or status may have evolved the concept of citywide asylum (and not just at the altar, a temporary measure).

35:1 YHWH spoke to Moshe, in the Plains of Moav,
    by Jordan-Jericho, saying:

2 Command the Children of Israel,
    that they may give over to the Levites, from their inherited
      holdings, towns to settle in,
    and pasture-land for the towns around them, give to the Levites.

3 The towns shall be for them to settle in,
    and their pasture-lands shall be for their cattle, their property and
      for all their animals.

4 And the pasture-lands of the towns that you give to the Levites
    (shall be)
    from the wall of the town and outward, a thousand cubits all
      around;

5 you are to measure outside the city, the eastern limit: two
      thousand by the cubit,
    and the Negev limit, two thousand by the cubit,
    and the seaward limit, two thousand by the cubit,
    and the northern limit, two thousand by the cubit,
    with the town in the middle.
    This shall be for them the pasture-lands of the towns.

6 And with the towns that you give to the Levites,
    with the six towns of asylum that you give for fleeing-to for the
      accidental-murderer—
    along with them you are to give forty-two towns.

7 All the towns that you are to give the Levites:
    forty-eight towns,
    them and their pasture-lands.

8 And the towns that you give (them) from the holdings of the
      Children of Israel—
    from those that have-many you are to take-many, from those that
      have-few you are to take-few,

35:2 **pasture-land:** Land for "driving" (Heb. *g-r-sh*) animals to graze in.
4 **the wall:** That is, its outer surface (Milgrom). **a thousand cubits:** About 1500 yards, or somewhat less than a mile.

5 **two thousand by the cubit:** This became the basis in later Jewish law for the maximum distance one could travel on the Sabbath (cf. Plaut for discussion).

each-one according to his inheritance that they receive-as-
inheritance
is to give of its towns for the Levites.

9 YHWH spoke to Moshe, saying:

10 Speak to the Children of Israel and say to them:
When you cross over the Jordan, into the land of Canaan:

11 You are to select for yourselves (certain) towns,
towns of asylum shall they be for you,
for fleeing-to for the accidental-murderer, one who strikes down a
life in error.

12 The towns shall be for you for asylum from the (blood) redeemer,
that the murderer not die
until he can come before the community for judgment.

13 And the towns that you provide—
six towns of asylum shall there be for you.

14 Three of the towns you are to provide across the Jordan,
and three of the towns you are to provide in the land of Canaan,
towns of asylum they are to be,

15 for the Children of Israel, for the sojourner and for the
temporary-settler among them,
these six towns are to be for asylum,
for fleeing-to for anyone who strikes down a person in error.

16 But if with an iron instrument he struck him down, so that he
died,
he is a murderer:
put-to-death, put-to-death must the murderer be!

17 And if with a stone in hand through which one can die he struck
him down, so that he died,
he is a murderer:
put-to-death, put-to-death must the murderer be!

18 Or with a wooden instrument in hand through which one can die
he struck him down,
so that he died,

---

16 **iron:** No one could be oblivious to what would likely result from hitting someone with such an instrument.

17 **in hand:** That is, large enough to fit in the hand.

he is a murderer:
put-to-death, put-to-death must the murderer be!

19 As for the blood redeemer—
he may put-to-death the murderer,
upon meeting him, he may put-him-to-death.

20 Now if in hatred he pushed him,
or threw (something) at him lying-in-wait, so that he died,

21 or in enmity struck him with his hand, so that he died,
put-to-death, put-to-death must be he who has struck,
he is a murderer:
the blood redeemer may put the murderer to death, upon
meeting him.

22 But if with suddenness, with no (previous) enmity, he pushed
him,
or threw at him any instrument, without lying-in-wait,

23 or with any stone instrument through which one can die,
without seeing (him),
he dropped it on him, so that he died
—now he was not his enemy, not one seeking his ill—

24 the community is to judge between the striker and the blood
redeemer,
according to these regulations;

25 the community is to rescue the murderer from the hand of the
blood redeemer,
and the community is to return him to his town of asylum, to
which he fled;
he is to stay in it until the death of the Great Priest
who was anointed with the oil of holiness.

26 But if the murderer goes out, yes, goes out
from the border of his town of asylum, whence he fled,

27 and the blood redeemer finds him, outside the border of his town
of asylum,

19 **meeting:** Or "coming across," "encountering."
25 **Great Priest:** High Priest.
27 **finds:** Or "catches" (Fishbane 1988). **he has no**

bloodguilt: And hence cannot himself be executed
for killing the murderer.

A Case of Inheritance: Daughters of Tzelofhad II (36): To round out both Part III and the entire book, the text returns to issues of inheritance, brought up first in Chap. 27. The decision rendered here (that the daughters of Tzelofhad may inherit their father's holdings, but that they must agree to marry within their tribe) ties the final loose end relating to the land, and so we are able to leave the wilderness narratives and laws with a sense that the future in the Promised Land is both assured and orderly. All that remains is for Moshe to die—but first he has a series of speeches to deliver to his charges of half a lifetime. These will be introduced by the opening verse of the next book, "These are the words/speeches . . . ."

Fishbane (1988) terms this chapter a "responsum," that is, an authoritative answer to a legal question, and notes how the original intent of the law in Chap. 27—to allow women to inherit property in certain circumstances—has been "subverted" by the ruling here. That is, male relatives ultimately inherit the land, as though there were no daughters! Thus the process of "inner-biblical interpretation," whereby already in the Bible itself passages are subject to later scrutiny and recasting, makes its appearance; it will be exemplified by much of the material in the next book, Deuteronomy.

the blood redeemer may murder the murderer,
he has no bloodguilt.

28 Indeed, in his town of asylum he must stay, until the death of the
   Great Priest;
   after the death of the Great Priest
   the murderer may return to the land of his holding.

29 These shall be for you
   as a law of procedure into your generations, throughout all your
   settlements:

30 whoever strikes down a person,
   at the mouth of witnesses (only) may a murderer be murdered;
   one witness (alone) may not testify against the person, to have-
   him-put-to-death.

31 You are not to accept a ransom for the life of a murderer,
   since he is culpable, (deserving) the death-penalty,
   indeed, he is to be put-to-death, put-to-death!

32 And you are not to accept a ransom
   for (him to) flee to his town of asylum,
   for (him to) return to settle in the land,
   until the death of the Great Priest.

33 You are not to corrupt the land that you are in,
   for the blood—it will corrupt the land,
   and the land will not be purged of the blood that has been shed
   upon it
   except through the blood of him who shed it.

34 You are not to make-*tamei* the land in which you are settling,
   in whose midst I dwell,
   for I am YHWH,
   Dweller in the midst of Israel!

36:1 Now there came-near the heads of the Fathers' (Houses) of a
   clan of the Sons of Gil'ad son of Makhir son of Menashe, of
   the clans of the Sons of Yosef,

30 **one witness (alone):** This became a central principle in later Jewish law (cf. also Deut. 19:15, where the
minimum number of witnesses is stipulated at
two).

33 **corrupt:** Murder is one of the major causes of such
biblical pollution (adultery is another).

they spoke before Moshe and before the leaders,
the heads of the Father(s' Houses) of the Children of Israel,

2   they said:

It is my lord that Y<small>HWH</small> has commanded to give out the land in
    inheritance, by lot, to the Children of Israel,
and my lord was commanded by Y<small>HWH</small> to give out the
    inheritance of Tzelofhad our brother, to his daughters.

3   Now should they be for one of the members of (another) tribe of
    the Children of Israel as wives,

their inheritance will be taken-away from the inheritance of their
    fathers
and be added to the inheritance of the tribe for whom they
    become (wives);
from our allotted inheritance it will be taken-away!

4   And when there is a Homebringing for the Children of Israel
and their inheritance is added to the inheritance of the tribe for
    which they are (wives)
from the inheritance of our fathers' tribe,
their inheritance will be taken-away!

5   So Moshe commanded the Children of Israel by order of Y<small>HWH</small>,
    saying:

Rightfully has the tribe of the Sons of Yosef spoken!

6   This is the word that Y<small>HWH</small> commands concerning the daughters
    of Tzelofhad, saying:

for those good in their eyes, they may become wives,
however, (only) for a clan from the tribe of their father, may they
    become wives.

7   The inheritance of the Children of Israel is not to go round from
    tribe to tribe;

indeed, each-one to the inheritance of his father's tribe is to
    cleave, (among) the Children of Israel.

36:4 **Homebringing:** Every fiftieth year, when the land re-
verts to its hereditary owner. Cf. Lev. 25:10 ff.

7 **each-one:** Each tribe.

8 And every daughter who comes-into-possession of inheritance
    from the tribes of the Children of Israel—
for someone from the clan of her father's tribe she must become
    a wife,
in order that the Children of Israel may remain-in-possession,
    each-man, of the inheritance of his fathers.

9 There shall not go round the inheritance of a tribe to another
    tribe,
indeed, each-one to his inheritance is to cleave, (among) the
    tribes of the Children of Israel.

10 As YHWH had commanded Moshe,
thus did the daughters of Tzelofhad.

11 They became, Mahla, Tirtza, Hogla, Milka and No'a, the
    daughters of Tzelofhad, wives for the sons of their uncles,

12 in the clans of the Sons of Menashe they became wives,
so that their inheritance went along with the tribe of the clan of
    their father.

13 These are the commandments and the regulations
that YHWH commanded by the hand of Moshe to the Children of
    Israel,
in the Plains of Moav, by Jordan-Jericho.

---

12 **clans:** Septuagint: "clan."

דברים

——⋄⋄⋄——

DEUTERONOMY

——⋄⋄⋄——

THESE ARE THE WORDS

ON THE BOOK OF DEUTERONOMY AND ITS STRUCTURE

DEUTERONOMY HOLDS A UNIQUE POSITION, AND SPEAKS WITH A UNIQUE VOICE, IN THE literature of the Torah. Up to this point, through the first four books, we have encountered a powerful mixture of literary genres; indeed, the books owe their characteristic stamp to the way in which they incorporate these genres. Genesis is predominantly narrative, punctuated by genealogies; Exodus begins with narrative and later proceeds with covenant-making and law, and then with the precise details of sanctuary building; Leviticus is composed almost entirely of cultic and then ethical and social law; and finally, Numbers alternates narrative and varied laws, under the structure of preparations for wilderness march, first encounters with the Promised Land, and preparations for entry. Except for Leviticus, the books also exhibit, at strategic points, striking examples of biblical poetry.

An ancient name for Deuteronomy, *mishne tora*—which means "copy of the Torah," but which was erroneously understood as "second Torah"—would seem to indicate more of the same combining of genres, and a not-too-close reading would support the idea of a rehashing of narrative, covenant-making, law, and poetry. But the reader who takes the time to weigh what stands before him or her will find much more. In its structure, style, content, and intent, Deuteronomy goes beyond what has preceded it. The image of Moshe addressing the assembled people on the Plains of Moab—the central setting of the book—provides the occasion for not merely a retelling, but a recasting of Israel's mission and destiny. No book of the Torah is truer to the idea of "instruction" (Deuteronomy uses the term numerous times), including an emphasis on teaching and learning, with assembled and yet-to-be-born children as much the audience as "elders."

From the book's opening phrase, "Now these are the words [or even "speeches"] that Moshe spoke to the Children of Israel / in (the country) across the Jordan," the basic premise of Deuteronomy is that the aged Moshe, personally and indeed in the first person, speaks for the last time to the assembled Israelites, before their triumphant entry into the land of Canaan. The setting affects the entire content of the book; no longer is the narrator in the background, as in most of the Torah, but instead he is presented as directly addressing a living audience, an audience composed not only of the ancient hearers portrayed in the text but also of contemporary listeners.

The image of a leader delivering a long public address on an auspicious occasion is well known from the ancient world, most familiarly from Greek historians (cf. Van Seters) but also abundantly in the ancient Near East (Weinfeld). The historian seeks to paint a vivid picture of the personality of his speaker and the high drama of the moment, and may go on at great length. While admitting to not having had the benefit of eyewitness sources, such chroniclers are nevertheless sincere in their desire to present what undoubtedly would have been said on such an occasion.

Deuteronomy, whenever it was composed and placed in the Torah, takes this approach a step further. It is a fantastic conceit, really: as Rosenberg (1975) notes, Moshe, the man who was "not a man of words" (Ex. 4:10), all of a sudden finds his voice. And as Polzin (1980) has shown in his forceful analysis, in Deuteronomy Moshe's voice functions fairly indistinguishably from God's own—and then closes off the text by stipulating that nothing in the future is to be added or subtracted to it. So we are dealing with a text of directly authoritative character, a series of speeches that in their own self-understanding already bore the status of "Torah." Hence Deuteronomy introduces into the Bible for the first time the concept of canon—a bounded, accepted body of authoritative literature.

Moshe's addresses, which include a historical review, repeated appeals to observe God's laws and dire warnings against their violation, a reworking of previous laws and the addition of new ones, and a poem designed to keep the appeals and warnings in popular memory, have about them a deep rhetorical urgency. As such they are stylistically quite different from most of what is found in the first four books of the Bible. To be sure, there are many moments of high rhetoric in the previous narratives, and the laws—including cultic ones—are also not lacking appeals to the emotions (cf., for instance, the repeated injunctions to not oppress the sojourner, "for you were sojourners in the land of Egypt"). But as an extended piece of argumentation and pleading, Deuteronomy holds pride of place in the Torah, with its specialized vocabulary (described in the notes and commentary below), its alternately pleading and warning tone, and its long, elegant phrases (as Gottwald notes, these phrases are most often cast in the form of subordinate clauses, not the typical syntactical form found in the previous books).

But not only does Deuteronomy provide an emotional capstone to the four books that precede it. It functions to link up with both the landed history of Israel in the narrative books to follow (Joshua through Kings) and the prophets' emotional speeches to the people and their leaders. In the words of G. Ernest Wright,

> the central purpose of Deuteronomy is to furnish Israel with a complete order of faith and life which is the prerequisite for a prosperous and secure existence on the God-given land. The historian [of the succeeding books] shows how Israel failed to keep it and what the consequences were.

It is in fact the monarchic setting that is commonly held to be the historical background to the compilation of Deuteronomy. While Moshe's last days and the people's being poised on the steppes opposite Jericho would certainly be a dramatic enough moment for our book's speeches to occur, its language, style, and many of its concerns point to a later time in the history of Israel as a likely venue for at least a good part of its emotional appeal.

That time, in the opinion of most biblical scholars over the past two centuries, was the middle of the reign of King Josiah (ruled 640–608 B.C.E.) of Judah, the southern kingdom (Israel, the north, had been overrun by Assyria a century previously). The Assyrian Empire, dominant in the region for three hundred years, was on the wane, and Josiah took advantage of this decline of power to expand his kingdom northward. He also—at about the time of the death of Ashurbanipal, the last powerful king of Assyria—began a wide-ranging reform that consisted largely of destroying the local "high places" of pagan worship that had figured so prominently in the reign of his grandfather, the notorious Manasseh (ruled 687–642). II Kings 23 describes the purge in great detail, noting both places and priests that were now rendered inoperative in favor of the centralization of the cult in Jerusalem.

It is within this setting that Chapter 22 reports the dramatic discovery of a scroll "of the Torah."

> The high priest Hilkiah said to Shaphan the secretary, "I have found the book of the law in the house of the LORD." . . . Shaphan then read it aloud to the king. When the king heard the words of the book of the law, he tore his clothes. Then the king commanded . . . saying: "Go, inquire of the LORD for me, for the people, and for all Judah, concerning the words of this book that has been found, for great is the wrath of the LORD . . . because our ancestors did not obey the words of this book, to do according to all that is written concerning us." (22:8, 10–13, New Revised Standard Version)

What precisely were the contents of the "book" we do not know; but it is usually taken to have been some form of Deuteronomy. The rhetorical force of the newly discovered text must have been considerable, for its reported result was that the king

> directed that all the elders of Judah and Jerusalem should be gathered to him. . . . he read in their hearing all the words of the book of the covenant that had been found in the house of the LORD. The king stood by the pillar and made a covenant before the LORD, to follow the LORD, keeping his commandments, his decrees, and his statutes, with all his heart and all his soul, to perform the words of this covenant that were written in this book. All the people joined in the covenant. (23:1–3)

The connections between these passages and the style of Deuteronomy will be obvious to anyone who reads the book, and it seems clear that Josiah's reforms are closely related to concerns expressed in Deuteronomy.

The Bible's portrayal of this background does not necessarily mean that Deuteronomy was composed for the occasion, or even that it originated in Judah. Several scholars (notably Ginsberg) have remarked on connections to the northern kingdom of Israel (e.g., affinities to the prophet Hosea), and so it is possible that at least some of our book was a series of traditions brought south by refugees fleeing the Assyrian onslaught. In any event, the text of Deuteronomy addresses its audience with such emotional immediacy that it may safely be presumed that a crisis of major proportions loomed, and the opportunity presented itself for a large-scale revival—or redefinition—of Israel's self-understanding. Similar crises later in Jewish history may have led to the editing and writing down (but not necessarily the composition) of other central texts, the Mishnah (c. 200) and the Babylonian Talmud (c. 450). Like these documents, and like the first four books of the Torah, Deuteronomy is written in such a way that it is difficult to pin down its precise background, which through additions and circumspection has been substantially obliterated. What is left to us are the many repetitions of "today" or "this day," which signal the desire to make the "Instruction" contemporary for the audience, whoever and whenever that may be.

The net effect of this process of creation and development was to establish the Torah's character as a text that shows signs of new life and new thinking within itself. Deuteronomy, by its inclusion as the final book of the five, officially began the practice of "explaining" (1:5) the traditions of Israel, and thus paved the way for the classic form of Jewish religious and intellectual activity: the interpretation of Scripture (cf. Fishbane 1988 for a definitive study on "inner-biblical exegesis," interpretation that appears within the Bible itself and hence becomes a legitimate part of its traditions). This activity strongly influenced Christianity and Islam as well, and is still a part of religious discourse and development in the Western world.

In its overall structure, Deuteronomy breaks down fairly easily; but it is perhaps best understood in the light of comparative ancient Near Eastern material. Weinfeld's lifetime of research has demonstrated the strong parallels between our book and certain Assyrian treaty texts (earlier Hittite texts have also been shown to be helpful in this regard; cf. Levenson 1985b for a useful summary). It is striking indeed that the Esarhaddon Treaty texts from the seventh century B.C.E., which also produced the final form of Deuteronomy, seem to prefigure the basic structure of what Moshe lays out in the book: a historical overview, an exhortation to keep the covenant, the laws—particulars of the covenant, a series of blessings and curses following upon observance or nonobservance of the covenant, and a ceremony ratifying it. A similar pattern, in abbreviated form, may be observed in the Sinai covenant in Ex. 19–24.

Weinfeld points out that such covenants or treaties were two-sided, with the suzerain granting his vassals certain favors in return for "love" (= loyalty), and threatening dire consequences if that loyalty were to become suspect. What is fascinating about the parallels is not so much that they exist, but that here, apparently, a political model from a hated enemy has been assimilated and transformed into a positive religious-national one. Such transformative power seems to be characteristic of biblical culture, which probably reworked known stories and poems, among other genres, into genuine Israelite creations (the Flood narratives of Genesis and Psalm 29 are two fruitful examples of the process).

Deuteronomy, then, focuses mainly on the relationship between God and Israel, a relationship that has been spelled out before (as in Exodus) but that forms in this book the very soul of the text. Every act that Israel performs as a community, and every one done by individuals, is to be seen in that light. As elsewhere in the Bible, breaking one of God's rules means not merely a violation of a statute but an affront to the suzerain, the sovereign Lord, and thus a grave risk to society's well-being and even to its very existence. And there is a unity of purpose and concept here: Gottwald summarizes the message of the book as "the indivisible unity of *one God* for *one people* in *one land* observing *one cult*" (italics his).

Given the treaty pattern that we have just referred to, an outline of the book might proceed along the following lines:

I Historical Overview (Moshe as Narrator; 1–4:43)
    A   Narrative of the Wilderness Journey (1–3)
    B   Transition: Beginning of the Exhortation (4:1–40) and Addendum on Towns of Asylum (4:41–43)
II Opening Exhortation (Moshe as Pleader; 4:44–11:36) Looking Back to the Revelation at Sinai
III The Terms of the Covenant (Moshe as Lawgiver; 12–28)
    A   The Laws (12–26)
    B   Covenant Ceremony; Blessings and Curses (27–28)
IV Concluding Exhortation (Moshe as Pleader; 29–30) Looking Ahead to Exile and Return
V Final Matters (31–34)
    A   Passing the Mantle (31)
    B   Moshe's Admonitory Poem (32)
    C   Moshe's Blessing to the Tribes (33)
    D   The End (34)

A few simple structural observations, based on a closer look at the text itself, may be made here. Parts I and V stress the role of Yehoshua (Joshua) in the future. Then, too, Parts II and IV use similar rhetorical formulas toward the end of each ("See, I set before you this day . . .," 11:26 and 30:15). Such a symmetry would suggest that Part III is the crucial one, and that is of course the case. Everything in Deuteronomy radiates out from the laws: a new humanism, a rethinking of tradition, and above all, a heartfelt appeal to "choose life" (30:19), a good life on the land under the blessing of God.

It is only when that appeal has been fully made, and when all of Deuteronomy's new material has been added (with no more to come, as the text sees it!), that Moshe can finally die, and the people of Israel can proceed into the

Promised Land. The book of Numbers proved to be a false ending, and indeed the report of Moshe's death was postponed from the end of that book to this, so that the biblical tradition could transform itself into a truly multifaceted and rich one. The Torah, which began in the nameless, unknowable past, ends in the limitless present and future, with a potential life ahead for the Israelite people as bountiful and as beautiful as the "good land" that Moshe is allowed to see from the summit of Pisga.

PART I

HISTORICAL OVERVIEW

(1–4:43)

IN THIS INTRODUCTORY SECTION, WHICH SOME SCHOLARS HAVE VIEWED AS A LATER addition to the core of the book, Moshe reviews the journey of the Israelites from Mount Sinai ("Horev") into the Negev, and from there up east of the Dead Sea to a spot opposite Jericho. Two things make this more than a mere itinerary: First, Moshe confines himself to the most important moments—the choosing of leaders, the sending of the spies (with all its disastrous consequences), the encounters with various nations, and the provisions made for the soon-to-occur conquest. Second, the text characterizes itself, not as a narrative per se, but as an "explanation" (1:5) of the "Instruction." In other words, history is made to function as lesson here. That the account ends with Bet (Baal) Pe'or in 3:29 is surely not accidental; as 4:3 reminds us, this was the site of Israel's great apostasy, the final negative act by a wayward generation that was not to live to enter the land of Israel. By means of this introduction, the new generation is warned about the failings of the old, and begins to be prepared for "entering and taking-possession of the land" promised to their ancestors (4:1).

The first four chapters of the book establish its character as a link: by recounting key events in Israel's wanderings, they summarize the narratives of Exodus and Numbers; by demonstrating that disaster resulted from the people's rebellions, they set the ideology that will permeate the so-called Deuteronomistic History, namely the books of Joshua, Judges, Samuel, and Kings (Nelson).

It should be realized that these chapters are not merely previous narratives repeated verbatim. They are in fact reworkings of earlier material, often with changes. Thus, to use Brettler's example, 1:9-18 retells Ex. 18:13-26, with the change that this time, as Moshe appoints lower-level leadership for the people, he does so without his father-in-law Yitro (who had helped in the Exodus version), and chooses them on the basis of their capabilities ("wisdom"), not their piety. Brettler also points to the frequent use of the phrase "at that time" as an indicator of later additions to the text. For a comprehensive discussion of how these opening chapters differ from earlier accounts, see Tigay.

Setting Out (1): After the narrator's brief introduction, which places the Israelites at the very borders of the Promised Land, Moshe's words bring the Israelites from Sinai to Kadesh, in the southern part of the land. He begins with his own problem, the burden of leadership; but the bulk of the chapter functions to explain why the Israelites that came out of Egypt were not privileged to enter the land itself. Stylistically interesting is Moshe's constant use of quotations—he cites God, himself, and the Israelites. The effect is to make the narrative vivid and also authoritative in tone (cf. Polzin 1980).

1:1 These are the words that Moshe spoke to all Israel
in (the country) across the Jordan
in the wilderness, in the plains near Suf,
between Paran and Tofel, Lavan, Hatzerot, and Di-Zahav—

2 eleven days (it is) from Horev, by the route of Mount Se'ir,
(going) by Kadesh-Barne'a.

3 And it was in the fortieth year,
in the eleventh New-Moon, on (day) one after the New-Moon,
Moshe spoke to the Children of Israel
according to all that YHWH had commanded him concerning
them,

4 after he had struck
Sihon king of the Amorite, who sat-as-ruler in Heshbon,
and Og king of Bashan, who sat-as-ruler in Ashtarot, in Edre'i.

5 In (the country) across the Jordan, in the land of Moav,
Moshe set about to explain this Instruction, saying:

6 YHWH our God spoke to us at Horev, saying:
Enough for you, staying at this mountain!

7 Face about, march on
and come to the Amorite hill-country and to all its dwellers
in the Plains, the Hill-Country and the Lowlands, the
Negev/Parched-Land and the shore of the sea,
the land of the Canaanite and the Lebanon,
as far as the Great River, the river Euphrates.

8 See,
I give before you the land,

1:1 **words:** Or "speeches."

2 **Horev:** Another biblical name for Mount Sinai.
Kadesh Barne'a: The "base camp" for Israel's wanderings after Num. 14, at the southern border of biblical Israel in the Negev.

3 **fortieth year:** Since the departure from Egypt.

4 **Sihon . . . Og:** Two kings vanquished by the Israelites in their march east and northeast of the Dead Sea (Num. 21).

5 **Instruction:** In Leviticus, this term (*tora*) referred to a priestly rule or ritual; here, however, it has a broader significance, and seems to refer to a good

part of the book of Deuteronomy. Only later does it come to mean The Five Books of Moses.

7 **Hill-Country:** The mountainous backbone running north to south in the center of the country, geographically including Shechem and Jerusalem.
the Plains: The Jordan Valley. **Lowlands:** The area west of the hill-country and east of the coastal plain. **Negev:** The southern region (south of Beersheba). **the Lebanon:** Usually including the definite article in the Bible, as here, this is approximately the region of modern Lebanon, a mountain range extending about 100 miles north of the land of Israel.

enter, take-possession of the land
about which YHWH swore to your fathers, to Avraham, to
 Yitzhak, and to Yaakov,
to give to them and to their seed after them.

9 Now I said to you at that time, saying:
I am not able, I alone, to carry you;

10 YHWH your God has made-you-many—
and here you are today, like the stars in the heavens for multitude!

11 YHWH, the God of your fathers, may he add to you as you are a
 thousand times,
and bless you, as he promised to you!

12 How can I carry, I alone, your load, your burden, your quarreling?

13 Provide yourselves (with) men, wise, understanding and
 knowledgeable, for your tribes,
and I will set them as heads-over-you.

14 And you answered me, you said:
Good is the word that you have proposed to do!

15 So I took heads of your tribes, men wise and knowledgeable,
and I placed them as heads over you,
as rulers of thousands, rulers of hundreds, rulers of fifties, and
 rulers of tens, and as officials for your tribes.

16 Now I commanded your judges at that time, saying:
hear-out (what is) between your brothers,
judge with equity between each-man and his brother or a
 sojourner.

17 You are not to (specially-)recognize a face in judgment,
as the small, so the great, you are to hear-them-out;
you are not to be-in-fear of any-man,
for judgment—it is God's!
And (any) legal-matter too hard for you, bring-near to me,
and I will hear-it-out.

---

8 **about which YHWH swore to your fathers:** Cited
many times in Exodus through Numbers.
9 **I said:** Switching back to Moshe as narrator.
13 **knowledgeable:** JPS "experienced."
15 **So I took heads:** As his father-in-law had advised
him in Ex. 18:21–22.

16 **(what is) between:** Legal disputes. **a sojourner:** A
noncitizen or temporary resident. The sojourner is
frequently protected in the Torah, as one whose experience parallels that of the Israelites in Egypt (cf.
Ex. 22:20).

18 So I commanded you at that time concerning all the matters that
 you should do.

19 We marched on from Horev
 and traveled through the whole wilderness, that great and awe-
  inspiring one that you saw,
 by the Amorite hill-country route
 as Y<small>HWH</small> our God commanded us,
 and we came as far as Kadesh-Barne'a.

20 And I said to you:
 You have come to the Amorite hill-country that Y<small>HWH</small> our God is
  giving us.

21 See,
 Y<small>HWH</small> your God has given before you this land,
 go up, take-possession (of it),
 as Y<small>HWH</small> the God of your fathers promised you.
 Do not be afraid, do not be dismayed!

22 Then you came-near to me, all of you, and said:
 Let us send men before us
 that they may explore the land for us
 and return us word
 about the route that we should (use to) go up against it
 and about the towns that we will come to.

23 The matter was good in my eyes,
 and so I took from among you twelve men, one man per tribe.

24 They faced about and went up into the hills, and came as far as
  the Wadi of Clusters
 and spied it out.

25 They took in their hand (some) of the fruit of the land and
  brought (it) down to us
 and returned us word, they said:
 Good is the land that Y<small>HWH</small> our God is giving us!

---

19 **great and awe-inspiring:** Or "great and fearsome." The phrase is used of the wilderness again in 8:15 but, interestingly, also of God in 7:21, 10:17, and 28:58.

21 **given before you:** This oft-used phrase is equivalent to "laid at your feet."

22 **Then you came-near:** In Num. 13, the incentive for sending the spies comes from God. Here is yet another indication of the more human-oriented viewpoint of Deuteronomy.

25 **they said: / Good:** In contrast to the Num. 13 narrative, where the majority report continues with an expression of the Israelites' considerable fears about the inhabitants of the land.

26 Yet you were not willing to go up,
   you rebelled against the order of YHWH your God.

27 You muttered in your tents, you said:
   Because of YHWH's hatred for us he took us out of the land of
      Egypt,
   to give us into the hand of the Amorites, to destroy us!

28 To where are we going up?
   Our brothers have made our hearts melt, saying:
   A people greater and taller than we,
   towns great and fortified to heaven,
   and even Children of the Anakites we saw there!

29 Now I said to you:
   Do not shake-in-fear, do not be afraid of them!

30 YHWH your God, who goes before you,
   he will wage-war for you,
   according to all that he did with you in Egypt, before your eyes,

31 and in the wilderness, where you saw
   how YHWH your God carried you
   as a man carries his child,
   on all the way that you went upon,
   until your coming to this place.

32 Yet in this matter
   you have been showing-no-trust in YHWH your God,

33 who goes before you on the way
   to scout out for you a place to pitch-your-camp,
   in fire by night, to have you see the way on which you should go,
   and in a cloud by day!

34 When YHWH heard the voice of your words,
   he became furious and swore, saying:

28 **Our brothers:** The spies. **Children of the Anakites:** The Anakites (the "Long-Necked") were seen as original inhabitants of Canaan but, more importantly, were regarded as giants, as human ancestors often were in antiquity. See, similarly, the fantastic ages of the primordial figures in Gen. 5.

29 **shake-in-fear . . . be afraid:** Deuteronomy has a large vocabulary of words connoting "fear"—oscil-

lating between shoring up the Israelites' military courage (as here) and warning them about the consequences of abandoning God (as, for instance, in 28:66).

33 **who goes before you:** An expression connoting military leadership. **fire . . . cloud:** Cf. Ex. 13:21–22.

34 **voice:** Or "sound."

35 If they should get-to-see—a (single) man of all of these men, of
    this evil generation—
    the good land that I swore to give to their fathers . . . !

36 Only Calev son of Yefunne, he will get-to-see it,
    to him will I give the land that he has tread upon, and to his
    children,
    in consequence that he fully-followed after YHWH.

37 At me also YHWH was incensed for your sakes, saying:
    You also will not enter there!

38 Yehoshua son of Nun, who stands before you, he will enter there;
    him (you are to) strengthen,
    for he will allot-it-as inheritance to Israel.

39 Now your little-ones, of whom you said: For plunder will they
    be,
    and your children who as of today do not (yet) know good or ill,
    they shall enter there,
    to them I will give it, they will take-possession of it!

40 As for you, face about, march into the wilderness, by the Reed
    Sea route.

41 But you spoke up, you said to me:
    We have sinned against YHWH,
    we will go up and wage-war,
    according to all that YHWH our God commanded us!
    So each-man girded on his implements of war
    and you made-bold to go-up to the hill-country.

42 But YHWH said to me:
    Say to them:
    You are not to go-up, you are not to wage-war,
    for I am not in your midst—
    that you not be smitten before your enemies!

---

35 **If they should get-to-see . . . !:** The ellipsis suggesting "No possibility!" as an answer.

36 **Calev:** Trad. English "Caleb." Cf. Num. 13:30; he and Yehoshua (trad. English "Joshua") are the only spies to encourage the people to undertake the conquest of Canaan. Notable in this text is the omission of Yehoshua (Plaut).

39 **little-ones:** Heb. *taf,* lit. "toddlers."

40 **Reed Sea:** The site of the drowning of the Egyptian army in Ex. 14; the precise location still eludes scholars.

Encountering the Nations (2, 3:1–22): Moshe's narrative moves the people toward their present location, east of Jericho, detailing their disappointments and triumphs in meetings with the indigenous peoples of the area. The account begins tentatively, with Israel warned not to antagonize their "cousins," the Children of Esav, but ends with a foreshadowing of the conquest of Canaan—the successful war-making of the two and a half tribes (cf. Num. 32) that received land east of the Jordan.

43 So I spoke to you,
but you did not hearken,
you rebelled against the order of YHWH,
brazenly going-up to the hills.

44 Now the Amorites came out, those who were settled in those
hills, to meet you,
they pursued you—as bees do!—
and they crushed you at Se'ir, as far as Horma.

45 When you returned, you wept before the presence of YHWH,
but YHWH did not hearken to your voice,
he did not give-ear to you.

46 So you stayed in Kadesh for many days, like the days you had
stayed (there before),

2:1 and we faced about and marched into the wilderness, by the Reed
Sea route,
as YHWH had spoken to me;
we circled around the hills of Se'ir for many days-and-years.

2 Now YHWH said to me, saying:

3 Enough for you, circling around these hills!
Face about, northward!

4 And as for the people, command (them), saying:
You are (about) to cross the territory of your brothers, the
Children of Esav, who are settled in Se'ir.
Though they are afraid of you,
take exceeding care!

5 Do not stir yourselves up against them,
For I will not give you of their land so much as the sole of a foot
can tread on,
for as a possession to Esav I gave the hill-country of Se'ir.

---

43 **brazenly:** The root (here in the form *va-tahinu*) occurs only once in the Bible, and its derivation and
meaning are uncertain; I concur with JPS here.

44 **Horma:** Recalled in Num. 14:45 as a stinging defeat,
but cited in Num. 21:3 as a victory.

2:1 **days-and-years:** Heb. *yamin* often means a long period of time, not simply "days."

5 **Se'ir:** Cf. Gen. 33:14–16, where Se'ir is mentioned as
the home of Esav (Esau).

6 Food you may market from them for silver, that you may eat;
  and also water you may purchase from them for silver, that you
    may drink.

7 For Y<small>HWH</small> your God has blessed you in all the works of your
    hands—
  he has known your travels in this great wilderness!
  (For) forty years is Y<small>HWH</small> your God with you;
  you have not lacked a thing!

8 So we crossed on by, away from our brothers, the Children of
    Esav, who are settled in Se'ir,
  (away) from the route of the Plain, from Eilat and from Etzion
    Gever,
  and we faced about and crossed the route of the Wilderness of
    Moav.

9 Y<small>HWH</small> said to me:
  Do not harass Moav,
  do not stir yourself up against them (in) war,
  for I will not give you (any) of their land as a possession,
  for to the Children of Lot I have given Ar as a possession.

10 —The Emites/Frightful-Ones were formerly settled there,
  a people great and many, and tall like the Anakites.

11 Like Refa'ites/Shades are they considered, as the Anakites (are),
  but the Moavites call them Emites.

12 Now in Se'ir the Horites were formerly settled;
  but the Children of Esav dispossessed them, destroying them
    from before them and settling in their place,
  (just) as Israel did to the land of their possession,
  which Y<small>HWH</small> gave to them.—

---

6 **silver:** Money in the form of coinage was not yet used; here weights (Heb. *shekels*) of silver are meant.

8 **Moav:** Trad. "Moab," the area to the southeast of the Dead Sea (today Jordan).

10 **Emites/Frightful-Ones:** A folk memory of earlier inhabitants of Canaan. **Anakites:** Another early Canaanite group according to biblical tradition. Cf. the note to 1:28, and the account in Num. 13.

11 **Refa'ites/Shades:** Like the previous two peoples, a part of folk memory; this is a term whose meaning has been subject to much scholarly debate, but is now taken to refer to the descendants of dead heroes.

13 Now, arise, cross you the Wadi Zered!
So we crossed the Wadi Zered.
14 And the days that we traveled from Kadesh Barne'a until we
crossed the Wadi Zered (were):
thirty-eight years,
until had ended in all that generation, the men of war, from
amid the camp,
as YHWH had sworn to them.
15 Yes, the hand of YHWH was against them, to panic them from
amid the camp,
until they had ended.
16 Now it was, when all the men of war had ended (their) dying
from amid the people,
17 YHWH spoke to me, saying:
18 You are crossing today the territory of Moav, Ar.
19 When you come-near, opposite the Children of Ammon,
do not harass them, do not stir yourself up against them,
for I will not give (any) of the land of the Children of Ammon to
you as a possession,
for to the Children of Lot I have given it as a possession.
20 It, too, is considered the land of the Refa'ites,
Refa'ites were settled in it in former-times,
but the Ammonites call them Zamzummites/Barbarians
21 —a people great and many, tall like the Anakites,
yet YHWH destroyed them from before them, and they
dispossessed them,
and settled in their place,
22 as he did to the Children of Esav who are settled in Se'ir,
that he destroyed the Horites from before them, and they
dispossessed them

---

13 **Wadi Zered:** The border between Edom and Moab, east of the lower end of the Dead Sea.
15 **panic them:** Paralleling the experience of the Egyptian army in Ex. 14:24.
20 **Zamzummites/Barbarians:** Lit. "mumblers," like the derivation of the English "barbarians" (so-called because the Greeks characterized other peoples as

speaking indistinctly). Gaster and others suggest an alternative interpretation taken from Arabic *za-mzama*, the low noise made by desert spirits; hence our phrase would refer to the supernatural, just as the Anakites and Refa'ites were seen as giants and shades.

♦ and settled in their place,
until this (very) day.

23 As for the Avvites who were settled in villages as far as Gaza,
Kaftorites who came from Kaftor destroyed them and settled in
their place.

24 Arise, march on and cross the Wadi Arnon!
See, I have given into your hand Sihon king of Heshbon, the
Amorite, and his land;
Start! Take-possession!
And stir yourself up against him (in) war!

25 This (very) day
I will start to put the terror of you and the awe of you
upon the peoples (that are) under all the heavens,
so that when they hear heard-rumors of you,
they will shudder and writhe before you.

26 Now I sent messengers from the Wilderness of Kedemot to
Sihon, king of Heshbon,
words of peace, saying:

27 Let me cross through your land;
on the main-route, on the main-route I will go,
I will not turn aside right or left.

28 As for food, for silver you may market (it) to me, that I may eat,
as for water, for silver you may give (it) to me, that I may drink,
only: let me cross on foot—

29 as the Children of Esav, who are settled in Se'ir, did for me,
and the Moavites, who are settled in Ar,
until I have crossed the Jordan
into the land that YHWH our God is giving us.

30 But Sihon king of Heshbon was not willing to let us cross
through him,

---

22 **until this (very) day:** This rather imprecise historical note occurs frequently in the Torah, especially in
Deuteronomy.
23 **Kaftor:** The island of Crete, understood in the Bible
as the place of origin of the Philistines, who figure
so prominently in Judges and Samuel as the archenemy of Israel.

24 **Heshbon:** Across the Jordan from Jericho. **Start!
Take-possession!:** In idiomatic English, "Start to
take possession."
26 **I sent messengers . . . to Sihon:** Cf. Num. 21:21ff.
30 **hardened his spirit and stiffened his heart:** Reminiscent of Pharaoh in the plagues narrative of Exodus.

for Y𝐻𝑊𝐻 your God hardened his spirit and stiffened his heart,
in order to give him into your hand, as (is) this day.

31 Now Y𝐻𝑊𝐻 said to me:
See, I have started to give before you Sihon and his land,
start, take-possession, to possess his land!

32 And Sihon went out to meet us, he and all his people in war, at
Yahatz,

33 but Y𝐻𝑊𝐻 our God gave him before us,
we struck him and his sons and all his people.

34 We conquered all his towns at that time,
we devoted-to-destruction every town: menfolk, women, and
little-ones;
we left no remnant.

35 Only the animals did we plunder for ourselves,
and the booty of the towns that we conquered.

36 From Aro'er, that is on the bank of the Wadi Arnon,
and the town that is in the Wadi, as far as Gil'ad,
there was not a city that was too lofty for us,
all (of them) Y𝐻𝑊𝐻 our God gave before us.

37 Only the land of the Children of Ammon you did not come-near,
all the environs of the Wadi Yabbok, and the towns in the hill-
country,
and all about which Y𝐻𝑊𝐻 our God commanded us.

3:1 We faced about and went up the route to Bashan,
and Og king of Bashan came out to meet us,
he and all his fighting-people in war, at Edre'i.

2 And Y𝐻𝑊𝐻 said to me:
Do not be afraid of him,
for into your hand I give him and all his fighting-people, and his
land,
you will do to him

---

34 **devoted-to-destruction:** Or "banned." According
to this biblical practice of *herem,* spoils of war were
confiscated for God/the sanctuary, and people so
designated were put to death. It is a concept of
"holy war," which seems to deny economic motives
for warfare. For a thorough discussion, see Stern.

3:1 **Bashan:** The region to the east and southeast of the
Sea of Galilee.

as you did to Sihon king of the Amorites, that sat-as-ruler in
　　Heshbon.
3　And YHWH our God gave into our hand
　　Og king of Bashan as well, and all his fighting-people,
　　we struck him until there was not left him any remnant.
4　We conquered all his towns at that time,
　　there was no city that we did not take from them,
　　sixty towns, all the region of Argov,
　　the kingdom of Og at Bashan.
5　All these (were) fortified towns (with) a high wall, doubled-
　　doored with a bar,
　　aside from the towns of the open-country-dwellers, exceedingly
　　many.
6　We devoted them to destruction,
　　as we had done to Sihon king of Heshbon,
　　devoting-to-destruction every town:
　　menfolk, women and little-ones,
7　while every (head of) cattle, and the plunder of the towns, we
　　took-as-plunder for ourselves.
8　And we took at that time the land
　　from the hand of the two kings of the Amorites that were in (the
　　country) across the Jordan,
　　from Wadi Arnon to Mount Hermon;
9　—Sidonians call Hermon Siryon,
　　but the Amorites call it Senir—
10　all the towns of the plateau and all of Gil'ad, and all of Bashan,
　　as far as Salkha and Edre'i,
　　towns of the kingdom of Og at Bashan.
11　For only Og king of Bashan was left of the rest of the Refa'ites
　　—here, his couch was a couch of iron,
　　is it not (still) in Rabba of the Children of Ammon,

8 **Mount Hermon:** The highest peak in the region (about 9,200 feet), located well northeast of the Sea of Galilee.

11 **Rabba:** Today's Amman, the capital of Jordan. **nine cubits:** Over thirteen feet in length!

nine cubits its length, four cubits its width, by the cubit of a
man?—

12   Now this land we possessed at that time,
from Aro'er which is by the Wadi Arnon;
half of the hill-country of Gil'ad and its towns I gave to the
Re'uvenites and to the Gadites.

13   And the rest of Gil'ad and all of Bashan, the kingdom of Og,
I gave to half of the tribe of Menashe, all the region of Argov,
including all of Bashan,
—it is called the Land of the Refa'ites.

14   Ya'ir son of Menashe took all of the region of Argov
as far as the territory of the Geshurites and the Maakathites,
and called them by his name, (the) Bashan (towns):
Havvot Ya'ir/Tent-Villages of Ya'ir,
until this (very) day.

15   Now to Makhir I gave Gil'ad,

16   and to the Re'uvenites and to the Gadites I gave from Gil'ad, as
far as Wadi Arnon, the middle of the Wadi as the boundary,
as far as Yabbok the Wadi,
the boundary of the Children of Ammon;

17   and the Plain and Jordan as (its) boundary
from the Kinneret as far as the Sea of the Plain, the Sea of Salt,
beneath the slopes of the Pisga (Range), toward sunrise.

18   And I commanded you at that time, saying:
YHWH your God has given you this land to possess;
you specially-drafted (men) are to cross over before their
brothers, the Children of Israel, all those of caliber.

19   Only your wives, your little-ones, and your livestock
—I know that you have many (head of) livestock—
are to settle in your towns that I am giving you,

---

12 **Re'uvenites . . . Gadites:** Along with half of the
tribe of Menashe (v.13), these tribes were granted
land on the east bank of the Jordan (cf. Num. 32).

15 **Makhir:** Like Ya'ir in the previous verse, a descendant ("son") of Menashe.

17 **Kinneret:** Some suggest a connection with the

shape of a lyre (Heb. *kinnor*); this is still the Hebrew
name for the Sea of Galilee. **Sea of Salt:** Likewise
the Hebrew name for the Dead Sea.

18 **specially-drafted:** Or "hand-picked." JPS, "shock
troops." **those of caliber:** Others, "warriors."

Moshe's Personal Plea (3:23–29): Before Moshe begins his appeal to the people of Israel to keep the covenant, he recalls his fervent prayer to God to be allowed into the land himself, a prayer that is, of course, answered in the negative. This recollection raises the emotional stakes of what is to come; the bulk of the book is now established as Moshe's last words.

20 until Yhwh gives-rest to your brothers as yourselves,
   and they take-possession, they as well, of the land that Yhwh
       your God is giving you, in (the country) across the Jordan.
   Then shall each-man return to his possession that I give you.
21 Now Yehoshua I commanded at that time, saying:
   Your eyes (it was) that have seen all that Yhwh your God did to
       these two kings;
   thus will Yhwh do to all the kingdoms into which you are
       crossing!
22 You are not to be afraid of them,
   for Yhwh your God,
   he is the one who wages-war for you!
23 Now I pleaded with Yhwh at that time, saying:
24 My Lord Yhwh,
   you yourself have started to let your servant see
   your greatness and your strong hand,
   that who is a god in heaven and on earth
   that can do according to your deeds and according to your power!
25 Pray let me cross over
   that I may see the good land
   that is in (the country) across the Jordan,
   this good hill-country, and the Lebanon!
26 But Yhwh was cross with me on your account,
   and he would not hearken to me,
   Yhwh said to me:
   Enough for you!
   Do not speak to me any more again about this matter!
27 Go up to the top of the Pisga (Range)
   and lift up your eyes—toward the sea, toward the north, toward
       the south, and toward sunrise;
   see (it) with your eyes,
   for you will not cross this Jordan!

---

21 **these two kings:** Sihon and Og.
26 **cross:** Playing on the oft-used "crossing over,"
   which appears here in vv.25, 27, and 28.

27 **Pisga:** The site where Moshe dies in Chap. 34 below.

Transition (4:1–40): Moshe, having narrated Israel's wilderness travels up to the spot where they are standing, now launches into the main set of speeches that characterize Deuteronomy's style, a series of exhortations to the people to follow God's laws. This section is connected to the previous material by its evocation of past events (the sin at Baal Pe'or and the revelation at Sinai/Horev), but it also points to the future, by means of its vision of exile and return. Not surprisingly, the words "hear/hearken," "see," "laws (and regulations)," and "command" are all key expressions; these become increasingly important in the chapters to follow.

Ironic is the repeated warning, which appears here for the first time, not to add anything to the Instruction. Yet Deuteronomy itself does just that. But, as we have noted above, by closing the Torah after the end of the book, Deuteronomy is able to introduce innovations with the force of tradition, and seemingly guard against further overt revision.

Levenson (1975) sees this section, along with material in chapters 28–32, as providing a framework for the book for the Israelite community in exile, suggesting that return to God is still possible through keeping the commandments laid out within the framework.

28 But command Yehoshua,
　　make-him-strong, make-him-courageous,
　　for he will cross over before this people
　　and he will cause them to inherit the land that you see.
29 And we stayed in the valley,
　　opposite Bet Pe'or.

4:1 And now, O Israel, hearken to the laws and the regulations
　　that I am teaching you to observe,
　　in order that you may live
　　and enter and take-possession of the land that YHWH, the God of
　　　　your fathers, is giving to you.
2 You are not to add to the word that I am commanding you,
　　and you are not to subtract from it,
　　in keeping the commandments of YHWH your God that I am
　　　　commanding you.
3 Your eyes (it is) that have seen what YHWH did at Baal Pe'or:
　　indeed, every man that walked after Baal Pe'or—
　　YHWH your God destroyed him from among you!
4 But you, the ones clinging to YHWH your God,
　　are alive, all of you, today!
5 See,
　　I am teaching you laws and regulations
　　as YHWH my God has commanded me, to do thus,
　　amid the land that you are entering to possess.
6 You are to keep (them), you are to observe (them),
　　for that (will be) wisdom-for-you and understanding-for-you in
　　　　the eyes of the peoples
　　who, when they hear all these laws, will say:
　　Only a wise and understanding people is this great nation!
7 For who (else) is (such) a great nation
　　that has gods so near to it

---

29 **Bet Pe'or:** Cf. "Baal Pe'or" in 4:3 below.
4:3 **Baal Pe'or:** Cf. Num. 25. This brief instance of Is-
　　raelite idolatry is remembered in the Bible as one of
　　the worst examples of its kind.

4 **But you** etc.: This verse is recited in synagogues on
　　Sabbath mornings, as the Torah scroll is about to be
　　read from.

as Y<small>HWH</small> our God
in all our calling on him?

8 And who (else) is (such) a great nation
that has laws and regulations so equitable
as all this Instruction
that I put before you today?

9 Only: take you care, take exceeding care for your self,
lest you forget the things that your eyes saw,
lest you turn-aside in your heart
all the days of your life;
make-them-known to your children, and to your children's
children:

10 The day that you stood before the presence of Y<small>HWH</small> your God at
Horev,
when Y<small>HWH</small> said to me:
Assemble the people to me,
that I may have them hear my words
that they may learn to hold me in awe
all the days that they are alive on the soil,
—and their children, they are to teach!—

11 you came-near, you stood beneath the mountain:
now the mountain was burning with fire,
up to the (very) heart of the heavens,
(in) darkness, cloud and fog.

12 And Y<small>HWH</small> spoke to you from the midst of the fire:
a voice of words you heard,
a form you did not see,
only a voice!

13 He announced to you his covenant
which he commanded you to observe,
the Ten Words,
and he wrote them down on two tablets of stone.

9 **self:** Or "life."
10 **hold me in awe:** Others, "fear me," "revere me."
13 **the Ten Words:** They are never called the "Ten

Commandments" in the Hebrew Bible—only in
subsequent Jewish and Christian tradition.

866

14 And me, YHWH commanded at that time
to teach you laws and regulations
for you to observe them
in the land that you are crossing into to possess.

15 Now you are to take exceeding care for your selves—
for you did not see any form
on the day that YHWH spoke to you at Horev from the midst of
the fire—

16 lest you wreak-ruin
by making yourselves a carved form of any figure,

17 (in the) pattern of male or female,
the pattern of any animal that is on earth,
the pattern of any winged bird that flies in the heavens,

18 the pattern of any crawling-thing on the soil,
the pattern of any fish that is in the waters beneath the earth—

19 or lest you lift up your eyes toward the heavens
and see the sun and the moon and the stars, all the forces of the
heavens,
and be lured-away to prostrate yourselves to them
and serve them,
whom YHWH has apportioned for all the (other) peoples beneath
all the heavens.

20 But you, YHWH took
and brought you out of the Iron Furnace, out of Egypt,
to be for him a people of inheritance,
as (is) this (very) day.

21 Now YHWH was incensed with me because of your words
and he swore not to let me cross the Jordan,
not to enter the good land that YHWH is giving you as an
inheritance.

22 For I am going to die in this land,
I will not cross the Jordan!

---

16 **lest:** This particle occurs frequently in Deuteron-omy, as part of its elaborate language of warning.

21 **and he swore** etc.: Here it is to the people's "words" (unspecified, but probably their refusal to enter the land in Num. 13–14), and not to Moshe's own rebel-lious act in striking the rock in Num. 20, that the narrator attributes God's barring the Promised Land to him.

But you (are the ones who) will cross over and take-possession of
    this good land.

23 Take you care,
    lest you forget the covenant of YHWH your God which he cut
        with you,
    and you make yourselves a carved-image, the form of anything
    about which YHWH your God commanded you!

24 For YHWH your God—he is a consuming fire,
    a jealous God!

25 When you beget children and children's children
    and you grow old in the land:
    should you wreak-ruin by making a carved-image in the form of
        anything,
    thus doing what is ill in the eyes of YHWH your God, vexing him:

26 I call-as-witness against you today the heavens and the earth,
    that you will perish, yes, perish quickly
    from off the land that you are crossing the Jordan thither to
        possess;
    you will not prolong days upon it,
    but you will be destroyed, yes, destroyed!

27 YHWH will scatter you among the peoples,
    you will be left as menfolk few-in-number
    among the nations whither YHWH will lead you.

28 You will serve there gods made by human hands, of wood and of
        stone,
    which cannot see and cannot hear, and cannot eat and cannot
        smell.

29 But when you seek YHWH your God from there
    you will find (him),
    if you search for him with all your heart and with all your being.

30 When you are in distress
    because there befall you all these things, in future days,
    you shall return to YHWH your God and hearken to his voice.

27 **menfolk few-in-number:** Echoing Jacob's fear in   36 **discipline:** Or "rebuke."
Gen. 34:30.

31 For a compassionate God is Yhwh your God;
   he will not weaken you, he will not bring-ruin on you,
   he will not forget the covenant (with) your fathers that he swore
      to them.

32 For inquire, pray, of past days, which were before you:
   from the day that God created humankind on the earth, and from
      one edge of the heavens to the (other) edge of the heavens:
   has there ever been such a great thing,
   or anything heard like it?

33 Has a people ever heard the voice of a god speaking from the
      midst of the fire
   as you have heard, yourself,
   and remained-alive?

34 Or has a god ever essayed to come and take himself a nation from
      within a nation,
   with trials, signs, portents and deeds-of-war,
   with a strong hand and an outstretched arm
   and with great awe-inspiring (acts),
   according as all that Yhwh your God did in Egypt before your eyes?

35 You yourself have been made-to-see, to know
   that Yhwh—he is God,
   there is none else beside him!

36 From the heavens he had you hear his voice, to discipline you;
   on earth he had you see his great fire,
   and his words you heard from the midst of the fire.

37 Now since he loved your fathers,
   he chose their seed after them
   and brought you out with his presence with great power from
      Egypt,

38 to dispossess nations greater and mightier than you from before
      you,
   by bringing you out, by giving you their land as an inheritance, as
      (is) this (very) day—

37 **since he loved your fathers:** Often given as the reason for God's mercy toward Israel; cf. Moshe's plea
in Ex. 32:13. **seed:** Meaning "offspring." **with his**

presence: Focusing on the direct intervention of
God (as opposed to angels, for instance), is characteristic of Deuteronomy (Tigay).

Towns of Asylum (4:41–43): In a brief passage that seems utterly out of place amid the deep rhetoric of this section, Moshe carries out a command he had received in Num. 35:9–34 to make sure that an accidental manslayer has a special place(s) to flee to from an avenging family. Perhaps this has been placed here because it is one of the few "laws and regulations" in the Torah whose observance is mandated on the east bank of the Jordan River—and hence is one of the few that Moshe personally gets to carry out.

39 know today and lay it up in your heart,
    that Yhwh—he is God
    in the heavens above and on the earth beneath,
    (there is) none else!
40 You are to keep his laws and his commandments that I command
        you today,
    that it may go-well with you and with your children after you,
    in order that you may prolong days on the soil
    that Yhwh your God is giving you,
    all the days (to come).

41 Then Moshe set apart three towns in (the country) across the
        Jordan, toward the rising of the sun,
42 for fleeing to (for) the (accidental) murderer who murders his
        neighbor with no forethought,
    where he did not bear-hatred toward him from yesterday and the
        day-before,
    and so can flee to one of these towns and stay-alive:
43 Betzer in the wilderness of the plateau land, belonging to the
        Re'uvenites,
    Ra'mot in Gil'ad, belonging to the Gadites,
    and Golan in Bashan, belonging to the Menashites.

PART II

OPENING EXHORTATION

(4:44–11:32)

THIS SECTION OF DEUTERONOMY IS A LONG PERSONAL AND EMOTIONAL PLEA ON BE-
half of the leader. Its rhetoric has become famous, as have several passages noted
below. It is in this section that Moshe appears in his most classic Deuteronomistic
mode, urging the people on to follow God's rules and warning them against violating the covenant.

Recurring phrases in the section include "Hearken O Israel," "And now, O
Israel," "When I bring you into the land . . . ," and "take-care." In addition, the
word "love," which as noted above carries the connotation of "loyalty," is important in these speeches.

After a brief geographical introduction in vv.44–49, which parallels the opening of the book and which, in the eyes of many, once served as the book's actual
beginning, the section presents a version of the so-called Ten Commandments,
and a short recapitulation of the circumstances surrounding their being given on
Sinai. In that sense, Chapter 5 is a continuation of the historical overview of the
beginning of the book.

Another famous passage here is in Chapter 6, where Israel is enjoined to "love"
God, warned about what will happen if they abandon him, and given a kind of
script as answer to their children's future question, "What (mean) the precepts,
the laws and the regulations that YHWH your God has commanded you?" (v.20).

Other important themes appear in these speeches. Israel is defined as a people
that is not to intermarry with the indigenous peoples of Canaan; as a people chosen, not for its military power or large population, but because God "loved" them,
and because he could not abide the Canaanites' behavior. To prove his point that
Israel possesses no inherent superiority, Moshe turns again to history, and retells
the story of the Molten Calf (Ex. 32–34).

He ends (in Chap. 11) by reiterating the motif of God's power and hence his
ability to reward faithfulness with the gift of the good land. Israel is promised
blessing and not curse, provided that they "take-care to observe" the laws which
are now to be set before them.

The Basic Rules (4:44–5:30): After a brief introduction, the text appears to begin the sequence of "laws and regulations" with the Ten Commandments. The latter, however, are quoted from Sinai (albeit in slightly altered form), and we are justified in viewing them, just as their counterpart in Ex. 20, as a kind of preamble to the laws themselves. They may even function as a narrated piece amid the pleas of Moshe. At any event, Chap. 5 uses key words we have previously encountered—"speak," "command," "hear"—but puts major emphasis on variations of the root "live." The message would seem to be that those who heard God speaking at Sinai miraculously survived, and now will survive into the long term if they keep God's covenant which he presented at the mountain.

The Ten Commandments, of course, form a cornerstone of Western civilization—although a glance at them will reveal that they have not been very well followed over the past two millennia. But their language and their message remain an ideal. They served for a time as part of Jewish liturgy, but were ultimately removed from the Prayer Book out of fear that it would be thought that ten rules were the limit of one's obligations to God.

As in Chap. 4, where the audience is warned not to add anything to the revealed Instruction, Chap. 5 also reminds them that nothing was added at Sinai.

44 This is the Instruction that Moshe set before the Children of
　　Israel,

45 these are the precepts and the laws and the regulations that
　　Moshe declared to the Children of Israel when they went out
　　from Egypt,

46 in (the country) across the Jordan, in the valley opposite Bet
　　Pe'or,
　　in the land of Sihon, king of the Amorites, who sat-as-ruler in
　　Heshbon,
　　whom Moshe and the Children of Israel struck, when they went
　　out from Egypt;

47 they took possession of his land and the land of Og king of
　　Bashan—
　　the two kings of the Amorites who (were) in (the country) across
　　the Jordan, (toward) the rising of the sun,

48 from Aro'er that is on the bank of the Wadi Arnon, as far as
　　Mount Si'on/Peak—that is Hermon,

49 and all the Plain across the Jordan, toward sunrise, as far as the
　　Sea of the Plain, beneath the slopes of the Pisga (Range).

5:1 Moshe called all of Israel (together) and said to them:
　　Hearken, O Israel,
　　to the laws and the regulations
　　that I am speaking in your ears today!
　　You are to learn them,
　　you are to take-care to observe them!

2 YHWH our God cut with us a covenant at Horev.

3 Not with our fathers did YHWH cut this covenant,
　　but with us, yes, us, those here today,
　　all of us (that are) alive!

4 Face to face did YHWH speak with you on the mountain,
　　from the midst of the fire

5 —I myself was standing between YHWH and you at that time,
　　to report to you the word of YHWH;

5:3 **but with us . . . here today:** The extreme irony of
this statement, if taken at face value, is apparent.
But religious texts and practice emphasize the here-
and-now of the religious experience.

for you were afraid of the fire,
and would not go up on the mountain—
saying:

6 I am YHWH your God
who brought you out of the land of Egypt, out of a house of
serfs.
7 You are not to have other gods beside my presence.
8 You are not to make yourself a carved-image of any form
that is in the heavens above, that is on the earth beneath, that is in
the waters beneath the earth.
9 You are not to prostrate yourselves to them, you are not to serve
them,
for I, YHWH your God, am a jealous God,
calling-to-account the iniquity of the fathers upon the sons to the
third and to the fourth (generation) of those that hate me,
10 but showing loyalty to thousands
of those that love me, of those that keep my commandments.

11 You are not to take up the name of YHWH your God for
emptiness,
for YHWH will not clear him that takes up his name for emptiness!
12 Keep the day of Sabbath, by hallowing it,
as YHWH your God has commanded you.
13 For six days you are to serve and to do all your work;
14 but the seventh day
(is) Sabbath for YHWH your God—
you are not to do any work:
(not) you, nor your son, nor your daughter,
nor your servant, nor your maid,
nor your ox, nor your donkey, nor any of your animals,
nor your sojourner that is in your gates—
in order that your servant and your maid may rest as one-like-
yourself.

11 **take up . . . for emptiness:** That is, use God's name
for a false purpose.

13 **serve:** Or "do serving-tasks," labor.

15 You are to bear-in-mind that serf were you in the land of Egypt,
     but YHWH your God took you out from there with a strong hand
          and with an outstretched arm;
     therefore YHWH your God commands you to observe the day of
          Sabbath.

16 Honor your father and your mother,
     as YHWH your God has commanded you,
     in order that your days may be prolonged,
     and in order that it may go-well with you on the soil that YHWH
          your God is giving you.

17 You are not to murder!
     And you are not to adulter!
     And you are not to steal!
     And you are not to testify against your neighbor as a lying
          witness!

18 And you are not to desire the wife of your neighbor;
     you are not to crave the house of your neighbor,
     his field, or his servant, or his maid, his ox or his donkey,
     or anything that belongs to your neighbor!

19 These words YHWH spoke to your entire assembly at the
          mountain
     from the midst of the fire, the cloud, and the fog,
     (with) a great voice, adding no more;
     and he wrote them on the two tablets of stone
     and gave them to me.

20 And it was, when you heard the voice from the midst of the
          darkness
     and (saw) the mountain burning with fire,
     you came-near to me, all the heads of your tribes and your elders,

16 **that your days may be prolonged:** That you may live long.

17 **And you are not to** etc.: The "and" is a change from the Ex. 20 version.

18 **desire:** As your own. **crave:** Added to the Exodus version here. Notable as a change from the earlier text is the characterization of the wife as an entity distinct from the "house."

The Centrality of Education (6): Deuteronomy places particular emphasis on transmitting the meaning and practice of the laws. Crucial here is the concept that constant recital of key ideas and experiences, and making sure to pass them on to new generations, will insure the observance of the commandments and hence Israel's good life on the promised soil. "Command" is the frequently used key word; the central passage is the so-called *Shema* ("Hearken [O Israel]"), already used in ancient times as both the core prayer in daily Jewish liturgy and the cry of martyrs (it is used as well as a prayer for retiring at night and as the core of the deathbed confession). Here memory is the key: the experience of slavery in Egypt, Israel's trying behavior in the wilderness, and, above all, the constant rescuing grace of God. The idea that there should be constant reminders of the covenant became a staple of Jewish ritual practice, from the early education of children in the biblical text, to the *tefillin* (see below) worn in daily prayer, to the *mezuza* (a small box containing passages from Deuteronomy) on the doorpost. All three are mentioned in vv.7–9.

Vv. 5–9 have an oral, liturgical ring to them, with the tenfold repetition of the sound *ekha* ("your"). A good many sections of Deuteronomy in fact utilize this style, providing the book, despite its emphasis on the phenomenon of writing, with a distinctive sound.

21 and you said:
　Here, YHWH our God has let us see all his Glory and his
　　greatness,
　and his voice we have heard from the midst of the fire.
　This day we have seen that God can speak to humans and they
　　can remain-alive!

22 But now, why should we die?
　For it will consume us, this great fire;
　if we continue to hear the voice of YHWH our God anymore,
　we will die!

23 For who is there (among) all flesh
　that has (ever) heard the voice of the living God speaking from
　　the midst of the fire, as we have,
　and remained-alive?

24 *You* go-near and hear all that YHWH our God says;
　and *you* speak to us all that YHWH our God speaks to you,
　we will hearken and we will do (it).

25 And YHWH hearkened to the voice of your words when you
　　spoke to me,
　YHWH said to me:
　I have heard the voice of this people's words that they have
　　spoken to you;
　it is well, all that they have spoken!

26 Who would give that this heart of theirs would (always) belong
　　to them, to hold me in awe and keep all my commandments,
　　all the days,
　in order that it might go-well with them and with their children,
　　for the ages!

27 Go, say to them:
　Return you to your tents!

28 As for you, remain-standing here beside me,
　that I may speak to you all the commandment, the laws and the
　　regulations that you are to teach them,

---

21 **Glory:** God's visible manifestation, his "aura." **they can remain-alive:** In the Bible (cf. Ex. 33:20) as elsewhere in the ancient world, the divine usually can- not be directly viewed by humans.

26 **all the days:** Or "every day."

◆ that they may observe (them) in the land that I am giving them to
possess.

29 You are to take-care to observe as YHWH your God has
commanded you;
you are not to turn-aside to the right or to the left.

30 In all the way that YHWH your God has commanded you, you are
to walk, in order that you may remain-alive, and it may be-well
with you,
and you may prolong (your) days in the land that you are
possessing.

6:1 Now this is the commandment, the laws and the regulations
that YHWH your God has commanded (me) to teach you
to observe in the land that you are crossing into to possess,

2 in order that you may hold YHWH your God in awe,
by keeping all his laws and his commandments that I command
you,
you, and your child, and your child's child,
all the days of your life;
and in order that your days may be prolonged.

3 You are to hearken, O Israel,
and are to take-care to observe (them),
that it may go-well with you,
that you may become exceedingly many,
as YHWH, the God of your fathers promised to you—
(in) a land flowing with milk and honey.

4 Hearken O Israel:
YHWH our God, YHWH (is) One!

6:3 **exceedingly many:** Fulfilling the promise made to
Abraham in Genesis on numerous occasions.
honey: Alternatively, "nectar," the syrup of dates.
4 **YHWH our God, YHWH (is) One!:** Despite the centrality of this phrase as a rallying cry in later Jewish
history and thought, its precise meaning is not clear.

It most likely stipulates that the Israelites are to worship YHWH alone; a secondary meaning might be reflected by the translation "YHWH is (but) one" —
that is, God has no partner or consort as in the
mythology of neighboring cultures.

5 Now you are to love YHWH your God
    with all your heart, with all your being, with all your substance!
6 These words, which I myself command you today, are to be upon
       your heart.
7 You are to inculcate them in your children
    and are to speak of them
    in your sitting in your house and in your walking in the way,
    in your lying-down and in your rising-up.
8 You are to tie them as a sign upon your hand,
    and they are to be for bands between your eyes.
9 You are to write them upon the doorposts of your house and on
       your gates.

10 Now it shall be
    when YHWH your God brings you to the land that he swore to
       your fathers, to Avraham, to Yitzhak, and to Yaakov, to give
       you,
    towns great and good that you did not build,
11 houses full of every good-thing that you did not fill,
    cisterns hewn out that you did not hew,
    vineyards and olive-groves that you did not plant,
    and you eat and you are satisfied,
12 take-you-care,
    lest you forget YHWH
    who brought you out of the land of Egypt, out of a house of
       serfs.
13 YHWH your God you are to hold-in-awe,
    him you are to serve,
    by his name you are to swear!

---

5 **heart:** The word is often the equivalent of "mind" in biblical language. **being:** Heb. *nefesh* carries a host of meanings: "life" or "life-essence," "breath," "self," and "appetite," to mention a few. The traditional English "soul," while stirring in these passages, gives the impression of something contrasted to the body—not an idea that appears in the Hebrew Bible. It should be mentioned that the couplet "heart and being," which occurs a number of times in Deuteronomy, might also indicate "mind and emotions." **substance:** Or "excess"; others, "might," "capacity." There are other examples of biblical Hebrew words for "strength" that also mean "wealth" (e.g., *hayil* in Deut. 33:11).

7 **inculcate . . . in:** Others, "teach diligently to," "repeat with."

11 **and you eat . . . satisfied:** Or "eat your fill."

Israel and the Canaanites (7): An important part of Israel's self-understanding in Deuteronomy, as elsewhere in the Torah, is separation from other peoples—particularly from the inhabitants of the land they are to conquer. This chapter emphasizes the absolute avoidance of the Canaanites which the Israelites are to practice (it begins and ends with "devotion-to-destruction," a kind of ritual ban or confiscation). The violence on the part of Israel spoken of in the opening verses, and the destruction wrought by God in the closing lines, frame a middle section that speaks of God's "love" and "loyalty" toward Israel—again, in the mode of an ancient Near Eastern overlord. The emotional tone of the chapter strongly suggests a period of intense nationalism.

14 You are not to walk after other gods
from the gods of the peoples that are around you,

15 for a jealous God is YHWH your God in your midst—
lest the anger of YHWH your God flare up against you
and he destroy you from off the face of the soil.

16 You are not to test YHWH your God
as you tested him at Massa/Testing!

17 Keep, yes, keep the commandment of YHWH your God,
and his precepts and his laws that he commanded you.

18 You are to do what is right and what is good in the eyes of YHWH,
in order that it may go-well with you,
so that you may come and take-possession of the good land that
YHWH swore to your fathers;

19 to push out all your enemies before you,
as YHWH has promised.

20 When your child asks you on the morrow, saying:
What (mean) the precepts, the laws, and the regulations that
YHWH our God has commanded you?

21 Then you are to say to your child:
Serfs were we to Pharaoh in Egypt,
and YHWH took us out of Egypt with a strong hand;

22 YHWH placed signs and portents, great and evil-ones, on Egypt,
on Pharaoh and all his house, before our eyes.

23 And us he took out of there
in order to bring us, to give us the land that he swore to our
fathers;

24 so YHWH has commanded us to observe all these laws,
to hold YHWH our God in awe,
to have it be-well with us all the days (to come),
to keep-us-alive, as (is) this day.

16 **Massa/Testing:** Cf. Ex. 17:1–7, where the people grumble against their leaders because of thirst.

20 **When your child** etc.: Children are to be taught the meaning of *all* the laws to follow, not just the Passover regulations as in Ex. 12:26–27 and 13:8–15 (Weinfeld). Nonetheless, vv.20–25 were used by the later rabbis to form a central part of the Passover ceremony. Many translate "son," in keeping with a didactic image (father to son) found in biblical wisdom such as the book of Proverbs. In Weinfeld's view, Deuteronomy originated in wisdom circles.

25 And righteous-merit will it be (considered) for us
    when we take-care to observe all this commandment
    before the presence of YHWH our God,
    as he commanded us.

7:1 When YHWH your God brings you to the land that you are
        entering to possess,
    and dislodges great nations before you
    —the Hittite, the Girgashite, the Amorite, the Canaanite, the
        Perrizite, the Hivvite, and the Yevusite—
    seven nations more numerous and mightier (in number) than you,
 2 and YHWH your God gives them before you and you strike them
        down:
    you are to devote-them-to-destruction, yes, destruction,
    you are not to cut with them a covenant, you are not to show-
        them-mercy!
 3 And you are not to marry (with) them:
    your daughter you are not to give to their son, their daughter you
        are not to take for your son—
 4 for they would turn-aside your son from (following) after me
    and they would serve other gods,
    and the anger of YHWH would flare up against you, and he would
        destroy you quickly.
 5 Rather, thus are you to do to them:
    their slaughter-sites you are to wreck,
    their standing-pillars you are to smash,
    their sacred-trees you are to cut-to-shreds,
    and their carved-images you are to burn with fire!
 6 For you are a people holy to YHWH your God,
    (it is) you (that) YHWH your God chose for him as a treasured
        people
    from among all peoples that are on the face of the soil.

---

25 **righteous-merit:** The word often means "right-
eousness," but here and elsewhere clearly indicates
merit in the eyes of God.
7:1 **Hittite** etc.: The first nation on this list is not to be
confused with the great Hittite empire of Anatolia
(modern Turkey), which historically preceded the
Israelites. The listing of seven nations here (Plaut

notes that it is the only time in the Torah they all appear on the same list) is an indication of completeness; seven was a number of perfection in the
ancient world. **Yevusite:** The inhabitants of Jerusalem.
6 **a treasured people:** As promised in Ex. 19:5.

7 Not because of your being many-more than all the peoples
has YHWH attached himself to you and chosen you,
for you are the least-numerous of all peoples!

8 Rather, because of YHWH's love for you
and because of his keeping the sworn-oath that he swore to your
fathers
did YHWH take you out, with a strong hand,
and redeem you from a house of serfs,
from the hand of Pharaoh, king of Egypt.

9 Know
that YHWH your God, he is God,
the trustworthy God,
keeping the covenant of loyalty with those who love him and
with those who keep his commandments,
to the thousandth generation,

10 and paying back those who hate him to his face, by causing them
to perish—
he does not delay (punishment) to those who hate him to his
face; he pays them back!

11 So you are to keep the command: the laws and the regulations
that I command you today, by observing them.

12 Now it shall be:
because of your hearkening to these regulations, keeping and
observing (them),
then YHWH will keep for you the covenant of loyalty that he
swore to your fathers;

13 he will love you, he will bless you, he will make-you-many,
he will bless the fruit of your belly and the fruit of your soil,
your grain, your new-wine, and your shining-oil,
the offspring of your cattle and the fecundity of your sheep,
upon the soil that he swore to your fathers, to give you.

14 Blessed shall you be above all peoples:
there shall not be among you (any) barren-male or barren-female,
nor among your animals.

13 **grain . . . new-wine . . . offspring . . . fecundity:**
The Hebrew terms for these products of the land,
as Tigay notes, were originally names of gods.

The Land (8): Moshe now recounts the past—God's care of Israel in the wilderness (the opening chapters stressed other aspects), in order to set up expectations for the future life of the people in the Promised Land. The reference to the past is to insure that Israel not attribute its success and happiness in the land to their own prowess; otherwise they will disappear like the peoples they are replacing.

Appearing here, as it does frequently elsewhere in the Bible, is the idea of the "merit of the Fathers"—the concept that God is beneficent and forgiving toward the Israelites chiefly owing to the deeds of their ancestors. It survived as a key idea in classical Judaism.

15 YHWH will remove from you all sickness
  and all evil illnesses from Egypt that you know, he will not put
    (any of) them upon you,
  but will place them upon all those who hate you.

16 You shall devour all the peoples that YHWH your God gives to
    you;
  your eye is not to pity them,
  you are not to serve their gods,
  for that is a snare to you!

17 If you should say in your heart:
  More numerous are these nations than I,
  how will I be able to dispossess them?

18 Do not be afraid of them;
  bear-in-mind, yes, in mind, what YHWH your God did to Pharaoh
    and to all Egypt—

19 the great trials that your eyes saw,
  the signs and the portents, the strong hand and the outstretched
    arm
  by which YHWH your God took you out—
  thus will YHWH your God do to all the peoples of whom you are
    afraid.

20 And also the hornet, YHWH your God will send-loose upon them,
  until they perish, those left and those hidden from you.

21 Do not be terrified before them,
  for YHWH your God is among you,
  a God great and awe-inspiring.

22 YHWH your God will dislodge these nations before you, little by
    little;
  you may not finish them off quickly, lest the wildlife of the field
    become too-many for you.

---

20 **the hornet:** A known threat in the ancient Near East (Weinfeld).

22 **you may not finish them off quickly:** An attempt to explain why the Canaanites still survived among the Israelites at a later date (cf. Judges 3:1). Here the reason, a weak one, is that genocide would have led to an unacceptable rise in the number of scavenging animals. Another tradition (Ex. 23:29–30) posits that the Canaanites were to function as a test for the Israelites' faithfulness to God (curiously, medieval Christianity was to use the same argument to explain the survival of the Jews).

23 YHWH your God will give them before you,
   he will panic them with a great panic
   until they are destroyed.
24 He will give their kings into your hand,
   so that you cause their name to perish from under heaven;
   no man will be able to take-a-stand against you
   until you have caused them to perish.
25 The carved-images of their gods, you are to burn with fire,
   you are not to come-to-yearn for (the) silver and gold on account
      of them,
   and so take it for yourself,
   lest you be ensnared by it—
   for it is an abomination to YHWH your God!
26 You are not to bring an abomination into your house
   —you would become devoted-for-destruction like it!—
   you are to hold-it-in-disgust, yes, disgust,
   you are to consider-it-abominable, yes, abominable,
   for it is (something) devoted-for-destruction!

8:1 All the commandment that I command you today,
   you are to take-care to observe,
   in order that you may live and become-many and enter and
      possess the land
   that YHWH swore to your fathers.
2 You are to bear-in-mind the route that YHWH had you go
   these forty years in the wilderness,
   in order to afflict you, by testing you,
   to know what was in your heart, whether you would keep his
      commandments, or not.
3 So he afflicted you and made-you-hungry,
   and had you eat the *mahn*

8:2 **the route:** The circuitous journey, in both geography and experience.
3 ***mahn:*** Trad. "manna," a vegetable substance that according to Ex. 16:14–15 sustained the Israelites in the wilderness. **not by bread alone** etc.: Trad. "Man does not live by bread alone." **at YHWH's order:** Lit. "from YHWH's mouth."

888

which you had not known and which your fathers had not
    known,
in order to make you know
that not by bread alone do humans stay-alive,
but rather by all that issues at Yhwh's order do humans stay-alive.

4   Your garment did not wear out from upon you,
your foot did not swell,
these forty years.

5   You are to know in your heart
that just as a man disciplines his child,
(so) Yhwh your God disciplines you.

6   So you are to keep the commandment of Yhwh your God,
to walk in his ways and to hold him in awe!

7   When Yhwh your God brings you into a good land,
a land of streams of water, springs and Ocean-flows,
issuing from valleys and hills;

8   a land of wheat and barley, (fruit of the) vine, fig, and
    pomegranate,
a land of olives, oil and honey,

9   —a land in which you will never eat bread in poverty,
you will not lack for anything in it—
a land whose stones are iron,
and from whose hills you may hew copper:

10 when you eat, and you are satisfied,
you are to bless
Yhwh your God
for the good land that he has given you.

11 Take-you-care,
lest you forget Yhwh your God,
by not keeping his commandments, his regulations, and his laws
    that I command you today,

12 lest (when) you eat and are satisfied,
and build goodly houses and settle (there),

---

7 **Ocean-flows:** The subterranean waters on which
the earth rests in ancient thinking.

10 **when you eat,** etc.: A phrase included by the ancient Rabbis in the Grace after Meals, and the basis
for its practice in Judaism.

13 and your herds and your flocks become-many
and silver and gold become-much for you,
with all that belongs to you becoming-much—

14 that your heart become haughty
and you forget YHWH your God,
the one who brought you out from the land of Egypt, from a
house of serfs,

15 the one who had you travel in the wilderness, great and awe-
inspiring,
(of) burning snakes and scorpions,
and thirsty-soil where there is no water;
the one who brought forth water for you, from the flinty rock,

16 the one who had you eat *mahn* in the wilderness,
which your fathers had not known,
in order to afflict you and in order to test you,
for it to go-well with you, in your future.

17 Now should you say in your heart:
My power and the might of my hand have produced all this
wealth for me;

18 then you must bear-in-mind YHWH your God,
that he was the one who gave you the power to produce wealth,
in order to establish his covenant that he swore to your fathers, as
(is) this (very) day.

19 Now it shall be
if you forget, yes, forget YHWH your God
and walk after other gods,
serving them and prostrating yourselves to them,
I call-witness against you today
that perish, you will perish;

20 like the nations that YHWH is causing to perish before you,
so shall you perish,
because you did not hearken to the voice of YHWH your God!

9:1 Hearken, O Israel:
You are today crossing the Jordan

---

15 **burning snakes:** Cf. Num. 21:6. **water . . . from the
flinty rock:** Cf. Ex. 17:6 and Num. 20:11.

to enter to dispossess nations greater and mightier (in number)
 than you:
towns great and fortified up to heaven;

2 a people great and tall, the Children of the Anakites,
of whom you yourself know, of whom you have heard (it said):
Who can take-a-stand before the Children of Anak?—

3 You are to know today
that Yhwh your God,
he is the one who is crossing over before you,
a consuming fire;
he will destroy them, he will subjugate them before you,
so that you dispossess them, so that you cause them to perish
 quickly,
as Yhwh promised you.

4 Do not say in your heart
when Yhwh has pushed them out before you,
saying:
Because of my righteous-merit did Yhwh bring me in to possess
 this land,
and because of the wickedness of these nations is Yhwh
 dispossessing them from before you!

5 Not because of your righteous-merit, or because of the
 uprightness of your heart, are you entering to possess their land,
but rather because of the wickedness of these nations
is Yhwh your God dispossessing them from before you,
and in order that he might uphold the word that Yhwh swore to
 your fathers, to Avraham, to Yitzhak, and to Yaakov.

6 You are to know
that not because of your righteous-merit is Yhwh your God
 giving you this good land to possess,
for a people hard of neck are you!

7 Bear-in-mind, do not forget
how you infuriated Yhwh your God in the wilderness;

9:6 **hard of neck:** Trad. "stiff-necked." The image is
that of a stubborn draft animal that will not yield to
do its master's work.

The Calf Incident (9–10:11): Continuing the argument of the last chapter—that Israel should take great care to remember who it was that led them—Moshe makes pointed reference to the great rebellion that took place at the foot of Sinai itself: the incident of the Golden ("Molten") Calf in Ex. 32–34. In this he is recapitulating the rhetoric of the opening chapters of the book, as well as of the great poem in Chap. 32, which utilize the past to inform the future. The calf incident, in fact, paves the way for the passages that immediately follow.

from the day that he took you out of Egypt until your coming to
 this place,
you have been rebellious against YHWH!

8 And at Horev you infuriated YHWH,
so that YHWH was incensed (enough) with you to destroy you!

9 When I went up the mountain
to receive the tablets of stone,
the tablets of the covenant that YHWH had cut with you,
I stayed on the mountain forty days and forty nights:
food I did not eat, water I did not drink;

10 but God gave to me the two tablets of stone, written on by the
 finger of God,
and upon them, corresponding to all the words that YHWH spoke
 with you on the mountain, from the midst of the fire,
on the day of the Assembly.

11 Now it was,
at the end of forty days and forty nights,
YHWH gave to me the two tablets of stone, the tablets of the
 covenant.

12 And YHWH said to me:
Arise, go down quickly from here,
for they have wrought-ruin, your people, whom you took out of
 Egypt,
they have quickly turned-aside from the path that I commanded
 them,
they have made themselves something-molten!

13 And YHWH said to me, saying:
I see this people, and here, it is a hard-necked people!

14 Let me be, that I may destroy them,
I will blot out their name from beneath the heavens,
and I will make of you a nation mightier (in number) and many-
 more than they!

8 **at Horev:** Referring to the incident of the molten
calf (trad. "Golden Calf").

◆ 15 And I faced about and went down from the mountain
—now the mountain was burning with fire—
the two tablets of the covenant in my two arms,

16 and I saw:
here, you were sinning against YHWH your God, you had made
yourselves a molten calf;
you had turned-aside quickly from the way that YHWH had
commanded you!

17 Now I grasped the two tablets
and threw them from my two arms
and smashed them before your eyes.

18 I lay-fallen before YHWH as at the beginning (of the) forty days
and forty nights;
food I did not eat, water I did not drink,
because of all your sins that you sinned, by doing what was ill in
the eyes of YHWH, to vex him.

19 For I was in dread of the anger and the venom with which YHWH
was furious with you, to destroy you;
and YHWH hearkened to me, also on that occasion.

20 But with Aharon, YHWH was exceedingly incensed, (enough) to
destroy him,
but I interceded also on behalf of Aharon at that time.

21 Now as for your sinful-thing that you had made, the calf:
I took (it) and burned it with fire,
I beat it, well ground-up, until it was crushed (into) fine-dust,
and I threw its dust into the stream that comes down the
mountain.

22 —And at Tav'era/Blazing and at Massa/Testing, and at Kivrot ha-
Taava/Burial-Sites of Craving,
you were infuriating YHWH,

23 and (also) when YHWH sent you on from Kadesh Barne'a, saying:
Go up, possess the land that I am giving to you,

---

20 **I interceded also on behalf of Aharon:** A detail not
mentioned in the Exodus version.

21 **I threw its dust into the stream:** The Exodus account has Moshe forcing the Israelites to drink it.

22 **Tav'era/Blazing:** Cf. Num. 11:1ff. **Kivrot ha-
Taava/Burial-Sites of Craving:** Cf. Num. 11:4–34.

you rebelled against the order of YHWH your God, and did not
  trust him and did not hearken to his voice.
24 Rebellious have you been against YHWH from the (first) day that I
  knew you!
25 Now when I lay-fallen before YHWH
for the forty days and the forty nights that I was fallen,
when YHWH said he would destroy you,
26 I interceded to YHWH and said:
My Lord, YHWH,
do not bring-ruin on your people, your inheritance
whom you redeemed in your greatness,
whom you took out of Egypt with a strong hand!
27 Bear-in-mind your servants, Avraham, Yitzhak, and Yaakov;
do not face toward the hard-heartedness of this people or toward
  their wickedness or toward their sin,
28 lest the (people of the) land out of which you took them say:
Because of YHWH's inability to bring them to the land which he
  had promised to them
and because of his hatred for them
did he take them out, to cause-their-death in the wilderness!
29 —And they are your people, your inheritance
whom you took out in your great power and with your
  outstretched arm!
10:1 At that time YHWH said to me:
Carve yourself two tablets of stone, like the first-ones,
and come up to me, on the mountain,
and make yourself a coffer of wood.
2 I will write on the tablets the words that were on the tablets, the
  first-ones, that you smashed,
and you are to put them in the coffer.
3 So I made a coffer of acacia wood,
I carved out two tablets of stone, like the first-ones,
and I went up, on the mountain, the two tablets in my arms.
4 And he wrote on the tablets according to the first writing,
the Ten Words
that YHWH spoke to you on the mountain, from the midst of the
  fire,

Concluding Exhortation (10:12–11:32): To conclude his long introduction to the laws, Moshe returns to the theme of YHWH's love for Israel, expanding it to include Israel's duty to love the stranger and also to love God. Once again the past is invoked, especially those parts of it that focus on God's might. The intimate connection between people and land is stressed through Moshe's wonderful description of Canaan (vv.11–12), and the polarity of blessing and curse rounds out his plea—just as a long blessing/curse cycle will round out the whole book in Chaps. 29 and 30. In fact, Chap. 11, both in its beginning ("you are to keep his charge, his laws, his regulations and his commandments") and its ending ("you are to take-care to observe all the laws and the regulations that I place before you today"), form a fitting lead-in to the long sequence of laws that is about to commence.

on the day of the Assembly,
and YHWH gave them to me.

5 Now when I faced about and came down the mountain,
I put the tablets in the coffer that I had made,
and they have remained there,
as YHWH had commanded me.

6 And the Children of Israel marched from the Wells of the
Children of Ya'akan to Mosera;
there Aharon died, and he was buried there;
so El'azar his son served-as-priest in his stead.

7 From there they marched to Gudgoda,
from Gudgoda to Yotvata, a land of streams of water.

8 At that time YHWH separated the tribe of Levi
to carry the coffer of YHWH's covenant, to stand before the
presence of YHWH, to attend on him and to give-blessing in his
name,
until this day.

9 Therefore Levi did not have an inheritable portion along with his
brothers;
YHWH is his inheritance,
as YHWH your God promised him.

10 Now I stood on the mountain
like the days, the first-ones, forty days and forty nights,
and YHWH hearkened to me also on that occasion—
YHWH did not consent to bring-ruin upon you.

11 YHWH said to me:
Arise, go on the march before the people,
so that they may enter and take-possession-of the land
about which I swore to their fathers, to give them.

12 And now, O Israel,
what does YHWH your God ask of you
except to hold YHWH your God in awe,

---

9 YHWH is his inheritance: A phrase used in later
Jewish memorial prayers, referring not to the
Levites but to the dead.

to walk in all his ways
and to love him
and to serve YHWH your God with all your heart and with all
    your being,

13 to keep the commandments of YHWH and his laws which I
    command you today,
to have it go-well for you?

14 Here, YHWH your God's are
the heavens and the heaven of heavens,
the earth and all that is on it!

15 Only to your fathers was YHWH attached, to love them, so he
    chose their seed after them,
you, above all (other) peoples,
as (is) this (very) day.

16 So circumcise the foreskin of your heart,
your neck you are not to keep-hard anymore;

17 for YHWH your God,
he is the God of gods and the Lord of lords,
the God great, powerful, and awe-inspiring,
he who lifts up no face (in favor) and takes no bribe,

18 providing justice (for) orphan and widow,
loving the sojourner, by giving him food and clothing.

19 So you are to love the sojourner,
for sojourners were you in the land of Egypt;

20 YHWH your God, you are to hold-in-awe,
him you are to serve,
to him you are to cling,
by his name you are to swear!

21 He is your praise, he is your God,
who did for you these great and awe-inspiring (acts) that your
    (own) eyes saw.

---

15 **Only to your fathers:** Read in conjunction with the previous verse, this means "Even though he is the universal God, he loved your ancestors in particular."

16 **circumcise the foreskin of your heart:** Figuratively, to peel away the "thick" part, thus enabling one to love / be loyal to God.

19 **you are to love the sojourner:** Moving beyond the command, found in Ex. 22:20–22 and 23:9, not to "afflict" him (Weinfeld).

20 **swear:** Take an oath.

22 As seventy persons your fathers went down to Egypt,
   but now YHWH your God has made you like the stars of the
      heavens for multitude!
11:1 So you are to love YHWH your God,
   you are to keep his charge, and his laws, his regulations and his
      commandments,
   all the days (to come).
2 You are to know today
   that it is not with your children
   who did not know, who did not see
   the discipline of YHWH your God,
   his greatness: his strong hand and his outstretched arm,
3 his portents and his deeds that he did in the midst of Egypt
   to Pharaoh king of Egypt and to all his land,
4 what he did to the army of Egypt, to its horses and its
      charioteers,
   how he caused the waters of the Red Sea to flow over their faces
      when they pursued you,
   so that YHWH caused them to perish, until this day;
5 and what he did concerning you in the wilderness
   up to your arrival, up to this place;
6 and what he did concerning Datan and Aviram, the sons of Eliav,
      son of Re'uven,
   how the earth opened up its mouth and swallowed them and
      their households and their tents
   and all existing-things that were under their feet
   in the midst of all Israel;
7 indeed, it is your eyes that were seeing
   all the great deeds of YHWH that he did.
8 So you are to keep all the commandment that I command you
      today,

---

22 **seventy persons . . . to Egypt:** Cf. Gen. 46:27 and Ex. 1:5. **like the stars of the heavens:** Cf. Gen. 15:5, God's promise to Abraham.
11:2 **the discipline:** God's punishment of the Egyptians.

6 **Datan and Aviram:** Principals in the great rebellion in Num. 16; note that the ringleader there, Korah, is not mentioned here, perhaps indicating a separate tradition.

in order that you may have the strength to enter and to take-
    possession of the land that you are crossing into to possess,

9 in order that you may prolong (your) days on the soil that YHWH
    swore to your fathers to give them and their seed,
a land flowing with milk and honey.

10 For the land that you are entering to possess:
it is not like the land of Egypt, from which you went out,
where you sow your seed
and water it with your foot like a garden of greens;

11 but the land that you are crossing into to possess (is) a land of
    hills and cleft-valleys;
from the rain of the heavens it drinks water;

12 a land whose (welfare) YHWH your God seeks:
regularly (are) the eyes of YHWH your God upon it,
from the beginning of the year until the afterpart of the year.

13 Now it shall be
if you hearken, yes, hearken to my commandments that I
    command you today,
to love YHWH your God and to serve him with all your heart and
    with all your being:

14 I will give forth the rain of your land in its due-time, shooting-
    rain and later-rain;
you shall gather in your grain, your new-wine and your shining-
    oil;

15 I will give forth herbage in your field, for your animals,
you will eat and you will be satisfied.

16 Take-you-care,
lest your heart be seduced,
so that you turn-aside and serve other gods and prostrate
    yourselves to them,

17 and the anger of YHWH flare up against you
so that he shuts up the heavens, and there is no rain,
and the earth does not give forth its yield,

---

10 **with your foot:** Apparently a reference to an ancient irrigating technique.

14 **shooting-rain:** In the fall. **later-rain:** The soaking
rains that fall in the winter.

and you perish quickly from off the good land that YHWH is
>   giving you!

18 You are to place these my words upon your heart and upon your
>   being;
>   you are to tie them as a sign on your hand,
>   let them be as bands between your eyes;

19 you are to teach them to your children, by speaking of them
>   in your sitting in your house, in your walking on the way,
>   in your lying-down, in your rising-up.

20 You are to write them upon the doorposts of your house, and on
>   your gates,

21 in order that your days may be many, along with the days of your
>   children
>   on the soil that YHWH swore to your fathers, to give them
>   (as long) as the days of the heavens over the earth.

22 Indeed, if you will keep, yes, keep all this commandment that I
>   command you to observe,
>   to love YHWH your God, to walk in his ways and to cling to him,

23 YHWH will dispossess all these nations from before you,
>   and you will dispossess nations greater and mightier (in number)
>   than you.

24 Every place that the sole of your foot treads, yours shall it be:
>   from the wilderness and the Lebanon,
>   from the River, the river Euphrates, as far as the Hindward Sea
>   shall be your territory.

25 No man will be able to take-a-stand against you;
>   terror of you and awe of you, YHWH your God will place upon all
>   the land upon which you tread,
>   as he promised to you.

---

18 **sign . . . bands:** Understood traditionally by Jews as *tefillin,* leather bands worn in daily morning prayer. They are connected to small boxes containing this passage, along with Ex. 13:9, 16 and Deut. 6:8.

18–20 **You are to place these words . . . upon your gates:** These three verses reiterate much of the wording of 6:5–9 above.

24 **from the wilderness** etc: The Hebrew here is unclear. **Hindward Sea:** The Mediterranean, "behind" the land of Israel, in the usual orientation of facing eastward (Heb. *kedma,* "frontward").

◆ 26 See,
    I place before you today a blessing or a curse:
27 the blessing,
    (provided) that you hearken to the commandments of Yhwh
        your God that I command you today,
28 and the curse,
    if you do not hearken to the commandments of Yhwh your God,
    and turn-aside from the way that I command you today,
    walking after other gods whom you have not known.
29 Now it shall be
    when Yhwh your God brings you into the land that you are
        entering to possess,
    you are to give the blessing on Mount Gerizim and the curse on
        Mount Eval
30 —are they not in (the country) across the Jordan, along the path
        of the coming in of the sun,
    in the land of the Canaanites, who are settled in the Plain,
        opposite the Gilgal/Stone-Circle, near the Oaks of Moreh?
31 For you are crossing the Jordan to enter to take-possession of the
        land that Yhwh your God is giving you;
    when you take-possession of it, when you settle in it,
32 you are to take-care to observe all the laws and the regulations
        that I place before you today.

---

29 **Gerizim . . . Eval:** Two mountains that frame the
important political and cultic center of Shechem
(today Nablus). Cf. 27:11–13 below.

PART III

THE TERMS OF THE COVENANT

(12–28)

AFTER LENGTHY EXHORTATION WE ARE BROUGHT AT LAST TO THE HEART OF DEU-teronomy. Just as its corresponding Exodus section, Chapters 19–24, stands at the center of that book, and Gen. 22, Lev. 19, and Num. 19–20 place dramatic narratives or important laws at their core, the laws that we now encounter focus our attention on the object of Moshe's main concern in Deut. 1–11 and 27–30: the "covenant" or pact between God and Israel. Israel is to demonstrate its love or loyalty to God by "taking-care to observe" the laws, and binds itself in a ceremony, at least in descriptive form, at the end of the section.

The subject matter of this long collection forms an interesting contrast to both the Covenant Code of Exodus (in the chapters just referred to) and other law collections in the ancient Near East. The Exodus material contains much that deals with property and damages, whereas Deuteronomy appears to focus more heavily on criminal and moral issues. Although neighboring civilizations had legal literature that parallels many of the cases before us (cf. Hallo for a discussion), Deuteronomy's particular emphases suggest a shift away from personal property as the central area of society's concern (Greenberg 1970). In addition, the biblical text here (as previously in the book) is generally cast in the second person singular, giving it a highly personal edge, and there is a higher percentage of "motive clauses"—explanations or justifications for the laws—than in other Near Eastern law codes. Sonsino has noted a strong similarity between the language of these chapters and the thrust of biblical "wisdom literature" such as the book of Proverbs; thus a major function of the material may well be didactic and not legal per se. This, interestingly, puts Deuteronomy more squarely within its Near Eastern setting; Fishbane (1988) characterizes both sets of systems as "stylized collections of typical cases."

Yet he also argues that whatever the original purpose of the laws in Chapters 12–26, they came already within the biblical period itself to be seen as actual "legislative texts," and as such, subject to later interpretation much as any law code might spawn (this multiple function of the laws was noted by Weinfeld 1972a). In this connection it is clear that new attitudes have been adopted and changes made in specific cases. It is usually accepted that Deuteronomy has introduced a markedly humanistic tone into Israel's legal system; in Weinfeld's words (1993):

> ... the author's purpose was not to produce a civil-law book like the book of the covenant, treating of pecuniary matters, but to set forth a code of laws securing the protection of the individual and particularly of those persons in need of protection.

Some of the changes from earlier laws are noted in the Commentary and Notes below.

Nelson has divided the laws into the following sections: Purity in Worship (12:1–14:21); Life in the New Land (14:22–16:17); The Structures of Society (16:18–20:20); and Interpreting Traditional Laws (21:1–26:19). In his view, the changes introduced into Israel's legal culture are responses to changes in Israelite society, whether economic, political, or religious—changes that may well reflect the monarchic period. The attempt to find a logical pattern to the structure of the laws, however, does not always succeed. Levinson has shown how a better understanding of the sequencing of the laws may be found in the principle of response to the centralization of worship, the event that historically may have accompanied Deuteronomy's promulgation. In this scheme, 12:1–16:17 is above all a response to how centralization affected the cultic (sacrificial worship) sphere, and 16:18–17:13 to how judicial process was similarly affected. At the same time, these changes appear to be woven into older material.

The phrase "And YHWH spoke to Moshe, saying: / Speak to the Children of Israel and say to them: ... ," so common in the legal and cultic sections of Leviticus and Numbers, does not appear here. Neither does it appear in the Covenant Code; but in the context of Deuteronomy, the absence of the phrase supports the emphasis on Moshe as the central figure (in Exodus the legal portions are followed by the Tabernacle instructions, which indeed use the quoted formula).

Chapter 12 begins with "These are the laws and the regulations that you are to take-care to observe"; Chapter 28 ends with "These are the words of the covenant. ... ." As in Exodus, the laws are the terms of the covenant, not merely a set of rules to be followed. This is further supported by the framework into which these chapters have been placed. The first two parts of the book serve as a classic ancient Near Eastern introduction to a treaty, with their historical look back. In addition, the section ends with both a covenant ceremony (Chap. 27) and a series of blessings and curses (28), also typical in this genre. So far from being merely a dry list of laws, the core of Deuteronomy, with its reasoned tone and wide-ranging scope, serves both as a summing-up and as a basis for Israel's life on the land. No wonder, then, that the exiles returning from Babylonia under Persian rule in the sixth century B.C.E. and later came to view the Torah as a real constitution.

On Worship and Meat-Eating (12:2–31): The extended section on laws begins with what sounds like a reference to Josiah's reform—the smashing of idols, the abolition of the "high-places" (the pagan shrines which dotted the ancient landscape of Canaan), and the centralization of the cult in the place that "God chooses to have his name dwell." Since this emphasis is central to the program of Deuteronomy in its final form, it is not surprising that it appears first in the legal section of the book—rather like the opening of the laws in Exodus 21-23, which centers around the situation of one of its central concerns and images, the slave (Levinson). A logical result of the centralization of the cult is the need to permit the eating of meat in local sites; previously it had been permitted only at the Dwelling (cf. Lev. 17), the portable sanctuary. But the old prohibition against eating blood, as symbolic of the life, is upheld.

Vv.29-31, which mark a transition to the next chapter, round out Chap. 12's stern proscription of improper worship—"indeed, even their sons and daughters they burn with fire to their gods!" (31).

Christensen (1986) notes a stylistic peculiarity of this chapter which is typical of Deuteronomy: a shift between second person plural and singular. While others have tried to use this phenomenon to point to evidence of editing, he sees it as a stylistic way of marking metrical sections of the chapter.

12:1 These are the laws and the regulations that you are to take-care to observe

in the land that Y HWH the God of your fathers has given you to possess,

all the days that you live on the soil:

2 You are to demolish, yes, demolish, all the (sacred) places

where the nations that you are dispossessing served their gods,

on the high hills and on the mountains

and beneath every luxuriant tree;

3 you are to wreck their slaughter-sites,

you are to smash their standing-pillars,

their Asherot/Sacred-Poles you are to burn with fire,

and the carved-images of their gods, you are to cut-to-shreds—

so that you cause their name to perish from that place!

4 You are not to do thus with Y HWH your God;

5 rather, to the place that Y HWH your God chooses from among all your tribes

to put his name there, to have it dwell,

you are to inquire and are to come there,

6 you are to bring there your offerings-up and your slaughter-offerings,

your tithings and the contributions of your hands,

your vow-offerings and your freewill-offerings,

the firstborn of your herds and of your flocks.

7 And you are to eat there, before the presence of Y HWH your God,

you are to rejoice in all the enterprises of your hand,

you and your households,

with which Y HWH your God has blessed you.

8 You are not to do—according to all that we are doing here today—

each-man, whatever is right in his (own) eyes,

12:2 **demolish,** etc.: Like several other lists of laws in the Torah (e.g., Ex. 21–23), this one begins with the topic of proper worship of God.

4 **do . . . with:** Or "act . . . toward" (Tigay).

7 **enterprises:** Lit. "putting-forth."

8 **whatever is right in his (own) eyes:** A theme in Deuteronomistic literature, usually denoting chaos. Cf. the phrase at the ending of the book of Judges (21:25).

9 for you have not come until now
 to the resting-place, to the inheritance that YHWH your God is
   giving you.

10 When you cross the Jordan
 and settle in the land that YHWH your God is causing you to
   inherit,
 and he gives-rest to you from all your enemies round about,
 and you settle (in it) in security:

11 it shall be, in the place
 that YHWH your God chooses to have his name dwell,
 there you are to bring all that I command you:
 your offerings-up and your slaughter-offerings,
 your tithings and the contribution of your hands,
 and all your choicest vow-offerings that you vow to YHWH.

12 And you are to rejoice before the presence of YHWH your God,
 you, your sons and your daughters,
 your servants and your maids,
 and the Levite who is within your gates,
 for he has no portion or inheritance with you.

13 Take-you-care,
 lest you offer-up your offerings-up
 in any place you might see.

14 Rather, in the place that YHWH chooses in one of your tribal-
   districts,
 there you are to offer-up your offerings-up,
 there you are to observe all that I command you.

15 Only: in all your appetite's craving you may slaughter
   (animals)
 and may eat meat according to the blessing of YHWH your God
 that he has given you within all your gates;
 the *tamei* and the pure (alike) may eat it,
 as (of) the deer, so (of) the gazelle.

---

12 **before the presence of Y**HWH: This phrase usually
denotes a location in the sanctuary.

13 **see:** Or "select" (cf. Gen. 22:8).

15 **[your] appetite's [craving]:** Heb. *nefesh* elsewhere
means "self" or "being," but also refers to the seat of
emotions and, as here, appetite. ***tamei:*** Polluted in a
ritual sense; a standard term in Leviticus. **deer . . .
gazelle:** Animals fit for consumption but not for
sacrifice (Plaut).

16 Only: the blood you are not to eat,
   on the earth you are to pour it out, like water.

17 You may not eat within your gates
   the tithe of your grain, your new-wine or your shining-oil,
   or the firstlings of your herd or of your flock,
   or any of the vow-offerings that you vow,
   or your freewill-offerings or the contribution of your hand;

18 rather, before the presence of YHWH your God you are to eat it,
   in the place that YHWH your God chooses:
   you, your son and your daughter,
   your servant and your maid,
   and the Levite that is within your gates;
   you are to rejoice before the presence of YHWH your God, in all
      the enterprises of your hand.

19 Take-you-care,
   lest you abandon the Levite,
   all your days on your soil.

20 When YHWH your God broadens your territory,
   as he promised you,
   and you say: I want to eat meat,
   because your appetite craves eating meat,
   according to all your appetite's craving you may eat meat.

21 If it is too far-away from you, the place that YHWH your God
      chooses to put his name there,
   you may slaughter (animals) from among your herds and your
      flocks
   that YHWH has given you, as I have commanded you,
   and you may eat within your gates, according to all your
      appetite's craving.

22 Mark,
   as the gazelle and the deer are eaten,
   thus you may eat it,

16 **blood you are not to eat:** It is considered to represent the life essence (cf. v.23 below).

Leading the People Astray (13): The subject is various scenarios under which Israelites might be lured to worship other gods; it has first been broached in Ex. 22:19, and will return in Deut. 17:2–7. Vv.2–6 deal with a religious visionary, 7–12 with a relative (both of whom seek to turn the Israelites to idols), and 13–19 with a whole town that has abandoned the covenant in favor of other gods. In all three cases, the penalty is death, with the chapter building up the sentences into a crescendo of destruction in vv.16–19. The opening verse of the chapter forms a fitting superscript for the bulk of the laws, and hints that Deuteronomy is a kind of final, closed, "canonical" dispensation.

the *tamei* and the pure,
together they may eat it.

23 Only: be strong not to eat the blood,
for the blood is the life;
you are not to eat the life along with the meat!

24 You are not to eat it,
on the earth you are to pour it out, like water.

25 You are not to eat it,
in order that it may go-well with you and with your children after
you;
indeed, you are to do what is right in the eyes of YHWH!

26 Only: your holy-offerings that you have, and your vow-offerings,
you are to lift-up
and are to come to the place that YHWH chooses.

27 You are to sacrifice your offerings-up, the meat and the blood
on the slaughter-site of YHWH your God:
the blood of your slaughter-offerings you are to pour out on the
slaughter-site of YHWH your God,
but the meat, you may eat.

28 Take-care to hearken to these words that I command you,
in order that it may go-well with you and with your children after
you, into the ages,
that you may do what is good and what is right in the eyes of
YHWH your God.

29 When YHWH your God cuts off the nations where you are
entering, to dispossess them from before you,
so that you dispossess them and settle in their land,

30 take-you-care,
lest you be ensnared (to go) after them,
after they have been destroyed from before you,
lest you inquire about their gods, saying:
How (exactly) do these nations serve their gods?
I will do thus, I too!

---

25 **what is right in the eyes of YHWH:** In contrast to
v.8.

26 **holy-offerings . . . vow-offerings:** Obligatory and
voluntary sacrifices (Levinson).

31 You are not to do thus with YHWH your God,
   for everything abominable to YHWH, which he hates, they do
      with their gods;
   indeed, even their sons and their daughters they burn with fire to
      their gods!

13:1 Everything that I command you,
   that you are to take-care to observe,
   you are not to add to it, you are not to diminish from it!

2 When there arises in your midst a prophet or a dreamer of
      dreams
   and he gives you a sign or a portent,

3 and it comes-about, the sign or the portent of which he spoke to
      you, saying:
   Let us walk after other gods—whom you have not known—and
      let us serve them,

4 you are not to hearken to the words of that prophet or to that
      dreamer of dreams,
   for YHWH your God is (only) testing you
   to know if you (truly) love YHWH your God
   with all your heart and with all your being.

5 After YHWH your God you are to walk,
   him you are to hold-in-awe,
   his commandments you are to keep,
   to his voice you are to hearken,
   him you are to serve,
   to him you are to cling!

6 Now that prophet or that dreamer of dreams is to be put-to-
      death,
   for he has spoken defection against YHWH your God
   —the one taking you out from the land of Egypt,
   the one redeeming you from a house of serfs—
   by leading-you-away from the way

13:6 **so shall you burn . . . :** This phrase, which occurs frequently in the legal section of Deuteronomy, puts responsibility for eradicating evil on the
community (Stulman). **midst:** elsewhere rendered
"amid, among."

on which Yhwh your God has commanded you to walk;
so shall you burn out the evil from your midst!

7 When he allures you, your brother, the son of your mother,
or your son or your daughter or the wife of your bosom
or your neighbor who is (one) like your (very) self
in secret, saying:
Let us go, let us serve other gods—whom you have not known,
  you and your fathers,

8 from the gods of the peoples that are around you,
those near to you or those far from you,
from the (one) edge of the earth to the (other) edge of the
  earth—

9 you are not to consent to him,
you are not to hearken to him,
your eye is not to take-pity on him,
you are not to show-mercy and you are not to condone him;

10 rather, you are to kill, yes, kill him,
your hand is to be against him from the beginning, to cause-his-
  death,
and the hand of the entire people at the end.

11 You are to stone him with stones, so that he dies,
for he sought to drive-you-away from Yhwh your God,
the one taking you out from the land of Egypt, from a house of
  serfs.

12 Now all Israel will hear and be awed,
so that they will not do any more according to this evil matter in
  your midst!

13 When you hear in one of your towns that Yhwh your God is
  giving you to settle in, saying:

14 Men, base-fellows men have gone out from among you
and have driven-away the settlers of their town, saying:
Let us go, let us serve other gods—whom you have not known:

15 then you are to inquire, to examine and to investigate well,
and (if) here: the claim is certain (and) true
this abomination was (indeed) done in your midst—

16 strike-down, strike-down the settlers of that town with the edge
  of the sword,

Holiness (14): Chap. 14 looks back to a major priestly concern. Indeed, the word "holy" appears in v.2, just as it did in conjunction with Israel the "special treasure" (mentioned here as well) in Ex. 19:5–6. Holiness includes banning Canaanite practices regarding the dead, distinguishing between pure and impure animals, avoiding carcasses as a major source of ritual pollution, and following the rules concerning tithes. In regard to the latter, what seems to matter most in the text is not precisely what is due God—a narrowly religious concern—but rather the care one must take that the powerless members of society (sojourner, widow, orphan) are provided for—a much broader one.

devote it to destruction, it and all that is in it, and its animals,
　　with the edge of the sword,
17　and all its booty, you are to gather to the middle of its (town)
　　　square,
　　and are to burn with fire
　　the town and all its booty, completely, to YHWH your God;
　　it shall be a mound for the ages,
　　you are not to build (on it) again!
18　And there is not to cling to your hand anything from what is
　　　devoted-to-destruction,
　　in order that YHWH may turn from the flaming of his anger
　　and show compassion to you,
　　having-compassion on you and making you many,
　　as he swore to your fathers.
19　Indeed, you are to hearken to the voice of YHWH your God,
　　by keeping all his commandments that I command you today,
　　by doing what is right in the eyes of YHWH your God.

14:1　Children are you to YHWH your God!
　　You are not to gash yourselves, you are not to put a bald-spot
　　　between your eyes for a dead-person.
2　For you are a people holy to YHWH your God,
　　(it is) you (that) YHWH has chosen to be for him a specially-
　　　treasured people
　　from all the peoples that are on the face of the soil.

3　You are not to eat any abominable-thing!
4　These are the animals that you may eat:
　　ox, lamb-of-sheep and lamb-of-goats,
5　deer, gazelle, and roebuck,
　　wild-goat, ibex, antelope, and mountain-sheep,
6　and every (other) animal having a hoof or cleaving in a cleft two
　　　hooves,

17　**mound:** The sign of a ruined city.
18　**there is not to cling** etc.: Cf. the story of Akhan in
　　Josh. 7, where such misappropriation of spoils leads
　　to the death of the offender.

14:1　**gash . . . put a bald-spot:** Biblical ideology opposed
　　mutilation in mourning; indeed, cults of the dead
　　were a prime target of biblical polemics.

bringing-up cud, among animals,
it you may eat.

7 However, these you are not to eat among those that bring-up
cud,
among those that have a hoof, that is cleft:
the camel, the hare, and the daman,
for they bring-up cud, but a hoof they do not have—
they are *tamei* for you!

8 And the pig—
for it has a hoof but does not (bring-up) cud—it is *tamei* for you;
from their flesh you are not to eat,
their carcass you are not to touch!

9 These you may eat from all that is in the sea:
every one that has fins and scales, you may eat.

10 But every one that does not have fins and scales, you are not to
eat,
it is *tamei* for you.

11 Every (ritually-)pure bird, you may eat.

12 But these (are they) from which you are not to eat:
the eagle, the vulture, and the black-vulture,

13 the kite, the falcon, and the buzzard after its kind,

14 every raven after its kind,

15 the ostrich, the nighthawk, and the hawk after its kind;

16 the little-owl, the great-owl, and the white-owl,

17 the pelican, the bustard, and the cormorant,

18 the stork and the heron after its kind,
the hoopoe and the bat.

19 Now every kind of swarming thing that flies:
it is *tamei* for you,
they are not to be eaten!

20 Every (kind) of pure flying-thing, you may eat.

---

12 **eagle:** others, "griffin vulture."
16 **little-owl, . . . great-owl, . . . white-owl:** Despite
the English, there is no sound connection between
these words in Hebrew.

21 You are not to eat any carcass.
To the sojourner that is within your gates you may give it, that he
may eat it,
or it may be sold to a foreigner;
for you are a people holy
to YHWH your God;
you are not to boil a kid in the milk of its mother!

22 You are to tithe, yes, tithe all the produce of your seed-sowing,
(of) what comes forth from the field, year (after) year.

23 You are to eat, before the presence of YHWH your God,
in the place that he chooses to have his name dwell,
the tithe from your grain, your new-wine and your shining-oil
and from the firstlings of your flock and your herd,
in order that you may learn to hold YHWH your God in awe,
all the days.

24 And if the journey be too much for you,
that you are not able to carry it,
for it is too-far for you, the place
that YHWH your God chooses to set his name,
indeed, YHWH your God will bless you:

25 you may make-the-gift in silver:
you may bind up the silver in your hand
and go to the place
that YHWH your God chooses.

26 You may give the silver for all that your appetite craves,
for herd and flock, for wine and intoxicant,
for all that your appetite may seek,
you may eat (it) there, before the presence of YHWH your God;
and you are to rejoice, you and your household.

21 **you are not to boil** etc.: This law appears three times in the Torah (cf. also Ex. 23:19 and 34:26). It appears to prohibit the mixing of life (milk) and death. Its distinctive appearance here focuses on the aspect of food in general; in Exodus it occurs in the more limited context of rules regarding the spring ritual.
22 **tithe:** To give a tenth of one's produce to the sanctuary. Cf. Num. 18.

25 **make-the-gift in silver:** JPS, "you may convert them into money."
26 **you may eat (it) there:** In the priestly texts, the tithe is given to the Levites, not to the people themselves. The concept adopted in Deuteronomy is that holiness "is not inherent, but must be willed" (Weinfeld).

The Number Seven and the Matter of Debt (15:1–18): In Lev. 25, the Sabbatical year was explained in great detail, principally in regard to letting the land lie fallow. Similarly, the cycle of seven-times-seven years (plus one), the Jubilee ("Home-bringing") Year, was characterized as a time of land returning to its original owners. While the Leviticus text talks a good deal about poverty from v.35 on, most of it is about land and money. In Deuteronomy, on the other hand, the issue of the needy jumps to the fore from the beginning of the chapter, and remains central throughout. The result of such care is "blessing" from God, a theme word in the chapter.

Vv.12–18 parallel Ex. 21:2–6, but utilize a more rational argument. They also include the freeing of female slaves, in effect recognizing their personhood in a way the Exodus passage does not (Weinfeld 1992).

27 Now the Levite that is within your gates, you are not to abandon
    him,
for he does not have a portion or an inheritance beside you.

28 At the end of three years
you are to bring out all the tithing of your produce,
in that year,
and you are to deposit (it) within your gates.

29 And when he comes, the Levite
—for he does not have a portion or an inheritance beside you—
and the sojourner, the orphan and the widow that are within
    your gates,
they will eat and be-satisfied,
in order that YHWH your God may bless you
in all the doings of your hand that you do.

15:1 At the end of seven years, you are to make a Release.

2 Now this is the matter of the Release:
he shall release, every possessor of a loan of his hand,
what he has lent to his neighbor.
He is not to oppress his neighbor or his brother,
for the Release of YHWH has been proclaimed!

3 The foreigner you may oppress,
and he who belongs to you;
as for your brother, your hand is to release (him).

4 However, there will not be among you any needy-person,
for YHWH will bless, yes, bless you in the land
that YHWH your God is giving you as an inheritance, to possess.

5 Only: if you hearken, yes, hearken
to the voice of YHWH your God,
by taking-care to observe all this commandment that I command
    you today,

6 indeed, YHWH your God will bless you
as he promised you;

15:1 **Release:** Or "Remission."

you will cause many nations to give-pledges,
but you will not (have to) give-pledges;
you will rule over many nations,
but over you they shall not rule.

7 When there is among you a needy-person
from any-one of your brothers, within one of your gates
in the land that YHWH your God is giving you,
you are not to toughen your heart,
you are not to shut your hand
to your brother, the needy-one.

8 Rather, you are to open, yes, open your hand to him,
and are to give-pledge, yes, pledge to him,
sufficient for his lack that is lacking to him.

9 Take-you-care,
lest there be a word in your heart, a base-one, saying:
The seventh year, the Year of Release, is nearing—
and your eye be set-on-ill toward your brother, the needy-one,
and you not give to him,
so that he calls out because of you to YHWH,
and sin be incurred by you.

10 You are to give, yes, give (freely) to him,
your heart is not to be ill-disposed in your giving to him,
for on account of this matter
YHWH your God will bless you in all your doings
and in all the enterprises of your hand!

11 For the needy will never be-gone from amid the land;
therefore I command you, saying:
You are to open, yes, open your hand to your brother, to your
afflicted-one,
and to your needy-one in your land!

---

6 **give-pledges:** That is, be in debt.
11 **the needy will never be-gone:** A recognition of the human condition, and an indication that this law, at least, is realistic, not utopian (as opposed to the confident pronouncement of v.4).

12 When your brother is sold to you, Hebrew-male or
Hebrew-female,
and serves you for six years:
now in the seventh year
you are to send-him-free, at liberty, from beside you.

13 Now when you send-him-free, at liberty, from beside you,
you are not to send-him-free empty-handed;

14 you are to adorn, yes, adorn him
from your flock, from your threshing-floor and from your vat,
(from) that which YHWH your God has blessed you, you are to
give to him.

15 You must bear-in-mind
that a serf were you in the land of Egypt,
and YHWH your God redeemed you,
therefore I command you this word today!

16 Now it shall be
if he says to you:
I will not go out from beside you,
for I love you and your household
—for it goes-well for him beside you—

17 you are to take a piercing-tool
and are to put it through his ear, into the door,
and he shall be your serf forever;
even to your maid you are to do thus.

18 You are not to let-it-be-hard in your eyes
when you send-him-free, at liberty, from beside you,
for double the hire of a hired-hand
did he serve you, six years.
Then YHWH will bless you
in all that you do.

---

12 **brother:** Viewing the affected person in closer rela-
tional terms than as merely a "serf" or slave, as in
Ex. 21:2 (Greenstein 1985a).

14 **adorn:** Lit. "make a necklace," here used rather figuratively. JPS, "furnish."

16 **love:** The connotation here, as often in Deuteronomy, is one of loyalty.

The Firstling (15:19–23): Linking up with the Passover passage that follows, this law combines the idea of the consecrated firstborn of animals with Deuteronomy's new rules about eating sacrificial meat at home.

Pilgrimage Festivals (16:1–17): To the other sacred calendars in Ex. 23:14–17, Ex. 34:18, 22–24, and Lev. 23, our passage adds the stipulation that the three harvest/pilgrimage festivals be observed exclusively "in the place that YHWH chooses / to have his name dwell" (v.2). "Blessing" and the individual's capacity for giving are other important points.

Vv. 1-7, which deal with Passover, make clear how Deuteronomy reinterprets tradition in the light of its new program of centralization. As Levinson points out, this holiday, whose origin is clearly in the setting of the clan, is here broadened away from exclusive home observance and toward the sanctuary. To that end, animals other than lambs are now allowed to be sacrificed, and they may be boiled, not just roasted. In addition, the protective aspect of the animal's blood, which was so central to the Exodus account, is de-emphasized.

19 Every firstling that is born in your flock and in your herd, the
      male-one,
   you are to hallow to YHWH your God;
   you are not to do serving-tasks with the firstling of your ox,
   you are not to shear the firstling of your sheep.
20 Before the presence of YHWH your God you are to eat (it), year
      after year,
   in the place that YHWH chooses—
   you and your household.
21 Now if there be in it a defect,
   lame or blind,
   any defect for ill,
   you are not to slaughter (it) to YHWH your God.
22 Within your gates you are to eat it,
   the *tamei* and the pure together,
   as the gazelle, so the deer.
23 Only: its blood you are not to eat,
   on the earth you are to pour it out, like water.

16:1 Keep the New-Moon of Aviv/Ripe-Grain.
   You are to observe Passover to YHWH your God,
   for in the New-Moon of Aviv
   YHWH your God took you out of Egypt, at night.
2 You are to slaughter the Passover-offering to YHWH your God,
      (from) flock and herd,
   in the place that YHWH chooses
   to have his name dwell.
3 You are not to eat it with leaven;
   seven days you are to eat it with *matzot*, bread of affliction,
   for with trepidation you went out from the land of Egypt,
   in order that you may bear-in-mind the day of your going-out
      from the land of Egypt,
   all the days of your life.

---

20 **you are to eat (it):** As in 14:26, the goods go to the offerer, not to the priests or Levites (for which, see Ex. 22:28 etc.) (Weinfeld).
16:1 **Passover:** The description here indicates one agri-cultural festival, as opposed to the two (including a shepherd's holy day) that appear together in Ex. 23:15, 18 (Weinfeld).
3 ***matzot***: Plural of *matza*, unleavened bread.

4 There is not to be seen with you (any) fermentation in all your
   territory
for seven days,
there is not to remain-overnight
(any) of the meat that you slaughter at sunset on the first day, till
   daybreak.
5 You may not slaughter the Passover-offering
within one of your gates that YHWH your God is giving you;
6 rather, in the place that YHWH your God chooses his name to dwell
you are to slaughter the Passover-offering, at setting-time,
when the sun comes in,
at the appointed-time of your going-out from Egypt.
7 You are to boil it and you are to eat it
in the place
that YHWH your God chooses.
Then you are to face about, at daybreak,
and go back to your tents.
8 For six days you are to eat *matzot*,
on the seventh day
is a (day of) Restraint to YHWH your God;
you are not to do (any) work.

9 Seven weeks you are to number for yourself;
from the start of the sickle in the standing-grain you are to start
   numbering,
seven weeks.
10 You are to observe a pilgrimage-festival of Weeks to YHWH your
   God
according to the sufficiency of the freewill-offering of your hand
   that you give,
as YHWH your God blesses you.
11 And you are to rejoice before the presence of YHWH your God,
you, your son, your daughter,

---

6 **setting-time:** Rendered elsewhere as "sunset."

8 **Restraint:** The final day of the Sukkot festival
(vv.13ff. below) is similarly designated.

your servant and your maid,
and the Levite that is within your gates,
and the sojourner, the orphan and the widow that are among
    you,
in the place
that YHWH your God chooses
to have his name dwell.

12 You are to bear-in-mind that a serf were you in Egypt;
so you are to take-care and observe these laws.

13 The pilgrimage-festival of Sukkot/Huts you are to observe for
    yourself, for seven days,
at your ingathering, from your threshing-floor, from your vat.

14 You are to rejoice on your festival,
you, your son, and your daughter,
your servant and your maid,
the Levite,
the sojourner, the orphan and the widow that are within your
    gates.

15 For seven days you are to celebrate-a-festival to YHWH your God
in the place that YHWH chooses,
for YHWH your God has been blessing you
in all your produce and in all the doings of your hands,
and you shall be, oh so joyful!

16 (At) three points in the year
are all your male-folk to be seen
at the presence of YHWH your God
in the place that he chooses:
on the Festival of *Matzot,*
on the Festival of Weeks,
and on the Festival of Huts;
and no one is to be-seen at the presence of YHWH empty-handed;

---

13 **ingathering:** The fall harvest, of grapes.
16 **males:** Nursing females would not have been able to make the three-times-a-year pilgrimage. They are, however, included in the great gathering described in Chap. 31, which was to occur every seven years (Gruber).

Justice (16:18–20): This aspect of communal life has been treated before (e.g., Ex. 23:2–3, 6–9), but not with quite the impassioned edge found in v.20.

Against Canaanite Cult Objects (16:21–22): The destruction of pagan shrines is once again demanded. Both the *Ashera* and the "standing-stone" were connected to the theme of fertility, which in Canaanite worship was related to the gods' generative power. Israelite thought, on the other hand, attributed fertility to a non- or meta-sexual God.

Improper Sacrifice (17:1): Related to 15:21, the text reiterates that YHWH must be worshiped only in perfection—meaning that a sacrificial animal must be free of defects.

The Process of Judgment (17:2–13): Ancient Israel's judicial process involved, not judge and jury, but elders or priests. In this setting, proper "inquiry" was crucial; the testimony of eyewitnesses was required in multiple; and priests provided a sort of appeals court, with their "instruction" serving as the final word on the case—on pain of death.

As part of the Deuteronomic program of centralizing authority, it should be noted that elders are replaced here by state officials in various matters of judgment (vv.8-11; see also 16:18) (Levinson).

17 (rather) each-man according to the giving-capacity of his hand,
   according to the blessing of YHWH your God that he has given
   you.

18 Judges and officials you are to provide for yourselves, within all
   your gates
   that YHWH your God is giving you,
   for your tribal-districts;
   they are to judge the people (with) equitable justice.

19 You are not to cast aside a case-for-judgment,
   you are not to (specially) recognize (anyone's) face,
   and you are not to take a bribe
   —for a bribe blinds the eyes of the wise,
   and twists the words of the equitable.
20 Equity, equity you are to pursue,
   in order that you may live
   and possess the land that YHWH your God is giving you!

21 You are not to plant yourself an Ashera (or) any-kind of tree-
   structure
   beside the slaughter-site of YHWH your God that you make
   yourself;
22 and you are not to raise yourself a standing-stone
   (such) as YHWH your God hates.

17:1 You are not to slaughter-an-offering to YHWH your God
   (of) an ox or a sheep that has on it a defect, anything ill,
   for it is an abomination to YHWH your God!

2 When there is found among you, within one of your gates
   that YHWH your God is giving you,
   a man or a woman that does what is ill in the eyes of YHWH your
   God,
   to cross his covenant,

20 **Equity:** Others, "justice."
22 **standing-stone:** These pagan structures are seen by
   some as phallic fertility symbols.

Laws of Kingship (17:14–20): Deuteronomy here introduces a new note into the Torah, one which becomes familiar from I and II Samuel on. Ancient Israel had an interesting and at times ambivalent attitude toward monarchy: on the one hand, it viewed God as the sole king (cf. Judg. 8:22–23), and could roundly condemn monarchy's excesses (cf. I Sam. 8:10–18). On the other hand, popular support for this common human institution was widespread in the face of the constant military threat, especially from the coast-dwelling and technologically superior Philistines. Once established, the monarchy was permanent.

Our passage clearly demonstrates the controls on the institution desired by the biblical writers: limits on wealth and the stipulation that the king study God's Instruction. The latter expectation, in varying forms, is found all over the ancient Near East (Weinfeld).

The Levites' Share (18:1–8): Their role established fully in the book of Numbers, the Levites functioned as assistants to their kinsmen, the priests, in a variety of capacities. In Deuteronomy, however, the Levite-priest distinction is not sharply drawn. As elsewhere, the Levites owned no land, and hence were supported by portions of various sacrifices and tithes.

3 going and serving other gods
  and prostrating oneself to them
    —to the sun or to the moon or to any of the forces of heaven
      that I have not commanded,
4 and it is told to you,
  you are to hear and you are to inquire well,
  and (if) here: true and correct is the matter
    —this abomination was done in Israel—
5 then you are to take out that man or that woman
  who did this evil thing, (out) to your gates,
  the man or the woman;
  you are to stone them with stones,
  so that they die.

6 On the statement of two witnesses or three witnesses shall the
    one worthy-of-death be put-to-death;
  he shall not be put-to-death on the statement of one witness.
7 The hand of the witnesses is to be against him, at the beginning,
    to put-him-to-death,
  and the hand of the entire people, afterward;
  so shall you burn out the evil from your midst!

8 When any legal-matter is too extraordinary for you, in justice,
  between blood and blood, between judgment and judgment,
    between stroke and stroke,
  in matters of quarreling within your gates,
  you are to arise and go up to the place
  that YHWH your God chooses,
9 you are to come to the Levitical priests and to the judge that
    there is in those days;
  you are to inquire, and they are to tell you
  the word of judgment.

17:3 **sun . . . moon . . . forces of heaven:** Indicating probable Assyrian influence.
7 **hand of the witnesses . . . at the beginning:** Perhaps to indicate the gravity of the accusation.

8 **between blood and blood** etc.: Different types of cases.

10 You are to do according to this word that is told you,
   in that place that YHWH chooses;
   you are to take-care to observe what they instruct you.
11 According to the instruction that they instruct you,
   by the regulation that they tell you,
   you are to do;
   you are not to turn-away from the word that they tell you,
   right or left.
12 Now the man who does presumptuously,
   by not hearkening to the priest that is standing in attendance
      there on YHWH your God,
   or to the judge:
   dead is that man,
   so you shall burn out the evil from Israel!
13 And all the people will hearken, and be awed,
   and will act-presumptuously no more.

14 When you enter the land
   that YHWH your God is giving you,
   and you possess it and settle in it,
   should you say:
   I will set over me a king
   like all the nations that are around me—
15 you may set, yes, set over you a king
   that YHWH your God chooses;
   from among your brothers you may set over you a king,
   you may not place over you a foreign man
   who is not a brother-person to you.
16 Only: he is not to multiply horses for himself,
   and he is not to return the people to Egypt in order to multiply
      horses,
   since YHWH has said to you:
   You will never return that way again!

---

12 **dead:** I.e., he is to be executed.
16 **horses:** Horses were used in biblical warfare, mostly for chariots; everyday riding was chiefly consigned to donkeys.

17 And he is not to multiply wives for himself,
that his heart not be turned-aside,
and silver or gold he is not to multiply for himself to excess.

18 But it shall be:
when he sits on the throne of his kingdom,
he is to write himself a copy of this Instruction in a
   document,
before the presence of Levitical priests.

19 It is to remain beside him,
he is to read out of it all the days of his life,
in order that he may learn to have-awe-for YHWH his God,
to be-careful concerning all the words of this Instruction
and these laws, to observe them,

20 that his heart not be raised above his brothers,
that he not turn-aside from what-is-commanded,
to the right or to the left;
in order that he may prolong (his) days over his kingdom,
he and his sons,
in the midst of Israel.

18:1 There is not to be for the Levitical priests
—the entire tribe of Levi—
any portion or inheritance with Israel;
the fire-offerings of YHWH, and his inheritance, they may eat.

2 But a (normal) inheritance he may not have, in the midst of his
   brothers,
YHWH is his inheritance,
as he promised him.

3 Now this shall be the regulated-share of the priests from the
   people,
from the slaughterers of slaughter-offerings, whether of ox or
   sheep:
the priest is to be given the shankbone, the jawbone and the
   rough-stomach.

---

17 **turned-aside:** To the worship of other gods.
18 **before the presence of:** Tigay: "that is in the charge of."

18:1 **Levitical priests:** A term confined to Deuteronomy.
2 **a (normal) inheritance:** A piece of territory.

Sorcery and False Prophecy (18:9–22): Picking up the theme of avoiding the magical practices of the Canaanites (cf. the briefer Ex. 22:17), the text continues into the topic of prophecy, which is viewed as the proper way to know the will of God. The safeguard against false prophecy, though—noting the nonfulfillment of the "prophet's" word—was too shaky a basis for a stable system. Deuteronomy as a whole has a better overall answer than the one it gives here: it establishes the text as the authority, a process that the book appears to have inaugurated and that became central to the three Western religions.

The passage on sorcery (vv.9–12) repeats "abomination" three times, to emphasize the Bible's abhorrence of the practices enumerated here. This is not to imply that the Israelites did not believe in the efficacy of such phenomena; they simply viewed them as an unacceptable way of learning the divine will.

Towns of Asylum (19:1–13): Num. 35 dealt at length with the same problem, the fate of the accidental murderer. There, however, the manslayer was confined to particular locations until the death of the High Priest, as a kind of atonement for the polluting of the land through bloodshed, whereas here it is primarily to escape family vengeance.

4 The premier-part of your grain, your new-wine and your shining-
oil,
the premier-part of the shearing of your sheep you are to give him.

5 For him YHWH your God has chosen from all your tribes,
for standing-in-service, for attending, in the name of YHWH,
he and his sons,
all the days (to come).

6 Now when the Levite comes from one of your gates, from all
Israel,
where he sojourns,
and he comes with all his appetite's craving
to the place that YHWH chooses,

7 and attends in the name of YHWH his God,
like all his brothers, the Levites
who are standing-in-service there before the presence of YHWH:

8 a share like the (usual) share they may eat,
apart from the sale-revenues of (their) fathers' (property).

9 When you enter the land
that YHWH your God is giving you,
you are not to learn to do according to the abominations of those
nations.

10 There is not to be found among you
one having his son or his daughter cross through fire,
an augurer of augury, a hidden-sorcerer, a diviner, or an
enchanter,

11 or a tier of (magical) tying-knots, or a seeker of ghosts or
favorable-spirits,
or an inquirer of the dead.

12 For an abomination to YHWH is anyone who does these-things,
and because of these abominations
YHWH your God is dispossessing them from before you!

---

5 **standing . . . attending:** Assisting the priests in a
variety of tasks.

8 **A share** etc.: Heb. difficult.

10 **cross through fire:** Apparently as a sacrifice; but see
the discussion in Tigay.

11 **tier of (magical) tying-knots:** Following Driver.
JPS, "one who casts spells."

12 **them:** The Canaanites.

13   Wholehearted shall you be with YHWH your God!

14   For these nations that you are coming-to-possess:
to sorcerers and augurers do they hearken,
but you—not thus has YHWH your God made you!

15   A prophet from your midst, from your brothers, like myself
will YHWH your God raise up for you,
to him you are to hearken,

16   according to all that you sought from YHWH your God at Horev
on the day of the Assembly, saying:
I cannot continue hearing the voice of YHWH my God, and this
great fire I cannot (bear to) see anymore,
so that I do not die!

17   And YHWH said to me:
They have done-well in their speaking;

18   a prophet I will raise up for them from among their brothers, like
you;
I will put my words in his mouth, and he will speak to them
whatever I command him.

19   And it shall be:
(any) man who does not hearken to my words which he speaks in
my name,
I myself will require (a reckoning) from him.

20   But: the prophet who presumptuously speaks a word in my name
that I have not commanded him to speak,
or that he speaks in the name of other gods:
die that prophet shall!

21   Now if you should say in your heart:
How can we know it is the word that YHWH did not speak?

22   Should the prophet speak in the name of YHWH
but the word not happen, not come-about—
(then) that is the word that YHWH did not speak;

---

13 **Wholehearted:** Used to describe Noah (Gen. 6:9) and Abraham (17:1). The identical word (Heb. *tamim*, "wholly-sound,") ascribes animals fit for sacrifice in their purity and perfection.

20 **presumptuously:** Speaking in God's name without having been addressed.

with presumption did the prophet speak it;
you are not to be-in-fear of him!

19:1   When Y<small>HWH</small> your God cuts off the nations
whose land Y<small>HWH</small> your God is giving you,
and you dispossess them and settle in their towns and in their
    houses:

2   three towns you are to separate for yourselves,
in the midst of your land
that Y<small>HWH</small> your God is giving you to possess.

3   Measure yourself the way
and divide-in-three the territory of your land
that Y<small>HWH</small> your God is causing you to inherit.
It shall be for fleeing there, for every (accidental) murderer.

4   Now this is the matter of the (accidental) murderer who flees
    there, that he may stay-alive,
who strikes down his neighbor with no foreknowledge,
nor did he bear-hatred-toward him from yesterday and the day-
    before;

5   or who comes upon his neighbor in the forest, chopping wood,
and his hand swings-away with an ax, to cut wood,
and the iron-part slips off the wood-part
and reaches his neighbor, so that he dies:
he may flee to one of these towns, so that he may stay-alive

6   —lest the blood redeemer pursue the murderer,
since his heart is hot-blooded,
and overtake him—since the journey is long—and strike his life,
though his is not a judgment of death;
since he has not borne-hatred toward him, from yesterday and
    the day-before.

7   Therefore I command you, saying:
Three towns you are to separate for yourself.

19:4 **foreknowledge:** That is, prior intent.

6 **blood redeemer:** The kinsman obligated to avenge
the victim's death.

The Moving of Borders (19:14): A society that put great store by land, as many still in the region today, ancient Israel saw family holdings and borders as basically sacred (in this text as in others, the "inheritance" comes from God).

Witnesses (19:15–21): The need for multiple witnesses and proper inquiry establishes the seriousness of what is at stake in the justice system. In keeping with the biblical idea of "equity" (Heb. *tzedek*), that is, fairness and balance in judgment, a false witness suffers the same punishment as would have befallen the innocent person whom he accused. The "eye for an eye" punishment is thus to serve as a deterrent for a most abhorrent crime.

Laws of War (20): As an example of Deuteronomy's thinking and often humane approach, the rules of war have a reasoned tone compared even to the contemporary world. Many of them occur elsewhere in the ancient Near East. The first four verses stress the frequently appearing idea that God fights on the Israelites' behalf. From there vv.5–7 help to maintain the values of an agricultural society by keeping new builders, new planters, and newlyweds at home for a while. Added to this are considerations of troop morale (vv.8–9), offers of peaceful surrender terms (10–11), and the end results of siege as commonly portrayed in the ancient world (12–14). A different outcome is to be striven for in the case of the native Canaanites, who are to be wiped out, that Israel not be led astray into their "abominable" practices (16–18). The latter passage, especially since it is followed by an ecologically compassionate one about fruit trees, seems genocidal and hence morally unacceptable today. Clearly it stems from a zealous time and strong feelings; whether it was carried out as described we do not know. Medieval Jews solved the problem of moral sensibilities for themselves by defining the Canaanites as long dead with no contemporary successors. But the troubling nature of the text remains.

8 Now if YHWH your God should broaden your territory
as he swore to your fathers,
and give you all the land
that he promised to give your fathers:

9 indeed, you are to keep all this commandment, by observing it,
that I command you today,
to love YHWH your God, and to walk in his ways, all the days;
and you are to add for yourself another three towns to these
three,

10 so that the blood of the innocent not be shed amid your land
that YHWH your God is giving you as an inheritance,
and there be blood-guilt upon you!

11 But if it should be (that) a man bears-hatred toward his neighbor
and waits-in-ambush for him
and rises up against him and strikes his life, so that he dies,
and he flees to one of these towns:

12 the elders of his town are to send and have him taken from there,
they are to give him into the hand of the blood redeemer, so that
he dies.

13 Your eye is not to take-pity on him!
So you shall burn out the innocent blood from Israel,
and it will be-well with you.

14 You are not to move back the border of your neighbor
that the first-ones set-as-border,
in your inheritance that you inherit
in the land that YHWH your God is giving you to possess.

15 One witness (alone) shall not rise up against a man
for any (case of) iniquity, for any (case of) sin,
in any sin that he sins;
at the mouth of two witnesses or at the mouth of three
witnesses, a legal-matter is to be established!

16 When there arises a witness of malice against a man,
testifying against him (by) defection (from God),

19:14 **the first ones:** The ancestors.   15 **legal-matter:** Or lawsuit.

17 and the two men who have the quarrel stand before the presence
of YHWH,
before the presence of the priests or the judges that are-there in
those days:
18 the judges are to inquire well;
and (if) here: a false witness is the witness, falsely has he testified
against his brother:
19 you are to do to him
as he schemed to do to his brother.
So you shall burn out the evil from your midst!
20 Those who remain will hear and will be-awed,
they will not continue to do any more according to this evil
practice in your midst.
21 Your eye is not to take-pity—
(rather) life for life, eye for eye, tooth for tooth, hand for hand,
foot for foot!

20:1 When you go out to war against your enemies
and you see horses and chariots, fighting-people many-more than
you,
do not be overawed by them,
for YHWH your God is with you,
the one who brought you up from the land of Egypt!
2 And it shall be:
when you draw-near for war,
3 the priest is to approach and speak to the people / and say to them:
Hearken, O Israel!
You are drawing-near today to war against your enemies.
Let not your heart be soft,
do not be afraid, do not be in-trepidation,
do not be-terrified before them!
4 For YHWH your God
is the one who goes with you, to wage-war for you against your
enemies,
to deliver you!
5 Then the officials are to speak to the people, saying:
Who is the man
that has built a new house and has not (yet) dedicated it?
Let him go and return to his house,

lest he die in the war
and another man dedicate it!

6 And who is the man
that has planted a vineyard and has not (yet) made-common-use
of it?
Let him go and return to his house,
lest he die in the war
and another man make-common-use-of it!

7 And who is the man
that has betrothed a woman and has not (yet) taken her (in
marriage)?
Let him go and return to his house,
lest he die in the war
and another man take her!

8 And the officers are to continue to speak to the people,
they are to say:
Who is the man,
the one afraid and soft of heart?
Let him go and return to his house,
so that he does not melt the heart of his brothers, like his heart!

9 And it shall be,
when the officials finish speaking to the people,
the commanders of the armed-forces are to count by head the
fighting-people.

10 When you draw-near to a town, to wage-war against it,
you are to call out to it terms-of-peace.

11 And it shall be:
if peace is what it answers you, and it opens (its gates) to you,
then it shall be that all the people that are found in it shall belong
to you as forced-laborers,
and they shall serve you.

20:9 **count by head:** A military census ("mustering the troops"), as at the opening of the book of Numbers. Alternatively, "appoint army commanders at the head of the people" (Tigay).

The Unsolved Murder (21:1–9): Another memorable addition to Israel's law corpus, the case described here stands in stark contrast to the way things are done in contemporary society. For us, an unsolved murder is a matter of intellectual curiosity, a puzzle to be unraveled on a television screen; in biblical Israel, innocent blood had to be atoned for by the entire group when the perpetrator went unfound. In the biblical view (as in that of other ancient societies), crime or wrongdoing was seen as completely disruptive, a threat to the well-being of the very cosmos. Here atonement is made via a public confession and the death of an animal—not with the usual "decontaminating" use of sacrificial blood but with a death that symbolically atones for the death of the murder victim.

The Fair Captive (21:10–14): The situation of the female captive recalls the opening chapters of the *Iliad,* where it forms a key motif. Here, though, rather than the pride and anger of great warriors being at stake, it is the woman's humanity that is central. She is allowed to mourn her family, and retains her dignity to the extent that she cannot be sold as a slave if her husband eventually rejects her.

Wives and Sons (21:15–17): A tension that is played out in the Jacob and Joseph stories in Genesis, the conflict between two wives and their sons must have been a troubling reality in the polygamous ancient Near East. This could be conventionally solved by a father's selection of the "firstborn," but note the brake put on the father's absolute control (Frymer-Kensky 1992a).

12 But if they do not make-peace with you, and make war against
     you,
   you may besiege it.
13 And when YHWH your God gives it into your hand,
   you are to strike-down all its males with the edge of the sword.
14 Only: the women and the infants and the animals,
   everything that is within the town, all its booty, you may take-as-
     plunder for yourself;
   you may consume the booty of your enemies
   that YHWH your God gives you.
15 Thus you are to do to all the towns,
   those exceedingly far from you,
   that are not of the towns of those nations.
16 Only: in the towns of those peoples
   that YHWH your God is giving you as an inheritance,
   you are not to leave-alive any breath;
17 but: you are to devote-them-to-destruction, yes, destruction,
   the Hittite, the Amorite, the Canaanite, the Perizzite, the Hivvite
     and the Yevusite,
   as YHWH your God has commanded you.
18 —In order that they not teach you to do
   according to all their abominations that they do with their gods,
   and you sin against YHWH your God.

19 When you besiege a town for many days,
   waging-war against it, to seize it:
   you are not to bring-ruin on its trees, by swinging-away (with) an
     ax against them,
   for from them you eat,
   them you are not to cut-down—
   for are the trees of the field human beings, (able) to come against
     you in a siege?

17 **devote-them-to-destruction:** Their lives are to be
forfeit, confiscated to God, so to speak.

20 Only those trees of which you know that they are not trees for
    eating,
them you may bring-to-ruin and cut-down,
that you may build siege-works against the town that is making
    war against you, until its downfall.

21:1 If there be found a corpse
on the soil that YHWH your God is giving you to possess,
fallen in the field,
(it) not having-become-known who struck-it-down,

2 your elders and your judges are to go out
and measure-the-distance to the towns that are around the
    corpse.

3 And it shall be that the town nearest to the corpse—
the elders of that town are to take a she-calf of the herd,
with which no work has (ever) been done, which has never pulled
    a yoke;

4 the elders of that town are to bring-down that she-calf to an ever-
    flowing wadi
which has never had work done on it, and has never been sown,
and are to break-the-neck of the she-calf there, in the wadi.

5 Then they are to approach, the priests, the Sons of Levi
—for YHWH your God has chosen (them) to attend on him and to
    give-blessing in YHWH's name,
and by their statement shall be (settled) every legal-quarrel and
    every case-of-assault—

6 and all the elders of that town, the ones nearest the corpse,
are to wash their hands
over the neck-broken calf at the wadi;

7 then they are to speak up and say:
Our hands did not shed this blood,
our eyes did not see!

8 O purge your people Israel that you redeemed, O YHWH,
do not put innocent blood amid your people Israel!
So shall they be atoned of the blood,

21:4 **wadi:** A riverbed, frequently dry — but not in this
case.

8 **atoned of:** Or "purged of," "ransomed of."

9 and so shall you yourself burn out the innocent blood from your
    midst—
for you are to do what-is-right in the eyes of YHWH!

10 When you go-out to war against your enemies
and YHWH your God gives him into your hand, and you take-
    captive his captives,
11 and you see among the captives a woman fair of form,
and you desire her,
and would take her for yourself as a wife:
12 you are to bring her into the midst of your house,
she is to shave her head and to do her nails,
13 she is to put off her garments of captivity from herself
and is to sit in your house,
weeping for her father and her mother, for a month of days;
after that you may come in to her and espouse her,
and she may become your wife.
14 Now it shall be:
If you are not pleased with her,
you must send-her-free, in her person,
but sell, you may not sell her, for silver,
you are not to deal-treacherously with her, since you have
    humbled her!

15 When a man has two wives, the one loved and the other hated,
and they bear him sons, the loved-one and the hated-one,
and the firstborn son is the hated-one's—
16 it shall be, at the time of giving-as-inheritance to his sons what he
    has,
he must not treat-as-firstborn the son of the loved-one,
in the living-presence of the son of the hated-one, the firstborn.
17 Rather, the (actual) firstborn, the son of the hated-one, he is
    to recognize (as such),
by giving him two-thirds of all that is found with him,

---

12 **shave . . . do her nails:** Apparently these acts were signs of mourning. In this case, "doing the nails" means cutting them.

16 **living-presence:** In a person's lifetime; cf. Gen. 11:28.

17 **two-thirds:** Based on a cognate in Akkadian.

The Rebellious Son (21:18–21): Part of creating any ordered society involves continuity between the generations. Even so, this law seems to us to be "cruel and unusual punishment." It becomes more understandable in the context of Deuteronomy's transfer of power from parents (who have a choice here to report their son) to elders, that is, to society at large (see Marcus). The behavior of this son is regarded as a threat, not only to his family, but to the entire community (Frymer-Kensky 1992a). The law may also be, in its intensity, a reflection of the God-Israel relationship (see Psalms 78:8, Jer. 5:23) (Greenstein, personal communication).

The Dignity of the Corpse (21:22–23): Not burying the corpse of an executed criminal results in the pollution of the land and eventual expulsion, as set forth graphically in Lev. 18:24–30.

The Wandering Animal (22:1–4): Ex. 23:4–5 exhorted people to attend to their neighbor's lost or overburdened animal. Here the law is expanded to include taking care of the animal, and indeed of any lost object, until the owner makes inquiry. At issue is loss of work for the owner.

for he is the firstfruit of his vigor,
for him is the regulation of the firstborn-right.

18 When a man has a son, a stubborn-one and a rebel
—he does not hearken to the voice of his father or to the voice of
his mother—
and they discipline him, but he (still) does not hearken to them,

19 his father and his mother are to seize him
and are to bring him out to the elders of his town, to the gate of
his place;

20 then they are to say to the elders of his town:
Our son, this-one, is a stubborn-one and a rebel
—he does not hearken to our voice—
a glutton and a drunkard!

21 Then all the men of the town are to pelt him with stones,
so that he dies.
So you shall burn out the evil from your midst,
and all Israel will hear and be-awed!

22 Now when a man has sin-guilt, (resulting in) a sentence of death,
and is put-to-death,
and you hang him up on a wooden-stake,

23 you are not to leave his carcass overnight on the stake,
rather, you are to bury, yes, bury him on that (very) day,
for an insult to God is a hanging-person
—that you not render your soil *tamei*
that YHWH your God is giving you as an inheritance.

22:1 You are not to see the ox of your brother or his sheep wandering-
away
and hide yourself from them;
you are to return, yes, return them to your brother.

---

18 **stubborn-one . . . discipline:** Heb. *sorer . . . yisseru.*
20 **a glutton and a drunkard:** "He is" is understood at
the beginning of the clause.

22 **hang him up:** As a deterrent.

Mixed Clothing (22:5): This prohibition touches on a frequent theme in Leviticus: the improper mixing of categories.

Mother Bird and Child Bird (22:6–7): Another indicator of the humane concerns of Deuteronomy. There is an obvious parallel between the language here and that of the Fifth Commandment (honoring parents): "prolonging days" and "going-well" as a result of following these laws.

The Safe Roof (22:8): Deuteronomy, with its concern for human life, prevents the shedding of innocent blood once again.

2 Now if your brother not be near to you
   or you do not know him,
   you are to bring it into the midst of your house,
   it is to be-there with you until your brother makes-inquiry about
      it,
   then you are to return it to him.
3 Thus you are to do with his donkey,
   thus you are to do with his garment,
   thus you are to do with anything lost of your brother, that is lost
      by him, and you find it:
   you are not allowed to hide yourself.
4 You are not to see the donkey of your brother, or his ox, fallen by
      the wayside,
   and hide yourself from them;
   you are to raise, yes, raise it up (together) with him.

5 There is not to be a man's item on a woman,
   a man is not to clothe himself in the garment of a woman,
   for an abomination to YHWH your God is anyone doing these!

6 When you encounter the nest of a bird before you in the way,
   in any tree or on the ground,
   (whether) fledglings or eggs,
   with the mother crouching upon the fledglings or upon the eggs,
   you are not to take away the mother along with the children.
7 Send-free, send-free the mother,
   but the children you may take for yourself,
   in order that it may go-well with you and you may prolong (your)
      days.

8 When you build a new house,
   you are to make a parapet for your roof,
   that you not put blood-guilt on your house
   if someone-falling falls from it.

22:3 **Thus you are to do . . . :** Fishbane (1988) sees this phrase as an inner-textual expansion of the preceding law.

4 **hide yourself:** JPS "remain indifferent."

More Forbidden Mixtures (22:9–11): As Greenstein (1984a) explains, hybrids in various areas were understood as appropriate only for God (or, in the case of clothing, the priests).

Fringes (22:12): Paralleling Num. 15:37–41—but this time with no rationale. In Numbers, the "tassels" were to serve as a constant reminder of the divine commandments.

The "Damaged" Wife (22:13–21): A law that alternately upholds a woman's dignity (making her husband pay if he has baselessly accused her) and may lead to taking her life (if the accusation is true). In the former case, they must remain married, and the husband has no possibility of divorcing her.

Virginity for women at marriage was an important value in ancient Israel as elsewhere. Frymer-Kensky (1992a) notes that this case parallels the one of the rebellious son above: the parents' status and welfare is jeopardized; the parents can bring about the child's death; and the elders have the authority to make a ruling, while the public has the power to put the offender to death.

9 You are not to sow your vineyard with two-kinds,
   lest you forfeit-as-holy the full-yield from the seed that you sow,
      and the produce of the vineyard.

10 You are not to plow with an ox and a donkey together.

11 You are not to clothe yourself (in) *shaatnez*,
   wool and flax together.

12 Twisted-cords you are to make yourself
   on the four corners of your tunic-covering with which you cover
      yourself.

13 When a man takes a woman (in marriage)
   and comes in to her, and (then) hates her,
14 and puts on her capricious charges,
   giving out against her an evil name,
   and says:
   This woman I took-in-marriage
   and came near her,
   but I did not find in her signs-of-virginity:
15 the father of the girl and her mother are to take her
   and bring out the signs-of-virginity of the girl to the elders of the
      town, to the gate.
16 Then the father of the girl is to say to the elders:
   I gave my daughter to this man as a wife, and he came-to-hate-
      her.
17 Now here: he has put out capricious charges,
   saying:
   I did not find in your daughter signs-of-virginity;
   but these are the signs-of-virginity of my daughter!
   He is to spread out the garment before the presence of the elders
      of the town;

---

9 **two-kinds:** A mixture. **forfeit-as-holy:** It would be confiscated for God ("become holy property") under these circumstances.
11 ***shaatnez:*** A word of foreign origin that the text felt duty-bound to explain in the next line.

14 **signs-of-virginity:** From v.17, it appears that this was a garment stained with the blood of the de-flowered virgin—a practice found in many cultures.

Adultery (22:22): The definition used here is the classic biblical one: a married woman and a man, married or not. In Mesopotamia it was possible to pay off the aggrieved husband, but not in ancient Israel, where adultery was seen as attacking the moral foundations of society and perhaps also the symbolism of the close relationship between God and Israel.

Rape—or Not (22:23–27): In this case a woman is all but married, yet a distinction is made between an urban and a rural setting in terms of her fate. Note that her consent is not an issue here; as a betrothed woman, she had no right to give it (Frymer-Kensky 1992a).

18 then the elders of that town are to take the man and discipline
     him.
19 They are to fine him a hundred units-of-silver,
     and are to give (it) to the father of the girl—
     for he gave out an evil name
     upon a virgin of Israel.
     His she is to remain as a wife,
     he is not allowed to send her away all his days.
20 But if this matter was true
     —there were not found signs-of-virginity on the girl—
21 they are to bring out the girl to the entrance of her father's house
     and are to stone her, the men of her town, with stones
     so that she dies,
     for she has done a disgrace in Israel
     by playing-the-whore in her father's house.
     So you shall burn out the evil from your midst!

22 When there is found a man lying with a woman espoused to a
     spouse,
     they are to die, the two-of-them,
     the man who lies with the woman and the woman.
     So you shall burn out the evil from Israel!

23 When there is a girl, a virgin, spoken-for to a man,
     and a(nother) man finds her in the town, and lies with her,
24 you are to take-out both of them to the gate of that town
     and are to stone them with stones
     so that they die
     —the girl because she did not cry out in the town
     and the man because he humbled the wife of his neighbor.
     So you shall burn out the evil from your midst!

18 **discipline:** JPS reads "flog."
19 **gave out an evil name:** Slandered. **send her away:**
     Divorce her.
23 **spoken-for:** Not "engaged" in the modern sense,
     but rather one for whom the bride-price has been
     paid (JPS).
24 **humbled:** Others, "violated," "raped."

Rape of an Unattached Woman (22:28–29): The difference here, of course, is that the woman does not "belong" to a man. The rape must result in marriage, but since no husband's privilege has been violated, the crime is neither a capital one nor even a criminal one. It is, however, seen as a "disgrace" (see Gen. 34:7).

An Improper Union (23:1): Instead of the long lists in Lev. 18 and 20, we are given only what is a paradigmatic case of people who must not have sexual relations.

Those Disqualified from the Community (23:2–9): A curious list of those not counted as part of the "holy people": one who cannot reproduce, one born of a forbidden union, and a descendant of two of Israel's traditional enemies to the east. In contrast, the Edomites, Israel's "cousins," are permitted into the community after a waiting period. While scholars have tried to date these passages on the basis of specific historical events, such attempts are probably fruitless.

25 But if (it is) in the field the man finds the spoken-for girl
and the man strongly-seizes her and lay with her,
then he is to die, the man who lay with her, he alone.
26 But to the girl you are not to do anything,
the girl did not (incur) sin (deserving) of death,
for just as (the case of) the man who rises up against his neighbor
and murders his life,
so is this matter:
27 for in the open-field he found her;
when the spoken-for girl cried out,
there was no deliverer for her.

28 When a man finds a girl, a virgin who has never been spoken-for,
and seizes her and lies with her, and they are found:
29 the man who lies with her is to give to the father of the girl fifty
units-of-silver;
his shall she be, as a wife,
because he has humbled her;
he is not allowed to send her away, all his days.

23:1 A man is not to take-in-marriage the wife of his father,
that he not expose the skirt of his father.

2 One-wounded by crushing, or cut-off (in the) sperm-organ, is not
to enter the assembly of YHWH.

3 A *mamzer* is not to enter the assembly of YHWH;
even (to) the tenth generation
no one from him is to enter the assembly of YHWH.

4 An Ammonite or a Moabite is not to enter the assembly of
YHWH;
even to the tenth generation
no one from them is to enter the assembly of YHWH, for the ages,

---

27 **cried out:** Because it is out in the country, her cry-
ing for help is presumed.
23:1 **expose the skirt:** Which covers his wife's nakedness," meant only for him (Ehrlich).
2 **crushing . . . cut off:** Procedures meant to produce
eunuchs, who served in ancient courts (Driver).

3 **mamzer:** Pronounced *mom-zare;* apparently one
born of a forbidden union (e.g., incest or adultery).
The child of two unmarried parents, while rare in
the Bible, is not condemned in the manner of this
verse.

The Purity of the Camp (23:10–15): The matter of bodily wastes, interestingly, did not enter the list of ritually "polluting" emissions enumerated in Lev. 12 and 15. Unlike blood and semen, they did not carry the connotation of life-death boundaries. At the same time, it is recognized here that a lapse in personal cleanliness on the part ot the Israelites will violate the purity of the camp, in which God "dwells."

The Fugitive Slave (23:16–17): Despite the accepted existence of slavery in Israelite society, Deuteronomy deemed it cruel to return fugitive slaves. This contrasts not only with ancient Near Eastern practice but also with some cases in the Bible (e.g., I Sam. 3:15, I Kings 2:39–40) (Greenstein 1985a).

5 on account that they did not greet you with food and with water
on the way, at your going-out from Egypt,
and because he hired against you Bil'am son of Be'or
from Petor, (in) Aram-of-the-Two-Rivers, to curse you.

6 But YHWH your God was not willing to hearken to Bil'am,
and YHWH your God turned for you the curse into a blessing,
for YHWH your God loves you.

7 You are not to seek their peace or their well-being, all your days,
for the ages!

8 You are not to abominate an Edomite,
for he is your brother;
you are not to abominate an Egyptian,
for you were a sojourner in his land.

9 Children that are born to them, in the third generation,
may enter from them the assembly of YHWH.

10 When you go out as a camp against your enemies,
take-you-care against anything evil.

11 If there should be among you a man
who is not ritually-pure, (because of) a night accident,
he is to go outside the camp;
he is not to come into the midst of the camp.

12 Now it shall be toward the turn of sunset:
he is to wash with water,
and when the sun has come in,
he may come (back) into the midst of the camp.

13 An area you should have, outside the camp,
where you may go, outside:

14 a spike you should have, along with your weapon;
and it shall be, when you sit outside (to relieve yourself),
you are to dig with it,

---

5 **Bil'am:** Cf. Num. 22–24.
7 **peace . . . well-being:** The phrase has an equivalent
in treaties in Akkadian (Tigay).

10 **evil thing:** In this case, bodily waste.
11 **night accident:** An involuntary emission of semen.

Pagan "Clergy" (23:18–19): The use of pointed slurs (the key term "abomination" appears again) makes it clear how such people were regarded in the biblical estimation. In Frymer-Kensky's view (1992b), these people were not "holy prostitutes," but the Bible regards their deeds as horrifying. Likewise, Tigay rejects the idea that sexuality figured as an official part of ancient Near Eastern religion.

Charging Interest (23:22–24): The law prohibits taking interest within the community as a damaging practice. The society in question, of course, was not predominantly a commercial one, and hence later interpretations, such as that of medieval Christians and Jews, were to attempt to read other things into it.

Making Vows (23:22–24): The issue of taking vows is treated extensively in the book of Numbers (cf. Chaps. 6 and 30), and was of major concern in the religious life of ancient Israel as an opportunity to make a more personal contribution to religious practice. The law also demonstrates the significance of the spoken word (through the use of "lips" and "mouth"), common to ancient societies and to many later one as well.

and when you return, you are to cover up your excrement.

15 For YHWH your God walks about amid your camp,
to rescue you, to give your enemies before you;
so the camp is to be holy,
so that he does not see among you anything of "nakedness"
and turn away from you.

16 You are not to hand over a serf to his lord
who has sought-rescue by you from his lord.

17 Beside you let him dwell, among you,
in the place that he chooses, within one of your gates (that)
seems good for him;
you are not to maltreat him!

18 There is to be no holy-prostitute of the daughters of Israel,
there is to be no holy-prostitute of the sons of Israel.

19 You are not to bring the fee of a whore or the price of a dog to
the house of YHWH your God,
for any vow;
for an abomination to YHWH your God are the two-of-them!

20 You are not to charge interest to your brother,
interest in silver, interest in food, interest in anything for which
you may charge-interest.

21 The foreigner you may charge-interest,
but your brother you may not charge-interest,
in order that YHWH your God may bless you
in all the enterprises of your hand
on the land that you are entering to possess.

22 When you vow a vow to YHWH your God,
you are not to delay paying it,

---

15 **anything of "nakedness":** Trad. "anything inde-
cent."
18 **holy-prostitute:** Pagan priests and priestesses were
associated by the Bible with sexual ceremonies.
19 **the fee of a whore** etc.: "Dog" is clearly a term of
derision for a pagan priest. The verse comes to
teach that tainted money is not acceptable in pay-

ment of a vow, which is, after all, a religious matter.
21 **the foreigner you may charge-interest:** This verse
became central to economic debates in the Middle
Ages, when the church banned the charging of interest but permitted Jews to do it, thus funding
many a state treasury or military campaign.

Reasonable Use (23:25–26): Establishing a boundary for farms and their produce, the law steers a path between a human need (food) and theft.

Laws of Remarriage (24:1–4): Continuing the concern for holiness in the area of sexuality, Deuteronomy prohibits what occasionally happens in Western society—a woman remarries her first husband after her divorce from another man. Such behavior was considered ritually polluting in ancient Israel. It may also have been connected to the fact that the first husband, if the woman remarried him, would thus be receiving property from another man's wealth (the second husband's).

indeed, YHWH your God will require, yes, require it of you,
and it shall be (reckoned) a sin in you.

23 But if you hold-back-from vowing,
it shall not be (considered) a sin in you.

24 What issues from your lips, you are to keep,
and you are to do
as you vowed to YHWH your God, willingly,
as you promised with your mouth.

25 When you come into the vineyard of your neighbor,
you may eat (the) grapes, according to your appetite, until your
being-satisfied,
but in your vessel you may not put (any).

26 When you come into the standing-grain of your neighbor,
you may pluck off ears with your hand,
but a sickle you are not to swing above the grain of your
neighbor.

24:1 When a man takes-in-marriage a woman and espouses her,
and it happens: if she does not find favor in his eyes
—for he finds in her something of "nakedness"—
he may write for her a Document of Cutoff;
he is to place (it) in her hand
and (thus) send-her-away from his household.

2 Now when she goes out from his house,
(if) she goes and becomes another man's,

3 and should he too come-to-hate her, the latter man,
(then) he (too) is to write her a Document of Cutoff,
placing it in her hand
and sending-her-away from his household;
or if he should die, the latter man, who took her for him as a wife,

25 **but in your vessel** etc.: You may not take what is more than needed to slake your momentary hunger.

26 **but a sickle** etc.: The same applies in this case.

24:1 **something of "nakedness":** The "defect" is not specified here; there is lively debate on this point in later Jewish tradition. **Cutoff:** Usually translated as "divorcement," which is its legal meaning.

6 **a handmill or an upper-millstone:** A major means of livelihood or survival in ancient Israel. This law, and the others regarding collateral in Deuteronomy (vv.11 and 17 below), expand the basic rule found in Ex. 22:25–26.

The New Wife (24:5): This humane military rule may stem from a tradition separate from the one in 20:7. In any event, it appears to acknowledge sexuality as a part of marriage separate from procreation.

Pledge I (24:6): Even debt is a situation that must be handled sensitively; unfair collateral is not to be taken.

Kidnapping (24:7): The capital crime here would appear to be the sale of specifically an Israelite as a slave.

A Reminder about Skin Disease (24:8–9): As detailed in Lev. 13–15, *tzaraat* was some kind of skin condition that rendered a person temporarily unfit to be in the sacred camp. It was formerly identified with, and translated as, leprosy, but that is now felt to be incorrect by virtually all scholars. The law recurs here, among examples of injustice, because the disease was often viewed as the result of a person's wrongful behaviors.

Pledge II (24:10–13): A parallel to Ex. 22:24–26, which, in contrast to other cases of comparison between the two legal collections, has the more emotional tone. On the other hand, our passage emphasizes the dignity due even a debtor.

4   he may not return, her first husband who sent-her-away,
    to take her to be his as a wife,
    since she has made-herself-*tamei*;
    for it is an abomination before the presence of YHWH,
    that you do not bring-sin-upon the land
    that YHWH your God is giving you as an inheritance!

5   When a man takes a new wife,
    he is not to go out to the armed-forces,
    he is not to cross over to them for any matter;
    (free-and-)clear let him remain in his house for one year,
    and let him give-joy to his wife whom he has taken.

6   There is not to be seized-for-payment a handmill or an upper-
        millstone,
    for (one's) life would (thus) be seized.

7   When a man is found to have stolen a person from his brothers,
        from the Children of Israel,
    and he deals-treacherously with him and sells him:
    die that thief shall;
    so shall you burn out the evil from your midst!

8   Be-careful regarding the affliction of *tzaraat,* take exceeding care
        to observe (the rules);
    according to all that the Levitical priests instruct you, as I have
        commanded them, you are to carefully observe.

9   Bear-in-mind what YHWH your God did to Miryam, on the way at
        your going-out of Egypt!

10 When you lend to your neighbor, a loan of anything,
    you are not to enter his house to take-his-pledge as a pledge.

11 Outside you are to stand,
    and the man to whom you have lent is to bring out the pledge to
        you, outside.

8   **priests:** In the Leviticus texts, they are the ones re-
    sponsible for identifying those with the disease and
    with ruling on the state of its progress.
9   **what God did to Miryam:** In Num. 12:10, God

strikes Miryam with *tzaraat* as punishment for
speaking against Moshe.
10 **pledge:** Typically one's cloak, which also served as a
    blanket.

Timely Payment (24:14–15): "Oppression" here consists of delaying the payment of a worker's wages. The "calling out" to YHWH recalls a similar cry of the oppressed in Ex. 22:22, 26. Overall, the rhetoric of the passage far exceeds that found in a parallel text in the Holiness Code (Lev. 19:13).

Fathers and Children (24:16): An issue of deep concern to the exiles in Babylonia, this questioning of free will is raised a number of times in the Bible. In Ex. 22:23, God was to punish oppressors by making their "wives widows, and [their] children orphans"; Deuteronomy has toned this down by punishing the evildoer and not his or her children. Cf. Fishbane (1988) for discussion.

The Oppressed Again (24:17–22): The three classic powerless groups in Israel and elsewhere have been mentioned before, but now receive help based on a particularly Israelite rationale: the people's historical experience of having been oppressed in Egypt. For a parallel passage, cf. Ex. 22:23–24.

12 And if he is an afflicted man, you may not lie down in his pledge;
13 you are to return, yes, return to him the pledge when the sun
    comes in,
  that he may lie down in his garment,
  and bless you,
  and yours will be righteous-merit, before the presence of YHWH
    your God.

14 You are not to withhold from a hired-hand, an afflicted and
    needy-one,
  (whether) from your brothers or from your sojourner that is
    within your land, within your gates.
15 On his payday you are to give his wage, you are not to let the sun
    come in upon him,
  for he is afflicted, for it he lifts his life-breath—
  that he not call out against you to YHWH, and there be sin upon
    you!

16 Fathers are not to be put-to-death for sons,
  sons are not to be put-to-death for fathers:
  every-man for his own sin (alone) is to be put-to-death!

17 You are not to cast aside the case of a sojourner (or) an orphan,
  you are not to seize-for-payment the clothing of a widow.
18 You are to bear-in-mind that serf were you in the land of Egypt,
  and YHWH your God redeemed you from there,
  therefore I command you to observe this word!

19 When you cut down your harvest in your field, and you forget a
    sheaf in the field,
  you are not to return to get it;
  for the sojourner, for the orphan and for the widow it shall be,
  in order that YHWH your God may bless you in all the doings of
    your hands.
20 When you knock off your olives, you are not to check-the-boughs
    after you;
  for the sojourner, for the orphan and for the widow it shall be.
21 When you cut off (grapes in) your vineyard, you are not to glean
    after you;
  for the sojourner, for the orphan and for the widow it shall be.

Corporal Punishment (25:1–3): Despite the predominance of "guilt" and "stroke / strike" in this passage, what is stressed in the end is more humanity than punishment.

The Laboring Ox (25:4): Parallel to the respect due human beings is that due a working animal. This may also reflect the Israelites' identification with certain animals in symbolic settings (cf. Eilberg-Schwartz).

Keeping a Man's Name Alive (25:5–10): A number of stories and laws in the Bible clarify how important the continuity of the generations, as represented by carrying on a man's name, was considered in ancient Israel. Here the law provides for the widow of a man who dies without heirs to provide one, through the institution of "levirate marriage"—whereby the man's brother or other close relative marries her, and the subsequent offspring bears the deceased brother's name. This institution vividly appears in the book of Ruth, which in fact contains a ceremony scene (4:1–11) of the kind set forth here.

22   You are to bear-in-mind that serf were you in the land of Egypt,
      therefore I command you to do this thing!

25:1   When there is a legal-quarrel between men,
      they are to approach the court-of-justice, and they are to render-
         justice to them;
      they are to declare-innocent the innocent-one, and to declare-
         guilty the guilty-one.

2   And it shall be:
      if deserving of strokes is the guilty-one,
      the judge is to have him lie-fallen and is to have him struck, in his
         presence,
      according to his guilt, by number.

3   Forty (times) he is to be struck, not adding (any),
      lest you add, by striking him, (too) many strokes to these,
      and your brother be worthy-of-insult in your eyes.

4   You are not to muzzle an ox while it is threshing (grain).

5   When brothers dwell together
      and one of them dies, and a son he does not have,
      the wife of the dead-man is not to go outside (in marriage), to a
         strange man:
      her brother-in-law is to come to her and take her for himself as a
         wife, doing-the-brother-in-law's-duty by her.

6   Now it shall be that the firstborn that she bears will be
         established under the name of his dead brother,
      that his name not be blotted-out from Israel.

7   But if the man does not wish to take his sister-in-law (in
         marriage),
      his sister-in-law is to go up to the gate, to the elders, and say:
      My brother-in-law refuses to establish for his brother a name in
         Israel,
      he will not consent to do-a-brother-in-law's-duty by me!

25:2 **strokes:** Of the whip, as punishment.
3 **forty:** The maximum number of strokes.
4 **You are not to muzzle an ox:** To prevent it from
eating while working.

5 **doing-the-brother-in-law's-duty:** One verb in the
Hebrew (y-b-m).

Improper Intervention in a Struggle (25:11–12): In a law literally protecting maleness, a wife loses her hand over an act understood by a patriarchal society to be completely intolerable. Not even the close ties of a woman to the males of her family may overrule this (Frymer-Kensky 1992a). But also at issue may be the idea that the convenant is passed on biologically, and hence damaging the genitals damages the covenant (Greenstein, personal communication).

True Weights (25:13–16): Not only violating "purity" in diet and worship are adjudged "abominations," but also the practice of falsifying weights and measures. Ethics in business is thus an aspect of serving God properly (as it is in other ancient Near Eastern cultures).

Amalek (25:17–19): Hearkening back to Ex. 17:8–16, this passage clarifies the crime of the Amalekites against the newly freed Israelites. The attack on the rear was remembered bitterly in the Bible; cf. I Sam. 15 and the book of Esther, where the villain, Haman, is portrayed as a descendant of the Amalekite king Agag.

The Declaration of the Farmer (26:1–15): In a climactic set of ceremonies, those who work the land are to acknowledge God's ownership of the soil. Through the offering of firstfruits, the memory of the Exodus and the gift of the land are kept immediate—"I have entered the land" (v.3). The descendants' rootedness in "a land flowing with milk and honey" (9) is made to contrast with the ancestors' wandering. This characterization of the land, and thanksgiving for its produce, is reiterated in the brief section about tithes (12–15). Thus the land is not taken for granted, and Israel celebrates, not the sexuality of the gods as the source of the soil's fertility, but rather the gift of a God who has intervened in human history.

This chapter is a fitting end to the sequence of laws in Deuteronomy; emphasizing the gift of the land (as Buber 1982 points out, "give" in various permutations occurs seven times) suggests that the gift may be revoked if the society does not uphold the covenant. Also notable is the sixfold use of the Hebrew root b-w-' (*bo'*), appearing here variously as "enter," "produce," "bring."

8 Then the elders of his town are to call for him and are to speak to
   him;
   and if he stands (there) and says: I do not wish to take her,
9 his sister-in-law is to approach him before the eyes of the elders,
   she is to draw off his sandal from his foot
   and is to spit in his face,
   then she is to speak up and say:
   Thus shall be done to the man that does not build up the house
   of his brother!
10 His name is to be called in Israel: The House of the (One with
   the) Drawn-Off Sandal.

11 When men scuffle together, a man and his brother,
   and the wife of one of them comes-near to rescue her husband
   from the hand of him that is striking him,
   and she stretches out her hand and seizes (him) by his genitals:
12 you are to chop off her hand, your eye is not to have-pity!

13 You are not to have in your purse stone-weight and stone-weight,
   (both) large and small.
14 You are not to have in your house *efa* and *efa*, (both) large and
   small.
15 A stone-weight perfect and equal shall you have, an *efa* perfect
   and equal shall you have,
   in order that your days may be prolonged on the soil that YHWH
   your God is giving you.
16 For an abomination to YHWH your God is everyone doing these,
   everyone committing corruption!

17 Bear-in-mind what Amalek did to you
   on the way, at your going-out from Egypt,
18 how he encountered you on the way
   and attacked-your-tail—all the beaten-down-ones at your rear—

---

9 **draw off his sandal . . . spit:** So the recalcitrant
kinsman is publicly shamed.
13 **stone-weight:** Used as a counterbalance on a scale.
16 **committing corruption:** JPS, "who deals dishon-
estly."

18 **beaten-down-ones:** Reading *nehelashim* for *nehe-shalim*, "stragglers."

◆ while you (were) weary and faint,
and (thus) he did not stand-in-awe of God.

19 So it shall be:
when Y HWH your God gives-you-rest from all your enemies
round about
in the land that Y HWH your God is giving you as an inheritance,
to possess it,
you are to blot out the name of Amalek from under the heavens;
you are not to forget!

26:1 Now it shall be:
when you enter the land
that Y HWH your God is giving you as an inheritance,
and you possess it and settle in it,

2 you are to take from the premier-part of all the fruit of the soil
that you produce from your land that Y HWH your God is giving
you;
you are to put it in a basket
and are to go to the place
that Y HWH your God chooses to have his name dwell.

3 You are to come to the priest that is (there) in those days,
and you are to say to him:
"I announce today to Y HWH your God
that I have entered the land that Y HWH swore to our fathers, to
give us."

4 Then the priest is to take the basket from your hand
and is to deposit it before the slaughter-site of Y HWH your God.

5 And you are to speak up and say, before the presence of Y HWH
your God:
"An Aramean Astray my Ancestor;
he went down to Egypt and sojourned there, as menfolk few-in-
number,

26:5 **An Aramean Astray my Ancestor:** Heb. *arami oved
avi,* a phrase clearly meant to be remembered, and
referring to Yaakov and his children in Genesis. It
has become part of the Passover ceremony, although its meaning there is changed ("an Aramean

[Laban in Gen. 28–31] sought to destroy my Ancestor [Jacob]").

9, 10 **he brought . . . I have brought:** The gift of the land
is answered by the gift of its produce to God (Buber
1982).

but he became there a nation, great, mighty (in number) and
  many.

6 Now the Egyptians dealt-ill with us and afflicted us,
  and placed upon us hard servitude.

7 We cried out to YHWH, the God of our fathers,
  and YHWH hearkened to our voice:
  he saw our affliction, and our strain, and our oppression,

8 and YHWH took us out from Egypt,
  with a strong hand and with an outstretched arm,
  with great awe-inspiring (acts)
  and with signs and portents,

9 and he brought us to this place
  and gave us this land,
  a land flowing with milk and honey.

10 So now—
  here, I have brought the premier-part of the fruits of the soil
  that you have given me, O YHWH!"
  Then you are to deposit it before the presence of YHWH your
    God
  and you are to prostrate-yourself before the presence of YHWH
    your God;

11 you are to rejoice in all the good-things that YHWH your God has
    given you and your household,
  you and the Levite and the sojourner that is in your midst.

12 When you finish tithing all the tithe of your produce
  in the third year, the year of the tithe,
  you are to give (it) to the Levite, to the sojourner, to the orphan
    and to the widow;
  that they may eat (it) within your gates, and be-satisfied.

13 And you are to say, before the presence of YHWH your God:
  "I have removed the holy-part from the house,
  I have also given (it) to the Levite, to the sojourner, to the orphan
    and to the widow,
  according to all your command that you have commanded me;
  I have not crossed-over away from your commandments, I have
    not forgotten:

Summary (26:16–19): The chapter, and the laws proper, end with the general observation that a two-way covenant has been made, as in Ex. 19:5–6. The result takes a high nationalistic turn in v.19, which once again seems to fit primarily an age of monarchy.

The Covenant Ceremony (27): As if to dramatize what has just concluded, the text at this point interpolates a ceremony that in location (Shechem) and theme anticipates what we find at the end of the book of Joshua (Chap. 24). It also encourages viewing Deuteronomy as a Northern document. Here the core is the series of curses uttered on Mount Eval in vv.25–26 (the blessings, curiously, do not appear). The curses, which do not introduce any new material as such, reflect the community's fear that someone will sin in secret and not be found out, and the entire community will suffer as a result (Bellefontaine). The public pronouncement of threats was not unusual at the sealing of an agreement in the ancient Near East. As in previous legal sections, we are presented with a mixture of areas—criminal, sexual, and ritual—ending with the general provision that the "words of this Instruction" are to be carefully observed.

14 I have not eaten of it while in sorrow,
I have not removed any of it (while) *tamei*,
I have not given any of it to the dead!
I have hearkened to the voice of YHWH my God,
I have done according to all that you have commanded me!

15 Look down from your holy abode, from heaven,
and bless your people, Israel,
and the soil that you have given us,
as you swore to our fathers,
a land flowing with milk and honey."

16 This day
YHWH your God commands you to observe these laws and the
regulations;
you are to take-care and observe them
with all your heart and with all your being.

17 YHWH you have declared today, to be for you a god,
to walk in his ways and to keep his laws, his commandments and
his regulations,
and to hearken to his voice.

18 And YHWH has declared you today, to be for him a specially-
treasured people,
as he promised you,
to be-careful (regarding) all his commandments,

19 and to set you most-high above all the nations that he has made,
for praise, for fame, and for honor,
for you to be a people holy to YHWH your God,
as he promised.

27:1 Now Moshe and the elders of Israel commanded the people,
saying:
Keep all this commandment that I command you today!

---

14 **(while) in sorrow:** At the time of mourning. **given
. . . to the dead:** As would have been customary in
the ancient Near East.

17 **declared:** JPS, "affirmed."
18 **to be-careful . . . :** The import of this phrase here is
unclear.

2 And it shall be:
at the time that you cross the Jordan
into the land that YHWH your God is giving you,
you are to set up for yourself great stones
and are to plaster them with plaster;

3 you are to write on them all the words of this Instruction, when
you cross over,
in order that you may enter the land that YHWH your God is
giving you,
a land flowing with milk and honey,
as YHWH, the God of your fathers, promised you.

4 Now it shall be, on your crossing the Jordan:
set up these stones
about which I command you today, on Mount Eval,
and plaster them with plaster.

5 You are to build there a slaughter-site to YHWH your God,
a slaughter-site of stones;
you are not to swing against them (any) iron.

6 (With) complete stones you are to build the slaughter-site of
YHWH your God,
you are to offer-up on it offerings-up to YHWH your God.

7 When you slaughter *shalom*-offerings, you may eat (them) there,
and you are to rejoice
before the presence of YHWH your God.

8 And you are to write on the stones
all the words of this Instruction,
explained well.

9 Now Moshe and the Levitical priests spoke
to all Israel, saying:
Be-silent and hearken, O Israel:
This day you are becoming a people to YHWH your God.

10 You are to hearken to the voice of YHWH your God,
you are to observe his commandments and his laws that I
command you today!

27:6 **complete stones:** In their natural and hence potentially holy state (Greenstein 1985a).

8 **explained well:** Ibn Ezra interprets this as "clearly
written."

11 And Moshe commanded the people at that time, saying:

12 These you are to stand to bless the people, on Mount Gerizim,
   when you have crossed the Jordan:
   Shim'on, Levi, and Yehuda,
   Yissakhar, Yosef, and Binyamin.

13 And these you are to stand for the curse, on Mount Eval:
   Re'uven, Gad, and Asher,
   Zevulun, Dan, and Naftali.

14 And all the Levites are to speak up and say to every man of Israel,
   (with) voice raised:

15 Damned be the man
   who makes a carved-image or molten-thing, an abomination to
      YHWH,
   made by the hands of an engraver,
   and sets (it) up in secret!
   And all the people are to speak up and say: Amen!

16 Damned be
   he that insults his father or his mother!
   And all the people are to say: Amen!

17 Damned be
   he that moves back the territory-marker of his neighbor!
   And all the people are to say: Amen!

18 Damned be
   he that leads-astray a blind-person in the way!
   And all the people are to say: Amen!

19 Damned be
   he that casts aside the case of a sojourner, an orphan, or a widow!
   And all the people are to say: Amen!

12–13 **Gerizim . . . Eval:** The two mountains framing the ancient and culturally significant city of Shechem (today Nablus).

15 **Damned:** Others, "cursed."

The Consequences (28): Following the dramatic ceremony of Chap. 27, which, as an event placed in the future, feels somewhat artificial, is the more conventional listing of blessings and curses, parallel to Lev. 26. The latter functionally ends the book of Leviticus (Chap. 27 is obviously a kind of appendix), and our chapter here ends the long legal portion of Deuteronomy. A further parallel is the summary verses in each; Lev. 26 ends with "These are the laws, the regulations and the instructions that YHWH gave / between himself and the Children of Israel at Mount Sinai, by the hand of Moshe," while v.69 of our chapter is "These are the words of the covenant / that YHWH commanded Moshe to cut with the Children of Israel / in the land of Moav, / aside from the covenant that he cut with them at Horev."

As is typical of this kind of literature, the curses seem to outweigh the blessings, not only in verse count (55 to 14) but in color of description as well. While later generations of Jews, horrified by the warnings of disaster, stipulated that this chapter be read in an undertone when it is a weekly public synagogue reading, it is fairly standard stuff in the context of ancient Near Eastern treaties.

20 Damned be
   he that lies with the wife of his father,
   for he has exposed the skirt of his father!
   And all the people are to say: Amen!

21 Damned be
   he that lies with any animal!
   And all the people are to say: Amen!

22 Damned be
   he that lies with his sister,
   the daughter of his father or the daughter of his mother!
   And all the people are to say: Amen!

23 Damned be
   he that lies with his mother-in-law!
   And all the people are to say: Amen!

24 Damned be
   he that strikes down his neighbor in secret!
   And all the people are to say: Amen!

25 Damned be
   he that takes a bribe,
   (thus) striking-down a life (through) innocent blood!
   And all the people are to say: Amen!

26 Damned be
   he that does not fulfill the words of this Instruction, to observe
      them!
   And all the people are to say: Amen!

28:1 Now it shall be:
   if you hearken, yes, hearken, to the voice of YHWH your God,
   taking-care to observe all his commandments that I command
      you today,
   then YHWH your God will make you most-high
   above all the nations of the earth.

24 **strikes down:** I. e., kills.

2 Then there will come upon you all these blessings, and overtake
 you,
 since you have hearkened to the voice of YHWH your God:
3 Blessed be you, in the town,
 blessed be you, in the (open) field;
4 blessed be the fruit of your womb, the fruit of your soil, and the
 fruit of your animals,
 the offspring of your cattle and the fecundity of your sheep.
5 Blessed be your basket and your kneading-bowl.
6 Blessed be you, in your coming-in,
 blessed be you, in your going-out.
7 May YHWH make your enemies, those that rise against you,
 be smitten before you;
 by one road they will go out against you,
 by seven roads they will flee before you.
8 YHWH will ordain for you the blessing
 in your storehouses,
 in all the enterprises of your hand,
 and he will bless you in the land that YHWH your God is giving
 you.
9 YHWH will establish you to be a people holy to him,
 as he swore to you,
 when you keep the commandments of YHWH your God
 and walk in his ways.
10 Now when all the peoples of the earth see
 that the name of YHWH is proclaimed over you,
 they will hold you in awe.
11 YHWH will leave-excess for you of good-things,
 in the fruit of your womb, the fruit of your animals, and the fruit
 of your soil,
 on the soil that YHWH swore to your fathers, to give them.
12 YHWH will open for you his goodly treasuries, the heavens,
 by giving the rain of your land in its set-time,
 and by blessing all the doings of your hand;
 you will lend to many nations,

28:8 **ordain:** Following JPS.

but you yourself will not have to take-a-loan.

13 YHWH will make you the head and not the tail,

you will be only top, you will not be bottom,

—if you hearken to the commandments of YHWH your God

which I command you today, by taking-care and by observing
    (them),

14 that you not turn-aside from all the words that I command you
    today,

to the right or to the left,

by walking after other gods, by serving them.

15 But it shall be:

If you do not hearken to the voice of YHWH your God,

by taking-care and by observing all his commandments and his
    laws

that I command you today,

then there will come upon you all these curses, and overtake you:

16 Damned be you, in the town,

damned be you, in the (open) field;

17 damned be your basket and your kneading-bowl,

18 damned be the fruit of your womb and the fruit of your soil,

the offspring of your cattle and the fecundity of your sheep;

19 damned be you, in your coming-in,

damned be you, in your going-out.

20 YHWH will send-forth against you

Curse, Confusion and Reproach,

against all the enterprises of your hand that you do,

until you have been destroyed, until you have perished quickly

because of the evil of your deeds by which you have abandoned
    me.

21 YHWH will make-cling to you the pestilence,

until it has finished you off from the soil that you are entering to
    possess.

22 YHWH will strike you

with consumption, with fever and with inflammation,

with violent-fever and with dehydration,

with blight and with jaundice;

they will pursue you until you are destroyed.

23 The heavens that are above your head will become bronze,
and the earth that is beneath you, iron.

24 Yhwh will make the rain of your land powder and dust;
from the heavens it will come-down upon you
until you perish.

25 Yhwh will cause you to be smitten before your enemies:
by one road you will go-out against them,
by seven roads you will flee before them—
you will become an object-of-fright to all the kingdoms of the
earth.

26 Your carcass will be for eating
for all the fowl of the heavens and for the beasts of the earth,
with none to make (them) tremble.

27 Yhwh will strike you
with boils of Egypt
and with tumors, with scabs, and with itching,
from which you cannot be healed;

28 Yhwh will strike you
with madness, with blindness, and with confusion of heart.

29 You will feel-about at noon
like a blind-person feels about in deep-darkness,
you will not make your way succeed;
you will be, oh so withheld-from and robbed all the days,
with no deliverer.

30 A woman you will betroth, but another man will lie with her,
a house you will build, but you will not dwell in it,
a vineyard you will plant, but you will not put-it-to-use,

---

27 **tumors:** Ancient scribes were uncomfortable with the text's *afolim*, "hemorrhoids," so they substituted *tehorim*, "tumors," for reading aloud. The original word is nevertheless printed in the text, with a marginal note (see v.30 below for a similar case).

29 **with no deliverer:** The emotional tone of the phrase, which is repeated in v.31 with the additional "for you," is captured by its first occurrence—in 22:23, where it refers to a rape victim being helpless.

30 **lie with:** The Hebrew text reads *yishgalenna*, which medieval commentators understood as "treat like a concubine" or the like, a meaning close to an Akkadian cognate. Scribes stipulated that it be read as *yishkevenna*, "lie with," which was seen as less upsetting (at least to the reader).

31 your ox (will be) slaughtered before your eyes, but you will not
    eat of it,
your donkey will be robbed (from you) in front of you, but it will
    not return to you,
your sheep will be given to your enemies,
with no deliverer for you.

32 Your sons and your daughters will be given to another people,
while your eyes look on and languish for them all the day,
with no God-power to your hand.

33 The fruit of your soil and all that-you-toil-for
will be consumed by a people that you have not known,
you will be only withheld-from and downtrodden all the days,

34 and you will go mad from the sight of your eyes that you see!

35 Yhwh will strike you
with evil boils upon the knees and upon the thighs,
from which you cannot be healed—
from the sole of your foot up to your crown.

36 Yhwh will drive you and your king whom you have raised over
    you
to a nation that you have not known, (either) you or your fathers,
you shall serve there other gods, of wood and of stone.

37 You will become an example-of-desolation, a proverb and a
    byword
among all the peoples to which Yhwh drives you.

38 Much seed you will take out to the field, but little will you gather
    in,
for locusts will ravage them.

39 Vineyards you will plant and till, but their wine you will not
    drink, nor will you store (it),
for the worm will devour them.

40 Olive trees you will have throughout all your territory, but oil you
    will not (get to) pour-for-anointing,
for your olives will drop off.

---

31 **with no deliverer:** The phrase breaks the sequence of "..., but..." that is characteristic of the previous verses; such a break in rhythm or structure is a common rhetorical flourish in biblical texts.

41 Sons and daughters you will beget, but they will not be yours,
for they will go into captivity.

42 All the trees and the fruit of your soil, the buzzing-cricket will
possess.

43 The sojourner that is in your midst
will rise-high above you, higher (and) higher,
while you descend lower and lower;

44 he will lend to you, but you will not lend to him;
he will become the head, but you will become the tail.

45 Now when there come upon you all these curses,
and pursue you and overtake you,
until you have been destroyed,
since you did not hearken to the voice of YHWH your God,
to keep his commandments and his regulations that I
commanded you,

46 they will be for you a sign and a portent,
and for your seed, for the ages—

47 because you did not serve YHWH your God in joy and in good-
feeling of heart out of the abundance of everything.

48 So you will have to serve your enemies, whom YHWH
will send-forth against you,
in famine and in thirst, in nakedness and in lack of everything;
he will put a yoke of iron upon your neck,
until he has destroyed you.

49 YHWH will raise up against you
a nation from afar, from the edge of the earth,
like an eagle swooping-down,
a nation whose language you do not understand,

50 a nation fierce of countenance
that does not lift up the countenance of the elderly
and (to) youths shows-no-mercy.

---

48 **he will put:** Referring to the enemy.

50 **countenance:** "Face," here altered so as not to clash
with "fierce."

51 It will devour the fruit of your animals and the fruit of your soil,
  until you have been destroyed;
  it will not leave for you grain, new-wine, or shining-oil,
  the offspring of your cattle or the fecundity of your sheep,
  until it has caused-you-to-perish.

52 It will besiege you within all your gates,
  until the collapse of your walls, high and fortified,
  in which you were feeling-secure throughout all your land,
  and will besiege you within all your gates, throughout all your
    land
  that Yнwн your God has given you.

53 You will consume the fruit of your womb,
  the flesh of your sons and of your daughters
  that he has given you, Yнwн your God,
  in the siege and in the straits with which your enemy puts-you-in-
    straits.

54 The tenderest man among you, the one exceeding daintiest—
  his eye shall be too set-on-evil toward his brother, toward the wife
    of his bosom,
  and toward the rest of his children that he has spared

55 to give to (even) one of them some of the flesh of his children
    that he eats,
  because he has nothing left of anything
  in the siege and in the straits with which your enemy puts-you-in-
    straits, within all your gates.

56 (She) tenderest among you, the daintiest-one,
  whose sole of foot has not essayed to be placed upon the earth
  out of daintiness and out of being-tender—
  her eye shall be set-on-evil against the husband of her bosom,
  against her son and against her daughter,

57 against her afterbirth that goes out from between her legs
  and against her children that she bears;
  indeed, she shall eat them, out of lack of everything, in secret,
  in the siege and in the straits with which your enemy puts-you-in-
    straits, within your gates.

58 If you do not carefully observe all the words of this Instruction,
  those written in this document,

to hold-in-awe the Name, this honored and awe-inspiring one,
YHWH your God,

59 then YHWH will make-extraordinary the blows (against) you
and the blows (against) your seed,
blows great and lasting,
sicknesses evil and lasting;

60 he will return upon you every illness of Egypt
from which you shrank-in-fear,
so that they cling to you;

61 also every sickness and every blow that is not written in this
document of Instruction
YHWH will bring up against you,
until you have been destroyed;

62 you will be left menfolk few-in-number,
in place of your having-been like the stars of the heavens for
multitude,
since you did not hearken to the voice of YHWH your God.

63 And it shall be:
as YHWH once delighted in you
by doing-good for you and by making-you-many,
thus will YHWH delight in you
by causing you to perish and by destroying you,
and you shall be pulled up from the soil that you are entering to
possess.

64 YHWH will scatter you among all the peoples,
from the edge of the earth to the (other) edge of the earth;
you will serve there other gods, whom you have not known,
(either) you or your fathers,
of wood and of stone.

65 Yet among those nations you shall not find-repose,
nor shall there be rest for the sole of your foot:
YHWH will give you there a shuddering heart, failing eyes and
languishing breath.

---

59 **blows:** The standard word for "plagues" (as in the Exodus story).
63 **delighted . . . in doing-good:** Tigay: "was determined. . . to do-good." **pulled up:** An idiom for "deport," as in Akkadian (Weinfeld 1972a).

66 Your life will hang-by-a-thread before you,
   you will be terrified night and day,
   and you will not trust in (the security of) your life.

67 At daybreak you will say: Who would make it sunset!
   And at sunset you will say: Who would make it daybreak!
   —out of the terror of your heart that you feel-in-terror,
   out of the sight of your eyes that you see.

68 YHWH will return you to Egypt in ships,
   by the route of which I had said to you:
   You shall not see it again any more!
   You will put yourselves up for sale there to your enemies as
      servants and as maids,
   with none to buy (you).

69 These are the words of the covenant
   that YHWH commanded Moshe to cut with the Children of Israel
   in the land of Moav,
   aside from the covenant that he cut with them at Horev.

---

66 **hang-by-a-thread:** Heb. difficult. Another possibility is "suffer-hardship."

67 **Who would make it:** Trad. "Would that it were."

daybreak . . . sunset: Or "morning . . . evening."

68 **put yourselves up for sale:** Following JPS.

PART IV

CONCLUDING EXHORTATION

(29–30)

THE FIRST TWO PARTS OF DEUTERONOMY RECALLED THE PAST IN SOME DETAIL; THE third envisioned the particulars of Israel's future life on its land—or, if we take the book in the context of Israelite monarchy, set forth a code of behavior for the present. The fourth part of the book, except for a few references to the wilderness experience, primarily places the future before the audience. Israel is warned, one last time, of the dire consequences of disregarding God's laws. At the same time, it is presented with a happy ending: even if they should go into exile for their disobedience, God is confident of their "turning" back to him, and in consequence will eventually "return" them to their land and prosperity.

This section appears to be extraneous in the context of Deuteronomy's basic structure. Perhaps it is a later addition, meant to address particular historical circumstances that presented a crisis situation.

Renewed Exhortation (29): Having concluded the covenant, Moshe now takes up his plea again, beginning the same way that God did when the people arrived at Mount Sinai (Ex. 19:4–6). Here, without the impressive backdrop of Sinai, Moshe goes on at some length, reviewing the past and then addressing both the "assembly" in front of him and those to come.

Much of the latter part of the chapter sounds like a reference to the fate of the Northern kingdom, Israel, which was overrun by Assyria a century before Josiah's discovery of the "book." Such may be the reason for the reference to "hidden" and "revealed" things in v.28—for the reason for the fall of the idolatrous North is certainly no mystery to the reader of Deuteronomy.

29:1 Now Moshe called all Israel (together) and said to them:
You yourselves have seen
all that YHWH did before your eyes in the land of Egypt,
to Pharaoh, to all his servants and to all his land,

2 the great trials that your eyes saw,
those great signs and portents.

3 But YHWH has not given you a mind to know or eyes to see or
ears to hear,
until this day.

4 Now I had you travel for forty years in the wilderness;
there did not wear-out your garments from upon you,
your sandal did not wear-out from upon your foot,

5 bread you did not eat,
wine and intoxicant you did not drink,
in order that you might know
that I am YHWH your God.

6 When you came to this place,
Sihon king of Heshbon and Og king of Bashan came-out to meet
you in war,
but we struck them down,

7 we took away their land and gave it as an inheritance
to the Re'uvenites and to the Gadites, and to half the Menashite
tribe.

8 So you are to be-careful regarding the words of this covenant,
and are to observe them,
in order that you may act-wisely in all that you do.

9 You are stationed today, all of you,
before the presence of YHWH your God:
your heads, your tribes, your elders and your officials,
all the men of Israel,

29:1 **You yourselves have seen:** Perhaps echoing
Ex. 20:19, which is also connected to covenant
warnings.
5 **bread . . . wine:** The lack of these staples supports

the characterization of Israel's wilderness experience as liminal—away from the everyday.
9 **your heads, your tribes:** Some ancient versions
read "your tribal heads."

10   your little-ones, your wives, your sojourner that is amid your
        encampments,
    from your woodchopper to your waterhauler,
11   for you to cross over into the covenant of YHWH your God, and
        into his oath-of-fealty
    that YHWH your God is cutting with you today—
12   in order that he may establish you today for him as a people,
    with him being for you as a god,
    as he promised you
    and as he swore to your fathers, to Avraham, to Yitzhak, and to
        Yaakov.
13   Not with you, you-alone
    do I cut this covenant and this oath,
14   but with the one that is here, standing with us today
    before the presence of YHWH our God,
    and (also) with the one that is not here with us today.
15   Indeed, you yourselves know
    how we were settled in the land of Egypt,
    and how we crossed amid the nations that you crossed;
16   you saw their detestable-things and their idol-clods,
    of wood and stone, of silver and of gold, that were with them—
17   (beware) lest there be among you a man or a woman, a clan or a
        tribe
    whose heart faces away today from YHWH our God
    by going to serve the gods of those nations,
    lest there be among you a root bearing-fruit of wormwood and
        poison-herb;
18   for it shall be
    when he hears the words of this oath
    and blesses himself in his heart, saying:
    I will have *shalom*,

---

10 **woodchopper . . . waterhauler:** Equivalent to "every man jack among you."

11 **cross over into the covenant:** The wording is a bit unusual. There may be a conscious play here on "crossing" in v.15 below. **oath-of-fealty:** Translated elsewhere as "oath-curse."

14 **our God:** Some ancient versions read "your God" here and in v.17.

16 **idol-clods:** A derogatory term for pagan gods.

18 **blesses himself in his heart:** JPS, "fancies himself immune." **"sweeping away the watered and the parched (alike)":** This seems to be an idiom denoting "total destruction."

though in the stubbornness of my heart I will walk—
with the result of "sweeping away the watered and the parched
    (alike),"

19 (that) YHWH will not consent to grant-him-pardon,
rather, then the anger of YHWH will smoke, along with his
    jealousy, against that man,
and there will crouch upon him all the oath-curse
that is written in this document,
and YHWH will blot-out his name from under the heavens.

20 YHWH will separate him for ill from all the tribes of Israel,
according to all the oath-curses of the covenant
that are written in this document of Instruction.

21 Then shall say a later generation,
your children who arise after you
and the foreigner that comes from a land far-off,
when they see the blows (dealt) this land
and its sicknesses with which YHWH has made-it-sick:

22 by brimstone and salt, is all its land burnt,
it cannot be sown, it cannot sprout (anything),
there cannot spring up in it any herbage—
like the overturning of Sedom and Amora, Adma and Tzvoyim
that YHWH overturned in his anger, in his venemous-wrath.

23 Then shall say all the nations:
For what (reason) did YHWH do thus to this land,
(for) what was this great flaming anger?

24 And they shall say (in reply):
Because they abandoned the covenant of YHWH the God of their
    fathers
that he cut with them when he took them out of the land of
    Egypt:

25 they went and served other gods and prostrated-themselves to
    them,

---

19 **anger:** Here, as usually in the Bible, the word literally means "nostrils." **crouch upon him:** That is, be
an unshakable burden.

22 **Sedom** etc.: Cf. Gen. 19:24–28 for a description of
that famous destruction.

Exile and Return (30): A chapter that is usually taken to be a late addition, 30 envisions a time after the curses have fallen upon the people of Israel and they finally return to God. This restorative vision is followed by Moshe's turning to his audience and finishing his exhortations with a rhetorically moving appeal (vv.11–20). In this section the key root is "life," occurring six times. It is a fitting ending to Moshe's regular speeches. Also noteworthy is the sevenfold use of Heb. *shuv* ("return / restore").

gods they had not known and that he had not apportioned to
    them.

26 So the anger of YHWH flared up against that land,
    to bring upon it all the curse that is written in this document.

27 So YHWH uprooted them from their soil
    in anger, wrath, and great fury,
    and he cast them into another land, as (is) this day.

28 The hidden things are for YHWH our God,
    but the revealed-things are for us and for our children, for the
        ages,
    to observe all the words of this Instruction.

30:1 Now it shall be:
    when there come upon you all these things,
    the blessing and the curse that I have set before you,
    and you take them to your heart
    among all the nations where YHWH your God has thrust-you-
        away,

2 and you return to YHWH your God and hearken to his voice,
    according to all that I command you today,
    you and your children,
    with all your heart and with all your being,

3 YHWH your God will restore your fortunes, and have-compassion
        on you:
    he will return to collect you from all the peoples
    wherein YHWH your God has scattered you.

4 If you be thrust-away to the ends of the heavens,
    from there YHWH your God will collect you, from there he will
        take you,

5 and YHWH your God will bring you
    to the land that your fathers possessed, and you shall possess it,
    he will do-well by you and make you many-more than your
        fathers.

25 **he:** God.
30:3 **restore your fortunes:** Heb. *shav . . . shevutekha;* continuing the use of the root *shuv* ("return") that echoes throughout the chapter.

6 YHWH your God will circumcise your heart and the heart of your
     seed,
   to love YHWH your God with all your heart and with all your
     being,
   in order that you may live.
7 YHWH your God will place all those threats upon your enemies
     and on those-that-hate-you, that pursue you;
8 and you, (if) you return and hearken to the voice of YHWH
   and observe all his commandments that I command you today:
9 YHWH your God will make you excel in all the doings of your
     hands,
   in the fruit of your womb and in the fruit of your animals, and in
     the fruit of your soil, to good-measure,
   indeed, YHWH will return to delighting in you, to (your) good,
   as he delighted in your fathers—
10 if you hearken to the voice of YHWH your God,
   by keeping his commandments and his laws—what is written in
     this document of Instruction—
   if you return to YHWH your God with all your heart and with all
     your being.
11 For the commandment that I command you this day:
   it is not too extraordinary for you,
   it is not too far away!
12 It is not in the heavens,
   (for you) to say:
   Who will go up for us to the heavens and get it for us
   and have us hear it, that we may observe it?
13 And it is not across the sea,
   (for you) to say:
   Who will cross for us, across the sea, and get it for us
   and have us hear it, that we may observe it?

---

6 **circumcise your heart:** See note to 10:16.

13 **across the sea:** An especially daunting proposition
    for the Israelites, who were not coast dwellers.

14 Rather, near to you is the word, exceedingly,
in your mouth and in your heart, to observe it!

15 See, I set before you today
life and good, and death and ill:

16 in that I command you today
to love YHWH your God,
to walk in his ways
and to keep his commandments, his laws and his regulations,
that you may stay-alive and become-many
and YHWH your God may bless you
in the land that you are entering to possess.

17 Now if your heart should face-about, and you do not hearken,
and you thrust-yourself-away and prostrate yourselves to other
gods, and serve them,

18 I announce to you today
that perish, you will perish,
you will not prolong days on the soil that you are crossing the
Jordan to enter, to possess.

19 I call-as-witness against you today the heavens and the earth:
life and death I place before you, blessing and curse;
now choose life, in order that you may stay-alive, you and your
seed,

20 by loving YHWH your God,
by hearkening to his voice and by cleaving to him,
for he is your life and the length of your days,
to be settled on the soil
that YHWH swore to your fathers, to Avraham, to Yitzhak and to
Yaakov,
to give them!

P A R T   V

FINAL MATTERS

(31–34)

As the four-book-long (Exodus through Deuteronomy) account of wanderings and laws draws to a close, there remain several pragmatic provisions for the future that must be attended to. Leadership must be passed on, so Moshe appears with his successor at the holiest spot in the encampment—the Tent of Appointment. It must be assured that the "Instruction" will be recited periodically in public, and that it be kept in safekeeping.

There are literary considerations as well. A number of biblical books or large units end with poetry (Genesis, the Deliverance Narratives of Exodus, the biography of King David in Samuel-Kings) and the editors of Deuteronomy have made use of the same device. As if to emphasize the majestic nature of the five books, not one but two poems make their appearance: the Song of Moshe, which serves as a final, memorable warning to the Israelites (and which, along with the laws, they are also supposed to remember), and his blessing, which makes use of the form that Yaakov used at the end of Genesis.

This business having been concluded, the Torah may finally draw to a close with the long-expected death of Moshe, who for his lifelong pains is literally rewarded with praise at the ending of the five books. But amid the reader's feelings about Moshe, the backdrop should not be forgotten: Israel has not—yet—entered the land. By ending "across" the Jordan (on the east bank), the Torah leaves the future open-ended, not filled with mourning for the past but rather full of hope for what is to come. This situation, not surprisingly, parallels the ending of the entire Hebrew Bible, which for the Jews of antiquity was located in II Chron. 36:

> Thus speaks Cyrus king of Persia:
> YHWH, the God of Heaven, has given me all the kingdoms of the
>   earth;
> he has commanded me to build him a House in Jerusalem, in Judah.
> Whoever there is among you of all his people, may his God be with
>   him! Let him go up!

Preparing for the Future (31): Having finished the bulk of his address to the people, Moshe now turns to his successor, Yehoshua—or rather, an anonymous narrator finally returns to have him do so. Yet Moshe takes care not only of the immediate future but also of the distant one, setting up the institutions of family teaching and reading the Instruction publicly every seven years (cf. Tigay for discussion). Depressingly, God couples his announcement of Moshe's impending death with a picture of the idolatry the people will commit thereafter. As a bulwark against this possibility, the text provides a "song," a long poetic chapter (32) that is to serve as a "witness" against aberrant behavior.

It should not be overlooked that Moshe writes down the "Instruction" and deposits it in the coffer (ark). Not only was this standard practice in the ancient Near East (Weinfeld), but in a narrative context it enables Israel to enter a new stage in its history, accompanied by strong words and symbols from the past.

31:1 Now Moshe went
and spoke these words to all Israel,

2 · he said to them:
A hundred and twenty years old am I today;
I am no longer able to go-out and to come-in,
and YHWH has said to me:
you are not to cross over this Jordan!

3 YHWH your God, he will cross over before you,
he will destroy those nations from before you, so that you may
dispossess them;
Yehoshua, he will cross over before you,
as YHWH has promised.

4 YHWH will do to them
as he did to Sihon and to Og, the kings of the Amorites, and to
their land,
that he destroyed them.

5 YHWH will give them before you
and you will do to them
according to all the command that I have commanded you.

6 Be strong, be courageous,
do not be overawed, do not be terrified before them,
for YHWH your God, he is the one who goes with you,
he will not let-go-of you, he will not abandon you!

7 Then Moshe called Yehoshua
and said to him, before the eyes of all Israel:
Be strong, be courageous,
for you yourself will enter with this people
the land about which YHWH swore to your fathers, to give them;
you yourself will allot-it-as-inheritance to them.

8 And YHWH, he is the one who goes before you,
he will be with you;
he will not fail you, he will not abandon you;
you are not to be overawed, you are not to be shattered!

31: 1 **went and spoke:** Ancient versions read "(When) Moshe finished speaking" (*vykl* instead of *vylk*).
2 **A hundred and twenty:** In the 60-based Mesopotamian number system, this number indicates the maximal duration of life (Tigay).

9 Now Moshe wrote down this Instruction
and gave it to the priests, the Sons of Levi,
those carrying the coffer of the Covenant of YHWH,
and to all the elders of Israel.

10 And Moshe commanded them, saying:
At the end of seven years,
at the appointed-time of the Year of Release, on the pilgrimage-
festival of Sukkot,

11 when all Israel comes
to be seen at the presence of YHWH your God,
at the place that he chooses,
you are to proclaim this Instruction
in front of all Israel, in their ears.

12 Assemble the people,
the men, the women, and the little-ones,
and your sojourner that is in your gates,
in order that they may hearken, in order that they may learn
and have-awe-for YHWH your God,
to carefully observe all the words of this Instruction;

13 and (that) their children, who do not know,
may hearken and learn
to have-awe-for YHWH your God,
all the days that you remain-alive on the soil
that you are crossing over the Jordan to possess.

14 YHWH said to Moshe:
Here, your days are drawing-near to die.
Call Yehoshua and station yourselves at the Tent of Appointment,
that I may command him.
So Moshe went, along with Yehoshua,
they stationed themselves at the Tent of Appointment.

14 **days . . . drawing near . . . die:** Despite the English,
the Hebrew here is not alliterative.

15 And Y<small>HWH</small> was seen at the Tent of Appointment, in a column of
   cloud,
   and the column of cloud stood over the entrance to the Tent of
   Appointment.

16 Now Y<small>HWH</small> said to Moshe:
   Here, you are about to lie beside your fathers;
   now this people will proceed
   to go whoring after the gods of the foreigner of the land
   that they are entering in his midst,
   they will abandon me
   and violate my covenant that I have cut with them.

17 And my anger will flare up against them on that day.
   I will abandon them and I will conceal my face from them;
   (they) will be (ripe) for devouring,
   and there will befall them many and troubling ills.
   And they will say on that day:
   Was it not because God was not in my midst
   (that) there have befallen me these ills?

18 But I, I will conceal, yes, conceal my face on that day,
   because of all the ill that they have done,
   for they faced-about to other gods!

19 But now, write yourselves down this song,
   teach it to the Children of Israel, putting it in their mouths,
   in order that this song may be for you as a witness against the
   Children of Israel.

20 When I bring them to the soil about which I swore to their
   fathers,
   a land flowing with milk and honey,
   and they eat, and are satisfied, and grow fat,
   and they face-about to other gods, and serve them,
   spurning me and violating my covenant:

21 it will be,
   when there befall them many and troubling ills,
   this song will speak up before their presence as a witness,

17 **conceal my face:** An oft-used biblical metaphor for
God's abandoning Israel.

19 **this song:** Which follows in 32:1–43.
21 **plans:** Suggesting evil ones; cf. Gen. 8:21.

The Song of Moshe (32:1–43): Especially in the ancient and medieval world, the death accounts of heroes tend to end with inspired visions. The inclusion of an ancient poem here is made to fit further into the context of Moshe's exhortations in Deuteronomy—as a final warning to and witness against the people whom he has led. The "song" emphasizes the power and caring nature of God, which is contrasted with Israel's pathetic response of unfaithfulness. God is likened to a nurturing parent and a protecting eagle; when Israel responds with idolatry, he turns into a destroyer. Much of this poem reminds one of other biblical literature, such as Psalm 78—also a reprise of Israel's history. That poem is recited as a proof of God's choosing the (southern) House of David; the political motivation behind Deut. 32, if there was one, is no longer clear to us.

Skehan notes that the number of verses in the song, 69, equals the number of letters in the Hebrew alphabet (23) times three. Similar or related schemes appear elsewhere in the Bible, often in the form of acrostics (cf. Lamentations).

The song, which may predate Deuteronomy, may have been placed here as a traditional poem that meaningfully deals with catastrophe (Tigay). Despite the obscurity of some of its phrases, it stands as a witness to Israel's self-understanding, albeit a negative one.

for it will not be forgotten from the mouths of their seed.
Indeed, I know the plans that they are making today,
(even) before I bring them into the land about which I swore!

22 So Moshe wrote down this song on that day,
and he taught it to the Children of Israel.

23 Now he commanded Yehoshua son of Nun
and said:
Be strong, be courageous,
for you will bring the Children of Israel
to the land about which I swore to them;
and I myself will be-there with you.

24 And it was, when Moshe had finished writing down the words of
this Instruction in a document, until they were ended,

25 Moshe commanded the Levites,
those carrying the coffer of the Covenant of Yhwh,
saying:

26 Take this document of Instruction
and place it beside the coffer of the Covenant of Yhwh your
God,
let it be there among you as a witness.

27 For I myself know your rebelliousness,
and your hard neck;
here, while I am yet alive with you today,
you have been rebellious against Yhwh—
even (more) so after my death!

28 Assemble to me all the elders of your tribes, and your officials,
that I may speak in their ears these words,
that I may call-to-witness against them the heavens and the earth.

29 For I know:
after my death, indeed, you will wreak ruin, yes, ruin,
turning-aside from the way that I have commanded you,
and calling down upon yourselves evil in future days;
for you will do what is evil in the eyes of Yhwh,
vexing him through the doings of your hands!

30 So Moshe spoke in the ears of the entire assembly of Israel
the words of this song, until they were ended:

32:1   Give ear, O heavens, that I may speak,
hear, O earth, the utterance of my mouth.

2   Let my teaching drip like rain,
let my words flow like dew,
like droplets on new-growth,
like showers on grass.

3   For the name of YHWH I proclaim,
give greatness to our God!

4   The Rock, whole-and-perfect are his deeds,
for all his ways are just.
A God steadfast, (with) no corruption,
equitable and upright is he.

5   His children have wrought-ruin toward him—a defect in
      them,
a generation crooked and twisted!

6   (Is it) YHWH whom you (thus) pay back,
O people foolish and not wise?
Is he not your father, your creator,
he (who) made you and established you?

7   Regard the days of ages-past,
understand the years of generation and generation (ago);
ask your father, he will tell you,
your elders, they will declare it to you:

8   When the Most-High gave nations (their) inheritances,
at his dividing the human-race,
he stationed boundaries for peoples
by the number of the gods.

9   Indeed, the portion of YHWH became his people,
Yaakov, the lot of his inheritance.

10   He found him in a wilderness land,
in a waste, a howling desert.
He surrounded him, he paid-him-regard,
he guarded him like the pupil of his eye;

32:2 **teaching:** Lit. "what is received."

3 **give:** Or "ascribe."

4 **The Rock** etc.: This verse forms the beginning of the traditional Jewish burial service.

5 **His children have wrought-ruin** etc.: An extremely difficult verse that has been much debated. The solution here is based on Dillmann, quoted by Driver. An emendation cited by Tigay yields "his non-children violated their loyalty."

8 **gods:** Ancient versions read "children of the gods."

10ff. **surrounded . . . paid-him-regard . . . guarded:** The sense is that God *kept on doing* these things (Rainey).

11   like an eagle protecting its nest,
      over its young-birds hovering,
      he spread out his wings, he took him,
      bearing him on his pinions.

12   YHWH alone did lead them,
      not with him any foreign god!

13   He had them mount on the high-places of the land,
      he fed them the crops of the field;
      he suckled them with honey from a boulder,
      with oil from a flinty rock;

14   on curds of cattle and milk of sheep,
      along with the milk of lambs and rams,
      of the young of Bashan and he-goats,
      along with the kidney fat of wheat,
      and blood of grapes, you drank fermented (wine).

15   But Yeshurun grew fat and kicked,
      you were fat, you were gross, you were gorged,
      he forsook the God that made him,
      and treated-like-a-fool the Rock of his deliverance.

16   They made-him-jealous with alien (gods),
      with abominations they vexed him.

17   They slaughtered (offerings) to demons, no-gods,
      gods they had not known;
      new-ones from nearby came,
      of whom your fathers had no idea.

18   The Rock that birthed you, you neglected,
      you forgot the God that produced-you-in-labor.

19   When YHWH saw, he spurned (you),
      from the vexation of his sons and daughters.

11 **protecting:** Following O'Connor.
13 **honey:** In Gaster's (1969) opinion, this and the appearance of the eagle in v.11 are an allusion to the folk motif of the Exposed Child (a child left to die in the wild is saved and succored by the gods and/or friendly animals).

15 **gorged:** Some read Heb. *casita* as *nashita*, "forgot."
17 **had no idea:** Driver suggests "did not shudder."
18 **produced-you-in-labor:** A reminder that God is not always perceived in exclusively male imagery in the Bible.

20 He said: I will conceal my face from them,
I will see what is their future.
Indeed, a generation of overturning are they,
children in whom one cannot trust.

21 They made-me-jealous with a no-god,
vexed me with their nothingnesses;
so I will make-them-jealous with a no-people,
with a nation of fools I will vex them!

22 For fire is kindled in my nostrils,
it burns (down) to Sheol, below,
devouring the earth and its yield,
setting-ablaze the hills' foundations.

23 I will sweep them away with evils,
my arrows I will spend against them.

24 Drained by Famine,
deprived-of-food by Fiery-Plague and Bitter Pestilence;
the teeth of beasts I will send out against them,
along with the hot-venom of crawlers in the dust.

25 Outside, the sword bereaves,
in rooms-within, Terror!
(Destroying) young-men and virgins alike,
nurselings along with men of gray-hair.

26 I would have said: I will cleave-them-in-pieces,
I will make their memory cease from mortals,

27 —except that I feared the vexation from the enemy,
lest their foes misconstrue,
lest they say: Our hand is raised-high,
not YHWH wrought all this!

28 For a nation straying from counsel are they,
in them there is no understanding.

29 If (only) they were wise, they would contemplate this,
they would understand their future!

---

24 **Fiery-Plague:** Or "fire-bolts."

26 **cleave . . . in pieces:** A difficult expression; I follow Driver here, who relates it to Arabic.

30 How can one pursue a thousand,
  two put a myriad to flight,
  unless their Rock had sold them out,
  YHWH had handed them over?

31 For not like their rock is our Rock,
  though our enemies so-assess-it;
  indeed, from the vine of Sedom is their vine,

32 from the fields of Amora,
  their grapes are grapes of poison,
  clusters bitter for them,

33 the hot-venom of serpents their wine,
  the cruel poison of vipers.

34 Is this not laid up in store with me,
  sealed up in my treasuries:

35 mine are vengeance and payback,
  at the time when their foot slips,
  for near is the day of their calamity,
  making haste, the things impending for them.

36 But YHWH will judge (in favor of) his people,
  regarding his servants he will relent,
  when he sees that strength-of-hand is gone,
  naught (left) of (both) fettered and free.

37 He will say: Where are its gods,
  the rock in whom it sought-refuge,

38 that devoured the fat of their slaughtered-offerings,
  drank the wine of their poured-offerings?
  Let them rise up and help you,
  let them be over you a shelter!

39 See now that I, I am he,
  there is no god beside me;
  I myself bring-death, bestow-life,
  I wound and I myself heal,
  and there is from my hand no rescuing!

---

31 **though our enemies . . . :** Heb. difficult. **Sedom . . . Amora:** The infamous Sodom and Gomorrah of Gen. 19.

36 **naught (left) of (both) fettered and free:** Perhaps a merism meaning "anybody."

Some Final Words (32:44–52): Moshe's last regular words to the people reiterate the theme of "life" noted earlier. On the other hand, God, at the end of Moshe's life, cannot refrain from reminding him (and us) of the reason that the great leader may not enter the Promised Land (v.51).

The Blessing of Moshe (33): As if to balance Yaakov's deathbed blessing of his sons at the end (Chap. 49) of Genesis, Moshe doubles his poetic vision and blesses Israel, tribe by tribe. The weighting of tribes is very different here from what it was in Genesis: Levi is quite strong, Shim'on has disappeared, and Yehuda, the tribe of David's royal lineage, has a reduced role. Some scholars are therefore inclined to see a background of Northern ascendancy behind this poem, perhaps the days of Jeroboam II (early eighth century B.C.E.).

For a useful comparison of this chapter with other tribal blessings in the Bible, see Plaut; for discussion of textual problems, Tigay is clear and helpful.

40 For I lift up my hand to the heavens,
and say: As I live, for the ages—

41 when I sharpen my lightning sword,
my hand seizes judgment,
I will return vengeance on my foes,
and those who hate me, I will pay back.

42 I will make my arrows drunk with blood,
my sword devour flesh,
with the blood of the slain and the captives,
from the head thick-with-locks of the enemy.

43 Shout-for-joy, O nations, (over) his people,
for the blood of his servants he will avenge.
Vengeance he will return upon his foes,
effecting-atonement for the soil of his people!

44 Moshe came
and spoke all the words of this song in the ears of the people,
he and Hoshe'a son of Nun.

45 When Moshe had finished speaking all these words to all Israel,

46 he said to them:
Set your hearts toward all these words which I call-as-witness
among you today,
that you may command your children
to carefully observe all the words of this Instruction.

47 Indeed, no empty word is it for you,
indeed, it is your (very) life;
through this word you shall prolong (your) days upon the soil
that you are crossing over the Jordan to possess.

48 Now YHWH spoke to Moshe on that same day, saying:

49 Go up these heights of Avarim / The-Region-Across, Mount Nevo
that is in the land of Moav,
that faces Jericho,

---

43 **avenge:** Or "exact retribution from." **effecting-atonement . . .:** Heb. difficult. **for the soil of his people:** Heb. likewise difficult; JPS note suggests "wipe away his people's tears."

44 **Hoshe'a:** An alternate version of "Yehoshua." Al-

though the names sound the same, the latter means "YHWH is noble," the former, "YHWH delivers."

47 **empty:** Not the same word as "emptiness" in 5:11. **word:** Alternatively, "matter" or "thing."

49 **holding:** Others, "land grant."

and see the land of Canaan
that I am giving to the Children of Israel for a holding.

50 You are to die on the mountain that you are going up,
and are to be gathered to your kinspeople,
as Aharon your brother died on Hill's Hill
and was gathered to his kinspeople

51 —because you (both) broke-faith with me
in the midst of the Children of Israel
at the waters of Merivat Kadesh, in the Wilderness of Tzyn,
because you did not treat-me-as-holy
in the midst of the Children of Israel.

52 Indeed, at-a-distance you shall see the land,
but there you shall not enter,
the land that I am giving to the Children of Israel.

33:1 Now this is the blessing
with which Moshe the man of God blessed the Children of Israel
before his death.

2 He said:

> YHWH from Sinai came,
> he shone forth from Se'ir for them,
> radiating from Mount Paran,
> approaching from Rivevot Kodesh,
> at his right-hand, a fiery stream for them.
>
> 3 Though he has-affection-for the peoples,
> all his holy-ones (are) in your hand,
> they place themselves at your feet,
> bearing your words.
>
> 4 Instruction did Moshe command us,
> a possession the assembly of Yaakov.

---

51 **at the waters of Merivat Kadesh:** Cf. Num. 20:1–13.

33:2 **Sinai:** Unusual here, since Deuteronomy tends to use "Horev" for Sinai. **at his right-hand** etc.: Another difficult phrase; O'Connor, "from his Southland, the slopes, which are his."

3 **the peoples:** The Septuagint reads "his people." **bearing your words:** O'Connor, "they honor your commands." The entire verse as we have it is enigmatic.

5   Now he became king in Yeshurun
when there gathered the heads of the people,
together, the tribes of Israel!

6   May Re'uven live and not die,
but let his menfolk be few-in-number.

7   And this to Yehuda, he said:

Hearken, O YHWH, to the voice of Yehuda,
to his kinspeople bring him,
his hands'-strength great for him.
A help against his foes may you be!

8   To Levi he said:

Your *Tummim* and your *Urim* for your loyal man,
whom you tested at Massa / Testing,
you quarreled with him by the waters of Meriva / Quarreling.

9   Who says of his father and of his mother: I have not seen
them,
his brother he does not recognize,
and his children he does not acknowledge—
for they have guarded your sayings,
your covenant they have watched over.

10   Let them instruct your regulations to Yaakov,
your Instruction to Israel,
putting smoking-incense in your nostrils,
and complete-offerings on your slaughter-site.

11   Bless, O YHWH, his wherewithal,
and the works of his hands, accept-with-favor;
smash the loins of those rising up against him,
those hating him, from rising up!

---

8 **quarreled:** Or "strove."
10 **complete-offerings:** Completely consumed by fire on the altar.

11 **from rising up:** Some understand as "who will arise?"

12 To Binyamin he said:

> The beloved of YHWH! He dwells securely upon him,
> he surrounds him every day,
> as between his shoulders he dwells.

13 To Yosef he said:

> Blessed by YHWH be his land,
> from the excellence of the heavens, from dew,
> from Ocean crouching below,

14 from excellence of the sun's produce,
> from excellence of the moon's crop.

15 And from the tops of the ancient hills,
> from the excellence of the age-old mountains,

16 from the excellence of the land and its fullness,
> the favor of the *Seneh*-bush Dweller;
> may it come on the head of Yosef,
> on the brow of the consecrated-one among his brothers.

17 His firstling bull—it has splendor,
> the horns of the wild-ox, his horns;
> with them he shall gore the peoples together, the ends of
> the earth.
> They are the myriads of Efrayim,
> they are the thousands of Menashe.

18 To Zevulun he said:

> Rejoice, O Zevulun, in your going-out,
> and Yissakhar, in your tents.

19 Peoples they will call to the hills,
> there they will slaughter slaughter-offerings of victory,
> for the abundance of the seas they will suck,
> the hidden treasures of the sand.

---

12 **He dwells securely upon him:** Avishur brings an iconographic parallel from Egypt, where a god, in the guise of a hawk, sits upon the shoulder or back of the one to be protected.

16 **consecrated-one:** The same phrase is used of Yosef in Gen. 49:26. It might also be rendered "the one set apart."

17 **together:** O'Connor reads as "incites," based on an Arabic cognate. **the ends of the earth:** Follow JPS.

20 To Gad he said:

> Blessed be he that expands Gad,
> like a king-of-beasts he dwells,
> tearing arm, yes, (and) brow.

21
> He selected a premier-part for himself,
> for there a portion for a ruler was reserved;
> he approached (with) the heads of the people,
> the justice of YHWH did he do,
> his regulations along with Israel.

22 To Dan he said:

> Dan is a whelp of lions
> leaping forth from Bashan.

23 To Naftali he said:

> Naftali is sated with favor,
> full with the blessing of YHWH;
> (of) sea and southland taking-possession!

24 To Asher he said:

> Most blessed of sons, Asher!
> May he be the favored-one of his brothers,
> dipping his foot in oil.

25
> Iron and bronze your bolts,
> and as your days, your strength.

26
> There is none like God, O Yeshurun,
> riding (through) the heavens to your help,
> in his majesty in the skies.

27
> A shelter is the Ancient God,
> beneath, the arms of the Ageless-One.
> He drove out from before you the enemy,
> saying, "Destroy!"

---

23 **sea:** Probably a reference to the Sea of Galilee.
25 **strength:** Another difficult word; the reading here is based on ancient versions.
26 **like God, O Yeshurun:** Some read "like the God of Yeshurun." **Yeshurun:** A poetic name for Israel, probably derived from *yashar,* "upright."
27 **Ageless-One:** Taking Heb. *olam* as a reference to the divine (Cross and Freedman).

The End (34): Genesis concluded with the death of Yosef; Joshua will end with the death of the victorious general. Moshe's passing provides the natural ending for the Torah; like that other great work of the first millennium B.C.E., the *Iliad*, a funeral marks the end of the old generation and old circumstances. Israel, the narrated audience of the book of Deuteronomy, is now armed for what lies ahead, thanks to the leader's orations that have comprised an entire book. The rhetorical force of Deuteronomy thus caps the stories, poems, and laws of Genesis through Numbers, and makes of the five books truly a "teaching" or Instruction.

28 So Israel will dwell in security,
alone, the fountain of Yaakov,
in a land of grain and new-wine;
yes, his heavens drop down dew.

29 O your happiness, Israel,
who is like you,
a people delivered by YHWH,
your helping shield,
who is your majestic sword!
Your enemies shall come-cringing to you,
and you—on their backs you will tread!

34:1 Now Moshe went up from the Plains of Moav
to Mount Nevo, at the top of the Pisga (Range)
that faces Jericho;
and YHWH let him see all the land:
Gil'ad as far as Dan,

2 and all Naftali, and the land of Efrayim and Menashe,
and all the land of Yehuda,
as far as the Hindmost Sea,

3 and the Negev
and the round-plain, the cleft of Jericho, the town of palms, as far
as Tzo'ar.

4 And YHWH said to him:
This is the land
that I swore to Avraham, to Yitzhak, and to Yaakov, saying:
To your seed I give it!
I have let you see it with your eyes,
but there you shall not cross!

5 So there died there Moshe, servant of YHWH,
in the land of Moav,
at the order of YHWH.

34:1 **as far as Dan:** The northern border of Israel.
2 **all the land of Yehuda:** The center of the country.
5 **at the order of YHWH:** He dies as he has lived. It
should also be noted that the literal meaning, "at

the mouth of YHWH," gave rise to a Jewish tradition
that, as the greatest religious figure in Israel's history, Moshe died by a divine kiss.

6 He buried him
  in a valley in the land of Moav,
  opposite Bet Pe'or,
  and no man has knowledge of the site of his burial-place until
      this day.
7 Now Moshe was a hundred and twenty years old at his death;
  his eye had not grown-dim,
  his vigor had not fled.
8 The Children of Israel wept for Moshe in the Plains of Moav for
      thirty days.
  Then the days of weeping in mourning for Moshe were ended.

9 Now Yehoshua son of Nun was filled with the spirit of wisdom,
  for Moshe had leaned his hands upon him,
  and (so) the Children of Israel hearkened to him
  and did as Yhwh had commanded Moshe.
10 But there arose no further prophet in Israel like Moshe,
  whom Yhwh knew face to face,
11 in all the signs and portents
  that Yhwh sent him to do in the land of Egypt,
  to Pharaoh and to all his servants, and to all his land;
12 and in all the strong hand
  and in all the great, awe-inspiring (acts)
  that Moshe did before the eyes of all Israel.

---

6 **no man has knowledge:** Apparently to prevent worship of the dead, which was quite familiar to the Israelites from an Egyptian context.

10 **knew:** JPS: "singled out," the likely meaning here.
12 **before the eyes:** Stressing that this is not second-hand information (Tigay).

Suggestions for Further Reading

The secondary literature on the Five Books of Moses, singly and as a group, is immense. Tradition-minded Jews and Christians will as a matter of course make use of ancient exegetes and their medieval successors to get a fuller understanding of specific words and passages. Much of this material is now available in English translation, whether of Midrashim, some of the medievals, the Church Fathers, or Luther. As far as modern commentaries go, here too the amount of material is vast. New works appear constantly (Tigay's JPS *Commentary on Deuteronomy,* for instance, will be appearing in 1996), and a full listing of appropriate works would take up several volumes on its own. The reader is therefore advised to consult the solid and extensive bibliographies found in the major commentaries such as Speiser (1964), Childs (1974), Sarna (1986), Milgrom (1991), Levine (1993), Weinfeld (1991), and Tigay (1996). As mentioned below, there is also a wealth of material to be gleaned from the numerous recent reference works, such as the *Anchor Bible Dictionary.*

The list below, which cites mainly English-language works, is intended to supplement *The Five Books of Moses* in terms of interpreting the text, providing ancient Near Eastern background, biblical history, and a literary approach to the Bible. It makes no pretense at being comprehensive, but is selective, including both those works which I found stimulating and those which are referred to in the Commentary and Notes (cited there by author and, if there is more than one work by the author, by date). The abbreviation "JPS," which appears numerous times in the notes, refers to the New Jewish Publication Society translation, listed as *The Torah* below.

Medieval Hebrew Commentaries

Abravanel	Isaac Abravanel, fifteenth-century Spain/Italy
Bekhor Shor	Joseph ben Isaac Bekhor Shor, twelfth-century France
Ibn Ezra	Abraham ibn Ezra, twelfth-century Spain
Redak (Kimhi)	David Kimhi, twelfth- to thirteenth-century France
Ramban	Moses ben Nahman, thirteenth-century Spain
Rashi	Solomon ben Isaac, eleventh-century France

A well-produced and useful Hebrew edition of most of the above commentaries is *Torat Hayyim* (Jerusalem, 1986–1993).

Modern Works

Aberbach, A. and Smolar, Levy. "Aaron, Jeroboam and the Golden Calves." *Journal of Biblical Literature* 86 (1967).

Abrahams, Israel. "Numbers, Typical and Important." *Encyclopedia Judaica*, vol. 12. Jerusalem, 1972.

Ackerman, James S. "The Literary Context of the Moses Birth Story." In *Literary Interpretations of Biblical Narratives*, eds. Kenneth R. R. Gros Louis, James S. Ackerman, and Thayer S. Warshaw. Nashville, 1974.

———. "Joseph, Judah, and Jacob." In *More Literary Interpretations of Biblical Narratives*, eds. Kenneth R. R. Gros Louis and James S. Ackerman. Nashville, 1982.

Albright, William F. "What Were the Cherubim?" In *The Biblical Archaeologist Reader I*, eds. G. Ernest Wright and David Noel Freedman. New York, 1961.

Alter, Robert. *The Art of Biblical Narrative*. New York, 1981.

Alter, Robert, and Kermode, Frank, eds. *The Literary Guide to the Bible*. Cambridge, MA, 1987.

Anchor Bible Dictionary, ed. David Noel Freedman. New York, 1992.

Andersen, Frances. *The Sentence in Biblical Hebrew*. The Hague, 1974.

Anderson, Gary A. "The Interpretation of the Purification Offering in the Temple Scroll (11QTemple) and Rabbinic Literature," *Journal of Biblical Literature* III:1 (Spring 1992).

Auerbach, Erich. *Mimesis*. New York, 1957.

Avishur, Yitzhak. "Expressions of the Type *byn ydym* in the Bible and Semitic Languages." *Ugarit-Forschungen* 12 (1980).

Bamberger, Bernard J. "Leviticus." In *The Torah: A Modern Commentary*, ed. W. Gunther Plaut. New York, 1981.

Bar Efrat, Shimon. *Narrative Art and the Bible*. Sheffield, England, 1989.

Baring, Anne, and Cashford, Jules. *The Myth of the Goddess: Evolution of an Image*. London, 1991.

Beck, Harrell F. "Incense." In *The Interpreter's Dictionary of the Bible*, vol. 2. New York, 1962.

Bellefontaine, Elizabeth. "The Curses of Deut. 27: Their Relationship to the Prohibitions." In Christensen, ed., op. cit., 1993.

Bird, Phyllis. "Images of Women in the Old Testament." In *Religion and Sexism*, ed. Rosemary Radford Ruether. New York, 1974.

Blenkinsopp, Joseph. *The Pentateuch*. New York, 1992.

Brettler, Marc A. *The Creation of History in Ancient Israel*. New York, 1995.

Brichto, Herbert Chanan. *Toward a Grammar of Biblical Poetics*. New York, 1992.

Brisman, Leslie. *The Voice of Jacob*. Bloomington, 1990.

Buber, Martin. *Israel and the World*. New York, 1948.

———. *The Prophetic Faith*. New York, 1949.

———. *Good and Evil*. New York, 1952.

———. *Moses*. New York, 1988.

———. *On the Bible*. New York, 1982.

Buber, Martin, and Rosenzweig, Franz. *Die fuenf Buecher der Weisung*. Heidelberg, 1976.

———. *Scripture and Translation*. Bloomington, 1994.

Burkert, Walter. *Structure and History in Greek Mythology and Ritual.* Berkeley, 1979.

Campbell, Joseph. *The Hero with a Thousand Faces.* Princeton, 1972.

Cassuto, Umberto. *A Commentary on the Book of Exodus.* Jerusalem, 1967.

———. *A Commentary on the Book of Genesis. Part One: From Adam to Noah.* Jerusalem, 1972. Part Two: From Noah to Abraham. Jerusalem, 1974.

Childs, Brevard W. *The Book of Exodus: A Critical, Theological Commentary.* Philadelphia, 1974.

———. *Introduction to the Old Testament as Scripture.* Philadelphia, 1979.

Christensen, Duane L. "The Numeruswechsel in Deuteronomy 12." In *Ninth World Congress of Jewish Studies.* Jerusalem, 1986.

———, ed. *A Song of Power and the Power of Song (Sources for Biblical and Theological Study,* Vol. 3). Winona Lake, IN, 1993.

Clements, Ronald E. *Exodus* (Catholic Bible Commentary). Cambridge, 1972.

Cohen, Harold R. (Chaim). *Biblical Hapax Legomena in the Light of Akkadian and Ugaritic* (*SBL* Dissertation Series 37). Missoula, MT, 1978.

Cohn, Robert L. *The Shape of Sacred Space: Four Biblical Studies.* Chico, CA, 1981.

Cross, Frank Moore. *Canaanite Myth and Hebrew Epic.* Cambridge, MA, 1973.

———, and Freedman, David Noel. "The Blessing of Moses," *Journal of Biblical Literature* 67 (1948).

Culley, Robert. *Studies in the Structure of Hebrew Narrative.* Philadelphia, 1976a.

———, ed. "Oral Tradition and Old Testament Studies." In *Semeia* 5 (1976b).

Daiches, David. *Moses: The Man and His Vision.* New York, 1975.

Damrosch, David. *The Narrative Covenant.* New York, 1987.

Daube, David. *Studies in Biblical Law.* Cambridge, 1947.

———. "Direct and Indirect Causation in Biblical Law." *Vetus Testamentum* 11 (1961).

———. *The Exodus Pattern in the Bible.* London, 1963.

Davidson, Robert. *Genesis 1–11* (Cambridge Bible Commentary). Cambridge, 1979.

———. *Genesis 12–50* (Cambridge Bible Commentary). Cambridge, 1979.

Davies, Douglas. "An Interpretation of Sacrifice in Leviticus." In Lang, ed., op. cit., 1985.

DeVaux, Roland. *Ancient Israel.* New York, 1965.

———. *The Early History of Israel.* Philadelphia, 1978.

Douglas, Mary. "The Forbidden Animals in the Old Testament." *Journal for the Study of the Old Testament* 59 (1993a).

———. *In the Wilderness: The Doctrine of Defilement in the Book of Numbers* (*JSOT* Supplement Series 158). Sheffield, England, 1993b.

———. *Purity and Danger.* London, 1966.

———. "Deciphering a Meal." In *Implicit Meanings.* London, 1975.

Driver, Samuel R. *Deuteronomy* (International Critical Commentary). Edinburgh, 1895.

———. *Exodus* (Cambridge Bible). Cambridge, 1911.

————. *The Book of Genesis*. New York, 1926.

Ehrlich, Arnold. *Miqra Ki-Pheshuto* (Hebrew). New York, 1969.

Eilberg-Schwartz, Howard. *The Savage in Judaism*. Bloomington, 1990.

Exum, J. Cheryl. "You Shall Let Every Daughter Live: A Study of Exodus 1:8–2:10." *Semeia* 28 (1983).

Falk, Marcia. *The Song of Songs: A New Translation and Interpretation*. San Francisco, 1990.

Fishbane, Michael. "Accusations of Adultery: A Study of Law and Scribal Practice in Numbers 5:11–31." *Hebrew Union College Annual* 45 (1974).

————. "The Sacred Center: The Symbolic Structure of the Bible." In *Texts and Responses: Studies Presented to Nahum N. Glatzer on the Occasion of His Seventieth Birthday by His Students*, ed. Michael Fishbane and Paul Flohr. Leiden, 1975.

————. *Text and Texture*. New York, 1979.

————. "Biblical Colophons, Textual Criticism and Legal Analogies." *Catholic Bible Quarterly* 42 (1980).

————. *Biblical Interpretation in Ancient Israel*. Oxford, 1988.

Fokkelman, J. P. *Narrative Art in Genesis*. Assen and Amsterdam, 1975.

Fox, Everett. "The Bible Needs to Be Read Aloud." *Response* 33 (Spring 1977).

————. "The Samson Cycle in an Oral Setting." *Alcheringa: Ethnopoetics* 4:1 (1978).

————. "A Buber-Rosenzweig Bible in English." In *Amsterdamse Cahiers voor exegese in bijbelse Theologie* 2. Kampen, Holland, 1980.

————. "Can Genesis Be Read as a Book?" *Semeia* 46 (1989a).

————. "Franz Rosenzweig as Translator." *Leo Baeck Institute Yearbook* 34 (1989b).

————. On the Bible and Its World." In *The Schocken Guide to Jewish Books*, ed. Barry W. Holtz. New York, 1992.

————. "Stalking the Younger Brother: Some Models for Understanding a Biblical Motif." *Journal for the Study of the Old Testament* 60 (1993).

Frankfort, Henri. *Before Philosophy*. New York, 1951.

Fredman, Ruth Gruber. *The Passover Seder*. New York, 1983.

Freedman, David Noel. "The Broken Construct Chain." *Biblica* 53 (1972).

————. "Deliberate Deviation from an Established Pattern of Repetition in Hebrew Poetry as a Rhetorical Device." In *Proceedings of the Ninth World Congress of Jewish Studies*. Jerusalem, 1986.

Frick, Frank S. *The City in Ancient Israel* (*SBL* Dissertation Series 36). Missoula, MT, 1977.

Friedman, Richard Eliot, ed. *The Poet and the Historian: Essays in Literary and Historic Biblical Criticism*. Chico, CA, 1983.

————. *Who Wrote the Bible?* New York, 1989.

Frymer-Kensky, Tikva. "Pollution, Purification, and Purgation in Biblical Israel." In *The Word of the Lord Shall Go Forth: Essays in Honor of David Noel Freedman in Celebration of His Sixtieth Birthday*, ed. Carol Meyers and Michael O'Connor. Winona Lake, IN, 1983.

————. "The Strange Case of the Suspected *Sotah*." *Vetus Testamentum* 34 (1984).

———. "Biblical Cosmology." In *Backgrounds for the Bible*, eds. Michael Patrick O'Connor and David Noel Freedman. Winona Lake, IN, 1987.

———. "Deuteronomy." In *The Women's Bible Commentary*, eds. Carol A. Newsom and Sharon H. Ringe. Louisville, 1992a.

———. *In the Wake of the Goddesses*. New York, 1992b.

Gaster, Theodor H. *Passover: Its History and Traditions*. New York, 1949.

———. *Thespis*. New York, 1961.

———. *Myth, Legend, and Custom in the Old Testament*. New York, 1969.

Geller, Stephen A. "The Struggle at the Jabbok: The Uses of Enigma in a Biblical Narrative." *Journal of the Ancient Near Eastern Society of Columbia University* (*JANES*) 14 (1982).

Ginsberg, H. L. *The Israelian Heritage of Judaism*. New York, 1982.

Ginzberg, Louis. *The Legends of the Jews*. Philadelphia, 1968.

Girard, Rene. *Violence and the Sacred*. Baltimore, 1977.

Glatzer, Nahum N. *Franz Rosenzweig: His Life and Thought*. New York, 1961.

Goldin, Judah. "The Youngest Son or Where Does Genesis 38 Belong." *Journal of Biblical Literature* 96 (1977).

Goodman, L. E. "The Biblical Laws of Diet and Sex." In *Jewish Law Association Studies II* (Jerusalem Conference Volume), ed. B. S. Jackson. Atlanta, 1986.

Gottwald, Norman K. *The Hebrew Bible: A Socio-Literary Introduction*. Philadelphia, 1985.

Gray, George Buchanan. *Numbers (International Critical Commentary)*. Edinburgh, 1903.

Greenberg, Moshe. "The Biblical Concept of Asylum." *JBL* 67 (1959).

———. "Crimes and Punishments." *The Interpreter's Dictionary of the Bible*, vol. 1. New York, 1962.

———. "The Thematic Unity of Exodus 3–11." In *Fourth World Congress of Jewish Studies I*. Jerusalem, 1967.

———. *Understanding Exodus*. New York, 1969.

———. "The Redaction of the Plague Narratives in Exodus." In *Near Eastern Studies in Honor of W. F. Albright*, ed. Hans Goedike. Baltimore, 1971.

———. "Exodus." *Encyclopedia Judaica*, vol. 6. Jerusalem, 1972.

———. "Some Postulates of the Biblical Criminal Law." In *The Jewish Expression*, ed. Judah Goldin. New York, 1976.

———. *Ezekiel 1–20 (Anchor Bible 22)*. New York, 1983.

Greenstein, Edward L. "The Riddle of Samson." *Prooftexts* 1:3 (September 1981).

———. "Theories of Modern Bible Translation." *Prooftexts* 8 (1983).

———. "Biblical Law." In *Back to the Sources*, ed. Barry W. Holtz. New York, 1984a.

———. "Medieval Bible Commentaries." In Holtz, *op. cit.*, 1984b.

———. "Understanding the Sinai Revelation." In *Exodus: A Teacher's Guide*, ed. Ruth Zielenziger. New York, 1984c.

———. "The Torah as She Is Read." *Response* 14 (Winter 1985a).

————. "Literature, The Old Testament as." In *Harper's Bible Dictionary*, ed. Paul J. Achtmeier. San Francisco, 1985b.

————. "The State of Biblical Studies, or Biblical Studies in a State." *Essays in Biblical Method and Translation*. Atlanta, 1989.

————, and Marcus, David. "The Akkadian Inscription of Idrimi." *JANES* 8 (1976).

Gruber, Mayer. "Breast-Feeding Practices in Biblical Israel and in Old Babylonian Mesopotamia." *JANES* 19 (Held Memorial Volume) (1989).

Gunn, David M. *The Story of King David: Genre and Interpretation*. Sheffield, England, 1978.

Hallo, William W. *The Book of the People* (Brown Judaic Studies 225). Atlanta, 1991.

Haran, Menahem. "The Nature of the 'Ohel Mo'edh' in the Pentateuchal Sources." *Journal of Semitic Studies* 5 (1960a).

————. "The Use of Incense in Ancient Israelite Ritual." *Vetus Testamentum* 10 (1960b).

————. "Books-Scrolls in Israel in Pre-Exilic Times." *Journal of Jewish Studies* 33:1-2 (*Essays in Honour of Yigal Yadin*) (Spring-Autumn 1982).

————. *Temples and Temple Service in Ancient Israel*. Winona Lake, IN, 1985.

Hendel, Ronald. *The Epic of the Patriarch: The Jacob Cycle and the Narrative Traditions of Canaan and Israel*. Atlanta, 1987.

Heschel, Abraham Joshua. *The Sabbath: Its Meaning for Modern Man*. New York, 1951.

Hertz, Joseph H. *The Pentateuch and the Haphtorahs*. London, 1960.

Hyatt, J. Philip. *Commentary on Exodus* (New Century Bible). London, 1971.

Interpeter's Dictionary of the Bible. New York, 1962.

Interpreter's Dictionary of the Bible: Supplementary Volume. New York, 1976.

Isbell, Charles. "The Structure of Exodus 1:1–14." In *Art and Meaning: Rhetoric in Biblical Literature*, eds. David J. A. Clines, David M. Gunn, and Alan J. Hauser. Sheffield, England, 1982.

Jackson, Bernard S. "The Ceremonial and the Judicial: Biblical Law as Sign and Symbol." *JSOT* 30 (October 1981).

Jacob, Benno. *Des erste Buch der Tora: Genesis*. Berlin, 1931.

Jacobson, Dan. *The Story of the Stories*. New York, 1982.

Janzen, J. Gerald. "On the Most Important Word in the Shema (Deuteronomy 6:4–5). *Vetus Testamentum* 37:3 (1987).

Jeansonne, Sharon Pace. *The Women of Genesis*. Minneapolis, 1990.

Jenson, Philip Peter. *Graded Holiness: A Key to the Priestly Conception of the World* (*JSOT* Supplement Series 106). Sheffield, England, 1992.

Kasher, Menahem M., ed. *Encyclopedia of Biblical Interpretation*, vols. 7–9. New York, 1967–1969.

Keil, Carl, and Delitzsch, Franz. *Commentary on the Old Testament in Ten Volumes*. Vol. 1, *The Pentateuch*. Grand Rapids, MI, 1968.

Kessler, Martin. *Voices from Amsterdam*. Atlanta, 1994.

Kikawada, Isaac. "Literary Convention of the Primeval History." *Annual of the Japanese Biblical Institute* 1 (1975).

Kirk, G. S. *Myth: Its Meaning and Functions in Ancient and Other Cultures.* Berkeley, 1970.

Kiuchi, N. *The Purification Offering in the Priestly Literature* (*JSOT* Supplement Series 56). Sheffield, England, 1987.

Knight, Douglas A., and Tucker, Gene, eds. *The Hebrew Bible and Its Modern Interpreters.* Phildelphia, 1985.

Knohl, Israel. "The Priestly Torah Versus the Holiness School: Sabbath and the Festivals." *Hebrew Union College Annual* 58 (1987).

Kosmala, Hans. "The 'Bloody Husband'." *Vetus Testamentum* 12 (1962).

Lang, Bernhard, ed. *Anthropological Approaches to the Old Testament.* Philadelphia, 1985.

Lauterbach, Jacob Z., ed. *The Mekilta de-Rabbi Ishmael.* Philadelphia, 1976.

Leach, Edmund. "The Logic of Sacrifice," in Lang, ed., *op. cit.*

Leibowitz, Nehama. *Studies in Shemot I and II.* Jerusalem, 1976.

Levenson, Jon D. "Who Inserted the Book of the Torah?" *Harvard Theological Review* 68 (1975).

———. *Creation and the Persistence of Evil.* San Francisco, 1988.

———. *Sinai and Zion.* San Francisco, 1985.

Levine, Baruch A. *In the Presence of the Lord.* Leiden, 1974.

———. "The Epilogue to the Holiness Code: A Priestly Statement on the Destiny of Israel." In *Judaic Perspectives on Ancient Israel*, eds. Jacob Neusner, Baruch A. Levine, and Ernest S. Frerichs. Philadelphia, 1987a.

———. "The Language of Holiness: Perceptions of the Sacred in the Hebrew Bible." In *Backgrounds for the Bible*, eds. Michael Patrick O'Connor and David Noel Freedman. Winona Lake, IN, 1987b.

———. *Leviticus* (The JPS Commentary). Philadelphia, 1989.

——— *Numbers 1–20* (Anchor Bible, vol. 4). New York, 1993.

Levinson, Bernard M. *The Hermeneutics of Innovation: The Impact of Centralization upon the Structure, Sequence, and Reformation of the Legal Material in Deuteronomy.* Brandeis University dissertation, 1991.

Licht, Jacob. *Storytelling in the Bible.* Jerusalem, 1978.

Lichtenstein, Murray H. "Biblical Poetry." In *Back to the Sources,* ed. Barry W. Holtz. New York, 1984.

Magonet, Jonathan. "The Korah Rebellion." *Journal for the Study of the Old Testament* 24 (1982).

Mann, Thomas W. *The Book of the Torah.* Atlanta, 1988.

Marcus, David. "Juvenile Delinquency in the Bible and the Ancient Near East." *JANES* 13 (1981).

Mayes, A. D. H. *Deuteronomy* (New Century Bible). London, 1979.

———. "Deuteronomy 4 and the Literary Criticism of Deuteronomy." In Christensen, ed., *op. cit.,* 1993.

Mendenhall, George. "Covenant Forms in Israelite Tradition." *Biblical Archaeologist* 17 (1954).

Meyers, Carol. *The Tabernacle Menorah* (*ASOR* Dissertation Series 2). Missoula, MT, 1976.

Milgrom, Jacob. *Studies in Cultic Theology and Terminology*. Leiden, 1983.

———. *Numbers* (The JPS Commentary). Philadelphia, 1990.

———. *Leviticus 1–16* (Anchor Bible, vol. 3). New York, 1991.

Miller, Alan. "Claude Levi-Strauss and Gen. 37–Ex. 20." In *Shiv'im*, ed. Ronald Brauner. Philadelphia, 1977.

Miller, J. Maxwell. *The Old Testament and the Historian*. Philadelphia, 1976.

Moore, Michael S. *The Balaam Traditions* (*SBL* Dissertation Series 113). Atlanta, 1990.

Moran, William L. "The Ancient Near Eastern Background of the Love of God in Deuteronomy." *Catholic Bible Quarterly* 25 (1963).

Muffs, Yochanan. *Love and Joy*. New York, 1992.

Nelson, Richard D. "Deuteronomy." In *Harper's Bible Commentary*. San Francisco, 1988.

Newsom, Carol A., and Ringe, Sharon H., eds. *The Women's Bible Commentary*. Louisville, 1992.

Niditch, Susan. *War in the Hebrew Bible*. New York, 1993.

Nohrnberg, James. "Moses." In *Images of Man and God: Old Testament Short Stories in Literary Focus*, ed. Burke O. Long. Sheffield, England, 1981.

O'Connor, M. *Hebrew Verse Structure*. Winona Lake, IN, 1980.

Olson, Dennis T. *The Death of the Old and the Birth of the New*. Chico, CA, 1985.

Orlinsky, Harry M. *Notes on the New Translation of the Torah*. Philadelphia, 1970.

Paran, Meir. *Forms of the Priestly Style in the Pentateuch* (Hebrew). Jerusalem, 1989.

Paul, Shalom M. *Studies in the Book of the Covenant in the Light of Cuneiform and Biblical Law* (*VT* Supplement 18). Leiden, 1970.

Plaut, W. Gunther. *The Torah: A Modern Commentary*. New York, 1981.

Polzin, Robert. "The Ancestress of Israel in Danger." *Semeia* 3 (1975).

———. *Moses and the Deuteronomist*. New York, 1980.

Lord Raglan. *The Hero*. New York, 1979.

Rainey, Anson F. "The Ancient Hebrew Prefix Conjugation in the Light of Amarnah Canaanite." *Hebrew Studies* 27 (1986).

Redford, Donald. *A Study of the Biblical Story of Joseph*. Leiden, 1970.

Rofe, Alexander. "The Laws of Warfare in the Book of Deuteronomy: Their Origins, Intent and Positivity." *Journal for the Study of the Old Testament* 32 (1985).

Rosenberg, Joel. "Meanings, Morals, and Mysteries: Literary Approaches to Torah." *Response* 9:2 (Summer 1975).

———. "The Garden Story Forward and Backward: The Non-Narrative Dimensions of Gen. 2–3." *Prooftexts* 1:1 (1978).

———. "Biblical Narrative." In *Back to the Sources*, ed. Barry W. Holtz, New York, 1984.

———. *King and Kin*. Bloomington, 1986.

Russell. Letty M., ed. *Feminist Interpretations of Biblical Narrative*. Philadelphia, 1985.

Ryken, Leland. "The Epic of the Exodus." In *Literature of the Bible*. Grand Rapids, MI, 1974.

Sakenfeld, Katherine Doob. "Numbers." In Newsom and Ringe, eds., *The Women's Bible Commentary* (1992).

Sarna, Nahum M. *Understanding Genesis*. New York, 1966.

———. *Exploring Exodus*. New York, 1986.

———. *Genesis* (JPS Torah Commentary). Philadelphia, 1989.

———. *Exodus* (JPS Torah Commentary). Philadelphia, 1991.

———. *Songs of the Heart*. New York, 1993.

Schneidau, Herbert N. *Sacred Discontent: The Bible and Western Tradition*. Berkeley, 1976.

Scholem, Gershom. *The Messianic Idea in Judaism*. New York, 1972, 1995.

Schwartz, Baruch J. *Selected Chapters of the Holiness Code—A Literary Study of Leviticus 17–19* (Hebrew). Jerusalem, 1987.

———. "How Does a Technical Term Differ from a Metaphor? 'Bearing Iniquity / Rebellion / Sin' in the Bible" (Hebrew), *Tarbitz* 63:2 (Winter 1994).

Segal, Ben-Zion, ed. *The Ten Commandments in History and Tradition*. Jerusalem, 1990.

Sellers, Ovid P. "Weights and Measures." In *The Interpreter's Dictionary of the Bible*, vol. 4. New York, 1962.

Skehan, Patrick W. "The Structure of the Song of Moses in Deut. 32." In Christensen, ed., *op. cit.*, 1993.

Skinner, John. *Genesis* (International Critical Commentary). New York, 1910.

Soler, Jean. "The Dietary Prohibitions of the Hebrews." *New York Review of Books* 26:10 (June 14, 1979).

Sonsino, Rifat. *Motive Clauses in Hebrew Law: Biblical Forms and Near Eastern Parallels* (SBL Dissertation Series 45). Chico, CA, 1980.

Speiser, Ephraim E. *Genesis* (Anchor Bible 1). New York, 1964.

Spiegel, Shalom. *The Last Trial*. New York, 1979.

Steinberg, Naomi. "The Genealogical Framework of the Early Stories in Genesis." *Semeia* 46 (1989).

Steinmetz, Devora. *From Father to Son: Kinship, Conflict, and Continuity in Genesis*. Louisville, 1991.

Stern, Philip D. *The Biblical Ḥerem: A Window on Israel's Religious Experience* (Brown Judaic Studies 211). Atlanta, 1991.

Stulman, Louis. "Sex and Family Crimes in the Deuteronomy Code: A Witness to Moves in Transition." *Journal for the Study of The Old Testament* 53 (1982).

Talmon, Shemaryahu. "The 'Desert Motif' in the Bible and in Qumran Literature." In *Biblical Motifs: Origins and Transformations*, ed. Alexander Altmann. Cambridge, MA, 1966.

Tedlock, Dennis. "Toward an Oral Poetics." *New Literary History* 7:3 (Spring 1977).

The Torah: A New Translation According to the Masoretic Text. Philadelphia, 1962.

Tigay, Jeffrey H. "On the Meaning of t(w)tpt," *JBL* 101:3 (1982).

———. *Deuteronomy* (JPS Torah Commentary). Philadelphia, 1996.

Trible, Phyllis. *God and the Rhetoric of Sexuality*. Philadelphia, 1978.

Tunyogi, Andrew C. "The Rebellions of Israel." *JBL* 81 (1962).

Turner, Victor. *The Ritual Process: Structure and Anti-Structure*. Chicago, 1969.

Ullendorff, Edward. *Is Biblical Hebrew a Langauge?* Wiesbaden, Germany, 1977.

Vansina, Jan. *Oral Tradition: A Study in Historical Methodology*. London, 1965.

Vawter, Bruce. *On Genesis: A New Reading*. New York, 1977.

Walzer, Michael. *Exodus and Revolution*. New York, 1985.

Wander, Nathaniel. "Structure, Contradiction, and 'Resolution' in Mythology: Father's Brother's Daughter Marriage and the Treatment of Women in Genesis 11–50." *Journal of the Ancient Near Eastern Society* 13 (1981).

Wegner, Judith Romney. *Chattel or Person?* New York, 1988.

———. "Leviticus." In Newsom and Ringe, eds., *The Women's Bible Commentary* (1992).

Weinfeld, Moshe. "Theological Currents in Pentateuchal Literature." In *Proceedings of the the American Academy for Jewish Research*. New York, 1969.

———. "The Covenant of Grant in the Old Testament and in the Ancient Near East." *Journal of the American Oriental Society* 90 (1970).

———. *Deuteronomy and the Deuteronomistic School*. Oxford, 1972a.

———. "Congregation." *Encyclopedia Judaica*, vol. 5. Jerusalem, 1972b.

———. "Covenant," *ibid.*

———. *Deuteronomy* (Anchor Bible 5). New York, 1991.

———. "The Present State of Inquiry." In Christensen, ed., *op.cit.*, 1993.

Wenham, Gordon J. *The Book of Leviticus* (The New International Commentary on the Old Testament). Grand Rapids, MI, 1979.

———. *Numbers* (Tyndale Old Testament Commentary). London, 1981.

Williams, James G. *Women Recounted: Narrative Thinking and the God of Israel*. Sheffield, England, 1982.

Wright, David P. *The Disposal of Impurity*. Atlanta, 1987.

———. "Holiness." In *The Anchor Bible Dictionary*. New York, 1992.

———. "Purification from Corpse-Contamination in Numbers XXXI 19–24." *Vetus Testamentum* 35:2 (1985).

Wright, G. Ernest. "Deuteronomy." In *The Interpreter's Bible*. Nashville, 1953.

Zornberg, Avivah Gottlieb. *Genesis: The Beginning of Desire*. Philadelphia, 1995.